Deconstruction

DECONSTRUCTION

A READER

Editor
Martin McQuillan

EDINBURGH UNIVERSITY PRESS

Introductions, selection and editorial
materials © Martin McQuillan, 2000

Edinburgh University Press
22 George Square, Edinburgh

Typeset in Sabon and Gill Sans
by Bibliocraft Ltd, Dundee, and
printed and bound in Great Britain
by The Cromwell Press,
Trowbridge, Wilts

A CIP record for this book is available
from the British Library

ISBN 0 7486 1255 6 (hardback)
ISBN 0 7486 1256 4 (paperback)

CONTENTS

ACKNOWLEDGEMENTS

If I were to list all of those who have explicitly, implicitly, consciously, unconsciously, deliberately, or accidentally helped in the construction of this book there would be little room left for the texts themselves. Since it is an obligation and a delight to name at least the obviously guilty, I would like to thank (in alphabetical order): Derek Attridge, Richard Beardsworth, Catherine Belsey, Geoffrey Bennington, Fred Botting, Paul Bowman, Scott Brewster, Pamela Brown, Peter Buse, Hélène Cixous, Simon Critchley, Jacques Derrida (*tout court*), Robert Eaglestone, Diane Elam, Marc Froment-Meurice, Rodolphe Gasché, Peggy Kamuf, Peter Krapp, Ernesto Laclau, Willy Maley, J. Hillis Miller, Christopher Norris, Eric Prenowitz, John Ronan, Phil Rothsfield, Nicholas Royle, Susan Sellers, Marq Smith, Scott Wilson, Julian Wolfreys, Robert Young and my friends and ex-colleagues at Staffordshire University. I would like to thank David Kammera, Christine Izzary and Ramona Fotiade for their fine translations. I would also like to thank Hilary Jenkins, Ruth Addison, Nancy Moufied and all the British Council staff in London and Cairo, as well as the members of the English departments in Menia, Al Shamps and Alexandria universities, for providing me with an opportunity to develop the introduction to this book before appreciative and inquisitive audiences. Finally, my sincerest thanks go to the skills, wisdom and patience of Jackie Jones. This book is dedicated to Ellie and Oscar, the McQuillan-Byrnes.

The editor and publishers would like to thank the following who have kindly given permission for the use of copyright material; every effort has been made to contact copyright holders; any queries should be addressed to Edinburgh University Press. Karl Marx, from *Capital*, trans. Ben Fowkes, reprinted by permission of Penguin Books; Sigmund Freud, 'A note upon the "mystic writing pad"', reprinted by permission of Hogarth Press; Georges Bataille, 'The meaning of general economy', reprinted by permission of Zone Books; Walter Benjamin, 'Critique of violence', reprinted by permission of Verso; Martin Heidegger, 'The task of destroying the history of ontology', reprinted by permission of Basil Blackwell; Edmond Jabes, 'The moment after', reprinted by permission of University of Chicago Press; Paul Valéry, 'In praise of water', reprinted by permission of Gallimard Press; Maurice Blanchot, 'Friendship', reprinted by permission of Stanford University Press; Jacques Derrida, 'A number of yes (Nombre de oui)', reprinted by permission of the author and *Qui Parle*; Christopher Norris, 'Deconstruction, post-modernism and the visual arts', from *What is Deconstruction?*, reprinted by permission of Academy Editions; Richard Rorty, 'Philosophy as a kind of writing: An essay on Derrida', reprinted by permission of *New Literary History*; Rodolphe Gasché, 'Deconstruction as criticism', reprinted by permission of the author and *Glyph*; Geoffrey Bennington, 'Genuine Gasché (perhaps)', reprinted by permission of the author and *Imprimatur*; Simon Critchley, 'Black Socrates? Questioning the philosophical tradition', reprinted by permission of the author and *Radical Philosophy*; Jean-François Lyotard, 'Discussions, or phrasing "After Auschwitz"', reprinted by permission of Andrew Benjamin; J. Hillis Miller, 'Derrida's topographies', reprinted by permission of Stanford University Press; Paul de Man, 'Autobiography as de-facement', reprinted by permission of Columbia University Press; Derek Attridge, 'Ghost writing', reprinted by permission of Anslem Haverkamp; Nicholas Royle, 'The phantom review', reprinted by permission of the author and *Textual Practice*; Catherine Belsey, 'Hamlet's dilemma', reprinted by permission of the author, Macmillan Press and St. Martin's Press; Peggy Kamuf, 'The ghosts of critique and deconstruction', reprinted by permission of the author; Geoffrey Bennington, 'Deconstruction is not what you think', reprinted by permission of *Art and Design*; Andrew Benjamin, 'Derrida, architecture and philosophy', reprinted by permission of *Architectural Design*; Bernard Tschumi, 'Violence of architecture', reprinted by permission of *Artforum*; Richard Beardsworth, 'Thinking technicity', reprinted by permission of *Cultural Value*; Avital Ronnel, 'Toward a narcoanalysis', from *Crack Wars: Literature, Addiction, Mania*, reprinted by permission of University of Nebraska Press, 1995; Judith Butler, 'Speech acts politically', from *Excitable Speech: A Politics of the Performative*, reprinted by permission of Routledge; Fred Botting and Scott Wilson, 'Homoeconopoesis I', appears at the authors' own pleasure and risk; Diane Elam, 'Unnecessary introductions', from *Feminism and Deconstruction: Ms. en Abyme*, reprinted by permission of Routledge; Robert Young, 'The Same Difference', reprinted by permission of the author and *Screen*; Barbara Johnson, 'Gender theory and the Yale School', reprinted by permission of *Genre*; Rachel Bowlby, 'Domestication', reprinted by permission of Routledge; Alexander Duttmann, 'Recognising the virus', from *At Odds with Aids: Thinking and Talking about a Virus*, reprinted by permission of Stanford University Press; Hélène Cixous, 'What is it o'clock? or The door (we never enter)', reprinted by permission of the author; Geoffrey Hartman, 'Psychoanalysis: The French connection', from *Saving the Text: Literature/Derrida/Philosophy*, reprinted by permission of Johns Hopkins University Press; Nicolas Abrahams and Maria Torok, from *The Wolf Man's Magic Word*, reprinted by permission of University of Minnesota Press; Samuel Weber, 'The sideshow, or: Remarks on a canny moment', reprinted by permission of *Modern Language Notes*; Nicholas Royle, 'The remains of psychoanalysis (i): Telepathy', from *After Derrida*, reprinted by permission of Manchester University Press; David Wills, 'Berchtesgaden', from *Prosthesis*, reprinted by permission of Stanford University Press; Michael Ryan,

'Marx and Derrida', from *Marxism and Deconstruction: A Critical Articulation*, reprinted by permission of Johns Hopkins University Press; Willy Maley, 'Spectres of Engels', reprinted by permission of the author, Macmillan Press and St. Martin's Press; Bill Readings, 'The deconstruction of politics', reprinted by permission of University of Minnesota Press; Gayatri Spivak, 'Practical politics of the open end', reprinted by permission of *Canadian Journal of Political and Social Theory/Revue canadienne de théorie politique et sociale*; Ernesto Laclau, 'Why do empty signifiers matter in politics?', reprinted by permission of Verso; Homi K. Bhabha, 'Of mimicry and man: The ambivalence of colonial discourse', reprinted by permission of Routledge; Emmanuel Levinas, 'Jacques Derrida: Wholly otherwise', from *Proper Names*, reprinted by permission of Stanford University Press; Robert Bernasconi, 'The trace of Levinas in Derrida', reprinted by permission of Northwestern University Press; Drucilla Cornell, 'Post-structuralism, the ethical relation and the law', reprinted by permission of *Cardozo Law Review*; Philipe Lacoue-Labarthe, 'In the name of . . .', and Jean-Luc Nancy, 'What is to be done', from *Retreating the Political*, reprinted by permission of Routledge; John D. Caputo, 'God is not différance', from *The Prayers and Tears of Jacques Derrida: Religion without Religion*, reprinted by permission of Indiana University Press; Jacques Derrida, '(In memorium) Paul de Man', reprinted by permission of the author and *Yale French Studies*; Jacques Derrida, 'Text read at Louis Althusser's funeral', reprinted by permission of the author and Verso; Jacques Derrida, 'Adieu: Emmanuel Levinas', reprinted by permission of the author and *Critical Enquiry*; Jacques Derrida, 'I'm going to have to wander all alone: Gilles Deleuze', reprinted by permission of the author and *Philosophy Today*; Jacques Derrida, 'Friendship-above-all: Jean-François Lyotard', reprinted by permission of the author and *Liberation*; Jacques Derrida and Pierre Mendes France, 'Open letter to Bill Clinton', reprinted by permission of the authors; Jacques Derrida, 'Telepathy', reprinted by permission of the author and *Oxford Literary Review*; Jacques Derrida, 'The deconstruction of actuality: An interview with Jacques Derrida', reprinted by permission of the author and *Radical Philosophy*.

A MAP OF THIS BOOK

If so much of deconstruction is concerned with the experience of aporia and impasse, then perhaps a map is not the most useful means by which to orientate oneself within the problems of deconstruction. However, the paralysis which comes with the conceptual difficulty of not knowing how to proceed does not necessarily preclude a knowledge of the terrain. For this reason then, a few 'manufacturer's instructions' on how to use this book. It is not another 'Derrida Reader'. It includes texts by Derrida, and deconstruction would not be what it now is without Derrida, but the book is not intended as an introduction or guide to the complex field of Derrida's writing. Rather, its purpose is to present the reader with as rich and diverse an introduction as possible to the entire work of deconstruction past and present. For all the reasons that will be given in this book, this goal is no doubt impossible. However, one day we will surely have to live without Derrida, just as surely as the work of deconstruction and the reading of Derrida's texts will continue in all their heterogeneity. While much deconstruction may seem like so many Talmudic glosses on Derrida's texts, this volume is motivated by the belief that for good or ill deconstruction has become a 'field of knowledge' in its own right. As such deconstruction – if it is to retain the name of deconstruction – must lose the inhibitions which tie it to the unreconstructed desire for presence which places Jacques Derrida (man and texts) at the centre of an academic discipline. Derrida himself has explained the difficulties of escaping such essential desires, but the day must inevitably come when we no longer rely on fathers. It is a matter of the greatest importance that Derrida's texts should be set up to be worked and reworked by others. At no stage should Derrida's writing be allowed to occupy a privileged or 'transcendental' space within the discourse of deconstruction. If this is allowed to happen deconstruction will indeed become a 'school', with 'paternal' status accorded to certain texts, a 'presence' and authority bestowed upon Derrida as a person, its own set of legal injunctions and rules of behaviour, its own prefects whose readings are favoured over others, and its own pedagogical hierarchy. The highest compliment that one could pay to the work of Derrida might be to see his name disseminated across a range of texts, each one signed and countersigned by Derrida and his readers, each signature becoming more illegible and indistinguishable with every reinscription. In short, one cannot forget Derrida, but there is more to deconstruction than merely Derrida.

This volume presents the reader (perhaps the singular reader of its title) with an introduction to a variety of work undertaken within the locus of deconstruction. It is not intended as a substitute for wide and rigorous reading within the ambit of deconstruction but, on the contrary, as a stimulus to the reader to explore beyond the confines of this selection and so to return to the text of Derrida itself. It goes without saying that this selection is partial, partisan, inadequate, and on the whole completely unjustifiable. However, as a rough rule of thumb, the eventualities which determined the cut of the decisions which included or excluded material were always pedagogical. The Reader assumes a student or novice audience, and is constructed with the demands of teaching in mind, but it is hoped that the range of its material (with new translations and previously unanthologised texts) will appeal to the researcher as a handy resource. The volume begins with a user-friendly introduction to some key ideas within deconstruction. It is followed by a prelude of sorts. The section 'Avant la Lettre' provides a selection of some of the important texts discussed by Derrida and deconstruction, texts which exemplify a deconstructive logic of their own without necessarily recognising themselves as such. This section could have been as long as the Reader itself: one could have easily added Condillac, Rousseau, Kant, Hegel, Flaubert, Nietzsche, Mallarme, Joyce, Celan, Ponge, Genet, Austin, etc. Perhaps this is the suggestion of a pedagogical text 'yet to come'.

With the progress of the Reader well established 'opening remarks' can begin. Derrida's essay 'A Number of Yes' has been described by Geoffrey Bennington as appearing 'to contain *the whole of Derrida* (if only you have read the rest) in a condensation that would demand hundreds of pages of commentary' (Bennington 1993: 202). This ought to make for an interesting seminar! The little text is metonymic of Derrida's place in this Reader: one must 'read the rest' *and* immerse oneself in the commentary for its own sake. Thereafter the Reader is divided into nine further sections, which represent the diversity of past and present work in/on deconstruction. Seven of these sections cover significant interests within deconstruction: Philosophy, Literature, Culture, Sexual Difference, Psychoanalysis, Politics and Ethics. The contents of individual sections attempt to stage a dialogue, which performs a particular line of argument. For example, in the 'Philosophy' section Rodolphe Gasché's essay responds to Richard Rorty's description of deconstruction as a theory of writing, while Geoffrey Bennington's review-essay offers a counterbalance to Gasché. The 'Literature' section gathers together a selection of texts on *Hamlet* as both a recognition of the diversity of opinion within deconstruction and as a pedagogical aid. Examples multiply within each section. Every text in these sections is accompanied by cross-references to other texts within the Reader. Because individual sections are ordered thematically, cross-references only refer to texts outside the section in which they appear. Given that there is potentially no limit to the interests of deconstruction, an accurate cross-referencing would involve listing all of the texts on every occasion. Indeed, in the manner of a Venn diagram, every section could be subsumed into every other section: the contamination of drugs being as relevant to the 'law of genre [gender]' as the question of God to the problem of spectrality. Derrida's idea of the 'invaginated fold' might provide a more descriptive model here. However, given the pedagogical pressures at work in this text, each essay or extract is followed by a select, if inadequate, number of cross-references. The sensitive reader will no doubt identify more striking and unconventional routes of reading for themselves. The Reader ends with three attempts at closure. First, a collection of memorial pieces by Derrida for his 'philosophical friends'. Secondly, a series of 'closing statements', each one a previously unanthologised text. Finally, two bibliographies: one listing texts by Derrida and one listing texts by the other thinkers collected in this volume. Such a comprehensive display of anxiety for closure can only serve to open the Reader out onto the textual field it attempts to encapsulate and so encourage its user to be a reader of deconstruction.

The first problem which *Deconstruction: A Reader* encounters is the impossibility of its own name. 'Deconstruction' is of course only one term among many which Derrida uses in his early texts to describe his 'adventure' in philosophy. The word 'deconstruction' has, however, taken on a set of not always welcome meanings related to Derrida's philosophical practice and the interdisciplinary work associated with it. In various contexts 'deconstruction' has come to mean a method or theory of reading, a school of philosophical investigation, what Derrida 'does', what Derrida's 'followers' 'do', the totality of the institutional discourse surrounding Derrida's texts, any relativising or 'radical' aspect of 'postmodern' critical theory. Certainly, the majority of these uses of the term need to be challenged and none of them is satisfactory. The idea of a 'theory', that idea which calls itself theory, hides its own institutionalised assumptions in its own constant reinvention. In using the term theory one may be in danger of reinscribing or being recuperated by the very political gesture of mimesis (of the question of the copy or likeness and the ideal form) which the deconstruction attempts to undo. Deconstruction is not a delimitable entity, reducible to a collection of named scholars or to a set of procedural manoeuvres in textual analysis. Rather, deconstruction takes place in a singularity (it is 'always applied'). Deconstruction is what happens in the event of a reading, which attempts to open a text or institution to the movement of *différance* forgotten within it. There is no incorporeal syntax of deconstruction separate from its constant acts of reading. To confuse these events of reading with a 'theory' would be to burden deconstruction with the very logocentric confusion it seeks to dispel.

As a name, like any other proper name, the word 'deconstruction' is replaceable and in fact its replacement is made necessary by the impossibility of the 'proper' identified by deconstruction itself. However, because the term is replaceable it does not need to be replaced precisely because of its own 'improperity'. What could be more improper than, as this Reader does, to place essays by Levinas, Lyotard, Rorty, Benjamin, Norris, Belsey and de Man together under the same umbrella term? What connects these texts is not a 'method' or a 'school' but an openness to reading which responds to the possibilities of difference. If 'deconstruction' is an inappropriate name for the interdisciplinary discourse which relates itself to Derrida's texts, then it is an equally impertinent (and therefore apposite) name for a reader which offers a collection of readings impossibly related by difference. The 'deconstruction' in the title of this volume therefore does not attempt to designate a school of thinkers or a canon of exemplary methodologies, rather it suggests an interest in a movement of reading which responds to the invitation made by the endless work of Derrida's texts.

This volume must also negotiate what Peggy Kamuf calls 'the impossibility of position' suggested in the term 'Reader'. The reader is a genre of academic publishing, it is a selection of texts to be read. The reader is also the person who reads, and who works and reworks the texts which they read, imbricated within these texts and displaced by the reading process. If deconstruction is an experience of a question of reading then the very idea of the 'reader' may have to be examined by this volume as a precondition of the volume being allowed to say anything at all. It may be necessary to address the topic of reading as an opening onto the effects of the trace and as an accession to a context of writing. Deconstruction cannot be disentangled from the problems of reading. However, it may also be necessary to 'deconstruct' the very idea of the reader *qua* genre. If *Deconstruction: A Reader* is to mean anything at all (not just another commercial product, not just another 'theoretical' tool) it must rethink the institutional assumptions of the reader genre from the ground up. The point would be not to remove the volume from this genre but to give the genre the possibility of being thought. The possibility of thinking through a deconstruction reader might necessarily involve a putting into question of everything within a reader to which deconstruction might be subjugated, namely, the values of categorisation, selection, pedagogy, translation, and so forth. All of which can be deconstructed but which do not in themselves constitute a deconstruction. Ultimately, there may be something unquestioned, and therefore problematic, in the very idea of a deconstruction reader. *Deconstruction: A Reader* must question the problem of the programme and the resistance to programme or to 'family resemblances' implied by the genre of 'reader'. It must also accept that in order for the book to succeed as a deconstruction it must fail as a reader.

INTRODUCTION: FIVE STRATEGIES FOR DECONSTRUCTION

Martin McQuillan

What deconstruction is not? Everything of course!
What is deconstruction? Nothing of course!

> Jacques Derrida, 'Letter To A Japanese Friend'

The difficult I'll do right now.
The impossible will take a little while.

> Billie Holiday, 'Crazy He Calls Me'

Philosophers 'do' 'it', literary critics 'do' 'it', even architects and psychoanalysts 'do' 'it', poets 'do' 'it', painters 'do' 'it', capital and the political are said to 'do' 'it', texts 'do' 'it' to themselves and justice is 'it', but what is this thing? The following pages are an introduction to the term which has come to act as a metonym for the work of Jacques Derrida and the substantial body of knowledge which has grown up around his texts in the form of an extensive commentary and dialogue. However, the word means more than this. It is a translation (and adaptation) into French, and then into the languages of the world, of the Heideggerian term '*Destruktion*' or '*Abbau*'. In this sense it suggests an operation performed in relation to the structure of the fundamental concepts of Western metaphysics. It is a translation – successful or not – which attempts to limit the connotations of 'destruction' implied by a straight transliteration of Heidegger's term into French. In French, it has both a grammatical and a mechanical meaning. It means both to disarrange the construction of words in a sentence and to disassemble a machine and transport it elsewhere. It also forms a reflexive verb [*se deconstuire*] meaning to lose one's own construction. However, this thing cannot be reduced to a semantic or a mechanical model. Indeed the term itself questions the architecture of such models, as well as the model of architecture.

This thing is most commonly associated with post-structuralism but has its contextual roots in the historical conjunction surrounding structuralism. Like structuralism it is concerned with a certain idea of structure but it also wishes to undo or desediment structures of all kinds, including the structure of structuralism as well as structures older than structuralism. This thing places all the terms of Western philosophy under erasure, while returning to those terms as absolutely necessary. It has been called a negative theology, but is incompatible with all theologies, even negative ones. It has been mistaken for a form of critique, but the undoing of such transcendental apparatus has been one of the key themes of the work done by this thing. It has been taken for a type of literary criticism, claimed as a mode of philosophy, and designated a movement in architecture. A record label has been called after it, and a fashionable moment in the fashion industry took its name in vain. It is called postmodern but is to be found in the texts of the ancients.

It takes place everywhere and this term has become a motif for the action it refers to (although it is too passive to deserve the name of action). Any attempt to define it will fail, or at least come undone, because all the defining concepts and means of articulation and signification are themselves open to the effects of this thing. This includes the term itself. The very term which denotes this thing is open to its own effects. This term is not equal to the thought it conveys. Perhaps the word will only prove to have been of strategic use in a particular moment in the history of Western thought. Certainly, it will prove as difficult to introduce as it is to translate.

Introductions can be formal and serve to make one better acquainted with someone or something. Introductions can be uncertain, if they are arranged blind through what are now called 'introduction agencies'. Introductions may seem marginal to a text (outside of its main body) but they are always preliminary for a deeper understanding of the text. Introductions can be deceptively simple but sometimes contain the greatest complexities: one might think here of the 'introduction' to a jazz score or the DJ Shadow album *Entroducing*. The word 'introducing' also suggests within its own etymology an impossible passage, combining both *intro* meaning 'inward' and *ducere* meaning 'to lead' – 'leading inward' seems something of a paradox if one usually 'leads out' or 'retreats inward'. As such perhaps an introduction (with its suggestions of rigour, unpredictability, marginality, deceptiveness and paradox) is the proper place for this thing, if it were not for the fact that it makes the 'proper' one of its abiding objects of study.

The last few paragraphs have been based on a wager. On telling a friend that I was preparing this book he set me the challenge of writing an introduction to *Deconstruction: A Reader* which did not use the word 'deconstruction'. He did so out of the concern that the word was too readily used in places where it was not appropriate and used lazily to cover an absence of real thinking. Certainly, we could all think of instances in which this was true. However, if 'deconstruction' is a catch-all term it is because, as I have suggested above, it is a metonymic concentration of a number of operations none of which can be reduced to the name of deconstruction (or indeed of an operation). To have continued writing this introduction without using the word 'deconstruction' may have constituted an excellent private joke but it would have been a purely academic exercise (particularly since the word has been named in the title and preface to the book, neither of which are 'outside the text'). This is not so much a philosophical point as a matter of technical uses of language. If I put my mind to it I could write an introduction without the use of the letter 'e' but it would be a sterile event. In fact, by not using the word 'deconstruction' I would be merely calling attention to its absence and so its insistent repetition. The less I used it, the more significant it would become. There are those who, for well-intentioned philosophical reasons, do not want to exhaust the term 'deconstruction', as if a word could wear itself out. However, if we are going to be remotely serious about all Derrida has said concerning both iteration and logocentrism then we cannot afford to be protective of a term, the rigorous purity of which cannot and should not be guarded. Instead, relax, learn to love the word in all its inelegance and impropriety. Let it float as a signifier inside and outside the shelter of the contextual strategies built for it by professionals. It is impossible to predict its fate or the effects it may produce. Here is an introduction to only five of its previous haunts.

DECONSTRUCTION, AN IMPOSSIBLE METHOD

Deconstruction, if such a thing exists and it is one, is not a method of literary criticism or even of reading. Deconstruction is not a method if we take 'method' to mean a general set of rules, practices, prescribed formulae and so on which will operate consistently every time (systematic, programmatic, hermeneutic). If we say we are going to do something 'methodologically' we mean that we are going to follow a set of rules or fixed procedures, which if followed through will yield the desired result. In this sense the idea of a 'method' presupposes the nature or route of inquiry and the result of that inquiry. For example, if there is a method for extracting iron from ore, it will involve a sequence of steps which, when each one has been gone through, will produce a fixed amount of iron. Similarly, if we speak of a method of reading or of criticism (although both of these words represent greatly overdetermined phenomena) then we must mean a set of procedures which if followed will produce a predetermined result. For example, a 'reading method' which we might call 'materialist' (although again the meaning of this word is up for grabs) could run as follows: before I even pick up a nineteenth-century novel I know that it is going to be an expression of bourgeois sensibility and a cultural inscription of middle-class dominance. It must be so: nineteenth-century novels were written by middle-class authors for a middle-class audience who had the education, wealth and leisure time to read them. All I need to do as a reader or critic to provide a materialist reading of the novel is to find evidence of this in the text. To this end I require a certain terminology ('base', 'superstructure', 'economic determination' and so on) and a sequence of steps which will take me through the novel matching my vocabulary to textual evidence (looking at the characterisation of the working-class might be a good place to start). This is not intended as a description, let alone a caricature, of any materialist critic's work: it is merely an example of what might be involved in describing an approach to reading as a 'method'. Examples could be multiplied following a certain Feminist, Post-Colonial or, say, a Formalist vocabulary.

As you can see, the problem with the idea of a method of reading is that it treats every text encountered in exactly the same way: *Madame Bovary* is 'an expression of bourgeois sensibility and a cultural inscription of middle-class dominance', *Hard Times* is 'an expression of bourgeois sensibility and a cultural inscription of middle-class dominance', *Middlemarch* is 'an expression of bourgeois sensibility and . . .': you get the idea. This may be an accurate description of all these novels but it hardly constitutes 'reading'. Indeed, I would not actually have to read any of these novels to come to this opinion of them. The whole of the nineteenth-century novel could be conveniently pigeon-holed along the lines of my methodological template. Any 'reading' I gave of such a text would merely involve me rummaging through the text looking for symptoms which proved my point – a point I had already decided upon before I ever approached the text. A point which must be true by the inexorable logic of my method, regardless of the facts of the novel. We might call this way of reading, although it is hardly worthy of the name, 'the sausage machine approach', in which a mix of heterogenous and conflicting material is placed in one end of the machine and identical, pre-set units come out the other end. This is not deconstruction.

There is no set of rules, no criteria, no procedure, no programme, no sequence of steps, no *theory* to be followed in deconstruction. This usually comes as something of a disappointment to scholars who want their reading to be like 'join the dots'. If I do x, y and z I will have a 'reading' and 3000 words to hand-in to my tutor; which they will mark; I will get a grade; I will add all my grades together; I will get a degree; I will get a job. Once we have overcome this naïve desire for a formula to academic and socio-economic success, and opened ourselves up to the possibility of another way of thinking about the act of reading, then we can begin to orient ourselves towards the questions raised by deconstruction. However, you may well ask, if deconstruction is not a method then how can you have a school of it, as in the 'Yale school of deconstruction'? (See Paul de Man, J. Hillis Miller and Geoffrey Hartman's essays in this volume.) Like the Konstanz school of *receptzionaesthetick* (reader-response theory) all of the participants of 'the school' have to be doing more or less the same thing and producing similar results. Perhaps we should jettison the term 'school' as an inaccurate label applied by the media to a phenomenon they did not understand. None of the so-called school members ever used the term as a description about themselves (see Barbara Johnson, 'Gender Theory and the Yale School', this volume, pp. 292–303).

However, it would be churlish to continue with this protest of deconstruction's non-methodology for too long. The intelligent reader will point out that there are deconstruction conferences, monographs, modules, textbooks, readers and other such academic merchandising. Therefore, how can one not speak of deconstruction as a method if so many people 'do' 'it' and I as a reader am being encouraged to take 'it' up. As we will discover about much of deconstruction both statements discussed here ('deconstruction is a method', 'deconstruction is not a method') are true at one and the same time, the condition of impossibility of one being the condition of possibility of the other. In his essay 'Living on: Borderlines' (contained in the volume of 'Yale School' essays *Deconstruction and Criticism*) Derrida describes deconstruction as *'pas de methode'*.[1] The word *pas* in French means both 'not' and 'step', so this ambiguous phrase can be translated as either 'not a method' or 'a methodological step'. Thus, deconstruction is simultaneously (neither of these English phrases on their own adequately translates Derrida's expression, they have to be taken together) not a method and a step in, or towards, a methodology. You will say, this is impossible, and you would be correct: deconstruction is impossible.

Deconstruction only ever happens once. Derrida 'does' deconstruction, Paul de Man 'does' deconstruction, J. Hillis Miller 'does' deconstruction, Diane Elam 'does' deconstruction, Gayatri Spivak 'does' deconstruction, Martin McQuillan 'does' deconstruction, but the 'doing' of it (if 'doing' is the correct verb to apply here) is unique in each case. Unique not only to Derrida or de Man or whoever, but unique in each text that they write. Not only is Derrida's reading of Rousseau different from de Man's reading of Rousseau, but Derrida's reading of Blanchot is different from his reading of Hegel, and his reading of Blanchot's novel *The Madness of the Day* is different from his reading of Blanchot's novel *The Death Sentence*, and his reading of *The Madness of the Day* in the essay 'The Law of Genre' is different from his reading of the same novel in the essay 'Title: To be specified'. Similarly, while de Man may read a series of texts by Rousseau each reading is unique, unrepeatable and irreducible to any of his other readings. A deconstructive reading (a term never used by Derrida, because it implies both the idea of a method and the idea of a 'doing' or an external application, but which I will employ here only provisionally) treats a text as if it were unique. To say that a text is unique and irreducible to any other text is not the same as saying that it is isolated or cut off from extra-textual concerns. As we will see in a moment it means quite the reverse. However, deconstruction reads a text in its singularity. Deconstruction does not bring to a text a pre-conceived methodology which can be applied to a textual difficulty as if it were an ointment being applied to an infected area, in order to 'clear up' the problem.[2] Rather, deconstruction is a reading which is sensitive to what is irreducible in every text, allowing the text to speak before the reader, and listening to what the text imposes on the reader. So, let us nail a frequent lie about deconstruction which is commonly mouthed without reflection by the most seemingly erudite of scholars, namely, that deconstruction is Humpty Dumpty criticism: 'a text means what I want it to mean'.

Nothing could be further from the truth. This is the least apt description of deconstruction because deconstruction must always be open to the other, which speaks in the text even before an act of reading has begun. Deconstruction cannot help but do this since the other always speaks before I do. Think of psychoanalysis for a moment. The other of the unconscious speaks in me before I have even begun to think about it. When I begin to think about the expression of the unconscious, it enters into consciousness, and its otherness is reduced or assimilated to the same as me (or my ego). It is impossible to know otherness as otherness (as soon as I think about it, it is reduced to sameness) but I cannot stop the other speaking in advance of me. In this way, the other of the unconscious interrupts and destabilises the set patterns of my conscious thinking and there is nothing I can do about it (either to control the other or make it an object of knowledge in its otherness). Therefore, being sensitive to the openings made possible by otherness is just about one of the most difficult things we can hope to do. Ultimately, any attempt to do so will fail, because we always end up reducing the other to the self-same. But that does not stop the unsettling effects of the other and does not absolve us of the responsibility of listening for those effects. Similarly, when reading we must be open to the otherness in and of a text.

A definition (if we really must have such things) of deconstruction might be that deconstruction is an act of reading which allows the other to speak. Two consequences of this, then an example. First, deconstruction is the singular act of reading itself, not a method applied to the text to produce the reading. Deconstruction is not a thing in this sense: it is a situation or an event of reading. Deconstruction is what happens. It does not exist separately from a text but only ever arises in the moment of reading. Derrida's reading of Blanchot is a deconstruction, de Man's reading of Proust is a deconstruction, Eleanor Byrne's reading of a Disney film is a deconstruction, but there is no deconstruction outside these moments or reading situations. This is what I mean when I say that deconstruction only ever happens once. Each deconstruction is unique and singular to the text it reads and to the moment in which it reads. If you will, there is no deconstruction outside the text. Secondly, deconstruction is impossible. If deconstruction allows the other to speak, then a 'proper' deconstruction (as we shall see nothing is 'proper' to deconstruction) would not be knowable because whenever we think we are hearing the other speak we are always reducing its otherness to the self-same. So, in fact Derrida's reading of Blanchot is not a deconstruction as such, but falls short of the idea of deconstruction while attempting to aspire to the condition of a deconstruction. Derrida's reading will inevitably reduce the otherness of Blanchot's text to an inscription of the self-same. However, the other continues to speak in Derrida's text (how can it be otherwise?) and so we must begin to read Derrida for the effects of otherness as well, and thus deconstruction will go in an endless act of reading. Hence, there is no limit to the task of deconstruction.

But what is actually meant by allowing the other to speak and how does this lead to reading in singularity? An example then, bearing in mind that this example is merely strategic (to explain this pedagogical point) and is therefore specific (or singular) to its context (or reading moment). When Derrida was asked to curate an exhibition from the collection of paintings in the Louvre in Paris he chose a selection of paintings which exemplified two things: blindness and self-portraiture.[3] If we think of this exhibition as a deconstruction of the collection of the Louvre (a reading of one particular text) it is singular because it only ever happened once. The exhibition was assembled from the collection, then was disbanded, leaving only the trace of its existence in the catalogue which Derrida wrote for it (which cannot be reduced to the actual exhibition of paintings itself). An infinite number of different exhibitions could be curated from the gallery's vast collection but this selection of twenty-one paintings was the unique and irreducible exhibition chosen by Derrida at a particular moment in time. On another occasion, say in a moment of political crisis, Derrida might have chosen completely different paintings, for example, on the topic of revolution, to respond to a different set of unique circumstances. The blindness and self-portraiture exhibition was not the best or perfect selection chosen from the gallery's collection, but was a singular and specific moment of reading. In choosing the theme of blindness, the exhibition allowed the other of painting to speak. Unlike reading or radio (or even film, television and theatre, which all involve voices of one kind or another) painting is a medium which relies solely on looking. A painting must be seen. What is unique and irreducible in each painting can only be appreciated by the experience of looking. Painting then, as an art form, privileges sight. What is other ('not-me', 'not-the-same') to painting, but blindness? The selection of paintings depicting blindness, chosen from thousands of possible paintings, destabilises and questions the whole idea of painting and of art galleries in general. With the accompanying group of self-portraits the question of blindness, as the other of painting, speaks from within the very centre of the Western tradition of art. Self-portraiture is a privileged category in the history of Western art, practised by all the great painters, but it is impossible to know exactly if the so-called self-portrait is indeed a painting of the artist or even by the artist. The fact that we are told that it is, by scholars or textbooks, is not grounds for certain knowledge. This ultimate undecidability can be thought of as a 'blindness' (we can never definitely 'see' if it is true) within self-portraiture as a genre. And yet we provisionally accept it as true whenever we look at such a painting (in order to experience it as a self-portrait) and so 'turn a blind eye' to its own impossibility. Thus the other of painting (blindness) speaks from within a painting at the very moment when we are attempting to deny or erase the existence of this other. Thinking one knows when in fact the very process of knowledge is showing us that we do not know, this is blindness.

Derrida's selection of paintings here might be thought of as 'deconstructive' but it certainly is not methodological. The only set rule involved in choosing the paintings was that the other, which speaks before me, should be allowed to speak. As we know this is impossible and so cannot be identified with the idea of a 'rule'. As de Man says of one of his own readings of Shelley:

> To monumentalize this observation into a method of reading would be to regress from the rigor exhibited by Shelley which is exemplary precisely because it refuses to be generalised into a system.[4]

Thus, we can say that deconstruction, if it is a method, is an impossible method.

DECONSTRUCTING BINARY OPPOSITIONS

Given that deconstruction is an impossible method (both not a method and nothing but a method) what sort of things are of interest to it? The short answer is that there is nothing which is not of interest to deconstruction. The long answer, and this might be another definition of the thing, is that the task of deconstruction is to rethink the conceptual and non-conceptual foundations of the Western tradition from the ground up. This, as you will appreciate, is quite an undertaking and the work of 'deconstruction' in the last forty years or so has only scratched the surface of this challenging enterprise. As a starting point (although as with any starting point it is strategic for a particular purpose and moment in time rather than essential) deconstruction examines the way in which Western thought is structured. In early texts such as *Of Grammatology*. Derrida suggests that the whole of Western thought since Plato and Aristotle is structured in terms of binary oppositions. This means that the Western tradition (philosophy, art, literature, culture and so on) tends to divide conceptual material into categories of binary terms (e.g. Man, Woman; Black, White; Voice, Silence; Speech, Writing etc.). However, these couplings are not true opposites, in which one term would be the equal but contrasting compliment to the other, rather one of these terms (in the list above, the first term of each) is always privileged over the other. For a thinker of the rigour and meticulous caution of Derrida, this is an extraordinarily bold claim to make. The justly famous example he gives in *Of Grammatology* is the suggestion that every single philosopher without exception in the Western tradition privileges the concept 'speech' over the concept 'writing' (thinks of speech as more important than and as logically prior to writing).

Binary thinking pervades Western thought. Thus any Western text caught up in this form of structuration depends upon a series of assumptions about binary oppositions. Hélène Cixous discusses the privileging of the term Man over Woman in Western thought (the conceptual foundation of the non-conceptual orders of patriarchy) in her essay 'Sorties':

Where is she?
Activity/passivity
Sun/Moon
Culture/Nature
Day/Night

Father/Mother
Head/Heart
Intelligible/Palpable
Logos/Pathos.
Form, convex, step, advance, semen, progress.
Matter, concave, ground–where steps are taken, holding- and dumping-ground.
Man

Woman
   Always the same metaphor: we follow it, it carries us, beneath all its figures, wherever discourse is organised. If we read or speak, the same thread or double braid is leading us throughout literature, philosophy, criticism, centuries of representation and reflection.[5]

The first term in each binary opposition is a masculine characteristic traditionally privileged ('throughout literature ... centuries of representation') over the feminine characteristic which accompanies it. The question 'where is she?' is a rhetorical one as the list clearly shows the position of woman in this tradition as subordinate to man. Men ('step') over women ('ground'). The history of Western thought, says Cixous, is the history of this constructed inequality passing for fact, and so the history of the West is a history of patriarchy or phallocentrism (privileging the phallus).

   It is necessary at this point to stress that such binary oppositions are not the way things really are but the way they are *represented* by Western thought and through the habitualisation and sedimentation of this thought are presented as natural. Another example might be the way that the West has traditionally considered its other, the East. The following list characterises the way in which the East (or the non-Western world) has been represented through centuries of discourse:

West	East
Rational	Irrational
Progressive	Backward
Recognisable	Exotic
Scientific	Mystical
Masculine	Feminine
Moral	Amoral

Reason	Superstition
Democracy	Despotism
Order	Chaos
Culture	Nature

Throughout Western culture the East has always been figured in this way by the West. Think of *The Arabian Nights*, think of a film like *Lawrence of Arabia*, think of the nightly news' reporting of politics in the Middle East (a term which demonstrates this very problem since those who live there do not think of themselves as east of anywhere, let alone in the 'middle' of something).

These representations of women and the non-Western world are not accurate descriptions of the lived experience of those who occupy these positions (woman, non-Western). However, the function of such descriptions is not to reflect lived reality but to construct the identity of the privileged term (in this instance either Man or the West). In order to retain his privileged position Man must present (and so convince himself) that this relation of inequality ('activity/ passivity') is the true or natural condition of human beings. This idea is posited in and maintained by the discourses and conceptual orders of Western thinking. For example, we can see that in the set of binaries which construct the West as a privileged term the West is figured as 'masculine' and the East as its subordinate other, 'feminine'. This privileging of terms is called logocentrism, *logos* being the Greek word for 'word', Greek being the founding Western language of philosophy (allegedly: see Simon Critchley, 'Black Socrates', in this volume, pp. 143–53). In Cixous' list we can see 'logos' (speech, meaning, sense) privileged over the feminine 'pathos' (emotions, feelings, non-sense). The history of Western thought is the history of logocentrism in which the inequality of binary oppositions (privileging one term to the detriment of another) depends upon the representation of such inequality within discourse (philosophical, literary, and so on).

The success of logocentrism or patriarchy (phallo-logocentrism) as a system of thought and real privilege depends upon the 'unreadability' of these discourses. The moment we recognise the inequality we are bound to question this way of thinking and so endanger the privileges of those who benefit by it. Fortunately for patriarchy and the *Logos* (Western thoughts' expression in language) these conceptual orders, which predicate the non-conceptual orders of lived reality, find their expression in language and users of language can be 'trained' into accepting these circumstances through its habitual use (see Diane Elam, 'Unnecessary introductions', in this volume, pp. 275–82). To this end the Logos is a particularly efficient organising principle, running as Cixous says like a 'double braid' (one thread for the privileged term, one for the subordinate) through whole cultural formations and histories of thought. The Logos is doubly efficient. De Man defines it as a mode of thought which:

> Divides the world into a binary system of oppositions organised along an inside/outside axis and then proceeds to exchange the properties on both sides of this axis on the basis of analogies and potential identities.[6]

First, it constructs a way of thinking which makes thought impossible without an appreciation of the 'inherent' superiority of one term over another, resulting in a cultural understanding of the importance of certain terms and according those terms a privileged value. For the moment let us call this value 'presence' (as in the visible presence of the male phallus, as opposed to the inferior invisible 'absence' of the female sexual organs). Secondly, the Logos has an uncanny (this should be understood in the full Freudian sense of that word: see Samuel Weber, 'The sideshow', in this volume, pp. 351–60) knack of recuperating any attempt to undo its own logic back into a system of thought which continues to rely on the dominant value of presence. Momentarily, let us call this action 'metaphysics' (also the name of the philosophical discourse of ontology or being, literally 'beyond nature or the physical'). The meaning of these two terms, 'presence' and 'metaphysics' will be the concern of much of the argument and performance of this volume.

However, it may be helpful to think about 'presence' for a moment in the following way (see also Christopher Norris, 'The metaphysics of presence', in this volume, pp. 109–20). Deconstruction, if it teaches anything, reminds us that we should not assume that the way we perceive the world is the same as the way the world actually is. Consider, if I were to say 'I exist here and now'. In uttering this linguistic statement I am proposing that I am a real person who exists in the present moment and articulate this present by affirming my existence *here* and *now*. However, due to the infinitesimally small split in time between my thinking or saying the words 'here and now' and the actual moment to which they refer, the 'here and now' of my statement is not identical with the one I refer to. The 'here and now' I refer to is always already past by the time I think about it, but I retain it as a regulatory principle by which I understand my present existence and so paradoxically it always remains in advance of me and part of the future. What is certain is that the 'here and now' of my statement does not correspond exactly in time and space with a real moment in the current present. However, we do not go around worrying about the asymmetry between our thoughts and their referents – that way madness lies! Instead, for conceptual purposes, we assume that the two 'presents' are indeed the same. This becomes a habitual mode of perception and we no longer give it a second thought. However, this necessary forgetting is 'presence', the assumption of a relation of the self-same between reference and phenomena. It is not the way things really are but it is the fiction we tell ourselves in order to live. The desire for presence is merely the understandable desire for stable and coherent origins. Sadly, we can't always get what we want.

Cixous suggests that phallologocentrism (the complicity between patriarchy and the operation of logocentrism) always employs 'the same metaphor: we follow it, it carries us, beneath all its figures, wherever discourse is organised'. Logocentrism is a form of metaphorisation. All words are metaphors in which one thing (say the sound or written word 'tree') stands for another (the concept 'tree' or a particular tree with bark, branches and leaves).

Similarly, the phallocentric conceptual order Cixous lists is also a series of metaphors in which reality is said to be like this list. The successful maintenance of this order depends upon users of language being unable or unwilling to recognise this list as a metaphor. In this way its metaphorical status goes undetected and it continues within language as a 'dead metaphor'. However, such metaphors are anything but 'dead' since their seeming morbidity (when we no longer think of them as metaphors, but take them to be the way things really are) allows them to produce powerful political and ideological effects. Philosophy has been particularly guilty of this gesture, often turning against figurative or literary uses of language in the name of scientific rigour. By contrast, for Geoffrey Hartman:

> Deconstruction is . . . a defense of literature [i.e. the figural dimension of language]. It shows, by close reading, (1) that there are no dead metaphors, (2) that literature is often more self-aware than those who attack it, and (3) that literary texts contain significant tensions that can be disclosed not resolved by analysis.[7]

Logocentrism is the mode of thought which works through the erasure of the metaphorical status of privileged terms within a binary opposition in order to support a conceptual order structured around the valuing of such terms as positive. Thus logocentrism constructs, or centres, sense and meaning around the identity of these terms, while disguising the unresolvable tensions within them.

From the two examples outlined above, patriarchy and orientalism (the discourse of the West about the East), it is not difficult to see the possible detrimental political effects of logocentrism. The history of the West as the history of logocentrism is a history of both patriarchy and racism. The task of deconstruction is to identify and undo the binary oppositions upon which logocentrism is predicated. There are two necessary stages in this process. First, the binary must be *reversed*. In a deconstruction it is necessary to show that a binary opposition is at work (for example the valuing of man over woman) and that the meaning of the text depends upon the assumption of this binary logic. This demonstration will involve adequately illustrating the ways in which the subordinate term is devalorised within the text's conceptual system even though there is no justification for this gesture outside logocentrism's own logic. In this way, the binary will be shown to be a false opposition working to serve a particular set of interests. However, it is not enough to stop here and simply privilege the other term to restore the balance, for this would be merely to repeat the binary structure upon which the initial inequality depends. To arrest your analysis at this point would only create another inequality and do nothing to disrupt the system responsible for producing inequality in general. So – and here is the second and necessary condition of a deconstruction – having reversed the binary it is necessary to then *displace* the whole system of binary thinking. The terms within the opposition must be thought in a way that does not involve binary logic at all. Only in this way can the binary be said to be undone because only by displacing binary logic altogether can we hope to escape being dragged back into another set of binary oppositions and their accompanying inequality. However, to say the least, this is difficult.

Deconstruction is at pains to point out that it is impossible in principle to escape from logocentric thinking. De Man states:

> For example, the idea of . . . the human subject as a privileged viewpoint, is a mere metaphor by means of which man protects himself from his insignificance by forcing his own interpretation on the entire universe, substituting a human-centred set of meanings that is reassuring to his vanity for a set of meanings that reduces him to being a mere transitory accident in the cosmic order. The metaphorical substitution is aberrant *but no human self could come into being without this error.*[8]

Given that logocentrism is the mode of Western thought (and Western thought is today extended all over the globe) then, for those who think in this way, escaping logocentrism will involve a way of thinking not yet thought. In order to reach this other kind of thinking it will be necessary to think about it in our current (logocentric) mode of thought. Another way of thinking will only be reached through logocentrism, and so this other thinking cannot help but be logocentric itself. It is similar to the question of the otherness of the unconscious. As soon as we recognise the unconscious our thinking about it is no longer unconscious as such but part of our conscious experience. Similarly, an escape from logocentric thinking would only be possible via logocentrism and so cannot avoid being logocentric itself. Furthermore, if logocentrism means a way of thinking which puts meaning or sense at the centre of human activity, then how can we ever escape such a system of thought and know that we have done so? To know that we have escaped would be to make sense of our new condition and this would once again lead us back to logocentrism. Or, if logocentrism is the way that we use language ('word-centrism') then how can we escape language through means of language? How can we begin to talk about language except via language itself and by so doing prove the impossibility of escaping it: as Hillis Miller suggests 'language cannot think itself or its own laws, just as a man cannot lift himself by his own bootstraps'.[9] Accordingly, for de Man the reintroduction of a metaphysical vocabulary into a deconstructive reading 'is not itself intentional but the result of a linguistic structure'.[10]

One of the key texts of Western culture, St John's Gospel, opens with the pronouncement, 'In the beginning was the Word, and the Word was with God' (John 1: 1). The Greek manuscript here states 'logos' and so could be translated as 'word' but also 'meaning' or 'sense': 'In the beginning was Meaning, and Meaning was with God'. Such a translation is suggestive of the ways in which Western thought is governed by an idea of stable or essential meaning, which is ultimately fixed by a 'transcendental signifier' (a signifier which escapes the play of meaning and against which all meaning is measured) such as God. For example, when we read literature or film or art, perhaps the most obvious thing we desire is to 'know' what the text means. In traditional literary criticism this desire to know (another way of saying 'logocentrism') has been associated with referring to the author as a transcendental signifier. A certain event happened in the author's life, therefore the text is about that event. The author said in an interview, or in his/her diaries, that the text is about his/her childhood therefore the text is indeed about his/her childhood. Here, the word 'author' demonstrates its etymology, being derived from the same root as 'authority'. Thus logocentrism, and this way of 'reading', is a theological activity because it presupposes and desires a single, fixed and authoritative centre. Such a concept also assumes that the question of who we are (subjectivity) is settled and stable: if the centre of authority is fixed then the question of who I am, defined in relation to that essential authority, is also fixed. Hence, logocentrism treats subjectivity or being as a matter of essential and stable meanings. In other words, logocentrism is a form of ontology (the science of being) and Western thought is a system of onto-theology (thinking the question of who we are in terms of an essential and fixed authoritative centre).

An example of how it is impossible to escape logocentric thinking may be required. The postcolonial critic Homi K. Bhabha offers a deconstruction of racial difference (see Homi K. Bhabha, 'Of mimicry and man', in this volume pp. 414–21).[11] Bhabha argues that racist or colonial discourse in the West is predicated upon a binary opposition between racial identities: West/East, white/black, coloniser/colonised, with the first term in each coupling privileged over the other. It is not difficult to demonstrate this binary logic at work in something like British colonial discourse or the political inequalities it gives rise to. In this way having reversed the binary (exposed its operation and demon-strated its non-validity) Bhabha sets out to displace it. In an unfortunate turn of phrase Bhabha proposes that the binary logic of racial difference can be dis-placed into a 'third space'. This is awkward since it seems to suggest that this 'space' is easily identified and stable, or, the mean point between the two terms of the binary. It also carries the dubious connotations of the political expediency of the so-called 'third way' – definitely not deconstruction! However, this third space is described by Bhabha as a moment of hybridity. The maintenance of colonial power depends upon continuing the illusion of binary difference while denying (or disavowing) the possibility of hybridity. A hybrid racial identity is one which breaks down the binary logic of separate ethnic conditions, mixing them up within the one individual, and 'contaminating' any easy notion of ethnic purity. For example, the children of those immigrants from the former colonies of the British Empire who came to Britain in the 1940s have a hybrid identity. They have both an English identity (being born and living in England) and through their parentage another ethnic identity (African, Caribbean, Indian, Pakistani and so on). At the same time they are neither purely English (in the way this term has been traditionally understood within a binary or racist logic) because they retain part of another ethnic or national identity (for example, they might be bilingual, or speak mainly in a language other than English). Nor are they purely, say, Indian because they were born and live in Britain. They are neither English nor not English, neither Indian nor not Indian. Their identity is hybrid (new, mixed, different, decentred, deconstructed) denoted by a neologism like Anglo-Indian, Afro-Caribbean and so on. In the 'melting pot' of North America where the make-up of the population has been so heavily influenced by immigration, this sense of hybridity is profound after generations of inter racial parentage. The golfer Tiger Woods rejects the label 'black', describing himself as 'cablinasian' (referring to a mixture of caucasian, black, native America (Indian) and Asian).

Bhabha's term, 'hybridity', is helpful because it shows the ways in which logocentrism works by maintaining a fiction of purity around its privileged terms. In presupposing the innate superiority of one term over another (man/woman, white/black) it is necessary to assume that one term is sealed against contamination by the other. In an essay entitled 'Racism's last word' Derrida argues that the practice of apartheid (racial segregation) in South Africa before 1994 was the ultimate logic of Western logocentrism.[12] 'Apartheid' literally means 'segregation', and logocentrism works by constructing false borders between concepts and assuming the rigorous purity of terms. Deconstruction is hybridity because it seeks to undo this logic of 'outside' and 'inside', showing the ways in which terms within a binary opposition are not independent of one another but rely on each other through mutual contamination.

However, if there is no end to the task of deconstruction we cannot be satisfied with declaring hybridity as the perfect state of being. On the contrary, we might well ask when does hybridity stop being hybridity and start to become colonial appropriation? This must be true, since by the logic of deconstruction there can be no simple or pure notion of hybridity either. For example, a hybrid identity might involve wearing a hajib (an Islamic headscarf) and drinking coke-a-cola, or wearing denim trousers. At what point does drinking coke or wearing denims constitute hybridity rather than colonial appropriation of one culture (Western) by another (Islamic)? In fact, hybridity is impossible. While aspiring to the condition of hybridity (a deconstructed racial identity) any identity, because it must be grounded in the logocentric orders of lived reality, will inevitably fall short of that condition and be caught up, or drawn back into, a logocentric and colonial logic. Once a hybrid identity has been established (American-Italian say) there is nothing to stop those characterised by that identity turning this hybridity into yet another privileged term within a binary logic. For example, American-Italians, defined in terms of a racial purity, might think of themselves as superior to the American-Irish or the American-Jews and so on. This does not mean that we should give up deconstructing racial identity. Rather it suggests that there can be no limit to this task because there is no limit to the recuperative effects of metaphysics.

This is not the end of the story. An understanding of what it might mean to deconstruct difference will allow us to suggest that hybridity is not an aberrant form of racial identity but the general condition of all identity. Binary oppositions rely on a fixed notion of difference: man is different from woman, white different from black and so forth. To take a trivial example, a binary logic, implicitly if not explicitly, recognises that tall people depend upon short people for their identity (tall people only being tall relative to – or different from short people). So, a system of binary oppositions depends upon a certain understanding of difference, even if it does not allow for the full play of the consequences of difference. To appreciate what it would mean to deconstruct the idea of difference upon which binary logic depends, let us read Derrida's early essay 'Différance'.[13] *Différance* is deconstructed difference (see Robert Young, 'The same difference' in this volume, pp. 283–91).

First, Derrida notes that, 'différance is literally neither a word nor a concept' ('Différance', p. 3). It is neither a word nor a concept in the traditional sense of these terms, as denoting a clear system of reference between a set signifier and a knowable signified. There is no phonetic difference in French between Derrida's *différance* with an 'a' and *différence* meaning difference, as in the phrase 'vive la différence'. The difference therefore between *différance* and *différence* is marked but not pronounced (written but not spoken). The difference is purely one of writing: it is legible or readable but cannot be spoken. As such Derrida's wordplay gets to the crux of the deconstruction of difference, the 'a' here remains silent, a secret 'a'. Therefore *différance* resists both the sensible (it cannot be heard) and the intelligible (it is a secret) and so resists 'one of the founding oppositions of philosophy, between the sensible and the intelligible' (p. 5). This founding binary in philosophy is one of the reasons why it was suggested earlier that speech (an empirical and verifiable act) has been privileged over writing (an action cut off from its author and which cannot easily be traced back to its source and origin). Accordingly, the 'a' in *différance* cannot become present or said to have Being. The moment we think it is there, when we say '*différance*', we cannot actually be sure that it is there because it is undecidable whether we have used the word *différance* or the French for 'difference'.

In Saussure's theory of the sign difference is the relation whereby the identity of each sign is produced.[14] Saussure states that there is no necessary link between the signified and the signifier and that the signifier is only connected to the signified in an arbitrary and conventional way. What stops Saussure's understanding of the sign system from collapsing is the value of difference, whereby the signifier 'dog' only refers to the signified 'dog' because it does not refer to the signifieds 'cat', 'house', 'money', 'love', 'Glasgow', 'moral philosophy' and so on. That is to say the relation between signs for Saussure is differential (constituted by difference). However, *différance* for Derrida is the structure which makes difference itself possible. He says *différance* 'makes possible the presentation of the being-present' (p. 6) although it is never presented a such. *Différance* produces appearance as it disappears and appears in its disappearance. If identity (the 'being-present' of whiteness, masculinity, tallness) is constructed through difference (to blackness, femininity, shortness) then *différance* is what makes possible the presentation of this system of difference. *Différance* produces the presentation of difference, but that presentation is not itself *différance*. Think once more about the impossibility of a deconstruction, just as we aspire to the condition of a deconstructed difference (*différance*) we fail to achieve it because the moment we fix the terms of this difference we are caught up once more in metaphysics and drawn back into a logocentric logic. Derrida's understanding of *différance* in this essay can be read as a polemic against Lacan's psychoanalytic approach to difference, which assigns the principle of determinability (and so transcendentality) to lack. Paraphrasing and inverting Lacan, Derrida calls absence 'a hole with indeterminable borders' (p. 6). For Lacan difference is defined in relation to the male and female sexual organs and so, although Lacan denies it, his idea of difference must depend upon the visual presence or absence ('lack' to use Lacan's term) of a penis. Hence, difference for Lacan is fixed by the value of presence and 'presence' and 'absence' becomes a founding binary opposition of Lacanian psychoanalysis, in which the female figure of lack is subordinate to the privileged male position of presence. It cannot be otherwise since for Lacan absence has 'determinable', and so fixed, borders. However, for Derrida *différance* makes being present while not being present itself and so its relation to the process by which being is made present is at best strategic and it is '[enmeshed] in a chain that in truth it never will have governed' (p. 7). It is strategic in the sense that it is only provisional and so can be changed.

Différance (as a word) is a play on the French verb *différer* meaning both 'to defer' and 'to differ'. *Différance* then involves an action of time (deferral) and action of spacing (differing) and is what Derrida calls 'the becoming-time of space and the becoming-space of time' (p. 8). In philosophy time is most often privileged as the transcendental horizon of being, that is, the question of human existence should be thought through in relation to the problem of time, as the fixed concept against which human activity ought to be measured. So *différance* then, within its very etymology, undoes the fundamental philosophical binary between time and space. This is particularly important since throughout the history of philosophy and literature time and space have been gendered as masculine and feminine traits (think of Cixous' binary between masculine 'step' – forward motion, linear temporality – and feminine 'ground' or space).

The first consequence of this is that, *contra* Saussure, in semiological difference (in language there are only differences without positive terms) the signified concept is never present in and of itself but is inscribed in a system within which it refers to other concepts by means of the systematic play of differences. For Saussure, the relation between signifiers is differential but the relation between signified and signifier, although arbitrary and conventional, is stable. However, for Derrida the signified concept 'tree' only exists, *as a concept*, in relation to other concepts expressed by signifiers. This does not mean that trees do not exist but that the idea of a tree (to which sycamores, oaks, poplars, the tree of knowledge, etc., actual and imagined trees, are all related) only makes sense by its differential relation to other concepts. For Saussure, the concept is fixed as the signified and has priority over its arbitrary and conventional mode of expression as a signifier; for Derrida, the concept is only meaningful through its expression as a signifier, and because the signifier is arbitrary and conventional the concept itself is unstable. *Différance* is not the difference between signifiers but is the system of play itself. Thus, *différance* is not a concept as such 'but rather the possibility of conceptuality, of a conceptual process and system in general' (p. 11). *Différance*, as the system that puts difference into play, is the means by which concepts are produced and so the means by which thinking can take place. This means, according to Derrida, that 'différance is the non-full, non-simple, structured and differentiating origin of differences. Thus, the name "origin" no longer suits' (p. 11).

Différance is the source of all difference, but it is not an origin in the traditional theological sense because it is not fixed (it is never entirely knowable or identifiable as a single point of authority because the moment we think we have it pinned down it is no longer *différance* but its logocentric inscription). Thus we cannot speak of it as an 'origin' in the traditional sense of that term: it can never be reached but is instead constantly deferred, always just out of reach. In this way *différance* both structures language (or any other system of difference) and makes the idea of structure impossible because structures depend upon a fixed point of origin. Following this Derrida goes on to say that *différance* can be designated as 'the movement according to which language, or any code, any system of referral in general, is constituted "historically" as a weave of differences' (p. 12). It is historical because of its deconstruction of the concept of time, but note that Derrida places 'historically' within scare-quotes here – we are no longer talking about History as it has been metaphysically understood. Differences are historic and if History as a practice and discipline were not synonymous with the repression of difference (Histories rely on single, authoritative and knowable origins) we might say that only differences can be historic. So *différance* is both structural and historic and no more historical than it is structural.

The point of such a description would be to allow us to say that, while the history of Western metaphysics is a history of 'an active indifference to difference' (p. 17), metaphysics as *a system of conceptuality* exists through *différance*. This is obviously true if *différance* is the means by which all systems and all concepts come into being. Thus *différance* is in fact not that which is different (it produces metaphysics, the very effacement of difference) but is that which is the same, even if this 'sameness' is not identical. The deconstruction of binary oppositions involves not an erasure of these oppositions but a consideration of what it is that makes each term of the opposition appear as the differed and deferred *différance* of the other (the same but different). Since only a displacement of a binary opposition can be said actually to undo that binary, then a deconstruction of binaries involves not a dissolution of binaries but a rigorous consideration of the system of thought which makes binary logic possible. This system is, of course, *différance*. So, when we say we are deconstructing a binary opposition what we mean is we are attempting to think through the complexities of this thing called *différance*.

This leads us to the most obscure aspect of *différance*. *Différance* is the economic action of delay in which the element of the same aims to come back to the deferred pleasure of presence, and it is the impossible relation to a presence which can never be. If *différance* makes all conceptual systems possible then it must also make metaphysics or logocentrism possible as well. Therefore, *différance* is responsible for the recuperative action of metaphysics, which manages to reclaim all otherness (difference) back into the logocentric schema. Hence, while *différance* makes all difference possible it also is responsible for reclaiming all difference back into the self-same of metaphysics. This recuperation always happens just when we think we have pinned down *différance* . In fact it is this desire to pin down which causes the recuperation of difference back into logocentrism. This is a desire for what we earlier termed 'presence' (the knowable, the sensible, the single-simple origin). *Différance* makes presence impossible (it produces the systematic play of differences) while instigating the desire for presence (to know *différance*) as a continually delayed desire because *différance* can never be 'pinned down' or known as such. Thus *différance* initiates logocentrism and makes it impossible. *Différance* is both the economical transfer and the expenditure without reserve which interrupts every economy. *Différance* makes every system possible and, simultaneously, impossible. An economy is merely a system of exchange based on differential relations. *Différance* at once enables those relations and interrupts any simple idea of them as stable. This is what Derrida calls elsewhere the logic of supplementarity: *différance* is the system of systematicity, the general economy of economy, the difference of difference.

A brief explanation of supplementarity is required (see also Richard Beardsworth 'Thinking technicity' in this volume, pp. 235–43). Consider the following universal system:

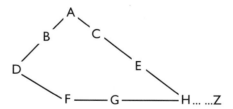

Imagine a system in which all the systems of the world (A to Z) are related. In order for this system to be a system (for it to be systematic) it must be closed. A to Z must be related in clear and predictable ways in order for their relation to be systematic and this means that there must be a discernible limit to the action of the system. Therefore, the system must be closed. So, let us call this system of systems the universal system and its aim is to relate all known systems to one another. There are two consequences from this description. First, if there is indeed a limit to the action of the system, something must exist outside the system. Whenever we draw a limit we are defining what is inside the limit by presupposing an outside of the limit. Thus, if there is something outside the limit of the universal system (and it must have a limit in order to be a system) then the system cannot be 'universal' because it leaves 'something' unaccounted for. Secondly, what is it that the universal system does not account for? Which system lies outside the closed field of systematic relations described by the 'universal system'? The answer is the universal system itself. The universal system cannot account for itself as a system. To do so would be to recognise the impossibility of maintaining the limit to the universal system and so to admit that it is neither systematic nor universal. In this way the universal system, far from regulating all systems, would have to admit that no system can be truly systematic because it is not possible to maintain the rigorous purity of a limit. The universal system demonstrates the impossibility of the system *per se*, and so undoes the logic of a 'properly' maintained inside and outside.

This deconstruction of an 'inside-outside' polarity is called 'supplementarity'. The 'supplement' is that which escapes the system and at the same time installs itself within the system to demonstrate the impossibility of the system. For example, consider the idea of metaphor. All words are metaphors because all words say that one thing (say, the concept 'tree' to use a favourite example) is like another (the sound-image 'tree' or *arbre* or whatever language you happen to be speaking). The concept 'metaphor' then can account for all words as metaphors and so for the universal phenomenon of metaphor. However, by the logic of supplementarity there is one metaphor which the idea of metaphor cannot account for and that is the idea of metaphor itself. The word 'metaphor' is a metaphor (a denotation through comparison) for the idea of denotation through comparison. Hence, the metaphor of 'metaphor' refuses a limit to the field of metaphor. The consequence of this is that metaphor is not a discrete unit of rhetoric but the general condition of language and thus of thought itself because thinking only ever takes place within language. If all thought is metaphorical (and there is no fixed limit to the field of metaphor) then there is no anchor of stable origin for any concept (beauty, fate, war, drugs, etc.) but merely a chain of metaphors constantly referring to other metaphors. What we think of as a set idea, say 'God', is not a stable concept but a metaphor (a denotation through comparison for all that the name of God represents – see John D. Caputo, 'God is not *différance*', in this volume, pp. 458–63) which only has meaning by reference to other metaphors (truth, teleology, death and so on). There is no limit to this field of reference, and language becomes not a system of metaphorical illustration in comparison to a stable 'reality' but an unbounded set of metaphors referring only to one another. And so the very idea of metaphor becomes problematic: we cannot say that 'the lion is the king of the jungle' is a metaphor (in the traditional way we have understood this term) because the idea of a 'lion' is itself metaphorical. This does not mean that lions do not exist, it would be difficult to reason with one on such grounds, but that the idea of metaphor is itself metaphorical and so demonstrates the difficulty of closing off our understanding of the effects of metaphor in thought and language. The supplement undoes bounded (i.e. all) systems just as it makes those systems possible.

Différance is this action of supplementarity. It is the condition of possibility of all systems and simultaneously makes all systems impossible, *as systems*. If supplementarity undoes the opposition between inside and outside then, given that this is a necessary if not sufficient condition of a deconstruction, we might say that supplementarity is deconstruction. Similarly, we can say that *différance* is deconstruction. All of these terms (hybridity would be another) are all related in a chain of non-identical substitutions in which any one word can substitute for any other (différance = supplementarity = deconstruction = hybridity = ...) without being equal to or reducible to that term. In this way no term in the chain should have greater importance than any other term and it is by historical (or perhaps metaphysical) accident that the term 'deconstruction' has imposed itself within this speculative discourse (this chain of substitutions was the basis for the wager with which this introduction began).

To conclude this lengthy, but necessary, detour around the topic of *différance*, let us note that *différance* is not a present thing. As a system of governance it does not and cannot govern any system but instead is that which makes any system impossible, as much as we all desire systems. Therefore, while ontological difference (the difference between the idea of Being and actual ('human') beings or the difference between 'presence' and 'the present') is put in play by *différance* this difference is one of the most difficult things to think because there is no essence of *différance*. It is not fixed but constantly defers the moment of presence and its final knowability. Ontological difference (the fundamental question of philosophy) remains part of the history of *différance* and history as *différance*. Therefore the word *différance* is a metaphysical name we give in our language for an operational operation which 'dislocates itself in a chain of differing and differing substitutions'. *Différance* is not a word, the word *différance* is not adequate to this system of play in which the unnameable makes possible certain nominal effects called 'names' in a chain of substitutions in which its own name is, as Derrida says, inscribed like 'a false exit' ('*Différance*' p. 27), both a name and not a name, both the description of the system and unable to adequately describe the system.

There is no easy escape from metaphysical thinking. Deconstruction is not about the facile denunciation of 'Western thought' or 'metaphysics' (if such things actually exist and are not themselves metaphors for the effects produced in the name of 'metaphysics' or whatever you wish to call the thing). Deconstruction questions all the assumptions of 'the Western tradition' from the ground up, but it is clearly part of that tradition. Let us not fall prey to the easy temptation to equate deconstruction with destruction or nihilism or 'relentless negativity', as so many hurried professors have done before us. Let us not give such 'thinkers' the excuse to say so by blithely calling for the end to all binary oppositions or any other such slogans, the existence of which merely demonstrates the recuperative power of the logos. Rather, deconstruction shows us the limits of our world only to turn them inside out so that we might not be duped by their claims to constitute the world. This is a truly affirmative gesture, not a destructive one.

To return to the example of Bhabha's term 'hybridity', it is the means by which 'newness enters the world' (to quote Salman Rushdie) and identities such as Anglo-Indian or Irish-American are created. However, a pure hybridity is impossible to sustain and can quickly collapse into yet another form of cultural imperialism. This is the action of escape from, and recuperation by, logocentrism that we have already identified. However, if we push our knowledge of *différance* a little, might we say hybridity (as a non-identical substitution for *différance*) is that which makes all identity possible just as it undoes the possibility of a pure identity. The idea of identity presupposes a strict sense of inside and outside: I am Scottish and these are the borders of my nation, language, religion, culture, etc. However, to know that I am a Scotsman (as opposed to just a man) then I automatically presuppose, as part of being Scottish, that there is something outside of those borders, for example Englishness. The moment I recognise the existence of this boundary its disintegration begins, because my Scottishness (that which is on the inside of the boundary and whose purity I wish to maintain) must depend upon the Englishness against which I have set my boundary and so define myself as Scottish. If Englishness is other to my Scottishness then it must already speak in advance of me, destabilising the purity of my Scottishness and demonstrating the permeability of the boundary I wish to remain fixed. An elementary example might be the very word 'Scotland' which is not a Scottish word at all (it is neither Gaelic nor so-called 'Scots' dialect) but the English language word for 'the land of the Scots' (Old English *Scottas*). Thus, from the very beginning my Scottish identity demonstrates the influence of another culture and so its own impurity.

Even the most 'rigorously pure' identity cannot help but be hybrid because all identity depends upon the construction of limits which must, by their nature, be permeable. Thus, any identity is always already haunted by the other it seeks to exclude. Anglo-Indian is only a dramatically visible example of the way in which one identity installs itself in another through a logic of neither/nor, but all identity works this way. Hybridity produces identity, 'Anglo-Indian', and makes that identity impossible, 'neither English nor Indian' because hybridity is the general condition of all identity. It is the identity of identity, the supplementary logic which predicates the system of identity and undoes identity's own sense of itself as a system of inside and outside. It would be possible to equate the Englishness of the word 'Scotland' with a colonial recuperation but this would merely demonstrate the difficulties of escaping the logos. Hybridity, like *différance*, produces appearance as it disappears and appears in its disappearance. In fact, hybridity is impossible but loses nothing in admitting that it is.

DECONSTRUCTION EMBRACES THE MARGINS

Having said all that we have about the reversal of binary oppositions it should come as no surprise that deconstruction is interested in the terms that constitute these binaries. The next two sections in this introduction deal with the two halves of the binary: first the 'dominated' or 'subservient' term. Another way to describe this term might be as the 'excluded' or 'marginal' term. In a binary opposition like Man-Woman, 'woman' is the excluded term as we saw in Cixous' description of the history of Western discourse as a tradition of patriarchy. The situation she describes is always:

$$\frac{\text{Man}}{\text{Woman}}$$

Man over Woman, man as more important than woman, man at the centre of discourse, woman at the margins. Or, in the example of Orientalism the West likes to think of itself as the 'centre' of the world (Greenwich is the zero meridian for a reason!) while the East is on the margins ('the Far East') of 'the known world'. These geographical metaphors (entirely relative to where you are standing) spill over into cultural and political discourses as well. In every binary opposition one of the terms will be figured as central to discourse, and one marginal; one will be 'included' within the concerns of discourse, one 'excluded' from them.

Deconstruction is interested in this so-called marginal term. Given that this exclusion does not reflect lived reality but is an operation of power enacted on behalf of certain politically constituted groups, then the recuperation of the margins is a necessary step in demonstrating the injustices which are disguised by the work of logocentrism. An elementary example in the study of literature might be a reading of Charlotte Bronte's *Jane Eyre* which took account of the character Bertha (the first Mrs Rochester). Ostensibly *Jane Eyre* is a love story, which tells of the encounter and eventual marriage of a governess (Jane) and her aristocratic employer (Mr Rochester). A superficial political reading of this text might make 'subversive' claims for the novel as a feminist text because Jane does not marry Rochester until she is professionally and financially independent of him. Thus the novel could be said to be about the emancipation of women from the subservient roles allotted to them by nineteenth-century patriarchy. This analysis is only true up to a point because such a reading would only be interested in what lies at the centre of the novel. The character of Bertha Mason lies at the margins of the text, literally locked away in the attic and almost forgotten, a female character whose fate would not square with this preliminary reading. Rochester is married to Bertha a Creole woman from the West Indies and this is a legal impediment to Rochester and Jane's marriage (and ultimately the novel's resolution). Bertha is pathologised as mad and locked away in the attic. She escapes on occasions, once attempting to set fire to Rochester's bed while he is still in it. The novel ends when Bertha succeeds in burning the entire house down, killing herself in the process and so clearing the way for Jane and Rochester (blinded and crippled trying to save Bertha from the fire) to be wed.

The point of reading around the character of Bertha would not be merely to reverse the operation of exclusion: valorising Bertha over Jane, just as Jane has been frequently privileged over Bertha. Rather it would be to interrogate the ways in which this act of exclusion (which predominately operates around the question of race) structures the entire text, raises questions about the nineteenth-century novel in general, and problematises traditional readings of this novel and literature as a whole. In fact, to quote Paul de Man's last reported words, the stakes are enormous.[15] Jane, as narrator, describes Rochester's smile 'such as a sultan might, in a blissful and fond moment, bestow on a slave his gold and gems had enriched'. This orientalist imagery of master and slave (in contrast to the master–employee relation of Rochester's patriarchy) leads to an extended racial discourse:

> 'I would not exchange this one little English girl for the Grand Turk's whole seraglio–gazelle-eyes, houri forms, and all!'
>
> The Eastern allusion bit me again. 'I'll not stand you not an inch in the stead of a seraglio,' I said; 'so don't consider me an equivalent for one. If you fancy for anything in that line, away with you, sir, to bazaars of Stamboul, without delay, and lay out in extensive slave-purchases some of the spare cash you seem at a loss to spend satisfactorily here.'
>
> 'And what will you do, Janet, while I am bargaining for so many tons of flesh and such an assortment of black eyes?'
>
> 'I'll be preparing myself to go out as a missionary to preach liberty to them that are enslaved – your harem inmates amongst the rest. I'll get admitted there, and I'll stir up mutiny; and you, three-tailed bashaw as you are, sir, shall in a trice find yourself fettered amongst our hands: nor will I, for one, consent to cut your bonds till you have signed a charter, the most liberal that despot ever conferred.[16]

It is beyond the scope of this short introduction to do justice to the full implications of this passage, but it will be clear from even the most cursory acquaintance with these paragraphs that the novel works by relating sexuality, desire and sexual difference to issues of race and economics. Rochester is married to Bertha and seems to have made his fortune on the back of the slave trade in the West Indies, but Jane eventually gains her economic independence by inheriting a legacy also made through Caribbean slavery. At one point in the novel Jane almost leaves England to marry a missionary in India.

The question of slavery may appear marginal to the text but in fact it is the question which both structures and undoes the entire work. Bertha never speaks for herself, we are never told where Rochester's fortune or Jane's inheritance comes from, but as we can see from the above passage the whole text wraps itself around the equation of sex and gender with race and economics. Jane refuses to be 'bought' by Rochester's wealth or to be 'imprisoned' as his servant, but her fortune and subsequent independence derives from colonialism in the West Indies, while Bertha is literally incarcerated in the attic of a house built on money made through slavery. These are the structuring principles around which the text operates even as the novel attempts to repress them, encouraging the reader to be complicit in the novel as love story. Jane's description of Bertha is particularly revealing, even as it attempts to efface Bertha:

> In the deep shade, at the farther end of the room, a figure ran backwards and forwards. What it was, whether beast or human being, one could not at first sight tell: it grovelled, seemingly, on all fours; it snatched and growled like some strange wild animal: but it was covered with clothing, and a quantity of dark, grizzled hair, wild as a mane, hid its head and face. (p. 321)

This is the first time Jane sees Bertha, it comes by way of an explanation after Rochester has revealed her existence and so his own attempted bigamy. Rochester contrasts Bertha with Jane 'look at the difference! Compare these clear eyes with the red balls yonder – this face with that mask – this form with that bulk' (p. 322). The text here offers us a set of binaries (man–woman, master–slave, Jane–Bertha) around which we should understand the necessary exclusion of Bertha as mad and undesirable. However, it is this last opposition (Jane–Bertha) which exemplifies best what we know about the way *différance* works and which undoes the binary logic of Rochester's patriarchy. The attempted contrast between Jane and Bertha is explicit: 'look at the difference!' However, this comparison fails in its intention to place Jane and Bertha in separate categories (white–black, sane–insane, civilised–animal) rather it calls the reader's attention to the similarities between Jane and Bertha, namely that they are both women. Jane will be a substitute for Bertha, both are imprisoned, both belong to Rochester. Jane is not Bertha but she has the potential to be Bertha; what this contrast shows is not difference but the ways in which the two women are identical.

Difference is recuperated into the self-same and it is our appreciation of this which begins to undo the other false binaries on which the novel depends. All of the oppositions which support Rochester's position (race, sanity, civilisation) collapse because they prove impossible to maintain in the light of our knowledge that the forced opposition between Jane and Bertha disguises a wider schema of political interests. The opposition white–black is constructed, maintained and naturalised for the same reasons – and as part of the same system – as the binary oppositions of gender and sexuality put in operation here. Western colonialism, patriarchy and capitalism all share in and benefit from the maintenance of a logocentric discourse. This discourse constructs itself around the equation of gender and race as marginalised terms, just as it is the exclusion of those terms which allows us to see how that wider logocentric schema works and so unpick its injustices. For example, after reading *Jane Eyre* in this way, what can be said about similar collusions between patriarchal, orientalist and capitalist discourses in the nineteenth-century novel? Examples for study might include Emma's comparison of women to slaves in Jane Austen's novel, or, the dark-skinned Heathcliff in *Wuthering Heights*. The question could then be widened (deconstruction would not acknowledge any legitimate limit to the scope of this question) to ask, in what ways do these discourses intersect in the non-conceptual order of world-trade and colonialism in the nineteenth-century and beyond? If we pushed the question still further we could ask, why has the institution of literary criticism in the Western academy been so slow to read this and other canonical texts in this way? What does this tell us about the academy, the English literary tradition and 'Englishness' in general? The stakes are enormous.

In this reading of Charlotte Bronte's novel, what seems unimportant – or marginal – to the narrative, is in fact the decisive indices in which it is possible to discern the true condition of the text and the textual system of the nineteenth-century novel in general. The point here is not that I have made the text mean whatever I want it to mean, picking on an obscure detail to build a baroque fantasy. Rather the text itself has displaced the relation between its marginal and privileged terms and turned those terms, set in play by the text, back against the textual system which puts them in operation. As a reader I have not set out to demonstrate my own cleverness or own moral superiority to the text (as the earlier materialist reading of the nineteenth-century novel does). Instead, I have been sensitive to the singularity of Bronte's text (treating it in the first instance as unique and particular, rather than paradigmatic of the general). I have read the text in close detail – we have the quotation and exemplification to prove the point. And in so doing I have brought out what was already in the text by listening to what the text imposed upon me as a reader. The text can be read in this way because the text presents itself to be read in this way. However, my reading is not the only or best possible deconstruction of this text. My deconstruction can only happen once because it is unique to the singular moment of affirmation, which is the event of my reading. What I have done is to produce a specific reading by imbricating myself within the text. This is my reading, it is unique to me and I leave a trace of myself in the text, in so far as my reading of the novel becomes my understanding of the novel and so represents a reading of the text (i.e. for me this reading is the text). Others can and will read the novel differently.

Further, to this, my reading has opened up the false limit between the text and the textual system which produces it, and my reading of the text has given me access to that textual system. My movement away from *Jane Eyre* into a consideration of the English literary tradition or the university curriculum is not an illegitimate transformation from the specific to the general (as we had in

the materialist method 'all nineteenth-century novels are expressions of bourgeois sensibility etc.') but a movement along a singular path of reading which
has taken us from the textual disruption of *Jane Eyre* to a displacement of the
logocentric system which put the text of *Jane Eyre* into play. The novel depends
upon the same binary assumptions about race and gender put in operation by
the Western culture from which it emerges. However, the text demonstrates the
provisional and unstable nature of these assumptions and so places their
certainty in crisis. The binary assumptions then begin to unravel not only in
the text itself but this unravelling overspills into the cultural system which put
them into operation. Thus, the text is doing the work of deconstruction by itself
– deconstruction is a situation, it is what happens – and my singular path of
reading merely follows this self-deconstruction down one particular route
among many possible routes.

In this way, we might say the text deconstructs itself (for a necessary
corrective to this see Rodolphe Gasché, 'Deconstruction as criticism', in this
volume, pp. 126–33). In a certain sense of course the text is not deconstructing
itself: it is the pressure of my reading which lays bare the operation of the text.
But in an other sense, I am only describing what is always already present in the
text whether a reader or author is conscious of it or not. De Man explains:

> I assume, as a working hypothesis (as a working hypothesis, because I
> know better than that), that the text *knows* in an absolute way what it's
> doing. I know this is not the case, but it is a necessary working hypothesis
> that Rousseau knows at any time what he is doing and as such there is no
> need to deconstruct Rousseau. In a complicated way, I would hold to the
> statement that 'the text deconstructs itself, is self-deconstructive' rather
> than being deconstructed by a philosophical intervention from outside of
> the text ... I do need [Rousseau] very badly because I never had an idea of
> my own, it was always through a text, through the critical examination of
> a text.[17]

So, my reading (or deconstruction) is nothing more than a matter of placing
myself within the operation of the text and being part of that operation (the
text's own self-deconstruction) for the singular duration of my reading. As
de Man describes his reading of Nietzsche in *Allegories of Reading*, 'the text
also establishes that deconstruction is not something we can decide to do or
not to do at will. It is co-extensive with any use of language, and this use is
compulsive, or ... imperative' (p. 125). I am not criticising or attacking
Charlotte Bronte for being racist, far from it. I am suggesting the ways in
which her text gives us access to the racist assumptions of Western culture and
enables the reader to begin to unpick the network of power relations and
injustices which are upheld by the conceptual and non-conceptual orders
which depend upon these assumptions.

If we still wish to look for something like a 'deconstructive method' I think
we will find it here. In the margins of a text can be found the most decisive

indices of what is at stake in that text, our example here suggesting that what is at issue in *Jane Eyre* is not a love story or even simply the question of the emancipation of women but the entire Western project of capitalism, colonialism and patriarchy. This reading gesture is one frequently repeated in deconstruction although it would not necessarily define a reading as a deconstruction. However, the situation described in this reading of *Jane Eyre* (the identification of a set of terms put in play by a textual system, being returned against that system to make the system tremble in the recognition of its own fragility) is a necessary but not sufficient condition of any deconstruction. Such a strategy (and it is strategic in the full sense of that word, as it is used in the title of this chapter to suggest the provisionality of necessary but not sufficient conditions for any deconstruction) would be one step along what I have called the singular path of a moment of reading. This moment can be called deconstructive. However, to demonstrate the ways in which this reading is not methodological but specific and 'situational', we might think of Jean Rhys' novel *Wide Sargasso Sea* which re-writes Jane Eyre from Bertha's point of view. It would not be unreasonable to call Rhys' novel a deconstruction of *Jane Eyre*, even though Rhys may never have heard of the word. Like the reading I offered of Bronte's novel, Rhys' narrative leaves a trace in the text it reads. It follows one particular path of reading (after all we could re-write *Jane Eyre* from the servants' point of view or from the point of view of the newly blinded Rochester) to transform the object it analyses by highlighting what is at stake in the ethical and political repressions of Bronte's novel. Deconstruction is always already in *Jane Eyre*, a deconstruction of Jane Eyre by Jean Rhys already precedes my reading, my deconstruction is only a citation of these gestures.

Examples of this reading movement can be found throughout the history of deconstruction. One might think of a recent text by Derrida such as *Spectres of Marx*, in which he reads *The Communist Manifesto*, *Das Kapital* and *The German Ideology* in terms of the seemingly marginal consideration of ghosts. Showing that the structure of haunting is in fact central to Marx's consideration of the commodity, history, revolution, and to the continuing relevance of Marx's texts today (See Nicholas Royle 'The Phantom Review', in this volume, pp. 178–89). Alternatively, one might look at Derrida's bravura reading of Heidegger in his early essay '*Ouisa* and *Gramme*: Note on a note from *Being and Time*', which examines one footnote in Heidegger's monumental text *Being and Time*, in order to demonstrate how the implications of the contradictions in this footnote make Heidegger's entire text tremble and with it Western philosophy's traditional understanding of temporality.[18] In this volume Nicholas Royle offers a powerful argument about the scientific claims of psychoanalysis based on a reading of Freud's treatment of the seemingly marginal concern of telepathy. Avital Ronell reads *Madame Bovary* through the almost invisible question of drugs, while Willy Maley analyses 'Marxism' in terms of its excluded author Engels.

In *Memoirs for Paul de Man*, Derrida provides a discussion of this tenacious pursuit of the margin, as an important strategy for deconstruction. He begins by quoting de Man who, in a discussion of Hegel, describes allegory (one of de Man's own non-identical substitutions for deconstruction) as being 'like the defective cornerstone of the entire system'.[19] This paradoxical phrase, 'defective cornerstone', seems to neatly describe the double action of the marginal term. Like a cornerstone it is something seemingly unimportant, pushed to the side or hidden from view. However, the cornerstone is in fact the most important stone, the one which is planted first and around which all the other stones are placed: it is the stone which supports the entire house. Yet, this is a 'defective' cornerstone, that is one which will cause the house to fall down. Its position is precarious and unstable, ready to fall at the slightest push. The reader would aid the work of the defective cornerstone by exerting leverage against the entirety of the architectonic system.

Derrida offers an extended commentary on this phrase of de Man's. After rejecting a seemingly irresistible but ultimately misleading metaphorical relation between deconstruction and the figures of architecture, he goes on to say:

> The very condition of a deconstruction may be at work, *within* the system to be deconstructed; it may already be located there, already at work, not at the centre but in an excentric [*sic* the pun here collapsing 'eccentric' with an 'ex-centre'] centre, in a corner whose eccentricity assures the solid concentration of the system, participating in the construction of what at the same time threatens to deconstruct. One might then be inclined to reach this conclusion: deconstruction is not an operation that supervenes *afterwards*, from the outside, one fine day; it is always already at work in the work; one must just know how to identify the right or wrong element, the right or wrong stone – the right one, of course, always proves to be, precisely, the wrong one. Since the disruptive force of deconstruction is *always already* contained within the architecture of the work, all one would finally have to do to be able to deconstruct, given this always already, is to do memory work [i.e. going over what the text has already done itself]. (Derrida, *Memoirs for Paul de Man*, p. 73)

Derrida neither accepts nor rejects a formulation based on these terms but leaves the question hanging, having flagged up the problem it leads to. He goes on to say by way of contrast (remember another important gesture of deconstruction is the impossible logic of the double-bind, yes and no, on the one hand/ on the other hand, neither-nor):

> If allegory [substitute here 'deconstruction' or 'marginality'] is 'the defective cornerstone of the entire system', it is also a figure for its most effective cornerstone. As a cornerstone, it supports it, however rickety it may be, and brings together at a single point all its forces and tensions. It does not do this from a central commanding point, like a *keystone*; but it also does it, laterally, in its corner. It represents the whole in a point and at every instant; it centres it, as it were, in a periphery, shapes it, stands for it. (pp. 73–4)

In other words, this defective cornerstone acts as a metonym for the entire system and so the whole schema is as 'defective' and unstable as it is. Thus we can offer two conclusions. First, that the deconstructive effects disseminated by the repression of the marginal term demonstrate that the entire system or text is deconstructive through and through. If deconstruction is interested in the instability of the margin it is not out of a perverse love of the marginal as such but because these 'defective cornerstones' demonstrate the unstable condition of the text in general. Secondly, the position of the margin follows the logic of the double-bind. It leads to deconstruction but only because it is responsible for the entire structuring principle of the text or system. Again, margins should not be valorised for their own sake: that would be just another reversal of binary logic. After all, what is marginal today might not be tomorrow – the margin of anything being entirely relative to where you stand – and so if the occupancy of the margins can change then there can be no end to the task of deconstruction.

DECONSTRUCTION IS HISTORY

Now, let us turn to the second component of the binary opposition, the privileged term. As suggested above, a textual system signifies by putting in play a set of terms around which the text is 'structured' ('structured' is placed in inverted commas here because a 'self-deconstructing' text can no longer retain the name of a structure as this term has been traditionally understood). One strategy for a deconstruction of a text might be to identify the privileged term(s) within this operation and demonstrate the genealogy of that term as a concept. In this way the term can be put to work against the textual system which wishes to privilege or limit its meaning. A few clarifications may be needed.

First, a genealogy is a kind of archaeology without limits. When I use the phrase 'conceptual order' I mean a system of terms or concepts, which are all produced in the same way and are all related to and dependent on one another (the word 'order' also suggests a hierarchy within that system). The metaphysical conceptual orders of Western culture, as we have seen, are produced by a system of logocentric thinking which at one and the same time establishes binary relations and the 'defective cornerstones' on which they are built, so ensuring their own deconstruction. The terms within this order are divided into binary oppositions with privileged and marginal terms. As we saw in the example of *Jane Eyre* the constellation of 'privileged' terms in Western culture are not arbitrary but set by the relations of power derived from the successful maintenance of a logocentric discourse: male, white, capital, West and so on. Despite pretensions to the contrary none of these terms are innocent or neutral (the same could equally be said of so-called 'marginal' terms). Rather, each of these terms has a history. That is to say that the privileged position such terms now occupy within Western discourse are the result of a long process of historical formation in which the meaning of terms may have changed or the value allotted to them may have changed. An important part of this process – and this is the essential action of metaphysics – is that the system covers the tracks of this historical formation, not allowing the concept to be read as historically constituted but presenting it as 'natural' or 'common sense'.

For example, throughout the history of European philosophy the 'subject' has been a privileged term: its corresponding binary opposite would be the 'object'. In contemporary critical theory we readily speak of the 'Freudian subject' or the 'Lacanian subject' or latterly the 'decentred subject' as if this term were a single, complete entity. However, the subject has a history and a specific context. For example, the idea (or concept) of the subject would become lost in translation if we were to attempt to translate from a 'Continental' philosophical idiom to an English philosophical vocabulary. There is no equivalent term in the English philosophical tradition, the idea of 'the self' is not an adequate translation. So, the concept of the subject is singular (it is not universal but specific to a certain context). However, it is also plural because it has a history. If we were to make a genealogy of its usage by working our way through the texts of Western philosophy we would see that the definition of what constitutes a subject has changed over time. Not only does the term mean different things in the French, German and Greek philosophical traditions but the limits of the subject have changed with the development of European philosophy. Descartes' Enlight-enment subject, (*cogito, ergo sum*, 'I think therefore I am') is not the same as the subject of Judeo-Christian theology which founds its 'I am' in its relation to God. Neither is Descartes' subject the same as Freud's which, as a result of the effects of the unconscious, 'is no longer master in its own house'. Previously, this idea of the subject has been class specific (its definition excluding the non-thinking masses), gender specific (women have not always been considered subjects) and racially inscribed (only the white European had subjectivity). Even today the concept of the subject is continuing to change. For example, if we think it is unethical to eat animals are we saying that an animal is also a subject? Since there is no necessary horizon which limits our thinking on this topic, the definition and redefinition of the subject is without limits. Similarly, there is no fixed point of origin for this concept, no pure idea of the subject in, say, Socrates from which all other definitions are merely embellishments. While Socrates may suppose an idea of the subject, the concept is not original to him and his definition although older than, say, Freud's is not the 'origin' of Freud's because it is not anymore essential than Freud's. This is what I mean by 'an archaeology without limits', a sense of historical accretion which does not depend upon a fixed point of origin against which 'development' can be measured.

You will recall that the powerful inertial set of inequalities which are predicated upon the conceptual orders of logocentrism depend upon the erasure of the readability of concepts as concepts. For patriarchy to succeed, for example, it is necessary that its exclusive definition of the subject should be thought of as natural rather than recognised as historically constituted, that is it should not be thought of as a concept at all. A deconstruction then might read this as patriarchy's philosophical pretension to non-philosophy (taking a philo-sophically determined term and presenting it as unproblematic common sense).

Part of the task of undoing the work of phallogocentrism here would be to reinscribe this so-called natural state back into the philosophical and meta-phorical conceptual order from which it came. In other words, not abandoning concepts or philosophy but making them do the work of their own deconstruc-tion. Given that it is différance which puts all concepts into play, this action will involve both a certain recuperation by the conceptual order and a leverage on the concept as the 'defective cornerstone' (every stone is a defective cornerstone) of that order.

A useful example provided by Derrida is that of 'Drugs'.[20] To understand drugs a history is required (see also Avital Ronell, 'Towards a narcoanalysis', in this volume, pp. 254–62). We need a political evaluation of the conceptual order which institutes the institutionalised definition of drugs. 'Drugs' are a concept – a word which signifies the intersection of a whole series of historically constituted philosophical and ethical discourses, all of which must be consid-ered as part of evaluating this term. To appreciate the idea of 'drugs' as a concept, a definition of its overdetermined network of discursive causes is required. This definition can not be a scientific one (for science itself cannot distinguish between heroin, aspirin and soap powder – to science they are all chemicals) but will be constituted by ethical and political considerations. Even to use the word 'drugs' in this sense and not actually the 'stuff' itself is to open yourself onto a performative and formalising context. The moment we use the term 'drugs' we enter into a discourse which is already established and which has created a certain meaning for the term 'drugs' (an ethical one) which we cannot help but be implicated in even if we wish to reject this use of the word. For example, both the position of 'natural freedom' ('it's my body and drugs occur naturally to relax or stimulate' or 'my drugs, say ecstasy, are illegal but you use legal drugs like alcohol or tobacco') and that of the 'preventativist', both start out from the same opposition of nature and institution and are therefore not radically exclusive: as Derrida says, 'naturalism is no more natural than conventionalism' ('Points', p. 229). The boundary between these two positions follows drugs' own logic of contamination and adulteration. The 'criminalised lifestyle' of the illegal drug user is not a private affair but is the inescapably political moment of a consumer transaction. The consumption of drugs is a social event and the buying and dealing of drugs is inscribed within the open market of a greater economy, so much so that drugs now account for 8 per cent of world trade. The production and distribution of drugs are inevitably organised by right-wing groups and by a form of capitalism, which is difficult to distinguish from recognised structures of capital. This ideological operation is masked by the paradoxical association of drug use and drug culture with an anti-establishment, often left-leaning outlook, while attempts to constrain that culture are a synonym for reactionary politics.

The political disavowal of the 'natural freedom' position places the user in the classic Liberal position of viewing the political and ideological as secondary or public adjuncts to the real, genuine and authentic private life. This apolitical stance is a strategy of depoliticization enrolled in the service of particular political interests. It denies the social consequence of drugs which is changing our very notion of the social space, namely AIDS (See Alexander Duttman, 'Recognising the virus', in this volume, pp. 311–20). Derrida calls Aids a 'world war' ('*Points*', p. 251). It affects our relation to desire and to the other: it thus challenges the integrity of the very idea of the body. The virus installs itself in every intersubjective relation changing fixed concepts of temporality, leaving the trace of the third party as a disruption of the social. The daily presence of AIDS then provides, what Derrida calls, 'a massive readability' (p. 251) of that trace of the third party as a 'destructuring structuration' (p. 251) of the social which the naturalistic-private discourse on drugs denies and must deny to retain its effect as a polemic.

'Drugs' and drug addiction emerge with Modernity as does the institution of Literature. The prohibition against the illegal use of narcotics is a prohibition against irresponsibility, against an activity which cuts the user off from social relations and from remembering. Writing, Derrida suggests, is exactly this drug which leads to irresponsibility: literature in particular has a suspended relation of reference to meaning and takes irresponsibility and forgetting as necessary conditions of its own activity. The drug user escapes into a simulacra of experience, an 'unreality'. The modern prohibition against drugs is not a legislation against pleasure but against a pleasure taken without reference to truth and to responsibility. Perhaps it is no accident that communities of drug users became visible in Britain in the 1980s when the State decreed that there was no such thing as society. It is a basic assumption of Western Modernity that there is some affinity between the experience of fiction and the use of drugs:

> Away! away! for I will fly to thee,
> Not charioted by Bacchus and his pards,
> But on the viewless wings of Poesy[21]

The poet may seek to 'leave the world unseen/And with thee fade away into the forest dim' but he always returns to restore the normative order of production. From Keats to Coleridge to De Quincey to Barrett-Browning to Baudelaire to Artaud to Ginsberg what the writer produces always results in a value. The emergence of literature *qua* institution is contemporaneous with an experience of socially acceptable drug addiction. In fact if cigarettes and coffee were to be included in the definition of drugs there might not be a thing we call Literature in the West without drugs: we might cite Pope, Addison, Blake, Balzac, Valéry. Writing is the process of opening up to the other and giving oneself over to the experience of the other. This form of possession is not unrelated to the experience of drugs. For example, we might ask what is the connection between writers who are said to be inspired by muses and writers (or indeed citizens) who take inspiration from the inspiration (inhalation) of drugs? And so a thinking about drugs cannot be separated from this thinking about the history of thought (writing) itself.

It is quite impossible to separate drugs from literature and thus the history of Western thought. What is at stake here is a metaphysical genealogy, which we must never stop analysing and distinguishing. The relation between drugs and literature encompasses questions of the self, consciousness, reason, freedom, social responsibility, the body, sexual difference, death, mourning, the law and the real, all of which must be thought through as part of a process of questioning. The concept 'drugs' does not stand on its own but is inscribed in the conceptual orders of Western thought and every time we use the term we are opening ourselves onto these orders. When we use the term 'drugs' we place our own discourse at the intersection of all of these concerns and are caught up in this network of traces and figures. This happens to a 'metaphysical' discourse, such as that of successive British governments, which takes the definition of drugs as fixed and forbids discussion or interrogation of the term as official policy. However, the différance which puts the concept into play also enables its own deconstruction. The governmental discourse produces ethical judgements whose effects it cannot control: for example, banning a discussion of drugs policy merely demonstrates the provisionality and fragility of that policy.

Just as the prohibition against drugs has a powerfully inscribed canon so does the naturalistic argument in favour of drugs. The place of this canon is in literature and includes those cited above along with Knut Hamsun, Burroughs, Huxley, Ginsberg, Kessey, Leary, Hunter Thompson, Trocchi and Irvine Welsh. On his return from an outlawed seminar in Prague the communist authorities planted drugs in Derrida's luggage; international pressure saved him from a two-year prison sentence. There is then also a connection between speech (freedom of speech) and the conceptual and nonconceptual orders which predicate the term 'drugs'. Drugs are inextricably linked to questions of litera-ture and to the very idea we have of democracy. It is impossible to think of drugs outside this conceptual order which is the very history of the West. While the deconstruction of a logocentric logic of inside ('drugs' as a pure, natural or self-evident term) and outside (all philosophical and ethical discourses supposed to be outside this term but which as we have seen cannot be separated from it) is itself suggestive of the pervasive strategies of ingestion and their prohibition which disguise all the unclassified and unclassifiable supplementary objects of compelled consumption such as chocolate, alcohol, coffee and cigarettes which install us all in our own singular relation to the concept of 'drugs'.

While the question of drugs as a concept opens itself onto an illimitable field of conceptual difficulty, in strictly schematic terms it is an 'easier' proposition than say the concepts of religion, politics, gender, race, economics and so on. Having had a small glimpse here into what might be involved in an understanding of 'drugs', one can imagine the work that will be required to deconstruct a concept like religion. Given that there is no limit to the potential interests of deconstruc-tion, deconstruction certainly has its work cut out. Perhaps this is a possible explanation for the resistance in some quarters to deconstruction, namely, that the casual adoption of a loose discursive formulation like 'drugs' is easier than doing the work involved in thinking through the questions raised by this term. This is frequently the case in literary and philosophical texts. We might think of someone like Irvine Welsh's quite banal treatment of drugs in *Trainspotting* which follows the 'natural freedom' route. Or, to change the conceptual mode, we can wonder at the repeated casual use of a term like History in literary criticism.

The common gesture of materialist criticism (be it Marxist, cultural materialist, or New Historicist) is 'always historicise'.[22] However, this injunction invokes History as both the cause of textual production and its explanation. That is to say, Marxism derives its legitimacy from the inevitable dialectical path of History. Therefore, History is the object, source and measure of inquiry. As such, History is beyond reproach and beyond interrogation. In other words History is beyond history: it is a concept whose invocation here bars us from examining its own genealogical status. History has a history: the annalists' idea of history was not the same as Tacitus, or Gibbon, or MacCauley, or Marx, or Benjamin, or Spengler, and so on. So, traditional Marxism compels us to understand History without being able to explain that term. This is a frequent metaphysical gesture: theology asks us to understand God although it is unable to explain the idea of God as a concept without undermining its own religious injunction which commands that we understand God – God, in theological terms, being the only thing worth understanding. It is what Geoffrey Bennington calls 'transcendental contraband', in which a term is smuggled into a text and used as a transcendental rule by which to measure the text even though the term is itself part of the text. We might compare this situation to police officers being asked to conduct an inquiry into police brutality. The officers are there to uphold the law but they are the structural cause of the law being broken. This situation may be unavoidable within discourse, and we might think of it as another example of the ways in which metaphysical thinking always manages to re-establish itself.

Hopefully, this section will have nailed another myth about deconstruction, namely, that it is 'ahistorical'. In fact since deconstruction insists on the non-identity of the present with itself, deconstruction is the most historical of discourses because it is always dealing with a past (or a future) which is non-recoverable, not even potentially so. If deconstruction historicises, it does so by means of a 'history without history'. That is to say an idea of the historical which has to be thought outside the logocentric conceptual schema which surround the traditional use of the term 'history'. In this way, deconstruction is both historical and cannot be assimilated to any easy historicism. Finally in this introduction, I will argue that deconstruction undoes the binary opposition between historicism and formalism.

THERE IS NOTHING TEXT-FREE

Perhaps the most misunderstood aspect of deconstruction is the memorable phrase 'there is nothing outside of the text'. This aphorism is Gayatri Spivak's

English translation of Derrida's expression '*il n'y a pas de hors-texte*' in *Of Grammatology*. The aphorism or sound bite is in general anathema to deconstruction because such slogans generalise what is irreducible and singular. The importance of this phrase for the reception and criticism of deconstruction was not planned by either Derrida or his translator. It is ironic that Derrida's text should fall prey to one of the truths of writing which his work has done most to explain. Namely, that cut off from its source and origin (an irretrievable source which can thus no longer carry the name of an origin) a text is caught up in set of interpretative contexts non-identical with authorial intention and so is open – not just potentially but as a necessary condition of its meaning – to misinterpretation and misappropriation. In other words, the full presence of authorial intention can never be realised. Or, in another memorable phrase, this time a paraphrase of Lacan, a letter never arrives at its destination, that is texts are always (mis)interpreted.[23]

It is perhaps as a consequence of the mnemonic qualities of Spivak's translation that this phrase has been seized upon as evidence of deconstruction's reckless abandonment of history, politics, reality, starving orphans and newborn kittens. Even if you have never read a word of Derrida you will be familiar with this phrase. Sadly those who use this phrase in a reckless way have usually never read a word of Derrida. To say that this aphorism – its aphoristic status being the result of its frequent citation by critics of deconstruction – characterised the whole of deconstruction would be like quoting Macbeth's line 'life is a tale told by an idiot' (V, i, 101) and suggesting that Shakespeare was an atheist, nihilist, moral relativist and old grump. Just as this facile charge could be countered by actually reading Shakespeare's play (and perhaps some more of his forty-one dramas) so the accusation that Derrida's phrase implies that deconstruction is an ahistorical discourse of radical nihilism can be countered by actually reading what he wrote. The full passage comes in a reading of the supplement in Rousseau's *Confessions* and runs as follows:

> Yet if reading must not be content with doubling the text, it cannot legitimately transgress the text toward something other than it, toward a referent (a reality that is metaphysical, historical, psychobiographical, etc.) or toward a signified outside the text whose content could take place, could have taken place outside of language, that is to say, in the sense that we give here to that word, outside of writing in general. That is why the methodological considerations that we risk applying here to an example are closely dependent on general propositions that we elaborated above; as regards the absence of the referent to the transcendental signified. *There is nothing outside of the text* [Derrida's italics] [there is no outside-text; *il n'y a pas de hors-texte*]. And that is neither because Jean-Jacques' life, or the existence of Mamma or Therese *themselves*, is not of prime interest to us, nor because we have access to their so-called 'real' existence only in the text and we have neither any means of altering this, nor any right to

neglect this limitation. All reasons of this type would already be sufficient, to be sure, but there are more radical reasons. What we have tried to show by following the guiding line of the 'dangerous supplement' is that in what one calls the real life of these existences 'of flesh and bone,' beyond and behind what one believes can be circumscribed as Rousseau's text, there has never been anything but writing; there has never been anything but supplements, substitutive significations which could only come forth in a chain of differential references, the 'real' supervening, and being added only while taking on meaning from a trace and from an invocation of the supplement, etc. And thus to infinity, for we have read, *in the text*, that the absolute present, Nature, that which words like 'real mother' name, have always already escaped, have never existed; that what opens meaning and language is writing as the disappearance of natural presence.[24]

This paragraph will bear some analysis.

Taking the quotation line by line a paraphrase – a dangerous strategy perhaps – might run something like this. While critical reading does not merely wishes to retell the narrative (of Rousseau's *Confessions*) it is an illegitimate move to turn the text into something that it is not. Criticism should pay attention to the singularity of Rousseau's text rather than producing 'a reading' by making reference to something extraneous to the text such as a metaphysical understanding of history or psychobiography. A reader cannot possibly say that they know these things (the historical basis of Rousseau's text or the state of Rousseau's mind) because such things are in the past and are absolutely irretrievable with any degree of certainty. Neither can one point to some 'outside world' to which the text refers, as if there were some 'outside world' which existed beyond language. Drawing a line in order to say 'this is the text and this is the real world to which it refers' is a false distinction. We can 'know' Rousseau's text but how can we know Rousseau's real world: it is of the irretrievable past. There is no stable point of origin to which we can refer in order to know the essence of Rousseau's text, only our own contexts of reading which are without absolute anchoring or proper limits. There is no 'transcendental signified' for Rousseau's text, nothing which exists beyond the text as a measure against which the events and meaning of the narrative can be calibrated. Nothing is text free. This is not because we are not concerned with the real existence of the characters who populate this autobiographical work. Nor is it because we could not possibly know this real existence anyway since we only have access to these characters through the text – how do I know if Rousseau is telling the truth about the events he narrates? That is not the point of reading this text as a text. These are good reasons but there are better ones.

Namely, that what we have been casually calling the real lives behind this narrative were themselves caught up in a textual network. These real lives were textual, real lives are textual. Rousseau, Mamma and Therese all had names, family histories, life stories, occupied positions within discourse, were affected by linguistic exchanges, constructed their own identities out of the things they read, heard and said. Rousseau's text in describing real lives was describing a set of textually inscribed existences. Traditionally criticism sets up a divide between the text and the author's life, with one firmly outside the other, but in truth one is supplementary to the other. We can identify the important points of a life because we claim they are transformed into text, but writing that text was part of the author's life, one which shaped and rearranged or caused events in that life. It is not life which precedes the text but it is the text which produces the life (as Oscar Wilde notes 'art does not imitate life, life at its most fortunate imitates art'). All texts work by a supplementary logic. We imagine a false limit to them as a way of conceptualising them but because texts are only visible examples of the textual processes which go on all the time (and in which we are engaged all the time) there is no proper limit between the literary text and the textuality of the life imbricated within it. Thus it is a mistake to distinguish between the events of a text and the events of a life as if the life were more 'real' than the text because those things which you imagine to exist in the real world never really existed in a proper present moment. Their full presence was never achieved and they have always been part of an irretrievable past even when they themselves thought they were present. If we say we know these events, we only 'know' them 'historically'. That is to say we do not 'know' them as such but as texts.

This argument is part of the complex architecture of Derrida's study of Rousseau and should be read in this context. However, this short introduction cannot elaborate all the intricacies of that work, rather I will conclude with a few observations about the paragraph just quoted. In short what the phrase *il n'y a pas de hors-texte* means is that one cannot read a text without acceding to its contextual opening. 'There is nothing outside of the text' does not mean that we should not pay attention to social, historical, political or biographical issues which affect the text. On the contrary, it means that when we read, all of these things are already inscribed within the text and we can access them through the text. It certainly does not mean that we should only pay attention to the written words on the page or to the formal characteristics of the prose – this is an elementary definition of 'text' which literary criticism has not found useful since before structuralism. Rather, it means that when reading a text there is nothing but context – it is doubly ironic then that this statement should have been taken so violently out of context. The text is constantly referring to the chain of differential traces, which give the text its meaning. Think of the reading of *Jane Eyre* above, which suggested that the novel was caught up in a conceptual order which included the history of colonialism and patriarchy. These histories were acceded to through the text and should not be thought of as 'outside' the text but as imbricated within the text. Furthermore, something like colonialism is textual through and through. It depends on laws, charters, policy statements, acts of parliament, slogans, propaganda, popular literature and so on. We could equally say that colonialism is conceptual through and through, being the intersection of numerous discursive (or textual) constructions: nation, money, civilisation, race, religion and so on. If we understand *Jane Eyre* through colonialism (and vice versa) it is because colonialism (the supposed 'real' or 'historical' outside) can never be text free. This is the translation of *hors-texte* which I offered as the subtitle to this final section. It relies, in part, on the phrase often seen at francophone airports, *hors taxe*, meaning 'duty free'. A literal translation might be 'beyond tax', such shopping areas following a rigorous prophylactic logic. They only exist in specially designated areas and are noteworthy because everywhere else in the country is not 'beyond tax', that is tax has to be paid everywhere. Similarly if we say there is nowhere text free – no *hors-texte*) – then everywhere is textual, no special dispensations.

This does not mean that deconstruction wishes to extended the paradigm of the text to cover the whole world, making the entire universe one big book. People suffer and bleed; only a fool would think otherwise; only a fool would suggest that deconstruction thinks otherwise. Rather, by expanding our understanding of textuality deconstruction makes us think about what is at stake in an everyday formulation like 'people suffer and bleed'. In employing this phrase I have bought into a humanist and humanitarian vocabulary, in which 'people' is an abstract understanding of a common humanity which I am enjoined to care for lest I betray myself as 'inhuman'. This is the same kind of discursive formulation which critics of deconstruction lazily adopt in which 'bleeding' (as a metonym for death through war or oppression) is invoked as a brutal 'real' outside to any textual consideration, its brutality deriving from its supposed absolute urgency in comparison with the self-indulgent reflection of thought. As we can see, however, this formulation does not in fact refer to real suffering – rather it is a quick way of dismissing real suffering – but is a rhetorial move in an argument designed to score points against another discourse. The urgency it alludes to is not absolutely urgent, as its tenor suggests, but merely one urgency among many. For example, we might think of other sufferings or injustices which do not involve symbolically significant 'bleeding' but which are equally important. However, comparing the supposed luxury of thought to the urgency of adult unemployment is not so rhetorically successful. This analysis could be carried on 'thus to infinity', as Derrida says.

It might be useful to think here of de Man's late understanding of materiality. In the essay 'The resistance to theory' he notes that

> literature is fiction not because it somehow refuses to acknowledge 'reality', but because it is not *a priori* certain that language functions according to principles which are those, or which are *like* those, of the phenomenal world. It is therefore not *a priori* certain that literature is a reliable source of information about anything but its own language' (p. 11).

Literature is of interest to de Man because the figurative dimension of language is more explicitly foregrounded in literature than in other verbal manifestations (p. 17). De Man suggests that we should not take it for granted that the language by which we understand the world works by the same rules as the world. Not taking anything for granted might be a useful rule of thumb in deconstruction. If our everyday assumptions about 'reality' are mediated through (and so complicated and displaced by) language then we cannot be certain that literature is useful for anything other than an appreciation of rhetoric and the study of tropes. The paradox here is that if we understand our world through the figurative dimension of language then literature will be useful precisely for comprehending the world because the materiality of the world is our visceral implication within language as the tangible medium of our being. We should not 'confuse the materiality of the signifier with the materiality of what it signifies' (p. 11) – de Man is not denying the existence of tables and chairs! No one would use the metaphorical resonances of the word 'day' (light, health, purity, consciousness and so on) to organise agricultural practice, but it would be inconceivable to imagine our lives (our past, present and future existence) without an idea of temporality which comes from fictional narratives rather than the phenomenal world. This does not mean that fictional narratives are not part of the world: on the contrary their effects on the world may be profound. Rather, it is the essential gesture of ideology to confuse 'linguistic with natural reality' (p. 11) and it is this sort of bafflement and disorientation which de Man wishes to avoid. Thus, de Man's critical-linguistic analysis can lay claim to a political pertinence:

> It follows that, more than any other mode of inquiry, including economics, the linguistics of literariness is a powerful and indispensable tool in the unmasking of ideological aberrations, as well as a determining factor in accounting for their occurrence. Those who reproach literary theory [i.e. deconstruction] for being oblivious to social and historical (that is to say ideological) reality are merely stating their fear at having their own ideological mystifications exposed by the tool that they are trying to discredit. They are, in short, very poor readers of Marx's *German Ideology*. (p. 11)

The impatience of many readers have caused them to overlook this fundamentally important aspect of de Man's work and rush to the conclusion – based on no evidence – that de Man's deconstruction is apolitical or at best 'the latest stage of a liberal scepticism'.[25] Nothing could be further from the truth, because de Man does not assume that the discourse of politics is identical with, or operates under the same rules as, phenomenal politics; he opens up a space (the gap between reference and phenomenon) for thinking about the political which is aware of, rather than dazzled by, ideology.

This entanglement in a textuality without borders or limits is the human condition, what I called above 'the very materiality of the world, our visceral implication within language as the tangible medium of our being'. We cannot escape language by means of language and we cannot pull language up by its own bootstraps. The point is not that war or oppression is not important but that there can be no rigorous purity between the facts of a war and the way it is understood, described and presented, that is its textual inscription. As Bill Readings puts it (See Bill Readings, 'The deconstruction of politics', in this volume, pp. 388–96):

> The literal, in its most rigorous sense, is a metaphor, and in that branch of Western philosophy named positivism [ensuring knowledge by referential verification with the 'real'], it has become the metaphor of metaphors. The literal is thus a trope among tropes, which is not to erase literality but to insist that the literal cannot ground itself outside rhetoric, in a referential real abstracted from the figural. Furthermore, the distinction between the figural and the literal must be read as a tropaic distinction in an order of rhetoric, rather than a literal one in an order of meaning.[26]

Deconstruction does not ignore war – it would not be difficult to construct an argument which showed that deconstruction only ever talks about war even if it does not talk only about war. Rather, it asks us to think very hard about what we mean when we use such a word and the consequences of its usage. It is this persistent challenge to thinking – a thinking that asks us to think about thought – which means that there is no end to the task of deconstruction, and perhaps explains why those complacent enough to refuse reflection have little time for deconstruction.

We have seen in this chapter that deconstruction is concerned with the most intricate parts of a text and rigorously pursues these parts in the most detailed of close readings. In this sense we might say that deconstruction is a 'super-formalism', a formalism which goes beyond formalism in its precise understanding of the metaphorical and conceptual construction of textuality and the figurality of thought. The decisive rigour of 'Yale school' readings have caused some to confuse deconstruction with mere formalism. In its American guise deconstruction has been mistakenly called the 'new New Criticism'. However, we have also seen the ways in which deconstruction opens up a text to contextual matters such as history, sociology, politics and so forth – there is nothing but context. Deconstruction then, if such a thing exists and is one, dismantles the opposition between contextual readings and formal readings which has riven the critical institution since its inception. This thing called deconstruction is not only a moment of reading but it deconstructs the moment of reading, refusing a limit to what is proper to reading and disturbing all the known classifications of reading.

Having made an attempt to open up the question of what deconstruction might be, let me conclude by saying what deconstruction certainly is not (See Geoffrey Bennington 'Deconstruction is not what you think' in this volume, pp. 217–19). Deconstruction is not a school or an 'ism'. There is no such thing as 'deconstructionism': this is a word used by idiots. Deconstruction is not a theory or a project. It does not present an idea of the world with which we should keep faith, nor does it offer rules for achieving that idea. Deconstruction is not an 'application' of the thought of Derrida or de Man or Hillis Miller or Barbara Johnson or . . . Deconstruction undoes the logic of outside-inside which the idea of an application presupposes. Deconstruction is not literary criticism. This would be like saying Shakespeare was a half-decent actor.

Deconstruction is not philosophy, deconstruction reads philosophy. Alternatively since the history of philosophy is the history of the appropriation of what was previously outside it, deconstruction's reading can only ever accomplish philosophy in its most traditional aspects.[27] Deconstruction is not postmodernism. Deconstruction *happens* in texts by Augustine, Chaucer, Duns Scotus, Rembrandt, Shelley, Rousseau, Woolf; it is not period or genre specific. Deconstruction is not a political ideology. It refuses the appropriative gesture of political discourses which wish to assimilate it to themselves, while opening up the question of what 'the political' itself might mean. Deconstruction is not solely about language, the so-called 'extension of the linguistic paradigm'. Rather deconstruction displaces and reinscribes our understanding of textuality. Deconstruction is not opposed to reality/history/the world. Deconstruction opens up reality/history/the world by not allowing us to think of it as detached or 'opposed to' anything. Deconstruction is not discourse. Discourse is a text and deconstruction reads texts. Deconstruction is not reading, unless we are prepared to displace the idea of reading in the same way that we have displaced the idea of text. It is possible that the most 'deconstructive' of work should happen in ignorance of Derrida or de Man or Miller or Spivak or Bhabha – think of Jean Rhys. To say that 'X' is deconstruction probably means that 'X' is not deconstruction and that deconstruction has gone elsewhere. A Deconstruction Reader is strictly impossible. Deconstruction produces appearance as it disappears and appears in its disappearance. This word 'deconstruction' is only the metaphysical name we give to the effects of an ethico-theoretico-political situation. Deconstruction is what happens.

NOTES

1. Jacques Derrida, 'Living on: Borderlines', trans. J. Hulbert, in H. Bloom et al. (eds), *Deconstruction and Criticism* (New York: Seabury Press, 1979), pp. 75–176 (96).
2. Geoffrey Bennington has some useful comments on this notion of deconstruction as application in his essay, 'X', in (eds), John Brannigan, Kate Robbins and Julian Wolfreys *Applying: to Derrida* (London: Macmillan, 1997), pp. 1–21.
3. See the text, Jacques Derrida, *Memoirs of the Blind*, trans. Pascale-Anne Brault and Michael Naas (Chicago: University of Chicago Press, 1993).
4. Paul de Man, 'Shelley disfigured', *The Rhetoric of Romanticism* (New York: Columbia University Press, 1984), pp. 93–125 (123).
5. Hélène Cixous, 'Sorties: Out and out: Attacks/ways out/forays', in Hélène Cixous and Catherine Clement, *The Newly Born Woman*, trans. Betsy Wing (Minneapolis: University of Minnesota Press, 1986), pp. 63–75 (63).
6. Paul de Man, *Allegories of Reading: Figural Language in Rousseau, Nietzsche, Rilke, and Proust* (New Haven and London: Yale University Press, 1979), p. 230.
7. Geoffrey Hartman, 'Looking back on Paul de Man' in (eds) Lindsay Walters Wlad Godzich *Reading de Man Reading* and (Minneapolis: University of Minnesota Press, 1989), pp. 3–25 (19).

8. Paul de Man, *Allegories of Reading*, p. 111, my italics.
9. J. Hillis Miller, *The Ethics of Reading: Kant, de Man, Eliot, Trollope, James, and Benjamin* (New York: Columbia University Press, 1987), p. 56.
10. Paul de Man, *Allegories of Reading*, p. 210.
11. Homi K. Bhabha, *The Location of Culture* (London: Routledge, 1994).
12. Jacques Derrida, 'Racism's last word', trans. Peggy Kamuf, *Critical Inquiry*, 12, 1985, pp. 290–9.
13. Jacques Derrida, 'Différance', in *Margins of Philosophy*, trans. Alan Bass (Chicago: University of Chicago Press, 1982), pp. 1–29.
14. Ferdinand de Saussure, *Course in General Linguistics*, eds Charles Ballay, Albert Sechehaye and Albert Riedlinger, trans. Wade Baskin (London: Fontana, 1974).
15. These are not de Man's actual 'last words', a topic on which he might have had a few things to say, but currently his last recorded words as described by J. Hillis Miller in 'An open letter to Professor John Wiener' (J. Hillis Miller, 'An open letter to Professor John Wiener', in Thomas Kennan, ed., *Responses to Paul de Man's Wartime Journalism 1940–1942* [Lincoln: University of Nebraska Press, 1989], 334–42) De Man was referring to an article by René Welleck in *The New Criterion* which accused him of 'destroying literary studies'.
16. Charlotte Bronte, *Jane Eyre* (Hammondsworth: Penguin, 1966 [1847]), pp. 197–8.
17. Paul de Man, 'An interview with Paul de Man', *The Resistance to Theory* (Minneapolis: Minnesota University Press, 1986), pp. 115–22 (118).
18. See Jacques Derrida, *Specters of Marx: The State of the Debt, the Work of Mourning, and the New International*, trans. Peggy Kamuf (London and New York: Routledge, 1994), and '*Ouisa* and *Gramme*: Note on a note from *Being and Time*', in *Margins of Philosophy*, pp. 29–69.
19. Quoted, Jacques Derrida, *Memoires for Paul de Man, Revised Edition* (New York: Columbia University Press, 1989), p. 72.
20. See Jacques Derrida, 'The rhetoric of drugs', in *Points: Interviews 1974–1994*, ed. Elisabeth Weber (Stanford: Stanford University Press, 1995), pp. 228–55.
21. John Keats, 'Ode to a Nightingale'.
22. If I seem unduly harsh on Marxism it is only out of my love for the text of Marx. This is a topic I have treated at length elsewhere: see Eleanor Byrne and Martin McQuillan, *Deconstructing Disney* (London: Pluto, 1999).
23. See Jacques Derrida, 'Le factuer de la vérité', *The Post Card: From Socrates to Freud and Beyond*, trans. Alan Bass (Chicago: University of Chicago Press, 1987), pp. 411–97.
24. Jacques Derrida, *Of Grammatology*, trans. Gayatri Chakravorty Spivak (Baltimore: Johns Hopkins University Press, 1976), pp. 158–9.
25. Terry Eagleton, *Literary Theory: An Introduction* (Oxford: Blackwell, 1983), p. 147.
27. See Geoffrey Bennington, *Jacques Derrida* (Chicago: University of Chicago Press, 1993).

PART I
AVANT LA LETTRE

1.1

FROM *CAPITAL*

Karl Marx

THE FETISHISM OF THE COMMODITY AND ITS SECRET

A commodity appears at first sight an extremely obvious, trivial thing. But its analysis brings out that it is a very strange thing, abounding in metaphysical subtleties and theological niceties. So far as it is a use-value, there is nothing mysterious about it, whether we consider it from the point of view that by its properties it satisfies human needs, or that it first takes on these properties as the product of human labour. It is absolutely clear that, by his activity, man changes the forms of the materials of nature in such a way as to make them useful to him. The form of wood, for instance, is altered if a table is made out of it. Nevertheless the table continues to be wood, an ordinary, sensuous thing. But as soon as it emerges as a commodity, it changes into a thing which transcends sensuousness. It not only stands with its feet on the ground, but, in relation to all other commodities, it stands on its head, and evolves out of its wooden brain grotesque ideas, far more wonderful than if it were to begin dancing of its own free will.[1]

The mystical character of the commodity does not therefore arise from its use-value. Just as little does it proceed from the nature of the determinants of value. For in the first place, however varied the useful kinds of labour, or productive activities, it is a physiological fact that they are functions of the human organism, and that each such function, whatever may be its nature or its

Source: Karl Marx, *Capital*, tr. Ben Fowkes (New York: Vintage, 1977), vol. 1, ch. 1, sect. 4, pp. 163–7.

form, is essentially the expenditure of human brain, nerves, muscles and sense organs. Secondly, with regard to the foundation of the quantitative determination of value, namely the duration of that expenditure or the quantity of labour, this is quite palpably different from its quality. In all situations, the labour-time it costs to produce the means of subsistence must necessarily concern mankind, although not to the same degree at different stages of development.[2] And finally, as soon as men start to work for each other in any way, their labour also assumes a social form.

Whence, then, arises the enigmatic character of the product of labour, as soon as it assumes the form of a commodity? Clearly, it arises from this form itself. The equality of the kinds of human labour takes on a physical form in the equal objectivity of the products of labour as values; the measure of the expenditure of human labour-power by its duration takes on the form of the magnitude of the value of the products of labour; and finally the relationships between the producers, within which the social characteristics of their labours are manifested, take on the form of a social relation between the products of labour.

The mysterious character of the commodity-form consists therefore simply in the fact that the commodity reflects the social characteristics of men's own labour as objective characteristics of the products of labour themselves, as the socio-natural properties of these things. Hence it also reflects the social relation of the producers to the sum total of labour as a social relation between objects, a relation which exists apart from and outside the producers. Through this substitution, the products of labour become commodities, sensuous things which are at the same time suprasensible or social. In the same way, the impression made by a thing on the optic nerve is perceived not as a subjective excitation of that nerve but as the objective form of a thing outside the eye. In the act of seeing, of course, light is really transmitted from one thing, the external object, to another thing, the eye. It is a physical relation between physical things. As against this, the commodity-form, and the value-relation of the products of labour within which it appears, have absolutely no connection with the physical nature of the commodity and the material [*dinglich*] relations arising out of this. It is nothing but the definite social relation between men themselves which assumes here, for them, the fantastic form of a relation between things. In order, therefore, to find an analogy we must take flight into the misty realm of religion. There the products of the human brain appear as autonomous figures endowed with a life of their own, which enter into relations both with each other and with the human race. So it is in the world of commodities with the products of men's hands. I call this the fetishism which attaches itself to the products of labour as soon as they are produced as commodities, and is therefore inseparable from the production of commodities.

As the foregoing analysis has already demonstrated, this fetishism of the world of commodities arises from the peculiar social character of the labour which produces them.

Objects of utility become commodities only because they are the products of the labour of private individuals who work independently of each other. The sum total of the labour of all these private individuals forms the aggregate labour of society. Since the producers do not come into social contact until they exchange the products of their labour, the specific social characteristics of their private labours appear only within this exchange. In other words, the labour of the private individual manifests itself as an element of the total labour of society only through the relations which the act of exchange establishes between the products, and, through their mediation, between the producers. To the producers, therefore, the social relations between their private labours appear as what they are, i.e. they do not appear as direct social relations between persons in their work, but rather as material [*dinglich*] relations between persons and social relations between things.

It is only by being exchanged that the products of labour acquire a socially uniform objectivity as values, which is distinct from their sensuously varied objectivity as articles of utility. This division of the product of labour into a useful thing and a thing possessing value appears in practice only when exchange has already acquired a sufficient extension and importance to allow useful things to be produced for the purpose of being exchanged, so that their character as values has already to be taken into consideration during production. From this moment on, the labour of the individual producer acquires a twofold social character. On the one hand, it must, as a definite useful kind of labour, satisfy a definite social need, and thus maintain its position as an element of the total labour, as a branch of the social division of labour, which originally sprang up spontaneously. On the other hand, it can satisfy the manifold needs of the individual producer himself only in so far as every particular kind of useful private labour can be exchanged with, i.e. counts as the equal of, every other kind of useful private labour. Equality in the full sense between different kinds of labour can be arrived at only if we abstract from their real inequality, if we reduce them to the characteristic they have in common, that of being the expenditure of human labour-power, of human labour in the abstract. The private producer's brain reflects this twofold, social character of his labour only in the forms which appear in practical intercourse, in the exchange of products. Hence the socially useful character of his private labour is reflected in the form that the product of labour has to be useful to others, and the social character of the equality of the various kinds of labour is reflected in the form of the common character, as values, possessed by these materially different things, the products of labour.

Men do not therefore bring the products of their labour into relation with each other as values because they see these objects merely as the material integuments of homogeneous human labour. The reverse is true: by equating their different products to each other in exchange as values, they equate their different kinds of labour as human labour. They do this without being aware of it. Value, therefore, does not have its description branded on its forehead; it rather transforms every product of labour into a social hieroglyphic. Later on, men try to decipher the hieroglyphic, to get behind the secret of their own social product: for the characteristic which objects of utility have of being values is as much men's social product as is their language. The belated scientific discovery that the products of labour, in so far as they are values, are merely the material expressions of the human labour expended to produce them, marks an epoch in the history of mankind's development, but by no means banishes the semblance of objectivity possessed by the social characteristics of labour. Something which is only valid for this particular form of production, the production of commodities, namely the fact that the specific social character of private labours carried on independently of each other consists in their equality as human labour, and, in the product, assumes the form of the existence of value, appears to those caught up in the relations of commodity production (and this is true both before and after the above-mentioned scientific discovery) to be just as ultimately valid as the fact that the scientific dissection of the air into its component parts left the atmosphere itself unaltered in its physical configuration.

NOTES

1. One may recall that China and the tables began to dance when the rest of the world appeared to be standing still – *pour encourager les autres*. 'To encourage the others'. A reference to the simultaneous emergence in the 1850s of the Taiping revolt in China and the craze for spiritualism which swept over upper-class German society. The rest of the world was 'standing still' in the period of reaction immediately after the defeat of the 1848 Revolutions.
2. Among the ancient Germans the size of a piece of land was measured according to the labour of a day; hence the acre was called *Tagwerk, Tagwanne (jurnale,* or *terra jurnalis,* or *diornalis), Mannwerk, Mannskraft, Mannsmaad, Mannshauet,* etc. See Georg Ludwig von Maurer, *Einleitung zur Geschichte der Mark-, Hof-, usw. Verfassung,* Munich, 1854, p. 129 ff.

See:

Jacques Derrida, *Spectres of Marx: The Work of Mourning, the State of the Debt, and the New international,* tr. Peggy Kamuf (London and New York: Routledge, 1994).
Jacques Derrida, 'Marx & Sons', in Michael Sprinkner (ed.), *Ghostly Demarcations: A Symposium on Jacques Derrida's Spectres of Marx,* (London: Verso, 1999).

'A NOTE UPON THE "MYSTIC WRITING PAD"'

Sigmund Freud

If I distrust my memory – neurotics, as we know, do so to a remarkable extent, but normal people have every reason for doing so as well – I am able to supplement and guarantee its working by making a note in writing. In that case the surface upon which this note is preserved, the pocket-book or sheet of paper, is as it were a materialized portion of my mnemic apparatus, which I otherwise carry about with me invisible. I have only to bear in mind the place where this 'memory' has been deposited and I can then 'reproduce' it at any time I like, with the certainty that it will have remained unaltered and so have escaped the possible distortions to which it might have been subjected in my actual memory.

If I want to make full use of this technique for improving my mnemic function, I find that there are two different procedures open to me. On the one hand, I can choose a writing-surface which will preserve intact any note made upon it for an indefinite length of time – for instance, a sheet of paper which I can write upon in ink. I am then in possession of a 'permanent memory-trace'. The disadvantage of this procedure is that the receptive capacity of the writing-surface is soon exhausted. The sheet is filled with writing, there is no room on it for any more notes, and I find myself obliged to bring another sheet into use, that has not been written on. Moreover, the advantage of this procedure, the fact that it provides a 'permanent trace', may lose its value for me if after a time the note ceases to interest me and I no longer want to 'retain it in my memory'. The alternative procedure avoids both of these

Source: Sigmund Freud, *The Standard Edition of the Complete Psychological Works of Sigmund Freud*, vol. 19, pp. 225–32, tr. James Strachey (London: Hogarth, 1957).

disadvantages. If, for instance, I write with a piece of chalk on a slate, I have a receptive surface which retains its receptive capacity for an unlimited time and the notes upon which can be destroyed as soon as they cease to interest me, without any need for throwing away the writing-surface itself. Here the disadvantage is that I cannot preserve a permanent trace. If I want to put some fresh notes on the slate, I must first wipe out the ones which cover it. Thus an unlimited receptive capacity and a retention of permanent traces seem to be mutually exclusive properties in the apparatus which we use as substitutes for our memory: either the receptive surface must be renewed or the note must be destroyed.

All the forms of auxiliary apparatus which we have invented for the improvement or intensification of our sensory functions are built on the same model as the sense organs themselves or portions of them: for instance, spectacles, photographic cameras, trumpets.[1] Measured by this standard, devices to aid our memory seem particularly imperfect, since our mental apparatus accomplishes precisely what they cannot: it has an unlimited receptive capacity for new perceptions and nevertheless lays down permanent – even though not unalterable – memory-traces of them. As long ago as in 1900 I gave expression in *The Interpretation of Dreams*[2] to a suspicion that this unusual capacity was to be divided between two different systems (or organs of the mental apparatus). According to this view, we possess a system *Pcpt.-Cs.*, which receives perceptions but retains no permanent trace of them, so that it can react like a clean sheet to every new perception; while the permanent traces of the excitations which have been received are preserved in 'mnemic systems' lying behind the perceptual system. Later, in *Beyond the Pleasure Principle* (1920g),[3] I added a remark to the effect that the inexplicable phenomenon of consciousness arises in the perceptual system *instead* of the permanent traces.

Now some time ago there came upon the market, under the name of the 'Mystic Writing-Pad', a small contrivance that promises to perform more than the sheet of paper or the slate. It claims to be nothing more than a writing-tablet from which notes can be erased by an easy movement of the hand. But if it is examined more closely it will be found that its construction shows a remarkable agreement with my hypothetical structure of our perceptual apparatus and that it can in fact provide both an ever-ready receptive surface and permanent traces of the notes that have been made upon it.

The Mystic Pad is a slab of dark brown resin or wax with a paper edging; over the slab is laid a thin transparent sheet, the top end of which is firmly secured to the slab while its bottom end rests on it without being fixed to it. This transparent sheet is the more interesting part of the little device. It itself consists of two layers, which can be detached from each other except at their two ends. The upper layer is a transparent piece of celluloid; the lower layer is made of thin translucent waxed paper. When the apparatus is not in use, the lower surface of the waxed paper adheres lightly to the upper surface of the wax slab.

To make use of the Mystic Pad, one writes upon the celluloid portion of the covering-sheet which rests on the wax slab. For this purpose no pencil or chalk is necessary, since the writing does not depend on material being deposited on the receptive surface. It is a return to the ancient method of writing on tablets of clay or wax: a pointed stilus scratches the surface, the depressions upon which constitute the 'writing'. In the case of the Mystic Pad this scratching is not effected directly, but through the medium of the covering-sheet. At the points which the stilus touches, it presses the lower surface of the waxed paper on to the wax slab, and the grooves are visible as dark writing upon the otherwise smooth whitish-grey surface of the celluloid. If one wishes to destroy what has been written, all that is necessary is to raise the double covering-sheet from the wax slab by a light pull, starting from the free lower end.[3] The close contact between the waxed paper and the wax slab at the places which have been scratched (upon which the visibility of the writing depended) is thus brought to an end and it does not recur when the two surfaces come together once more. The Mystic Pad is now clear of writing and ready to receive fresh notes.

The small imperfections of the contrivance have, of course, no importance for us, since we are only concerned with its approximation to the structure of the perceptual apparatus of the mind.

If, while the Mystic Pad has writing on it, we cautiously raise the celluloid from the waxed paper, we can see the writing just as clearly on the surface of the latter, and the question may arise why there should be any necessity for the celluloid portion of the cover. Experiment will then show that the thin paper would be very easily crumpled or torn if one were to write directly upon it with the stilus. The layer of celluloid thus acts as a protective sheath for the waxed paper, to keep off injurious effects from without. The celluloid is a 'protective shield against stimuli'; the layer which actually receives the stimuli is the paper. I may at this point recall that in *Beyond the Pleasure Principle* [p. 298 ff.] I showed that the perceptual apparatus of our mind consists of two layers, of an external protective shield against stimuli whose task it is to diminish the strength of excitations coming in, and of a surface behind it which receives the stimuli, namely the system *Pcpt.-Cs.*

The analogy would not be of much value if it could not be pursued further than this. If we lift the entire covering-sheet – both the celluloid and the waxed paper – off the wax slab, the writing vanishes and, as I have already remarked, does not reappear again. The surface of the Mystic Pad is clear of writing and once more capable of receiving impressions. But it is easy to discover that the permanent trace of what was written is retained upon the wax slab itself and is legible in suitable lights. Thus the Pad provides not only a receptive surface that can be used over and over again, like a slate, but also permanent traces of what has been written, like an ordinary paper pad: it solves the problem of combining the two functions *by dividing them between two separate but interrelated component parts or systems*. But this is precisely the way in which, according to the hypothesis which I mentioned just now, our mental apparatus performs its perceptual function. The layer which receives the stimuli – the system *Pcpt.-Cs.* – forms no permanent traces; the foundations of memory come about in other, adjoining, systems.

We need not be disturbed by the fact that in the Mystic Pad no use is made of the permanent traces of the notes that have been received; it is enough that they are present. There must come a point at which the analogy between an auxiliary apparatus of this kind and the organ which is its prototype will cease to apply. It is true, too, that once the writing has been erased, the Mystic Pad cannot 'reproduce' it from within; it would be a mystic Pad indeed if, like our memory, it could accomplish that. None the less, I do not think it is too far-fetched to compare the celluloid and waxed paper cover with the system *Pcpt.-Cs.* and its protective shield, the wax slab with the unconscious behind them, and the appearance and disappearance of the writing with the flickering-up and passing-away of consciousness in the process of perception.

But I must admit that I am inclined to press the comparison still further. On the Mystic Pad the writing vanishes every time the close contact is broken between the paper which receives the stimulus and the wax slab which preserves the impression. This agrees with a notion which I have long had about the method by which the perceptual apparatus of our mind functions, but which I have hitherto kept to myself.[4] My theory was that cathectic innervations are sent out and withdrawn in rapid periodic impulses from within into the completely pervious system *Pcpt.-Cs.* So long as that system is cathected in this manner, it receives perceptions (which are accompanied by consciousness) and passes the excitation on to the unconscious mnemic systems; but as soon as the cathexis is withdrawn, consciousness is extinguished and the functioning of the system comes to a standstill.[5] It is as though the unconscious stretches out feelers, through the medium of the system *Pcpt.-Cs.*, towards the external world and hastily withdraws them as soon as they have sampled the excitations coming from it. Thus the interruptions, which in the case of the Mystic Pad have an external origin, were attributed by my hypothesis to the discontinuity in the current of innervation; and the actual breaking of contact which occurs in the Mystic Pad was replaced in my theory by the periodic non-excitability of the perceptual system. I further had a suspicion that this discontinuous method of functioning of the system *Pcpt.-Cs.* lies at the bottom of the origin of the concept of time.[6]

If we imagine one hand writing upon the surface of the Mystic Writing-Pad while another periodically raises its covering-sheet from the wax slab, we shall have a concrete representation of the way in which I tried to picture the functioning of the perceptual apparatus of our mind.

NOTES

1. [This notion is expanded in Chapter III of *Civilization and its Discontents* (1930a), P.F.L., **12**, 276–7.]
2. [P.F.L., **4**, 689. As Freud mentions in *Beyond the Pleasure Principle* (1920g), p. 296 above, this distinction had already been drawn by Breuer in his theoretical section of *Studies on Hysteria* (1895d), P.F.L., **3**, 263 a.]

3. [The method by which the covering-sheet is detached from the wax slab is slightly different in the current form of the device; but this does not affect the principle.]
4. [It had in fact been mentioned in *Beyond the Pleasure Principle*, p. 299 above. The notion reappears at the end of the paper on 'Negation' (1925*h*), below, pp. 440–41. It is already present in embryo at the end of Section 19 of Part I of the 'Project' of 1895 (Freud 1950*a*).]
5. [This is in accordance with the 'principle of the insusceptibility to excitation of uncathected systems', which is discussed in an Editor's footnote to the metapsychological paper on dreams (1917*d*), pp. 234–5 above.]
6. [This also had been suggested in *Beyond the Pleasure Principle*, p. 300 above, and hinted at earlier, in 'The Unconscious' (1915*e*), p. 191 ff. above. It is restated in 'Negation' (1925*h*), pp. 440–41 below, where, however, Freud attributes the sending out of feelers to the ego.]

See:

Jacques Derrida, 'Freud and the scene of writing', in *Writing and Difference*, trans. Alan Bass (London: Routledge & Kegan Paul, 1978).

'THE MEANING OF GENERAL ECONOMY'

Georges Bataille

The Dependence of the Economy on the Circulation of Energy on the Earth

When it is necessary to change an automobile tyre, open an abscess or plough a vineyard, it is easy to manage a quite limited operation. The elements on which the action is brought to bear are not completely isolated from the rest of the world, but it is possible to act on them as if they were: one can complete the operation without once needing to consider the whole, of which the tyre, the abscess or the vineyard is nevertheless an integral part. The changes brought about do not perceptibly alter the other things, nor does the ceaseless action from without have an appreciable effect on the conduct of the operation. But things are different when we consider a substantial economic activity such as the production of automobiles in the United States, or, *a fortiori*, when it is a question of economic activity in general.

Between the production of automobiles and the *general* movement of the economy, the interdependence is rather clear, but the economy taken as a whole is usually studied as if it were a matter of an isolatable system of operation. Production and consumption are linked together, but, considered jointly, it does not seem difficult to study them as one might study an elementary operation relatively independent of that which it is not.

Source: Georges Bataille, *The Accursed Share: An Essay on General Economy*, vol. 1, *Consumption*, tr. Robert Hurley (New York: Zone Books, 1988), pp. 19–26.
La Part maudite, I: La Consommation was first published by Editions de Minuit in 1949, and re-edited in a 1967 edition.

This method is legitimate, and science never proceeds differently. However, economic science does not give results of the same order as physics studying, first, a precise phenomenon, then all studiable phenomena as a co-ordinated whole. Economic phenomena are not easy to isolate, and their general co-ordination is not easy to establish. So it is possible to raise this question concerning them: shouldn't productive activity as a whole be considered in terms of the modifications it receives from its surroundings or brings about in its surroundings? In other words, isn't there a need to study the system of human production and consumption within a much larger framework?

In the sciences such problems ordinarily have an academic character, but economic activity is so far reaching that no one will be surprised if a first question is followed by other, less abstract ones: In overall industrial develop-ment, are there not social conflicts and planetary wars? In the global activity of men, in short, are there not causes and effects that will appear only provided that *the general data of the economy* are studied? Will we be able to make ourselves the masters of such a dangerous activity (and one that we could not abandon in any case) without having grasped its *general* consequences? Should we not, given the constant development of economic forces, pose the *general* problems that are linked to the movement of energy on the globe?

These questions allow one to glimpse both the theoretical meaning and the practical importance of the principles they introduce.

The Necessity of Losing the Excess Energy that Cannot be Used for a System's Growth

At first sight, it is easy to recognize in the economy – *in the production and use of wealth* – a particular aspect of terrestrial activity regarded as a cosmic phenomenon. A movement is produced on the surface of the globe that results from the circulation of energy at this point in the universe. The economic activity of men appropriates this movement, making use of the resulting possibilities for certain ends. But this movement has a pattern and laws with which, as a rule, those who use them and depend on them are unacquainted. Thus the question arises: is the general determination of energy circulating in the biosphere altered by man's activity? Or rather, isn't the latter's intention vitiated by a determination of which it is ignorant, which it overlooks and cannot change?

Without waiting, I will give an inescapable answer.

Man's disregard for the material basis of his life still causes him to err in a serious way. Humanity exploits given material resources, but by restricting them as it does to a resolution of the immediate difficulties it encounters (a resolution which it has hastily had to define as an ideal), it assigns to the forces it employs an end which they cannot have. Beyond our immediate ends, man's activity in fact pursues the useless and infinite fulfilment of the universe.[1]

Of course, the error that results from so complete a disregard does not just concern man's claim to lucidity. It is not easy to realize one's own ends if one must, in trying to do so, carry out a movement that surpasses them. No doubt these ends and this movement may not be entirely irreconcilable; but if these two terms are to be reconciled we must cease to ignore one of them; otherwise, our works quickly turn to catastrophe.

I will begin with a basic fact: the living organism, in a situation determined by the play of energy on the surface of the globe, ordinarily receives more energy than is necessary for maintaining life; the excess energy (wealth) can be used for the growth of a system (e.g., an organism); if the system can no longer grow, or if the excess cannot be completely absorbed in its growth, it must necessarily be lost without profit; it must be spent, willingly or not, gloriously or catastrophically.

THE POVERTY OF ORGANISMS OR LIMITED SYSTEMS AND THE EXCESS WEALTH OF LIVING NATURE

Minds accustomed to seeing the development of productive forces as the ideal end of activity refuse to recognize that energy, which constitutes wealth, must ultimately be spent lavishly (without return), and that a series of profitable operations has absolutely no other effect than the squandering of profits. To affirm that it is necessary to dissipate a substantial portion of energy produced, sending it up in smoke, is to go against judgements that form the basis of a rational economy. We know cases where wealth has had to be destroyed (coffee thrown into the sea), but these scandals cannot reasonably be offered as examples to follow. They are the acknowledgement of an impotence, and no one could find in them the image and essence of wealth. Indeed, involuntary destruction (such as the disposal of coffee overboard) has in every case the meaning of failure; it is experienced as a misfortune; in no way can it be presented as desirable. And yet it is the type of operation without which there is no solution. When one considers the *totality* of productive wealth on the surface of the globe, it is evident that the products of this wealth can be employed for productive ends only insofar as the living organism that is economic mankind can increase its equipment. This is not entirely neither always nor indefinitely possible. A surplus must be dissipated through deficit operations: the final dissipation cannot fail to carry out the movement that animates terrestrial energy.

The contrary usually appears for the reason that the economy is never considered *in general*. The human mind reduces operations, in science as in life, to an entity based on typical *particular* systems (organisms or enterprises). Economic activity, considered as a whole, is conceived in terms of particular operations with limited ends. The mind generalizes by composing the aggregate of these operations. Economic science merely generalizes the isolated situation; it restricts its object to operations carried out with a view to a limited end, that of economic man. It does not take into consideration a play of energy that no particular end limits: the play of *living matter in general*, involved in the movement of light of which it is the result. On the surface of the globe, for *living matter in general*, energy is always in excess; the question is always posed in terms of extravagance. The choice is limited to how the wealth is to be squandered. It is to the *particular* living being, or to limited populations of living beings, that the problem of necessity presents itself. But man is not just the separate being that contends with the living world and with other men for his share of resources. The general movement of exudation (of waste) of living matter impels him, and he cannot stop it; moreover, being at the summit, his sovereignty in the living world identifies him with this movement; it destines him, in a privileged way, to that glorious operation, to useless consumption. If he denies this, as he is constantly urged to do by the consciousness of a *necessity*, of an indigence inherent in separate beings (which are constantly short of resources, which are nothing but eternally *needy* individuals), his denial does not alter the global movement of energy in the least: the latter cannot accumulate limitlessly in the productive forces; eventually, like a river into the sea, it is bound to escape us and be lost to us.

WAR CONSIDERED AS A CATASTROPHIC EXPENDITURE OF EXCESS ENERGY

Incomprehension does not change the final outcome in the slightest. We can ignore or forget the fact that the ground we live on is little other than a field of multiple destructions. Our ignorance only has this incontestable effect: It causes us to *undergo* what we could *bring about* in our own way, if we understood. It deprives us of the choice of an exudation that might suit us. Above all, it consigns men and their works to catastrophic destructions. For if we do not have the force to destroy the surplus energy ourselves, it cannot be used, and, like an unbroken animal that cannot be trained, it is this energy that destroys us; it is we who pay the price of the inevitable explosion.

These excesses of life force, which locally block the poorest economies, are in fact the most dangerous factors of ruination. Hence relieving the blockage was always, if only in the darkest region of consciousness, the object of a feverish pursuit. Ancient societies found relief in festivals; some erected admirable monuments that had no useful purpose; we use the excess to multiply 'services' that make life smoother,[2] and we are led to reabsorb part of it by increasing leisure time. But these diversions have always been inadequate: their existence *in excess* nevertheless (in certain respects) has perpetually doomed multitudes of human beings and great quantities of useful goods to the destruction of wars. In our time, the relative importance of armed conflicts has even increased; it has taken on the disastrous proportions of which we are aware.

Recent history is the result of the soaring growth of industrial activity. At first this prolific movement restrained martial activity by absorbing the main part of the excess: the development of modern industry yielded the period of relative peace from 1815 to 1914.[3] Developing in this way, increasing the resources, the productive forces made possible in the same period the rapid demographic expansion of the advanced countries (this is the fleshly aspect of the bony proliferation of the factories). But in the long run the growth that the technical changes made possible became difficult to sustain. It became productive of an increased surplus itself. The First World War broke out before its limits were really reached, even locally. The Second did not itself signify that the system could not develop further (either extensively or in any case intensively). But it weighed the possibilities of a halt in development and ceased to enjoy the opportunities of a growth that nothing opposed. It is sometimes denied that the industrial plethora was at the origin of these recent wars, particularly the first. Yet it was this plethora that both wars exuded; its size was what gave them their extraordinary intensity. Consequently, the general principle of an excess of energy to be expended, considered (beyond the too narrow scope of the economy) as the effect of a movement that surpasses it, tragically illuminates a set of facts; moreover, it takes on a significance that no one can deny. We can express the hope of avoiding a war that already threatens. But in order to do so we must divert the surplus production, either into the rational extension of a difficult industrial growth, or into unproductive works that will dissipate an energy that cannot be accumulated in any case. This raises numerous problems, which are exhaustingly complex.[4] One can be sceptical of arriving easily at the practical solutions they demand, but the interest they hold is unquestionable.

I will simply state, without waiting further, that the extension of economic growth itself requires the overturning of economic principles – the overturning of the ethics that grounds them. Changing from the perspectives of *restrictive* economy to those of *general* economy actually accomplishes a Copernican transformation: a reversal of thinking – and of ethics. If a part of wealth (subject to a rough estimate) is doomed to destruction or at least to unproductive use without any possible profit, it is logical, even *inescapable*, to surrender commodities without return. Henceforth, leaving aside pure and simple dissipation, analogous to the construction of the Pyramids, the possibility of pursuing growth is itself subordinated to giving: the industrial development of the entire world demands of Americans that they lucidly grasp the necessity, for an economy such as theirs, of having a margin of profitless operations. An immense industrial network cannot be managed in the same way that one changes a tyre ... It expresses a circuit of cosmic energy on which it depends, which it cannot limit, and whose laws it cannot ignore without consequences. Woe to those who, to the very end, insist on regulating the movement that exceeds them with the narrow mind of the mechanic who changes a tyre.

NOTES

1. Of the materiality of the universe, which doubtless, in its proximate and remote aspects, is never anything but a beyond of thought. *Fulfilment* designates that which *fulfils itself*, not that which *is fulfilled*. *Infinite* is in opposition both to the limited determination and to the assigned *end*.
2. It is assumed that if industry cannot have an indefinite development, the same is not true of the 'services' constituting what is called the tertiary sector of the economy (the primary being agriculture and the secondary, industry), which includes specialized insurance organizations as well as the work of artists.

3. See this volume, pp. 194–5.
4. Unfortunately, it is not possible to discuss all these problems within the framework of a first – theoretical and historical – essay.

See:

Jacques Derrida, 'From restricted to general economy: A Hegelianism without reserve', in *Writing and Difference*, trans. Alan Bass (London: Routledge & Kegan Paul, 1978).

1.4

'CRITIQUE OF VIOLENCE'

Walter Benjamin

The task of a critique of violence can be summarized as that of expounding its relation to law and justice. For a cause, however effective, becomes violent, in the precise sense of the word, only when it bears on moral issues. The sphere of these issues is defined by the concepts of law and justice. With regard to the first of these, it is clear that the most elementary relationship within any legal system is that of ends to means, and, further, that violence can first be sought only in the realm of means, not of ends. These observations provide a critique of violence with more – and certainly different – premises than perhaps appears. For if violence is a means, a criterion for criticizing it might seem immediately available. It imposes itself in the question whether violence, in a given case, is a means to a just or an unjust end. A critique of it would then be implied in a system of just ends. This, however, is not so. For what such a system, assuming it to be secure against all doubt, would contain is not a criterion for violence itself as a principle, but, rather, the criterion for cases of its use. The question would remain open whether violence, as a principle, could be a moral means even to just ends. To resolve this question a more exact criterion is needed, which would discriminate within the sphere of means themselves, without regard for the ends they serve.

The exclusion of this more precise critical approach is perhaps the predominant feature of a main current of legal philosophy: natural law. It perceives in the use of violent means to just ends no greater problem than a man sees in his

Source: Walter Benjamin, *One Way Street and Other Writings* (London: Verso: 1985), pp. 132–43.

'right' to move his body in the direction of a desired goal. According to this view (for which the terrorism in the French Revolution provided an ideological foundation), violence is a product of nature, as it were a raw material, the use of which is in no way problematical, unless force is misused for unjust ends. If, according to the theory of state of natural law, people give up all their violence for the sake of the state, this is done on the assumption (which Spinoza, for example, states explicitly in his *Tractatus Theologico-Politicus*) that the individual, before the conclusion of this rational contract, has *de jure* the right to use at will the violence that is *de factor* at his disposal. Perhaps these views have been recently rekindled by Darwin's biology, which, in a thoroughly dogmatic manner, regards violence as the only original means, besides natural selection, appropriate to all the vital ends of nature. Popular Darwinistic philosophy has often shown how short a step it is from this dogma of natural history to the still cruder one of legal philosophy, which holds that the violence that is, almost alone, appropriate to natural ends is thereby also legal.

This thesis of natural law that regards violence as a natural datum is diametrically opposed to that of positive law, which sees violence as a product of history. If natural law can judge all existing law only in criticizing its ends, so positive law can judge all evolving law only in criticizing its means. If justice is the criterion of ends, legality is that of means. Notwithstanding this antithesis, however, both schools meet in their common basic dogma: just ends can be attained by justified means, justified means used for just ends. Natural law attempts, by the justness of the ends, to 'justify' the means, positive law to 'guarantee' the justness of the ends through the justification of the means. This antinomy would prove insoluble if the common dogmatic assumption were false, if justified means on the one hand and just ends on the other were in irreconcilable conflict. No insight into this problem could be gained, however, until the circular argument had been broken, and mutually independent criteria both of just ends and of justified means were established.

The realm of ends, and therefore also the question of a criterion of justness, is excluded for the time being from this study. Instead, the central place is given to the question of the justification of certain means that constitute violence. Principles of natural law cannot decide this question, but can only lead to bottomless casuistry. For if positive law is blind to the absoluteness of ends, natural law is equally so to the contingency of means. On the other hand, the positive theory of law is acceptable as a hypothetical basis at the outset of this study, because it undertakes a fundamental distinction between kinds of violence independently of cases of their application. This distinction is between historically acknowledged, so-called sanctioned violence, and unsanctioned violence. If the following considerations proceed from this it cannot, of course, mean that given forms of violence are classified in terms of whether they are sanctioned or not. For in a critique of violence, a criterion for the latter in positive law cannot concern its uses but only its evaluation. The question that concerns us is, what light is thrown on the nature of violence by the fact that such a criterion or distinction can be applied to it at all, or, in other words, what is the meaning of this distinction? That this distinction supplied by positive law is meaningful, based on the nature of violence, and irreplaceable by any other, will soon enough be shown, but at the same time light will be shed on the sphere in which alone such a distinction can be made. To sum up: if the criterion established by positive law to assess the legality of violence can be analysed with regard to its meaning, then the sphere of its application must be criticized with regard to its value. For this critique a standpoint outside positive legal philosophy but also outside natural law must be found. The extent to which it can only be furnished by a historico-philosophical view of law will emerge.

The meaning of the distinction between legitimate and illegitimate violence is not immediately obvious. The misunderstanding in natural law by which a distinction is drawn between violence used for just and unjust ends must be emphatically rejected. Rather, it has already been indicated that positive law demands of all violence a proof of its historical origin, which under certain conditions is declared legal, sanctioned. Since the acknowledgment of legal violence is most tangibly evident in a deliberate submission to its ends, a hypothetical distinction between kinds of violence must be based on the presence or absence of a general historical acknowledgement of its ends. Ends that lack such acknowledgement may be called natural ends, the other legal ends. The differing function of violence, depending on whether it serves natural or legal ends, can be most clearly traced against a background of specific legal conditions. For the sake of simplicity, the following discussion will relate to contemporary European conditions.

Characteristic of these, as far as the individual as legal subject is concerned, is the tendency not to admit the natural ends of such individuals in all those cases in which such ends could, in a given situation, be usefully pursued by violence. This means: this legal system tries to erect, in all areas where individual ends could be usefully pursued by violence, legal ends that can only be realized by legal power. Indeed, it strives to limit by legal ends even those areas in which natural ends are admitted in principle within wide boundaries, like that of education, as soon as these natural ends are pursued with an excessive measure of violence, as in the laws relating to the limits of educational authority to punish. It can be formulated as a general maxim of present-day European legislation that all the natural ends of individuals must collide with legal ends if pursued with a greater or lesser degree of violence. (The contradiction between this and the right of self-defence will be resolved in what follows.) From this maxim it follows that law sees violence in the hands of individuals as a danger undermining the legal system. As a danger nullifying legal ends and the legal executive? Certainly not; for then violence as such would not be condemned, but only that directed to illegal ends. It will be argued that a system of legal ends cannot be maintained if natural ends are anywhere still pursued violently. In the first place, however, this is a mere dogma. To counter it one might perhaps consider the surprising possibility that the law's interest in a monopoly of violence vis-à-vis individuals is not explained by the intention of preserving legal ends but, rather, by that of preserving the law itself; that violence, when not in the hands of the law, threatens it not by the ends that it may pursue but by its mere existence outside the law. The same may be more drastically suggested if one reflects how often the figure of the 'great' criminal, however repellent his ends may have been, has aroused the secret admiration of the public. This cannot result from his deed, but only from the violence to which it bears witness. In this case, therefore, the violence of which present-day law is seeking in all areas of activity to deprive the individual appears really threatening, and arouses even in defeat the sympathy of the mass against law. By what function violence can with reason seem so threatening to law, and be so feared by it, must be especially evident where its application, even in the present legal system, is still permissible.

This is above all the case in the class struggle, in the form of the workers' guaranteed right to strike. Organized labour is, apart from the state, probably today the only legal subject entitled to exercise violence. Against this view there is certainly the objection that an omission of actions, a non-action, which a strike really is, cannot be described as violence. Such a consideration doubtless made it easier for a state power to conceive the right to strike, once this was no longer avoidable. But its truth is not unconditional, and therefore not unrestricted. It is true that the omission of an action, or service, where it amounts simply to a 'severing of relations', can be an entirely non-violent, pure means. And as in the view of the state, or the law, the right to strike conceded to labour is certainly not a right to exercise violence but, rather, to escape from a violence indirectly exercised by the employer, strikes conforming to this may undoubtedly occur from time to time and involve only a 'withdrawal' or 'estrangement' from the employer. The moment of violence, however, is necessarily introduced, in the form of extortion, into such an omission, if it takes place in the context of a conscious readiness to resume the suspended action under certain circumstances that either have nothing whatever to do with this action or only superficially modify it. Understood in this way, the right to strike constitutes in the view of labour, which is opposed to that of the state, the right to use force in attaining certain ends. The antithesis between the two conceptions emerges in all its bitterness in face of a revolutionary general strike. In this, labour will always appeal to its right to strike, and the state will call this appeal an abuse, since the right to strike was not 'so intended', and take emergency measures. For the state retains the right to declare that a simultaneous use of strike in all industries is illegal, since the specific reasons for strike admitted by legislation cannot be prevalent in every workshop. In this difference of interpretation is expressed the objective contradiction in the legal situation, whereby the state acknowledges a violence whose ends, as natural ends, it sometimes regards with indifference, but in a crisis (the revolutionary general strike) confronts inimically. For, however paradoxical this may appear at first sight, even conduct involving the exercise of a right can nevertheless, under certain circumstances, be described as violent. More specifically, such conduct, when active, may be called violent if it exercises a right in order to overthrow the legal system that has conferred it; when passive, it is nevertheless to be so described if it constitutes extortion in the sense explained above. It therefore reveals an objective contradiction in the legal situation, but not a logical contradiction in the law, if under certain circumstances the law meets the strikers, as perpetrators of violence, with violence. For in a strike the state fears above all else that function which it is the object of this study to identify as the only secure foundation of its critique. For if violence were, as first appears, merely the means to secure directly whatever happens to be sought, it could fulfill its end as predatory violence. It would be entirely unsuitable as a basis for, or a modification to, relatively stable conditions. The strike shows, however, that it can be so, that it is able to found and modify legal conditions, however offended the sense of justice may find itself thereby. It will be objected that such a function of violence is fortuitous and isolated. This can be rebutted by a consideration of military violence.

The possibility of military law rests on exactly the same objective contradiction in the legal situation as does that of strike law, that is to say, on the fact that legal subjects sanction violence whose ends remain for the sanctioners natural ends, and can therefore in a crisis come into conflict with their own legal or natural ends. Admittedly, military violence is in the first place used quite directly, as predatory violence, toward its ends. Yet it is very striking that even – or, rather, precisely – in primitive conditions that know hardly the beginnings of constitutional relations, and even in cases where the victor has established himself in invulnerable possession, a peace ceremony is entirely necessary. Indeed, the word 'peace', in the sense in which it is the correlative to the word 'war' (for there is also a quite different meaning, similarly unmetaphorical and political, the one used by Kant in talking of 'Eternal Peace'), denotes this a priori, necessary sanctioning, regardless of all other legal conditions, of every victory. This sanction consists precisely in recognizing the new conditions as a new 'law', quite regardless of whether they need *de facto* any guarantee of their continuation. If, therefore, conclusions can be drawn from military violence, as being primordial and paradigmatic of all violence used for natural ends, there is inherent in all such violence a law-making character. We shall return later to the implications of this insight. It explains the above-mentioned tendency of modern law to divest the individual, at least as a legal subject, of all violence, even that directed only to natural ends. In the great criminal this violence confronts the law with the threat of declaring a new law, a threat that even today, despite its impotence, in important instances horrifies the public as it did in primeval times. The state, however, fears this violence simply for its law-making character, being obliged to acknowledge it as law-making whenever external powers force it to concede them the right to conduct warfare, and classes the right to strike.

If in the last war the critique of military violence was the starting point for a passionate critique of violence in general – which taught at least one thing, that violence is no longer exercised and tolerated naïvely – nevertheless, violence was not only subject to criticism for its law-making character, but was also judged, perhaps more annihilatingly, for another of its functions. For a duality in the function of violence is characteristic of militarism, which could only come into being through general conscription. Militarism is the compulsory, universal use of violence as a means to the ends of the state. This compulsory use of violence has recently been scrutinized as closely as, or still more closely than, the use of violence itself. In it violence shows itself in a function quite different from its simple application for natural ends. It consists in the use of violence as a means of legal ends. For the subordination of citizens to law – in the present case, to the law of general conscription – is a legal end. If that first function of violence is called the law-making function, this second will be called the law-preserving function. Since conscription is a case of law-preserving violence that is not in principle distinguished from others, a really effective critique of it is far less easy than the declamations of pacifists and activists suggest. Rather, such a critique coincides with the critique of all legal violence – that is, with the critique of legal or executive force – and cannot be performed by any lesser programme. Nor, of course – unless one is prepared to proclaim a quite childish anarchism – is it achieved by refusing to acknowledge any constraint toward persons and declaring 'What pleases is permitted'. Such a maxim merely excludes reflection on the moral and historical spheres, and thereby on any meaning in action, and beyond this on any meaning in reality itself, which cannot be constituted if 'action' is removed from its sphere. More important is the fact that even the appeal, so frequently attempted, to the categorical imperative, with its doubtless incontestable minimum programme – act in such a way that at all times you use humanity both in your person and in the person of all others as an end, and never merely as a means – is in itself inadequate for such a critique.[1] For positive law, if conscious of its roots, will certainly claim to acknowledge and promote the interest of mankind in the person of each individual. It sees this interest in the representation and preservation of an order imposed by fate. While this view, which claims to preserve law in its very basis, cannot escape criticism, nevertheless all attacks that are made merely in the name of a formless 'freedom' without being able to specify this higher order of freedom, remain impotent against it. And most impotent of all when, instead of attacking the legal system root and branch, they inpugn particular laws or legal practices that the law, of course, takes under the protection of its power, which resides in the fact that there is only one fate and that what exists, and in particular what threatens, belongs inviolably to its order. For law-preserving violence is a threatening violence. And its threat is not intended as the deterrent that uninformed liberal theorists interpret it to be. A deterrent in the exact sense would require a certainty that contradicts the nature of a threat and is not attained by any law, since there is always hope of eluding its arm. This makes it all the more threatening, like fate, on which depends whether the criminal is apprehended. The deepest purpose of the uncertainty of the legal threat will emerge from the later consideration of the sphere of fate in which it originates. There is a useful pointer to it in the sphere of punishments. Among them, since the validity of positive law has been called into question, capital punishment has provoked more criticism than all others. However superficial the arguments may in most cases have been, their motives were and are rooted in principle. The opponent of these critics felt, perhaps without knowing why and probably involuntarily, that an attack on capital punishment assails, not legal measure, not laws, but law itself in its origin. For if violence, violence crowned by fate, is the origin of law, then it may be readily supposed that where the highest violence, that over life and death, occurs in the legal system, the origins of law jut manifestly and fearsomely into existence. In agreement with this is the fact that the death penalty in primitive legal systems is imposed even for such crimes as offenses against property, to which it seems quite out of 'proportion'. Its purpose is not to punish the infringement of law but to establish new law. For in the exercise of violence over life and death more than in any other legal act, law reaffirms itself. But in this very violence something rotten in law is revealed, above all to a finer sensibility, because the latter knows itself to be infinitely remote from conditions in which fate might imperiously have shown itself in such a sentence. Reason must, however, attempt to approach such conditions all the more resolutely, if it is to bring to a conclusion its critique of both law-making and law-preserving violence.

In a far more unnatural combination than in the death penalty, in a kind of spectral mixture, these two forms of violence are present in another institution of the modern state, the police. True, this is violence for legal ends (in the right of disposition), but with the simultaneous authority to decide these ends itself within wide limits (in the right of decree). The ignominy of such an authority, which is felt by few simply because its ordinances suffice only seldom for the crudest acts, but are therefore allowed to rampage all the more blindly in the most vulnerable areas and against thinkers, from whom the state is not protected by law – this ignominy lies in the fact that in this authority the separation of law-making and law-preserving violence is suspended. If the first is required to prove its worth in victory, the second is subject to the restriction that it may not set itself new ends. Police violence is emancipated from both conditions. It is law-making, for its characteristic function is not the promulgation of laws but the assertion of legal claims for any decree, and law-preserving, because it is at the disposal of these ends. The assertion that the ends of police violence are always identical or even connected to those of general law is entirely untrue. Rather, the 'law' of the police really marks the point at which the state, whether from impotence or because of the immanent connections within any legal system, can no longer guarantee through the legal system the empirical ends that it desires at any price to attain. Therefore the police intervene 'for security reasons' in countless cases where no clear legal situation exists, when they are not merely, without the slightest relation to legal ends, accompanying the citizen as a brutal encumbrance through a life regulated by ordinances, or simply supervising him. Unlike law, which acknowledges in the 'decision' determined by place and time a metaphysical category that gives it a claim to critical evaluation, a consideration of the police institution encounters nothing essential at all. Its power is formless, like its nowhere tangible, all-pervasive, ghostly presence in the life of civilized states. And though the police may, in particulars, everywhere appear the same, it cannot finally be denied that their spirit is less devastating where they represent, in absolute monarchy, the power of a ruler in which legislative and executive supremacy are united, than in democracies where their existence, elevated by no such relation, bears witness to the greatest conceivable degeneration of violence.

All violence as a means is either law-making or law-preserving. If it lays claim to neither of these predicates, it forfeits all validity. It follows, however, that all violence as a means, even in the most favourable case, is implicated in the problematic nature of law itself. And if the importance of these problems cannot be assessed with certainty at this stage of the investigation, law nevertheless appears, from what has been said, in so ambiguous a moral light that the question poses itself whether there are no other than violent means for regulating conflicting human interests. We are above all obligated to note that a totally non-violent resolution of conflicts can never lead to a legal contract. For the latter, however peacefully it may have been entered into by the parties, leads finally to possible violence. It confers on both parties the right to take recourse to violence in some form against the other, should he break the agreement. Not only that; like the outcome, the origin of every contract also points toward violence. It need not be directly present in it as law-making violence, but is represented in it insofar as the power that guarantees a legal contract is in turn of violent origin even if violence is not introduced into the contract itself. When the consciousness of the latent presence of violence in a legal institution disappears, the institution falls into decay. In our time, parliaments provide an example of this. They offer the familiar, woeful spectacle because they have not remained conscious of the revolutionary forces to which they owe their existence. Accordingly, in Germany in particular, the last manifestation of such forces bore no fruit for parliaments. They lack the sense that a law-making violence is represented by themselves; no wonder that they cannot achieve decrees worthy of this violence, but cultivate in compromise a supposedly non-violent manner of dealing with political affairs. This remains, however, a 'product situated within the mentality of violence, no matter how it may disdain all open violence, because the effort toward compromise is motivated not internally but from outside, by the opposing effort, because no compromise, however freely accepted, is conceivable without a compulsive character. "It would be better otherwise" is the underlying feeling in every compromise.'[2] Significantly, the decay of parliaments has perhaps alienated as many minds from the ideal of a non-violent resolution of political conflicts as were attracted to it by the war. The pacifists are confronted by the Bolsheviks and Syndicalists. These have effected an annihilating and on the whole apt critique of present-day parliaments. Nevertheless, however desirable and gratifying a flourishing parliament might be by comparison, a discussion of means of political agreement that are in principle non-violent cannot be concerned with parliamentarianism. For what parliament achieves in vital affairs can only be those legal decrees that in their origin and outcome are attended by violence.

NOTE

1. One might, rather, doubt whether this famous demand does not contain too little, that is, whether it is permissible to use, or allow to be used, oneself or another in any respect as a means. Very good grounds for such doubt could be adduced.

See:

Jacques Derrida, 'Force of law: The mystical foundations of authority', tr. Mary Quaintance, in Drucilla Cornell, Michael Rosenfield and David Gray Carlson (eds) *Deconstruction and the Possibility of Justice* (New York: Routledge, 1992).

'THE TASK OF DESTROYING THE HISTORY OF ONTOLOGY'

Martin Heidegger

All research – and not least that which operates within the range of the central question of Being – is an ontical possibility of Dasein. Dasein's Being finds its meaning in temporality. But temporality is also the condition which makes historicality possible as a temporal kind of Being which Dasein itself possesses, regardless of whether or how Dasein is an entity 'in time'. Historicality, as a determinate character, is prior to what is called 'history' (world-historical historizing).[1]

'Historicality' stands for the state of Being that is constitutive for Dasein's 'historizing' as such; only on the basis of such 'historizing' is anything like 'world-history' possible or can anything belong historically to world-history. In its factical Being, any Dasein is as it already was, and it is 'what' it already was. It *is* its past, whether explicitly or not. And this is so not only in that its past is, as it were, pushing itself along 'behind' it, and that Dasein possesses what is past as a property which is still present-at-hand and which sometimes has after-effects upon it: Dasein 'is' its past in the way of *its* own Being, which, to put it roughly, 'historizes' out of its future on each occasion.[2] Whatever the way of being it may have at the time, and thus with whatever understanding of Being it may possess, Dasein has grown up both into and in a traditional way of interpreting itself: in terms of this it understands itself proximally and, within a certain range, constantly. By this understanding, the possibilities of its Being are disclosed and regulated. Its own past – and this always means the past of its

Source: Heidegger, Martin, *Being and Time*, tr. John McQuarrie (Oxford: Blackwell, 1988), pp. 41–9.

'generation' – is not something which *follows along after* Dasein, but something which already goes ahead of it.

This elemental historicality of Dasein may remain hidden from Dasein itself. But there is a way by which it can be discovered and given proper attention. Dasein can discover tradition, preserve it, and study it explicitly. The discovery of tradition and the disclosure of what it 'transmits' and how this is transmitted, can be taken hold of as a task in its own right. In this way Dasein brings itself into the kind of Being which consists in historiological inquiry and research. But historiology – or more precisely historicity[3] – is possible as a kind of Being which the inquiring Dasein may possess, only because historicality is a determining characteristic for Dasein in the very basis of its Being. If this historicality remains hidden from Dasein, and as long as it so remains, Dasein is also denied the possibility of historiological inquiry or the discovery of history. If historiology is wanting, this is not evidence *against* Dasein's historicality; on the contrary, as a deficient mode[4] of this state of Being, it is evidence for it. Only because it is 'historical' can an era be unhistoriological.

On the other hand, if Dasein has seized upon its latent possibility not only of making its own existence transparent to itself but also of inquiring into the meaning of existentiality itself (that is to say, of previously inquiring into the meaning of Being in general), and if by such inquiry its eyes have been opened to its own essential historicality, then one cannot fail to see that the inquiry into Being (the ontico-ontological necessity of which we have already indicated) is itself characterized by historicality. The ownmost meaning of Being which belongs to the inquiry into Being as an historical inquiry, gives us the assignment [Anweisung] of inquiring into the history of that inquiry itself, that is, of becoming historiological. In working out the question of Being, we must heed this assignment, so that by positively making the past our own, we may bring ourselves into full possession of the ownmost possibilities of such inquiry. The question of the meaning of Being must be carried through by explicating Dasein beforehand in its temporality and historicality; the question thus brings itself to the point where it understands itself as historiological.

Our preparatory Interpretation of the fundamental structures of Dasein with regard to the average kind of Being which is closest to it (a kind of Being in which it is therefore proximally historical as well), will make manifest, however, not only that Dasein is inclined to fall back upon its world (the world in which it is) and to interpret itself in terms of that world by its reflected light, but also that Dasein simultaneously falls prey to the tradition of which it has more or less explicitly taken hold.[5] This tradition keeps it from providing its own guidance, whether in inquiring or in choosing. This holds true – and by no means least – for that understanding which is rooted in Dasein's ownmost Being, and for the possibility of developing it – namely, for ontological understanding.

When tradition thus becomes master, it does so in such a way that what it 'transmits' is made so inaccessible, proximally and for the most part, that it rather becomes concealed. Tradition takes what has come down to us and delivers it over to self-evidence; it blocks our access to those primordial 'sources' from which the categories and concepts handed down to us have been in part quite genuinely drawn.[6] Indeed it makes us forget that they have had such an origin, and makes us suppose that the necessity of going back to these sources is something which we need not even understand. Dasein has had its historicality so thoroughly uprooted by tradition that it confines its interest to the multiformity of possible types, directions, and standpoints of philosophical activity in the most exotic and alien of cultures; and by this very interest it seeks to veil the fact that it has no ground of its own to stand on. Consequently, despite all its historiological interests and all its zeal for an Interpretation which is philologically 'objective' ['sachliche'], Dasein no longer understands the most elementary conditions which would alone enable it to go back to the past in a positive manner and make it productively its own.

We have shown at the outset (Section I) not only that the question of the meaning of Being is one that has not been attended to and one that has been inadequately formulated, but that it has become quite forgotten in spite of all our interest in 'metaphysics'. Greek ontology and its history – which, in their numerous filiations and distortions, determine the conceptual character of philosophy even today – prove that when Dasein understands either itself or Being in general, it does so in terms of the 'world', and that the ontology which has thus arisen has deteriorated [verfällt] to a tradition in which it gets reduced to something self-evident – merely material for reworking, as it was for Hegel. In the Middle Ages this uprooted Greek ontology became a fixed body of doctrine. Its systematics, however, is by no means a mere joining together of traditional pieces into a single edifice. Though its basic conceptions of Being have been taken over dogmatically from the Greeks, a great deal of unpretentious work has been carried on further within these limits. With the peculiar character which the Scholastics gave it, Greek ontology has, in its essentials, travelled the path that leads through the *Disputationes metaphysicae* of Suarez to the 'metaphysics' and transcendental philosophy of modern times, determining even the foundations and the aims of Hegel's 'logic'. In the course of this history certain distinctive domains of Being have come into view and have served as the primary guides for subsequent problematics: the *ego cogito* of Descartes, the subject, the 'I', reason, spirit, person. But these all remain uninterrogated as to their Being and its structure, in accordance with the thoroughgoing way in which the question of Being has been neglected. It is rather the case that the categorial content of the traditional ontology has been carried over to these entities with corresponding formalizations and purely negative restrictions, or else dialectic has been called in for the purpose of Interpreting the substantiality of the subject ontologically.

If the question of Being is to have its own history made transparent, then this hardened tradition must be loosened up, and the concealments which it has brought about[7] must be dissolved. We understand this task as one in which by taking *the question of Being as our clue*, we are to *destroy* the traditional content of ancient ontology until we arrive at those primordial experiences in which we achieved our first ways of determining the nature of Being – the ways which have guided us ever since.

In thus demonstrating the origin of our basic ontological concepts by an investigation in which their 'birth certificate' is displayed, we have nothing to do with a vicious relativizing of ontological standpoints. But this destruction is just as far from having the *negative* sense of shaking off the ontological tradition. We must, on the contrary, stake out the positive possibilities of that tradition, and this always means keeping it within its *limits*; these in turn are given factically in the way the question is formulated at the time, and in the way the possible field for investigation is thus bounded off. On its negative side, this destruction does not relate itself towards the past; its criticism is aimed at 'today' and at the prevalent way of treating the history of ontology, whether it is headed towards doxography, towards intellectual history, or towards a history of problems. But to bury the past in nullity [Nichtigkeit] is not the purpose of this destruction; its aim is *positive*; its negative function remains unexpressed and indirect.

The destruction of the history of ontology is essentially bound up with the way the question of Being is formulated, and it is possible only within such a formulation. In the framework of our treatise, which aims at working out that question in principle, we can carry out this destruction only with regard to stages of that history which are in principle decisive.

In line with the positive tendencies of this destruction, we must in the first instance raise the question whether and to what extent the Interpretation of Being and the phenomenon of time have been brought together thematically in the course of the history of ontology, and whether the problematic of Temporality required for this has ever been worked out in principle or ever could have been. The first and only person who has gone any stretch of the way towards investigating the dimension of Temporality or has even let himself be drawn hither by the coercion of the phenomena themselves is Kant. Only when we have established the problematic of Temporality, can we succeed in casting light on the obscurity of his doctrine of the schematism. But this will also show us *why* this area is one which had to remain closed off to him in its real dimensions and its central ontological function. Kant himself was aware that he was venturing into an area of obscurity: 'This schematism of our understanding as regards appearances and their mere form is an art hidden in the depths of the human soul, the true devices of which are hardly ever to be divined from Nature and laid uncovered before our eyes.' Here Kant shrinks back, as it were, in the face of something which must be brought to light as a theme and a principle if the expression 'Being' is to have any demonstrable meaning. In the end, those very phenomena which will be exhibited under the heading of 'Temporality' in our analysis, are precisely those *most covert* judgments of the 'common reason' for which Kant says it is the 'business of philosophers' to provide an analytic.

In pursuing this task of destruction with the problematic of Temporality as our clue, we shall try to Interpret the chapter on the schematism and the Kantian doctrine of time, taking that chapter as our point of departure. At the same time we shall show why Kant could never achieve an insight into the problematic of Temporality. There were two things that stood in his way: in the first place, he altogether neglected the problem of Being; and, in connection with this, he failed to provide an ontology with Dasein as its theme or (to put this in Kantian language) to give a preliminary ontological analytic of the subjectivity of the subject. Instead of this, Kant took over Descartes' position quite dogmatically, notwithstanding all the essential respects in which he had gone beyond him. Furthermore, in spite of the fact that he was bringing the phenomenon of time back into the subject again, his analysis of it remained oriented towards the traditional way in which time had been ordinarily understood; in the long run this kept him from working out the phenomenon of a 'transcendental determination of time' in its own structure and function. Because of this double effect of tradition the decisive *connection* between *time* and the '*I think*' was shrouded in utter darkness; it did not even become a problem.

In taking over Descartes' ontological position Kant made an essential omission: he failed to provide an ontology of Dasein. This omission was a decisive one in the spirit [im Sinne] of Descartes' ownmost Tendencies. With the '*cogito sum*' Descartes had claimed that he was putting philosophy on a new and firm footing. But what he left undetermined when he began in this 'radical' way, was the kind of Being which belongs to the *res cogitans*, or – more precisely – the *meaning of the Being of the 'Sum'.*[8] By working out the unexpressed ontological foundations of the '*cogito sum*', we shall complete our sojourn at the second station along the path of our destructive retrospect of the history of ontology. Our Interpretation will not only prove that Descartes had to neglect the question of Being altogether; it will also show why he came to suppose that the absolute 'Being-certain' ['Gewisssein'] of the *cogito* exempted him from raising the question of the meaning of the Being which this entity possesses.

Yet Descartes not only continued to neglect this and thus to accept a completely indefinite ontological status for the *res cogitans sive mens sive animus* ['the thing which cognizes, whether it be a mind or spirit']: he regarded this entity as a *fundamentum inconcussum*, and applied the medieval ontology to it in carrying through the fundamental considerations of his *Meditationes*. He defined the *res cogitans* ontologically as an *ens*; and in the medieval ontology the meaning of Being for such an *ens* had been fixed by understanding it as an *ens creatum*. God, as *ens infinitum*, was the *ens increatum*. But createdness [Geschaffenheit] in the widest sense of something's having been produced [Hergestelltheit], was an essential item in the structure of the ancient conception of Being. The seemingly new beginning which Descartes proposed for philosophizing has revealed itself as the implantation of a baleful prejudice, which has kept later generations from making any thematic ontological analytic of the 'mind' ['Gemütes'] such as would take the question of Being as a clue and would at the same time come to grips critically with the traditional ancient ontology.

Everyone who is acquainted with the middle ages sees that Descartes is 'dependent' upon medieval scholasticism and employs its terminology. But with this 'discovery' nothing is achieved philosophically as long as it remains obscure to what a profound extent the medieval ontology has influenced the way in which posterity has determined or failed to determine the ontological character of the *res cogitans*. The full extent of this cannot be estimated until both the meaning and the limitations of the ancient ontology have been exhibited in terms of an orientation directed towards the question of Being. In other words, in our process of destruction we find ourselves faced with the task of Interpreting the basis of the ancient ontology in the light of the problematic of Temporality. When this is done, it will be manifest that the ancient way of interpreting the Being of entities is oriented towards the 'world' or 'Nature' in the widest sense, and that it is indeed in terms of 'time' that its understanding of Being is obtained. The outward evidence for this (though of course it is *merely* outward evidence) is the treatment of the meaning of Being as παρονσία or ούσία, which signifies, in ontologico-Temporal terms, 'presence' ['Anwesenheit'].[9] Entities are grasped in their Being as 'presence'; this means that they are understood with regard to a definite mode of time – the 'Present'.[10]

The problematic of Greek ontology, like that of any other, must take its clues from Dasein itself. In both ordinary and philosophical usage, Dasein, man's Being, is 'defined' as the ζῷον λόγον ἔχον – as that living thing whose Being is essentially determined by the potentiality for discourse.[11] λέγειν is the clue for arriving at those structures of Being which belong to the entities we encounter in addressing ourselves to anything or speaking about it [im Ansprechen und Besprechen]. This is why the ancient ontology as developed by Plato turns into 'dialectic'. As the ontological clue gets progressively worked out – namely, in the 'hermeneutic' of the λόγος – it becomes increasingly possible to grasp the problem of Being in a more radical fashion. The 'dialectic', which has been a genuine philosophical embarrassment, becomes superfluous. That is *why* Aristotle 'no longer has any understanding' of it, for he has put it on a more radical footing and raised it to a new level [aufhob]. λέγειν itself – or rather νοεῖν, that simple awareness of something present-at-hand in its sheer presence-at-hand,[12] which Parmenides had already taken to guide him in his own interpretation of Being – has the Temporal structure of a pure 'making-present' of something.[13] Those entities which show themselves in this and for it, and which are understood as entities in the most authentic sense, thus get interpreted with regard to the Present; that is, they are conceived as presence (ούσία).[14]

Yet the Greeks have managed to interpret Being in this way without any explicit knowledge of the clues which function here, without any acquaintance with the fundamental ontological function of time or even any understanding of it, and without any insight into the reason why this function is possible. On the contrary, they take time itself as one entity among other entities, and try to grasp it in the structure of its Being, though that way of understanding Being which they have taken as their horizon is one which is itself naïvely and inexplicitly oriented towards time.

Within the framework in which we are about to work out the principles of the question of Being, we cannot present a detailed Temporal Interpretation of the foundations of ancient ontology, particularly not of its loftiest and purest scientific stage, which is reached in Aristotle. Instead we shall give an interpretation of Aristotle's essay on time, which may be chosen as providing a way of *discriminating* the basis and the limitations of the ancient science of Being.

Aristotle's essay on time is the first detailed Interpretation of this phenomenon which has come down to us. Every subsequent account of time, including Bergson's, has been essentially determined by it. When we analyse the Aristotelian conception, it will likewise become clear, as we go back, that the Kantian account of time operates within the structures which Aristotle has set forth; this means that Kant's basic ontological orientation remains that of the Greeks, in spite of all the distinctions which arise in a new inquiry.

The question of Being does not achieve its true concreteness until we have carried through the process of destroying the ontological tradition. In this way we can fully prove that the question of the meaning of Being is one that we cannot avoid, and we can demonstrate what it means to talk about 'restating' this question.

In any investigation in this field, where 'the thing itself is deeply veiled' one must take pains not to overestimate the results. For in such an inquiry one is constantly compelled to face the possibility of disclosing an even more primordial and more universal horizon from which we may draw the answer to the question, 'What is "*Being*"?' We can discuss such possibilities seriously and with positive results only if the question of Being has been reawakened and we have arrived at a field where we can come to terms with it in a way that can be controlled.

NOTES

1. 'weltgeschichtliches Geschehen'. While the verb 'geschehen' ordinarily means to 'happen', and will often be so translated, Heidegger stresses its etymological kinship to 'Geschichte' or 'history'. To bring out this connection, we have coined the verb 'historize', which might be paraphrased as to 'happen in a historical way'; we shall usually translate 'geschehen' this way in contexts where history is being discussed. We trust that the reader will keep in mind that such 'historizing' is characteristic of all historical entities, and is *not* the sort of thing that is done primarily by historians (as 'philosophizing', for instance, is done by philosophers).
2. 'Das Dasein "ist" seine Vergangenheit in der Weise *seines* Seins, das, roh gesagt, jeweils aus seiner Zukunft her "geschieht".'
3. 'Historizität'.
4. 'defizienter Modus'. Heidegger likes to think of certain characteristics as occurring in various ways or 'modes', among which may be included certain ways of 'not occurring' or 'occurring only to an inadequate extent' or, in general, occurring 'deficiently'. It is as if zero and the negative integers were to be thought of as representing 'deficient modes of being a positive integer'.

5. '... das Dasein hat nicht nur die Geneigtheit, an seine Welt, in der es ist, zu verfallen und reluzent aus ihr her sich auszulegen, Dasein verfällt in eins damit auch seiner mehr oder minder ausdrücklich ergriffenen Tradition.' The verb 'verfallen' is one which Heidegger will use many times. Though we shall usually translate it simply as 'fall', it has the connotation of *deteriorating, collapsing,* or *falling down.* Neither our 'fall back upon' nor our 'falls prey to' is quite right: but 'fall upon' and 'fall on to', which are more literal, would be misleading for 'an ... zu verfallen'; and though 'falls to the lot of' and 'devolves upon' would do well for 'verfällt' with the dative in other contexts, they will not do so well here.

6. In this passage Heidegger juxtaposes a number of words beginning with the prefix 'über-'; 'übergibt' ('transmits'); 'überantwortet' ('delivers over'); 'das Überkommene' ('what has come down to us'); 'überlieferten' ('handed down to us').

7. '... der durch sie gezeitigten Verdeckungen.' The verb 'zeitigen' will appear frequently in later chapters.

8. We follow the later editions in reading *'der Seinssinn des "sum"'*. The earlier editions have an anacoluthic 'den' for 'der'.

9. The noun οὐσία is derived from one of the stems used in conjugating the irregular verb εἶναι, ('to be'); in the Aristotelian tradition it is usually translated as 'substance', though translators of Plato are more likely to write 'essence', 'existence', or 'being'. Heidegger suggests that οὐσία is to be thought of as synonymous with the derivative noun παρουσία ('being-at', 'presence'). As he points out, παρουσία has a close etymological correspondence with the German 'Anwesenheit', which is similarly derived from the stem of a verb meaning 'to be' and a prefix of the place or time at which ('an-'). We shall in general translate 'Anwesenheit' as 'presence', and the participle 'anwesend' as some form of the expression 'have presence'.

10. 'die *"Gegenwart"'*. While this noun may, like παρουσία or 'Anwesenheit', mean the *presence* of someone *at* some place or on some occasion, it more often means the *present*, as distinguished from the past and the future. In its etymological root-structure, however, it means a *waiting-towards*. While Heidegger seems to think of all these meanings as somehow fused, we shall generally translate this noun as 'the Present', reserving 'in the present' for the corresponding adjective 'gegenwärtig'.

11. The phrase ζῷον λόγον ἔχον is traditionally translated as 'rational animal', on the assumption that λόγος refers to the faculty of *reason*. Heidegger, however, points out that λόγος is derived from the same root as the verb λέγειν ('to talk', 'to hold discourse'); he identifies this in turn with νοεῖν ('to cognize', 'to be aware of', 'to know'), and calls attention to the fact that the same stem is found in the adjective διαλεκτικός ('dialectical'). He thus interprets λόγος as 'Rede', which we shall usually translate as 'discourse' or 'talk', depending on the context.

12. '... von etwas Vorhandenem in seiner puren Vorhandenheit ...' The adjective 'vorhanden' means literally 'before the hand', but this signification has long since given way to others. In ordinary German usage it may, for instance, be applied to the stock of goods which a dealer has 'on hand', or to the 'extant' works of an author; and in earlier philosophical writing it could be used, like the word 'Dasein' itself, as a synonym for the Latin *'existentia'*. Heidegger, however, distinguishes quite sharply between 'Dasein' and 'Vorhandenheit', using the latter to designate a kind of Being which belongs to things *other* than Dasein. We shall translate 'vorhanden' as 'present-at-hand', and 'Vorhandenheit' as 'presence-at-hand'. The reader must be careful not to confuse these expressions with our 'presence' ('Anwesenheit') and 'the Present' ('die Gegenwart'), etc., or with a few other verbs and adjectives which we may find it convenient to translate by 'present'.

13. '... des reinen *"Gegenwärtigens"* von etwas'. The verb 'gegenwärtigen', which is derived from the adjective 'gegenwärtig', is not a normal German verb, but was used by Husserl and is used extensively by Heidegger. While we shall translate it by

various forms of 'make present', it does not necessarily mean 'making physically present', but often means something like 'bringing vividly to mind'.

14. 'Das Seiende, das sich in ihm für es zeigt und das als das eigentliche Seiende verstanden wird, erhält demnach seine Auslegung in Rücksicht auf – Gegen-wart, d.h. es ist als Anwesenheit (οὐσία) begriffen.' The hyphenation of 'Gegen-wart' calls attention to the structure of this word in a way which cannot be reproduced in English. See note 10. The pronouns 'ihm' and 'es' presumably both refer back to λέγειν, though their reference is ambiguous, as our version suggests.

See:

Jacques Derrida, 'Ousia and Gramme: Note on a note from Being and Time', in Margins of Philosophy, tr. Alan Bass (Brighton: Harvester Press, 1982).

Jacques Derrida, 'Geschlect II: Heidegger's Hand', tr. John P. Leavey Jr, in John Sallis (ed.), Deconstruction and Philosophy: The Texts of Jacques Derrida (Chicago: Chicago University Press, 1987).

Jacques Derrida, Of Spirit: Heidegger and the Question, tr. Geoffrey Bennington and Rachel Bowlby (Chicago: University of Chicago Press, 1989).

Jacques Derrida, 'Heidegger's Ear: Philopolemology (Geschlect IV)', tr. John P. Leavey Jr, in John Sallis (ed.), Reading Heidegger: Commemorations (Bloomington: Indiana University Press, 1993).

1.6

'THE MOMENT AFTER'

Edmond Jabes

[1]

'The eye captures what it will destroy. It ca'n not perceive what escapes death, what is invisible,' he said.

'The eye is human. It made Adam mortal.
'When Adam opened his eyes God trembled.
'Adam's fall is the triumph of the eye.'
'God is eyeless,' he also said.

God knows: He is blind. Man comes to know what his eyes destroy. All knowledge passes through choice. Choice guarantees murder.

'Thou shalt not kill,' commands God. Did he hope that man would turn blind again?

'Ah Lord, why make me a murderer by giving me the sense of sight and then damn me for opening my eyes?' wrote a rabbi I met shortly after writing the last page of the *Book of Questions*.

'God created the world on the scale of the creature's glance so that they would die of one another,' he had noted.

'God created the world, that is, God created Himself, in order to face up to the eyes of man and to show His power by escaping them,' he had noted elsewhere.

Source: Edmond Jabes, *The Book of Margins*, tr. R. Waldrop (Chicago: University of Chicago Press, 1993), pp. 33–48.

The best proof of love the creature could give God was to accept His Invisibility.

The world will go out with the eye. Everything will have been said, as at the beginning.

[2]

'... the lethal opening of the eye.'

Jacques Derrida

[3]

The eye is a blank page. It succumbs to seeing.

You turn into writing what you see; what sees you, into reading.

The eye means oblivion. Both oblivion of things seen and the muted glace of oblivion.

You will do nothing. You will disintegrate.

LETTER TO JACQUES DERRIDA ON THE QUESTION OF THE BOOK

'... I have regularly tried to put philosophy on stage, on a stage it cannot upstage.'

Jacques Derrida

To speak, to keep silent, already invokes difference.
Where totality is a blank, the fragment must also be.
A drop of blood, the book's sun.)

To the incendiary letter we have granted the right to set fire.
The word is a world in flames.

God burns forever in the four fires of His Name.

O day everlasting within ephemeral day.

'Tonight, like every night, by the light of my candle, I am filling a few unquenched pages with exhumed words.

'God, on the other side of my table, composes His book whose smoke envelops me: for the flame of my candle is His pen.

'What will my book be, shortly, but a bit of ash on one of His pages?

'There is no protected preserve of writing,' an unappreciated rabbi, whose name I will not reveal, wrote three centuries ago.

He also wrote: 'In every word, a wall of fire separates me from God, and God, together with me, is this word.'

The fire cannot die in the word it writes. Eternity of the book, from conflagration to conflagration ...

There will never be more than one single book promised to the fire to which all books are sacrificed. Thus time is written in the ashes of time, and the book of God, in the mad flames of our books.

(*Fire: virginity of desire.*)

If, in reply to the invitation to participate in an issue of the magazine *L'Arc* devoted to you, I have decided to address you directly in its pages, it is because I have reached a crucial point in the practice of writing, the heart – and often darkest night – of an incessant questioning of letter and sign (caught at the perilous point of becoming word and book) where I can speak to – or of – others only in the intimate voice of dialogue, a voice charged with all our listening for a voice that, as we know, once broke the silence for itself.

But it is also in order to control my irritation at the fact that, for many, questioning the word has suddenly become a rigged game of surface boldness, a clever appropriation of what cannot be taken head-on.

The code is known, transmitted, and our reading is based on it, on this knowledge, this confidence in the written. A reading called open at the level of the text. But of which text? since, once drafted – of this reading I shall make my writing – the text is nothing but the application of a theory accepted in advance, of a method adopted with all its subtle combinations and schemes, whose consequences for us we cannot even gauge, but on which we nevertheless build our books.

The blank page is not a grid we must adapt to. It will surely become so, but at what price?

Thus the important works of our time are most often approached as part of a current craze and, above all, in terms of what we have gotten out of them and remembered, of what we can cheerfully refer to.

At the farthest outpost of the coast, we erect a lighthouse: stone tower and beacon. We become its honorable keeper, but forget that the only purpose of the beacon is to sweep its beam across the ocean and direct ships through the night toward anchor in safe harbor.

The movement of the book is that of amorous and aggressive waves lit by the pen as by searchlights in the dusk where writing unfolds, and whose sighs, growls, cries, and gasps are recorded from a distance by the lighthouse keeper and the writer.

This is why there is no *pleasure* – alone – *of the text*, nor boredom, terror, or rage. We cannot cling exclusively to one of those equivocal instants when the duration of the text – and otherwise the text would not be text – is sovereign testimony to all the hate and lust felt, all the sperm and blood spurted and spilled by wave and word as our share.

We always start out from a written text and come back to the text to be written, from the sea to the sea, from the page to the page. The ship, too, is perhaps an obsessive word caught by the searchlight, glimpsed, followed, then vanishing, but still haunting us as it haunts the rectangle of paper or the part of the ocean turned white with its passage, with spindrift secreted from a wound.

Light beams! My mind has always connected the image of the lighthouse keeper with that of the fireman up on his ladder: one tries to douse a fire, the other, to light up the sea. Both make us see death.

So many buildings burn beneath the water.
Day and night are one and the same wager of ashes.

Leaving the book, we do not leave it: we inhabit its absence. Likewise, outside their shared space, readable only to them, the keeper at the foot of his lighthouse and the writer away from his desk.

The absence of the book is located both before and beyond the word. But it is also written in the margin of writing, as its erasure.

The gesture of writing is, first, a movement of arm and hand entering into an adventure under the sign of thirst. But the throat is dry, body and thought all attention. Only much later we realize that our forearm on the page marks the boundary between the writing and ourselves. On one side, the words, the work; on the other, the writer. In vain do they search to communicate. The page remains witness to two interminable monologues, and once there is silence on either side, it is the abyss.

Our forearm constrains and inhibits us. All around, words go to waste. We thought that in taking up the pen we could reach a kind of comforting fullness and unity. But afterwards nothing is ever the same. Cut off from ourselves by our own daring, stripped of our belongings, the male gut reaction is to try to master this rebellious voice of ink and to appropriate it.

But the transcribed word, which we naively thought we had arrested and handcuffed, keeps its freedom for the space of its perennial night. Dazzled freedom which frightens and worries us.

Behind the bars, the lines of the book, we watch the word spread its wings in the vast realm that is its own. So that it confronts us first of all with the void; not, certainly, to reduce it, but in order to feel its infinite vertigo. Inside and outside any imaginary enclosure, there begins and ends writing in its perpetual beginning, begins and ends our passionate questioning of an absolute – the book – which is finally but the white ground beyond time on which the shadows of our numbered words have been dancing since daybreak. Death has its heyday where everything remains to be said.

Reading a text involves several degrees of violence; this is sufficient warning that there is danger in the house.

Only in fragments can we read the immeasurable totality. Hence it is with reference to a fabricated totality that we tackle a fragment, which always represents the accepted, traditional part of the totality, yet at the same time renews its challenge of the beginning and, taking its place, becomes the beginning of all possible beginnings that can be brought to light.

The eye is guide and beacon for this fertile 'deconstruction' which works in two directions: from totality toward the ultimate fragment, and from the tiniest fragment, through its own rescinding, its own gradual fading into the void of preponderant fragmentation, toward restoration of this very totality. The eye lays down – and is – the law. The invisible claims us behind all that is seen, as if its absence were only what hides at the heart of the manifest – or else hides from us what is nevertheless manifest – and silence, what is unsaid within the uttered word.

To which move, which deportment – or deportation – of writing do we owe our awareness of this invisibility, this silence? What remains to be seen, what promises a voice after silence, fascinates us. The field of writing is twofold. The place of the book is a place forever lost.

Thinking of you, of your questioning and questioned approaches to the book, of your ways that are all one, yet marked by significant twists and turns, as if we could really advance only by accepting, from the start, that we must return to our point of departure, which would be the point of all departures, and asking myself, in turn, the burning question: What is the book? I came across the answer proposed by a kabbalistic rabbi to this most pertinent and pressing question. (A rabbi who, I assure you, knew more about what we now call writing than you imagine, or perhaps knew nothing about it, being more preoccupied with symbolism, but what matter?) An answer that I would divert from its original mystical sense and submit to your literal reflection: that the Book is 'what the black of fire carves into the white of fire.' Black fire on white fire. Endless consuming of sacred parchment and profane page given over to signs, as if what is consigned – co-signed – to writing were only a play of flames, fire of fire, 'word-fires,' you said in a recent interview. Confidence in what dies purified to be reborn of the desire for purifying death, thanks to which words add to their own the readability of a time advanced to the 'deferred' reading, which we now know is the reading of all reading; time forever preserved within abolished time.

Could it be that for the writer everything happens in a forebook whose end he cannot see, whose end is in his book? But nothing happens that has not already happened. The book is at the threshold. This also confirms your cherished project, your declared course, whose ambition might strike us as paradoxical since it is a matter both of undermining the road and of continuing it, as if it could exist only in and through these successive continuations.

Your 'deconstruction' would then simply be starting countless fires, which your philosophers, your thinkers, your favorite writers help spread in their writing: 'Valéry reminds us that philosophy is written.' Plato, for whom writing is both 'remedy' and 'poison,' a 'poison-remedy,' considers it suspect, but his suspicion is in writing.

Everything is again set in motion – called into question – by writing. As we *speak*, nothing is ever said so completely that it could not be said over, differently. So that saying is a revelation, with the promise of further saying. Deconstruction functions at this level also, arranging and preparing those moments when utterance splits apart and is neutralized by its reconciled opposites:
  'For the unlimited itself has become the limit proclaimed by the neutral affirmation which, speaking always from the other side, speaks in the word.'
  Thus all your books reflect one another and reflect, back to back, your favorite examples.

You always, and with unequaled rigor, question anything that is taken for granted. What immediately won me over in your writings and the resolve they convey, what commands our respect in your profound attempt to overcome all obstacles and grasp the ungraspable, is the total acceptance of risk that runs through all your work and quickly wears out those who would nail you down. It is precisely the kind of risk that the book in process of being made and unmade forces us to take at each stage of its evolution, its articulation, and its abandonment.

If, starting from Hegel, the 'last philosopher of the book and first thinker of writing,' from Husserl, Nietzsche, Freud, Heidegger (both closest and most remote), you stop quite naturally on your way as you encounter Mallarmé, Bataille, Artaud, it is not so much, I think, to widen the field of your investigations, of your inscribed and transcribed anxieties, in the mad hope of one day closing the loop, as to increase the sense of the unfathomable in your questioning. For the question of writing truly arises on abyssal ground – the question of being likewise, the two being riveted to one another.

Everything seems to happen as in a game of chess. But what strategy can we resort to when, as with Mallarmé, the chessboard is all white? What game is conceivable where all possibility of play is taken from the players? Here, at this point, begins the adventure.

White is not a color of rest. You know. You have said so. So much virgin blood in whiteness. Desire and wound, kiss and combat fuse in it and drown. Whenever the page we hold on to is not itself the void, it is the 'hymen' or 'tympanum' of an ecstatic or fearful incarnation of emptiness pierced by the pen. The moment of pleasure or sacrifice consummated, the carnal act continues, and silence is henceforward filled with strange and tenuous sonorities.

A kind of counter-writing carried, however, by writing – its irksome contrary or contrariety, with which it collides and breaks – attempts to lord it where reflexion overflows the foaming wave. But there is already the beach, the sand, the progressive erosion of a reproduced trace that was but the daring imprint of a question left open. The beach is flooded with the 'white blood' of the sea; the trace, drowned in blood. Obliteration is but waves of blood on an abandoned wharf all written, all covered with footprints.

'In breaking the silence, language realizes what silence wanted and could not obtain,' writes Merleau-Ponty. So it is out of breakage – breakage in death, of death – but of the fatal fissure that renders it mortal while bringing it about, that the question of the book is born. Question put to nothingness, to the void. Question of the void around which swarm mad words that, though impotent, are yet master of the question.

'To question means to be able to wait an entire lifetime,' writes Heidegger. To write the question, to question the writing of the question, is even more demanding. It demands going beyond, beyond light, beyond life, into the very light and life, but into their desert regions – are deserts not the dust of questions? – harried to death by panting interrogations, by the recluse clarity of thought and man's arrant word.

Sand responds only to sand, and death, only to death.

Your 'margins' are without reassuring contours; your 'positions,' 'disseminating.' To hope to be soothed means turning away from you. You burn what stood just outside the flame. Rare, very rare, to live writing with such intensity. 'An entire lifetime' is indeed not enough to appease the fire.

You are against all repression and especially, on behalf of the book, against that of the letter; because the letter is perhaps an origin diverted from the origin by its tie to a signified whose weight it must help carry.

So one letter, the seventh, of the word *différence* was secretly, silently exchanged against the first of the alphabet. This was enough to change the text.

You have often explained this new word. It destroys and creates a space where everything is canceled as it faces, as it opens to, its potential difference by deferring it (*différant*); that is, as it opens to what forever opposes and unites it with itself in its textual manifold.

The word 'differance' (*différance*) is here a synonym of *mine*. Mine, graphite to draw with; mine, underground riches; mine, explosive.

So the space created by 'differance' is at the same time a space for leaving traces, a pyramid to bury the Pharaoh – 'pyramid silence of graphic difference,' 'tomb that we cannot make resonate,' but which we have violated, gutted with dynamite, so that going down into the mine means a descent into death, into the night of the word, in order to make off with its riches – and, 'playing with a word that has no word, a name that has no name,' a black, blinding absence giving birth to signs – 'signs represent the present in its absence' – in the time that is a fold in time, a golden time, where writing moves.

Moreover, this word 'differance,' deferring (*différant*) presence – 'when the present does not present itself we signify, we take the detour of the sign. We take in or make a sign' – is here also an equivalent of the Greek coin, *mine*, and – why not – also of *mines* in the French sense of features, play of physiognomy, tics, and all the word denotes.

As 'an origin not full, not simple, the structured and deferring origin of differences,' 'differance' compromises presence by dissociating it from time. The time of presence is not the present tense, but the chance, expectation, and torment of time, the attention paid to time whose vice is writing.

And where it is currency: a place of hoarding and wasting of signs thus simplified.

A single letter may contain the entire book, the universe. Reading the book means, in these pages, excessive reading of a letter that takes us to most remote points. So that it is in the distance where we embrace our differences, in the detours, the backs and forths where we come up against 'differance,' that the book presents itself as a book printed on an absence dis seminated by the page. Absence of an absence dismissed and unraveled by presence.

A glance divides. On one side, fire; on the other, fire. The 'black of fire' is the conflagration of evening facing the white conflagration of morning. Between these two fires – for the space of a fraction of a second, the time of fiery nuptials – emerges a familiar face. The sound of words in the book is but the sound made by fire, gestures become the jumbled voices of flames.

'Philosophical discourse always gets lost at a certain moment. Perhaps it is nothing but an inexorable way of losing and getting lost. Of this also we are reminded by the degrading murmur: *it goes its way*.'

Maurice Blanchot

... it just goes its inky way.

See:

Jacques Derrida, 'Edmond Jabes and the question of the book', in *Writing and Difference*, tr. Alan Bass (London: Routledge & Kegan Paul, 1978).

'IN PRAISE OF WATER'

Paul Valéry

So many have sung the praise of WINE. Countless drunken poets have reached up to lyrical heights and held out to the gods the goblet of strong WINE that their souls awaited.

WINE is most precious and deserves those praises. But how ungrateful and mistaken were those who cursed WATER ...

Divine lucidity, transparent Rock, marvelous Agent of life, universal WATER, to you I would gladly pay my respects with an endless litany.

Let me sing the stillness of WATER, luxuriating in sites of absolutely calm expanses, pure plane in whose mirror all becomes more perfect than it is. All of nature turns into Narcissus there, and loves itself ...

WATER MOVES, soft and strong, and, sweating, grinding with stupendous slowness, by sheer weight, unstoppable currents and swirls, misty and raining, streaming, cascading in cataracts, water shapes the rocks, polishes granite, wears down marble, rounds pebbles indefinitely, cradling the wealth of sand she has made then laying it out like the train of a gown, making soft beaches. She labors and diversifies, sculpts and decorates the hard ground's harsh, sullen figure.

WATER IS MULTIFORM; she lives in clouds and fills abysmal depths; she lands as snow on sun-drenched heights, which let her flow away, pure again; and following paths she knows, blindly, with strange, confident assurance, she descends invincibly toward the sea, her greatest quantity.

Source: Paul Valéry, *Oeuvres* (Paris: Gallimard, 1957–60), vol. 2, pp. 202–3.

Sometimes she runs away, visible and clear, fast or slow, with a mysterious murmur which suddenly changes into the bellow of a leaping torrent, only to melt into crushing and dazzling waterfalls with their perpetual thunder and their rainbows borne in vapors.

But at times she steals away and, underground, she crawls concealed and pervasive. She scrutinizes mineral masses, into which she seeps and scouts the strangest course. Self-seeking during harsh nights, she becomes one again, joined to herself, piercing, transuding, searching, dissolving, cleaving, acting without getting lost in her self-made maze; later she quietly feeds buried lakes with the long flow of her tears, which freeze into alabaster columns, in somber cathedrals, from which hellish rivers spring, full of blind fish and antediluvian molluscs.

What strange adventures WATER has known, and what a great number of things! ... But her ways of knowing are singular. Her substance becomes memory: she grabs and eats a trace of all she has skimmed, bathed, rolled: from the limestone she has dug out to the shelters she has washed, and the rich sands that served as her filters. Should she spout into the daylight, she is charged with primitive powers of the rocks through which she traveled. She carries away bits of atoms, elements of pure energy, bubbles of subterranean gases, and even at times the earth's intimate heat.

At last she springs out, pregnant with the treasures her race has earned, an offering to Life's needs.

Who wouldn't worship her, LIFE's essential element? And yet how few can conceive that LIFE is nothing but organized WATER?

Consider a plant, look up to a large tree, and your mind will see that it is just an upright river spilling into the air in the sky. Through the TREE, WATER goes to meet light- WATER molds each day into amorous forms with the salt of the earth. She tends and extends toward the universe fluid, powerful arms and weightless hands.

Man will settle where WATER is. Is a very fresh nymph not most necessary? A nymph and a spring, source of water, mark the sacred place where Life alights and takes a look.

And so we come to realize that WATER does inebriate. To drink! ... To drink ... It is well known that only pure water slakes a real thirst. There is a je ne sais quoi and a genuine agreement between the body's true desire and the primeval liquid. An altered course distills us, and leads to corruption; thus we still our thirst and are repaired, by having recourse to water, life's requirement.[1]

Language itself is filled with the praise for WATER. We say that we THIRST FOR TRUTH. We speak of CLEAR speeches. We spill STREAMS of words at times ...

Times itself has sought in running WATER the likeness of its figurative progress.

I adore WATER.

Translated Christine Izzary

NOTE

1. Etre altéré, c'est devenir autre: se corrompre. Il faut donc se désaltérer, redevenir, avoir recours à ce qu'exige tout ce qui vit.

See:

Jacques Derrida, 'Qual quelle: Valéry's sources', in *Margins of Philosophy*, tr. Alan Bass (Brighton: Harvester Press, 1982).

I.8

'FRIENDSHIP'

Maurice Blanchot

How could one agree to speak of this friend? Neither in praise nor in the interest of some truth. The traits of his character, the forms of his existence, the episodes of his life, even in keeping with the search for which he felt himself responsible to the point of irresponsibility, belong to no one. There are no witnesses. Those who were closest say only what was close to them, not the distance that affirmed itself in this proximity, and distance ceases as soon as presence ceases. Vainly do we try to maintain, with our words, with our writings, what is absent; vainly do we offer it the appeal of our memories and a sort of figure, the joy of remaining with the day, life prolonged by a truthful appearance. We are only looking to fill a void, we cannot bear the pain: the affirmation of this void. Who could agree to receive its insignificance - an insignificance so enormous that we do not have a memory capable of containing it and such that we ourselves must already slip into oblivion in order to sustain it – the time of this slippage, the very enigma this insignificance represents? Everything we say tends to veil the one affirmation: that everything must fade and that we can remain loyal only so long as we watch over this fading movement, to which something in us that rejects all memory already belongs.

I know there are the books. The books remain, temporarily, even if their reading must open us to the necessity of this disappearance into which they withdraw themselves. The books themselves refer to an existence. This existence, because

Source: Maurice Blanchot, *Friendship*, tr. E. Rottenberg (Stanford: Stanford University Press, 1999), pp. 120–33.

it is no longer a presence, begins to be deployed in history, and in the worst of histories, literary history. Literary history, inquisitive, painstaking, in search of documents, takes hold of a deceased will and transforms into knowledge its own purchase on what has fallen to posterity. This is the moment of complete works. One wants to publish 'everything,' one wants to say 'everything,' as if one were anxious about only one thing: that everything be said; as if the 'everything is said' would finally allow us to stop a dead voice, to stop the pitiful silence that arises from it and to contain firmly within a well-circumscribed horizon what the equivocal, posthumous anticipation still mixes in illusorily with the words of the living. As long as the one who is close to us exists and, with him, the thought in which he affirms himself, his thought opens itself to us, but preserved in this very relation, and what preserves it is not only the mobility of life (this would be very little), but the unpredictability introduced into this thought by the strangeness of the end. And this movement, unpredictable and always hidden in its infinite imminence – that of dying, perhaps – arises not because its term could not be given in advance, but because it never constitutes an event that takes place, even when it occurs, never a reality that can be grasped: ungraspable and henceforth entirely in the ungraspable is the one destined to this movement. It is this unpredictable that speaks when he speaks, it is this which in his lifetime conceals and reserves his thought, separates and frees it from all seizure, that of the outside as well as that of the inside.

I also know that, in his books, Georges Bataille seems to speak of himself with a freedom without restraint that should free us from all discretion – but that does not give us the right to put ourselves in his place, nor does it give us the power to speak in his absence. And is it certain that he speaks of himself? The 'I' whose presence his search seems still to make manifest when it expresses itself, toward whom does it direct us? Certainly toward an I very different from the ego that those who knew him in the happy and unhappy particularity of life would like to evoke in the light of a memory. Everything leads one to think that the personless presence at stake in such a movement introduces an enigmatic relation into the existence of him who indeed decided to speak of it but not to claim it as his own, still less to make of it an event of his biography (rather, a gap in which the biography disappears). And when we ask ourselves the question 'Who was the subject of this experience?' this question is perhaps already an answer if, even to him who led it, the experience asserted itself in this interrogative form, by substituting the openness of a 'Who?' without answer for the closed and singular 'I'; not that this means that he had simply to ask himself 'What is this I that I am?' but much more radically to recover himself without reprieve, no longer as 'I' but as a 'Who?,' the unknown and slippery being of an indefinite 'Who?'

We must give up trying to know those to whom we are linked by something essential; by this I mean we must greet them in the relation with the unknown in which they greet us as well, in our estrangement. Friendship, this relation without dependence, without episode, yet into which all of the simplicity of life enters, passes by way of the recognition of the common strangeness that does not allow us to speak of our friends but only to speak to them, not to make of them a topic of conversations (or essays), but the movement of understanding in which, speaking to us, they reserve, even on the most familiar terms, an infinite distance, the fundamental separation on the basis of which what separates becomes relation. Here discretion lies not in the simple refusal to put forward confidences (how vulgar this would be, even to think of it), but it is the interval, the pure interval that, from me to this other who is a friend, measures all that is between us, the interruption of being that never authorizes me to use him, or my knowledge of him (were it to praise him), and that, far from preventing all communication, brings us together in the difference and sometimes the silence of speech.

It is true that at a certain moment this discretion becomes the fissure of death. I could imagine that in one sense nothing has changed: in the 'secret' between us that was capable of taking place, in the continuity of discourse, without inter-rupting it, there was already, from the time in which we were in the presence of one another, this imminent presence, though tacit, of the final discretion, and it is on the basis of this discretion that the precaution of friendly words calmly affirmed itself. Words from one shore to the other shore, speech responding to someone who speaks from the other shore and where, even in our life, the measurelessness of the movement of dying would like to complete itself. And yet when the event itself comes, it brings this change: not the deepening of the separation but its erasure; not the widening of the caesura but its leveling out and the dissipation of the void between us where formerly there developed the frankness of a relation without history. In such a way that at present, what was close to us not only has ceased to approach but has lost even the truth of extreme distance. Thus death has the false virtue of appearing to return to intimacy those who have been divided by grave disagreements. This is because with death all that separates, disappears. What separates: what puts authentically in relation, the very abyss of relations in which lies, with simplicity, the agreement of friendly affirmation that is always maintained.

We should not, by means of artifice, pretend to carry on a dialogue. What has turned away from us also turns us away from that part which was our presence, and we must learn that when speech subsides, a speech that for years gave itself to an 'exigency without regard,' it is not only this exigent speech that has ceased, it is the silence that it made possible and from which it returned along an insensible slope toward the anxiety of time. Undoubtedly we will still be able to follow the same paths, we can let images come, we can appeal to an absence that we will imagine, by deceptive consolation, to be our own. We can, in a word, remember. But thought knows that one does not remember: without memory, without thought, it already struggles in the invisible where everything sinks back to indifference. This is thought's profound grief. It must accompany friendship into oblivion.

See:

Jacques Derrida, *Politics of Friendship*, tr. George Collins (London: Verso, 1998).

PART 2
OPENING REMARKS

'A NUMBER OF YES (NOMBRE DE OUI)'

Jacques Derrida

Yes, in a foreign land. We must have come across each other most often in a foreign land. These encounters retain an emblematic value for me. Perhaps because they took place elsewhere, far away, but more surely because we never separated without a promise; I have not forgotten. Nor have I forgotten what Michel de Certeau writes of writing in the mystical text: through and through, it is also a promise.[1]

To me, it is as if these encounters in the other's country (by which I also mean the interruption immediately marking them, the separation which tears apart their very event) described in their own way the paths taken by thought as it intermingles with the word given in writing: at the heart of the same time, of a single time, the opening *and* the cut. And this is already a citation from *La Fable mystique*.[2]

> Angelus Silesius ... identifies the graph of the Separate (*Jah, or Jahveh*) with the boundlessness of the 'yes' (*Ja*). The same phoneme (*ja*) makes the cut and the opening coincide, the *No Name* of the Other and the *Yes* of the Will, absolute separation and infinite acceptance:
> > *Golt Spricht nur immer Ja*
> > God says nothing but Yes [or: I am].

A chance encounter in the singularity of a 'graph,' the coincidence of the cut and the opening. We will have to come back to this again and again.

Source: Jacques Derrida, 'A number of yes (Nombre de oui)', tr. B. Holmes, *Qui Parle*, 2 (2), 1988, pp. 120–33.

Of these encounters which from the start were separations, I will say nothing, that is, nothing directly. Instead I will go on murmuring, for myself, a few place names. I remember the California sun, in San Diego and in Irvine. I remember Cornell, Binghamton, New York, and finally I remember Venice, in the snow, in December of 1983. How can I gather all this memory together into a cipher where it is no longer distinct itself from what I have learned, and still learn, reading Michel de Certeau? If memory had to inhabit but a single word, and one which resembled it, perhaps that word would be *yes*.

What he has said to us *about* the *yes* was not simply a discourse on a particular element of language, a theoretical metalanguage bearing on a possible utterance, one scene of the utterance among others. For essential reasons, it is always risky to say '*the* "yes",' to make just another name or word of the adverb 'yes,' an object *about* which constative statements might pronounce the truth. Because a *yes* doesn't suffer any metalanguage, it engages the 'performative' of an originary affirmation and thus is supposed by every utterance *about* the *yes*. Indeed – to put it aphoristically – for Michel de Certeau there is no subject of any kind which does not arise from the scene of the *yes*. The two types of *yes* which we have just discerned (but why are there always two? we will ask ourselves this again) are not homogeneous and yet they are deceptively similar. That a *yes* should each time be presupposed, not only by every statement about the *yes* but also by every negation and every opposition, dialectical or not, between the *yes* and the *no*, this is perhaps what immediately gives the affirmation its essential, irreducible *infinity*. Michel de Certeau insists on this infinity. He sees in it the 'mystic postulate.' It 'posits the boundlessness of a "yes".' The excellent analysis he then proposes seems to me to hold at least four questions. I will ask them, and then will sketch out a *quasi* transcendental or ontological analytic of *yes* – but beforehand, as if to prolong an interrupted colloquy, I will quote a long passage from '*The Scene of the Utterance*' in *La Fable mystique*:

> In a more discreet but insistent tradition, the 'performance' of the subject also gives itself the mark of the *yes*. A *yes* just as absolute as a *volo*, with neither objects nor ends. Whereas knowledge de-limits its contents according to a procedure which is essentially that of the 'no,' a process of distinction, ('this is not that') the mystic postulate posits the bound-lessness of a 'yes.' Naturally, this is a postulate of principle, as unfettered by circumstances as the intention which would seek 'all,' 'nothing' or God. It has its model in a surprising saying of St. Paul about Christ: 'In him there is only yes (*nai*).' This paradox of a limitless 'yes' within the circumscription of a singular entity (Jesus) sketches out a contradictory and atopical theory of the (Christly) Subject; an in-finite yes pierces the field of separations and distinctions utilized by all of Hebraic epistemol-ogy. This 'yes' then repeats itself. The same lapsus of history (the same forgetting) is reproduced. In the 17th century, Angelus Silesius goes even

further. He identifies the graph of the Separate (*Ja, Jahveh*) with the boundlessness of the 'yes' (*Ja*). In the place of the sole proper Name (a name which distances from all beings) he installs disappropriation (by assenting to everything). The same phoneme (*Ja*) makes the cut and the opening coincide, the *No Name* of the Other and the Yes of the Will, absolute separation and infinite acceptance:

> Gott spricht nur immer Ja
>
> God never says but Yes [or: I am].

Identity between the Christly 'yes' and the 'I am (the Other)' of the burning bush. The Separate returns as exclusion of the exclusion. Such is the cipher of the mystic subject. Figure of 'abandon' or 'detachment,' the 'yes' names, in the end, the 'interior.' In that region, a population of intentions cries from all sides 'yes, yes,' like the God of Silesius. Is this space divine or Nietzschean? The word (*Wort*) which institutes this place (*Ort*) participates in the 'essence' which, according to Evagre, 'has no contrary.'[3]

I will leave the four questions open or suspended. The responses will not come, not from me in any case, but that hardly matters. That's what I would like to explain. Not that the response matters less here than the question. It's the question which matters less than a certain *yes*, the one that resounds in the question so as to always come *before* it. What interests us here is a *yes* which, opening the question, always lets itself be supposed by it, a *yes* affirming prior to, before and beyond any possible question.

First question. Why does repetition belong to the destiny of the *yes*? Michel de Certeau makes two allusions to two repetitions which apparently do not have the same significance in his eyes. He does not compare the one to the other and does not linger on them. There is first 'this "yes"' which, he says, 'then repeats itself. The same lapsus of history (the same forgetting) is reproduced.' This reproduction seems not to have the same value as the 'yes, yes' of Silesius's God. Perhaps. But what could be the common root of these two repetitions or reproductions? And what if, curiously, they repeated themselves or implied each other? Does the *quasi* transcendental or ontological structure of the *yes* not prescribe this double destiny, which is also a destiny of duplicity?

Second question. Why is it necessary to choose between a 'divine' and a 'Nietzschean' space? Michel de Certeau is not doubt alluding to numerous texts by Nietzsche, for example *The Seven Seals* (or *The Song of Yes and of Amen*) in *Thus Spake Zarathustra*. And in fact Nietzsche himself opposes the light, dancing, ethereal Ja of the innocent affirmation to the Ja, Ja of the Christian ass suffering or sighing beneath the burden of a gravely assumed responsibility ('*But at that, the ass brayed I-A.*') (*The Awakening*). Repetition and memory (*Ja, Ja*) seem to be assigned to the Christian *yes* which would thus be a *yes* of finitude. The infinite *yes*, in its very innocence, would be excessive in the face of this finitude, and it is probably for this reason that Michel de Certeau poses his question in the form of an alternative ('divine or Nietzschean') thus perhaps referring to 'the vast unbounded Yes – and Amen – saying' of *Thus Spake Zarathustra (Before Sunrise)*. But once again, is there not in the *quasi* transcendental or ontological experience of the *yes* a common root which, without annulling the alternative, prescribes its derivation from a more 'ancient' possibility?

Third question. Concerning this boundless *yes*, Michel de Certeau says that it *simultaneously* 'pierces the field of the separations and distinctions utilized by all of Hebraic epistemology' and reminds us of 'the identity between the Christly "yes" and the "I am (the Other)" of the burning bush.' These two propositions do not contradict each other, of course. A 'Hebraic epistemology' of separation is not necessarily harmonious or homogeneous with the infinite affirmation. And in any case, the boundless *yes* does not exclude separation. On the contrary. Between the Judaic affirmation and the Christian affirmation we will certainly not speak of affinity, even less of affiliation. But does the 'identity between the Christly "yes" and the "I am (the Other)" of the burning bush' not touch, once again, on an event or an advent of the *yes* which might be *neither* Judaic *nor* Christian, not yet or no longer simply one or the other? And does this *neither-nor* bring us, not to some ontological or transcendental condition of possibility, but to the 'quasi' which I've been insinuating for some time now ('quasi transcendental' or 'quasi ontological'), which could harmonize the originary eventness of the event with the fabulous narrative or with the fable inscribed in the *yes* as the origin of every word (*fari*)? One can ask, for example, if Franz Rozenzweig still speaks as a Jew, or as the already over-Christianized Jew he has been accused of being, when he calls upon us to heed the originary *yes* in certain texts whose status remains by nature uncertain, texts which waver – like everything saying (the) *yes* – between the theological, the philosophical (transcendental or ontological) and the song of praise or the hymn. Let's not forget that the Hebrew *yes* (*ken*) can always inscribe itself in the Shekinah whose tradition is often invoked in *La Fable mystique*.[4] Since Michel de Certeau does not, to my knowledge, quote Rozenzweig (whose *Star of Redemption* was in fact not yet translated at the time he published *La Fable mystique*), perhaps it's best to first read these few lines:

> Yea is the beginning. Nay cannot be the beginning; for it could only be a Nay of the Nought. This, however, would presuppose a negatable Nought, a Nay, therefore, that had already decided on a Yea ... This non-Nought is, however, not independently given, for nothing at all is given except for the Nought. Therefore the affirmation of the non-Nought circumscribes as inner limit the infinity of all that is not Nought. An infinity is affirmed: God's infinite essence, his infinite actuality, his Physis ... Such is the power of Yea that it adheres everywhere ... It is the arch-word (*Urwort*) of language, one of those which first makes possible, not sentences, but any kind of sentence-forming words at all, words as parts of the sentence. Yea

is not a part of a sentence, but neither is it a shorthand symbol for a sentence, although it can be employed as such. Rather it is the silent accompanist of all parts of a sentence, the confirmation, the 'sic!' The 'Amen' behind every word. It gives every word in the sentence its right to exist, it supplies the seat on which it may take its place, it 'posits.' The first Yea in God establishes the divine essence for all infinity. And this first Yea is 'in the beginning.'[5]

As originary word (*Urwort*), the *yes* doubtless belongs to language. It's definitely a word. It can always be a word, and translatable. And yet, implied by all the other words whose source it figures, it also remains silent, a 'silent companion' (somewhat like the 'I think' which, according to Kant, 'accompanies' all our representations), and thus in a certain way foreign to language, heterogeneous to the sum of terms thus bound within and by its power. It is therefore a kind of inaudible term, inaudible even as a determined *yes* is pronounced, in one language or another, within a given sentence counting as an affirmation. Language without language, it belongs without belonging to that totality which it simultaneously institutes and opens. It exceeds and incises language, to which it remains nonetheless immanent: like language's first dweller, the first to step out of its home. It *brings to being* and *lets be* everything which can be said. But its intrinsic double nature is already discernable, or more precisely, it is already confirmed. It is and is not of language, it both merges and does not merge with its utterance in a natural language. For if it is 'before' language, it marks the essential exigency, the promise, the engagement to come to language, in a given language. Such an event is required by the very force of the *yes*. Insofar – says Rozenzweig – as it approves or confirms every possible language, the 'sic' or the 'amen' which it institutes doubles with an acquiescence the arche-originary *yes* which gives the first breath to every utterance. The 'first' is already, always, a confirmation: *yes, yes*, a *yes*, which goes from *yes to yes* or which comes from *yes to yes*. Something of this acquiescence speaks also a certain cruel tranquility, a 'cruel rest' (*immanem quietem*) to which we will refer again later.[6] Can one reckon with, give an explanation for, attempt the enumeration of this redoubling of the *yes*? Why can its analytic only be 'quasi' transcendental or ontological?

Fourth question. Michel de Certeau analyzes the performance of the *yes* in the course of an interpretation of the *volo* ('a "yes" just as absolute as the *volo*, with neither objects nor ends' p. 239), in the particularly beautiful pages devoted to *A Preface: the 'volo' (from Meister Eckhart to Mme. Guyon).*[7] Is the thinking of this *yes* coextensive with that of the *volo*? Does the originary consent which thus lets itself be articulated or heard in this wordless word belong to the 'absolute volitive' which, suggests Michel de Certeau, is 'the equivalent of what Jacob Boehme places at the origin of all existence: the violence, even the fury, of a will'?[8] Must it then be said that this determination of the *yes* remains imprisoned by what Heidegger calls a metaphysics of the will, in other words by the interpretation of being as the unconditional will of a subjectivity whose hegemony marks all modernity, at least from Descartes to Hegel and Nietzsche? And if this were so, would it not be necessary to detach the experience and the description of the *yes* from the *volo*? Of course, it would then become a matter of experience without experience, of description without description: there would be no determinable presence, no object, no possible theme. As I am unable to enter here into the immensity of this daunting problematic, I shall only situate three possible points of orientation.

A. Having upheld, throughout an almost thirty-year course of inquiry, the irreducible privilege of the questioning attitude, having written that questioning (*Fragen*) was the piety (*Frömmigkeit*) of thought, Heidegger at least had to complicate this axiom. First by recalling that piety should from the start have been understood as the docility of listening, thus making the question, before anything else, into a modality of reception, a trusting attention to what gives itself to be understood rather than – or prior to – the enterprising, inquisitorial activity of a request or an inquest. Secondly by insisting, for the future, on a more originary dimension of thought, the *Zusage*, a confident acceptance, an assent to the proffered word (*Zuspruch*) without which no question is possible, a *yes* in short, a sort of pre-engagement presupposed by every language and by every type of speech (*Sprache*).[9] This dimension of experience clearly resonates, in his later texts, with the one described in *Gelassenheit*.[10] I bring up the word not only because of the major role it plays in Heidegger's texts but also to evoke Meister Eckhart, of whom Heidegger was, doubtless even more so than he said, an assiduous reader. Michel de Certeau names Heidegger from the first page of *La Fable mystique*,[11] and alludes to Meister Eckhart's *Gelâzenheit* in the chapter with which we are preoccupied. What he says of it brings me to my second point of orientation.

B. The *Gelâzenheit* speaks the non-will in the most unconditional will. Such that the very unconditionality of an act of will with neither end nor object turns will into a-will. Once again it will be necessary to quote at length:

> because it has no particular object and holds to *nothing*, this *volo* turns itself into its contrary – willing nothing – and thus occupies the entire field, both positive and negative, of will. Will only stabilizes itself (in affirmation or in negation) if it is attached to a particular object ('I want' or 'I don't want' *that*) and, consequently, if there is a distinction between a particular subject ('I') and a particular object ('that'). As soon as this link to singularity has been taken away, will turns on itself and identifies itself with its contrary. 'Wanting everything' and 'wanting nothing' coincide. The same for 'wanting nothing' and 'not wanting.' When it is no longer the will to have something and when it no longer stays in the orbits organized by constellations of distinct subjects and objects, the *volo* is also an act of 'renunciation of one's will.' It is equally a *non-will*, for example with

Meister Eckhart's 'releasement' (*Gelâzenheit*) and 'detachment' (*Abegescheidenheit*). The annihilation of the predicate (*I want nothing*) also spills back onto the subject: in the end, *who* wants? What is the 'I' who wants? What remains, cast out of its orbit, is the act of will, a force which is born. The verb is 'linked to nothing' and is appropriable by no-one. It passes through moments and places. In the beginning there is the verb to want. It posits immediately that which will repeat itself in the mystic discourse with man other verbs (to love, to hurt, to search, to pray, to die, etc.), itinerant acts amid actors placed now in the position of subjects, position of subjects, now in the position of predicates: who loves whom? who hurts whom? who prays to whom? Now God, now the believer . . . [12]

C. The consequences are measureless. Particularly for everything in the Heideggerian discourse which attempts to discern *epochs* within the history of being. The very thought of a history of being finds itself affected by this internal *epokhê* which thus distributes, divides or suspends the *yes*. If the very unconditionality of willing turns it into non-will, and this according to an internal necessity, then no 'metaphysics of the will' remains rigorously *identifiable*. Will is not identical to itself. Nor is everything with which Heidegger constantly associates it: subjectness, objectness, the *cogito*, absolute knowledge, the *rationality principle (Principium reddendae rationis: nihil est sine ratione)*, calculability, etc. And among so many other things, the one which here interests us before all others: the 'explanation' to be given, the 'reckoning' to be done, the countability and the computability, indeed the imputability of the innumerable *yes*. The *yes* gives or promises *just that*, it gives it with the promise: the incalculable itself.

You can sense it now: a transcendental or ontological analytic of the *yes* can only be fictive or fabulous, completely given over to the adverbial dimension of a *quasi*. Let's take things up again from the start, naively. The arche-originary *yes* resembles an absolute performative. It does not describe and does not state anything, but engages a kind of arche-engagement, a kind of alliance or consent or promise lost in its acquiescence to the utterance which it always accompanies, albeit silently, and even if this utterance is radically negative. Since this performative is presupposed as the condition of possibility for all other performatives, it is not one performative among others. One can even say that, as a *quasi* transcendental, silent performative, it is removed from any science of the utterance and from any speech act theory. It is not, *stricto sensu*, an act, it is not assignable to any subject nor to any object. If it opens the eventness of every event, it is not itself an event. It is never *present* as such. That which translates this non-presence into a present *yes*, in the act of an utterance or in any act, dissimulates the arche-originary *yes* in the very motion which reveals it. The reason which thus retracts it from any linguistic theory (but not from any theory of its linguistic effects) likewise tears it from the grasp of all knowledge, and in particular from all history. Precisely because it is implied in all writing of history.

That being the case, the analytic of an unpronounceable 'yes' which is neither present, nor object, nor subject, could no more be ontological (a discourse on the being of a presence) than it could be transcendental (a discourse on the conditions of an object – theoretical, practical, esthetic – for a subject). All ontological or transcendental statements suppose the *yes* or the *Zusage*. Thus they can only fail in the attempt to thematize it. And yet, *one must* – yes – uphold the ontological-transcendental exigency in order to uncover the dimensions of a *yes*. which is neither empirical nor ontic, which does not fall within the province of any specific science, ontology or phenomenology, nor finally of any predicative discourse. Presupposed by every proposition, it cannot be confused with the position, thesis or theme of any discourse. It is through and through the fable which, almost [*quasiment*] before the act and before the *logos*, remains *almost* at the beginning: 'Par le mot *par* commence donc ce texte' (*Fable*, by Ponge).

Why *almost* at the origin? And why a transcendental-ontological quasi-analytic? We have just seen why the *quasi* concerns the ontological-transcendental pretension. Now let me stress that it is a *quasi analytic*. An analytic must return to *simple* structures, principles or elements. But the *yes* never lets itself be reduced to any ultimate simplicity. Here we rediscover the fatality of *repetition*, and of repetition as an *incisive opening*.[13] Let us suppose a first *yes*, the arche-originary *yes* which engages, promises and acquiesces before all else. On the one hand it is originarily, in its very structure, a response. It is *firstly, second*, coming after a demand, a question or another *yes*. On the other hand, as an engagement or a promise, it must *at least* bind itself beforehand to a confirmation in a next *yes*. *Yes* to the next, or to the other *yes*, already there but nonetheless yet to come. The 'I' does not pre-exist this movement, nor does the subject: they are instituted in it. I ('I') can only say yes (yes-I) by promising to keep the memory of the *yes* and to confirm it immediately. Promise of memory and memory of promise. This 'second' *yes* is *a priori* enveloped in the 'first.' The 'first' would not take place without the project, the bet or the promise, the mission or the emission, the send-off of the second which is already there in it. This last, this first, doubles itself in advance: *yes, yes*, previously assigned to its repetition. Since the second *yes* resides in the first, the repetition augments and divides, distributing *in advance* the arche-originary *yes*. This repetition, which figures the condition of an opening of the *yes*, menaces it as well: mechanical repetition, mimetism, therefore forgetting, simulacrum, fiction, fable. Between the two repetitions, the 'good' and the 'bad', there is a cut and a contamination, simultaneously. 'Cruel tranquility,' cruel acquiescence. The criterion of conscience or subjective intention has no pertinence here, it is itself derived, instituted, constituted.

Promise of memory, memory of promise in a place of eventness which precedes all presence, all being, all psychology of the *psyche*, as well as all morality. But memory itself must forget in order to fulfill what is, since the *yes*, its mission. Promised simultaneously with the 'first,' the 'second' *yes* must come as an absolute renewal, again absolutely, once again absolutely inaugural and 'free,' failing which it could only be a natural, psychological or logical consequence. It must act as if the 'first' were forgotten, far enough past to require a new, initial *yes*. This 'forgetting' is not *psychological* or accidental, it is structural, the very condition of fidelity, of both the possibility and the impossibility of a signature; it is the divisibility against which a signature extends. Volontarily and involontarily, the non-will of the unconditional will, the second first *yes* splits from the first *yes* (which was already double), it *cuts itself off* from the other so as to be that which it must be, 'first,' unique, uniquely unique, opening *in its turn, in vicem, vice versa,* in its day, each time the first time (*vices, vez, volta, fois, Mal,* etc.). Thanks, if this may be said, to the menace of forgetting, the memory of the promise, the promise itself can take its first step, that is to say the second. A *yes* always *renders thanks* to this danger – and is it not here that, as Michel de Certeau says, the same *yes* 'repeats itself again' in 'the time same lapsus of history (the same forgetting)' and that 'the same phoneme (Ja) makes the cut and the opening coincide'?

Already but always a faithful countersignature, a *yes* can never be counted. Promise, mission, emission, it always sends itself off in numbers.

NOTES

1. 'This act does not postulate a reality or a knowledge anterior to that which it says. Even in its linguistic form it has the force of a beginning. Among the performatives, it fits more precisely into the class of the "commissives." The examples which Austin gives of this class (I promise, am determined to, pledge myself, dedicate myself to, declare my intention, etc.) bring up in review the terms which mark the social manifestation of the initial *volo* in mystical texts.' Michel de Certeau, *La Fable mystique, XVIe–XVIIe siècle* (Paris: Gallimard, 1982) 237.
2. *La Fable mystique*, 239.
3. *La Fable mystique*, 239–40.
4. 'The *Sekina* implies an inhabitation, a presence, a glory and, subsequently, a femininity of God, themes which have a great role to play in the Christian mysticism of the time.' (*La Fable mystique*, 11, n. 3; c.f. as well 187.) On this affinity between affirmation and femininity, I will have the liberty of referring to *Eperons* (Paris: Flammarion, 1987), to *Parages* and to *Ulysse Gramophone* (Paris: Galilée, 1986 and 1987) and will again quote *The Madness of the Day* by Blanchot: 'But I have encountered beings who never told life to be quiet or death to go away – usually women, beautiful creatures.' [Previously quoted in Derrida's 'The Law of Genre,' trans. Avital Ronell, *Glyph* 7 (Baltimore: The Johns Hopkins University Press, 1980) 223. TN]
5. Franz Rozenzweig, *The Star of Redemption*, translated by W. W. Hallow (New York: Holt, Rinehart and Winston, 1971) 26–27.
6. *La Fable mystique*, notably 193 and 197.
7. *La Fable mystique*, 225ff.
8. *La Fable mystique*, 231.
9. Cf. *Unterwegs zur Sprache* (Neske, 1959) 175 ff.; translated as *On the Way to Language* (New York: Harper and Row, 1971). I have taken up these questions on the *yes*, in *Ulysse Gramophone*; as to the Heideggerian movement to which I here allude, in *De l'esprit. Heidegger et la question* (Paris: Galilée, 1987).
10. [Published in English under the title *Discourse on Thinking* (New York: Harper and Row, 1976). The translators of this work, J. M. Anderson and E. H. Freund, have

proposed to render the word *Gelassenheit* by 'releasement,' a solution which I have also adopted. TN]

11. 'When this situation comes to be said, it can still adopt the language of the ancient Christian prayer. "May I not be separated from you." Not without you. *Nicht ohne.*' At this point, Michel de Certeau adds in a note: 'This Heideggerian category had seemed to me to permit a reinterpretation of Christianit.' Cf. Michel de Certeau, 'La rupture instauratrice,' in *Esprit* (June 1971): 1177–1214.

12. *La Fable mystique*, 232–33.

13. Alliance and cut, Mt. Carmel, whose name 'means the *science of circumcision.*' Here one would have to cite the pages devoted to the language of circumcision and the circumcision of language in mystical texts (cf. *La Fable mystique*, 185 ff.). Concerning the 'bloody signature of the body' which, according to Michel de Certeau, 'marks the access to the name of the father (to virility) by a submission to paternal power: As Abraham raised his knife over his son Issac to sacrifice him to Yahweh, that is to say, to make sense ("sacer facere"), in the same way John of the Cross cuts to the quick of the flesh to describe the path of union. To sever is the process of alliance when it is a matter of the absolute tracing itself through that which it takes away. A sculptural work, dear to John of the Cross. Negative theology: it *signifies* by that which it *removes.*' (*La Fable mystique*, 189).

PART 3
PHILOSOPHY

3.1

'DECONSTRUCTION, POST-MODERNISM AND THE VISUAL ARTS'

Christopher Norris

THE METAPHYSICS OF PRESENCE: PLATO, ROUSSEAU, SAUSSURE

To 'deconstruct' a text is to draw out conflicting logics of sense and implication, with the object of showing that the text never exactly means what it says or says what it means. This approach was first developed by the French philosopher Jacques Derrida (born 1921), whose ideas were then taken up by numerous (mainly American) literary critics. Derrida's writings have been predominantly concerned with philosophical, rather than literary texts, although he would certainly reject the very terms of this distinction, arguing that philosophy – like literature – is a product of *rhetorical* figures and devices. What defines philosophy as a discipline, he argues, is precisely its reluctance to face this fact; its desire to ignore the omnipresence of figural language in the texts of its own past and present. Deconstruction is the process of rhetorical close-reading that seizes upon those moments when philosophy attempts – and signally fails – to efface all knowledge of this figural drift.

Thus Derrida reads philosophical texts very much against the grain of their overt meanings and intentions. He is proposing what amounts to a psycho-analysis of Western 'logocentric' reason, that reason which aims at a perfect, unmediated access to knowledge and truth. The 'unconscious' of philosophy – to pursue this comparison – could then be read in all the signs and symptoms of its own (long repressed) rhetorical dimension. This is why Derrida regards the opposition between *speech* and *writing* as among the most basic determinants

Source: Christopher Norris with Andrew Benjamin, *What is Deconstruction?* (London: Academy Editions, 1989), pp. 7–16.

of Western philosophical tradition. From Plato to Hegel, from Rousseau to Saussure and the modern (structuralist) sciences of man, speech is always privileged over writing, since spoken language is thought to possess a unique authenticity, a truthfulness deriving from the intimate relation between word and idea. The ambiguity of the French phrase *s'entendre-parler* – meaning both 'to hear' and 'to understand oneself speak' – best conveys the logic of this potent belief. Speech enjoys priority by virtue of its issuing from a self-present grasp of what one means to say in the moment of actually saying it. And when we listen to the words of another such speaker, we are supposedly enabled to grasp their true sense by entering this same, privileged circle of exchange between mind, language and reality. Communication thus becomes ideally a kind of reciprocal 'auto-affection', a process that depends on the absolute priority of spoken (self-present) language over everything that threatens its proper domain. And *writing* constitutes precisely such a threat in so far as it is cut off at source from the authorising presence of speech. Writing is condemned to circulate endlessly from reader to reader, the best of whom can never be sure that they have understood the author's original intent. Its effect is to 'disseminate' meaning to a point where the authority of origins is pushed out of sight by the play of a henceforth limitless interpretative freedom.

Thus writing is condemned as a mere 'parasite', a debased, fallen mode of utterance, one that philosophers *must* perforce use (since otherwise their thoughts would be lost to posterity), but only on condition that they recognise these dangerous effects. To write is to risk having one's ideas perverted, wrenched out of context and exposed to all manner of mischievous reinterpretation. Socrates was wise enough to write nothing down but entrust his wisdom to a circle of initiates willing to listen and inwardly commemorate his words. Among those disciples was Plato, himself privileged (or condemned) to record *in writing* the various dialogues and scenes of instruction through which Socrates imparted his wisdom. There is an obvious irony in Plato's predicament, continuing as he does (in the *Phaedrus* and elsewhere) to denounce the wayward, subversive effects of writing, textuality or rhetoric. And this irony is yet more sharply underlined as Derrida brings out the strange double logic which comes into play whenever Plato touches on the vexed topic of written language. For it seems that he is unable to argue his case for the superior truth-claims of speech without falling back on metaphors of writing – notably a mystic 'writing in the soul' – in order to explain how authentic wisdom comes about. These metaphors complicate the logic of Plato's dialogue beyond any hope of sorting them out into a clear-cut pattern of thematic development.

This kind of brief summary can scarcely do justice to Derrida's brilliant and meticulously argued account of the *Phaedrus*. But it does give some idea of the strategies involved in a 'classic' deconstructionist reading. One begins by locating those key-points in the text where its argument depends on some crucial opposition of terms, as between speech and writing. Then it is a matter of showing: 1. that these terms are hierarchically ordered, the one conceived as derivative from, or supplementary to, the other; 2. that this relation can in fact be inverted, the 'supplementary' term taking on a kind of logical priority; and 3. that the pattern of unstable relationships thus brought to light is characteristic of the text in every last detail of its rhetorical organisation. What Plato manifestly *means to say* is that writing is at best a poor substitute for speech and at worst a corrupter of authentic, first-hand wisdom. What his text actually turns out to mean – if read with an eye to this uncanny double logic – is that writing (or a certain idea of writing) is indispensable to philosophy and any reflection on the nature and limits of language.

In *Of Grammatology*, his best-known text, Derrida turns to Rousseau as a striking case of how these logical complications can inhabit an author's work and disrupt any semblance of unified, coherent sense. Rousseau holds that *nature* is the pattern and the source of everything good in human life. As *culture* begins to develop – as societies evolve toward 'higher', more complex forms of organisation – so man loses touch with those primitive virtues. Language acquires more sophisticated means for expressing abstract ideas, but it also comes to lack any sense of its authentic (natural) origin in the speech-song of passionate feeling. In music, the spontaneous nature of *melody* gives way to a decadent modern style where *harmony* prevails, and where the multiplication of lines and notes demands that music be *written down*. Then there is the writing of Jean-Jacques himself, compulsively recounting his own life-history in the *Confessions* and guiltily aware of the constant temptation to falsify the record, disguise his faults, make himself appear a more complex, intriguing character. This bad habit exerts a contaminating influence, not least upon Rousseau's sexual indentity. In the 'natural' state of things, sex (like speech) is the passionate exchange of genuine, unselfconscious feeling between partners who perfectly reciprocate each other's desire. To indulge in auto-erotic fantasy or other kinds of solitary vice is for Rousseau a perversion of nature, a 'summoning up of absent beauties' that denies the living presence of sexual encounter. Like writing – and indeed as one effect of too much writing – this habit turns instinct from its natural path and induces all kinds of psychic disorder.

So writing is a 'dangerous supplement', the product of a decadent culture whose symptoms Rousseau discovers deep within and all around. In fact, as Derrida shows, this word 'supplement' appears with remarkable frequency whenever Rousseau is in the process of denouncing some further manifestation. But it is also a distinctly ambivalent word, and one whose double logic can again be shown to deconstruct all normative assumptions. On the one hand a 'supplement' is that which may be added to something already complete in itself and thus having no need of such optional extras. On the other, it is a necessary addition, one that supplies (makes up for) some existing lack and must henceforth be counted an integral part of the whole. The various 'supplements' to a standard work of reference like the *Oxford English Dictionary* might be taken in either sense, depending on whether the 'complete' *OED* is the original twenty-volume set or the set including its subsequent updates.

What Derrida discerns in Rousseau's text is the functioning of a 'supplementary' logic which repeats this curious twist of implication at every level. Thus Rousseau's theory of the origin of language – that it started as a kind of pre-articulate chant, then gradually declined into system and structure – breaks down as soon as he comes to examine its premises. Language can only communicate on the basis of shared conventions which in turn presuppose and articulate *systems* of distinctive sounds and meanings. Rousseau is sufficiently a structuralist *avant la lettre* to perceive, like Saussure, that a grasp of this system is prerequisite to any understanding of individual speech-acts. It is impossible to sustain the idea of a language so close to its primitive natural) roots that no such effects would yet have overtaken its development.

A similar drastic reversal of values seems to befall those other loaded oppositions that characterise Rousseau's discourse. Society itself is strictly inconceivable except at a stage of historical advance far beyond its putative 'natural' origin. Quite simply, there is no social order – even the most primitive – which doesn't participate in 'culture' at least to the extent of displaying kinship-systems, distinctions of rank, codes of acceptable behaviour and so forth. What Rousseau *means to say* about the origins of society – that nature is the source of all human good – is effectively undone by what the logic of his text *constrains him to mean*. It is the same with his writings on music, where the notion of a pure melodic style – as yet untouched by the bad supplement' of harmony – cannot be sustained in the end. For melody is unthinkable except in terms of a certain harmonic context, a background of overtones, chordal progressions, implicit cadences, etc., which define our very sense of melodic continuity and shape. This applies even to a single (unaccompanied) vocal line, in so far as we perceive it to possess musical character. Once again, Rousseau is forced up against the limits of his nature/culture opposition; constrained to admit that there is always already a 'supplement' (or swerve from natural origins) perversely in at the source.

This is nowhere more apparent than in Rousseau's autobiographical writing. It is not simply that he has missed out on real-life experience by devoting so much time and effort to the reconstruction of his own past history. What is worse is the fact that this narrative – always ambivalently placed between truth and fiction – increasingly confounds any attempt to distinguish the one from the other. Rousseau confesses that he has always been awkward in company, unable to do himself justice by saying what he genuinely means and feels at any given time. His experience only comes alive, so to speak, in the act of writing it down, narrating what (supposedly) happened from a standpoint of idealised retrospective grasp. Thus Rousseau's *Confessions* take on this uncanny power to usurp the very nature and privileged value of real-life experience. Writing – that 'dangerous supplement' – perverts the natural order of things by substituting fictions and lifeless signs for the authentic living presence of speech. And this is most evident in the psychopathology of Rousseau's sexual desires, given over (as he ruefully confesses) to the realm of erotic fantasy and substitute pleasure. So far has he gone down this dangerous path that even the experience of 'natural' intercourse falls far short of his solitary dreams. Rousseau's instincts are perverted to the point where he needs to 'supplement' such real-life pleasures by imagining some other woman in the place of his actual, flesh-and-blood partner. And for Rousseau this habit is one more evil consequence of a writing that tends increasingly to blur the distinction between dream and reality.

What is remarkable in Derrida's readings of Plato and Rousseau is the way these effects become manifest at every level of the text. He is not simply offering new interpretations, or seizing on those passages that offer some hold for ingenious revisionist treatment. Derrida's claim is that language itself – or the language of Western 'logocentric' tradition – is always subject to the dislocating forces at work in these texts. On the one hand it is marked by that primordial 'metaphysics of presence' which subordinates writing in the name of an authentic, natural speech. On the other it bears involuntary witness to the conflicts, tensions and paradoxes created by a writing whose effects are everywhere inscribed within the language and history of Western culture. This 'writing' is not confined to the standard (restricted) definition which works to preserve the contrast between speech and secondary inscriptions, mere written marks on a page. In *Of Grammatology*, writing is the name of whatever resists the logocentric ethos of speech-as-presence. In the texts of that tradition it becomes a kind of scapegoat, a 'wandering exile', cast out from the garden of innocent, natural origins but exerting a constant disruptive pressure from the margins of discourse. Derrida employs the term *archi-écriture* to signify writing in this massively extended or generalised sense. Its domain thus includes the whole range of deplorable effects that Rousseau attributes to 'culture' as the active antithesis of everything genuine, spontaneous and natural in human affairs.

Two further examples may help to explain what Derrida is driving at here. When a modern anthropologist (Claude Lévi-Strauss) celebrates the virtues of a primitive life-style, it is *writing* that he sees as the chief corrupting influence thrust upon an innocent oral culture by the emissaries of Western civilisation (himself unhappily included). The gift of writing is a double-edged, treacherous gift. It brings along with it the power to dominate others through possession of a secret, mandarin skill; the authority to lay down laws and prohibitions which are always those of a privileged class, and can thus be used to prop up a system based on arbitrary differences of rank. Writing becomes the precondition for every kind of social injustice that marks the progressive falling-away from a state of communal grace. And when a linguist (Saussure) asserts the priority of spoken over written language, it is likewise in terms of the corrupting effects that are brought about by substituting lifeless inscriptions for living sounds. Speech is the proper, authentic form of language; writing not merely derivative from speech but in some sense a parasite, an alien body which exploits and perverts the very nature of language. It is the sheer exorbitance, the hyperbolic character of these charges against writing that Derrida asks us to recognise.

Saussure and Lévi-Strauss are representative figures in a modern (structuralist) line of descent which undoubtedly looks back to Rousseau for its informing myths and values.

But their texts, like his, bear all the marks of an opposite, complicating tendency at work. Lévi-Strauss provides copious evidence that the tribe in question – the Nambikwara – already practised a great variety of laws, customs and social taboos which may not have been literally *written down*, but which yet had the force of articulate prescriptions. In short, these people were far from enjoying that state of idyllic communal existence that Lévi-Strauss identifies with the absence of writing. Once again, it is the Rousseauist mystique of origins that underwrites this notion of a small-scale, organic community, one where the face-to-face medium of speech suffices for all genuine social needs. If this were the case then writing would indeed be unable to assert its hold. But one only has to look more closely at Lévi-Strauss's text – at the detail of his trained ethnographic observation – to remark how many are the visible signs of a power that is exerted through the system of codified rules and regulations. And the same applies to Saussure's idea that the linguist should concentrate (at least as far as possible) on spoken rather than written language. For it is an axiom of Saussurian linguistics that meaning is the product of *differential* features – contrasts at the level of sound and sense – and not of any one-to-one identity between signifier and signified. And at certain crucial points in his argument Saussure falls back on analogies with writing as the best – perhaps the only – means to explain how this economy of difference operates. If modern linguistics has achieved some of its best results in analysing the sound-structure of language, this doesn't at all justify the phonocentric bias that equates 'natural' language with speech as self-presence and requires that writing be kept firmly in its place.

FRAMING THE TEXT: KANT AND HEGEL

It will be seen, therefore, that deconstruction is first and foremost an activity of textual close-reading, and one that resists the kind of summary account which I am here trying to present. Derrida himself has made a point of refusing all requests for a snap definition. If there is one 'truth' about deconstruction, he asserts, it is the fact that no statement of the form 'deconstruction is x' can possibly claim any warrant or genuine explanatory power. Definitions are reductive in the sense that they assume some ultimate, one-for-one match between signifier and signified, some point at which the text (or the detailed activity of reading) would yield up a meaning ideally possessed of its own self-authenticating truth. And it is precisely this assumption that Derrida is out to subvert by insisting on the non-self-identical nature of the linguistic sign, its involvement in a process of unlimited semiosis (or *différance*) which cannot be arrested by any such stipulative limit.

'Différance' in French is a kind of strategic neologism compounded to the two verbs 'to differ' and 'to defer'. What it signifies – in brief – is the fact that meaning can never be accounted for in terms of punctual self-presence; that language is not only (as Saussure argued) a *differential* structure of contrasts and relationships 'without positive terms', but also that meaning is endlessly *deferred* along the chain of linguistic substitutions and displacements that occur whenever we seek to define what a given term signifies in context. It would therefore be wrong to treat the term 'deconstruction' as uniquely exempt from this general condition, or to offer a summary account of it as involving some pre-given sequence of arguments, strategies or moves. For this is to assume – against all the evidence of Derrida's writings – that concepts can exist in an ideal realm of self-identical meaning and value which somehow transcends the contingent fact of their existing in written or textual form. So one can well understand Derrida's impatience with those purveyors of short-cut intellectual fashion who demand to know what deconstruction 'is', how it works or what results it will standardly produce when applied to any text.

All the same it is possible to push too far with this purist attitude and ignore the very real *philosophical* cogency and rigour of Derrida's arguments. What he does most often – in a move familiar to philosophers at least since Kant – is interrogate the grounds (or 'conditions of possibility') that underwrite the truth-claims of this or that discourse. Take for instance his commentary on Husserl's essay 'The Origin of Geometry', where Husserl sets out to establish the fact that geometrical truths are ideal, that they exist – once discovered by a thinker like Euclid – in a realm of absolute, intuitive self-evidence, unaffected by the vagaries of written transmission. What Derrida brings out through a close reading of Husserl's text is the way that his argument turns out to undermine (deconstruct) its own working premises. Hence the strict *impossibility* of conceiving geometry in terms of some primordial grounding intuition achieved repeatedly from age to age by everyone capable of grasping such truth. On the contrary, as Derrida argues: for truths to be 'ideal' in Husserl's sense it is necessary that they *not* be confined to the realm of intuitive self-evidence but conserved in a form of historically transmissible knowledge which writing alone is able to achieve. Indeed, Husserl himself (like Rousseau and Saussure) has passages that covertly acknowledge this necessity, even though he seeks to ground geometry in a realm of pure, self-present intuition where writing would figure as at most an ancillary device for reminding us of truths that we always in some sense already knew.

What Derrida is asking in each of the above cases (Plato, Rousseau, Saussure and Husserl) is something much akin to the Kantian question: namely, how it is possible for thinking to proceed at all when faced with certain ultimate problems in the nature of its own constitution as a self-reflective, self-critical project of enquiry. In Kant, these questions receive three kinds of answer according to the different forms or modalities of knowledge. *Understanding* is the province of epistemological critique, of a knowledge that deals with phenomena falling under the laws of objective cognition, causal explanation or other such perceived regularities of real-world experience. Its powers and limits are best established (Kant argues) by marking it off from all forms of speculative reason, all 'ideas' that go beyond any possible grounding in the data of intuitive self-evidence. So it is that, from the standpoint of theoretical understanding, 'intuitions without concepts are blind; concepts without intuitions are empty.' For *practical reason* (or ethics), on the contrary, what has to be preserved is the freedom or autonomy of human will, its capacity to legislate over actions and choices which must obey some ultimate categorical imperative, but which cannot be reduced to the level of natural necessity or rule-governed behaviour. Ethics is precisely that domain of reason where thinking gives itself the rule by appealing to a realm of 'supersensible' ideas whose source lies beyond all strictly theoretical understanding. And *aesthetic judgement* – his topic in the third *Critique* – has its own complex role to play in this Kantian structure of argument since it figures at crucial moments as a source of enabling transitions or analogies between one faculty and another. Thus the 'Transcendental Aesthetic' is Kant's title for that section of the first *Critique* which explains how sensuous intuitions are brought under concepts in order to provide the essential link betwen experience and *a priori* knowledge. And a similar connection exists between ethics and aesthetics, in so far as Kant seeks an analogy for moral law in our experience of art as calling forth powers of appreciative judgement that go beyond mere personal taste and demand universal assent.

Such knowledge cannot be legitimised in the manner of theoretical understanding, that is, by means of a cognitive appeal to objects of which we possess both a concept and a corresponding sensuous intuition. For it is, according to Kant, the very hallmark of aesthetic judgement that it cannot be 'brought under' a concept or reduced to any set of necessary or sufficient properties attaching to the object itself. What the beautiful brings about – whether in nature or in art – is a 'free play' of the faculties wherein they discover a sense of harmonious cooperative balance unattainable through any other mode of experience. And the sublime comes yet closer to providing an analogue for the absolute, unconditioned character of ethical reason. It involves (as with many of the best-known passages in Wordsworth, Coleridge or Shelley) an essentially twofold movement of thought: a sense of the mind being at first overwhelmed by the sheer awesomeness of nature and its own incapacity to grasp or represent it, followed by the realisation that precisely this lack of any adequate objective correlative signals the existence of imaginative powers that go beyond the realm of phenomenal cognition to that of 'supersensible' ideas. It is for this reason that Kant finds a kinship between ethics and that moment of sublime overreaching where intelligence responds to a call that would otherwise defeat all its powers of self-understanding.

It will help if we bear these arguments in mind when attempting to grasp how Derrida's work relates to the project of Kantian enlightened critique. Deconstruction is philosophical' in the sense that it deploys a distinctive mode of argument in raising certain problems about knowledge, meaning and representation. It suspends our commonsense-intuitive attitude and asks what ultimate grounds exist, in the nature of experience or *a priori* knowledge, for those items of belief we standardly take on trust. Moreover, it does this by always pursuing such judgements back a further stage, demanding what might be the 'conditions of possibility' that enable thought to get started on the process of examining its own claims to truth. Thus Derrida will ask of Plato, Rousseau and Saussure: how is it that these thinkers can on the one hand denounce writing as a parasite, a 'dangerous supplement', an obtrusive and usurping substitute for speech, while on the other conducting their arguments through a whole series of analogies and metaphors whose covert referent is writing itself? Of course it must be true that speech precedes writing as a matter of historical development, at least in so far as writing is identified with that form of phonetic-alphabetical transcription which prevails within our own culture. But there is no good reason to suppose that this contingent fact about *some* languages can be erected into a generalised precondition for language in general. It is this habit of moving surreptitiously from *de facto* to *de jure* orders of argument, or from local observations to universal truth-claims, that Derrida finds everywhere at work in the texts of Western 'logocentric' tradition. Thus it is taken for granted by thinkers from Plato and Aristotle to Kant, Hegel, Husserl and Saussure that there exists a wholly natural order of priorities where ideas must first be articulated in speech and then – if neccessary – speech be recorded in the purely conventional and arbitrary signs that make up a written language. Writing is seen as a bad necessity, a precondition for conserving and transmitting ideas from one generation to the next, but a recourse that can only be justified in so far as it obeys the imperative that *speech comes first*, and that writing must faithfully transcribe the elements of phonetic-alphabetical language.

This prejudice comes out with particular force in Hegel's insistence that no form of purely symbolic notation – no 'universal characteristic' of the kind proposed by a thinker like Leibniz – can possibly give rise to genuine, authentic philosophy. For it is essential to Hegel's argument in the *Phenomenology of Mind* that thinking should proceed through a recapitulation of those various stages in its own prehistory that bear witness to a consciousness struggling to achieve the condition of lucid self-knowledge. This can only come about if the texts of that tradition give access to a realm of spiritualised conflicts and dramas whose expression may depend upon writing – since otherwise we would possess no record of them – but whose essential meaning must remain unaffected by the vagaries of written language. For Hegel, the only good (philosophically acceptable) kind of writing is that which respects the priority of self-present speech, and which therefore confines itself to a form of phonetic-alphabetical notation where writing must faithfully preserve and transcribe the character of oral discourse. Hence Derrida's reiterated question: *by what right*, or according to what self-evident law of reason, must writing be consigned to this strictly subservient role in relation to speech? For there exist, after all, a great many striking counter-examples, from the various forms of non-European pictographic or ideogrammatical writing which he discusses at length in *Of Grammatology*, to those systems of formalised notation that have often been proposed, by philosophers from Leibniz to Ferge, as a means of overcoming the vagueness and imprecision of natural language. It is against this background that Hegel's gesture of exclusion takes on its wider significance. For it brings out very clearly the link that exists between Western logocentric assumptions and a certain deep-laid phonocentric bias, an attitude which holds that writing is at best a poor substitute for speech, but one which can attain some measure of truth so long as it properly reproduces those speech-sounds that in turn give access to the realm of self-present thought.

Derrida's *Glas* is undoubtedly the text where this argument is presented to maximum effect through a writing – a practice of spatial and graphic inscription – which cannot be reduced to any order of philosophic concepts. It has thus achieved something of a scandalous reputation as the *ne plus ultra* of philosophy's undoing at the hands of rhetoric or intertextual 'freeplay'. In fact this idea is demonstrably wide of the mark, since Derrida is here just as much concerned with issues in the province of post-Kantian (and especially Hegelian) philosophy. But they are addressed in a style – a typographical as well as a literary' style – whose effect is to provoke the greatest possible resistance among mainstream academic philosophers. The text is laid out in a running series of columns, commentaries and inset paragraphs, all of which the reader is supposed to take in by treating them on equal terms and not looking for some 'meta-language' or privileged voice of authorial truth. The two main sources are Hegel and Genet; on the one hand the philosopher of Absolute Reason, of the State, Christianity and the bourgeois family as embodiments of universal truth, on the other the homosexual thief-turned-writer whose aim was to tear those values apart by every means at his disposal.

At one level the effect of juxtaposing these utterly incongruous texts is to bring philosophy up against the limits of its own conceptual resources, to transgress all the margins and juridical border-lines that philosophy has established for the conduct of serious, responsible debate. Thus Hegel's dialectic is inscribed within a system of self-regulating concepts and values which ensure that truth is passed down through the channels of properly *authorised* thinking and teaching. This system connects in turn with the sexual division of labour where reason is exclusively a male prerogative, a power exercised by virtue of the husband's joint access to the domestic and civil spheres, while woman remains duty-bound to her role as wife, mother and family helpmeet. Derrida goes various ways around to deconstruct this covert gender-politics everywhere at work in the texts of Hegelian philosophy. He incorporates passages on love, marriage and the family from Hegel's letters and other biographical material; examines the way that his reading of Sophocles' *Antigone* turns upon this same dialectical overcoming of woman's interests in the name of male reason and political order. He then goes on to show, through a series of elaborately staged intertextual readings, how other philosophers (including Kant) have likewise managed to repress or to sublimate woman's voice while claiming to speak in the name of universal humanity and absolute reason. All this in counterpoint with the passages from Genet (chiefly *Our Lady of the Flowers* and *The Thief's Journal*) which supply not so much an ironic gloss as an adversary language which progressively invades and disfigures the discourse of Hegelian reason. Thus *Glas* opens up the domain of male dialectical thought to a series of complicating detours and aporias that cannot be subsumed by any logic of speculative reason.

There is so much going on at every stage in this extraordinary text that a brief account can really offer no more than a few suggested points of entry. One recurrent topos is the question of names, signatures and the way that such marks of authorial presence and origin can always be dissolved through what Derrida calls the 'disseminating' power of language, its capacity to graft them onto new contexts of meaning where they no longer function as 'proper' names but as signifying terms that generate all kinds of allusive cross-reference from text to text. Another is the distinction between 'literal' and 'figurative' sense, a difference that philosophers have often been concerned to hold securely in place, but which nonetheless continues to vex and elude their best efforts of conceptual clarification. There is a whole running subtext of allusions (*via* Genet) to the so-called 'flowers' of rhetoric, the seductive tropology of metaphor and other such figures that exert their unsettling influence on the discourse of philosophic reason. And this goes along with Derrida's insistence on the stubborn *materiality* of language, the way that effects of meaning come about through chance collocations, unlooked-for homonyms and everything that holds out against reduction to a stable economy of words and concepts.

Hegelian logic thinks to overcome such resistance by assimilating language, history and thought to the terms of an all-embracing dialectic that moves ever onward and up through stages of repeated conflict and tension, to the point of an ultimate reconciliation in the name of Absolute Reason. This movement involves a twofold process of subsuming and transcending whatever stands in its way, a process of conceptual 'raising' (*Aufhebung*) which also requires that reason should sublimate those previous stages on the path to enlightenment that reflected an as-yet imperfect grasp of the relation between thought, self-knowledge and reality. What Derrida asks us to read in his assemblage of intertextual echoes and allusions is the resistance that writing continues to offer in the face of this relentless totalising drive. Thus *Glas* draws attention to those episodes in Hegel's text where the narrative encounters something alien to the dominant (Graeco-Christian) tradition of idealised conceptual grasp. What is repressed at these moments is another history, one that Hegel attempts to bring under his grand teleological scheme of things, but which nonetheless continues to exert a steady disruptive pressure from the margins of his text.

Thus the progress of Hegelian dialectic is paralleled in his account of how Christianity (as revealed religious truth) supersedes and incorporates its Jewish source-texts, and again in his view of the bourgeois patriarchal family as the highpoint and natural, self-authorised foundation of present-day civil and socio-political order. 'What is consciousness', Derrida asks, 'if its ultimate power is achieved by the family?' And again, what is at stake in this repeated scenario of dialectical ascent or *Aufhebung* if one of its forms is the presumed overcoming of Jewish by Christian religion?

> To raise the pharisaic letter of the Jew would also be to constitute a symbolic language wherein the literal body lets itself be animated, aerated, roused, lifted up, benumbed by the spiritual intention. Now the Jew is incapable of this in his family, his politics, his religion, his rhetoric. If he became capable of it, he would no longer be Jewish. When he will become capable of it, he will have become Christian.

This passage should make it clear that there is more to Derrida's 'wordplay' than a simple desire to take philosophy down a peg or two by exposing its arguments to the dislocating force of a Joycian paronomasia pushed to the giddy extreme. What he is broaching in *Glas* is the deconstruction not only of certain tenacious philosophical ideas, but also of the way those ideas have worked to reinforce the predominant values and assumptions of Western ethnocentric discourse.

See also:

Bennington (5.1)
Beardsworth (5.4)
Readings (8.3)
Bernasconi (9.2)

'PHILOSOPHY AS A KIND OF WRITING: AN ESSAY ON DERRIDA'

Richard Rorty

Here is one way to look at physics: there are some invisible things which are parts of everything else and whose behavior determines the way everything else works. Physics is the search for an accurate description of those invisible things, and it proceeds by finding better and better explanations of the visible. Eventually, by way of microbiological accounts of the mental, and through causal accounts of the mechanisms of language, we shall be able to see the physicists' accumulation of truths about the world as itself a transaction between these invisible things.

Here is another way of looking at physics: the physicists are men looking for new interpretations of the Book of Nature. After each pedestrian period of normal science, they dream up a new model, a new picture, a new vocabulary, and then they announce that the true meaning of the Book has been discovered. But, of course, it never is, any more than the true meaning of *Coriolanus* or the *Dunciad* or the *Phenomenology of Spirit*, or the *Philosophical Investigations*. What makes them physicists is that their writings are commentaries on the writings of earlier interpreters of Nature, not that they all are somehow 'talking about the same thing,' the *invisibilia Dei sive naturae* toward which their inquiries steadily converge.

Here is a way of thinking about right and wrong: the common moral consciousness contains certain intuitions concerning equality, fairness, human dignity, and the like, which need to be made explicit through the formulation

Source: Rorty Richard, 'Philosophy as a kind of writing: An essay on Derrida', *New Literary History*, 10, 1978, pp. 141–5.

of principles – principles of the sort which can be used to write legislation. By thinking about puzzle-cases, and by abstracting from differences between our (European) culture and others, we can formulate better and better principles, principles corresponding ever more closely to the moral law itself.

Here is another way of thinking about right and wrong: the longer men or cultures live, the more *phronēsis* they may, with luck, acquire – the more sensitivity to others, the more delicate a typology for describing their fellows and themselves. Mingling with others helps; Socratic discussion helps; but since the Romantics, we have been helped most of all by the poets, the novelists, and the ideologues. Since the *Phenomenology of Spirit* taught us to see not only the history of philosophy, but that of Europe, as portions of a *Bildungsroman*, we have not striven for moral knowledge as a kind of *epistēmē*. Rather, we have seen Europe's self-descriptions, and our own self-descriptions, not as ordered to subject matter, but as designs in a tapestry which they will still be weaving after we, and Europe, die.

Here is a way of looking at philosophy: from the beginning, philosophy has worried about the relation between thought and its object, representation and represented. The old problem about reference to the inexistent, for example, has been handled in various unsatisfactory ways because of a failure to distinguish properly philosophical questions about meaning and reference from extraneous questions motivated by scientific, ethical, and religious concerns. Once these questions *are* properly isolated, however, we can see philosophy as a field which has its center in a series of questions about the relations between words and the world. The recent purifying move from talk of ideas to talk of meanings had dissipated the epistemological skepticism which motivated much of past philosophy. This has left philosophy a more limited, but more self-conscious, rigorous, and coherent area of inquiry.

Here is another way of looking at philosophy: philosophy started off as a confused combination of the love of wisdom and the love of argument. It began with Plato's notion that the rigor of mathematical argumentation exposed, and could be used to correct, the pretensions of the politicians and the poets. As philosophical thought changed and grew, inseminated by this ambivalent *eros*, it produced shoots which took root on their own. Both wisdom and argumentation became far more various than Plato dreamed. Given such nineteenth-century complications as the *Bildungsroman*, non-Euclidean geometries, ideological historiography, the literary dandy, and the political anarchist, there is no way in which one can isolate philosophy as occupying a distinctive place in culture or concerned with a distinctive subject or proceeding by some distinctive method. One cannot even seek an essence for philosophy as an academic *Fach* (because one would first have to choose the country in whose universities' catalogs one was to look). The philosophers' own scholastic little definitions of 'philosophy' are merely polemical devices – intended to exclude from the field of honor those whose pedigrees are unfamiliar. We can pick out 'the philosophers' in the contemporary intellectual world only by noting who is commenting on a certain sequence of historical figures. All that 'philosophy' as a name for a sector of culture means is 'talk about Plato, Augustine, Descartes, Kant, Hegel, Frege, Russell . . . and that lot.' Philosophy is best seen as a kind of writing. It is delimited, as is any literary genre, not by form or matter, but by tradition – a family romance involving, e.g., Father Parmenides, honest old Uncle Kant, and bad brother Derrida.

There, then, are two ways of thinking about various things. I have drawn them up as reminders of the differences between a philosophical tradition which began, more or less, with Kant, and one which began, more or less, with Hegel's *Phenomenology*. The first tradition thinks of truth as a vertical relationship between representations and what is represented. The second tradition thinks of truth horizontally – as the culminating reinterpretation of our predecessors' reinterpretation of their predecessors' reinterpretation . . . This tradition does not ask how representations are related to nonrepresentations, but how representations can be seen as hanging together. The difference is not one between 'correspondence' and 'coherence' theories of truth – though these so-called theories are partial expressions of this contrast. Rather, it is the difference between regarding truth, goodness, and beauty as eternal objects which we try to locate and reveal, and regarding them as artifacts whose fundamental design we often have to alter. The first tradition takes scientific truth as the center of philosophical concern (and scorns the notion of incommensurable scientific world-pictures). It asks how well other fields of inquiry conform to the model of science. The second tradition takes science as one (not especially privileged nor interesting) sector of culture, a sector which, like all the other sectors, only makes sense when viewed historically. The first likes to present itself as a straightforward, down-to-earth, scientific attempt to get things right. The second needs to present itself obliquely, with the help of as many foreign words and as much allusiveness and name-dropping as possible. Neo-Kantian philosophers like Putnam, Strawson, and Rawls have arguments and theses which are connected to Kant's by a fairly straightforward series of 'purifying' transformations, transformations which are thought to give clearer and clearer views of the persistent problems. For the non-Kantian philosophers, there are no persistent problems – save perhaps the existence of the Kantians. Non-Kantian philosophers like Heidegger and Derrida are emblematic figures who not only do not solve problems, they do not *have* arguments or theses. They are connected with their predecessors not by common subjects or methods but in the 'family resemblance' way in which latecomers in a sequence of commentators on commentators are connected with older members of the same sequence.

To understand Derrida, one must see his work as the latest development in this non-Kantian, dialectical tradition – the latest attempt of the dialecticians to shatter the Kantians' ingenuous image of themselves as accurately representing how things really are. Derrida talks a lot about language, and it is tempting to view him as a 'philosopher of language' whose work one might usefully compare with other inquiries concerning the relations between words and the world. But it would be less misleading to say that his writing about language is an attempt to show why there should be no philosophy of language. On his view, language is the last refuge of the Kantian tradition, of the notion that there is something eternally present to man's gaze (the structure of the universe, the moral law, the nature of language) which philosophy can let us see more clearly. The reason why the notion of 'philosophy of language' is an illusion is the same reason why philosophy – *Kantian* philosophy, philosophy as more than a kind of writing – is an illusion. The twentieth-century attempt to purify Kant's general theory about the relation between representations and their objects by turning it into philosophy of language is, for Derrida, to be countered by making philosophy even more impure – more unprofessional, funnier, more allusive, sexier, and above all, more 'written.' Thus, insofar as he has an attitude towards, for example, the mini-tradition which stretches from Frege to David-son, it is the same as his attitude towards Husserl's discussion of language. The attitude, roughly, is that most twentieth-century concern with language is Kantian philosophy in extremis, a last desperate attempt to do on a pathetically small scale what Kant (and before him Plato) attempted to do on a large scale – show how the atemporally true can be contained in a spatio-temporal vehicle, regularize the relation between man and what man seeks by exhibiting its 'structure,' freezing the historical process of successive reinterpretations by exhibiting the structure of all possible interpretation.

Derrida, then, has little to tell us about language, but a great deal to tell us about philosophy. To get a handle on his work, one might take him as answering the question, 'Given that philosophy *is* a kind of writing, why does this suggestion meet with such resistance?' This becomes, in his work, the slightly more particular question, 'What must philosophers who object to this characterization think *writing* is, that they should find the notion that that is what they are doing so offensive?' Whereas Heidegger, Derrida's great father-figure, was the first to 'place' (or if you prefer, 'transcend' or 'castrate') Hegel by giving a historical characterization of Hegel's historicism, Derrida wishes to 'place' (or whatever) Heidegger by explaining Heidegger's distrust of writing. Heidegger, it is true, wrote a lot, but always (after the 'turn') in the interests of urging us to be still and listen to the single line of verse, the individual Greek word. Derrida is suspicious of Heidegger's preference for the simplicity and splendor of the word spoken on the hill, and also of his contempt for the footnote scribbled in the ergastulum, down in the valley. The preference, he thinks, betrays a fatal taint of Kantianism, of the Platonic 'metaphysics of presence.' For it is characteristic of the Kantian tradition that, no matter how much writing it does, it does not think that philosophy *should* be 'written,' any more than science should be. Writing is an unfortunate necessity; what is really wanted is to show, to demonstrate, to point out, to exhibit, to make one's interlocutor stand at gaze before the world. The copy theory of ideas, the spectator theory of knowledge, the notion that 'understanding representation' is the heart of philosophy, are expressions of this need to substitute an epiphany for a text, to 'see through' representation. In a mature science, the words in which the investigator 'writes up' his results should be as few and as transparent as possible. Heidegger, though struggling manfully against this cluster of notions, and especially against the notion of the 'research-project' as model for philosophical thinking, in the end succumbed to the same nostalgia for the innocence and brevity of the spoken word. His substitution of auditory for visual metaphors – of listening to the voice of Being for being a spectator of time and eternity – was, Derrida thinks, only a dodge. The Kantian urge to bring philosophy to an end by solving all its problems, having everything fall into place, and the Heideggerian urge towards *Gelassenheit* and *Unverborgenheit*, are the same urge. Philosophical writing, for Heidegger as for the Kantians, is really aimed at putting an end to writing. For Derrida, writing always leads to more writing, and more, and still more – just as history does not lead to Absolute Knowledge or the Final Struggle, but to more history, and more, and still more. The *Phenomenology*'s vision of truth as what you get by reinterpreting all the previous reinterpretations of reinterpretations still embodies the Platonic ideal of the Last Reinterpretation, the *right* interpretation at last. Derrida wants to keep the horizontal character of Hegel's notion of philosophy without its teleology, its sense of direction, its seriousness.

See also:

Miller (4.1)
De Man (4.2)
Attridge (4.3)
Bennington (5.1)

3.3

'DECONSTRUCTION AS CRITICISM'

Rodolphe Gasché

In science, conceptual progress as well as 'the wandering off into different fields,' without which there is no such progress, leads to the impossibility of asking questions and explaining problems which were essential to the previous theoretical configuration. Indeed, such a loss is not considered a serious one for 'there is no need to possess such knowledge,' as the only *one* thing legitimately to be demanded of a theory 'is that it should give us a correct account of the world, i.e., of the totality of facts *as constituted by its own basic concepts.*'[1] What is true of science is in principle also true of literary criticism. If 'the context of discovery' comes into conflict with 'the context of justification,'[2] if the reading devices produce discoveries that the previous theories can no longer account for, and if in the eyes of the traditional critic it becomes undecidable 'whether a new view *explains* what it is supposed to explain, or whether it does not wander off into different fields,'[3] then one may speak of what Paul Feyerabend calls the *incommensurability* of approaches. Yet, is this incommensurability as securely established as some of the Newer Critics – the so-called deconstructive critics – and most of their opponents would like to believe? Implicitly, a distinction such as Wayne C. Booth's between monism and limited pluralism (i.e., liberalism) acknowledges already that the seemingly mutually exclusive approaches to literature are about the same. What Booth's conceptual system vouches for – an intimate affinity of traditional academic criticism in all its forms and deconstructive criticism, a commensurability

Source: Rodolphe Gasché, 'Deconstruction as criticism', *Glyph*, 6, 1979, pp. 177–215.

without the knowledge of the critics (Booth included) – is one of the presuppo-sitions of this article. However, rather than representing a conciliatory gesture in the direction of a 'critical commonwealth' whose access depends on the critics' statements seen as 'a passport into the country of debate'[4] and far from being a belief into the continuity of tradition, the stand taken here is critical of deconstructive literary criticism, and maintains that it is incapable of living up to its pretensions. For the problem of either thematic criticism and/or New Criticism (only disguised by a new and sometimes fashionable vocabulary) still dominates the post-structuralist approaches,[5] in spite of their rhetoric. Apart from this rhetoric there is no trace of what Bachelard called an episte-mological break.[6] In no way does such a judgement disqualify or impair the contributions of modern deconstructive criticism. On the contrary: in the wake of New Criticism deconstructive criticism has developed now indispensable insights into the very object of literary criticism, the text. But just as science textbooks represent a sort of obstruction within the ongoing activity of scien-tific research,[7] much of what appears as deconstructive criticism contributes more to prolonging the impasses of traditional academic criticism than to opening up new areas of research. Hence the generalized discomfort about, in particular, deconstructive criticism. But the critical malaise of modern critics that makes them long for a 'beyond-deconstruction' and simultaneously allows the attacks of the rear-guard, stems in the first place from a mutual misunder-standing of the notion of deconstruction. It is precisely this misinterpretation that makes its accommodation by American criticism possible, and, by the same token, transforms it into a mechanical exercise similar to academic thematism or formalism.

Before trying to clarify the misinterpretation of the notion of deconstruction, some of the *evidence* guiding so-called deconstructive criticism has to be pointed out.[8] In the wake of New Criticism, which rightly showed that literary criticism was not derivative and was not simply a parasitic response to litera-ture, but an autonomous discipline, it has become fashionable to conceive of literary criticism as *theory*. Yet, what does theory mean in this context except the all too often naive and sometimes even, for its uncontrolled and unwanted side-effects, ridiculous *application* of the *results* of philosophical debates to the literary field? It is on this unproblematized and rarely justified application, as well as the lack of any questioning of the applicability of such philosophemes to the specific levels of texts, that the theory rests. It rests especially on a generally intuitive understanding of conceptual systems situated as it is in the (institu-tionally motivated) absence of all rigorous formation in pilot sciences such as anthropology, linguistics, psychoanalysis, and especially philosophy.[9] With this, *theory* is no different from the impressionistic approaches and loose conceptual instruments of traditional academic criticism which seldom reflects its own presuppositions. In fact, the unproblematized application of borrowed tools to the analysis of literary texts already proves the affinity of deconstructive and traditional criticism. Indeed, the newly fashionable *a-theoretical* stand which in the present configuration pretends to come to the rescue of literary, aesthetic, and ethical values is by its very definition not only *violently* theoretical, but this hypocritical innocence in matters of theory stems from its blindness and an ignorance of its own presuppositions that are in the end all dependent on various extra-literary disciplines such as psychology, history, and philosophical aesthetics. The origins of these disciplines in nineteenth-century philosophy are never admitted or made explicit.

If deconstructive criticism does not simply coincide with such an ill-founded application of conceptual tools borrowed from certain pilot sciences to the analysis of literary texts, its theoretical pretensions end with the elaboration of the cognitive aspects of these texts. Such an approach, however masterful it may be, by taking the information and knowledge explicitly or implicitly displayed by a text for granted or by taking the reflections a text confers about itself literally, not only fosters a theoretical eclecticism that raises the critic to the status of characters like Bouvard and Pecuchet, but also makes him subject to the same kind of criticism that Levi-Strauss directed against Mauss: to have tried to explain the melanesian notion of *mana* with the help of a native theory.[10]

A second evidence predominant in deconstructive criticism is the conviction that everything is literature, text or writing. This evidence of Newer Criticism only radicalizes the purely aesthetic and a-historical vista of its academic antecedents. It also continues the conservative function of traditional criticism by neutralizing and blurring the capital differences and critical functions between different kinds of discourses. In the case of the so called deconstructive criticism, this evidence originates in an illicit application of the Derridean notion of *écriture* to all forms of discourses. This precipitated application in question is made possible – as always – through a confusion of levels in a specifically philosophical debate with Husserl's phenomenology. These levels are in fact distinguished carefully by Derrida himself. The notion of *writing* (of text, and of literature, as well) as used by modern deconstructive criticism refers in general only to the *phenomenological experience of writing* as something present in all discourses and texts. Yet, in *Of Grammatology* Derrida clearly warned of mistaking writing (as arche-writing) for the colloquial meaning of writing. Indeed, writing as arche-writing 'cannot occur *as such* within the phenomenological experience of a *presence.*' The notion of the trace, he adds, 'will never be merged with a phenomenology of writing.'[11] Derrida's notion of writing and of the trace presupposes a phenomenological reduction of all the mundane regions of sensibility (but also of the intelligible). Being anterior (yet not as an essence) to the distinctions between the regions of sensibility, and consequently to any experience of presence, the trace or writing is not something which can be said to be *present* in all discourses. The regions of sensibility and of presence are 'only' the regions where writing as arche-writing appears *as such*, becomes present by occulting itself. Thus, the evidence in question, since it confuses and is unaware of distinctions as important as those between appearance and appearing, between appearance and signification, consists of a fall back into a phenomenological apprehension of writing as something readable, visible, and significant in an empirical medium open to experience. However, criticizing this evidence does not entail (as will be shown) that there is a tangible outside to literature, to the text, and to writing, nor does the rejection of such an exteriority necessarily imply one's entanglement in the pure immanence of the text.

The major evidence of deconstructive criticism, also shared by its opponents, is its understanding of the operation of deconstruction. The evidences already mentioned, the priority of theory and the universalization of literature, are linked to modern criticism's understanding of deconstruction. According to these presuppositions, Derrida's philosophical work can be turned into a theory to be applied to the regional science of literary criticism as well as to the literature it deals with, without the categories of literature and criticism (and the institutions supporting them) being put into question. This naive and intuitive reception of Derrida's debate with philosophy, its reduction to a few sturdy devices for the critic's use, represents nothing less than an extraordinary blurring and toning-down of the critical implications of this philosopher's work.

Since it requires only a little more than skimming Derrida's major works to know what deconstruction *is not*, let us briefly enumerate what it certainly cannot be identified with. Deconstruction is *not* to be mistaken for a nihilism, nor for a metaphysics of absence, nor for a negative theology. It is *not* a demolition and a dismantling to be opposed by or calling for a rebuilding and a reconstruction.[12] It is *not* to be taken for what Heidegger calls *destruction*. At the same time, deconstruction is not what is asserted by positive definitions in Newer Criticism. Here deconstruction is said to represent the moment where in a text the argument begins to undermine itself; or, in accordance with Jakobson's notion of the poetic and aesthetic function, the relation of a message of communication to itself that, thus, becomes its own object; or, finally the self-revelation and indication by the text of its own principles of organization and operation. Consequently, deconstructive criticism seldom appears to be more than a very sophisticated form of structural analysis. The only difference with structural analysis is that the diacritical principal of meaning, that is to say its dependence on differentially determined opposites, on the correspondence and reciprocity of coupled terms, is applied in a negative fashion. Meaning, as well as the aesthetic qualities of a text, then spring forth from the self-cancelling of the text's constituting oppositions.[13] But not only is this interplay of binary terms that parody and debunk one another called deconstructive, to increase the confusion it is often also said to be dialectical.[14] Yet, in terms of logic, the diacritical relations do not even represent the threshold to (negative or not) dialectics, not to speak of deconstruction.

As a negative diacritical approach to literature and the text, deconstructive criticism consequently asserts and simultaneously depends on the idea of the self-reflexivity and the autonomy of the text. It is this rationale of almost all of modern criticism that, as the third evidence, totally distorts the notion of deconstruction.

Here again, in order to avoid some all too hasty conclusions, a few remarks are indispensable. The self-reflexivity with its idea of a more or less infinite *mise en abyme* of the text, as well as the idea of its autonomy assumed by modern criticism is not to be criticized from an, if you will, extrinsic approach. Besides, such an approach, historical, sociological, psychological, psychoanalytical, and so forth, goes perfectly with the assumption of the text's self-reflexivity and self-referentiality as constitutive of its autonomy. Nonetheless, the contributions based on such a notion of the text cannot be minimized. Compared to the traditional approach which, in spite of its erudition is scarcely more than an unflagging effort to avoid the object of literary studies, modern deconstructive criticism has shown itself to be able to investigate the manifold linguistic density of the *work of literature itself*. Moreover, the self-reflexivity of the text is in no way to be denied. Undoubtedly, its self-reflexive stratas *almost* constitute its entirety. But what is at stake here is this *almost*, the point of nonclosure of the reflexive space of the text.

In general, modern deconstructive criticism attributes this self-reflexivity of the text to certain specific totalizing emblems such as tropes, images, similes, and so on. Never questioning the nature and the status of *representation in the text*, deconstructive criticism conceives of these emblems of the whole as hyperbolically reinscribing the act of writing.[15] Through such images, the text *itself* (or the writer) is said to perceive 'the act of constituting – that is, of writing – (its, or) his nascent *logos*.'[16] This is certainly true, but this is precisely the problem as well. Indeed, as an especially modern aesthetic device this self-reflexivity of texts depends on the totalizing consciousness of an author, or on an equally questionable assertion of a consciousness or unconsciousness of the text. Thus a textual reading would precisely have to account for these cognitive functions of the text, for the images or scenes where its production is staged and for its self-reflexive stratas, by inscribing them into the *global* functioning of the text. As the self-perceiving function of the text is subject to the same aporias which haunt perception and consciousness in general, as the act of production of the text will never coincide with its reflection through totalizing emblems (or concepts), such a move toward a global apprehension of the functions of the text becomes imperative. Yet since the (neither *de facto* nor *de iure*) overlapping of the two languages – writing on the one hand and its reflection on the other – never takes place, that overlapping or that identity, which is supposed to engender the text, would also call, in a global apprehension of the functions of the text, for another notion or concept of the text. The current notion of the text's autonomy and self-reflexivity only continues the claim of American formalism to a totalizing principle, to what is called the integrity of the literary form. The idea of self-reflexivity indeed reconfirms, but also – and this is its historical importance – represents the development of what makes the idea of contextual unity possible. Modern deconstructive criticism, a faithful offspring of New Criticism, significantly enough was able to think the mode of totalization of texts in terms of what makes such a unity possible by borrowing from European thematic criticism.[17]

A compromise between formal and thematic criticism on the one hand and on the other hand a radical development of the metaphysical implications of the formalist's idea of contextual unity, deconstructive criticism cannot hope to escape the, it is true, usually dull critique of its opponents. A more radical critique, however, is to be directed against deconstructive criticism (a critique that affects traditional criticism so much the more), which by erroneously mistaking the reflexive stratas and the cognitive functions of the text that it describes for the text as a whole, seriously reduces and restricts the play of the text, a play it was one of the first to take into account.

Reassessing deconstruction thus faces several tasks. Besides the necessity of restoring its rigorous meaning against its defenders as well as against those who argue against it, deconstructive criticism will have to break away from its formalist past and to resituate its loans from thematic criticism, in order to open the notion of the text to its outside. That will not, however, mean that the text is to be precipitously connected to the real and empirical outside.[18] It is true, that far from being an operation *in the limits* of the text, deconstruction proceeds *from and at the limit* of the text. But the outside of the text, that which limits its reflexive stratas and cognitive functions, is not its empirical and sensible outside. The outside of the text is precisely that which *in* the text makes self-reflexion possible and at the same time limits it. While on the one hand, the position which consists of criticizing the self-reflexivity of a text from one of its possible sensible and empirical outsides is still privy to what it criticizes, deconstructive criticism, on the other hand, is incommensurate with one of these corresponding alternatives. Proceeding from that limit that traverses the text in its entirety, deconstructive criticism reasserts literariness and the text as *play*: as the unity of chance and rule. In this perspective, the reflexive strata which constitute *almost* all of the text, appear as *almost* parasitical in relation to the text and its play. In short, such a deconstructive criticism reaffirms all of the text. More complex than a totality solely based on a self-reflexive autonomy, the global situation of the text encompasses both the text's reflexive inside and that outside from which it proceeds, an outside that it harbors in its core. This approach to the play of the text (still called literature in the absence of a better term[19]), which unlike conventional criticism inevitably limits this very play by its mere investigation, accounts for its own desire to limit and induce changes in this play.[20]

Thus, in the pages that follow, one aspect of deconstruction only will be analyzed. Indeed, if Derrida's work can already provide a superficial reader with enough material to invalidate most of the critic's contentions, this one aspect in particular has misled philosophically untrained readers. This one aspect, more than obvious to the philosopher, is that deconstruction in the first place represents a critique of reflexivity and specularity. It is the unawareness of this essential feature of deconstruction that has caused the easy accommodation of deconstruction by contemporary American criticism.

NOTES

1. Paul Feyerabend, *Against Method* (London: Verso, 1978), pp. 283–84.
2. Ibid., p. 167.
3. Ibid., p. 283.
4. Wayne C. Booth, 'Preserving the Exemplar: or, How Not to Dig Our Own Graves,' in *CI* (1977): 420.
5. Post-structuralism is an exclusively American label that reveals more about the departmentalizing spirit in power or in search for power than about the phenomenon in question if we accept that there is such a thing as post-structuralism at all.
6. The notion of the epistemological break as a passage from sensible to scientific knowledge is not only a much more complex notion than is usually believed, but also cannot serve to conceptualize the incommensurability between theories. We will try to show this elsewhere.
7. See, Edward W. Said, *Beginnings* (New York: Basic Books, 1975; Baltimore: Johns Hopkins University Press, 1978), pp. 202–3.
8. It is with the evidence of modern criticism that I am concerned here and not with the at least as questionable evidences of literary criticism in general. Of these evidences one can assert that they belong 'to the deepest, the oldest, and apparently the most natural, the least historical layer of our conceptuality, that which best eludes criticism, and especially because it supports that criticism, nourishes it, and informs it; our historical ground itself.' Jacques Derrida, *Of Grammatology*, trans. Gayatri Chakravorty Spivak (Baltimore: Johns Hopkins University Press, 1976), pp. 81–82.
9. See for instance the 'Polemical Introduction' by Northrop Frye to his *Anatomy of Criticism* (Princeton: Princeton University Press, 1973).
10. Claude Lévi-Strauss, 'Introduction à l'oeuvre de Marcel Mauss,' in Marcel Mauss, *Sociologie et Anthropologie* (Paris: Presses Universitaires de France, 1968).
11. Derrida, *Of Grammatology*, p. 68.
12. In this context Lionel Abel commits a philosophical blunder. Abel's contention that deconstruction is identical with Husserl's notion of *Abbau* is particularly revealing since it provides the philosophical base, so to speak, of all the misinterpretations of deconstruction. See Lionel Abel, 'It Isn't True and It Doesn't Rhyme. Our New Criticism' in *Encounter* 51:1 (1978): 40–42.
13. It is precisely this self-undermining and self-cancelling of the text's constituting oppositions that brings about what J. Hillis Miller in a first attempt to analyze the anti-deconstruction's rhetoric calls 'strong language' ('The Critic as Host,' in *CI* [1977]: 442). Indeed, the modern critic's approach to the text as a self-reflexive totality fills the traditional critic with strong moral, political, and religious indignation. The apocalyptic titles such as Abrams' 'The Deconstructive Angel' and Booth's 'Preserving the Exemplar: or, How Not to Dig Our Graves' (in the same issue), speak for themselves. Booth, moreover, in analyzing criticism in terms of a pluralistic (yet limited) community of critics, accuses the deconstructionists of a sacrilegious claim to superiority – a superiority which would spring forth from their nihilistic destruction of moral and aesthetic values. Booth, consequently, demands the banishment (as foreign agents) of those who from the very beginning refuse the openess demanded of them from the 'country of debate' (Booth, pp. 420–23).
14. Besides this naive confusion as to the nature of deconstruction, Derrida foresaw in *Of Grammatology* the philosopher's critique of deconstruction as dialectics: as 'the enterprise of deconstruction always in a certain way falls prey to its own work ... the person who has begun the same work in another area of the same habitation

does not fail to point [this] out with zeal. No exercise is more widespread today and one should be able to formalize its rules' (*Of Grammatology*, p. 24). We might at this point note the erroneousness of the nonphilosopher's common identification of deconstruction with dialectics. Since it is precisely an operation *on* dialectics, this mistake nevertheless confers an inkling of the rigors of deconstruction. Deconstruction indeed vies with dialectics in what Hegel called the seriousness and the work of the concept.

15. Though not using the notion of deconstruction Cary Nelson's approach in 'Reading Criticism' (*PMLA* 91:5 [1976]) to reading critical language as literary language rests also on the idea of the self-referentiality of language. Cary Nelson's analysis provides provocative insights into the nature of criticism as a discourse, no doubt. Yet, since this approach leads, in particular in Nelson's analysis of the critical works of Susan Sontag, to a definition of criticism as an endless process of self-appropriation and self-actualization through the object and the other at distance, consequently to dialectics in a genuinely Hegelian way (pp. 807–8), it is therefore an excellent example of the presuppositions and implications of the so-called deconstructive criticism.

16. Said, *Beginnings*, p. 237.

17. The major critics in question are Auerbach and Poulet. Poulet's notion of a harmony of vision that gives a sense of unity to the work of each individual writer, as well as Auerbach's germinal notion of a self-referring, self-interpreting, and self-criticizing text (see, in particular, *Mimesis* [Princeton: Princeton University Press, 1953] p. 486) allowed for the transformation of the totalizing mode of formalism into a contextual unity based on the self-reflexivity of the text.

18. 'Chaque fois que, pour brancher précipitamment l'écriture sur un dehors rassurant ou pour rompre très vite avec tout idéalisme, on en viendrait à ignorer telles acquisitions théoriques récentes (…), on regresserait encore plus surement dans l'idéalisme avec tout ce qui … ne peut que s'y accoupler, singulièrement dans la figure de l'empirisme et du formalisme.' Derrida, *La Dissémination* (Paris, Seuil, 1972), p. 5.

19. See also Derrida, *La Dissémination*, p. 62.

20. Derrida, *Of Grammatology*, p. 59.

See also:

Miller (4.1)
De Man (4.2)
Johnson (6.3)
Hartman (7.1)

3.4

'GENUINE GASCHÉ (PERHAPS)'

Geoffrey Bennington

A review of Rodolphe Gasché, *Inventions of Difference: On Jacques Derrida*, Harvard University Press, 1994 Paperback ISBN O–674–46443–5

The Tain of the Mirror established Rodolphe Gasché as the undisputed moral consciousness (or let's say the super-ego) of all Derrideans (and maybe even Derrida himself). There was something inexorable and unavoidable about the book, probably because in almost every detail it was so clearly *right*. Any temptation we, or some of us, may have had to get playful or, especially, 'literary' about Derrida was sternly put in its place as irresponsible, because philosophically ill-informed, and this judgement could be felt, immediately and a little dispiritingly, stretching into all our Derridean futures, condemning us to at least Kant, Hegel and Heidegger if we wanted to earn the right to keep following the master. The book was essentially, explicitly and unashamedly a *rephilosophising* of Derrida, the beginning of a systematic and potentially exhaustive[1] transcription of Derrida's work back into something more 'properly' philosophical than Derrida's work itself seemed always to be. Derrida did deconstruction, and Gasché was doing the philosophy of deconstruction. Derrida, the book seemed to imply, *always might* be seducing us, leading us astray, especially if we were 'literary' people, because the *apparently* literary feel of some of his work *always might* hide its *true or genuine* philosophical import. Gasché offered no such prospects of seduction and wandering, keeping us firmly away from temptation, on a rather puritanical straight and narrow

Source: Geoffrey Bennington, 'Genuine Gasché (perhaps)', *Imprimatur*, 1(2/3), Spring 1996, pp. 252–7.

that looked as though it would require constant vigilance, lots of honest hard work and a good deal of self-denial. The gesture of the book was one of reclaiming rightful property from irresponsible tenants or borrowers, or of rescuing Derrida from being misused or even abused outside the home of philosophical tradition.

Inventions of Difference, which Gasché describes as a 'companion volume of sorts' (p. 2) to *The Tain of the Mirror*, has no qualms whatsoever about pursuing this project. Not only does Gasché repeat and indeed reinforce the fundamental gesture of the earlier book by maintaining the view that Derrida's work is formalisable as a set of 'infrastructures' (ignoring any explicit attempts that have been made to show that this is, both conceptually and philologically, an extremely unhappy term to use in the way he uses it),[2] but also he tells us repeatedly that even Derrida's 'later', reputedly more 'playful' texts (largely left to one side in the earlier book, and maybe still, or so we might have thought, a refuge for the literary) 'belong to philosophy'.[3]

This 'belonging to philosophy' is, as in the earlier book, still essentially argued against the possibility of a possible rival 'belonging to literature', although Gasché does also make more traditional philosophical gestures, separating the properly philosophical from the 'merely empirical', or the domain of the human sciences.[4] He also spends several pages in his introduction refuting Rorty's view of Derrida's later work as giving up on the public and the philosophical in favour of the private and ironical because it does indeed refute it convincingly, but Rorty makes an easy target in this respect (if only because he has, along with many other professional philosophers, such a philosophical idea of the non-philosophical and its supposed joys or advantages), and there are much more 'serious' ways of trying to talk about the relationship of Derrida and philosophy than Rorty's. It is easy to argue that Derrida 'belongs to philosophy' if the only other possibility is to lose him to the sort of alternative Rorty describes, or to some soft and non-specific 'literary criticism'. But the point here is to claim that 'philosophy' (and this is just what Derrida will have helped us to understand) is, in its permanent efforts to secure belongings in general, properties, proprieties, adequacies, authenticities and genuinenesses, also the permanent witness to the 'logic' of impropriety that makes those efforts both possible and necessary, and necessarily endless. Gasché's particular insistence on Derrida's 'belonging to philosophy' paradoxically does more (helpful) damage to *philosophical ap*propriations or criticisms of Derrida as non- or anti-philosophical (Habermas, Marion, Rorty, Taylor, Vattimo, Zizek[5] all fare more or less badly at Gasché's hands) than to the vaguely invoked 'literary' commentators whom Gasché clearly thinks he has put in their place once and for all in the 1979 essay 'Deconstruction as Criticism', reprinted here as Chapter 1, and whom he tends not to deign to name. But being very philosophical like this, *more* philosophical about Derrida than other philosophers, however admirable and necessary that is – and it is admirable and necessary – involves an inevitable reappropriative limitation of what in Derrida is ultra-philosophical:

Derrida's work, as I have tried to argue elsewhere, is both the most and the least philosophical discourse imaginable, at one and the same time; Gasché is thus paradoxically enough oh so philosophical, but *not philosophical enough to* traverse philosophy in the non-belonging way that Derrida does explicitly, and has done at least since *La voix et le phénomène* and the *Grammatology*. This point also has institutional and professional implications for the 'ownership' of philosophy by 'philosophers': Derrida's work may annoy philosophers by being so disciplinarily promiscuous, so *available*, despite its very real difficulty, to readers of all sorts – including literary ones – but dealing with that annoyance by making a claim for proper ownership is always likely to be reactively metaphysical. It also leaves open the possibility that some less professionally philosophical readings of Derrida might be *more* philosophical than Gasché's, *opening philosophy up* (in the sense both of democratic accessibility and anatomical dissection) in ways he cannot.

This problematic of 'belonging', and all that it implies, communicates more or less explicitly with an insistence on the *proper*,[6] the *genuine*[7] and the adequate[8] which underpins all of Gasché's discussions as their ultimate appeal and guarantee. A familiar if subterranean Germanic thread of words in *eigen*[9] links a concern to establish what is philosophy's property with what is proper in general, it just being proper to philosophy – and this is inseparable from its concern with truth[10] – to worry as to what is proper to everything and especially to itself.[11] Gasché cannot but invoke the genuine once he has made his claim to (proper) property over Derrida's work. What has to be genuine or adequate here is a *response* (or an encounter with alterity), and here that problem separates into two aspects: 1) Derrida's 'response' to metaphysics; 2) 'our' (Gasché's) 'response' to Derrida. (The problem of 'our' [my] response to Gasché does not appear in the book as *Gasché*'s problem, but it is clearly enough our problem.)

The problem of Derrida's response to metaphysics justifies the tenor and approach of Gasché's (re-)philosophising of his work. Derrida's work, for Gasché, *just is* a response to metaphysics in its most challenging and difficult aspects (especially Hegel and Heidegger). So, for example, the motif of difference so prevalent in recent criticism must be understood, according to 'The Eclipse of Difference' (Chapter 3), via Heidegger's meditations on the ontico-ontological difference; the motif of infinity or interminability in Derrida, according to 'Structural Infinity' (Chapter 5), must be read as a response to Hegel's account of 'good' and 'bad' infinity; Derrida's stress on affirmation as reading the Hegelian speculative 'yes' ('Yes Absolutely', Chapter 8). Let us spend a moment on this last example and its extension in the following chapter ('Responding Responsibly'), for it is here that Gasché most clearly and helpfully thematises the issues of response and responsibility, which have indeed been given extensive treatment in some of Derrida's recent work.[12] A 'genuine response', he tells us in three descriptions on page 199, is sudden, unexpected, unpredictable and spontaneous: that is, it has the character of an *event*. In

Hegel, the 'yes' that appears in religious consciousness then moves on to the sublation of its own finite irruption in the 'absolute yes' of the Notion, setting a problem for reading which Gasché unpacks admirably as follows:

> How is one to respond to Hegel's all-inclu*sive yes*, by sublating up to the finite event of its eruption, has also forgone its nature as a response [insofar as a response, or at least a genuine response, is marked by just that irruptive finitude]? More precisely, how does one relate to a *yes* that not only is all-encompassing but that by virtue of its all-inelusiveness consists in his having attempted to demonstrate that all finitude sublates *itself*, and that the reconciling *yes, the yes* between the extremes erupts into a relation of Otherness to self? Evidently, whatever such a response may prove to be, in order to be that response – both responsive and responsible – it must respond to the absolute *yes*. Yet, to make such a response, one must first read and hear Hegel to the end – to the eruption of the resounding *yes*. There can be no responsible debate with Hegel without the recognition that all the Hegelian developments take place in view of, and are always already predetermined by, the telos of absolute knowing, or the Notion, that is, by the thought of a figureless and nonrepresenta-tional thinking in which thought can say *yes* to itself in a mode in which even saying is no longer different from what is said. In other words, any genuine response to Hegel must say *yes* – and not in the mode of parrotlike repetitive affirmation – to the call of the Other by the speculative *yes* itself, which, as the event of the positive assimilation of all Otherness, addresses itself as a whole to Other. The *yes* of genuine response is, at its most elementary, a *yes* to it in its all-embracing affirmation of self and Other in absolute identity. But such a response, precisely because it is presupposed, requested by the *yes* of Hegel's thought, falls out of its range and power. While the responding yes comes to meet the demand for recognition, it necessarily escapes what it thus lets come into its own: the speculative *yes*. Indeed, any genuine response to the Hegelian *Yes* implies not only that it be formulated in its most powerful and demanding articulation – that of the end of *Phenomenology of Spirit* and the *Greater Logic* – rather than in disembodied or decapitated versions, but also that it resist *corresponding* to the demand and the call of the all-encompassing yes. Although the *yes* must stand up to the demand to respond to the speculative yes it must fail to keep the appointment. Only thus is it a genuine response. (pp. 201–2)

The – difficult – logic of this passage is exemplary of the positions Gasché espouses in his book. But also, or so I shall try to show, of the unthought aporia that underlies his whole project of reclaiming Derrida for philosophy. If Derrida is to respond 'genuinely' to metaphysics (of whom Hegel is here the exemplary representative), he must take the measure of its most powerful and resourceful articulations, read them according to their own programme (insofar as every text programmes something of its own reading, and philosophy in its metaphysical guise attempts to programme that reading as the only possible or appropriate reading – Hegel's system being at the limit an interminable reading of itself), in order then to do something different. If a genuine response is to be a surprise, as Gasché says it must be, then it cannot simply be the response called for by that to which it responds.

The 'genuineness' of the genuine response, then, involves a measure of infidelity to the text to which the response is made. Gasché makes this clear at the end of the chapter:

> Without the possibility of slippage, no response to the call to say *Yes to yes* is thinkable to begin with. In addition, genuine response to the call to say *yes to yes*, and thus to a mode of thinking that is both encyclopedic and self-inclusive, is genuine only if it remains different . . . *The yes* of response must be a *yes* that can always be denied. Its singularity is constituted both by the possibility that it might not occur and by the possibility that if it does, its response recedes out of the reach of that to which it consents. (p. 226)

This is what Gasché explains under the head of responsibility at the beginning of the following chapter, 'On Responding responsibly' (Ch. 9). Responsibility cannot responsibly be thought of as following a programme of ethical (or political) correctness: responsibility can be taken only when such programes are exceeded or surprised by the event of the advent of the other. Responsibility occurs on the occasion of a singular event which escapes prior normative preparations. Responsibility is responsibility to the other, but is also *of* the other: the responsive decision 1 must take is not mine but a measure of 'my' originary de-propriation in the advent of the other and the other other. The other, we might say, signs my responsibility for me and only thus might I take a responsibility upon myself *as* other.

Gasché's response to this structure is to displace it into the 'demanding *question of* responsibility' (p. 227, my emphasis).[13] He wants to 'speak responsibly about responsibility' (ibid.), to say responsibly what responsible responsibility is. As he quite rightly shows, this commits him on the one hand to an investigation of the inherited concept of responsibility, and, on the other, to some unpredictable break with that concept. There is, then, an essential risk that, *through its very responsibility*, the responsible response to the question of responsibihty will appear irresponsible. It cannot but 'lead to something anethical' (non-ethical opening of ethics, as Derrida's 'early' work already said) that, 'because it does not coincide with a given ethics, will invariably be called anti-ethical' (p. 228). Whence the need to assert responsibility 'in the mode of a "perhaps"', marking 'an essential lack of dogmatic certitude' (ibid.).[14]

This 'mode of a perhaps' is the most difficult challenge posed by someone responding to Gasché's response, and articulation of the logic of response. The last thing it implies is the false or feeble – irresponsible – modesty of saying

'perhaps he's right (but then again perhaps he isn't)'. We *know* (can demonstrate) that Gasché is right about almost everything he says in his book (there's
room for a small amount of scholarly murmuring here and there, the odd
complaint about lack of clarity or clumsy prose): the 'perhaps' affects not that,
nor even the tone of the writing which can seem at times overbearing. Let's
imagine that there were no such problems. How can we hear a 'perhaps' in
Gasché now? Where is the 'invention' here? Or, how can we register the *event* of
Gasché's book (if it 'is' one?). Not of course, by simply looking in it for
something 'opaque, silent or immediate in a nondialectical sense' (p. 14).[15]
But this, perhaps: Gasché's book asserts a *perhaps* with such a clear, serious
honesty, such an admirable sense of responsibility, such a willing acceptance of
pedagogical burdens, that the perhaps 'itself' escapes, perhaps in the call, here
so generously transcribed and transmitted to *reading*. Reading as such *always*
engages a radical perhaps – and thereby a responsibility – insofar as it must *open*
the book to get started. Gasché's rigorous insistence on philosophy as the true
home of Derrida's work, his immeasurably helpful precision around the
tradition Derrida reads, curiously refers us in its interstices to that 'perhaps'.
A *certain* silence in Gasché calls irresistibly for our further unrepentant inventions of a still unread Derrida to come.

One way of elaborating this problem is to concentrate on the question of the
tradition itself. In 'Deconstruction and the Philosophers' I complained about
Gasché's historicising of Derrida's work on the grounds that Derrida's thinking
of historicity and traditionality exceeded all historicist determination, making it
very difficult to situate deconstruction 'in' history, for example as coming 'after'
Heidegger. 'Plato's Pharmacy', for example, showed deconstruction happening
in fifth-century bc Athens at least as much as in '70s Paris. In 'The Law of
Tradition' (Chapter 2), Gasché picks up this point, arguing now that the
impossibility of situating deconstruction in a history of ideas does not mean
that it does not need to be related to tradition as a 'whole', or to the
traditionality of tradition (p. 62).[16] This is in fact an analytic consequence of
what Derrida calls the 'déjà', that we are always *already* in a language that we
neither create nor initiate. Oddly enough, however, and this is where Gasché
does not go, this means not that we are therefore forever condemned to reworking that tradition, but that Derrida's loving and meticulous readings of
texts from the tradition partially liberate indebtedness to Heidegger (but also
Plato, Hegel, Marx or Blanchot), and this does not so much indebt us in our turn
to those same texts, as in part (whence our gratitude and indebtedness to
Derrida 'himself', who is, however, just this liberatory reading machine) open
us to other, always different debts and engagements. It is precisely Derrida's
endless negotiation of the tradition that generates the possibility of reading
Derrida *outside* the law of tradition he thus formulates, for example as a sort of
'system' whose permanent debt to tradition is already inscribed within it and is
thereby in part already paid off on our account. This inscription is such that,
for example, the Hegel column in *Glas* is at one and the same time utterly

dependent ('parasitic') on Hegel, and radically free from Hegel, to the extent that 'Hegel' becomes something like a fictional character in Derrida's work, someone whom we read in reading Derrida.[17] Gasché thinks we ought to read Hegel and Heidegger to read Derrida and thereby locate his singularity with respect to them: but we, who have read Derrida, have *thereby* read a Hegel and a Heidegger to whom we would not otherwise have access (not least, but not only, in that Derrida's own pedagogical generosity makes them *easier*), and who are henceforth *part of* the singularity of 'Derrida'. This does not at all *exclude* our continuing to read Hegel, Heidegger, or anybody else, and in fact encourages it by lifting from that reading certain academic taboos, but enables a reading that could not have *preceded* Derrida. By giving us to read the traditionality of the tradition of metaphysics, Derrida simultaneously frees up a non-traditional and essentially non-academic relation to tradition and its traditionality that is the chance of tradition's no longer determining what futures are now to come, and therefore also the chance of responsibility and invention. The 'perhaps' in Derrida, the moment of risk at which the best and the worst are always possible, is also the mark of this strictly *unprece*dented (non-traditional) relation to tradition, which is as far as can be from the Heideggerian thinking of tradition to which Gasché brings it so close. This liberatory (not liberationist) 'perhaps', which is not the mere lack of dogmatic certainty that Gasché thematises, is opened every time a book – including a book of philosophy – is opened for *reading*, and philosophy, which is com-mitted – that's tradition – to the *reduction* of reading, cannot have any thematic grasp of it, and cannot fail to be professionally unsettled by it. Traditionality is allergic to reading – its own condition. The vertiginous perspective this opens up (one that is, as such, radically indifferent to academic or editorial guarantees, shot through with ambivalence, desire and duplicity, more originary than truth) cannot possibly 'belong' to philosophy, and is just the sort of thing Gasché cannot but anathematise as 'literary', though it cannot possibly 'belong' to literature or literary criticism either. Anyone can understand this – perhaps.

NOTES

1. This is confirmed rather than challenged by the remarkable frequency in these essays of the rhetorical gesture which consists in saying things like, 'I must here *limit* myself to . . .' See for example The Tain of the Mirror: Derrida and the Philosophy of Reflection (Cambridge, MA: Harvard University Press, 1986), pp. 181, 183, 185, 195, 206.
2. I make this argument in 'Deconstruction and the Philosophers (The Very Idea)', in *Legislations: The Politics of Deconstruction* (London: Verso, 1994), 11–60, pp. 26–7, and urge the superiority of 'quasi-transcendental', which has the advantage of marking its nonpropriety from the start. Gasché in his Introduction 'recalls' that his earlier use of 'infrastructure' was 'strategic', 'Other terms would have served equally well, "undecidables," or "the law of the law," for example' (p. 5), and refers the reader to Derrida's own comments on the use of the term in *Acts of Literature*, ed. Derek Attridge (New York and London: Routledge, 1992), pp. 70–2, where Derrida says the term 'troubles me a bit', and 'I think it has to be avoided'.

3. Cf. p. 231, 'Although "Ulysses Gramophone" certainly performs what it establishes through its argumentative procedures and thus has "literary" features, there is also ample evidence that this text belongs to philosophy', and, p. 234, 'A genuine philosophical question is at the center of "Ulysses Gramophone".'

4. E.g. pp. 83 and 144.

5. Note 14 to Chapter 8 shows how Zizek's rather feeble attempt at a Hegelian refutation of Derrida relies on a basic misreading of the structure of the *Greater Logic*.

6. 'For what mode of relating do [these texts] most properly call?' (p. 1).

7. 'Any genuine response ... a genuine response ... the *yes* of the genuine response ... any genuine response ... any genuine response ... the essential risk of failing to genuinely respond ... a genuine response ... a genuine response ...' (pp. 199–204).

8. 'Truly achieve an adequate encounter ... Any adequate response' (pp. 153, 228).

9. *Eigen*, proper, one's own; *Eigenheit*, particularity, property; *eigentlich*, proper, true, genuine, etc. Derrida has of course drawn attention to these terms and their implications in Heidegger, around the latter's *Eigentlichkeit* (authenticity); cf. 'The Ends of Man' in *Margins of Philosophy* (Chicago: Chicago UP, 1982), pp. 109–36.

10. Cf. Heidegger's link of the question of truth and the question of the proper and the genuine at the beginning of 'On the Essence of Truth', tr. John Sallis, in D. F. Krell, ed., *Martin Heidegger: Basic Writings* (London and Henley: RKP, 1978), pp. 117–42 (p. 119).

11. As one example among many, cf. Kant, *Critique of Pure Reason*, A235–6/B294–5: 'We have now not merely explored the territory of pure understanding, and carefully surveyed every part of it, but have also measured its extent, and assigned to everything in it its rightful place. This domain is an island, enclosed by nature itself within unalterable limits. It is the land of truth – enchanting name! – surrounded by a wide and stormy ocean, the native home of illusion, where many a fog bank and many a swiftly melting iceberg give the deceptive appearance of farther shores, deluding the adventurous seafarer ever anew with empty hopes, and engaging him in enterprises which he can never abandon and yet is unable to carry to completion. Before we venture on this sea, to explore it in all directions and to obtain assurance whether there be any ground for such hopes, it will be well to begin by casting a glance upon the map of the land which we are about to leave, and to enquire, **first**, whether we cannot in any case be satisfied, inasmuch a there may be no other territory upon which we can settle; and secondly, by what title we possess even this domain, and can consider ourselves as secured against all opposing claims'.

12. Cf. most recently 'Foi et Savoir' in Derrida and Vattimo, eds., *La religion* (Paris: Seuil, 1996), pp. 9–86 (pp. 39ff). In a complex argument, Derrida tries to show how this structure 'mechanically' generates God and religion, which would thus have the same root as reason and techno-science – and I unpack this more fully in a forthcoming discussion of recent work by Richard Beardsworth and Bernard Stiegler.

13. In fact, as Derrida's work since *Of Spirit* has shown, the time or place of responsibility, and the nexus of 'concepts' accompanying it (pledge, promise, faith, hope, affumation, etc.) precedes that of the question. To that extent, making responsibility into a *question* already guarantees an *irresponsible* response.

14. This 'perhaps' just is what is marked in the, 'quasi-' of the quasi-transcendental, and is exposed more explicitly in Derrida's *Politiques de l'amitid* (Paris: Galilée, 1994), pp. 46ff., where Derrida also invokes an essay by Gasché not included in the present volume, and goes on to show how the *question* is secondary to the 'perhaps'.

15. Even this, which is part of Gasché's critique of Mark Taylor, is probably too rapid. It is, for example, tempting to seek something 'opaque' and singular in what we might naively call Gasché's *style*, with its discreet but insistent marks of linguistic alterity. Although the book is thus *signed* on every page, Gasché's own text nowhere provides for such an approach to his work.

16. Gasché's new attempt to correct his earlier presentation, however, is still historicist through and through: although he is quite correct to insist on the naivety of trying to present Derrida's work as an absolute break with the tradition (he has no difficulty in showing in dialectical style that this is in fact the most traditional presentation (pp. 59–60)), he nowhere elaborates on the curious (ancient and unprecedented) structure whereby 'Derrida' as the othering of tradition is everywhere in the tradition. What we might call for shorthand the non-historical becoming-Derrida of Plato is both funnier and spookier than Gasché's account allows for.

17. This is why, shockingly enough, none of Derrida's arguments really depends on the historical accuracy of any of his comments on the authors he reads. It is at least sometimes a salutary exercise to read Derrida as though Plato, Hegel and the rest were his inventions, and wonder what difference it would make.

See also:

De Man (4.2)
Bennington (5.1)
Benjamin (5.2)
Levinas (9.1)

3.5

'BLACK SOCRATES? QUESTIONING THE PHILOSOPHICAL TRADITION'

Simon Critchley

Inconsiderateness in the face of tradition is reverence for the past.

Martin Heidegger, *Sophistes*

Funk not only moves, it can remove.

George Clinton, *P. Funk (Wants to Get Funked Up)*

Philosophy tells itself stories.[1] One might go further and claim that the life of philosophy, the memory that ensures its identity and its continued existence as something to be inherited, lived and passed on, consists in the novel repetition of certain basic narratives. And there is one story in particular that philosophy likes to tell, which allows philosophers to reanimate, theatrically and sometimes in front of their students, the passion that founds their profession and which, it seems, must be retold in order for philosophy to be capable of inheritance. It concerns, of course, Greece – or rather, as General de Gaulle might have said, a certain idea of Greece – and the passion of a dying Socrates.

PHILOSOPHY AS DE-TRADITIONALIZATION

Socrates, the philosopher, dies. The significance of this story is that, with it, we can see how philosophy constitutes itself as a tradition, affects itself with narrative, memory and the chance of a future, by repeating a scene of radical *de-traditionalization*. For Hegel and Nietzsche, to choose two examples of philosophers who affect themselves with a tradition – although from seemingly opposed perspectives – the historical emergence of philosophy, the emergence

Source: Simon Critchley, 'Black Socrates? Questioning the philosophical tradition', *Radical Philosophy*, 69, January/February 1995, pp. 17–26.

of philosophy into history, that is to say, the decisive break with mythic, religious or aesthetic world-views, occurs with Socrates' death.[2]

Who is Socrates? So the story goes, he is an individual who claims that the source of moral integrity cannot be said to reside in the traditional customs, practices and forms of life of the community, what Hegel calls *Sittlichkeit*: nor, for Nietzsche, in the aesthetico-religious practices that legitimate the pre-philosophical Greek polis, that is to say, attic tragedy. Rather, Socrates is an individual who demands that the source of moral legitimacy must lie in the appeal to universality. It must have a universal form: what is justice? The philosopher does not ask 'What is justice for the Athenians?' or 'What is justice for the Spartans?', but rather focuses on justice in general, seeking its *eidos*. Socrates announces the vocation of the philosopher and establishes the lines of transmission that lead from individuality to universality, from the intellect to the forms – a route which by-passes the particular, the communal, the traditional, as well as conventional views of ethical and political life.

The vocation of the philosopher is *critique*, that is, an individual interrogation and questioning of the evidence of tradition through an appeal to a universal form. For Hegel and Nietzsche, Socrates' life announces the death of tragedy, and the death of the allegedly *sittlich* (ethical) community legitimated through the pre-philosophical aesthetico-religious practices. In Hegel's words, Socrates' death marks the moment when tragedy comes off the stage and enters real life, becoming the tragedy of Greece.[3] Socrates' tragic death announces both the beginning of philosophy and the beginning of the irreversible Greek decline that will, for Hegel and Nietzsche, take us all the way from the legalism of the Roman Republic to the eviscerated *Moralität* (abstract morality) of post-Kantian Germany. Of course, one's evaluation of Socrates' death will vary, depending on whether one is Hegel or Nietzsche. For the former (not without some elegaic regret for the lost Sophoclean *polis*) it is the first intimation of the principle of subjectivity; for the latter, Socrates' death ignites the motor that drives (Platonic-Christian) nihilism. But, despite these differences of evaluation, the narrative structure is common to Hegel and Nietzsche; the story remains the same even if the moral is different: Socrates' death marks the end of tragic Greece and the tragic end of Greece.

It is a beautiful story, and as I recount it I am once again seduced by its founding passion: the historical emergence of philosophy out of the dying Socrates is the condition of possibility for the traditionalization. It announces the imperative that continues to drive philosophy, *critique*, which consists in the refusal to recognize the legitimacy of tradition without that tradition having first submitted itself to critical interrogation, to dialogue *viva voce*.

PHILOSOPHY AS TRADITION

However, if on my view philosophy is de-traditionalization, that which calls into question the evidence of tradition, then what is philosophy's relation to its own tradition? What is the relation of philosophy to the stories it tells about itself?

With the admittedly limited examples given above, one might say that the philosophical tradition is a tradition of de-traditionalization, of stories where the authority of tradition is refused. As Descartes famously writes, 'I will devote myself sincerely and without reservations to the general demolition of my opinions'.[4] As we will see presently with reference to Husserl and Heidegger, the philosopher's appeal to tradition is not traditional, it is, in Derrida's words, 'an appeal to tradition which is in no way traditional'.[5] It is a call for a novel repetition or retrieval of the past for the purposes of a critique of the present, often – for example, in Husserl – with a view to the construction of an alternative ethical teleology. But, slightly getting ahead of myself, should we believe the stories that philosophy tells to itself? Should these stories themselves be exempt from philosophical critique? More particularly, what about the story of the dying Socrates? What more can I say about this story apart from feeling its beauty and pathos despite (or perhaps because of) its being so often recounted?

To ventriloquize a little: 'One might point out that the story of Socrates' death is a *Greek* story, a narrative that recounts and reinforces the Greek beginning of philosophy. Indeed, it is a story that can be employed to assert the exclusivity of the Greek beginning of philosophy: Philosophy speaks Greek and only Greek, which is to say that philosophy does not speak Egyptian or Babylonian, Indian or Chinese and therefore is not Asian or African. Philosophy can only have one beginning and that beginning has to be the Greek beginning. Why? *Because we are who we are*. We are Europeans and Europe has a beginning, a birthplace, that is both geographical and spiritual, and the name of that birthplace is Greece. What takes place in Greece, the event that gives birth to our theoretical-scientific culture, is *philosophy*. By listening to the story that philosophy tells to itself, we can retrieve our beginning, our Greek beginning, the Greek beginning or the European Spiritual adventure. Further-more, by appropriating this beginning as our own we will be able to come into our own as authentic Europeans, to confront the crisis of Europe, its spiritual sickness, a malaise which consists in the fact that we have forgotten who we are, we have forgotten our origins and immersed ourselves unquestioningly in tradition. We must de-traditionalize the tradition that ails us and allows us to forget the crisis – be it the crisis of objectivism (Husserl), rationalization (Weber), commodification (Marx), nihilism (Nietzsche) or forgetfulness of Being (Heidegger). We must project another tradition that is truly our own. The only therapy is to face the crisis as a crisis, which means that we must tell ourselves the story of philosophy's Greek beginning, of philosophy's exclusively Greek beginning – again and again. If philosophy is not exclusively Greek, we risk losing ourselves as Europeans, since to philosophize is to learn how to live in the memory of Socrates' death.'

This troubling ventriloquoy is very loosely based on Husserl's 1935 Vienna Lecture, 'Philosophy and the Crisis of European Humanity',[6] which in many ways perfectly exemplifies the concerns of this paper and the position I am seeking to question. We could also quote examples from Hegel, Nietzsche, Heidegger, Merleau-Ponty, Arendt, Gadamer, and an entire German and English romantic tradition. What such remarks testify to, I believe, is the importation of a certain model of ancient history, centred on the exclusivity of Greece, into philosophy as the foundation stone of its legitimating discourse. I would briefly like to explore and question the historical basis for this belief.

PHILOSOPHY AS INVENTED TRADITION

One of the most challenging consequences of reading Martin Bernal's *Black Athena*[7] – regardless of its many alleged scholarly infelicities, which I am simply not in a position to judge – is the way in which he traces the genealogy of the invented historical paradigm upon which Husserl bases his remarks; the 'Aryan Model' of ancient history, which (astonishingly) only dates from the early decades of the nineteenth century and was developed in England and Germany. Prior to this period, and indeed for most of Western history, what Bernal calls 'The Ancient Model' of classical civilization had been dominant. The latter model believed, amongst other things, that the Egyptians invented philosophy, that philosophy was essentially imported into Greece from Egypt, and that Egypt – and remember Plato visited there around 390 b.c.e. – was the font of all philosophical wisdom. In addition to the Egyptian influence on Greek civilization, it was also widely assumed that Greece was subject to colonization and extensive cultural influence from Phoenician traders and mariners, and that, therefore, Greek civilization and the philosophy expressed by that civilization was largely a consequence of the influence of near-eastern cultures on the African and Asian continents. That is to say, Greek culture – like all culture – was a *hybrid ensemble*, a radically impure and mongrel assemblage, that was a result of a series of invasions, waves of immigration, cultural magpieism and ethnic and racial mixing and crossing.

Contesting this picture of the African and Asiatic roots of classical civilization given in the Ancient Model, a picture that Bernal wants to revise and defend, the Aryan Model claims that Greek civilization was purely Indo-European and a consequence of either the autonomous genius of the pre-Hellenes – resulting in what is sometimes called 'The Greek Miracle', the transition from *mythos* to *logos* – or of alleged invasions from the north by shadowy Indo-European peoples. Bernal's polemical thesis is that the displacement of the Ancient Model by the Aryan Model was not so much driven by a concern for truth as by a desire for cultural and national purity which, for chauvinistic, imperialist and ultimately racist reasons, wanted to deny the influence of African or Semitic culture upon classical Greece, and by implication upon nineteenth century northern Europe.

The influence of this Aryan Model in philosophy can be seen in the way the canon of the history of philosophy was transformed at the beginning of the nineteenth century.[8] Up until the end of the eighteenth century, the history of philosophy was habitually traced back to multiple so-called 'wisdom traditions' in Egyptian, Hebraic, Babylonian, Mesopotamian and Sumerian cultures. However, from the early 1800s, these traditions were generally excluded from the canonical definition of 'philosophy' either because of their allegedly mythical or pre-rational status or because they were largely anonymous, whereas the Greeks, like Thales, had names. The individual thinker rather than a body of thought becomes the criterion for philosophy. The consequence of this transformation of the canon is the belief that philosophy begins exclusively amongst the Greeks; which is also to say that philosophy is indigenous to the territory of Europe and is a result of Europe's unique spiritual geography – setting aside the unfortunate geographical location of certain pre-Socratics on the Ionian coast, which is usually explained away by calling them Greek colonies, an explanation that conceals a slightly anachronistic projection of the modern meaning of colonialism back into the ancient world.

The hegemony of the Aryan model can also be seen in the development of the discipline of Classics in England in the nineteenth century based on the German model of *Altertumswissenschaft*. Both are premised upon a vision of the Greeks as quasi-divine, pure and authentic. What Bernal shows is the way in which this vision was complicit with certain northern European nationalisms and imperialisms (particularly in England and Germany), where contemplation of the Greeks was felt to be beneficial to the education of the future administrators of empire. It is on this point of a possible link between culture and imperialism that one can perhaps link Bernal's analysis to the wider problematic of the invention of tradition in the nineteenth century, as diagnosed by Eric Hobsbawm and others.[9] Hobsbawm shows that traditions were invented with extraordinary rapidity in this period by various states (notably Britain, France, Germany and the USA) in order to reinforce political authority and to ensure the smooth expansion of electoral democracy – for males at least.

More specifically, the traditions invented in this period, which in Britain were as grand as the fabrication of a modern monarchy complete with its jubilees and public processions, or as small as the invention of the postage stamp complete with image of the monarch as symbol of the nation; or, more widely, the proliferation of public statuary in France and Germany, with the ubiquitous image of Marianne in the former and Bismarck or Kaiser Wilhelm in the latter, or the spread of national anthems and national flags – culminate, claims Hobsbawm, in the emergence of *nationalism*. It was nationalism that became the quasi-Rousseauesque civic religion of the nineteenth century, and which, crucially, ensured social cohesion and patterns of national identification for the newly hegemonic middle classes, providing a model which could then be extended to the working classes, as and when they were allowed to enter the political process. The power of invented tradition consists in its ability to inculcate certain values and norms by sheer ritualization and imposed repetition, and to encourage the belief that those traditions are rooted in remotest antiquity, in the case of English nationalism in the sentimental myth of 'a thousand years of unbroken history'.

My concern, as someone who teaches philosophy, is the extent to which the version of tradition that is operative and goes largely unquestioned in much philosophical pedagogy and post-prandial parley (the belief in the exclusivity of the Greek beginning of the philosophy and the centrality and linear continuity of the European philosophical tradition) remains tributary to an invented historical paradigm, barely two centuries old, in which we have come to believe by sheer force of inculcation and repetition. Is the vision of philosophy offered by those, like myself, working on the geographical and spiritual edges of the Continental tradition, tributary to the Aryan model of ancient history and thereby complicit with a Hellenomania that buttresses an implicit European chauvinism? Indeed – although this is not my direct concern here – might one not be suspicious of the nationalist motives that lead to the retrieval within an Anglo-American tradition suspicious of the high metaphysics of 'Continental-ists' of a specifically 'British' empiricist tradition in the 1950s to justify either an Anglicized logical positivism or Oxford ordinary language philosophy?[10] Or the self-conscious retrieval of pragmatism or transcendentalism as distinctively and independently *American* traditions in the work of thinkers as diverse as Stanley Cavell, Richard Rorty and Cornel West?[11]

All of which brings me to some critical questions: must the Greco-European story of the philosophical tradition – from ancient Greece to modern northern Europe, from Platonism to its inversion in Nietzsche – be accepted as a legiti-mating narrative by philosophers, even by those who call themselves philoso-phers only in remembrance? Must philosophy be haunted by a compulsion to repeat its Greek origin? And if so, what about the possibility of other traditions in philosophy, other beginnings, other spiritual adventures? Could philosophy, at least in its European moment, ever be in the position to repeat another origin, announce another beginning, invent another tradition, or tell another story?

More gravely, and with reference to Bernal and also to David Theo Gold-berg's *Racist Culture*,[12] is there perhaps a racist logic intrinsic to European philosophy which is founded on a central *paradox*, hinted at above in the coin-cidence of the geographical and the spiritual or the particular and the universal in Husserl? That is, philosophy tells itself a story which affirms the link between individuality and universality by embodying that link either in the person of Socrates or by defining the (European) philosopher as 'the functionary of humanity',[13] but where at the same time universality is delimited or confined within one particular tradition, namely the Greco-European adventure? Philo-sophy demands universal validity, or is defined by this demand for universal validity, yet it can only begin here, in Europe. We are who we are, and our supra-national cultural identity as Europeans is founded in the universality of our claims and the particularity of our tradition; a tradition that, for Husserl, includes 'the English dominions', i.e. the USA, but does not extend to the gypsies, 'who constantly wander across Europe',[14] like some living memory trace of Egypt. No other culture could be like us, because we have exclusive rights to philosophy, to the scientific-theoretical attitude.

In the light of Edward Said's work, such philosophical sentiments do not seem far from the core belief of imperialism: namely, that it is the responsibility or *burden* of the metropolitan powers to bring our universal values to bear on native peoples, that is, to colonize and transform other cultures according to our own world-view and to conceal oppression under the cloak of a mission. As Said puts it, why are most professional humanists unable or unwilling to make the connection between, on the one hand, the prolonged cruelty of practices such as slavery, colonialism, imperial subjection and racial oppression, and, on the other hand, the poetry, fiction and philosophy of the societies that engage in such practices?[15]

However, if we provisionally admit that there is a racist or imperialist logic in philosophy – and this is as much an accusation against myself as against Husserl – then could it ever be otherwise? That is, would it be conceivable for philosophy, or at least for 'we European philosophers', to be in a position to repeat another origin? Wouldn't this be precisely the fantasy of believing oneself to speak from the standpoint of the excluded without being excluded, of wishing to speak from the margins whilst standing at the centre, that is to say, the fantasy of a romantic anti-Hellenism or Rousseauesque anti-ethno-centrism? If so, where does this leave us? How do we proceed? As a way of sharing my perplexity, rather than resolving it, I shall try to illuminate these questions by taking a slightly different tack.

SEDIMENTATION, REACTIVATION, DECONSTRUCTION

Tradition can be said to have two senses: (1) as something inherited or handed down without questioning or critical interrogation; (2) as something made or produced through a critical engagement with the first sense of tradition, as a de-traditionalization of tradition or an appeal to tradition that is in no way traditional. Of course, this distinction is artificial insofar as it could be claimed that the consciousness of tradition *as such* only occurs in the process of its destruction, that is to say, with the emergence of a *modernity* as that which places in question the evidence of tradition.

However, it is this second sense of tradition, the philosophical sense, that is shared – not without some substantial differences – by Husserl and Heidegger. For the Husserl of the *Crisis of the European Sciences*, the two senses of tradition correspond to the distinction between a *sedimented* and a *reactivated* sense of tradition. Sedimentation, which in one passage of the *Crisis* Husserl compares to 'traditionalization',[16] and which it is helpful to think of in geo-logical terms as a process of settling or consolidation, would consist in the forgetfulness of the origin of a state of affairs. If we take Husserl's celebrated example of geometry, a forgetfulness of the origin of geometry leads to the forgetfulness of the historicity of such a discipline, of the genesis of the theo-retical attitude expressed by geometry, and the way in which the theoretical attitude belongs to a determinate *Lebenswelt*. What is required to counter the sedimentation of tradition is the *reactivation* of the origin in what Husserl calls 'a teleological-historical reflection upon the origins of our critical scientific and philosophical situation'.[17] Thus, philosophy in the proper sense of the word, i.e. transcendental phenomenology, would be the product of critical-historical reflection upon the origin of tradition and the (re)active making of a new sense of tradition against the pernicious naivetés of objectivism and naturalism.

Matters are not so different with the early Heidegger's conception of *Destruktion*, the deconstruction of the history of ontology, which is precisely not a way of burying the past in nullity, but rather of seeking the positive tendencies of the tradition. *Destruktion* is the production of a tradition as something made and fashioned through a process of repetition or retrieval, what Heidegger calls *Wiederholung*. The latter is the assumption of the tradition as a genuine repetition, where the original meaning of a state of affairs (the temporal determination of the meaning of Being, to pick an example at random) is retrieved through a critical-historical reflection. In the period of *Being and Time*, Heidegger articulates the difference between a received and destroyed tradition in terms of the distinction between tradition (*Tradition*) and heritage (*Überlieferung*), where the possibilities of authentic existing are delivered over and disclosed.[18]

It is important to point out that the target of Husserl's and Heidegger's reflections on tradition – and this is equally true of Hegel's reflection on the history of Spirit and Nietzsche's conception of nihilism – is not the past as such, but the *present* and precisely the *crisis* of the present. The true crisis of the European sciences (Husserl) or distress of the West (Heidegger) is felt in the absence of distress: 'crisis, what crisis?' At the present moment, when the Western techno-scientific-philosophical adventure is in the process of globaliz-ing itself and reducing humanity to the status of happy consumers wearing Ronald McDonald Happy Hats, we are called upon to reactivate the origin of the tradition from which that adventure sprang, and to do this precisely in order to awaken a sense of crisis and distress. Thus, a reactivated sense of the tradition permits us a critical, perhaps even *tragic* consciousness of the present. As Gerald Bruns points out in an essay on tradition,

> On this line of thinking a good example of the encounter with tradition would be the story of Oedipus and his discovery of the truth of what has been said about him by seers, drunks, and oracles, not to mention what his own awakened memory can tell him. I mean that from a hermeneutical standpoint the encounter with tradition is more likely to resemble satire than allegory, unmasking the past rather than translation of the past. Or, as I've tried to suggest, the hermeneutical experience of what comes down to us from the past is structurally *tragic* rather than comic. It is an event that exposes us to our own blindness or the limits of our historicality and extracts from us *an acknowledgement of our belongingness to something different*, reversing what we had thought. It's just the sort of event that might drive us to put out our eyes.[19]

The Husserlian-Heideggerian sense of reactivated tradition which destroys the past in order to enable us to confront the present achieves this by consigning us, as Derrida puts it,[20] to the security of the Greek element with a knowledge and confidence which are not comfortable, but which permit us to experience crisis, distress and tragedy.

But we must proceed carefully here: on the one hand, it seems that the Husserlian-Heideggerian demand for the reactivation of a sedimented tradition is a necessary and unavoidable move, it is the step into philosophy and critique, that is, into the realization of tradition as something made or fashioned (re)actively as a way of confronting the tragedy of the present. However, on the other hand, the problem here is that the tradition that is retrieved is uniquely and univocally Greek; it is only a Greek tragedy that will permit us to confront the distress of the present. The way in which globalized techno-scientific ideology is to be confronted is by learning to speak Greek. My problem with this conception of tradition, as pointed out above, is that it might be said to presuppose implicitly an imperialist, chauvinist or racist logic. One recalls the remark that Heidegger was reported to have made to Karl Löwith in 1936, where he asserted that his concept of historicity was at the basis of his political engagement with National Socialism.[21]

It is with this problem in mind that I want to make an excursion into Derrida's 1964 essay, 'Violence and Metaphysics', which deals with the thought of Emmanuel Levinasinsofar as that work might be said to offer an ethical challenge to the Heideggerian and Husserlian conceptions of tradition. I think it is justified to claim that Derrida's thinking of tradition, at least in the early work, is dominated by the problem of closure, that play of belonging and non-belonging to the Greco-European tradition, which asserts both the necessity and impossibility of such a tradition. Broadly stated, the problem of closure describes the duplicitous or ambiguous historical moment – *now* – when our language, institutions, conceptuality and philosophy itself show themselves both to belong to a metaphysical (or logocentric) tradition that is theoretically exhausted, while at the same time searching for the breakthrough from that tradition.[22] The problem of closure describes the liminal situation of late modernity out of which the deconstructive problematic arises, and which, I believe, Derrida inherits from Heidegger. Closure is the double refusal of both remaining within the limits of the tradition and of transgressing that limit. Closure is the hinge that articulates the double movement between the philosophical tradition and its other(s).

In 'Violence and Metaphysics', Derrida's general claim is that Levinas's project cannot succeed except by posing the question of closure, and that because this problem is not posed by Levinas in *Totality and Infinity*,[23] his dream of an ethical relation to the Other which is linguistic but which exceeds the totalizing language of the tradition, remains just that, a *dream*. Derrida calls it the dream of pure empiricism that evaporates when language awakens. Levinas's discourse – and Derrida repeats this strategy with regard to all discourses that claim to exceed the tradition, those of Foucault, Artaud, Bataille or whoever – is caught, unbeknownst to itself, in an economy of betrayal, insofar as it tries to speak philosophically about that which cannot be spoken of philosophically.

Now, one conservative way of understanding the problem of closure is to argue that Derrida demonstrates the irresistibility of the claims of the Greco-Roman tradition and the impossibility of claiming any coherent position outside of this tradition – 'Hegel, Husserl and Heidegger are always right!' Although this interpretation is to some extent justified, it is by no means the whole story. The logic of closure works within a double bind, that is, if there is no outside to the philosophical tradition from which one can speak in order to criticize its inside, then, by the same token, there is no inside to the tradition from which one can speak without contamination by an outside. This is why closure describes the *liminal* situation of late modernity, and why it is a *double* refusal of both remaining within the limits of the tradition and of transgressing those limits. Thus, there is no pure Greek inside to the European tradition that can be claimed as an uncontaminated origin in confronting the crisis. This, I believe, explains Derrida's strategy when confronted with a unified conception of tradition, when he works to show how any such conception is premised upon certain exclusions which cannot be excluded. One thinks, for example, of his unpicking of Heidegger's reading of Nietzsche or of Foucault's reading of Descartes, or again in *Glas*, where the focus is on that which refuses the dialectical-historical logic of *Aufhebung*, and in *La carte postale*, where Heideggerian unity of the Greek sending of Being (*envoi de l'être*) is undermined and multiplied into a plurality of sendings (*envois*).

NOTES

1. These thoughts were first assembled for a conference on the theme of de-traditionalization held at Lancaster University in July 1993. They were extensively reworked for a conference on the work of Edward Said held at Warwick University in March 1994. But their real source lies in conversations with Robert Bernasconi over the past few years and, more recently, with Homi Bhaba. I am particularly grateful for the careful comments of Jonathan Rée and Peter Osborne, although I don't think I have fully responded to either of their criticisms.
2. See Hegel, 'Tragedy and the Impiety of Socrates', from *Hegel on Tragedy*, eds. A. and H. Paolucci (Harper and Row, New York, 1975), pp. 345–66; and Nietzsche, *The Birth of Tragedy*, tr. W. Kaufmann (Vintage, New York, 1967); and 'The Problem of Socrates', in *Twilight of the Idols*, tr. R. J. Hollingdale (Penguin, Harmondsworth, 1968), pp. 29–34.
3. 'Tragedy and the Impiety of Socrates', p. 364.
4. 'Meditations on First Philosophy, *The Philosophical Writings of Descartes*, Vol. II, trs. J. Cottingham *et al.* (Cambridge University Press, Cambridge, 1984), p. 12.
5. 'Violence and Metaphysics', in *Writing and Difference*, tr. A. Bass (Routledge, London and New York, 1978), p. 81.
6. In *The Crisis of the European Sciences and Transcendental Phenomenology: An Introduction to Phenomenological Philosophy*, tr. D. Carr (Northwestern University Press, Evanston, 1970), pp. 269–99.

7. Martin Bernal, *Black Athena: The Afroasiatic Roots of Classical Civilization*, Vol. I 'The Fabrication of Ancient Greece 1785–1985' (Vintage, London, 1991 [1987]).
8. I rely here on Robert Bernasconi's paper, 'Heidegger and the Invention of the Western Philosophical Tradition', *Journal of the British Society for Phenomenology*, forthcoming.
9. *The Invention of Tradition*, eds. E. Hobsbawm and T. Ranger (Cambridge University Press, Cambridge, 1983); see esp. pp. 1–14 and 263–307.
10. See Jonathan Rée, 'English Philosophy in the Fifties', *Radical Philosophy* 65, p. 15.
11. In this regard, see especially Cornel West, *The American Evasion of Philosophy* (Macmillan, London, 1989).
12. David Theo Goldberg, *Racist Culture, Philosophy and the Politics of Meaning* (Blackwell, Oxford, 1993), p. 6. Also see in this regard Harry M. Bracken's 'Philosophy and Racism', *Philosophia*, Vol. 8 (1978), pp. 241–60. In an innovative and provocative discussion of racism and empiricism, it is argued that Lockean (and, to a lesser extent, Humean) empiricism facilitate 'the expression of racist ideology *and* that Locke was actively involved in formulating policies (compatible with those theories) and encouraging practices (e.g. the African slave trade and perpetual racial slavery) which were racist in character' (p. 255). In contrast to empiricism, and by way of a covert defence of the Cartesianism of Chomsky's linguistic theory, Bracken argues that Cartesianism contains 'a modest conceptual barrier to racism' (p. 254).
13. *Crisis of the European Sciences*, p. 17.
14. Ibid., p. 273.
15. Edward Said, *Culture and Imperialism* (Chatto and Windus, London, 1993), p. xiv.
16. *Crisis of the European Sciences*, p. 52.
17. Ibid., p. 3.
18. *Being and Time*, trs. J. Macquarrie and E. Robinson (Blackwell, Oxford, 1962); German pagination, p. 395; English pagination, p. 447.
19. Gerald L. Bruns, *Hermeneutics Ancient and Modern* (Yale University Press, New Haven and London, 1992), p. 204 (my emphasis).
20. 'Violence and Metaphysics', p. 82.
21. Karl Löwith, 'My Last Meeting with Heidegger in Rome, 1936', in *The Heidegger Controversy*, ed. R. Wolin (MIT, Cambridge, Mass. and London, 1993), p. 142.
22. For a detailed discussion of the problem of closure in Derrida, see my *The Ethics of Deconstruction* (Blackwell, Oxford, 1992), pp. 59–106. For an illuminating discussion of tradition in Derrida in comparison with Walter Benjamin, see Alexander Garcia Düttmann's 'Tradition and Destruction' in A. Benjamin and P. Osborne, eds., *Walter Benjamin's Philosophy* (Routledge, London and New York, 1993), pp. 33–58.
23. I argue that matters become much more complicated in Levinas's later work, *Otherwise than Being or Beyond Essence*; in this regard, see my 'Eine Vertiefung der ethischen Sprache und Methode', *Deutsche Zeitschrift für Philosophie*, Vol. 42, no. 4 (1994), pp. 643–51.

See also:

Spivak (8.4)
Bhabha (8.6)
Levinas (9.1)
Bernasconi (9.2)

'DISCUSSIONS, OR PHRASING "AFTER AUSCHWITZ"'

Jean-François Lyotard

The following remarks, transcribed by Jean-François Lyotard, are taken from the discussion which took place after the reading of 'Phrasing "After Auschwitz"' at Cerisy.

Derrida states that he finds himself in agreement with the talk, that he does not want to 'yield to this pathos' (of agreement), that he seeks to 'link on, no, not to link on, but to add phrases'. He wonders if 'the question' is not that of 'the multiplicity of proper names', if 'the very grave stakes of what Lyotard has given to think' are not 'the fact that there are several proper names'. He wonders, first of all, about the 'schema' presupposed by Lyotard's discourse centred upon Auschwitz; and he thinks he perceives that 'in referring to this nameless name, in making a model of it, that discourse risks reconstituting a kind of centrality', a *we* for this occasion, one which is certainly not that of speculative dialectics, but which is related to the unanimous privilege 'we Western Europeans' grant Auschwitz in 'the combat or the question' we oppose to speculative dialectics, to 'a certain kind of Western reason, etc.'. The risk is that this *we* 'would consign to oblivion or would brush aside (*latéraliserait*) proper names other than that of Auschwitz and which are just as abhorrent as it', names which have names, and names which don't. 'And my worry', says Derrida, 'is that a certain *we*, reconstitutes itself in reference to what you have said so admirably about Auschwitz.'

Source: Andrew Benjamin, ed., *The Lyotard Reader* (Oxford: Blackwell, 1989), pp. 386–9.

Derrida then formulates 'another worry', which resembles the less dramatic or 'more formal' one he feels when he reads Levinas: 'Despite all the indisputable things he says about the utterly-other (*le tout-autre*), about the hiatus, the relation to the utterly-other gives rise to linkings of phrases.' This difficulty, Derrida calls in a text devoted to Levinas, '*sériature*'. By the same token, we have 'to make links historically, politically, and ethically with the name, with that which absolutely refuses linkage'. Derrida asks: 'If there is today an ethical or political question and if there is somewhere a *One must*, it must link up with a *one must make links with Auschwitz ... (Il faut enchaîner sur Auschwitz).* Perhaps Auschwitz prescribes – and the other proper names of analogous tragedies (in their irreducible dispersion) prescribe – that we make links. It does not prescribe that we overcome the un-linkable, but rather: because it is unlinkable, we are enjoined to make links. I do not mean to say that one must make links in spite of the linkable; I mean to say that the unlinkable of Auschwitz prescribes that we make links.' If Lyotard was able to move us, it is because the presupposition shared by all is that Auschwitz is intolerable and therefore that one must say and do something, so that it does not, for instance, start over again ...

Finally a couple of 'ancillary' words on difference. Refusing the nascent pathos of this subject, Derrida states:

> I would say with a smile that of course the word seems to imply some nostalgia. It is nonetheless an economical word which has a *Zweideutigkeit* upon which I do not wish to dwell but with which I can reckon (*compter*). One of the two senses can imply nostalgia, but the other does not imply nostalgia very much, if at all; I have explained myself on this point elsewhere. I do not say this in order to correct an interpretation – that would be absolutely ridiculous here – I say it in order to break with the kind of pathos of agreement in which I have been up until a little while ago, and in order to try to understand, no matter how far this agreement may be pursued, what the fundamental difference of tone or affect is between what you say and what I would say. In regards to nostalgia, I said that I wanted to break with it, but I guard (and I assume this guardedness because that's the way it is), I guard a nostalgia for nostalgia, and that is perhaps a sign that when I say, 'Nostalgia would be better', I continue to, etc. You, on the other hand – and I was very sensitive to this again today, I have always been sensitive to this in reading you, but I was again even today when I have never felt myself closer to you – you have a style, a mode and a tone of rupture with nostalgia (and with everything it brings or connotes) that is resolute, trenchant, wilful, etc., and I thought to myself that perhaps this, and nothing more, was what was fundamentally at play in this question.

Lyotard recalls, first of all, that he was tempted to suggest, perhaps in 'too resolute' a fashion, that 'every phrase, if it is apprehended as an occurrence in the strong sense of the term, can become a model' (German: *Modell* (*mold*) specifies Maurice de Gandillac). In this sense, there can be innumerable name-models, and Derrida is right to underscore this because there ensues a considerable displacement in how one thinks about history. Then, to the objection of breaking too quickly with dialectics, Lyotard answers: 'On the contrary, while working on this talk, I had the feeling of making an enormous effort to try not to break with dialectics.' Whence the accent on the 'One must make links', presented as the sole necessity and sole enigma. He strove not to let this 'One must' slip into a philosophy of the will. But neither does he believe that it arises (*relève*) from ethics: 'the "One must" is much more stupid than that'. One must make links after Auschwitz, but without a speculative result. As for the question about the *we*, he is inclined to think in the Hassidic tradition reported by *Gog and Magog*, in the sense of the impossibility for a community to conceive the following: 'We would merely be hostages of the "One must make links"', '*we* are not in possession of its rule, *we* seek it, *we* make links in seeking it; it is thus the stakes but not the rule for the linkage'. This *we* works, or has to work no matter where 'to vary all the rules of linkage whatever they might be, in music, in painting, in film, in political economy' in a way not unrelated to Derridean dissemination. This quest for the rule of linkage is a quest for the intelligible. Adorno speaks of the legible, Derrida of the illegible. This is a radical divergence, and yet 'if *we* are the community of hostages of the "One must make links", it is that we are learning to read, therefore that we do not know how to read, and that for *us*, to read is precisely to read the illegible'.

As for the question of nostalgia, Lyotard says to Derrida: 'I will not intervene because, after all, you have turned it into an affair of idiosyncrasy.' Derrida: 'Something like that.' Lyotard: 'Then, I would be indiscreet if I were to intervene in your nostalgia just as you were indiscreet to intervene in my resoluteness' (laughter). Derrida: 'It was a little more than an idiosyncratic comparison ... in the resolute break with nostalgia, there is a psychoanalytic-Hegelian logic, a rigid relation, not very well regulated' (laughter); 'there is perhaps more nostalgia in you than in me' (laughter). 'This is the suspicion rooted in the question about style' (laughter). Lyotard: 'Do you have the right rule then?' Derrida: 'No.' Lyotard observes that he did not speak about Heidegger, even though ontology is evidently what is implicated in the idea of a phrase game wherein what is at stake is that a phrase present the entailed presentation. This omission is not due to an excess of 'resolution'; rather, it is that the interest of phrases (in the Kantian sense of the interest of reason) does not appear to him to be on the side of ontology. The notion of interest is a little narrow, but it introduces what is at stake in a justice or justness (*justesse*) where one did not expect to find it. Derrida observes that the relation to nostalgia is always badly regulated, and that 'to dismiss it purely and simply' is a case of a bad rule. Lyotard says he had hoped to evoke Derrida's agreement by proposing a less nostalgic acceptation of difference (laughter), which he sees emerging in the development of his work. Derrida acknowledges this shift, but he repeats that 'in your case it is the face that breaks away from nostalgia' that is mostly seen.

See also:

Tschumi (5.3)
Benjamin (5.2)
Laclau (8.5)
Derrida (10.5)

PART 4
LITERATURE

4.1

'DERRIDA'S TOPOGRAPHIES'

J. Hillis Miller

> about this place where I am going, I know enough
> to think, with a certain terror, that things are not
> going well there and that, considering everything,
> it would be better not to go there.
>
> Jacques Derrida[1]

This chapter is about Derrida and literature. I use deliberately the blandest, most innocent, least question-begging conjunction. I want to put my remarks in the context of an ideological story that is making the rounds. Of course it does not have currency with you and me, dear reader. We know better. But the traces of this story's force are widely visible. A recent book by Jonathan Loesberg, *Aestheticism and Deconstruction: Pater, Derrida, de Man*[2] defends Derrida and de Man from the claim that they are ahistorical by arguing that neither is really interested in reading works of literature. Of Derrida, Loesberg says: 'Because Derrida embeds his analysis of literary language within his analysis of founda-tional philosophy, it has as little relevance to the interpretation of actual literary works as his philosophical discussion has to the status of particular proposi-tions' (106). Later he asserts categorically that 'de Man's theory of literary language will no more produce practical criticism than does Derrida's' (116). Where did this strange contrary-to-fact story about Derrida's and de Man's lack of interest in doing literary criticism come from, and what is its ideological function?

Source: J. Hillis Miller, *Topographies* (Stanford: Stanford University Press, 1994), pp. 291–301.

Rodolphe Gasché was the first to argue in detail that Derrida is a technical philosopher in the wake of Husserlian phenomenology and that de Man, myself, and other American 'deconstructionists' have falsified his work by using it in literary criticism.[3] We have made it, so the story goes, into nothing more than a new New Criticism. In fact, the Yale group were more influenced by William Empson and Kenneth Burke than by John Crowe Ransom or Allen Tate. And they were by no means ignorant of Continental phenomenology. Derrida's teaching at Yale was spectacularly forceful and original, but it entered a context there that was far from foreign to it. Why then does Gasché's argument so much appeal still today to Loesberg and others, for example, to Jeffrey T. Nealon and to Mas'ud Zavarzadeh?[4] Gasché's reading is part of an ideological narrative that plays an essential part these days in the reassertion of thematic and mimetic readings of literature, in the return to 'history,' and in the reinstatement of traditional ideas about personal identity, agency, and responsibility. As Thomas Cohen has recognized in incisive diagnoses,[5] what has happened is the following: deconstruction or post-structuralism, some people have thought, has to be denigrated ('abjected' is Cohen's word) in order to justify certain ways of turning or returning to history, to thematic and mimetic interpretations of literature, to the social, to multiculturalism, to the widening of the canon, to cultural studies, and to 'identity politics.' This has by no means happened universally. Works by Judith Butler, Diane Elam, Alex Garcia Düttmann, and many others appropriate deconstruction for new work. Nevertheless, others have falsely identified deconstruction as nihilistic, as concerned only with an enclosed realm of language cut off from the real world, as destroying ethical responsibility by undoing faith in personal identity and agency, as ahistorical, quietistic, as fundamentally elitist and conservative. The Yale 'Deconstructors' can then be dismissed as made-over New Critics who are presumed to have shared the politics of the Southern agrarians. The discovery of de Man's wartime writings doubly justifies writing him off. He has come to be seen as both a new New Critic *and* someone with a tainted past, however the early writings are read in relation to the later.

That leaves Derrida. To argue, as Loesberg does, following Gasché, that Derrida is really a philosopher, whose work has little or no relevance to literary studies, is to recuperate him from the 'abjection' of American deconstruction. It is hard to make Derrida either a fascist or a New Critic, though his abiding interest in Heidegger puts him, for some people, under suspicion of the former, while his evident interest in reading works of literature puts him in danger of being seen as a strange, Continental, crypto-New Critic. Calling him a phenomenological philosopher in the tradition of Husserl avoids both bad names. But this recuperation is performed at the cost of neutralizing Derrida. It puts him out of literature departments and back in the philosophy department. So anyone in literature, anyone doing cultural studies, feminist studies, studies of popular culture, 'new historicism,' or multicultural studies can, if she or he wants to, breathe a sigh of relief, and say: 'Thank God. I don't have to take

Derrida seriously any more. He is just a philosopher, after all.' Given what interests most members of American philosophy departments these days, the last thing most of them would be likely to take seriously is Derrida's theories about the contradictory founding moments of philosophical thinking.

This narrative, like all such ideologemes, like ideology in general, is extremely resistant to being put in question or refuted. It takes many forms and is used in aid of many different arguments, including those by people who consider themselves friendly to Derrida, such as Loesberg or Nealon. However cogently this story is shown to be a linguistic construct based on a whole set of radical misreadings, it is still likely to be unconsciously assumed, taken as a natural truth. It fits Althusser's definition of ideology as a set of unconscious assumptions that obscure one's real material conditions of existence or de Man's definition of ideology as 'the confusion of linguistic with natural reality, of reference with phenomenalism.'[6]

The result of this handy bit of ideological storytelling is to underwrite the return to unreflective mimetic, thematic, and biographical readings of literature so widespread today. One unfortunate result of this return is that wherever it is accepted it disables the crucially necessary political and intellectual work being attempted today in the name of a better democracy by cultural studies, women's studies, ethnic studies, studies in 'minority discourse,' and so on. The disabling might be defined by saying that the left, whenever it (perhaps unconsciously) reassumes the old, traditionalist ideological presuppositions of the right about mimesis, about the acting and responsible self, about thematic ways to read literature and other cultural forms, is cooperating in the return to a neoconservative and nationalist atmosphere that is occurring in many places now and that the 'left' means to be trying to forestall and contest. Another way to put this is to say that a discourse that reaffirms these assumptions is unable to contest the power of what Marx called 'bourgeois ideology' and what is today called 'the hegemony of the dominant discourse' because it is, in its essence, bourgeois ideology all over again. This reaffirmation leaves the dominant discourse as dominant as ever because it is another form of it. It is vulnerable to the same critique Marx made of Feuerbach or of 'German ideology' generally, that it is no more than a theoretical or mental rearrangement of the terms it challenges and has therefore no means of touching the material world. It is incapable of producing historical events. Only a materialist inscription can do that.

What about Derrida and literature, then? Take, for example, the following passage from Derrida's description of a crypt in 'Fors: The Anglish Words [*mots anglés*] of Nicolas Abraham and Maria Torok': 'Caulked or padded [*calfeutré ou capitonné*] along its inner partition, with cement or concrete [*ciment ou béton*] on the other side, the cryptic safe [*le for cryptique*] protects from the outside the very secret of its clandestine inclusion or its internal exclusion.'[7]

Are these words literal or figurative, referential or fictional, philosophical or literary? What do these words name? How would one verify answers to these questions? This essay is an attempt to account for Derrida's language use in this sentence.

Calfeutré ou capitonné? Ciment ou béton? These words describe or name everyday objects, things ready to hand in our collective perceptual world. They belong to the technical vocabulary of the construction trades. A building contractor would order so many cubic yards of cement to pour the foundation for a new house, or, for that matter, to build a new crypt in a cemetery. Padding or caulking are also construction materials. To what strange use is Derrida putting these words here? The words do not seem to refer to any 'real' cement, caulking, or padding. Could they be 'literary'? What would that mean? How is the literary related to the topographical in Derrida's work?

A comparison may be made with the use made of words in works conventionally designated 'literature.' Examples would be the following two descriptions of other cryptic enclosures, secret places, like the crypt in 'Fors,' where something or someone both dead and alive is buried, where something has happened without having happened. The first is from Thomas Hardy's description of the Fawkes Fires on the top of Rainbarrow in *The Return of the Native*, the second from a translation of the opening description of the burrow in Franz Kafka's 'The Burrow':

> It was as if these men and boys had suddenly dived into past ages, and fetched therefrom an hour and deed which had before been familiar with this spot. The ashes of the original British pyre which blazed from that summit lay fresh and undisturbed in the barrow beneath their tread. The flames from funeral piles long ago kindled there had shone down upon the lowlands as these were shining now. Festival fires to Thor and Woden had followed on the same ground and duly had their day.[8]

> I have completed the construction of my burrow and it seems to be successful. All that can be seen from the outside is a big hole; that, however, really leads nowhere; if you take a few steps you strike against natural firm rock.[9]

'Ashes,' 'barrow,' 'rock,' 'burrow': are these words used by Hardy and Kafka in the same way as Derrida uses *ciment* and *béton?* Derrida's writing, it would seem, is primarily philosophical and theoretical. It is only intermittently and contingently concerned with literature or written 'as literature.' It may be that literature enters into Derrida's work only when he 'does literary criticism,' that is, when he writes about one or another work generally assumed to be literature – Mallarmé, Joyce, or Baudelaire; Celan, Shakespeare, or Melville, and many others. Writing about literature could then be opposed to writing about philosophy, anthropology, political science, theology, architecture, and so on, but the stylistic texture of Derrida's own work would never be 'literary.' Its ground or starting place would certainly not be literature but philosophical reflection, as Gasché and Loesberg argue.

What, for Derrida, distinguishes a literary use of language from other uses, if indeed there is such a distinction, or if indeed such a thing as literature exists? I shall approach this question indirectly, by a roundabout route, namely by way of an attempt to map Derrida's topographies, or, more precisely, in order to account for that sentence I cited from 'Fors.'

'Derrida's topographies': this is an immense domain, requiring a virtually interminable mapping procedure for its full graphing. New topographies are constantly being added in new work, for example, Derrida's current seminars in Paris and at the University of California at Irvine (beginning in 1992) on 'the secret and responsibility.' Some invitation to the reader to place things and concepts within an imaginary space has been a feature of his work from the beginning, for example, in the early image of the 'closure of metaphysics,' or in the spatial figures indicated in the titles of *Marges*, *Parages*, or *Khôra*, or in the theory of invention, with its image of extrapolation in *Psyché: Inventions de l'autre*, or in the strange topography of 'Fors,' or in the geographical figures (if they *are* figures) of *L'Autre Cap*, or in the many places where the words 'topography,' 'topology,' 'toponymy,' 'frontier,' 'places,' 'topoi,' 'margin,' 'limit,' or the like appear. The immense, intertwined problematics of politics, of exemplarity, of nationalism, and of translation, not to speak of literature, in Derrida are inseparable from images of some definite place, 'this place here' with all its geographical and social particularity.

The chief obstacle to a complete cartography of Derrida's topographies, however, is not the extent and complexity of the terrain but the presence within any place on his map – inside it, outside it, intestine, clandestine, deep buried, and yet on the surface – of a place that cannot be mapped. This place resists toponymy, topology, and topography, all three. Somewhere and nowhere in every Derridean topography is a secret place, a crypt whose coordinates cannot be plotted. This place exceeds any ordinary topographical placement. What is the relation, for Derrida, between literature and the secret place-without-place hidden in every topography?

Far from being peripheral to Derrida's work, just one more topic approached from perspectives that are properly 'philosophical,' literature, it can be argued, is his main concern throughout. For Derrida, everything begins with the question of literature and is approached from that place. In 'Ponctuations: Le Temps de la thèse' ('Punctuations: The Time of the Thesis'; written in 1980), Derrida recalls that about 1957 he had '"deposited" as they say,' a thesis subject entitled 'L'Idéalité de l'objet littéraire' ('The Ideality of the Literary Object'). A little later he indicates something of what that thesis might have contained. The title, he says, is to be understood in the context of Husserl's thought, much in the air in the fifties:

> It was a question, then, for me, to deploy, more or less violently, the techniques of transcendental phenomenology in the elaboration of a new theory of literature, of this very particular type of ideal object that is the

literary object, an ideality 'concatenated' [enchaînée], Husserl would have said, concatenated with so-called natural language, a non-mathematic or non-mathematizable object, but nevertheless different from music or works of plastic art, that is to say, from all the examples privileged by Husserl in his analyses of ideal objectivity. For I must recall a little globally and simply, my most constant interest, I would say even before the philosophical interest, if that is possible, went toward literature, toward the writing called literary.

What is literature? And first of all, what is writing? How does writing come to upset even the question 'What is?' [Qu'est-ce que?] and even 'What does that mean?' [Qu'est-ce que ça veut dire?]. Put otherwise – and this is the putting otherwise that is important for me – when and how does inscription become literature and what happens then? To what and to whom does that return? [À quoi et à qui cela revient-il?] What happens between [Qu'est-ce qui se passe entre] philosophy and literature, science and literature, politics and literature, theology and literature, psychoanalysis and literature, there in the abstraction of its label is the most insistent question.[10]

If Derrida's most insistent question, reaffirmed here in a text of 1980, goes toward literature, and if science, politics, theology, psychoanalysis, and even philosophy are to be approached, for him, from the point of view of the question 'What is literature?,' much hangs, in comprehending his work, on understanding just what he means by literature or by saying 'l'objet littéraire' is an 'objet idéal.'

Could it be that though Derrida never wrote that thesis, all his work from one end to the other, in all its amplitude and diversity, has been obliquely preliminary notes toward that unwritten thesis on 'l'idealité de l'objet littéraire'? These notes have often been based on readings of specific literary texts. Passages from three recent works, '"This Strange Institution Called Literature": An Interview with Jacques Derrida,' Donner le temps (Given Time), and Passions, give provisional answers to the question 'What is literature?' In the first and third of these he says that literature is a modern institution that begins at a certain moment in history and is tied in complex ways to history, politics, law, and society. There could be and have been cultures with no concept of literature in the sense the modern West means the word. Literature, for example, cannot exist outside democracy and the complete freedom of speech permitted in principle in a democracy, though of course never yet fully permitted in fact. Democratic freedom guarantees the 'right to say everything.'[11] Literature, that is, goes along with a certain irresponsibility. Democratic freedom of speech gives me the right to say anything and everything and not be held accountable for it, not to have to respond when questioned about it. This irresponsibility is the basis of the most exigent responsibility. Derrida in the interview is unequivocal on this last point:

The writer can just as well be held to be irresponsible. He can, I'd even say that he must sometimes demand a certain irresponsibility, at least as regards ideological powers, of a Zhdanovian type for example, which try to call him back to extremely determinate responsibilities before socio-political or ideological bodies. This duty of irresponsibility, or refusing to reply for one's thought or writing to constituted powers, is perhaps the highest form of responsibility. To whom, to what? That's the whole question of the future or the event promised by or to such an experience, what I was just calling the democracy to come. Not the democracy of tomorrow, not a future democracy which will be present tomorrow but one whose concept is linked to the to-come [à-venir, cf. avenir, future], to the experience of a promise engaged, that is always an endless promise.[12]

Irresponsibility vis-à-vis constituted ideological powers is sometimes the only way to begin to fulfill an infinitely more exigent responsibility toward the democracy to come. Our responsibility to that democracy to come takes the form of a promise that is endless because it can never be declared fulfilled. It always remains future. This future makes the most imperative demands on our actions today. For example, it requires our refusal under certain circumstances to accept responsibility before constituted authorities. But just what does this freedom to say everything have to do with literature? Why is this freedom enacted especially in literature? What Derrida says in an important footnote in *Passions* will help answer that question:

Something literary [*Quelque chose de la littérature*] will have begun when it will not have been possible to decide if, when I speak of something [*quelque chose*] I speak of some thing, of the thing itself [*de la chose même*], this one here, for itself, or if I give an example, an example of something, or an example of the fact that I am able to speak of some thing, of my way of talking of something, of the possibility of speaking in general of something, or again of writing these words, etc. (89)

If literature is a historical phenomenon, an institution that began at a certain moment in certain Western societies and that could disappear entirely, literature is also a permanent and inalienable possibility in language, in signs generally, or in what Derrida calls the 'trace.' The conditions of the possibility of literature have always already been there, not only ever since there have been human beings and language but even before that, in a preverbal realm.

About Derrida's idea of the preverbal there would be much to say.[13] His notion of the preverbal contradicts everything people think they know about Derrida and about so-called 'deconstruction' generally. He and 'it,' we are told, give absolute priority to language. Deconstruction holds that language makes everything in the human world. For humankind, 'it's all language.' On the contrary, what Derrida calls literature paradoxically does not depend on letters or on language in the ordinary sense. The impossibility of deciding whether a sign or a trace is about something or is only an example of a word, sign, or trace begins already in animal gesture or play, for example, when a kitten pretends that a ball of paper is a mouse. What Derrida says about this is clear and without reservation: 'What I have just said about something [*quelque chose*] does not need to wait for speech, that is to say discursive enunciation and its written transcription. It is valid already for every trace in general, even a preverbal one, for example, a mute pointing [*déictique muet*], or animal gestures or games' (*Passions*, 90).

As can be seen, the possibility of literature depends on the strange structure of exemplarity, on the fact that every example at one and the same time is just one example out of many, perhaps innumerable, examples of the same thing that might be given and is always at the same time the example of examples, the exemplary example, unique and singular.[14] To put this another way, it is impossible to tell when an example ceases to be an example and becomes something to be taken seriously, something for which the one who gives the example must take responsibility. The dependence of literature on the possibility of giving examples is evident not only in Derrida's formulations about when literature will have begun but also in the way it seems impossible to talk about this concept of literature without giving examples. You cannot talk about exemplarity except by way of examples, for example, my example of the playing kitten or Derrida's example of 'un déictique muet, le geste ou le jeu animal,' phrases introduced by Derrida with the words *par exemple*.

What does this have to do with the connection of literature and democracy, the fact that democracy, which accords the right to say everything, is a condition for literature to appear as an institution in history and in specific societies? The answer is given in what Derrida says about the 'I' as an example of the literary. If literature begins when it is impossible to decide, when I speak of something, whether I am indeed speaking of something – this thing here – or whether I am giving an example of something or of the fact that I can speak of something, the same thing can be said of the 'I' in any utterance. It is impossible to decide whether 'I' am speaking for myself or whether I am giving an example of the possibility of using the word 'I': 'No one could seriously contradict me if I say (or write, etc.) that I do not write about me but about "me," about some other me [*un moi quelqonque*] or about the me in general, by proposing an example: I am only an example or I am exemplary' (*Passions*, 89). If this is the case, then I can never be held responsible for anything 'I' say because I can always claim it was not 'I' speaking but that I was only giving an example of the possibility of saying whatever I said or indeed of saying anything at all. Another way to put this, as Derrida observes, is to say that literature is inseparable from irony. If the 'I' can always be 'literary,' then I cannot be held responsible for what I say. I can always say what I have said is literature. Therefore everything can be said, irresponsibly. Democracy with its right to free speech is indeed the indispensable condition for the appearance of literature as an institution, with all its legal, social, and pedagogical circumstances, even though the conditions of possibility for literature to begin have always begun, even in the preverbal trace, even in the prehuman state, even in animal gesture or play, and even though the freedom to say everything has never in fact been granted in any democracy.

NOTES

1. 'Ponctuations: Le Temps de la thèse,' *Du droit à la philosophie* (Paris: Galilée, 1990), 442–43. Translations in this chapter are my own unless otherwise noted.
2. Princeton: Princeton University Press, 1991.
3. Rodolphe Gasché, *The Tain of the Mirror: Derrida and the Philosophy of Reflection* (Cambridge, Mass.: Harvard University Press, 1986). See, for example, the categorical statements in the introduction: 'More over, deconstructionist criticism is the offspring of a heritage that has little in common with that of Derrida's thought. Deconstructionist criticism must be understood as originating in New Criticism; it is a continuation of American-bred literary scholarship' (3). Gasché's book is invaluable for its investigation of Derrida's relation to European phenomenology, but it is too lacking in detail in its treatment of American literary criticism to be persuasive in its claim that American deconstructionists are doing something that has little in common with what Derrida is doing. The question-begging genetic figures in 'offspring of a heritage,' 'originating,' and 'American-bred' ignore the fact that the influence of phenomenology on American literary criticism, including, among many others, three members of the so-called Yale School (de Man, Hartman, and myself), had already made a decisive break in the continuity of American New Criticism in the 1950s, prior to any influence of Derrida in America.
4. See Jeffrey Nealon, 'The Discipline of Deconstruction,' *PMLA* 107, no. 5 (October 1992), 1266–79, and Mas'ud Zavarzadeh, 'Pun(k) deconstruction and the Postmodern Political Imaginary,' *Cultural Critique*, vol. 14, no. 22 (Fall 1992): 5–47.
5. In the introduction to *Anti-Mimesis*, forthcoming from Cambridge University Press, and in 'Diary of a Deconstructor Manqué; Reflections on Post "Post-Mortem de Man,"' forthcoming in *Minnesota Review*.
6. Paul de Man, 'The Resistance to Theory,' *The Resistance to Theory* (Minneapolis: University of Minnesota Press, 1986), 11.
7. Jacques Derrida, 'Fors,' in Nicolas Abraham and Maria Torok, *Cryptonymie: Le Verbier de L'Homme aux loups* (Paris: Aubier Flammarion, 1976), 13. Jacques Derrida, 'Fors: The Anglish Words of Nicolas Abraham and Maria Torok,' foreword to Nicolas Abraham and Maria Torok, *The Wolf Man's Magic Word: A Cryptonymy*, trans. Nicholas Rand (Minneapolis: University of Minnesota Press, 1986), xiv. Further references will be indicated in the text by 'F' and 'E,' respectively, followed by the page numbers. In places, I have altered the translation to more directly reflect the original.
8. Thomas Hardy, *The Return of the Native* (London: Macmillan, 1974), 44–45.
9. Franz Kafka, 'The Burrow,' *The Great Wall of China*, trans. Willa and Edwin Muir (New York: Schocken, 1948), 79.
10. Jacques Derrida, 'Ponctuations,' 443.
11. *Passions* (Paris: Galilée, 1993), 65. Later citations will be given by page number in the text.
12. '"This Strange Institution Called Literature": An Interview with Jacques Derrida,' *Acts of Literature*, ed. Derek Attridge (New York: Routledge, 1992), 38.
13. See, for example, 'Fors': 'It is in fact precisely *because* the verbal instance is only a derivative effect that the word-thing [*mot-chose*] could constitute itself as such, rebecome a kind of thing after the repression that cast it out. It is the topographical possibility [*possibilité topique*] of the crypt, the line of demarcation that it institutes between the process of introjection and the fantasy of incorporation, which would account for, but is not restricted to, the verbal function.' (Exxxix; F58.)

14. For an exemplary discussion of the structure of exemplarity in Derrida's work, see Michael B. Naas's brilliant introductory essay to the English translation of Derrida's *L'Autre Cap*, 'Introduction: For Example,' in Jacques Derrida, *The Other Heading*, trans. Pascale-Anne Brault and Michael B. Naas (Bloomington: Indiana University Press, 1992), vii–lix.

See also:

Gasché (3.3)
Johnson (6.3)
Hartman (7.1)
Royle (7.4)

'AUTOBIOGRAPHY AS DE-FACEMENT'

Paul de Man

The theory of autobiography is plagued by a recurrent series of questions and approaches that are not simply false, in the sense that they are farfetched or aberrant, but that are confining, in that they take for granted assumptions about autobiographical discourse that are in fact highly problematic. They keep therefore being stymied, with predictable monotony, by sets of problems that are inherent in their own use. One of these problems is the attempt to define and to treat autobiography as if it were a literary genre among others. Since the concept of genre designates an aesthetic as well as a historical function, what is at stake is not only the distance that shelters the author of autobiography from his experience but the possible convergence of aesthetics and of history. The investment in such a convergence, especially when autobiography is concerned, is considerable. By making autobiography into a genre, one elevates it above the literary status of mere reportage, chronicle, or memoir and gives it a place, albeit a modest one, among the canonical hierarchies of the major literary genres. This does not go without some embarrassment, since compared to tragedy, or epic, or lyric poetry, autobiography always looks slightly disreputable and self-indulgent in a way that may be symptomatic of its incompatibility with the monumental dignity of aesthetic values. Whatever the reason may be, autobiography makes matters worse by responding poorly to this elevation in status. Attempts at generic definition seem to founder in questions that are both pointless and unanswerable. Can there be autobiography before the eighteenth century or is it

Source: Paul de Man, *The Rhetoric of Romanticism* (New York: Columbia University Press, 1984), pp. 67–72.

a specifically preromantic and romantic phenomenon? Generic historians tend to think so, which raises at once the question of the autobiographical element in Augustine's *Confessions*, a question which, despite some valiant recent efforts, is far from resolved. Can autobiography be written in verse? Even some of the most recent theoreticians of autobiography categorically deny the possibility though without giving reasons why this is so. Thus it becomes irrelevant to consider Wordsworth's *The Prelude* within the context of a study of autobiography, an exclusion that anyone working in the English tradition will find hard to condone. Empirically as well as theoretically, autobiography lends itself poorly to generic definition; each specific instance seems to be an exception to the norm; the works themselves always seem to shade off into neighboring or even incompatible genres and, perhaps most revealing of all, generic discussions, which can have such powerful heuristic value in the case of tragedy or of the novel, remain distressingly sterile when autobiography is at stake.

Another recurrent attempt at specific circumscription, certainly more fruitful than generic classification though equally undecisive, confronts the distinction between autobiography and fiction. Autobiography seems to depend on actual and potentially verifiable events in a less ambivalent way than fiction does. It seems to belong to a simpler mode of referentiality, of representation, and of diegesis. It may contain lots of phantasms and dreams, but these deviations from reality remain rooted in a single subject whose identity is defined by the uncontested readability of his proper name: the narrator of Rousseau's *Confessions* seems to be defined by the name and by the signature of Rousseau in a more universal manner than is the case, by Rousseau's own avowal, for *Julie*. But are we so certain that autobiography depends on reference, as a photograph depends on its subject or a (realistic) picture on its model? We assume that life *produces* the autobiography as an act produces its consequences, but can we not suggest, with equal justice, that the autobiographical project may itself produce and determine the life and that whatever the writer *does* is in fact governed by the technical demands of self-portraiture and thus determined, in all its aspects, by the resources of his medium? And since the mimesis here assumed to be operative is one mode of figuration among others, does the referent determine the figure, or is it the other way round: is the illusion of reference not a correlation of the structure of the figure, that is to say no longer clearly and simply a referent at all but something more akin to a fiction which then, however, in its own turn, acquires a degree of referential productivity? Gérard Genette puts the question very correctly in a footnote to his discussion of figuration in Proust. He comments on a particularly apt articulation between two patterns of figuration – the example being the image of flowers and of insects used in describing the encounter between Charlus and Jupien. This is an effect of what Genette calls a 'concommitance' (right *timing*) of which it is impossible to say whether it is fact or fiction. For, says Genette, 'it suffices to locate oneself [as reader] outside the text (*before* it) to be able to say that the timing has been manipulated in order to produce the *metaphor*. Only a situation supposed to have been forced upon the author from the outside, by history, or by the tradition, and thus (for him) not fictional . . . imposes upon the reader the hypothesis of a *genetic* causality in which the metonymy functions as cause and the metaphor as effect, and *not* the *teleological* causality in which the metaphor is the end (*fin*) and the metonymy the means toward this end, a structure which is always possible within a hypothetically pure fiction. It goes without saying, in the case of Proust, that each example taken from the *Recherche* can produce, on this level, an endless discussion between a reading of the novel as fiction and a reading of the same novel as autobiography. We should perhaps remain *within* this whirligig (*tourniquet*).'[1]

It appears, then, that the distinction between fiction and autobiography is not an either/or polarity but that it is undecidable. But is it possible to remain, as Genette would have it, *within* an undecidable situation? As anyone who has ever been caught in a revolving door or on a revolving wheel can testify, it is certainly most uncomfortable, and all the more so in this case since this whirligig is capable of infinite acceleration and is, in fact, not successive but simultaneous. A system of differentiation based on two elements that, in Wordsworth's phrase, 'of these [are] neither, and [are] both at once' is not likely to be sound.

Autobiography, then, is not a genre or a mode, but a figure of reading or of understanding that occurs, to some degree, in all texts. The autobiographical moment happens as an alignment between the two subjects involved in the process of reading in which they determine each other by mutual reflexive substitution. The structure implies differentiation as well as similarity, since both depend on a substitutive exchange that constitutes the subject. This specular structure is interiorized in a text in which the author declares himself the subject of his own understanding, but this merely makes explicit the wider claim to authorship that takes place whenever a text is stated to be *by* someone and assumed to be understandable to the extent that this is the case. Which amounts to saying that any book with a readable title page is, to some extent, autobiographical.

But just as we seem to assert that all texts are autobiographical, we should say that, by the same token, none of them is or can be. The difficulties of generic definition that affect the study of autobiography repeat an inherent instability that undoes the model as soon as it is established. Genette's metaphor of the revolving door helps us to understand why this is so: it aptly connotes the turning motion of tropes and confirms that the specular moment is not primarily a situation or an event that can be located in a history, but that it is the manifestation, on the level of the referent, of a linguistic structure. The specular moment that is part of all understanding reveals the tropological structure that underlies all cognitions, including knowledge of self. The interest of autobiography, then, is not that it reveals reliable self-knowledge – it does not – but that it demonstrates in a striking way the impossibility of closure and of totalization (that is the impossibility of coming into being) of all textual systems made up of tropological substitutions.

For just as autobiographies, by their thematic insistence on the subject, on the proper name, on memory, on birth, eros, and death, and on the doubleness of specularity, openly declare their cognitive and tropological constitution, they are equally eager to escape from the coercions of this system. Writers *of* autobiographies as well as writers *on* autobiography are obsessed by the need to move from cognition to resolution and to action, from speculative to political and legal authority. Philippe Lejeune, for example, whose works deploy all approaches to autobiography with such thoroughness that it becomes exemplary, stubbornly insists – and I call his insistence stubborn because it does not seem to be founded in argument or evidence – that the identity of autobiography is not only representational and cognitive but contractual, grounded not in tropes but in speech acts. The name on the title page is not the proper name of a subject capable of self-knowledge and understanding, but the signature that gives the contract legal, though by no means epistemological, authority. The fact that Lejeune uses 'proper name' and 'signature' interchangeably signals both the confusion and the complexity of the problem. For just as it is impossible for him to stay within the tropological system of the name and just as he has to move from ontological identity to contractual promise, as soon as the performative function is asserted, it is at once reinscribed within cognitive constraints. From specular figure of the author, the reader becomes the judge, the policing power in charge of verifying the *authenticity* of the signature and the consistency of the signer's behavior, the extent to which he respects or fails to honor the contractual agreement he has signed. The transcendental authority had at first to be decided between author and reader, or (what amounts to the same), between the author *of* the text and the author *in* the text who bears his name. This specular pair has been replaced by the signature of a single subject no longer folded back upon itself in mirror-like self-understanding. But Lejeune's way of reading, as well as his theoretical elaborations, show that the reader's attitude toward this contractual 'subject' (which is in fact no longer a subject at all) is again one of transcendental authority that allows him to pass judgment. The specular structure has been displaced but not overcome, and we reenter a system of tropes at the very moment we claim to escape from it. The study of autobiography is caught in this double motion, the necessity to escape from the tropology of the subject and the equally inevitable reinscription of this necessity within a specular model of cognition.

NOTE

1. Gerard Genette, *Figures III* (Paris: Editions du Seuil, 1972), p. 50.

See also:

Gasché (3.3)
Johnson (6.3)
Hartman (7.1)
Derrida (10.1)

4.3

'GHOST WRITING'

Derek Attridge

I saw a ghost last night. More important, I heard a ghost. I was addressed by a ghost, we were addressed by a ghost.

Was it the ghost of William Shakespeare? The ghost of Karl Marx? The ghost of deconstruction (yet again risen from the dead)? Or of deconstruction in America?

Or even the ghost of Jacques Derrida? One of the many ghosts of Jacques Derrida?

It said many things, but in saying everything that it had to say it also said: 'Remember me!'

During yesterday afternoon's session, Philip Lewis posed a question to Hillis Miller, who had been discussing the responsibility entailed in the act of reading. Where does this responsibility come from? he wanted to know. Who lays it upon me? Who *calls* me to be responsible? And *to* whom, *for* whom, *before* whom am I responsible?

Called upon to identify the source of the responsibility that calls upon him when he reads, Miller gave a somewhat evasive answer, talking about fidelity to the original text and his Protestant upbringing. This evasiveness was not surprising; it *is* a discomfiting question, without a single or a simple answer.

Last night, Derrida gave one answer (or reminded us that we already know one answer – if we know the best-known work in English literature).

Responsibility comes from a ghost, or the ghost; the revenant which is also an *arrivant*. The ghost lays me under an obligation to recognize my responsibility.

Source: Anslem Haverkamp (ed.), *Deconstruction Is/in America: A New Sense of the Political* (New York: New York University Press, 1995), pp. 223–8.

The ghost says to Hamlet, 'Remember me' – once in so many words but by implication continuously throughout the play. 'Remember me' is an injunction, in this context, to *act*, to kill a man, a 'high public official' a king. It is a call to justice.

The peculiar institution we know as 'literature' is haunted by many ghosts, which appear to the living to remind them of their responsibility, to test them, to demand justice. Think only of the ghost in *Beloved*, and what it calls for and recalls. Or the ghostlike figure of Melville's Bartleby, which the narrator terms an 'apparition.' (Both of these are important texts for 'deconstruction in America.')

But not only is it possible to talk about the ghost *in* literature; we can say that the ghost *is* literature (as long as we're cautious about that word 'is'). Literature appears to us, calls on us, recalls us to our task, lays us under an obligation. The ghost is *prosopopoeia* and *apostrophe* in their most violent form.

This is not the place to elaborate in detail on the connection between literature and ghosts, but I want to make four points about ghosts which are also points about literature.

1) The ghost is as much *event* as *object* (the word 'apparition' holds both of these together). The ghost speaks performatively – it is itself a performative – nothing will be the same again after it has appeared and spoken.

(It is also a citation, of course, or else it would not be recognized as a ghost.) And it is an event which demands a *response*.

2) It is more than an event demanding a response, however: it is an event *already constituted* by that response. Hamlet's response to the ghost's narrative is 'Oh my prophetic soul!' (I.v.40). What he has heard is and is not news to him. Although, as literary critics often point out, Shakespeare exteriorizes the ghost in the first scene (in which Hamlet plays no part), the ghost will *speak* only to Hamlet. Its injunction is for Hamlet's ears alone (like the door before which the man from the country waits in Kafka's 'Before the Law').

The otherness of the ghost, so powerfully conveyed in the play, is not opposed to its familiarity. The ghost is borderline creature, an insider as well as an outsider. A certain *virtuality*, a *relation* to the other, as Rodolphe Gasché might put it. The ghost is Hamlet, after all, another Hamlet, Hamlet as the other.

So Hamlet's responsibility is not laid upon him by means of a *punctual* injunction, nor is it just a question of accountability or answerability. As Derrida reminded us last night, Hamlet complains that he was *born* to set right the out-of-joint time. One is born, thrown, into responsibility; one inherits it. In 'The Politics of Friendship,' Derrida observes that the moment I speak I am '*pris, surpris*' by responsibility (634).

The very question 'Where does responsibility come from?' arises out of responsibility; responsibility is prior to subjectivity, to questioning.

3.) Hamlet's immediate response is that there is no way of knowing whether this is a good spirit or an evil spirit (a reasonable response in early seventeenth-century Europe):

Angels and ministers of grace defend us!
Be thou a spirit of health or goblin damn'd,
Bring with thee airs from heaven or blasts from hell,
Be thy intents wicked, or charitable . . .

(I.iii.39)

Nothing is certain here. There are no rules. Hamlet has to read the ghost with no assured codes of reading.

Hamlet has to *judge*, to *decide*; he has to take a *risk*, indeed, to risk everything. In responding to the ghost's summons, he asserts: 'I do not set my life at a pin's fee' (I.iv.65). He has to *trust*, and trust is only possible when there are no grounds for it. Trust is always trust in the future, an attitude which Hamlet adopts – or rather finds himself adopted by – towards the end of the play: 'If it be now, 'tis not to come; if it be not to come, it will be now; if it be not now, yet it will come – the readiness is all'(V.ii.220).

4.) The ghost comes back. The *arrivant* is also a *revenant*. 'Perchance 'twill walk again,' says Hamlet to Horatio after hearing about the ghost's appearance, but Horatio is in no doubt: 'I warr'nt it will' (I.ii.242). If we fail to remember it, it will remember us. And as we cannot not forget it, it cannot not return.

We have been summoned by many ghosts at this conference – all the talks have been performative events calling for active responses, reminding us of our responsibilities. Their demands have been impossible ones, as all real demands are, since they demand that which is impossible, justice. Derrida's litany of reasons for thinking that our own time is out of joint is a reminder of the scale of the obligations we are under, but his work, and deconstruction in America, deconstruction around the globe, reminds us too that we still have the ghost of a chance – the chance of a ghost.

BIBLIOGRAPHY

Attridge, Derek. 'Trusting the Other: Ethics and Politics in J. M. Coetzee's *Age of Iron*.' *South Atlantic Quarterly* 93 (1994): 59–82.

Derrida, Jacques. *Aporias*. Trans. Thomas Dutoit. Stanford: Stanford UP, 1993.

——. 'Force of Law: The "Mystical Foundation of Authority."' *Deconstruction and the Possibility of Justice*. Ed. Drucilla Cornell, Michel Rosenfeld, and David Gray Carlson. New York: Routledge, 1992. 3–67.

——. 'The Politics of Friendship.' *The Journal of Philosophy* 85 (1988): 632–645.

——. *Spectres de Marx: L'État de la dette, le travail du dueil et la nouvelle Internationale*. Paris: Galilée, 1993.

Ellmann, Maud. 'The Ghosts of Ulysses.' *The Languages of Joyce*, eds. R. M. Bollettieri Bosinelli, C. Marengo Vaglio, and Chr. van Boheemen. Philadelphia/Amsterdam: John Benjamins, 1992.

See also:

Marx (1.1)
Royle (7.4)
Weber (7.3)
Maley (8.2)

4.4

'THE PHANTOM REVIEW'

Nicholas Royle

Jacques Derrida, *Spectres of Marx: The State of the Debt, the Work of Mourning, and the New International*, trans. Peggy Kamuf (New York: Routledge, 1994), 198 pp.

The Nag Hammadi Library in English, trans. and introduced by members of the Coptic Gnostic Library Project of the Institute for Antiquity and Christianity at Claremont, California, ed. James M. Robinson, 3rd, completely revised edn (New York: HarperCollins, 1990), 549 pp.

> Like a pair of spectacles, Christianity enables you to see things more clearly.
>
> (Peter Lilley)

No book review without phantoms. It is difficult to conceive of trying to review Jacques Derrida's *Spectres of Marx* without engaging with the strangeness of the 're-' (repetition, viewing again, return, revenance) inscribed in the word 'review' and thus with a questioning of the very institution of the book review. 'What, has this thing appear'd again tonight?' I have a feeling that perhaps corresponds in some way with the feeling Derrida claims to have about Marx and ghosts in *Spectres of Marx*: as he puts it, 'everyone reads, acts, writes with *his* or *her* ghosts' (p. 139). Impossible, at least for me, to review this book about apparitions, phantoms, spectres, without feeling a need to respond in kind. In

Source: Royle, Nicholas, 'Phantom review', *Textual Practice*, 11 (2), 1997, pp. 386–98.

what follows, then, I propose to consider not only what *Spectres of Marx* has to say about spectrality and phantoms (for example, in relation to the university, politics and religion), but also what it does *not* say, or says (perhaps) without saying. A phantom book calls for a phantom review.[1]

Spectres of Marx is concerned with another thinking of the spaces of academic research and scholarship. Scholars and phantoms make strange bedfellows. As Derrida remarks, near the beginning of the book:

> There has never been a *scholar* who really, as such, deals with phantoms [*fantômes*]. A traditional *scholar* does not believe in phantoms – nor in all that one might call the virtual space of spectrality. There has never been a *scholar* who, as such, does not believe in the sharp distinction between the real and the unreal, the actual and the inactual, the living and the non-living, being and non-being ('to be or not to be', in the conventional reading), in the opposition between what is present and what is not, for example in the form of objectivity. Beyond this opposition, there is, for the *scholar*, only the hypothesis of a school of thought, theatrical fiction, literature, and speculation.
>
> (pp. 11/33)[2]

This quotation provides, in a sense, the framework of Derrida's book. The context, as indicated by the parenthetical reference 'to be or not to be', is that of a reading of Shakespeare's *Hamlet*. Derrida is meditating on Marcellus's words in the face of the Ghost of Hamlet's father: 'Thou art a scholar, speak to it, Horatio.' He describes this member of the King's Guard as suffering from the 'Marcellus complex', that is to say a blindness to, or ignorance of, that 'singularity of a place of speech, of a place of experience, and of a link of filiation, places and links from which alone one may address oneself to the phantom' (p. 12). Derrida is here focusing on something which has become, I think, particularly evident in his more recent writing, namely the uncanniness of solitude, the experience of the impossible, the aporias of what happens in 'my life' as 'what only happens to me'. ('It only happens to me' is an insistence made in the autobiothanatoheterographical text entitled 'Circumfession'.[3])

'"Thou art a scholar, speak to it, Horatio" …' (p. 279): these are also the last words of *Spectres of Marx* and they mark, in effect, a turning back to the reader or listener, a return to or revenance of the Marcellus complex but now, perhaps, in a more critical, even deconstructive form. Marcellus's apostrophe, then, provides the curtain on Derrida's book, on his 'essay in the night' (p. xviii) as he calls it. It is with the notion of the phantom that the book concludes. Derrida asks:

> Could one *address oneself in general* if already some phantom did not come back? If he [*sic*] loves justice at least, the 'scholar' [*Le 'savant'*] of the future, the 'intellectual' of tomorrow should learn it and from the phantom. He should learn to live by learning not how to make conversation with the phantom but how to talk with him, with her, how to let it

speak or how to give it back speech, even if it is in oneself, in the other, in the other in oneself: they are always *there*, spectres, even if they do not exist, even if they are no longer, even if they are not yet. They give us to rethink the 'there' as soon as we open our mouths.

(pp. 176/279)

These passages from *Spectres of Marx* suggest why one might want to describe Derrida as both scholarly and unscholarly. On the one hand, like the traditional scholar, he upholds 'the sharp distinction between the real and the unreal, the actual and the inactual, the living and the non-living, being and non-being'. It is in this context that he says of phantoms: 'of course they do not exist' (p. 174). On the other hand, unlike the traditional scholar, Derrida looks towards a new notion of scholarship, other spaces of intellectual thinking, spaces that can be called affirmatively spectral or phantomistic. It is in this context that he says of phantoms: 'of course they do not exist, *so what?*' (p. 174, my emphasis); and that he argues that 'the logic of spectrality' is 'inseparable from the very motif . . . of deconstruction' (p. 178, n. 3). There *are* phantom effects, even if phantoms do not exist. The unscholarly or perhaps one should say the ascholarly dimensions of deconstruction are linked to this spectrality or phantomistics. If beyond 'the opposition between what is present and what is not . . . there is, for the *scholar*, only the hypothesis of a school of thought, theatrical fiction, literature, and speculation', deconstruction would be concerned with new ways of thinking about 'schools of thought', 'theatrical fiction', 'literature' and 'speculation'. What today are the chances of writing *as* phantom effect or phantom effects?

Everything begins by coming back to the question of mourning. Of mourning Derrida writes:

> It consists always in attempting to ontologize remains, to make them present, in the first place by *identifying* the bodily remains and by *localizing* the dead (all ontologization, all semanticization – philosophical, hermeneutical, or psychoanalytical – finds itself caught up in this work of mourning but, as such, it does not yet think it; we are posing here the question of the spectre, to the spectre, whether it be Hamlet's or Marx's, on this near side of such thinking). One has to know . . . *who* and *where*, to know whose body it really is and what place it occupies – for it must stay in its place. In a safe place . . . Nothing could be worse, for the work of mourning, than confusion or doubt: one *has to know* who is buried where – and *it is necessary* (to know – to make certain) that, in what remains of him, *he remain there*. Let him stay there and move no more!

(p. 9)

This passage signals towards a certain phantomistic topography in *Spectres of Marx*, concerning what Derrida does *not* say in this book, areas of silence, unspoken or unspeakable. In a sense what I want to do here is elucidate in another way what has been called symptomatic reading, to unfold in a perhaps new way Pierre Macherey's thesis that 'The speech of a book comes from a certain silence ... [T]he book is necessarily accompanied by a *certain absence*, without which it would not exist'.[4] Such a phantomistic topography may not have a name, as yet: neither 'subtext' nor 'intertext', neither 'source' nor 'precursor' seem to me appropriate critical vocabulary for the identification and localization of what would be, perhaps, encrypted in this topography. In a text called 'Living on/ border lines', dating from 1979, Derrida declared: 'One text reads another ... Each "text" is a machine with multiple reading heads for other texts.'[5] *Spectres of Marx* provokes an elaboration on this claim and in particular it leads us towards an exploration of the effects or effectivities of *texts which do not exist*. It is a question of a feeling, to begin with, a feeling I have about the passage on mourning just cited and about the strange 'place' (atopical topos) of the work of Nicolas Abraham and Maria Torok in relation to this. In particular, my feeling has to do here with Abraham's notion of anasemia as what is on the 'near side' (to pick up Derrida's phrase) of meaning, as what in some sense precedes 'all semanticization', 'psychoanalytical' or otherwise.

Although Derrida has written a book about spectres, spirits, ghosts and phantoms, nowhere in *Spectres of Marx* does he discuss the writings of Nicolas Abraham and Maria Torok.[6] Given the amount of attention he devotes to their work elsewhere, Derrida's apparent silence on Abraham and Torok in *Spectres of Marx*, and in particular his silence about Abraham's so-called theory of the phantom, and even more particularly Abraham's theory as expounded specifically in relation to *Hamlet*, seems rather remarkable. Let me stress that I am not interested here in making hypothetical pronouncements about Derrida's 'debt' to or swerve away from Abraham, or about Abraham's theory of the phantom as a precursor, or even as an intertext, for Derrida's book. Rather I am interested in the way in which Abraham's theory might itself be said to constitute a phantom which, in motioning us towards a spectral topography in *Spectres of Marx*, might serve as a sort of model for thinking about texts in general in terms of phantom effects. It is a question, then, of phantom texts – textual phantoms which do not necessarily have the solidity or objectivity of a quotation, an intertext or explicit, acknowledged presence and which do not in fact come to rest *anywhere*. Phantom texts are fleeting, continually moving on, leading us away, like Hamlet's Ghost, to some other scene or scenes which we, as readers, cannot anticipate.

In his essay 'Notes on the phantom: a complement to Freud's metapsychology', Abraham begins with the idea that 'the theme of the dead – who, having suffered repression by their family or society, cannot enjoy, even in death, a state of authenticity – appears to be omnipresent (whether overtly expressed or disguised) on the fringes of religions and, failing that, in rational systems' (*The Shell and the Kernel*, p. 171). His emphasis is on the fact that 'the "phantom", whatever its form, is nothing but an invention of the living'. His argument is that phantom-effects can arise if (and, it would seem, only if) 'the dead were shamed during their lifetime or ... took unspeakable secrets to the grave'. The phantom is an invention of the living insofar as it embodies 'the gap produced in us by the concealment of some part of a loved object's life ... what haunts are not the dead, but the gaps left within us by the secrets of others' (p. 171).

Abraham puts strange flesh on, or perhaps takes strange flesh off this argument in 'The phantom of Hamlet' (*The Shell and the Kernel*, pp. 191–205), his posthumously published fictional supplementary Sixth Act to Shakespeare's play. 'The phantom of Hamlet' was written, Abraham tells us in his introductory statement ('The intermission of "Truth"', pp. 187–90), in response to his sense that 'The final scene of the *Tragedy of Hamlet* does not close the dramatic action, it simply cuts it off' (p. 187). He proposes that the characters in Shakespeare's play are, in fact, the 'puppets of a phantom' (p. 188). 'The phantom of Hamlet' is a short text, composed in decasyllabic verse, in which the ghost of Hamlet's father returns and this time is obliged to confirm that the secret he took to the grave was not his death at the hands of his brother Claudius but another secret, namely the fact that, in collusion with Polonius, he had thirty years earlier murdered the father of Fortinbras. With this fictional supplement Abraham seeks to expose and transform that 'state of mind' which in Shakespeare's play (he says) 'forces itself upon us like an inescapable necessity emanating from some unknown source' (pp. 187–8). 'The phantom of Hamlet' is Abraham's attempt to 'reduce the phantom'; 'to "cure" the *public* of a covert neurosis [which] the *Tragedy of Hamlet* has, for centuries, inflicted upon it' (p. 190); to exorcise the crypto-phantomatic power imposed on our culture by the silences in Shakespeare's play.

Abraham's account of the phantom, especially in the form of this poetic supplement to Shakespeare's *Hamlet*, is very different from Derrida's. I would suggest that there are at least four ways in which it would be necessary to distinguish between Abraham and Derrida here:

1   Derrida's conception of revenants, spirits, ghosts or phantoms is specifically bound up with an experience of language as an experience of the impossible. If, as he says in *Spectres of Marx*, 'one cannot speak of generations of skulls or spirits ... except on the condition of language' (p. 9), this speech is caught up in a ghostly prosopopoeia: we are ourselves spoken by skulls and spirits. Whereas for Abraham and Torok, in *The Wolf Man's Magic Word*, there is the supposition of a magic word ('tieret') at the heart of a psychoanalytic treatment or case history, for Derrida there is rather what he calls 'the *cryptic* structure of the ultimate "referent"'.[7] If deconstruction is inseparable from a logic of spectrality, it is because the trace or *différance* is ghostly: all language, every manifestation of meaning, is the phantom effect of a trace which is neither present nor absent, but which is the condition of possibility of the opposition of presence and absence. The trace cannot become present, or absent, in its essence: it is the revenant at the origin.

2 In his essay 'Notes on the phantom', Abraham's emphasis is quite heavily on what passes down from generation to generation – for example, he speaks of '"phantomogenic" words' that can 'rule an entire family's history and function as the tokens of its pitiable articulations'. He contends that 'the "phantom effect" progressively fades during its transmission from one generation to the next and that, finally, it disappears' (p. 176). Derrida's position appears less teleological and less fixed. As if in passing, he remarks at one point in *Spectres of Marx* that ghosts 'trick consciousness and skip generations' (p. 30). However tacitly, Derrida's account breaks up the family, interrupts the logic of the linear, skips successiveness. His focus in *Spectres of Marx* is rather on anachronism, contretemps, time out of joint.[8]

3 Derrida's conception of the logic of exorcism is in many respects less benign than Abraham's. In 'The phantom of Hamlet', for example, Abraham is concerned with an 'exorcism' that may lead (as he puts it) to 'a higher wisdom about oneself and the world of humans at large' (p. 189). Derrida's account of ghosts and phantoms in *Spectres of Marx* would call, in effect, for a subsuming of the Abrahamic conception within a broader, distinctly less humanist and more troubling perspective in which ghosts do not die and exorcism is in some sense impossible. For Derrida, 'to exorcise' is 'to attempt to destroy and to disavow' – 'exorcism consists in repeating in the mode of incantation that the dead man [or woman] is really dead . . .' (p. 48). We may here recall the shocking case reported in January 1996 of a 61-year-old woman in Cambridgeshire, Daphne Banks, pronounced dead by her GP, but discovered, in 'her' body bag, to be still breathing.[9] To 'pronounce dead' is, like exorcism, a performative. As Derrida points out in *Spectres of Marx*: it is 'a performative that seeks to reassure but first of all to reassure itself by assuring itself, for nothing is less sure, that what one would like to see dead is indeed dead. It speaks in the name of life, it claims to know what that is' (p. 48). At issue here, among other things, is a new definition and 'concept' of murder. It is a question of rethinking the teleological work of mourning, such as one encounters in the writings of Freud or in Hamlet's uncle Claudius (mourning must have an end, it is something that we should know how to 'throw to earth', as Claudius says [I, ii, 106]). As Derrida observes in a related essay on *Hamlet*, entitled 'The time is out of joint', such a notion of mourning 'presumes . . . that mourning depends on us, in us, and not on the other in us. It presumes above all a knowledge, the knowledge of the date. One must indeed know *when*: *at what instant* mourning began. One must indeed know *at what moment* death took place, really took place, and this is always the moment of a murder.'[10] To pronounce dead is to collude in murder. To pronounce dead or to exorcise, for Derrida, is '*effectively* a performative. But here effectivity phantomalizes itself' (p. 48). To exorcise is not to escape from phantom-effects, rather the reverse.[11]

4 There are at the same time various respects in which Derrida's account of ghosts and phantoms is perhaps *more* benign, more open than Abraham's.

This distinction is perhaps most evident in relation to the temporality of the phantom or ghost. For Abraham the phantom comes from the past. For Derrida it comes at least as much from the future: 'It is a proper character-istic of the spectre, if there is any, that no one can be sure if by returning it testifies to a living past or to a living future ... [A] phantom never dies, it remains always to come and to comeback' (p. 99). 'The thinking of the spectre', he proposes, 'contrary to what good sense leads us to believe, signals toward the future' (p. 196, n. 39).

With these four distinctions in mind, I want to ask: What happens if one lets Abraham's account of the phantom come back, filtering itself through the singularity of Derrida's account, into a space which does not exist but which might be said nevertheless to appear 'through' *Spectres of Marx*? Into what phantomistic scene might a reading of Abraham-through-Derrida lead us? In particular, what happens if one follows the sense that *Spectres of Marx* is to a large degree silently, but perhaps all the more powerfully on that account, a book as much about Christianity as about Marxism, and above all a book that fastens on the notion of Jesus Christ as the most spectral force in politics today, in the 'world war', as Derrida calls it, that is all around us, even if it has its most concentrated focus on the question of 'the appropriation of Jerusalem' (p.58)?

If there is a publication which (alongside *The Interpretation of Dreams* or *Finnegans Wake* or *Of Grammatology*) has claims to being among the most devastating texts to have appeared this century, it might be *The Nag Hammadi Library*. It consists of twelve books, plus eight leaves taken from a thirteenth, altogether amounting to fifty-two tractates. The manuscripts themselves are now in the Coptic Museum in Cairo and some readers may already be familiar, for example through the work of Elaine Pagels, with the bizarre history of the discovery of these texts in December 1945 by a cannibalistic murderer called Muhammad Ali of the al-Samman clan in the Naj Hammadi region of Upper Egypt.[12] Among the more striking details of the process by which these fourth-century papyrus books came to be disseminated across the world and finally brought back together in Cairo and eventually published in a single volume in English are the fact that most of Codex I was acquired in May 1952 by the Jung Institute in Zurich and initially published as the 'Jung Codex' (the history and legacies of psychoanalysis are thus already implicated here, in the most material fashion) and the fact that Muhammad's mother, Umm-Ahmad, later admitted that she'd used up a fair amount of the papyrus for (one hastens to add, non-cannibalistic) cooking purposes at home.

The Nag Hammadi Library is in Coptic, though it is thought to have been originally written in Greek. There is evidence in the texts themselves that they were intended to have been preserved in a jar in a mountain until the end of time. They are, in Freudian terms perhaps, uncanny texts *par excellence* – texts which ought to have remained secret and hidden but have come to light. The texts in *The Nag Hammadi Library* transform the history and conception of

Gnosticism and early Christianity. Of particular interest in the present context is the evidence furnished by some of these tractates showing that certain features originally thought to be characteristic of Christian Gnosticism are in fact non-Christian in their provenance. James M. Robinson refers to two of the tractates, 'The three steles of Seth' and 'The paraphrase of Shem', as being 'without Christian ingredients' (p. 7). Perhaps most dramatic, however, is the double-tractate published as 'Eugnostos the blessed' and 'The Sophia of Jesus Christ' (pp. 220–43), in which the latter emerges in a particularly explicit fashion as a fictional reworking into a Christian discourse of the pre-Christian discourse of the former.

Theologians have not, to date, rushed into the breach or into the strange aporias hereby generated. Thus Elaine Pagels, for example, argues that the Nag Hammadi Library enables us to 'begin to see that what we call Christianity – and what we identify as Christian tradition – actually represents only a small section of specific sources, chosen from among dozens of others' (p. xxxv). While acknowledging that the discovery of the Nag Hammadi texts makes it more difficult than ever to argue the case for which of the sayings of Jesus may or may not be 'genuinely authentic' (p. 148) – in other words, while implicitly recognizing that the Nag Hammadi Library fundamentally disturbs and even (I would argue) phantomizes the basis on which the teachings of Jesus have been read and understood – Pagel's account in her book *The Gnostic Gospels* remains a curiously static and conservative one. In her Conclusion she asserts that 'the discoveries at Nag Hammadi reopen fundamental questions. They suggest that Christianity might have developed in very different directions or that Christianity as we know it might not have survived at all' (p. 142). History, in the eyes of Elaine Pagels, is finished, achieved, already written. Rather than speculate on the 'very different directions' in which Christianity 'might [or might not] have developed', would it not be more critical and productive to consider how the discoveries at Nag Hammadi *change* history by transforming our conception of Christianity *to date* and *in the present*? The history of Christianity in this sense would lie in 'the opening of the future itself' (to borrow a phrase from Derrida).[13]

I would like to illustrate this in a specific, if perverse (and thus perhaps necessarily impish or spectrally grafting) way. There can be little doubt that the Nag Hammadi Library constitutes a scandal in its own right: it phantomizes our reading of the New Testament and suspends the possibility of Christianity 'as we know it'. I would like to conclude with the evocation (in the strong sense of that word: to evocalize or call up from the dead) of another, perhaps differently scandalous text, a phantom text generated out of Abraham, Derrida and *The Nag Hammadi Library*. This text, let me emphasize, does not exist. It does not even have a name. It is a product (if it can be called a product at all) of the spectral topography I have been trying to describe in this review. If I were to try to figure the materiality of this text I would think of ashes in the wind – like the ashes of Umm-Ahmad's fire or Derrida's ashes, in the wind.

This phantom text is fragmentary. Like 'The Sophia of Jesus Christ' (pp. 220–43), it presents us with a revelation discourse spoken by Christ to Mary Magdalen after coming back from the dead. And like 'The Gospel of the Egyptians' (pp. 208–19) and 'Allogenes' (pp. 490–500), it refers to the idea of the text itself being concealed in a mountain until the end of time or until the coming of the 'dreadful one'. The fragment reads as follows:

> And Jesus came back and appeared unto Mary Magdalen and this woman was greatly afraid. Fear not, Mary, saith the Lord; I am come as a spirit to comfort you and tell – [text missing] – thunder – [text missing] – and [why] this stone was rolled away, with trembling of the earth three days and nights, and why I now appear in cloth as fresh and smelling sweet as when my body was anointed for the tomb. Let the word pass to [the chosen?]: I am a spirit come back to tell the secrets of my time on earth – [text missing] – The heaven and the earth will be rolled up in your presence. Know now that I am not he who died on the cross, but I replaced and hid myself. The one who died in my place was unknown, a stranger. I ask for your forgiveness, as I have asked forgiveness of my father, – [text missing] – Write down the things that I tell you and place this book in the mountain. Then you shall adjure the Guardian, 'Come Dreadful One'.

This fragment would presuppose a rereading of Christianity in its biblical and related contexts as the story of a phantom or phantom effects at once inaugurated and revealed, legible in a new way. It would constitute a sort of futuristic ur-text for Abraham's account of the phantom, and more specifically a possible sense of what Derrida calls the *arrivant* ('a thinking of the past, a legacy that can come only from that which has not yet arrived' (*Spectres of Marx*, p. 196, n. 39)).

Two remarks by way of cutting things off:

1   As Geza Vermes has argued, if there is a single thing about which there would appear to be consensus regarding the death of Jesus, it is 'the one disconcerting fact ... that the women who set out to pay their last respects to Jesus found to their consternation, not a body, but an empty tomb'.[14] The various Gospel, Nag Hammadi and other accounts of seeing the dead Jesus alive again, together with the discovery of an empty tomb, constitute a testimony to what can be described, in Abraham's terms, as a vast phantom effect. Christian belief would be structured by the phantom effect of a figure whose reappearances beyond the grave, bolstered by the disappearance of his corpse, testify to unspoken or unspeakable secrets. In this context we might turn round Elaine Pagels's question: 'Why does faith in the passion and death of Christ become an essential element – some say, *the* essential element – of orthodox Christianity?' (p. 75) Rather than, like Pagels, wonder at it, wonder at our supposed wonder, might we not then reflect and elaborate in a critical, even deconstructive fashion on the passion, death and resurrection scene as precisely cryptic and phantomatic?

Jesus did not die on the cross but rather had himself substituted – an unknown man, an anonymous stranger, perhaps someone who looked similar to him, was taken away and crucified in his place. This shameful secret will have been at the heart of the ghost story called Christianity. The crucifixion might then call to be rethought as the passion of (to borrow Maurice Blanchot's fragmentary formulation) 'The unknown name, alien to naming'.[15]

2 At the same time, we would be impelled to read this phantom text in terms of the way Derrida in *Spectres of Marx* seeks to situate the significance of Jesus Christ for Marxism and deconstruction. Following Marx and Max Stirner, Derrida declares: 'Christ is the most spectral of spectres. He tells us something about absolute spectrality' (p. 144). Marx, like Stirner, was concerned to dissolve 'the mirages of Christian onto-theology' (p. 191, n. 14). Derrida is willing to describe this as a work of deconstruction. But Marx's and Stirner's attempts to dispose of 'that arch-ghost in flesh and blood that is ... Christ, God made Man in the incarnation' are themselves haunted, Derrida suggests:

> Their 'deconstruction' is limited at the point at which they *both* oppose this spectral onto-theology ... to the hyper-phenomenological principle of the flesh-and-blood presence of the living person, of the being itself, of its effective and non-phantomatic presence, of presence in flesh and blood.
>
> (pp. 191–2, n. 14)

Spectres of Marx delineates a Marxist deconstruction of Christian onto-theology but suggests that the Marxist conception is itself still too much bound up in another kind of mirage, namely that of 'non-phantomatic presence, of presence in flesh and blood'. To be mere 'flesh and blood', to have 'ears of flesh and blood', is to be a ghost. The word 'Christ' is Greek for Messiah. *Spectres of Marx* calls for a de-Christification of experience, for 'a messianism without religion' (p. 59). Derrida stresses the notion of 'the *messianic* rather than *messianism*, so as to designate a structure of experience rather than a religion' (pp. 167–8). His messianic is concerned with a 'formal structure of promise' that at once 'exceeds' and 'precedes' both Marxism and the religions it criticizes (p. 59). This messianic is 'irreducible to any deconstruction', he suggests; it entails a 'suspension', 'trembling' or 'hesitation' that is 'essential to the messianic in general', a 'thinking of the other and of the event to come'. He writes: 'what remains irreducible to any deconstruction, what remains as undeconstructible as the possibility itself of deconstruction is, perhaps, a certain experience of the emancipatory promise' (p. 59). The 'perhaps', as elsewhere in Derrida's writing, testifies to the trembling that *is* the messianic. The messianic 'would no longer be messianic if it stopped hesitating' (p. 169). This hesitation is the destabilization of every identification and localization, and it is promised, if one can say this, by mourning.

The phantom text I have evoked here concerns the logic of what Derrida speaks of as the 'furtive passage' (p. 168): trembling in the unspoken of *Spectres of Marx* and the writings of Nicolas Abraham, it does not *belong*, it does not rest, perhaps, anywhere. The fragment would constitute a phantom effect of what Derrida elsewhere describes as the project of an 'internal critique' of Christianity and the 'putting on trial' of a 'fabricated mystery', the deconstruction of what is private, of privacy as such.[16] leave some provisional last words on fragments to Maurice Blanchot, who writes: 'Fragmentary writing is risk, it would seem: risk itself. It is not based on any theory, nor does it introduce a practice one could define as *interruption*.'[17] And to the politicians, those 'marionettes' of 'televisual rhetoric' (*Spectres of Marx*, p. 80), those 'puppets of a phantom': *Paddy Ashdown*: 'I conduct my life according to a code of Christian values ... My religion is a private affair'; *John Major*): 'The Conservative Party is founded on principles flowing from the Christian faith', 'I don't pretend to understand all of the complex parts of Christian theology, but I simply accept it'; *Tony Blair*: 'the idea of the individual and their place in society is to me ... the distinguishing feature of the Christian religion, and it [is also] my political belief.'[18]

NOTES

1. Permit me to refer here to 'This is not a book review', *Angelaki*, 2:1 (1995), pp. 31–5, where I discuss the relation between book reviews and phantoms at greater length.
2. The translation/untranslatability of '*fantôme*' in Derrida's text is ultimately perhaps indissociable from that of the '*es spukt*' (it spooks, it apparitions, it phantoms) on which Derrida meditates in relation to Freud's 'The uncanny': see *Spectres*, pp. 172–4. For reasons which I hope may become more apparent as I go on, I have preferred to translate '*fantôme*' as 'phantom' rather than as 'ghost' (Peggy Kamuf's translation). It will also already be evident that I have taken the liberty of translating Routledge's US spelling of 'specters' into its conventional British form. Otherwise I have generally followed Kamuf's fine translation throughout. Where appropriate, references to the French text, *Spectres de Marx: L'État de la dette, le travail du deuil et la nouvelle Internationale* (Paris: Galilée, 1993), are given in brackets, following the English translation page number and a slash.
3. Jacques Derrida (with Geoffrey Bennington), *Jacques Derrida*, trans. Bennington (Chicago and London: Chicago University Press, 1993), p. 305.
4. Pierre Macherey, *A Theory of Literary Production*, trans. G. Wall (London: Routledge & Kegan Paul, 1978), p. 85.
5. 'Living on', trans. James Hulbert, in Harold Bloom *et al.*, *Deconstruction and Criticism* (New York: Seabury Press, 1979), p. 107.
6. There is a footnote reference on p. 178 but this is to Derrida's '*Fors*: the Anglish words of Nicolas Abraham and Maria Torok', rather than to the book to which that essay formed the foreword, viz. *The Wolf Man's Magic Word: A Cryptonymy*, trans. Nicholas Rand (Minneapolis: University of Minnesota Press, 1986). In what follows I will also be referring to Nicolas Abraham and Maria Torok, *The Shell and the Kernel*, vol. 1, ed., trans. and with an Introduction by Nicholas T. Rand (Chicago and London: Chicago University Press, 1994): further page references are given in brackets in the main body of the review.
7. '*Fors*: The Anglish words of Nicolas Abraham and Maria Torok', p. xxvi.

8. If there is what he calls the 'tableau of an ageless world' (the subtitle of Chapter 3 of *Spectres of Marx*), the 'ageless' here is not a reference to some putatively ahistorical notion of the 'timeless' but rather to a punctual anachronism – a two-timing or split-time that comports the very old and the very new *at the same time*. For comparison one might think here of the proposition, in *Memoirs of the Blind: The Self-Portrait and Other Ruins*, trans. Pascale-Anne Brault and Michael Naas (Chicago: Chicago University Press, 1993), that love is 'an ageless ruin – at once originary, an infant even, and already old' (pp. 68–9).

9. See Edward Pilkington, 'Thwarting the Grim Reaper', *The Guardian*, Saturday 6 January 1996, p. 1.

10. Jacques Derrida, 'The time is out of joint', trans. Peggy Kamuf, *Deconstruction is/in America: A New Sense of the Political*, ed. Anselm Haverkamp (New York: New York University Press, 1995), p. 20.

11. As with his observation (quoted earlier) about mourning's enigmatic commitment to 'identifying the bodily remains and . . . localizing the dead', Derrida's conception of the place and time of death – and therefore of the place and time of life, of presence, of experience itself – is perhaps best described as a trembling, a trembling conception and trembling of the concept. His thought is oriented by a sense of the injustice and even impossibility of 'localizing the dead' or of knowing 'at what instant mourning began'. This thought is not to be confused, however, with mere 'confusion' or 'doubt' ('Nothing could be worse, for the work of mourning, than confusion or doubt: one *has to know* who is buried where' (p. 9)): knowledge itself is spectralized. Similarly, it is not a matter of mourning as something to be thought 'merely' within us. As he suggests, in a related context, in *Mémoires*: 'thought is not bereaved interiorization; it thinks at boundaries, it thinks the boundary, the limit of interiority' (*Mémoires; for Paul de Man*, trans. Cecile Lindsay, Jonathan Culler and Eduardo Cadava (New York: Columbia University Press, 1986), p. 71).

12. See Elaine Pagels, *The Gnostic Gospels* (New York: Vintage, 1979), pp. xiii–xvi. Further references to Pagels' book are given in the main body of this review.

13. Jacques Derrida, 'Afterw.rds: or, at least, less than a letter about a letter less', trans. Geoffrey Bennington, in *Afterwords*, ed. Nicholas Royle (Tampere, Finland: Outside Books, 1992), p. 200.

14. Geza Vermes, *Jews the Jew: A Historian's Reading of the Gospels*, 2nd edn (London: Collins, 1983), p. 41.

15. Maurice Blanchot, *The Writing of the Disaster*, trans. Ann Smock (Lincoln: Nebraska University Press, 1986), p. 47.

16. See Jacques Derrida, *The Gift of Death*, trans. David Wills (London and Chicago: Chicago University Press, 1995), especially pp. 109–12.

17. *The Writing of the Disaster*, p. 59.

18. *Belief in Politics*, Interviews by Roy McCloughty, ed. Huw Spanner (London: Hodder & Stoughton, 1996), pp. 20, 133, 126, 50.

See also:

Marx (1.1)
Royle (7.4)
Maley (8.2)
Caputo (9.6)

'HAMLET'S DILEMMA'

Catherine Belsey

Ever since the publication of *Specters of Marx*, though perhaps as a minor and unintended consequence, English departments have been looking at *Hamlet* with renewed attention. The play, we now recognise, begins in mystery, with an enigma, a Ghost, which cannot be classified with certainty as either alive or dead, and thus exceeds the frame of what we seem to know. This apparition, a 'thing' that presents a puzzle for epistemology and defies both semantics and ontology,[1] also prompts within the play an ethical question that I want, very tentatively, to pursue.

The Ghost itself, it must be said, is not tentative at all. On the contrary, the Ghost consistently addresses Hamlet in the imperative: 'Mark me', it urges (1.5.2); 'lend thy serious hearing/To what I shall unfold' (1.5.5–6); 'Now, Hamlet, hear' (1.5.34).[2] Hamlet, who is all ears, barely needs these injunctions, or, when the tale is told, the further imperative, 'Remember me' (1.5.91). Finally, from an invisible place below the stage, 'Swear', the Ghost insists, not once, but four times in succession (1.5.157, 163, 169, 189). This is evidently a spectre which intends to be obeyed, and the main purpose of its encounter with Hamlet is to deliver the specific command which both names the genre and inaugurates the action of the play: 'If thou didst ever thy dear father love – ... Revenge his foul and most unnatural murder' (1.5.23–5).

The Ghost sustains the enigma of its own being. A ghost is not a person, but the ghost of a person. This spectre initially affirms a distinction between itself and Old Hamlet: 'I am thy father's spirit' (1.5.9), but it moves on to a sequence of

Source: Catherine Belsey, *Shakespeare and the Loss of Eden: Family Values in Early Modern Culture* (London: Macmillan, 1999).

possessives which collapse the two identities in references to 'my death', (1.5.37) 'my ... queen' (1.5.47), 'my orchard' (1.5.59). By speaking in the name of the father, the spirit lays claim to the authority of the paternal law. Fathers, who socialise and civilize their sons, who, by inculcating the proprieties of their culture, prepare little boys to take their own place in due course, are entitled to expect obedience. Filial piety consists in a proper respect for the father and his surrogates, the tutor, the teacher. When Hamlet indicates, by promising to 'sweep' to his revenge, that he has duly internalised his lesson, the Ghost comments approvingly, 'I find thee apt' (1.5.31), for all the world as if it were delivering a school report. Eager to act, the pupil, we are invited to believe, is neither lazy nor stupid. On the contrary:

> ... duller shouldst thou be than the fat weed
> That roots itself in ease on Lethe wharf,
> Wouldst thou *not* stir in this.
>
> (1.5.32–4)

The educational authority of the father is reinforced by the love that is due within the family, and the Ghost invokes that emotion as well as Hamlet's duty: 'If thou didst ever thy dear father love ...' To this day, family values have not lost their rhetorical power. The Ghost of Hamlet's father can count on filial and familial feeling to motivate a son who has been brought up to recognise the authority of nature in allegedly creating a relation of love between parents and children, and between the siblings who share their blood. Even now, despite any number of counter-examples, we continue to suppose that genetic inheritance produces affection as well as obligation. Claudius contravenes the law of nature in repeating the sin of Cain: fratricide is 'foul and most unnatural murder'; he also breaks it by seducing his brother's wife. But the Ghost wants Hamlet to act in accordance with his natural impulses in order to prevent the criminal's continued enjoyment of the fruits of his unnatural deeds:

> If thou hast nature in thee, bear it not,
> Let not the royal bed of Denmark be
> A couch for luxury and damned incest.
>
> (1.5.81–3)

Hamlet *has* nature in him, and passion too: 'O most pernicious woman!/O villain, villain, smiling, damned villain!' (1.5.105–6). But he also has a problem, which paradoxically reproduces with a difference, which is to say repeats, the very terms of his obligation. Revenge means killing his uncle and his king; it entails a breach of both family values and the authority structure of a patriarchalist Renaissance regime, where the king lays claim to the obedience due precisely to a father. Uncles in general, as everyone knows, are (or ought to be) indulgent incarnations of familial feeling, embodiments of the father's affection, without his fearful power to forbid. And the Claudius of Act 1 outwardly conforms to type, even though his sulky nephew refuses to respond (1.2.104–12).

But if the murder of an uncle is pernicious, regicide is the act of a traitor and incurs damnation.[3] Half a century after the first performance of the play, Cromwell was to experience the greatest difficulty in inducing his Parliamentarian colleagues to sign the death warrant of Charles I, even though the law had been rewritten to legitimate the King's legal execution as a traitor to the people of England. The Ghost confronts Hamlet with an impossible dilemma: nature, love and duty require an act which constitutes the repudiation of nature, love and duty.

The play registers the ethical undecidability of Hamlet's obligation in the imagery of its period, the effect of centuries of Christian iconography. What it withholds – both from the hero and from the audience – is the place of origin which in conventional Christian terms would specify the moral identity of the Ghost. At its first appearance to Hamlet, he approaches it in the explicit recognition of this uncertainty:

> Be thou a spirit of health or goblin damn'd,
> Bring with thee airs from heaven or blasts from hell,
> Be thy intents wicked or charitable,
> Thou com'st in such a questionable shape
> That I will speak to thee.
>
> (1.4.40–4)

What is a 'questionable shape'? A shape, perhaps, which prompts a question, a signifier whose significance is unknown? Does the term 'shape' imply the possibility of alternatives, of other shapes? Has a shape no shape of its own, no proper shape? Or might this figure change its shape at will, on the basis that there is behind the appearance a substantial, if immaterial, identity, whether angel or demon?

The Romantic critics, locating the cause of Hamlet's delay in the character of the sensitive prince, too imaginative, too intellectual, too 'poetic', as indeed they were themselves, to be capable of direct intervention in the affairs of a violent world, tended to disregard the questionable shape of a spectral figure from outside the frame of what it is possible for human beings to know. And Hamlet, caught up in the immediate intensity of filial propriety and family values, at the moment of the encounter disregards it too. But his first anxiety recurs throughout the play, as the hero repeatedly reopens the 'question' of an injunction from the Ghost of a loving father who commands an action which might incur his son's damnation. 'The spirit that I have seen', he reflects,

> May be a devil, and the devil hath power
> T'assume a pleasing *shape*, yea, and perhaps,
> Out of my weakness and my melancholy,
> As he is very potent with such spirits,
> Abuses me to damn me. I'll have grounds
> More relative than this.
>
> (2.2,594–600)

An analysis of the play as a record Hamlet's quest for the grounds on which to base an ethical decision represents an alternative reading to the Romantic story of the sensitive, suicidal prince. And if the eschatological imagery locates the play firmly in its moment at the end of the sixteenth century, there is, I want to suggest, a sense, nevertheless, in which Hamlet's moral deliberations recapitulate a history, or rather one possible, tentative history, of ethics.

The grounds Hamlet seeks will be, he says, 'more relative than this'. More relative, we must assume, than the questionable shape of the ambiguous spirit who is (perhaps) a devil, and who (perhaps) abuses Hamlet's credulity in order to lure him to hell. But how are we to understand 'more relative'? More *related* to the immediate circumstances, more pertinent to Hamlet's own situation, to *this* world, in which the eternal conflict between good and evil is perpetually re-enacted at the level of human choice? 'The play's the thing', he goes on, 'Wherein I'll catch the conscience of the King' (2.2.600–1). But possibly, too, in a meaning marginally in advance of its time, more relative because less absolute, since the Ghost, for all its apparently insubstantial spectrality, despite its questionability, is uncompromising, and its injunction is unconditional. It owes its absolute authority precisely to its supernatural character, to the defiance of epistemology, semantics and ontology which locate it beyond the reach of what it is possible to understand. It is not easy to conduct a moral debate with a shape that might or might not be something quite different, and different not only from itself but from anything you could hope to know. In the intensity of the moment Hamlet does not even try, any more than Moses made serious efforts to negotiate with the Burning Bush.[4] But now, in shifting the grounds he seeks for an ethical decision to his own judgment, the student from Wittenberg registers a doubt about blind submission to the exclusive and absolute spiritual authority of an external source, even one that wants to be addressed as 'Father'. As the Renaissance hero of a Protestant culture, Hamlet wants to know for himself and so to be responsible for his own decision.

In the event, knowing the facts does not solve the problem. Claudius, it will turn out, is guilty, but this does not resolve the question of the moral authority of the imperatives delivered by the questionable shape. Three or four years later another of Shakespeare's tragedies was to demonstrate throughout its length that 'oftentimes, to win us to our harm,/The instruments of Darkness tell us truths' (*Macbeth* 1.3.123–4).[5] In the following scene Hamlet places the ethical grounds he seeks elsewhere, in the nature of true nobility:

> ... that is the question:
> Whether 'tis nobler in the mind to suffer
> The slings and arrows of outrageous fortune,
> Or to take arms against a sea of troubles.
>
> (3.1.56–9)

By reformulating the ethical problem as a question of value (what is nobler) rather than truth (Claudius's guilt), this hero on the threshold of the

Enlightenment, who could not have read Hume, reveals that he hesitates, after all, to move from *is* to *ought*. The reformulated question counterposes Stoical endurance of wrong with violent resistance, when overwhelming odds will almost certainly ensure the protagonist's death: 'To take arms against a sea of troubles/And by opposing end them. To die' (3.1.59–60). The treason the Ghost requires of Hamlet is no small crime, and regicide can hardly be kept secret. But death is not the problem: 'To die – to sleep,/No more' (3.1.60–1). Hamlet, who repeatedly castigates himself for cowardice, is not afraid of dying. In a Christian cosmos, however, if treason is not justified, and at this historical moment there is some debate about whether it ever is,[6] the penalty remains to be paid beyond execution: 'in that sleep of death what dreams may come?' (3.1.66). Hamlet's anxiety is 'the dread of something after death' (3.1.78), which 'puzzles the will' (3.1.80) and makes us cowards in all conscience (3.1.83).

The nature of true nobility gets relatively short shrift here, after all, though it recurs in the soliloquy on Fortinbras's army. Within the framework of Christianity, ethics cannot be disentangled from religion, which requires, despite all Hamlet's efforts to take responsibility for his own decision, a choice that is delimited by the prospect of inevitable but essentially inscrutable consequences for infringement of the moral law. The Ghost withholds the secrets of his prison-house from ears of flesh and blood (1.5.13–22), but Hamlet has every reason to suppose that the price he would pay for ethical miscalculation is not loss of integrity, but the sacrifice of his immortal soul.

And yet the proximity in Hamlet's Renaissance account of the secular question and the theocratic order may be read as hinting at the degree to which the Enlightenment project of finding grounds of right action independent of Christianity will continue to bear the trace of religion, in its allusion to an independent moral law, which defines what ought to be done or specifies the ethical imperative. Inscrutability simply shifts from the eternal consequences to the nature of the imperative itself, which is, after all, where in practice it was to begin with. Hamlet faces damnation if he kills Claudius *and* if it is wrong to kill a usurper and a murderer who is also a king. The Romantic critics, who interpreted this speech as a meditation on suicide by a prince too sensitive to act, betrayed in the process their own understanding of right action: two revolutions had by now demystified monarchy; regicide was no longer quite so special; and evidently it was obvious to them that real men do not hesitate to solve moral problems by violence. At the same time, their intense sympathy with Hamlet surely also implies a more complex, if unacknowledged, reading of the play. 'I have a smack of Hamlet myself, if I may so so', Coleridge famously commented,[7] distancing himself in the process from the violent imperatives of his culture. The ethical problem, which they seem to disregard, returns to inform the ambivalent relationship of the Romantics to the prince they both despise and identify with.

Hamlet does not give up the ethical struggle easily. Just how resolutely he pursues it is in practice partly a textual question. Modern editions have tended to conflate three distinct texts, the first quarto of 1603, the second, much longer quarto of 1604, and the Folio (F).[8] No wonder Hamlet's delay seems protracted: it is, in the versions we read, more prolonged than it probably was in any early modern performance. Among other differences, his self-castigating soliloquy over Fortinbras's army ('How all occasions do inform against me' 4.4.33–66) is omitted from F, leaving a relatively more decisive figure at the centre of the play. Meanwhile, F develops the case for action in more specific detail by adding four critical lines in the final act (5.2.67–70). Hamlet's renewed attempt to formulate the question posed by the questionable shape of the Ghost is addressed to Horatio, in the light of the new evidence that the King has tried to have his nephew killed in England. 'Does it not', Hamlet asks – and the modality remains interrogative –

> Does it not, think thee, stand me now upon –
> He that hath kill'd my king and whor'd my mother,
> Popp'd in between the election and my hopes,
> Thrown out his angle for my proper life
> And with such coz'nage – is't not perfect conscience
> To quit him with this arm? And is't not to be damn'd
> To let this canker of our nature come
> In further evil?
>
> (5.2.63–70)

The reference to conscience and the lines that follow are new. If, as seems possible, F is closer to the text that was actually performed in the theatre, the early modern stage Hamlet was a good deal less indecisive than the Romantic prince. The framework of his reflections is still Christian and eschatalogical, though both conscience and damnation have changed sides in this new reformulation of the question. But the case against Claudius is now political. The issue is justice: in the light of such crimes, is it not more than perfect conscience, but an obligation, to quit him (requite him, bring about a situation in which to call it quits)? When justice is at stake the gap between *is* and *ought* is by no means so clearcut. The issue is also the prevention of crime. The question posed by the questionable shape from the past also bears on the future, as Claudius threatens to come in further evil. And in addition the issue is collective: no longer a matter of personal revenge or individual integrity, the question concerns public safety, 'our nature', which faces the possibility of evil still to come.[9] Redefined in this way, the argument is about a tyrant's abuse of power; it is only residually religious; and it is only very residually ethical.

In the Folio version of the play, Hamlet has found possible grounds for action, for killing Claudius with a clear conscience, though the grounds are tentative, rather than total or conclusive, and they may not be decisive. But politically, as Ernesto Laclau has argued, we make decisions in a framework of 'constitutive incompletion', acknowledging undecidability, while not investing it with an alternative metaphysics of ground*lessness*.[10] Hamlet does, in the event, kill Claudius, in the instant after he has received his own death wound, and without, therefore, the opportunity for further reflection. But we are not necessarily invited to see the action, decisive though it is, as the outcome of his deliberations, in the sense that the moment of decision is incommensurable with the thought that leads up to it. Urgency, Derrida argues, in a passage that might serve as a commentary on *Hamlet*, is the law of the decision. 'Centuries of preparatory reflection and theoretical deliberation – the very infinity of a knowledge – would change nothing in this urgency. It is absolutely cutting, conclusive, decisive, heartrending; it must interrupt the time of science and conscience, to which the instant of decision will always remain heteroge-neous.'[11] It is not clear whether the grounds Hamlet has identified determine the act. Nor is it certain whether the act is ethically right, whether he is *entitled* to a clear conscience, and to the angelic 'rest' that Horatio wishes for him (5.2.365). On this issue, the play as whole retains, I believe, the questionable shape imposed on it by the apparition in Act 1: the undecidable Ghost inhabits the decision it prompts, deconstructing any certainty we might lay claim to.[12]

For all his proleptic insight into matters that the twentieth century has yet to come to terms with, Hamlet has not read Derrida's *Politics of Friendship*. He believes he knows, that is to say, the difference between his Stoical friend, Horatio, and his murderous enemy, Claudius: Claudius the traitor, who contra-vened both family values and the law by poisoning his brother, the King. Innocent of deconstruction's scepticism towards binary oppositions, Hamlet identifies himself and Claudius as 'mighty opposites' (5.2.62). And yet, in the event, he kills his uncle, amid cries of 'Treason! treason!' (5.2.328), with the poisoned sword he snatches from Laertes the revenger: 'The point envenom'd too! Then, venom, to thy work' (5.2.327). And to make doubly sure, he forces Claudius the poisoner to drink the poisoned wine. These are not the conven-tional actions of a political hero with a clear conscience. They are, however, quite possibly, and always questionably, the best he can do in the circumstances.

The villain of *The Mousetrap*, the play that Hamlet stages to catch the con-science of Claudius, poisons the King and marries the Queen. He is, as Hamlet triumphantly explains to the stage audience, the king's nephew (3.2.239). In the play within the play, poisoner and nephew are one and the same. In Shakespeare's tragedy uncle and nephew are antagonists. But as he pursues the ethical question posed by the Ghost's absolute and unconditional identi-fication of his enemy, Hamlet, who is responsible, directly or indirectly, for the deaths of Polonius, Rosencrantz and Guildenstern, Ophelia, Laertes and Claudius, comes to bear an uncanny resemblance to the antagonist whose violence initiates the entire sequence of events that constitutes the action of the play.

The twentieth century, in which mighty opposites, whether superpowers, European states or ethnic groupings at war, or Christians and Muslims, have come to resemble each other in certain dispiriting ways, might have something to learn from that. It is not clear to me that ethics, which implies an absolute imperative, which was not in the event much help to Hamlet, which led him in contradictory directions and towards an unsustainable opposition, has any significant part to play in resolving the issues we too confront in an equally complex present. Our dilemmas have more to do with power and resistance than good and evil: they are, in my view, political.

NOTES

1. Jacques Derrida, *Specters of Marx: The State of the Debt, the Work of Mourning, and the New International*, trans. Peggy Kamuf (New York: Routledge, 1994), p. 6.
2. William Shakespeare, *Hamlet*, ed. Harold Jenkins, The Arden Shakespeare (London: Methuen, 1982).
3. In Beaumont and Fletcher's *The Maid's Tragedy* (1610) Amintor, however wronged, cannot contemplate killing the king.
4. Exodus 3 and 4. Moses asks a series of questions, which God answers with the inscrutable affirmation, 'I AM THAT I AM'; when Moses expresses a doubt about his own likely success, God proves with a series of miracles the fact that his will is beyond human understanding (and scepticism).
5. William Shakespeare, *Macbeth*, ed. Kenneth Muir, The Arden Shakespeare (London: Methuen, 1964).
6. Catherine Belsey, *The Subject of Tragedy: Identity and Difference in Renaissance Drama* (London: Methuen, 1985), pp. 93–125; Quentin Skinner, *The Foundations of Modern Political Thought* (Cambridge: Cambridge University Press, 1978), 2 vols, vol. 2.
7. S. T. Coleridge, *Table Talk*, Collected Works, 14, ed. Carl Woodring (Princeton, NJ: Princeton University Press, 1990), 2 vols, vol. 2, p. 61.
8. The parallel texts are laid out clearly in Paul Bertram and Bernice W. Kliman, eds, *The Three-text 'Hamlet'* (New York: AMS Press, 1991).
9. The audience already knows, though Hamlet does not, that the further evil takes the form of suborning Laertes to kill Hamlet.
10. Ernesto Laclau, *Emancipation(s)* (London: Verso, 1996), p. 79.
11. Jacques Derrida, *Politics of Friendship*, trans. George Collins (London: Verso, 1997), p. 79. Cf. Jacques Derrida, *The Gift of Death*, trans. David Wills (Chicago: Chicago University Press, 1995), p. 77.
12. Cf. Jacques Derrida, 'Force of Law: "The Mystical Foundation of Authority"', *Deconstruction and the Possibility of Justice*, ed. Drucilla Cornell, Michael Rosenfeld and David Gray Carlson (New York: Routledge, 1992), pp. 3–67 (pp. 24–5).

See also:

'THE GHOSTS OF CRITIQUE AND DECONSTRUCTION'

Peggy Kamuf

To begin with that beginning we call a title, I will point out that my title uses an ambiguous plural. By grammar alone and without much context, one cannot decide whether to read the plural 'ghosts' as the two ghosts of critique and deconstruction, each having or being its own ghost, or whether to read a plural plurality: both critique and deconstruction having or being more than one ghost and even more than one kind of ghost. Both of these plurals are possible, which means that there is yet another kind of plurality to be reckoned with in the title's phrasing: a plurality of kinds of pluralization other than the pluralization of separable, identifiable ones. There would be a possible plurality of not just the more than one but also a plurality of modes of plurality: the other than one.

In French, there is an expression that says at the same time more than one and other than one: *plus d'un*. Depending on whether or not one pronounces the 's': 'plus/plus,' the expression shifts its register from that of counting by ones to that of counting without number one, or of taking account of the other than one. In French, then, it is possible to say all that at once, or rather to write it, because this pluralization of the same time has its effect only if voice itself is muted so as to suspend the final 's' of 'plus/plus' between its two possibilities.

Jacques Derrida has frequently made use of this fortunate possibility in the French idiom, to the perpetual torment, perhaps, of his translators. But it is also

Source: Peggy Kamuf, 'The ghosts of critique and deconstruction', first appeared in *Tympan*, www.tympanum.usc.edu/Kamuf

[This essay was first written as a lecture for a conference organized by Geoff Bennington in July 1998 at the University of Sussex on the topic 'Critique and deconstruction'. Marks of the original occasion are still legible on this somewhat rewritten version.]

the chance his texts give to the work of translation between languages and idioms: the chance of pluralization of another language. Here it is the chance of posing at the same time the other time that is not counted by beginning with one. For example, in *Specters of Marx*, which deploys Derrida's most concentrated reflection on a certain plurality of ghosts, the phrase 'plus d'un/plus d'un' regularly rhythms the opening pages. When these conjunctions occur in the text, translation encounters or makes apparent a sudden pluralization of the features it must attempt to project into the other language, with all its idiomatic differences. There is immediately more than one translation called for.

I should explain why I thought a conference titled 'Critique and Deconstruction' offered the best opportunity I would likely ever find to revisit the opening pages of *Specters of Marx*, and to read them as if for the first time.

I have always been unsure what is strictly meant by 'critique' when it is distinguished from deconstruction. Doubtless this is because of my lack of formal philosophical training. For me, 'critique' has always shaded quickly into the indistinct area of 'criticism,' and thus into what is called 'literary criticism.' There is, of course, no more indistinct 'thing' than literary criticism; just about anything and everything written in the vicinity of the literary can and has been called criticism. As for the boundaries of the 'literary,' these are, of course, even more imprecise than the boundaries of criticism. But I do know this much about critique in the Kantian sense: it is all about setting down clear boundaries between things.[1] Hence, I must assume that critique should not be equated with criticism, and certainly not with literary criticism.

So, although I know that 'critique and deconstruction' sets up some strict, philosophical questions, I'm going to invoke the altogether looser discourse of criticism. This discourse, however, has at least the advantage of being somewhat more familiar since it is not confined to the publications or classrooms of formal philosophy, but spills over into mass-circulated newspapers in the form, for example, of supplemental Sunday 'Book Review' sections. Moreover, that deconstruction has been frequently assimilated to the discourse of criticism is something anyone in these very broadly defined intellectual circles may easily observe. It has been repeated over and over again that deconstruction is a kind of literary criticism, even a discipline of reading, which is, we are told, why it has been most extensively imported by departments of literature in our universities. As anyone can tell you who has had some recent experience in these departments, such an assertion is neither simply true nor false. But by force of repetition, it seeks to authorize itself as true, to perform and to produce its truth. One thing that will have been observed about the operations of this discourse is that the performing assertion predicating deconstruction as criticism is almost invariably accompanied by the manifest pronouncement that the said deconstruction is now dead and buried in these same departments of literature or wherever else one wishes to locate its grave. However, because the predicating discourse continues to be neither simply true nor false, which is to say not definitively or solely constative but performative as well, it also induces its own repetition, the necessity of repeatedly performing what otherwise has no certain truth. It is a matter, we might say, of having to reassert, reaffirm, or re-verify the death of deconstruction.

One way to understand this necessity is to invoke a logic of spectrality. That is, there would be a haunting effect observable in the discourse of deconstruction-as-criticism. It is as if criticism repeatedly had to exorcise a ghost, and even one that it seems to recognize as its own ghost. Take the example of the *New York Review of Books (NYRB)*, a journal in which a certain discourse of criticism materializes on a bimonthly basis, like some ghost that regularly returns. In a recent issue (June 25, 1998), the *NYRB* printed the report of one of its hired guns who had been sent out to read some recent books by Derrida so as to put to rest rumors that the ghost still walked. Mark Lilla, the ghostbuster-for-hire, did so very dutifully, although without much originality. If one took the time to read this report, one would quickly see how it strings together almost all the known incantatory formulae of the critical exorcism of deconstruction, including the *de rigueur* 'deconstruction-as-criticism-confined-to-literature-departments-where-it-is-now-dead.' Lilla thus earns his fee by confirming that deconstruction remains buried in these departments, the graveyard of the university. But if one had access to the archives of the *NYRB*, one would also notice that this magazine has had to print similar articles, which do more or less the same job, at regular intervals of about every four or five years. On these occasions, it has called in all the best exorcisors, political philosophers and even philosophers of speech acts, but the thing keeps reappearing somewhere, rumors get back to New York, the capital of speculative capital and skeptical criticism, that 'this thing has appeared again tonight.' For twenty or twenty-five years at least, the *NYRB* appears to have been haunted but it knows not by what.

One ought to try to put it out of its misery, if one had the power to do so. Perhaps, however, the power needed is not the exorcist's, with which to rid criticism of the deconstruction that haunts it, but the power of a *possibility* made available by the logic of ghosts, more precisely, by what *Specters of Marx* calls *hauntology* and which is not an ontology precisely because it does not begin by posing the ontological existence of ghosts. One might then have the means not only to account for the phenomenon of the *NYRS*'s repetition compulsion, but to address the haunting figure without succumbing to the paralyzing fear that the figure really exists somewhere.

It might thus be an act kindness to submit Lilla's *NYRB* article to a hauntological analysis, but it would also be rather tedious. This particular representative of critical discourse too often resembles bad journalism. And however loose the common notion of literary criticism may be, we still think we can distinguish between journalism and scholarly criticism. It is this category of the 'scholarly' that is going to permit us to return as promised to *Specters of Marx* and to the plurality of ghosts. First, however, we will take one more and longer detour through the very vague terrain of criticism, this time scholarly criticism.

By scholarly criticism, what do we generally mean? Perhaps nothing more than criticism practiced from within the school, criticism that therefore is accompanied by an injunction to teach and to study. This injunction, in other words, would locate the performative aspect of scholarly criticism. Whereas journalistic criticism performs under a different compulsion (in our example, it is the compulsion to exorcise deconstruction, either to kill it or to pronounce it dead), scholarly criticism, at least in theory, performs under the injunction to teach or to study, for example, deconstruction or not. It would not be too difficult, however, to locate many places where these injunctions or gestures cannot be radically distinguished from each other. That is why it is best to try to formalize the distinction in a strictly minimal fashion: scholarly criticism, we'll say, is criticism that is supported by the apparatus of the 'school,' which includes the classroom and the seminar room, sites of scholarly publication, research, and so forth. The school apparatus would be that which, like a prosthetic body, houses the spirit or the idea of scholarly criticism. Like any body, this prosthetic apparatus can be interpreted as displaying its symptoms on the various surfaces that support critical writing. The innumerable entries through which this body writes its symptoms come to be ordered and ordered like a body, from head to toe or from the top down. That is, the 'school' apparatus, the prosthetic body of scholars or of scholarship, is also – and this is something we are told everyday we must take into account – ranked from the top down. The school embodies itself in a more or less rigidly hierarchized differentiation, a trait that can therefore never be strictly excluded from the scholarly criticism produced or supported by the apparatus. How this trait of hierarchical ranking gets remarked in the work of scholarly criticism would be a vast area of study, and would even be very interesting if undertaken without the presuppositions of Bourdieu-style sociology, which disallows any spectral possibility from the analysis. A hauntological analysis, on the other hand, would have to address also the possibility that the hierarchy of the school's prosthetic body is the effect of a haunting by some *spirit* of scholarly criticism.

Which spirit? Whose spirit? And is this spirit a ghost?

Like the journalistic criticism of the *NYRB*, scholarly criticism has to do with the specter of spirit. But if indeed it is a specter or a ghost, that is, if it indeed materializes in the world of phenomena, then the body it assumes is also *someone's body, the body of some one.* That is the difference we can make out between spirit and specter.[2] The spirit has no one's body, no one body, it is the spirit of all in a collectivity: a spirit of nation, of language, of literature, of history, of philosophy, of criticism, and so forth. We even speak of a school spirit. However, if scholarly criticism acknowledges that, first of all and perhaps even above all, it has to do with the *specter* of spirit, then it is put to work on the question: whose specter is it? That is, whose ghost haunts the critical spirit?

Specters of Marx, as I'll try to show in a moment, has taken up this task of criticism as one which requires a deconstruction of the spectral spirit by which criticism has let itself be guided. The deconstruction of criticism occurs in this text not as a discarding of that notion but as its inheritance. There is an affirmation of the necessity to inherit and to inherit affirmatively, that is, by selecting and differentiating that which presents itself to be inherited, in all the different forms the inherited corpus may present itself. Derrida's gesture is to demonstrate the necessity to inherit from criticism the question: whose spirit? whose body? whose ghost? – but then to undertake to inherit it affirmatively, that is, deconstructively, by transforming the presuppositions of the question. Because the question 'whose ghost?' implies that there is only one of them, it presupposes the singular unity of the one at the origin and determines the form of the question. But, Derrida will wonder whether it is not possible to *speak to ghosts, always more than one, and to speak to them without questioning them.* I have tried to analyze elsewhere the significance of this suspension of the interrogative in *Specters of Marx.*[3] For our purposes here, I will simply under-score once again that a suspension or bracketing of any question to the ghost is the final gesture of the book. The last line of *Specters of Marx* quotes yet again the words spoken by Marcellus, in Act I, sc. ii of *Hamlet*, to the scholar Horatio, as both stood on the rampart before the apparition. He turns to Horatio and enjoins him: 'Thou art a scholar; speak to it, Horatio.' In the play, Marcellus adds: 'question it,' but Derrida cuts short the quotation and does not repeat the injunction to question it.

Now, anybody can quote *Hamlet* and millions do so every day. So there's not necessarily any significance to be noted when another scholar selects the same phrase, truncated at the same point, to conclude an essay on a certain ghost of literature, for example, the Ghost of *Hamlet*. However, the essay in question, Stephen Greenblatt's 'What is the History of Literature?', shows many other potential parallels with Derrida's, at least with its interest in haunting and conjuring as modalities of our relation to literature. Both, we could say, set out from the recognition that this relation is spectral and not just spiritual. These parallels, however, remain only potential because, although Greenblatt's admittedly brief essay was published subsequently, it makes no reference to Derrida's book. The omission is disappointing for whoever may have wished to understand in Greenblatt's own terms what difference he would make out, if any, between the ghost of literature he is talking about or to and the ghosts or specters Derrida entertains in his book. The ghosts they are talking about (or to) seem at once altogether other and yet oddly conjoined in spirit. Anyone might be led to conclude that they haunt each other's analyses.

Greenblatt's omission is puzzling since it seems unlikely that it could have been accidental and therefore utterly without some intent backing it up. This absence, when one might have reasonably expected something else, raises at least the possibility that, whatever else he wanted to do in this essay, Greenblatt sought to dissociate his discourse from that of Derrida or of deconstruction. He therefore took no risk of misunderstanding on this score and went so far as to silence any reference to *Specters of Marx*, even though he would no doubt have found much there to fuel his own thinking, both positively and negatively, about ghosts, literature, *Hamlet*, history, the difference between spirit and specter, and so forth and so on. We all know how distressing it can be when we discover that someone else has been working in a very similar vein, perhaps even on the same texts. The last thing we want to do is read their work, but it is of course usually the first thing we do as soon as we have the chance. When the work we must read is that of someone like Derrida, we may even have to arm ourselves in advance against him since we fear the power of his arguments or his readings. Perhaps this is what happened to Greenblatt, but the chronology of publication suggests that he had more than two years to read what he didn't want to have to read. Since Stephen Greenblatt is no slouch, it is hard to believe he simply forgot to do his scholarly work. That is why one is left trying to puzzle out the sense of this marked absence to the book that he all but quotes when he ends his essay with the same truncated line from the play: 'Thou art a scholar; speak to it, Horatio.'

With this omission, one is left to determine the significance of that gesture by the way it gets inscribed on the surface of the scholarly apparatus, the apparatus of the 'school' and of the school that defines itself through competing schools of criticism. It is on this apparatus that his gesture is able to signify in a minimally differential, way: not-deconstruction. That is, it is for the school in which 'deconstruction' is the name of a school of criticism that there can be something significant about omitting its name or any name associated with it.

We will take advantage of Greenblatt's omission in order to talk about the essay as if it could embody this negative thing that is criticism-but-not-deconstruction. It is doubtful that Stephen Greenblatt would accept to describe what he is doing as 'criticism,' but what matters for our purposes is that he quite pointedly removes what he is doing from the purview of deconstruction. More specifically, I would suggest that he removes it, attempts to set it out of view of, Derrida's reading of *Hamlet* and of Marx in *Specters of Marx*. The conjunction of *Hamlet* and Marx, a certain Marx or a certain Marxism that one wishes to inherit from Marx, is the conjunction that has been worked by the wide vein of criticism labeled loosely New Historicism or, as Greenblatt prefers to call it, cultural poetics. It is in the spirit of a certain Marx that Shakespeare critics, first of all and above all, have set about to reinherit or reinvent the inheritance of the whole of literature in English. By the criterion of the school's body-prosthetic and its ranked system of value, New Historicism or cultural poetics is to be differentiated as a competing school within the one school of the critical spirit, as one of the schools competing to define the terms of this critical spirit. The omission marking Greenblatt's essay is thus perhaps the trait of this competition, which would play itself out as a competition for the conjoined inheritance from the very heady spirits of Shakespeare and Marx. At stake would be the position at the head of the body of scholars. But to reach the head, the essay does not undertake crudely to try to 'kill' its chosen adversary or to announce, once again, that deconstruction is dead. Rather, it proceeds in a more *scholarly* fashion, even though it thereby runs the risk that someone might remark the omission and fault its scholarship. In any case, if there is some such competitive urge dictating the silence, it must at the same stroke disavow itself since the spirit of scholarly criticism, we believe, should have nothing to do with such urges, which therefore cannot be avowed.

At this point, one should point out that this structure of differential marking seems to affect no less Derrida's text than Greenblatt's. The fact is *Specters of Marx* likewise makes no reference to anything Greenblatt has written, notably anything he has written on Shakespeare, which is quite a lot. But it also makes little or no reference to Shakespeare criticism before or since Greenblatt, which is quite a lot more. So like Greenblatt, Derrida lets his text take form around a more or less symmetrical omission. It will take some space (and a little patience) to explain why these omissions should not be understood as mirror reflections of each other, a mutual disavowal and dismissal of two competing schools of criticism. The difference between them, however, nowhere resembles a line of demarcation that can be pointed out, shown, or demonstrated. Nevertheless, what I will be trying to make apparent is a difference between these two mobilizations of the ghost of *Hamlet*, and therefore of literature, that cross at the point of their disjointed inheritance. In brief, what I will be trying to show is this: whereas criticism, with its undeconstructed question as to the identity of the ghost, keeps alive a certain spirit of competition or dispute over the ghost's property, deconstruction moves to pluralize the spirit by pluralizing the ghost and therefore the possible scenes of inheritance. In order to describe criticism and deconstruction as two different or even opposed and competing ways of inheriting, which comes down to assimilating them to the same critical spirit, one has to dismiss the possibility that the pluralization in question in deconstruction comprehends, or at least *wishes to comprehend*, the critical inheritance, which it would not therefore oppose. But since it moves to pluralize the spirit from which, or in (the name of) which one inherits, it also displaces possible comprehension out of any totalizing unity or identity and onto multiple stages.

Or so we would try to argue by reading some scenes from *Hamlet* with Greenblatt and Derrida.

A certain logic of exemplarity, which I cannot summarize here,[4] leads Greenblatt in the final pages of his essay to the supreme example of *Hamlet* and to the Ghost in *Hamlet*, who is the chief or head ghost of English letters. When this subtly argued essay acknowledges its crowning example, two pages before its close, it does so in startling terms that strike with great force. After having quoted the line with which the Ghost begins his apostrophe to Hamlet in Act I, sc. v, 'I am thy Fathers Spirit,' Greenblatt writes: 'There is no more powerful claim in literature to an absolute attention, a complete investment of uncritical belief, than the dead king's horrific tale of his death.'[5] This is a striking, indeed a doubly striking affirmation. The striking, almost paralyzing force of the statement comes from the impossibility of deciding which of the two claims it contains is the more powerful one. Is it the claim said to be made by 'the dead king's horrific tale of his death' or is it rather the claim being *performed* here, which claims that the other claim, the claim made by a ghost and then repeated, is the most powerful claim 'in literature to an absolute attention, a complete investment of uncritical belief'? Is it even possible to separate the two claims or the two performances? Since what is claimed is that this tale of the dead father has the power to suspend our disbelief, then the extraordinary thing that is claimed is that we cannot but believe both claims as having absolute sway over our attention, which is powerless to resist its call or its claim.

Greenblatt, of course, will not let this absolute claim stand unchallenged. He proceeds immediately, in the next sentence, to take apart the rhetorical basis on which the Ghost grabs our attention. The essay carefully unpacks the line with which the King's Ghost explains his restless appearance among the not-yet-dead-and-buried. He was, he still is, as Shakespeare phrased it, 'Unhous'led, disappointed, unanel'd,' that is, buried without communion, without confession, and without anelement or anointing of the seven places of his dying body. Greenblatt retrieves the historical, non-rhetorical use of these terms in Church rituals governing the passage into the realm of the dead, which would be the realm of the spirit and not of ghosts only on the condition of the proper burial of bodies. He then remarks: 'The rituals that governed the passage of a person from the living to the dead had been changed, and the words that signified these rituals had been unmoored, making them the objects of a prolonged and murderous struggle. In *Hamlet* they have become a piece of spectral poetry, a weird pentameter line, voiced by a "questionable shape"' (ibid.). The scholar of the English Renaissance, who knows to read the line against the background of the 'prolonged and murderous struggle' called English history, questions the 'questionable shape' as to the *bona fide* claim made by a doctrine of religious faith. His philological exercise dismantling the Ghost's claim is performed in the very best tradition of enlightenment, even Kantian enlightenment. Greenblatt himself describes this philological commentary as 'a form of conjuration' (481) that dispels or exorcises the Ghost by disputing the faith to which it appeals.

However, this post-Enlightenment, post-Kantian criticism does not only evacuate the claims of religious faith; it also reaffirms the claim of what Greenblatt calls here 'the imagination's power.' As a result, this literary criticism or literary historicism (for it is not certain that this scholarship would differentiate them) sets itself up in a certain way to inherit the ghost and from the ghost called literature. I quote Greenblatt's conclusion to this reading of the Ghost in *Hamlet*: 'The Ghost in *Hamlet* is the *genius literarius* come to excite the literary historian's wonder at the imagination's power to invent and unsettle the real and to cross the boundary from death to life' (481). The power of ghosts is attributed to or appropriated by the power of what is called imagination, which is to say a specular structure. It is this structure that governs or watches over the scene of the strictly *filial* inheritance of literature that Greenblatt is recalling and calling upon us to renew.[6]

But cannot this inheritance also be enacted otherwise, more critically, more affirmatively, more deconstructively? And even, one might add, more historically? For one may easily be struck by the way in which Greenblatt's own appeal to the power of imagination seems to be carried forward by the history (that is, the legacy) of romanticism, such that it has little or no leverage on that history. It inherits above all from romanticism and the romantic configuration of literature as power of imagination, and it does so automatically, as it were, without questioning the very scene in which it is inscribed as son and heir to romanticism's realm. Criticism is unhistorical to the extent that is not urged to question the scene of its own inheritance, for example, its inheritance from the figure of the romantic imagination. If it is not urged to do so, then perhaps that is because the interests of criticism, in body or spirit, are best served by leaving fundamentally unquestioned or unchallenged the provenance, the origin, or the identity of the Ghost whose inheritors it would be or claim to be.

Whereas Greenblatt, the historical, philological scholar, easily disputes the King's claim to have been buried 'Unhous'led, disappointed, unanel'd,' what he does not question is the King's claim to be 'thy Father's spirit.' It is because that claim to the identity of spirit is accepted *at face value* that it has the force Greenblatt remarks and repeats, performs by repeating: 'There is no more powerful claim in literature to an absolute attention, a complete investment of uncritical belief, than the dead king's horrific tale of his death.' The striking force of this double claim, we may now see, is the force of a son's belief that he is addressed by the spirit of his father. The historical, philological apparatus the scholar will immediately deploy to counter this belief has above all an apotropaic function. That is, it serves to remind the one who wields it that the father is indeed dead and buried, hence his son need not fear the spirit that he sees, or reads, before him; not only need he not fear it, but it is a sign of his own power, the power of his own imagination, the fearsome father is not a castrating agent but an agent of his own excitement: 'The Ghost in *Hamlet* is the *genius literarius* come to *excite* the literary historian's wonder at the imagination's power to invent and unsettle the real and to cross the boundary from death to life.'

I am suggesting, then, that this historical scholarship is *not yet* historical, *not yet* historical enough because it raises its shield against the *impossibility* of knowing whose ghost addresses us. This impossibility is set at the limit of history understood as historical knowledge, that which it is possible to know. When historical scholarship is limited in this fashion to what it is possible to know, one renounces for it any thinking of the possibility of history itself, the becoming-historical of that of which one can have no knowledge until it happens. One renounces, that is, the necessity of thinking a certain *impossibility as also possibility*, as that which shelters possibility and gives it its chance. When the shield of scholarship is raised, when the whole armor of the prosthetic body is wielded, it is also wielded against the necessity of thinking this other possibility, the possibility of other histories, in all their plurality, and even the possibility of other pluralities. The fundamentally apotropaic gesture of scholarship is put in place as a protection against the *trope* of plurality, against the *more than one* but also the *other than one*.

The question, then, is whether there can be another scholarship, if not another scholar, one which or who would deploy a different shield. It would have to be a shield that, unlike Jason's, did not immediately deflect away the effects of looking into the face of plural possibility, so to speak, and that did not therefore have the same power to reflect back only the image of the one who wields it. A shield that is not a mirror, a shield that could shield, protect plurality, a shielded plurality and thus plural shields. What would such a body of scholarship look like? In what kind of body could it appear that would be able to hold together or stand up as a body has to do? Whose body? The ghost of whose body or of whose spirit?

Early in the first chapter of *Specters of Marx*, after Derrida has quoted for the first time Marcellus's injunction to Horatio the scholar, he wonders about the possibility of this other scholarly body. He has just rehearsed the scene between Marcellus and Horatio, and put the reader on guard against what he calls the Marcellus complex, in which the credulous eye witnesses to an unheard-of event call upon a scholar to verify, as only scholars know how to do, what the non-scholars think they have seen. Their claim to have seen 'the same figure, like the King that's dead' is what needs to be authenticated by the scholar who is enjoined to 'speak to it,' and more specifically to 'question it.' The illiterate Marcellus calls a witness who can ask the Ghost to identify himself. This implies that literacy is the capacity to speak with the ghosts of the dead. In other terms, to be able to hear oneself being addressed by the dead would be the mark of the scholar.

Horatio's scholarship, however, consists in charging the Ghost to speak its name before the court of reason. Here is how *Specters of Marx* describes the scene:

> 'Thou art a Scholler speake to it, Horatio,' [Marcellus] says naively, as if he were taking part in a colloquium. He appeals to the scholar or to the learned intellectual, to the man of culture as a spectator who better understands how to establish the necessary distance or how to find the appropriate words for observing, better yet, for apostrophizing the ghost, which is to say also for speaking the language of kings or of the dead. (p. 12)

It is tempting to read these lines, or indeed the whole of *Specters of Marx*, almost as stage directions for a representation of this scene in *Hamlet*. If one gives into that temptation, however, then one must also recognize that Derrida's analysis takes part in the scene it describes, as director but also as actor; it even plays all the roles, a plurality of roles. What the Scholar is called on to do by his naïve compatriot Marcellus is to verify that this plurality comes together under one, under one body, the body of the 'the king that's dead.' But as soon as this scholar comes on stage, the scene embeds another one within it, another play within the play being performed. Marcellus speaks, remarks Derrida, 'as if he were taking part in a colloquium,' and we recall that *Specters of Marx* first took part, played a part in a colloquium. Horatio, who is only one of the scholars being represented here, finally speaks to the thing when it returns, but he speaks to it by charging it, by commanding it to speak so that it may speak its own name: 'By heaven I charge thee speake!' This scholar, in Heaven's name, conjures the Ghost to identify itself and to arrest the frightening plurality of possible ghosts, the crowd of ghosts that comes on stage under the trope, or the figure of the King: 'the same figure, like the King that's dead.' As enacted by Horatio, the scholar's function is to question the Ghost so as to be able to identify it. Again, Derrida's stage directions are very precise: 'By charging or conjuring [the Ghost] to speak, Horatio wants to inspect, stabilize, *arrest* the specter in its speech.' And then the line is quoted in which Horatio vainly tries to arrest the departure of the Ghost – 'Stay and speake' – before he turns back to Marcellus and commands him to intervene: 'Stop it Marcellus.'

'Stop it Marcellus.' In Derrida's staging of the scene, this imperative gives the command to intervene with force so as to arrest the retreating Ghost. It would probably be somewhat perverse to hear it any other way. And yet, this re-staging also tempts me at least to wonder about another possible intonation. What if Horatio, or someone in Horatio, had meant to say, with a certain annoyance in his tone: 'Stop it, Marcellus, you are getting on my nerves with your credulity concerning the power of father-kings to rule even from beyond their graves. Not every ghost that walks before or beside you is the ghost of a father-king, get that through your thick skull. Learn that, learn how to live with that, learn how to live with all the other ghosts, your own ghosts; learn that every ghost is altogether another and another's ghost. This is what I would have to teach you, for you are not yet literate and therefore cannot see the difference between a body and its prosthesis, a body and a body of letters.'

This scene of an irascible scholar faced with his thick-headed illiterate student is not, however, the only one that Derrida's re-staging allows his readers to envision. For he asks whether it is not also possible to hear Marcellus, in his very naiveté, calling for another scholar to come, other than the irascible, charging, arresting, conjuring, exorcising scholar who is Horatio. Marcellus, to whom Derrida, like Greenblatt, is going to leave the last word of his lecture, would have thereby anticipated, as he puts it,

> the coming, one day, one night, several centuries later, of another 'scholar.' The latter would finally be capable, beyond the opposition between presence and non-presence, actuality and inactuality, life and non-life, of thinking the possibility of the specter, the specter as possibility. Better (or worse) he would know how to address himself to spirits. He would know that such an address is not only already possible, but that it

will have at all times conditioned, as such, address in general. In any case, here is someone mad enough to hope to *unlock* the possibility of such an address. (ibid.)

As he has done elsewhere in a similar way, Derrida is signaling here to the situation of someone giving what is called the 'keynote address' at a conference or colloquium. He thereby signals once again his own inclusion in the scene he is describing or anticipating. But one should not rush to conclude that there is some kind of facile self-reference here or there. With the phrase 'here is someone mad enough' the translator was translating 'voilà en tout cas quelqu'un d'assez fou'. 'Voilà' can always be translated as either here or there, but more often one hears it as 'there,' as a deictic that points not to the place from which one speaks, and therefore not first of all to oneself, but to another place and to the place of another over there. By translating it as 'here,' the translator perhaps *wanted to make believe* that Derrida was speaking about himself and announcing his own arrival as this other scholar, mad enough to believe he brings the key to unlock the possibility of all possibilities of address. If so, this may be a serious fault of the translation, because it once again arrests under one figure the plurality of ghosts and therefore the plurality of scholars who are speaking to ghosts here and there.

But where, here or there? So many scenes and acts are embedded at once, at the same time, as soon as a ghost can come on stage like any one of the other actors. And even if one now tried to own up to this faulty translation, the only way to do so would be to appeal again to an original one, thereby essentially repeating the fault whereby plurality, the plurality of possible translations, is referred back to just one. One would end up by doing nothing but multiplying all the scenes of the fault, and therefore all the stages on which a ghost may walk with the other actors. Perhaps, however, that is the point of doing what we call deconstruction: to end up doing nothing else but multiplying the scenes. The deconstructive scholar, the scholar whom Marcellus may have anticipated, for better or worse, is one who, we read, 'would know how to address himself to *spirits*.' The translation here cannot make any mistake about this plural. The scholar would know how to address himself 'aux esprits.' This pluralization of address, of the scenes of address, is altogether what deconstruction is, that is to say, what it does, what is done, and what happens. There is always more than one scene in deconstruction because deconstruction deconstructs the stage on which only one scene can be played at any time; the stage on which there is only one time in play.

This would be the point at which to recall Derrida's very *scholarly* reading of Hamlet's phrase after the Ghost has left the stage: 'the time is out of joint.' *Specters of Marx* is placed under the surveillance of this phrase, which, in its English version at least, is printed as a separate epigraph to the book as a whole. Hamlet's phrase thus commands, overlooks, and determines everything put forward between the book's covers, including everything Marx is made to think or to say when he comes back on stage later. This is to say that the book is not only a staging of the play but a prolonged translation into French (and a few other languages) of the event that Hamlet names 'time-out-of-joint.' With this translation, the phrase can be heard naming something like the event of history itself, and not just history repeating itself as either farce or the tragic call to vengeance.

Now, any critic who has the good fortune to be able to encounter Shakespeare in English may very well conclude that if indeed *Specters of Marx*, as I have just claimed, essentially retranslates bits of *Hamlet* into another language, then he or she does not need any such intermediary to read this scene. Perhaps that is what Stephen Greenblatt concluded; perhaps that is why he proceeded headlong as if he were a son listening without any intermediary to the voice of the father's spirit. If, however, he had been allowed or allowed himself to take account of this new translation, he might have noticed the effect of what is translated there as the 'visor.' It is the effect of that piece of the armor which allows someone to see without being seen. Noticing this effect, he would possibly not have been so ready to take the phrase 'I am thy Father's Spirit' at face value, meaning to *take it for* a face, in the place of the face one cannot see. All of that is possible. But it is also possible, of course, that Greenblatt did not notice this effect when he read Derrida's translation, or that he did notice it and decided he did not have to take account of it. Or that he simply decided he did not have to take account of anything Derrida might have to say about Shakespeare's ghost and therefore he did not read this staging of a new trans-lation. But in each of these possible cases, the visor effect would have operated all the more surely.

Specters of Marx recalls that 'The one who says "I am thy Father's Spirit" can only be taken at his word' because the visor effect is in place. We therefore 'feel ourselves seen by a look which it will always be impossible to cross,' meaning both a look we cannot look in the eyes or the face, and a look that is a command we cannot cross or disobey. The visor effect in this way conditions the very basis of inheritance from the law, it makes for the law of inheritance. By overlooking the visor effect, the scholar's historical criticism remains written into this scene always in the same place: the place of the legitimate son and heir. There can be only one, there should be only one. But of course there never is just one, the visor effect being also a prior pluralization of every one, everyone. If the visor effect can regulate the law as inheritance by only sons, it has this effect only to the extent that something can be made to play along the hinges or the joints of the law's power to reproduce its will through filiation. These hinges link the visor to a helmet, which bears the symbol or insignia of the king's power, a coat of arms as it is called, a coat of arms carried on a coat of armor. There is thus a visor effect, a helmet effect, and what hinges them together.

Historical criticism, and perhaps especially New Historicism, would appear to see clearly enough the helmet, that is, the chief prosthesis of power, but does not notice the visor. No doubt this is so because Horatio is taken as scholarly witness. When asked by Hamlet whether he saw the face of the Ghost, Horatio does not hesitate: yes, he saw it, because 'My Lord, he wore his Beaver up.' With this response, Horatio implies that because the Ghost wore his beaver or visor up, the spectator that he was had a clear view of whose head was protected beneath the helmet. He also implies that it would have been a different matter had the visor been worn not up but down. In this way, Horatio demonstrates that his kind of scholarship is essentially that of the spectator, one who believes, as Derrida puts it, 'that looking is sufficient' and that he need not speak to the Ghost or listen as it speaks to him. He is the traditional scholar, because he is the scholar who assures tradition by supposing, but only supposing, the body of the dead king beneath its prosthetic armor.

That is what the traditional scholar does, but is there any other? Any other possible scholar? A scholar of possibilities, perhaps, rather than a factual scholar or a critical scholar? For the scholar of possibilities, what should count is not whether the visor was in fact up or down, but that a hinge, a joint puts both possibilities into play in an articulation. This articulation moves or plays in its joint with a prosthetic panoply of power that seeks to make itself invulnerable. As Derrida writes, 'For the helmet effect, it suffices that a visor be *possible* and that one play with it. Even when it is raised, *in fact*, its possibility continues to signify that someone, beneath the armor, can safely see without being seen or without being identified.' This suggests that between the traditional scholar and this other possible scholar there is not *in fact* any difference, since it is indeed this status of *fact* that is in question. Thereby in question as well is what is called history, the facts or the events of history. Between the traditional criticism of fact and this other possible scholarship, there is not a factual or actual division: rather, there would be the effect of a prosthetic membrane opening and closing, in play between them.

Between all of them, who are many. I remember that I said somewhere closer to the beginning of this essay that I wanted to do little more than re-read the inscription of perhaps the most idiomatic mark on *Specters of Marx*, a common enough phrase: 'plus d'un/plus d'un.' I said that this phrase mutes its voice as soon as one attempts to translate it. But one could have said just as well that translation is straining there to hear a voice, so that it can decide which of all the possible plural translations is closest to the original, supposing always that the original is a single voice. In this way, translation is also a philology of voice, at least until it has to admit or take account of the visor effect under which it performs. But a visor effect refers one to vision, whereas here the effect affects voice, and therefore speech, logos, reason, the law of reason. So one would have to find another name for an apparatus that mutes all the tropes and notes of voice, thereby multiplying voice in a disseminating trait, a voice that is not one. What would one call such an apparatus? And if one calls king, for example, the one who can see without being seen behind a visor, then what would we call one who speaks without being heard, at least without being heard by those who are called scholars? We call them ghosts, perhaps, those beings whom no scholars have ever seen or heard because, as Derrida observes, 'A traditional scholar does not believe in ghosts nor in all that could be called the virtual space of spectrality. There has never been a scholar who, as such, does not believe in the sharp distinction between the real and the unreal, the actual and the inactual, the living and the non-living, being and non-being . . . in the opposition between what is present and what is not, for example in the form of objectivity' (11). As for the apparatus that can operate as the prosthetic armor of voice, perhaps we do not have to search very far for its name; perhaps it's simply what we call the 'school.'

That both Derrida and Greenblatt chose to end their text with the exact same words of Marcellus has been the *fact*, the textual fact which I've followed a certain minimal distance into each work. This fact, which anyone may quickly verify, is the very small jot of scholarship I've presumed to add to a conference on 'Critique and Deconstruction.' It's possible, however, that at the same time I have been heard to say that Greenblatt is the traditional critic and Derrida the scholar of possibilities. If so, then I cannot end without trying to correct that impression. For Greenblatt, no less than for Derrida, it is possible that the scholar he wants to hear addressed by Marcellus, the one to whom he no less than Derrida consigns his text by readdressing and repeating Marcellus's words in conclusion, be a scholar of possibilities. For Greenblatt as well the scholar must deal above all with possibility, with what he calls 'the possibility of literature.' He writes: 'literary history is always the history of the possibility of literature.' This absolutely abyssal phrase is inscribed twice in the essay as if in answer to the ontological question of its title: 'What is the History of Literature?' It suggests that, even though this historical critic aligns himself in the most traditional way with romantic criticism, for which ghosts are only figments of one's own imagination, even though he finds there the benefit of joining the chief school of criticism under its apotropaic armor, he may be no less ready to welcome a new scholar of possibilities. Indeed, I would say that he too is issuing an urgent call to reread *Hamlet*, and quite a few other texts, from the place of Marcellus, in the spirit, as we say, of Marcellus.

Conversely, I would argue that Derrida's gesture of inheriting not only *Hamlet* but everything that follows in European and American letters, all the visor effects or school effects conditioning the power relations called history, is a critical gesture. It is, in other words, a gesture that would respond to Marcellus by speaking to the ghosts that appear to appear behind a visor. The gesture is critical insofar as it remarks the apparatus raised and lowered at the limit between the scholar and that which he can know, that which he can teach and learn in school. But if it would also be more than that or other than that, if it would be deconstructive and not just critical-skeptical, if it would, in other words, deconstruct as well the traditional scholar's skepticism at the idea that one can speak to ghosts without first checking their ontological identity, then it will have to multiply the scenes of inheritance: of Shakespeare, of Marx, of literature, of Marxism, and thus of quite a few others. It will have to turn its critical armor into the shield of plurality, of the more than one/other than one: 'le plus d'un/le plus d'un …' And, as well, the 'plus d'une': more than one translation, no more of one translation.

NOTES

1. See Geoffrey Bennington's essays on Kant and frontiers: 'La frontière infranchissable,' in *Le passage des frontières: Autour du travail de Jacques Derrida*, ed. Marie-Louise Mallet (Paris: Galilée, 1994), and 'The Frontier Between Kant and Hegel,' in Bennington, *Legislations: The Politics of Deconstruction* (London: Verso, 1994).
2. See Derrida's characterization of Marx's own distinction between *Geist* and *Gespenst* as regards Hegelian idealism: 'For there is no ghost, there is never any becoming-specter of the spirit without at least an appearance of flesh, in a space of invisible visibility, like the dis-appearing of an apparition. For there to be ghost, there must be a return to the body, but to a body that is more abstract than ever. The spectrogenic process corresponds to a paradoxical incorporation.' *Specters of Marx: The State of the Debt, the Work of Mourning, and the New International*, trans. Peggy Kamuf (New York: Routledge, 1994), p. 126.
3. See my 'Violence, Identity, Self-Determination, and the Question of Justice: On *Specters of Marx*,' in Hent De Vries and Samuel Weber, eds., *Violence, Identity, Self-Determination* (Stanford: Stanford University Press, 1997).
4. I have done so in an unpublished essay, 'Undying Literature,' delivered at University of Wales, Cardiff, May, 1998.
5. Stephen Greenblatt, 'What is the History of Literature?' in *Critical Inquiry*, vol. 23, no. 3, Spring 1997, p. 478.
6. Greenblatt has earlier situated his essay as a response to just such a call for renewal: 'the time has come,' he writes, 'to renew on our own terms … the reason, if we have one, to study literature' (462).

See also:

Gasché (3.3)
Royle (7.4)
Weber (7.3)
Maley (8.2)

PART 5
CULTURE

5.1

'DECONSTRUCTION IS NOT WHAT YOU THINK'

Geoffrey Bennington

1.   Deconstruction is not what you think.

[...]

1.3.   Deconstruction is not what you think. If what you think is a content, present to mind, in 'the mind's presence-room' (Locke). But that you think might already be Deconstruction.

2.   Deconstruction is not (what you think if you think it is) essentially to do with language.

2.1.   Nothing more common than to hear Deconstruction described as depending on 'an extension of the linguistic paradigm'. 'There is nothing outside the text' (Derrida): proves it, obviously.

2.1.1. Everybody also knows this is not quite right. 'Text' is not quite an extension of a familiar concept, but a displacement or reinscription of it. Text in general is any system of marks, traces, referrals (don't say reference, have a little more sense than that). Perception is a text.

2.2.   Think of recognition. Two requirements: that the object of recognition be in principle repeatable as the same object in a different context; that in the given context it be identifiable as different from the other elements of that context. (If it helps, think of the first as a temporal requirement, the second as spatial: but space and time do not determine the text, they are made possible by it.)

Source: Geoffrey Bennington, 'Deconstruction is not what you think', *Art and Design*, 4 (3/4), 1988, pp. 6–7.

2.2.1. Presence would be that there be no difference, nor referral, no trace. Which is impossible. So presence would not be were there no difference, or referral, or trace. Presence is made possible by the trace, which makes pure presence impossible: each present moment is essentially constituted by its retention of a trace of a past moment. This is just as true of the 'first' present moment as of any other, which thereby has a relation with a past that never was present: absolute past.

2.3. 'Referral' is not reference in the linguistic sense. Deconstruction does not have a place for language over here, and a world over there to which it refers. Elements in the language refer to one another for their identity, and refer to non-linguistic marks which refer in turn for their identity and difference. There is no essential difference between language and the world, the one as subject, the other as object. There are traces.

2.3.1. Think of Deconstruction as extending the world paradigm if you like. It makes no difference, so long as you don't think of the world set up out there over against.

2.4. Of course text does not mean discourse. Perception is not a discourse, it is a text. Discourse is a text. (But nobody thinks you can separate Deconstruction from language. Nor from the world. Text is not a mediation between language and world, but the *milieu* in which any such distinction might be drawn.)

3. Deconstruction is not a theory or a project. It does not prescribe a practice more or less faithful to it, nor project an image of a desirable state to be brought about.

3.1. Deconstruction is necessary.

[...]

4. Painting. Not just that painting is probably unthinkable without language. Certainly not that painting is 'like a language'. But there's no trouble thinking about painting as difference and trace. The 'event of presence' (Lyotard) which a painting presents would be quite unpresentable otherwise.

4.1. A painting is a text, of course. The problem is that of knowing what sort of text. Deconstruction is not at all to do with treating a painting like a 'written' text, 'reading' it etc. (Unless 'reading' is displaced in the same way as text.)

4.1.1. Reading is not a simple process of deciphering, nor of interpreting, for Deconstruction. It is neither entirely respectful nor simply violent. 'Secure production of insecurity' (Derrida). Reading is not performed by a subject set against the text as object: reading is imbricated in the text it reads. Leave a trace in the text if you can.

4.2. Write about the way painting has been written about (in its supposed relation to the truth, especially), more on painting's side than on the attempts to speak its truth. That's one thing to do.

4.3.   But be very careful before writing on painting.

4.3.1.   Writing on painting is easy if you think writing and painting don't mix. So long as painting's not writing and writing's not painting, easy enough to keep writing (or painting). But it's just as bad to think that writing and painting are simply the same sort of thing (*ut pictura poesis*).

4.3.2.   But in the referrals of the text, the security of the divisions gives way and with it the security of the passages across those divisions. It's not great drama to cross a frontier so long as you know where it is.

4.3.3.   Writing can no doubt do things painting can't, and vice versa. But don't make too much of iterability and ideality on the side of writing, singularity and materiality on the side of painting. Of course there are differences between a literary text and a painting: but the latter is also essentially reproducible. The age of mechanical reproduction (Benjamin) does not befall painting like a catastrophe: aura is always already being lost.

[...]

5.   Colour. Where is the colour in Deconstruction?

5.1.   Colour is a question of differential values, and therefore traces. This is not a point about colour vocabulary, but about colour. Deconstruction is not linguistic relativism. Colour is, in Deconstruction.

[...]

6.   'Deconstructionist painting' could not be the result of a successful 'application' of Derrida's theory (see 3.)

6.1.   Deconstruction in painting has always already begun.

6.2.   Of course painting can be 'influenced' by Derrida's writing. This does not *ipso facto* make it 'Deconstructive'.

6.2.1.   It is quite possible that the most 'Deconstructive' painting should (have) happen(ed) in ignorance of Derrida's work, though knowledge of Derrida's work might help us to talk about that painting, and others.

[...]

7.   A painting could try to be a 'reading' of texts by Derrida. Adami. Leave a trace in the text if you can.

See also:

Derrida (2.1)
Norris (3.1)
Bennington (3.4)
Elam (6.1)

5.2

'DERRIDA, ARCHITECTURE AND PHILOSOPHY'

Andrew Benjamin

The history of philosophy has always demonstrated a two-fold concern with architecture. The first is by philosophy either addressing architecture as an aesthetic form (e.g. in Hegel's *Aesthetics*), or deploying architectural examples in a more general discussion of aesthetics or art (e.g. Heidegger's discussion of the Greek temple in *The Origin of the Work of Art*). The second is the presence of architectural forms (e.g. Kant's architectonic) or architectural metaphors in the development or construction of a philosophical argument. The second of these is, in this instance, the more relevant. To delimit a specific terrain of discussion into which Derrida's writings on architecture can be articulated, I will concentrate on the justly famous architectural metaphor developed by Descartes in the second part of the *Discourse on Method*. Despite the length of this passage I will quote it in full in order that its force may be made clear:

> ... there is not usually so much perfection in works composed of several parts and produced by different craftsmen as in the works of one man. Thus we see that buildings undertaken and completed by a single architect are usually more attractive and better planned than those which several have tried to patch up by adapting old walls built for different purposes. Again, ancient cities which have gradually grown up from mere villages into large towns are usually ill proportioned, compared with those orderly towns which planners lay out as they fancy on level ground. Looking at buildings of the former individually, you will often find as much art in

Source: Andrew Benjamin, 'Derrida, architecture and philosophy', *Architectural Design*, 58 (3/4), 1988, pp. 8–12.

them if not more than in those of the latter; but in view of their arrangement – a tall one here, a small one there – and the way they make the streets crooked and irregular you would say it is chance rather than the will of men using reason, that placed them so. And when you consider that there have always been certain officials whose job it is to see that private buildings embellish public places you will understand how difficult it is to make something perfect by working only on what others have produced.[1]

This passage refers, if only initially, to Descartes' attempt to justify both his own philosophical project as well as establishing the necessity of its being undertaken by a single philosopher working alone. Descartes is attempting neither a reworking nor a refurbishing of past philosophy but a radical departure that thereby establishes a new and original philosophical system. Descartes' aim therefore is two-fold. On the one hand he wants to establish a total and unified system, and, on the other, one that breaks fundamentally with past philosophical systems (in particular, of course, the Scholastics) and is thus not tainted by earlier mistakes and prejudices. It is this two-fold aim that is expressed in his metaphor of the activity of architects and builders.

The elaborate metaphor opens with a juxtaposition of the one and the many. Works produced by one craftsman have a greater degree of 'perfection' than those produced by a number. Buildings designed and built by a single architect are, as a consequence, far more attractive than buildings whose refurbishing has involved the participation of a collection of architects working over a number of years and inevitably with different intentions. Having made this point Descartes then extends the range of the metaphor, moving from a single construction to a city. Here the contrast is between a city which has developed through time, through consecutive and perhaps overlapping stages and which therefore contains ill-proportioned and irregular components, and a city or town conceived and built within an extended single moment. The force of this opposition is then reinforced by the further opposition between chance and reason. If there is anything attractive about the buildings, or even the quarters of an ancient city, then it is the result of chance. The beauty of a city designed and built during the single extended moment is the result of the application of reason. Before taking up the important opposition between reason and chance, it is essential to dwell on this single extended moment.

The moment is the enactment of that which reason dictates. The regulation of reason extends through the conception, the enactment and its completion. Reason has what could amount to a universal and to that extent an atemporal extension. The singularity of the construction (a singularity excluding plurality), the singularity of the architect (excluding pluralism and thereby erecting the architect as God – one replacing the other within similar hierarchic principles) is reinscribed within the singularity of this moment.

The lack of order in the ancient city is marked by – as well as being the mark of – the lack of reason. It has the consequence that not only is the city in some sense 'mad',[2] it can also be thought within the totalising purview of reason, except of course as mad. Therefore when taken to its logical extreme the architectural metaphor indicates both the possibility of a unified totality – to be provided by the application of reason – as well as that which stands opposed to this possibility, namely, madness; presented here as the untotalisable plurality of the ancient city. The opposition between reason and madness is introduced by, and within, an architectural metaphor.

The triumph of reason over madness, Descartes is insisting, is the path to be followed by the philosopher as architect and the architect as philosopher. The activity of each is delimited not by reason as such, but by the oppositions between reason and chance, and reason and madness. There is of course an imperative within Descartes' metaphor. It indicates his understanding of the philosophical task. For Descartes the totality and necessary unity engendered by reason can be attained. Within the metaphor the old city can be razed to the ground. The new city will emerge without bearing the traces of the old. There will be no traces of the old to be remarked. As will be seen it is precisely the possibility of the absence of any remark, or rather the impossibility of its absence that is taken up, amongst other things, when Derrida writes of 'maintaining'. The chance of architecture is maintained by the 'interruption' between the traditional and the affirmative. This point will be pursued.

There are two important components of Descartes' architectural metaphor and the ensuing philosophical practice to which it gives rise. The first is the functional opposition between reason and chance (reason and madness). The second, far more difficult to discern, involves the opposition between the inside and the outside. The metaphor of the city, in order that it further Descartes' philosophical end, must be understood as a structured space, and therefore as a place to be re-deployed in the construction of the city of reason. Furthermore it must be constructed to allow the philosopher or architect the possibility of a place outside its own wall. Regulation and control must take place from the outside. The metaphor of the city is therefore also ensnared within the further opposition of inside and outside (as well as the one between theory and practice). I want to develop these two elements.

The intriguing element that can be seen to emerge from within the metaphor of the city is the implicit recognition that if the city of reason has an outside, then it is madness. The haphazard chance of *déraison* is constrained to take place outside the city walls. The consequence of this is that the architect must be written into the city in order to avoid madness and yet the philosopher or architect must be outside the gates in order to exert control. The architectonic needs to be regulated from outside. Present here is the problem of the before and in front of. The philosopher (or architect) would seem therefore to be placed – and to have placed themselves – within a double-bind, that can, in historical terms, perhaps only be resolved by God.

The importance of the description of the opposition between reason and chance (reason and madness) as functional lies in the fact that it indicates that the opposition is neither arbitrary nor simply a result or conclusion, but plays a structuring role in the text. However in the present context it is the second component that is the more relevant. In spatial terms the distinction between the inside and the outside is perhaps best understood in relation to the labyrinth. The labyrinth is obviously the sign of the city. It is also the sign of writing.[3] Both the labyrinth and writing are concerned with, if only because they give rise to, firstly the problem of the place, and secondly an epistemology of the place. A philosophy of totality and unity positions itself, of necessity, outside the place – outside the labyrinth and writing – and as such, knowledge is invariably linked to the transcendental. In Cartesian terms this distinction finds its most adequate formulation in terms of the distinction between the understanding and the imagination. Only the understanding working with transcendental rules can determine and yield certainty. The understanding is always positioned outside and then comes to be applied in the world. This is not to suggest that for Descartes knowledge is empirical; rather knowledge is of the empirical. The conditions for the possibility of knowledge – the method to be applied and the rules governing clear and distinct perception, etc. – are themselves transcendental. The imagination on the other hand is trapped in the labyrinth. The problem of the imagination is that in itself it lacks a limit. The imagination is essential for knowledge but only when its results can be controlled by the understanding. For Descartes the typology of consciousness necessitates a divide between the domain of the understanding and the domain of the imagination. It is clear that this distinction – one that is repeated and reinforced in other of his writings in terms of the distinction between the understanding and the will – has specific ontological and temporal considerations.

In tracing the implications of the architectural metaphor in Descartes' *Discourse on Method* what has emerged is a series of oppositions that play a structuring role within the presentation of his philosophical position. It is quite literally constructed in terms of them. It is of course precisely in relation to these oppositions that the force of Deconstruction can be located. It is by tracing through their implications – allowing their unstable logic to unfold – that the work of Deconstruction begins to take place. Derrida details this aspect of Deconstruction in the following terms:

> De-construction ... analyses and compares conceptual pairs which are currently accepted as self-evident and natural, as if they had not been institutionalised at some precise moment, as if they had no history. Because of being taken for granted they restrict thinking.[4]

Deconstruction, in this instance, is therefore a beginning. However, Deconstruction is not the simple reversal of the dominant term within an opposition. This becomes increasingly clear in Derrida's writing on the work of Bernard Tschumi.[5] A fundamental strategy of that paper (*Point de folie – Maintenant l'architecture*) is the retention of both madness and chance and yet they are not part of a simple opposition. They are not merely the other side of reason.

The work of Tschumi under consideration by Derrida is his plan of the *Parc de la Villette*, and in particular a series of constructions within the park known as *Les Folies*. Of this title, name, signature, Derrida makes the important point that they are not 'madness (*la folie*), the allegorical hypostasis of Unreason, non-sense, but the madnesses (*les folies*)'. In sum what makes Derrida's writings on architecture of particular interest is the way he tries to indicate in what sense a philosphical argument or position can be incorporated into a different activity. Two elements need to be stated in advance. The first is that Derrida is emphatic that despite appearances Deconstruction is not itself an architectural metaphor. Not only is he suspicious of metaphors; it is also the case that Deconstruction does not amount to a simple dismantling, it is at the same time – and in the Nietzschean sense – affirmative.

The second point is that logocentrism is evident in the way in which architecture, habitation, dwelling, living, etc. are understood within both philo-sophical and architectural thinking. It is the evident presence and structural force of logocentrism that provides a possible entry for Deconstruction. It enters via the rearticulation of metaphysics. It is of course a rearticulation that is housed architecturally and yet extends beyond architecture. It is at home in the history of Western metaphysics. As Derrida suggests, the 'architectonics of invariable points . . . regulates all of what is called Western culture, far beyond its architecture.' However it also takes place – and finds a place – in its architecture. It is this that makes a Deconstruction of architectural thinking possible. It is furthermore what makes an affirmative architecture possible. Derrida says of Tschumi's *folies* that they: '. . . affirm, and engage their affirma-tion beyond this ultimately annihilating, secretly nihilistic repetition of meta-physical architecture.'[6]

There is an interesting parallel here between Derrida's discussion of archi-tecture and his discussion of literature. Without returning to the question – what is literature? – it is essential to point out that in Derrida's work there is no privileging of the literary as opposed to the philosophical. Both can be and usually are logocentric. They are both sites, inhabitated and constructed by the repetition of metaphysics. For Derrida literature is something to-come. It is this element that he locates in the work of the French writer Roger Laporte. Derrida writes of his work *Fugue* that '. . . in inscribing itself in an historically, libid-inally, economically, politically determined field . . . no meta-language is powerful enough today to dominate the progress [*la marche*] or rather the un-folding [*la dé-marche*] of this writing.'[7] He goes on to add: '*Fugue* . . . takes away in advance all metalinguistic resources and makes of this quasi-operation an unheard music outside of genre.'[8]

Taking into consideration Derrida's own writings on genre[9] his Decon-struction of the possibility of genres as all-inclusive – further serves to indicate that in the place of texts dominated by logocentrism and which therefore count as a rearticulation of metaphysics, as well as themselves being inscribed within 'conceptual pairs', Laporte's text *Fugue* is, in the sense alluded to above, affirmative. It is *as* a work – and *in* its work – the literature to-come. There is therefore, within Derrida's own philosophical undertaking, an important connection between the works/writings of Tschumi and Laporte. Their futural dimension, their being works to-come, is located in their connection to that which proceeded. The hinge connecting them marks a type of sublation.

What has to be traced in Derrida's understanding of Tschumi is this affirmative dimension. The point of departure is provided by the oppositions between reason and chance, and reason and madness. It is already clear in what sense these 'conceptual pairs' are operative in Descartes' architectural metaphor. The question is how are madness and chance taken over by Derrida?

The first point to note is that Tschumi's *folies* are not, as has already been mentioned, simply the other side of reason. They are marked by the opposition reason/madness and yet not articulated in terms of it. Connected to the act of affirmation is the equally important process of what could be called a form of displacement or distancing. The process of distancing is found in Derrida's description of the *folies*:

> Tschumi's 'first' concern will no longer be to organise space as a function or in view of economic, aesthetic, epiphanic, or techno-utilitarian norms. These norms will be taken into consideration, but they will find themselves subordinated and reinscribed in one place in a text and in a space that they no longer command in the final instance. By pushing architecture towards its limits, a place will be made for 'pleasure'; each *folie* will be destined for a given 'use', with its own cultural, ludic, pedagogical, scientific and philosophical finalities.[10]

The distancing or displacement – and indeed the hinge marking or remarking their connection to logocentrism/metaphysics/ 'conceptual pairs' – is captured by Derrida when he writes of 'norms' being 'taken into consideration'; being 'reinscribed'; present but no longer in 'command'. Norms become, in Nietzsche's sense, 'fictions'[11] – thereby opening up, though always in a way to be determined, the possibility gestured at in what Derrida calls 'trans-architecture'.

Distancing is still connective. There is no pure beyond. In any adventure there is still the remark. The Cartesian desire for the absolutely new, for the completely unique, is, for Derrida, an impossibility. It forms part of logo-centrism's desire for a self-enclosed totality. The remark can always be remarked upon. It is in terms of 'maintaining' that this interplay is described. In addition however it is also exemplified, stylistically, in the aphorisms which Derrida chose to preface a collection of recent papers on philosophy and architecture. The uniqueness and self-referring nature of the aphorism is deconstructed via that aphorism itself. Self-reference is an impossibility. Perhaps even the act of citing the following aphorism (its citation rather than its contents, especially as it is incomplete) is sufficient to make this point:

An authentic aphorism must never refer to another. It is sufficient unto itself; world or monad. But whether it is wanted or not, whether one sees it or not, the aphorisms interlink here as aphorisms, and in number, numbered. Their series yields to an *irreversible* order ... [12]

Derrida locates the work of Tschumi within a paradox and also within the *maintenant*. The presence of what could be described as a logic of paradox within Derrida's work is too large a theme to be taken up here. It is, however, at work in his discussion of Tschumi. When, for example, he argues that the 'red points' (deployed by Tschumi as part of his project) both disperse and gather, they become and articulate this logic. However the dispersal and gathering is held together and is maintained: 'The red points space, maintaining architecture in the dissociation of spacing. But this *maintenant* does not only maintain a past and a tradition: it does not ensure a synthesis. It maintains the interruption, in other words the relation to the other *per se*.' [13] It is of course precisely in terms of 'maintaining' that an affirmative conception of architecture is allowed to take place. Furthermore it is one that involves and deploys chance and madness in the 'interruption' with the 'conceptual pairs' within which the history of philosophy has placed them. Chance becomes the wager. And madness, that which by a fascinating etymological gamble is freed from one madness, becomes, amongst other things, the 'madness of an asemantics'. The importance of chance lies in its breaking of a conceptual closure. 'Disassociation' takes place – yet it takes place in the 'space of reassembly'. Maintained, it could be argued, within a logic of paradox.

The oppositions within which Descartes' architectural metaphor took place are no longer either authoritative or central. Madness and chance have been freed not just from their subordinate place within those oppositions, they have also emerged as affirmative 'concepts' within which to think the possibility of a Deconstructive architecture. The nature – and, it must be added, a nature beyond essentialism – of such an architecture is described by Peter Eisenman in the following way:

> What is being proposed is an expansion beyond the limitation presented by the classical mode to the realisation of architecture as an independent discourse, free from external values; that is, the intersection of the meaningful, the arbitrary and the timeless in the artificial. [14]

The challenge presented by Deconstruction to architecture is the 'same' as the challenge it presents to all the arts, and of course to philosophy, literary criticism, etc. It is a challenge that, initially, takes place on the level of thinking; here in the example of architecture thinking maintaining. Thinking that comes to be enacted – or can be seen to be enacted – in the architectural work of Eisenman and Tschumi amongst others.

Having come this far it is worth pausing to try and place Deconstruction before architecture, or architectural thinking before Deconstruction. In either case the 'before' does not mark the presence of a universal and transcendental law – e.g. the work of the understanding within the Cartesian texts, or Hegelian 'absolute knowledge' – that would regulate architecture or Deconstruction as philosophy. Does Deconstruction allow for what within traditional aesthetics is of fundamental philosophical importance; namely, evaluation? Derrida has tried to delimit the relationship between Deconstruction and architectural thinking: 'Architectural thinking can only be Deconstructive in the following sense: as an attempt to visualise that which establishes the authority of the architectural concatenation in philosophy.'[15]

The 'architectural concatenation' is itself repeated within the history of metaphysics. A repetition that is found throughout the texts – and in part structures the texts – that are included within the history of philosophy. (It has been observed in Descartes' *Discourse on Method*, though it could just have easily been traced in a diverse range of texts, including Aristotle, Kant, Hegel and Heidegger.) Its authority is precisely the object of Deconstruction. Deconstructed authority is retained but without its authority, although when it comes to the question of evaluation, the criteria are themselves articulated in terms of that authority. In *The Critique of Judgement* Kant subsumes the evaluation of architecture under the rubric of design which is then joined to taste. Taste becomes the universal and self-referential form of legitimation working before, during and after the construction: 'In painting, sculpture, and in fact in all the formative arts, in architecture and horticulture, so far as fine arts, the design is what is essential. Here it is not what gratifies in sensation but merely what pleases by its form, that is the fundamental prerequisite for taste.'[16]

In other words the vocabulary of evaluation – the language of aesthetics – does itself form part of the philosophical architectonic. The consequence of this is that if there is to be a language of evaluation stemming from Deconstruction then it will necessitate what Nietzsche described as a 'revaluation of all values'. Even though Derrida may appear to privilege the uniqueness of a specific work, this is not a recourse to a fundamental pragmatism. In fact the thing/event can never be unique and self-referential; hence gathering and dispersal; hence *maintenant/maintenir*; hence the always already-present remark. A Deconstructive aesthetic and the plurality of a Deconstructive criteria for evaluation are yet to be written. Derrida's writings on architecture, while on architecture, are also an aesthetics to-come. The potential for a Deconstructive aesthetics is to that extent always already written.

NOTES

1. R. Descartes, 'Discourse on Method', in *The Philosophical Writings of Descartes*, Vol 1, Cambridge University Press, 1985, p 116.
2. Derrida has written a number of texts on 'madness', including critiques of Foucault's *Madness and Civilisation* and Blanchot's *La folie du jour*.
3. Derrida makes similar points in an interview, 'Architetture ove il desiderio può abitare', *Domus*, No 671, April 1986. While it is perhaps a transgression, I have rewritten some of the arguments he presents so as to link them with more general, if not conventional, philosophical concerns. Perhaps, again, this is translation as transgression.

4. A point made by Derrida in the above-mentioned interview.
5. 'Point de folie', trans Kate Linker, *AA Files*, No 12, 1986.
6. *ibid*, p 69.
7. J. Derrida, 'Ce qui reste à force de musique', *Psyché*, Galilée, 1987, p 96, (my trans). For an amplification of the point made about literature see R. Gasché, *The Tain of the Mirror*, Harvard University Press, 1986, pp 255–318. I have discussed the importance of Gasché's book in 'Naming Deconstruction', *History of the Human Sciences*, Vol 1, No 2, 1988.
8. *ibid*, p 96.
9. J. Derrida, 'The Law of Genre', *Glyph*, 7, 1980.
10. Derrida, *op cit*, p 69.
11. See F. Nietzsche, *Beyond Good and Evil*, trans by W. Kaufman, Vantage Books, New York, 1966, Section 21.
12. J. Derrida, 'Cinquante-deux aphorismes pour un avant-propos', *Psyché*, Galilée, 1987, p 513 (my trans). This text formed the preface to *Mesure pour mesure: Architecture et philosophie*, Cahiers du CCI (Centre Georges Pompidou), 1987, a book emerging from a meeting between philosophers and architects organised by the Centre International de Philosophie.
13. Derrida, *op cit*, p 75.
14. P. Eisenman, 'The End of the Classical', *Perspecta*, No 21, 1984. Derrida has written on Eisenman in, 'Pourquoi Peter Eisenman écrit de si bons livres', *Psyché*, pp 496–508. For an introduction to Eisenman's work see *Investigations in Architecture: Eisenman Studies at the GSD: 1983–85*, Harvard University, 1986, and P. Eisenman, *Fin d'Ou T Hou S*, Architectural Association, 1985.
15. See the interview with Derrida mentioned above.
16. I. Kant, *The Critique of Judgement*, trans J. Meredith, Oxford University Press, 1986, p 67.

See also:

Norris (3.1).
Lyotard (3.6)
Wills (7.5)
Bernasconi (9.2)

5.3

'VIOLENCE OF ARCHITECTURE'

Bernard Tschumi

There is no architecture without action, no architecture without events, no architecture without program. By extension, there is no architecture without violence.

The first of these statements runs against the mainstream of contemporary architectural thought, whether 'modernist' or 'post-modernist,' by refusing to favor space at the expense of action. The second statement argues that although the logic of objects and the logic of man are independent in their relations to the world, they inevitably face one another in an intense confrontation. Any relationship between a building and its users is one of violence, for any use means the intrusion of a human body into a given space, the intrusion of one order into another. This intrusion is inherent in the idea of architecture; any reduction of architecture to its spaces at the expense of its events is as simplistic as the reduction of architecture to its facades.

By 'violence,' I do not mean the brutality that destroys physical or emotional integrity, but a metaphor for the intensity of a relationship between individuals and their surrounding spaces. The argument is not a matter of style: 'modern' architecture is neither more nor less violent than classical architecture, or than Fascist, Socialist or vernacular variations. Architecture's violence is fundamental and unavoidable, for architecture is linked to events in the same way that the guard is linked to his prisoner, the police to the criminal, the doctor to the patient, order to chaos. This also suggests that actions qualify spaces as much as spaces qualify actions; that space and action are inseparable and that

Source: Bernard Tschumi, 'Violence of architecture', *Artforum*, 20(1), September 1981, pp. 44–7.

no proper interpretation of architecture, drawing or notation can refuse to consider this fact.

What must first be determined is whether this relation between action and space is symmetrical – opposing two camps (people versus spaces) that affect one another in a comparable way – or asymmetrical, a relation in which one camp, whether space or people, clearly dominates the other.

BODIES VIOLATING SPACE

First, there is the violence that all individuals inflict on spaces by their very presence, by their intrusion into the controlled order of architecture. Entering a building may be a delicate act, but it violates the balance of a precisely ordered geometry (do architectural photographs ever include runners, fighters, lovers?). Bodies carve all sorts of new and unexpected spaces, through fluid or erratic motions. Architecture, then, is only an organism engaged in constant inter-course with users, whose bodies rush against the carefully established rules of architectural thought. No wonder the human body has always been suspect in architecture: it has always set limits to the most extreme architectural ambi-tions. The body disturbs the purity of architectural order. It is equivalent to a dangerous prohibition.

Violence is not always present. Just as riots, brawls, insurrections, and revolutions are of limited duration, so is the violence a body commits against space. Yet it is always implicit. Each door implies the movement of someone crossing its frame. Each corridor implies the progression of movement that blocks it. Each architectural space implies (and desires) the intruding presence that will inhabit it.

SPACE VIOLATING BODIES

But if bodies violate the purity of architectural spaces, one might rightly wonder about the reverse: the violence inflicted by narrow corridors on large crowds, the symbolic or physical violence of buildings on users. A word of warning: I do not wish to resurrect recent behaviorist architectural approaches. Instead, I wish simply to underline the mere existence of a physical presence and the fact that it begins quite innocently, in an *imaginary* sort of way.

The place your body inhabits is inscribed in your imagination, your uncon-scious, as a space of possible bliss. Or menace. What if you are forced to abandon your imaginary spatial markings? A torturer wants you, the victim, to regress, because he wants to demean his prey, to make you lose your identity as a subject. Suddenly you have no choice; running away is impossible. The rooms are too small or too big, the ceilings too low or too high. Violence exercised by and through space is spatial torture.

Take Palladio's Villa Rotonda. You walk through one of its axes and as you cross the central space and reach its other side you find, instead of the hillside landscape, the steps of another Villa Rotonda, and another, and another, and another. The incessant repetition at first stimulates some strange desire, but soon becomes sadistic, impossible, violent.

Such discomforting spatial devices can take any form: the white anechoic chambers of sensory deprivation, the formless spaces leading to psychological destructuring. Steep and dangerous staircases, those corridors consciously made too narrow for crowds, introduce a radical shift from architecture as an object of contemplation to architecture as a perverse instrument of use. At the same time it must be stressed that the receiving subject – you or I – may wish to be subjected to such spatial aggression, just as you may go to a rock concert and stand close enough to the loudspeakers to sustain painful – but pleasurable – physical or psychic trauma. Places aimed at the cult of excessive sound only suggest places aimed at the cult of excessive space. The love of violence, after all, is an ancient pleasure.

Why has architectural theory regularly refused to acknowledge such pleasures and always claimed (at least officially) that architecture should be pleasing to the eye, as well as comfortable to the body? This presupposition seems curious when the pleasure of violence can be experienced in every other human activity, from the violence of discordant sounds in music to the clash of bodies in sports, from gangster movies to the Marquis de Sade.

VIOLENCE RITUALIZED

Who will mastermind these exquisite spatial delights, these disturbing architectural tortures, the tortuous paths of promenades through delirious landscapes, theatrical events where actor complements decor? Who ...? The architect? By the seventeenth century, Bernini had staged whole spectacles, followed by Mansart's fêtes for Louis XIV and Albert Speer's sinister and beautiful rallies. After all, the original action, the original act of violence – this unspeakable copulating of live body and dead stone – is unique and unrehearsed, though perhaps infinitely repeatable, for you may enter the building again and again. The architect will always dream of purifying this uncontrolled violence, channeling obedient bodies along predictable paths and occasionally along ramps that provide striking vistas, ritualizing the transgression of bodies in space. Le Corbusier's Carpenter Center, with its ramp that violates the building, is a genuine movement of bodies made into an architectural solid. Or the reverse: it is a solid that forcibly channels the movement of bodies.

The original, spontaneous interaction of the body with a space is often purified by ritual. Sixteenth-century pageants and the reenactment of the storming of the Winter Palace in Leningrad, for example, are ritualistic imitations of spontaneous violence. Endlessly repeated, these rituals curb all aspects of the original act that have escaped control: the choice of time and place, the selection of the victim ...

A ritual implies a near-frozen relationship between action and space. It institutes a new order after the disorder of the original event. When it becomes necessary to mediate tension and fix it by custom, then no single fragment must escape attention. Nothing strange and unexpected must happen. Control must be absolute.

Such control is, of course, not likely to be achieved. Few regimes would survive if architects were to program every single movement of Individual and society in a kind of ballet mécanique of architecture, a permanent Nuremberg Rally of everyday life, a puppet theater of spatial intimacy. Nor would they survive if every spontaneous movement were immediately frozen into a solid corridor. The relationship is more subtle and moves beyond the question of power beyond the question of whether architecture dominates events, or vice versa. The relationship, then, is as symmetrical as the ineluctable one between guard and prisoner, hunter and hunted. But both the hunter and the hunted also have basic needs to consider, which may not relate to the hunt: sustenance, food, shelter, etc. Hunter and hunted enjoy these needs independent of the fact that they are engaged in a deadly game. They are respectively self-sufficient. Only when they confront each other's reality are their strategies so totally interdependent that it becomes impossible to determine which one initiates and which one responds. The same happens with architecture and the way buildings relate to their users, or spaces relate to events or programs. For any organized repetition of events, once announced in advance, becomes a program, a descriptive notice of a formal series of proceedings.

When spaces and programs are largely independent of one another; one observes a strategy of indifference in which architectural considerations do not depend on utilitarian ones, in which space has one logic and events another. Such were the Crystal Palace and the neutral sheds of the 19th-century's Great Exhibitions, which accommodated anything from displays of elephants draped in rare colonial silks to international boxing matches. Such, too – but in a very different manner – was Gerrit Rietveld's house in Utrecht, a remarkable exercise in architectural language, and a not unpleasant house to live in, despite, or perhaps because of the fortuitous juxtaposition of space and use.

At other times, architectural spaces and programs can become totally interdependent and fully condition each other's existence. In these cases, the architect's view of the user's needs determines every architectural decision (which may, in turn, determine the user's attitude). The architect designs the set, writes the script, and directs the actors. Such were the ideal kitchen installations of the twenties' Werkbund, each step of a near-biochemical housewife carefully monitored by the design's constant attention. Such were Meyerhold's biomechanics, acting through Popova's stage sets, where the characters' logic played with and against the logic of their dynamic surroundings. Such also is Frank Lloyd Wright's Guggenheim Museum. It is not a question of knowing which comes first, movement or space, which molds the other, for ultimately a deep bond is involved. After all, they are caught in the same set of relationships; only the arrow of power changes direction.

(If I outline these two relations of independence and interdependence, it is to insist on the fact that they exist regardless of the prescriptive ideologies – modernism versus humanism, formalism versus functionalism, etc. – which architects and critics are usually keen to promote.)

Most relations, of course, stand somewhere in between. You can sleep in your kitchen. And fight and love. These shifts are not without meaning. When the typology of an 18th-century prison is turned into a 20th-century city hall, the shift inevitably suggests a critical statement about institutions. When an industrial loft in Manhattan is turned into a residence, a similar shift occurs, a shift that is undoubtedly less dramatic. Spaces are qualified by actions just as actions are qualified by spaces. One does not trigger the other; they exist independently. Only when they intersect do they affect one another. Remember Kuleshov's experiment where the same shot of the actor's impassible face is introduced into a variety of situations, and the audience reads different expressions into each successive juxtaposition. The same occurs in architecture: the event is altered by each new space. And vice versa: by ascribing to a given, supposedly 'autonomous' space a contradictory program, the space attains new levels of meaning. Event and space do not merge, but affect one another. Similarly, if the Sistine Chapel were used for pole-vaulting events, architecture would then cease to yield to its customary good intentions. For a while the transgression would be real and all-powerful. Yet the transgression of cultural expectations soon becomes accepted. Just as violent Surrealist collages inspire advertising rhetoric, the broken rule is integrated into everyday life, whether through symbolic or technological motivations.

If violence is the key metaphor for the intensity of a relationship, then the very physicality of architecture transcends the metaphor. There is a deep sensuality, an unremittent eroticism in architecture. Its underlying violence varies according to the forces that are put into play – rational forces, irrational forces. They can be deficient or excessive. Little activity – hypo-activity – in a house can be as disturbing as hyper-activity. Asceticism and orgiastic excesses are closer than architectural theorists have admitted, and the asceticism of Gerrit Rietveld's or Ludwig Wittgenstein's house inevitably implies the most extreme bacchanals. (Cultural expectations merely affect the perception of violence, but do not alter its nature; slapping your lover's face is perceived differently from culture to culture.)

Architecture and events constantly transgress each other's rules, whether explicitly or implicitly. These rules, these organized compositions, may be questioned, but they always remain points of reference. A building is a point of reference for the activities set to negate it. A theory of architecture is a theory of order threatened by the very use it permits. And vice versa.

The integration of the concept of violence into the architectural mechanism – the purpose of my argument – is ultimately aimed at a new pleasure of architecture. Like any form of violence, the violence of architecture also contains the possibility of change, of renewal. Like any violence, the violence of architecture is deeply Dionysian. It should be understood, and its contradictions maintained in a dynamic manner, with their conflicts and complementarity.

In passing, two types of partial violence should be distinguished, types which are *not* specifically architectural. The first is *formal violence*, which deals with the conflicts between objects. Such is the violence of form versus form, the violence of Giovanni Battista Piranesi's juxtapositions. Kurt Schwitters' Merz-bau collages and other architectural collisions. Distortions, ruptures, compressions, fragmentations, and disjunctions are inherent in the manipulation of form. This is also the disruption inflicted by any new construction on its surroundings, for it not only destroys what it replaces, but violates the territory it occupies. It is the violence of Adolf Loos' House for Tristan Tzara in the context of vernacular 19th-century suburban Paris or, alternatively, the disruptive effect of an historical allusion in a curtain-wall avenue. This contextual violence is nothing but the polemical violence of difference. To discuss it is the task of sociology, psychology, and esthetics.

A door flanked by broken Corinthian columns supporting a twisted neon pediment, however, suggests farce rather than violence. Yet James Joyce's 'doorlumn' was both a pun and a comment on the cultural crisis of language. *Finnegans Wake* implied that particular transgressions could attack the constituent elements of architectural language – its columns, stairs, windows, and their various combinations – as they are defined by any cultural period, whether Beaux-Arts or Bauhaus. This formal disobedience is ultimately harmless and may even initiate a new style as it slowly loses the excessive character of a violated prohibition. It then announces a new pleasure and the elaboration of a new norm, which is in turn violated.

The second type of partial violence is not a metaphor. *Programmatic violence* encompasses those uses, actions, events, and programs which, by accident or by design, are specifically evil and destructive. Among them are killing, internment, and torture, which become slaughterhouses, concentration camps or torture chambers.

See also:
Benjamin (1.4)
Lyotard (3.6)
Miller (4.1)
Wills (7.5)

5.4

'THINKING TECHNICITY'

Richard Beardsworth

THE STAKES OF TECHNICITY

One of the major concerns of philosophical and cultural analysis in recent years has been the need to reflect upon the reduction of time and space brought about by contemporary processes of technicization, particularly digitalisation. Such a reduction radically reorganises classical and modern understandings of time and space, having effects in previously divergent, but now ever converging domains of experience. The recent return, for example, of religious faith and organisation is to be situated within these processes of technicization, the search for 'identity' and the desire for the 'pure' being predicated upon an uprooting movement of de-localisation and de-temporalization that is inextricably linked to present technico-economic invention. If this movement also accounts for the present upsurge in nationalist and ethnic-based politics, it calls at the same time for a re-elaboration of national and international law and political symbolisation (particularly the concept of citizenship) that would progressively articulate nternationalisation beyond present predominantly neo-liberal affirmations of 'globalization'. How can philosophy help us in these re-inventions? Without grounding a particular political programme, how can philosophical reflection assist future orientation in and, ultimately, beyond this world?

To give a sense of direction to these two questions from out of the preceding comments, I wish to stress first:

Source: Beardsworth, Richard, 'Thinking technicity', *Cultural Value*, 2(1), 1988, pp. 70–86.

- that time and space are today explicitly political issues. Since this has always been the case (from the Athenian *polis* to the First International, politics has always been a matter of organising time and space), the contemporary technicization of the world is significant because it has brought time and space out of their ideological formations within the domain of the political. It locates them, instead, *as* the very question *of* the political;

- that as contemporary processes of technicization (most evidently the tele-technologies) are radically affecting our experience of time and space, they are revealing more than any other technical processes within history that there is an essential, inextricable relation between time and space *as such* and technics *as such*;

- that, therefore, if the question of the political today can be considered as the question of time and space, this question cannot be rehearsed and articulated *without articulating what the relation between technics*, on the one hand, *and time and space*, on the other is;

- that the general tenor of this articulation calls for a *philosophical* analysis of the relation;

- that, finally, given the now immediately political nature of time and space, this analysis necessarily carries a political dimension, concerned, perhaps, with what we might understand from a world perspective by political locality and temporality.

Now, if these proposals demand a great deal of analysis in themselves, they already suggest that an answer to the above questions concerning philosophy's place in future orientation may lie, most immediately, *in thinking and developing our understanding of technicity*. What I wish to do here is show how, and in what terms, the thinking of technicity indeed gives us access to these questions and takes philosophy towards thinking actuality. The following is in this sense preliminary, preparing the stage for further reflection rather than rehearsing a particular response to the questions asked. That said, new directions in philosophical reflection that have a purchase on contemporary and future actuality, allowing thereby a sense of critical orientation in this world, are implied by the very staging of the argument.

I wish first to show why the thinking of technicity is a necessary consequence today of Continental Philosophy's 'mourning' of metaphysics, re-articulating it within a broader movement of technical supplementarity. To this effect it would be useful to concentrate on Plato's aporia of memory in the *Meno*. For the text is considered by many to represent the starting point of the transcendental method in philosophy and the place where the oppositional logic pertaining to metaphysical thought is inaugurated. To show that it can best be understood in terms of technical supplementarity will have important implications for the very status and terms of philosophical reflection upon technical actuality as such.

THE APORIA OF MENO

We recall that *Meno*'s initial question in the dialogue, 'Can virtue be taught?', becomes for Socrates that of the *topos* of the universal Virtue informing all particular virtues such that one can recognise each *as* a virtue. The question is in other words that of the origin of universals which becomes through the course of the history of philosophy the question of transcendence, of *a priori* conditions of experience, or indeed of thinking as such (the ecstasis, in Heideggerian terms, of the apophantic 'as' (Heidegger, 1967, I.V., pp. 32–33). Socrates expounds the question as an 'aporia' of thought, literally thinking's 'lack of passage'. Socrates says near the beginning of the dialogue:

> It is impossible for a man to discover either what he knows or what he does not know. He could not seek what he knows, for since he knows it there is no need of the inquiry, nor what he does not know, for in that case he does not even know what he is to look for. (Plato, 1961, 80e)

With Plato, the aporia of thought becomes an aporia of memory that is taken up by Socrates and resolved by the myth of recollection or reminiscence (*ana-mnesis*). Socrates continues a moment later:

> The soul, since it is immortal and has been born many times, and has seen all things both here and in the other world, has learned everything that is. So we need not be surprised if it can recall the knowledge of virtue or anything else which, as we see, it once possesses. All nature is akin, and the soul has learned everything, so that when a man has recalled a single piece of knowledge – *learned* it, in ordinary terms – there is no reason why he should not find out all the rest, if he keeps a stout heart and does not grow weary of the search; for seeking and learning are in fact nothing but recollection [*anamnesis*]. (Plato, 1961, 81d)

The original question posed by *Meno* whether virtue can be taught becomes, then, the more general question of re-cognition – of the universal (Virtue) in the particular (virtues) – in turn answered by the Platonic Socrates in terms of memory: to learn is to remember. The thesis necessitates in turn – or rather institutes for the first time – an axiomatic distinction between two domains of experience: that of the immortal soul and that of the body condemned to corruption and death. The distinction is rapidly accompanied both in the *Meno* and the following Platonic dialogues by other oppositions that now characterise what we call 'metaphysics': the opposition between the infinite and finite, the transcendental and empirical, *logos* and *techne*, form and matter. In other words, the myth of *anamnesis* institutes metaphysical logic as such: that is, it is nothing but the forgetting of the aporia *as* the logic of opposition.

This aporia sets the terms in which the axiomatic of the transcendence and the transcendental in the Western philosophical tradition is posed. It lies, for example, behind the question of being in Greek philosophy, behind the ontological argument of God in mediaeval and rationalist philosophy and haunts the question of transcendental method in both Kantian critique and modern phenomenology and hermeneutics. From this perspective, whatever the differences between these philosophies, their history (as a 'history') acquires form in the gesture which turns the aporia of memory into a phantasmatic opposition between two types of being (the ontico-ontological difference), two types of life and intelligence (the infinite and the finite, the soul and the body, the noumenal and the phenomenal) and, perhaps most interestingly, *two modalities of time* (the eternal present and the passing flux of time, transcendental apperception and the manifold, etc.). From out of the aporia, and in the very way in which the Platonic Socrates resolves it, emerge both the *decision* to turn an impasse of thought into a series of oppositions and the question of *finitude*.

THE MOURNING OF THE APORIA

It is this oppositional logic, together with its normative nature, that twentieth century thought in its various continental guises has set itself the task of mourning. It is, in this sense, a thinking of finitude. Its destruction and deconstruction of metaphysics can be considered as propelled by the wish to re-collect, re-cognize in turn that which the Platonic myth of recollection forgets in order to institute itself as such. Continental thought can consequently be seen to situate itself on the aporia of thought *qua* the other of thought, thereby wishing to get behind metaphysics and open up what *lies prior to oppositional thinking*. This mourning of metaphysics has been pursued since at least Nietzsche (to whom I will return in the conclusion); it nevertheless marks very particularly, both in its style and in its implications, continental philosophy from Martin Heidegger to Jacques Derrida. Let us take the three examples of Heidegger, Emmanuel Levinas and Derrida to see how:

- In *Being and Time* Heidegger's existential analytics of being-in-the-world and *Mitdasein* can be seen to reorganize *Meno*'s aporia of memory in terms of the being-thrownness of Dasein (Heidegger, 1967, I.III and IV). What will have become in the tradition the soul whose content is to be infinitely recollected – the modern form of which is to be found in the Kantian ideas of reason – is re-articulated in *Being and Time* as the worldness of Dasein, one which, in his destruction of traditional ethics, Heidegger goes on to develop in the second part of the book as the existentiale of originarily 'being-in-debt' (*Schuldigsein*). This indebtedness is prior to, and constitutive of, Platonic and Christian understandings of lack, guilt and sin. *Being and Time* constitutes accordingly, from out of the aporia of thought, a philosophical re-inscription of modern subjectivity and classical and Kantian ethics.

- In *Totality and Infinity*, Levinas's ethical re-inscription of the Western philosophical tradition constitutes in turn an *anamnesis* of the alterity of the other forgotten in the ontological determination of the world. As such it may also be considered to reorganise the aporia of *Meno*, this time, in part *contra* Heidegger, in terms of the 'other' that always precedes the 'sameness' of thinking. Although *Totality and Infinity* does not make reference to *Meno*, Levinas often speaks of the Socratic *maieutic*. Its ironic structure is conceived of as an ethical dilemma (Levinas, 1969, pp. 194–216). Levinas's understanding of teaching can thus be seen to re-articulate the Socratic aporia of thought as the *ethical* relation to the other, a relation disavowed in the oppositional thought of ontology, including that informing Heidegger's own distinction between primordial and vulgar temporalization. The temporalization of time disavows the other. The other that precedes me is my teacher: the law of the other is that I must learn 'my' past which is given to me through another. Levinas's 'mourning' of Greek re-collection re-situates metaphysics upon the alterity of the other as law, thought since *Totality and Infinity* increasingly in terms of the suspension of temporalization.

- In both *Of Grammatology* and 'Plato's Pharmacy' Derrida re-organizes the aporia in terms of *arche-writing*, maintaining that the condition of truth is the possibility of writing (Derrida, 1976 and 1981). It is here, following the thesis of Husserl's last major writing 'The Origin of Geometry' (Derrida, 1989), that technics is for the first time explicitly introduced behind the transcendental logic instituted by *Meno*.[1] Rather than the inscription of writing reflecting the truth – the argument which sets up 'logocentrism': the soul outside material supports, what we named earlier 'the desire of the pure' – its possibility is constitutive of truth as such. In *Of Grammatology* Derrida writes:

> Writing is not only an auxiliary means in the service of science – and possibly its object – but first, as Husserl in particular pointed out in the *Origin of Geometry*, the condition of the possibility of ideal objects and therefore of scientific objectivity. Before being its object, writing is the condition of episteme ... Historicity itself is tied to the possibility of writing; to the possibility of writing in general, beyond those particular forms of writing in the name of which we have long spoken of peoples without writing and without history. Before being the object of history – of an historical science – writing opens the field of history – of historical becoming. And the former (*Historie* in German) presupposes the latter (*Geschichte*). (Derrida, 1976, p. 27)

Thus, for Derrida, following Husserl's major insight, the exteriority of a technical object 'writing' is the very condition of the *logos*. When *Meno* situates the *logos* outside the world, thereby opposing the non-worldly nature of thinking and the soul to the worldly contingency of material inscription, it is, for Derrida, the finitude of human memory, that is, its exteriorization in 'supports' of memory is forgotten. The constitutive nature of technics concerning the trans-temporal nature of memory therefore implies that metaphysical thinking forms its oppositions by expelling into one term of the opposition the very possibility of the condition of such oppositions. Derrida calls this *general possibility* of inscription 'arche-writing' or the 'trace'. Both signal an irreducible arche-synthesis 'which connects within the same possibility, and they cannot be separated except by abstraction, the structure of the relationship with the other, the movement of temporalization and language as writing' (Derrida, 1976, p. 47; and Gasché, 1979). This arche-synthesis is what articulates the aporia of thought *as* what is radically other to thought: the form of the aporetic impasse thus represents a displaced symptom of the ex-posed nature of thought. In this sense, the quasi-concept not only represents a careful amalgamation of both Heidegger and Levinas's above mourning of metaphysical forgetting (Beardsworth, 1996), it addresses at the same time the originary 'technicity' of life in its attention to the supplementary nature of all living systems (what *Of Grammatology* will call, from out of a deconstruction of Rousseau's thinking on the distinction between nature and society, 'originary supplementarity').

Seen from the aporia of *Meno* the move from Heidegger to Derrida is one of an ever deeper articulation of what lies behind-metaphysics. In Derrida's work this ends up with a quasi-concept, arche-writing, that explicitly reworks the relation between material inscription and transcendence and at the same time generalises this relation, as one of a radical opening prior to the formation of the inside or outside, across all forms of life. A profound re-organization of metaphysical thinking ensues, the consequences of which are, as I argued in *Derrida and the Political*, severely underestimated if the concept is kept to the domain of literature and writing (Beardsworth, 1996).

Our ultimate interest in returning to the aporia of *Meno* has been to show:

1. that technics – i.e., technical objects/material inscription – conditions the movement of the transcendental; and
2. that technics is itself an effect of a movement of supplementarity, what I am calling 'technicity', namely, the very condition of life.

Following Derrida's deconstruction of oppositional thinking, technics (writing) emerges as the condition of transcendence, and technicity (arche-writing) as the 'structure' of the mind or organism in general that makes possible the relation between technical supplements and the mind. Neither technics nor the structure of technicity can be *opposed*, therefore, to thinking *without repeating the logic informing the myth of recollection*. Since, on the one hand, Heidegger himself makes this opposition when he argues that the essence of technics is not technical, and when he separates the movement of *physis* from that of *techne* (Heidegger, 1959 and 1977) – and since, on the other, Levinas's other of metaphysics is thought exclusively from out of the relation between the human and the divine, to the detriment of an analysis of matter and its evolution – the re-articulation of metaphysical thinking through the quasi-concept of arche-writing has clearly important implications, of an ontological, ethical and political nature, both for present orientation within continental philosophy and for its purchase upon the real.

DERRIDA'S AMBIVALENCE AND THE DEVELOPMENT OF TECHNICITY

And yet, that said, the emergence from behind the aporia of the thought of technics and technical supplementarity within philosophical reflection is ambivalent in Derrida's work. This ambivalence, given the very importance of his thinking, has had rather impoverishing intellectual and cultural consequences in the last twenty years which a return to the question of technics and technicity behind metaphysical thought can, precisely, begin to re-address.

On the one hand, Derrida derives in *Of Grammatology* and texts like 'Plato's Pharmacy' the oppositions of metaphysical thinking from phenomenal writing, considering the expulsion of writing from out of thinking as a gesture of the desire to set up qualitative distinctions between the inside and the outside, an expulsion that 'conceals' the originary and irreducible synthesis between inside and outside. Arche-writing is therefore developed better than elsewhere from out of (the expulsion of) writing. Writing is considered to be a form of support that betrays the radical exteriority of any interiority (a soul, for example) whilst intensifying the very belief in that interiority *qua* the external recording of its movements (the understanding of the soul that emerges with monotheism is only possible *through* writing). Since the 1960s Derrida's thinking has played on these various registers of exposition according to the context.

On the other hand – not that this implies a qualitative distinction between the two: there is, however, a shift of emphasis, one of consequence – Derrida will read what lies behind the institution of oppositional logic in terms of an 'excess' that precedes and conditions all determination (Derrida, 1993a, p. 37). During the 1980s and early 1990s, he works through this excess from out of Levinasian ethics, negative theology and the Platonic conception of the *khôra* (Derrida, 1993a, 1993b and 1993c). Following Plato's description of the *khôra* in the *Timaeus*, Derrida situates, for example, the non-place of the *khôra* behind the Platonic oppositions instituted, or at least stabilised, by the myth of recollection. This non-place is neither intelligible nor sensible, allowing for their separation in the first place. It lies prior to the distinction between the Forms and their copies and is, for Derrida, most interestingly described by Plato in terms of a 'maternal' receptacle (given that any archaeology of the opposition would derive the latter from a [paternal] origin).

CONCLUSION

At the beginning of this article I asked the question how philosophy might assist future orientation in a world increasingly articulated through explicit processes of technicization, processes that appeared to be severely reducing our experience of time and space. I then suggested that time and space had become the very question of the political given these processes, an event which implied in fact that there was an essential relation between time, space and technics that needed to be developed for us to understand the contemporary world and assume a critical and experimental position towards it. The preceding has staged a progression of argument concerning the impasse of thought from the aporia of memory in

Meno to the question of spirit in Nietzschean energetics. It has shown that this impasse conceals the other of thought and that, rather than freezing this other as the 'other of metaphysics', it is incumbent upon us to develop it in terms of an 'originary technicity' of life and in terms of this technicity's historical differentiations. A preliminary answer to our question, then, is that *it is precisely such a development that will allow us a more informed, more sober and, therefore, more inventive purchase on technical actuality*. Developing what lies behind metaphysical thought will give us the very terms in which orientation in the present and future world can be experimented upon. These terms cannot and should not be legislated upon: they come from the future. That said, and finally, in my brief allusions to the question of the incalculable and to the relation between technics, time and energy, we have nevertheless also argued *that it is the very giving of time and energy that forms the horizon of the development of technicity*. Developing technicity connotes, in the very terms of its own analysis, an 'ethics' of giving time (one, moreover, rooted in the practice of finitude). In this light, then, and in conclusion, rather than opposing thought to *techne*, our philosophical detour through the *Meno* has shown, in, as it were, quasi-Kantian terms, how 'morality' *is* compatible, but also in tension with 'technics'. For *both are concerned with the production and organisation of time*. Philosophical reflection on future orientation must also prepare our understanding of this compatibility.

NOTE

1. There are of course precedents: notably Karl Marx, Friederich Nietzsche and Henri Bergson. With Derrida's reading of Husserl technicity is explicitly articulated, however, through the philosophical problematic of transcendence.

REFERENCES

Beardsworth, Richard 1996: *Derrida and the Political*. London: Routledge.
Derrida, Jacques 1976: *Of Grammatology*. Gayatri Spivak trans. Baltimore, MD: John's Hopkins Press.
Derrida, Jacques 1981: Plato's Pharmacy. In Jacques Derrida *Dissemination*. Barbara Johnson trans. Chicago: Chicago University Press, pp. 61–171.
Derrida, Jacques 1989: *Edmund Husserl's 'Origin of Geometry'. An Introduction*. John P. Leavey trans. Lincoln and London: Nebraska Press.
Derrida, Jacques 1993a: Khôra. Paris: Galilée.
Derrida, Jacques 1993b: Passions. Paris: Galilée.
Derrida, Jacques 1993c: Sauf le nom. Paris: Galilée.
Gasché, Rodolphe 1979: Deconstruction as Criticism. In *Glyph*, 6, pp. 177–216.
Heidegger, Martin 1959: *An Introduction to Metaphysics*. Ralph Manheim trans. New Haven: Yale University Press.
Heidegger, Martin 1967: *Being and Time*. J. Macquarrie and E. Robinson trans. Oxford: Blackwell.
Heidegger, Martin 1977: The Question Concerning Technology. In M. Heidegger *The Question Concerning Technology and Other Essays*. William Lovitt trans. New York: Harper and Row, pp. 3–35.
Leroi-Gourhan, André 1993: *Gesture and Speech*. Anna Bostock Berger trans. Cambridge, MA: M.I.T. Press.

Levinas, Emmanuel 1969: *Totality and Infinity: An Essay on Exteriority*. Alphonso Lingis trans. Pittsburgh: Duquesne University Press.
Plato, 1961: *Meno*. In Edith Hamilton and Huntington Cairns (eds) *The Collected Dialogues*, Bollingen Series LXX. Princeton: Princeton University Press.

See also:

Freud (1.2)
Norris (3.1)
Wills (7.5)
Derrida (11.3)

5.5

'TOWARD A NARCOANALYSIS'

Avital Ronell

This work does not accord with literary criticism in the traditional sense. Yet it is devoted to the understanding of a literary work. It could be said to reside within the precincts of philosophical endeavor. Indeed, it tries to understand an object that splits existence into incommensurable articulations. This object resists the revelation of its truth to the point of retaining the status of absolute otherness. Nonetheless, it has given rise to laws and moral pronouncements. This fact, in itself, is not alarming. The problem is signaled elsewhere, in the exhaustion of language. Where might one go today, to what source can one turn, in order to activate a just constativity? We no longer see in philosophy the ultimate possibilities for knowing the limits of human experience. And yet we began this study by citing Nietzsche. There were two reasons for this selection. In the first place, Nietzsche was the philosopher to think with his body, to 'dance,' which is a nice way of saying also to convulse, even to retch. And then, Nietzsche was the one to put out the call for a supramoral imperative. This summons in itself will urge us on – for we are dealing in a way with the youngest vice, still very immature, still often misjudged and taken for something else, still hardly aware of itself . . .

What follows, then, is essentially a work on *Madame Bovary*, and nothing more. If it were another type of work – in the genre of philosophical essay, psychoanalytic interpretation, or political analysis – it would be expected to make certain kinds of assertions which obey a whole grammar of procedure and

Source: Avital Ronell, *Crack Wars: Literature, Addiction, Mania* (Lincoln: University of Nebraska Press, 1995), pp. 47–65.

certitudes. The prestige and historical recommendation of those methods of inquiry would have secured the project within a tolerably reliable frame. However, it is too soon to say with certainty that one has fully understood how to conduct the study of addiction and, in particular, how it may bear upon drugs. To understand in such a way would be to stop reading, to close the book, as it were, or even to throw the book at someone.

I cannot say that I am prepared to take sides on this exceedingly difficult issue, particularly when the sides have been drawn with such conceptual awkwardness. Clearly, it is as preposterous to be 'for' drugs as it is to take up a position 'against' drugs. Provisionally they may be comprehended as master objects of considerable libidinal investment, whose essence still remains to be determined. As it happens, literature is on drugs and about drugs – and here I retain the license to open the semantic range of this term (which does not even amount to concept). I shall come back to the many fluctuations of meaning and usage in the course of my argument. For the present, 'drugs' can be understood to involve materially (1) products of a natural origin, often known in antiquity; (2) products evolved from modern pharmaceutical chemistry; and (3) parapharmacological substances, or products prepared by and for the addict. This says nothing as yet for the symbolic values of drugs, their rootedness in ritual and the sacred, their promise of exteriority, the technological extension of supernatural structures, or the spaces carved out in the imaginary by the introduction of a chemical prosthesis.

Under the impacted signifier of drugs, America is fighting a war against a number of felt intrusions. They have to do mostly with the drift and contagion of a foreign substance, or of what is revealed as foreign (even if it should be homegrown). Like any good parasite, drugs travel both inside and outside of the boundaries of a narcissistically defended politics. They double for the values with which they are at odds, thus haunting and reproducing the capital market, creating visionary expansions, producing a lexicon of body control and a private property of self – all of which awaits review.

Drugs resist conceptual arrest. No one has thought to define them in their essence, which is not to say 'they' do not exist. On the contrary. Everywhere dispensed, in one form or another, their strength lies in their virtual and fugitive patterns. They do not close forces with an external enemy (the easy way out) but have a secret communications network with the internalized demon. Something is beaming out signals, calling drugs home.

The complex identity of this substance, which is never as such a substance, has given rise to the inscription of a shameful history. This is not the place to trace its intricate contours, for it is an open history whose approach routes are still blocked; nonetheless, the necessity of pursuing such an endeavor still stands. On some level of thinking's probity it is either entirely self-canceling or far too *easy* to treat drugs. Precisely because they are everywhere and can be made to do, or undo, or promise, anything. They participate in the analysis of the broken word, or a history of warfare: methedrine, or methyl-amphetamine, synthesized in Germany, had a determining effect in Hitler's Blitzkrieg; heroin comes from *heroisch*,[1] and Göring never went anywhere without his supply; Dr. Hubertus Strughold, father of space medicine, conducted mescaline experiments at Dachau – indeed, it would be difficult to dissociate drugs from a history of modern warfare and genocide. One could begin perhaps in the contiguous neighborhood of the ethnocide of the American Indian by alcohol or strategic viral infection, and then one could never end ...

The contagious spread of the entity described as drugs is discursively manifest. Drugs cannot be placed securely within the frontiers of traditional disciplines: anthropology, biology, chemistry, politics, medicine, or law, could not, solely on the strength of their respective epistemologies, claim to contain or counteract them. While everywhere dealt with, drugs act as a radically nomadic parasite let loose from the will of language.

While they resist *presentation*, drugs are still too readily appropriable. One problem dragging down thought is that the drug wars might scan well with the present atmosphere of consensual reading. It is actually becoming impolite to enter areas of conflict. Anyone who has not been prudent in thinking through this fragile zone where non-knowledge dominates knowledge has in any case been burned.

I refer in particular to the professional history of Sigmund Freud who, for the sake of some unplumbable purpose, staked his early career entirely on cocaine and on the essays devoted to cocaine. As a result of *Über Coca* – this text and the subsequent defense, 'Remarks on Craving for and Fear of Cocaine,' are not included in the *Standard Edition of the Complete Psychological Works* – Freud was publicly reprimanded and privately assailed. Why he willfully ignored the underside of cocaine usage researched by Dr. Louis Lewin, shall have to maintain its status as enigma. His altogether favorable disposition toward cocaine (he recommended it for combating fatigue, against aging, as a local anaesthetic) earned him the published reproof of the famous Berlin psychiatrist, Albrecht Erlenmeyer. Such attacks upon his scientific integrity for promoting the cause of cocaine might have cost a lesser ego its destiny. The personal aspect of disaster brought about by this impassioned research concerned his intimate friend, Von Fleischi, who was the first morphine addict to be treated by cocaine; our first European cocaine addict. Freud attended his friend through a night of paranoid terror, where he witnessed the felt invasion and devouring of Von Fleischl by endless insects and tireless demons. At great cost to himself, his friends, and his father (who was treated with cocaine by his son's prescription), Freud may have discovered something about the toxic drive that could not obtain immediate clearance. In his own work, the cocaine drama broke the ground for the study of hysterical neurosis.

If anything, Freud serves here as a warning system. He never, it seems to me, shook the trouble that cocaine advocacy earned him. This is not the place to analyze that fatal encounter, nor certainly would it be appropriate to concoct foolish moralizations as if one already understood what addiction is all about. There are good and bad addictions, and anything can serve the function of a drug. 'Drugs,' in any case, make us face the gaping chasms of *Beyond the Pleasure Principle*, where death drive and desire round up their victims.

In his more restrained estimations, Freud has characterized the addict as evoking the charm of cats and birds of prey with their inaccessibility, their apparent libidinal autonomy. This is not very far from his description, in another context, of women. (The place where the addict meets the feminine in a desperate attempt at social renarcissization is carefully marked in *Madame Bovary*.) Natcissistic withdrawal equally introduces a scandalous figure into the society of humans by removing the addicted subject from the sphere of human connectibility. But perhaps the hint of libidinal autonomy, or what Félix Guattari describes as 'the second degree of solitude,' furnishes the most menacing among social attributes. Jacques Lacan appears to confirm the conviction that drug addiction belongs to the domain of a post-analytical era reserved perhaps for schizoanalysis and the like; indeed, he sees the addict as constituting a hopeless subject of psychoanalysis: 'Addiction (*la toxicomanie*) opens a field where no single word of the subject is reliable, and where he escapes analysis altogether.' This is giving up quickly. William Burroughs shares quite the same opinion from the other side of experience: 'Morphine addiction is a metabolic illness brought about by the use of morphine. In my opinion psychological treatment is not only useless it is contraindicated.' A collusion on the parts of Lacan and Burroughs does not mean, however, that the psychotreatability of the addict is wholly out of the question, or that psychoanalysis would offer a useless or archaic access code for unlocking the whole problem. For, to the extent that addiction was at one point within the jurisdiction of *jouissance* – indeed, we are dealing with an epidemic of misfired *jouissance* – the major pusher, the one who gave the orders to shoot up, was surely the superego. In order to urge this point with some sustainment of clarity we shall have to enter the clinic of phantasms that Flaubert chose to call *Madame Bovary*.

The modern history of the attempt to stabilize a definition of drugs comprises long, dense, and contradictory moments (Queen Victoria waged war twice, for instance, in order to ensure the free commerce of opium)[2] The legal history of drugs compels analyses of the means by which drugs have been enlisted to erode the American criminal justice system. Airports now establish the clearest rhetorical space for reading the consequences of what Justice Brennan had once projected as the 'unanalyzed exercise of judicial will.' State control towers have effected the merger between air and drug traffic, instituting the airport as a premonitory law-free zone where the subject's orifices are kept open to investigation. No probable cause is necessary here. *Droit de la drogue*, a significant French study of the problem, clarifies the prohibitionist spell under which America continues to conduct its interventions. The study does not fail to analyze the effects of the xenophobic, racist and economic calculations that have commanded moral, legal, and military discourses. Its theoretical propositions derive from constructions concerning the freedom of the legal subject and his right to be protected from the condition of enslavement that drugs are said unavoidably to produce. It is a matter of determining at what point the object takes possession of the subject. We shall leave these terms to flood their undeconstructed history.

I can make no pretense to possessing legal competence more elaborate than that of any literate person. I would suggest only that one consider the degree to which the literary object has itself been treated juridically as a drug. In one case it fell to the favor of the literary work to be handled as a medicinal substance, possibly indeed by an 'unconscious' legal manipulation. This is the case of James Joyce's *Ulysses*, where the work's fate was considerably advantaged by its classification as emetic function rather than as pornographic inducement. These were the terms upon which it was performatively granted entry rights into the U.S. Be that as it may, *Ulysses*, whether legally conceived as emetic formula or as aphrodisiac philtre, was in the first place distilled down to its essence as a drug.

Naked Lunch evinces a similar collapse of the boundary between obscenity and drugs. In *Attorney General* v. *A Book Named 'Naked Lunch'*, the court finds the following:

> The Supreme Court of the United States has held that, to justify a holding of obscenity, 'three elements must coalesce: it must be established that (a) the dominant theme of the material taken as a whole appeals to a prurient interest in sex; (b) the material is patently offensive because it affronts contemporary community standards ... and (c) the material is *utterly* without redeeming social value' [emphasis supplied]; *A Book Named 'Johns Cleland's Memoirs of a Woman of Pleasure'* v. *Attorney General of Mass.* 383 U.S. 413, 418–421 ... As to whether [*Naked Lunch*] has any redeeming social value, the record contains many reviews and articles in literary and other publications discussing seriously this controversial book portraying the hallucinations of a drug addict. Thus it appears that a substantial and intelligent group in the community believes the book to be of some literary significance.

The slippage from obscenity to the representation of hallucination – in other words, the representation of representation – cannot fail to raise questions about the veilings that both literature and drugs cast. This order of questioning had already penetrated to the case of *Madame Bovary*, where it was held that the curtain of non-representation (the carriage scene) exploded hallucinatory rage in the open space of the socius. The menace of literature in these cases consists in its pointing to what is not there in any ordinary sense of ontological unveiling. The court is not wrong to institute the proximity of hallucination and obscenity as neighboring territorialities, since both put in question the power of literature to veil its insight or to limit its exposure. Literature is most exposed when it stops representing, that is, when it ceases veiling itself with the excess that we commonly call *meaning*.

The question comes down to the way literature dresses up the wound of its non-being when it goes out into the world. On this point, the cases of *Madame Bovary* and *Naked Lunch* are only to a certain degree different (it is all a matter of dosage), but the matter of representation continues to be the same: the court keeps a close watch on creatures of the simulacrum.

There can be no doubt about it. *Naked Lunch* gets out of trouble only when the social veil of literary review has been thrown over it. Literature has to be seen wearing something external to itself, it cannot simply circulate its non-being, and almost any article will do. This would affirm at least one value of the book review as that legal force which covers up the work.

Well, then. It is not so much a question of scientific knowledge. Nor certainly can it be a question of confidence in writing. There are certain things that force your hand. You find yourself incontrovertibly obligated: something occurs prior to owing, and more fundamental still than that of which any trace of empirical guilt can give an account. This relation – to whom? to what? – is no more and no less than your liability – what you owe before you think, under-stand, or give; that is, what you owe from the very fact that you exist, before you can properly owe: You do not have to *do* anything about your liability, and most finitudes don't. Still, it copilots your every move, planning your every flight, and it remains the place shadowed by the infinite singularity of your finitude.

The obligation that can force your hand resembles something of a historial compulsion: you are compelled to respond to a situation which has never as such been addressed to you, where you can do no more than run into an identificatory impasse. Nonetheless, you find yourself rising to the demand, as if the weight of justice depended upon your inconsequential advance.

It did not seem advantageous to put at risk the peculiar idiom of this work by installing ethical tonalities that may in the end correspond only weakly to its critical punch (Flaubert: 'The worth of a book can be judged by the strength of the punches it gives and the length of time it takes you to recover from them.'). The task of producing an introduction made me hesitate, the way a translator hesitates over the prospects of a sacrificial economy that will nevertheless dominate the entire work. Might as well face it: Some hesitations are rigorous. They own up to the fact that no decision is strictly possible without the expe-rience of the undecidable. To the extent that one may no longer be simply guided – by Truth, by light or logos – decisions have to be made. Yet I wanted neither to protect Emma B. from what was about to happen (she had to remain exposed) nor to pervert her further. I certainly did not want to create a dis-posable limit, an explanatory phase that, at lift off, could easily fall behind. This would have come too close to repeating a structure of dejection with which drugs have been associated – a structure where there is neither introjection nor even incorporation, but which posits the body as the no-return of disposability: the trash-body, pivoted on its own excrementality. Doubling for the remainder, however, this moment in my argument would occupy the terrifying position of quasi-transcendence because it can be made to determine the value of the inside from which it is ejected. And yet, one is liable, and one has to find a way of thinking this liability as if one were concluding an affirmative contract with an endlessly demanding alterity.

More so perhaps than any other 'substance,' whether real or imagined, drugs thematize the dissociation of autonomy and responsibility that has marked our epoch since Kant. Despite the indeterminacy and heterogeneity that character-ize these phenomena, drugs are crucially related to the question of freedom. Kant himself devotes pages of the *Anthropology* to contemplating the values of civic strength as they are affected by intoxicating foods (under which he comprehended mushrooms, wild rosemary, acanthus, Peruvian chicha, the South Sea Island's ava, and opium). The questions attending drugs disclose only a moment in the history of addiction. As such, drugs have accrued a meager hermeneutics in proportion to a considerable mobilization of force.

No one has so much as defined drugs, and this is in part because they are non-theorizable. Still, they have globalized a massive instance of destructive *jouis-sance*, they assert desire's mutation within a post-analytic phrasing, or put another way, drugs name the exposition of our modernity to the incompletion of *jouissance*. Perhaps the quality of these stakes explains in part why they have become the elusive objects of planetary warfare at the very moment when 'democracy' is on the rebound. The intersecting cut between freedom, drugs and the addicted condition (what we are symptomatologizing as 'Being-on-drugs') deserves an interminable analysis whose heavily barred doors can be no more than cracked open by a solitary research.

Narcotic desire's implications for freedom did not entirely escape Kant's gaze (hence the need for prescriptions in general). But it was not until Thomas De Quincey that drugs were pushed toward a philosophy of decision. The *Confessions of an English Opium Eater* can be shown to perturb an entire ontology by having drugs participate in a movement of unveiling that is capable of discovering no prior or more fundamental ground. Unveiling and unclouding, opium, on De Quincey's account, brings the higher faculties into a kind of legal order, an absolute legislative harmony. If it perturbs ontology this is in order to institute something else. The ontological revision which it undertakes would not be subject to the regime of *alèthia*, or rather, the clarity which opium urges is not dependent upon a prior unveiling. Where the warring parts of the *Confessions* refuse to suture, one detects the incredible scars of decision. Always a recovering addict, Kant's subject was not particularly pathological in the pursuit of his habits; De Quincey's addict has been exposed to another limit of experience, to the promise of exteriority. Offering a discreet if spectacular way out, an atopical place of exit, drugs forced *decision* upon the subject.

Self-dissolving and regathering, the subject became linked to the possibility of a new autonomy, and opium illuminated in this case (Baudelaire, though under De Quincey's influence, was to use it differently) an individual who finally could not identify with his ownmost autonomy but found himself instead subjected to heroic humiliation in the regions of the sublime. Opium became the transparency upon which one could review the internal conflict of freedom, the cleave of subjectivity where it encounters the abyss of destructive *jouissance*.

The ever-dividing self was transported on something other than the sacred, though the effects of revelation were not unrelated. Decisions would have to be met, one had to become a master strategist in the ceaseless war against pain. The most striking aspect of De Quincey's decision resides in the fact that it resists regulation by a telos of knowledge. To this end his elaboration has uncovered for us a critical structure of decision to the extent that it has been tinctured by non-knowledge, based largely upon a state of anarchivization. This leaves any future thinking of drugs, if this should be possible, in the decidedly fragile position of system abandonment. There is no system that can presently hold or take 'drugs' for long. Instituted on the basis of moral or political evaluations, the concept of drugs cannot be comprehended under any independent, scientific system.

These observations do not mean to imply that a certain type of narcotic supplement has been in the least rejected by metaphysics. To a great degree, it is all more or less a question of dosage (as Nietzsche said of history). Precisely due to the promise of exteriority which they are thought to extend, drugs have been redeemed by the conditions of transcendency and revelation with which they are not uncommonly associated. But qualities such as these are problematic because they tend to maintain drugs on 'this side' of a thinking of experience. Sacralized or satanized, when our politics and theories prove still to be under God's thumb, they install themselves as codependents; ever recycling the transcendental trace of freedom, they have been the undaunted suppliers of a metaphysical craving.

There can be no doubt about it. What is required is a genuine ethics of decision. But this in turn calls for a still higher form of drug.

Madame Bovary I daresay is about bad drugs. Equally, it is about thinking we have properly understood them. But if the novel matches its reputation for rendering its epoch – our modernity – intelligible, then we would do well to recall that *epoch* also means interruption, arrest, suspension and, above all, suspension of judgment. *Madame Bovary* travels the razor's edge of understanding/reading protocols. In this context understanding is given as something that happens when you are no longer reading. It is not the open-ended Nietzschean echo, 'Have I been understood?' but rather the 'I understand' that means you have ceased suspending judgment over a chasm of the real. Out of this collapse of judgment no genuine decision can be allowed to emerge. Madame Bovary understood too much; she understood what things were supposed to be like and suffered a series of ethical injuries for this certitude. Her understanding made her legislate closure at every step of the way. She was her own police force, finally turning herself in to the authorities. She understood when the time had come to end it all, whereupon she executed a brutal coincidence of panic and decision. She was no brooding Hamlet, whose tendency to read and re-read and to write down what he heard had granted him the temporal slack he needed to bring the whole house down. No doubt, Hamlet ends up sending himself the poisoned point by return mail and, like Emma, finally commits himself to a writing of suicide. But if they share the same poison, and even the banquets of the uneaten, one should not mix these up too readily, for *Madame Bovary* opens herself to an altogether different history of intelligibility, in fact, to another suicide pact, cosigned by a world that no longer limits its rotting to a singular locality of the unjust. This is not to say that Hamlet and his phantom have been dealt with definitively, but they have been left in suspension by an interrogating openness, a kind of ontological question or futural transmission running interference with the most serene channels of forgetfulness. Emma Bovary, she has been understood. And the material proliferation of critical works surrounding the novel does not refute this statement. On the contrary: No one has claimed to be puzzled by this enigma – she has been the clearing space, the translating machine through which an epoch renders itself intelligible, if not quite above itself.

Hamlet, De Quincey, Emma Bovary, Balzac, Baudelaire, William Burroughs, Artaud (and scores of others) urged upon us a thinking of human nourishment. If they were not quite vegetarians, they tried to nourish themselves without properly eating. Whether injecting themselves or smoking cigarettes or merely kissing someone, they rerouted the hunting grounds of the cannibalistic libido. In a certain manner of conscious monitoring, they refused to eat – and yet they were always only devouring, or drinking up the toxic spill of the Other. Drugs make us ask what it means to consume anything, anything at all. This is a philosophical question, to the extent that philosophy has always diagnosed health, that is, being-itself or the state of non-alienation, by means of its medico-ontological scanners. Where does the experience of eating begin? What of the remains? Are drugs in some way linked to the management of remains? How has the body been drawn into the disposal systems of our technological age?

It is perhaps not surprising that every utterance linked to drugs has something to say about what is appropriable. In his introduction, William Burroughs writes, 'The title means exactly what the words say: NAKED Lunch – a frozen moment when everyone sees what is on the end of every fork.' Prior to this frozen moment, Baudelaire, the first worthy reader of *Madame Bovary* according to Flaubert, remarked: 'In order to digest natural as well as artificial happiness, it is first necessary to have the courage to swallow; and those who would most deserve happiness are precisely the ones upon whom cheerfulness, as conceived by mortals, has always had an emetic effect (*l'effet d'un vomitif*).'

The possibility of an altogether other health, pointing as it does to the great vomiter, Nietzsche, has to do with the properly *improper* character of the body. We seem to be dealing with forces of inscription that relieve the body of itself while resisting its sublation into ideality, spirit, or consciousness. The *purification* of the body described by Baudelaire paradoxically maintains the body in its material, corruptible state of dis-integrity. As that which can swallow and throw up – naturally or artificially – the body rigorously engages the dynamics of becoming, surpassing itself without reducing itself to a passageway. These observations in fact model age-old concerns whose subscription to thought has been renewed by the way drugs negotiate the paracomestible substance.

Why should I begin my study of *Madame Bovary* in the mode of fiction? To fill a prescription; namely, that the provisions of the simulacrum be doubled. It is a method similar to the one I used three centuries ago for editing *The Sorrows of Young Werther*. There was another, more timely motive, which I did not discover until reading a passage from Gilles Deleuze in *Difference and Repetition*:

> On the one hand a book of philosophy ought to be a very particular kind of crime story, and on the other hand it should resemble science fiction. By crime story (*roman policier*) we mean that concepts should intervene, driven by a zone of presence, in order to resolve a local situation.

This places our inquiry on the outer precincts of the detective genre, in the tradition of Sherlock Holmes, who was reputed, alas, to suffer from cocaine addiction.

NOTES

1. In fact, heroin was first produced in 1874 at St Mary's Hospital in London. It was reinvented or 'discovered' in Germany in the 1890s and marketed by Bayer under the trade name 'heroin,' which derives from *heroisch* (cf. Virginia Berridge and Griffith Edwards, *Opium and the People* [New Haven and London: Yale University Press, 1987], p. xx).
2. Involved in the Indian opium trade with China, Britain fought two 'opium wars' against China, in 1839–42 and again in 1856–58.

See also:

Valéry (1.7)
Miller (4.1)
Duttmann (6.5)
Royle (7.4)

'SPEECH ACTS POLITICALLY'

Judith Butler

The implicit operation of censorship is, by definition, difficult to describe. If it operates within a bodily understanding, as Taylor and Bourdieu suggest, how do we understand the bodily operation of such a linguistic understanding? If censorship is the condition of agency, how do we best understand linguistic agency? In what does the 'force' of the performative consist, and how can it be understood as part of politics? Bourdieu argues that the 'force' of the performative is the effect of social power, and social power is to be undertood through established contexts of authority and their instruments of censorship. Opposed to this social account of performative force, Derrida argues that the breaking of the utterance from prior, established contexts consitutes the 'force' of the utterance.

In the introduction I maintained that the speech act is a bodily act, and that the 'force' of the performative is never fully separable from bodily force: this constituted the chiasm of the 'threat' as a speech act at once bodily and linguistic. Felman's contribution to speech act theory underscores that speech, precisely because it is a bodily act, is not always 'knowing' about what it says. In other words, the bodily effects of speech exceed the intentions of the speaker, raising the question of the speech act itself as a nexus of bodily and psychic forces. In the preceding discussion, I noted that foreclosure, in its revised sense, inaugurates or forms the subject, delimiting the limits of speakable discourse as the viable limits of the subject. Foreclosure implies that the

Source: Judith Butler, *Excitable Speech: A Politics of the Performative* (New York: Routledge, 1997), pp. 141–52.

normative production of the subject takes place prior to an overt act of censoring a subject, and ought to be undertood as a modality of productive power in Foucault's sense. The question now emerges: how is it that the norms that govern speech come to inhabit the body? Moreover, how do the norms that produce and regulate the subject of speech also seek to inhabit and craft the embodied life of the subject?

Pierre Bourdieu offers one account of how norms become embodied, suggesting that they craft and cultivate the *habitus* of the body, the cultural style of gesture and bearing. In the final discussion, then, I hope to show how Bourdieu offers a promising account of the way in which non-intentional and non-deliberate incorporation of norms takes place. What Bourdieu fails to understand, however, is how what is bodily in speech resists and confounds the very norms by which it is regulated. Moreover, he offers an account of the performativity of political discourse that neglects the tacit performativity of bodily 'speech,' the performativity of the *habitus*. His conservative account of the speech act presumes that the conventions that will authorize the performative are already in place, thus failing to account for the Derridean 'break' with context that utterances perform. His view fails to consider the crisis in convention that speaking the unspeakable produces, the insurrectionary 'force' of censored speech as it emerges into 'official discourse' and opens the performative to an unpredictable future.

Pierre Bourdieu writes that 'modalities of practices . . . are powerful and hard to resist precisely because they are silent and insidious, insistent and insinuating.' He makes clear what he means by this in a number of works, but perhaps most precisely in his essay, 'Censorship and the Imposition of Forms.' There he writes of specialized languages, indeed, the specialized languages of the academy, and suggests that they are not only based on censorship, but also on a sedimentation and skewing of everyday linguistic usage – 'strategies of euphemization,' to use his phrase. Focusing on the work of Heidegger, Bourdieu argues that Heidegger's language consistently engages strategies that produce the illusion that it has broken with ordinary language. Codes of legitimacy are established precisely through the invocation of non-ordinary words in ways that appear to have a systematic relation to one another. 'Once transformed and transfigured in this way,' Bourdieu writes, 'the word loses its social identity land its ordinary meaning in order to assume a distorted meaning.' 'Every word,' he writes, 'carries the indelible trace of the *break* which separates the authentically ontological sense from the ordinary and vulgar one . . .' He suggests not only that such philosophical discourse depends upon the distinction between sacred and profane knowledge, but that the codification of that distinction must itself be an instance of its sacred exercise.

Bourdieu's task, however, is not simply to return us to a world of ordinary locutions. Indeed, he offers us a theoretical reconstruction of the split that Heidegger's discourse is said to institutionalize, and refuses to treat ordinary language as primary and irreducible. Ordinary language, in his view, is 'moulded politically': 'the objectively political principles of opposition (between social groups) are recorded and preserved in ordinary language.'

According to Bourdieu, then, a philosophical discourse apparently opposes itself to ordinary language, and an ordinary language is structured by political and sociological oppositions between groups, and the latter are structured in part by what he calls the market, understood as an objective field. Ordinary language records and preserves social oppositions, and yet it does so in a way that is not readily transparent. Those oppositions are sedimented within ordinary language and a theoretical reconstruction of that very process of sedimentation is necessary in order to understand them at all. A philosophical discourse such as Heidegger's thus distances itself from both ordinary language and the possibility of theoretically reconstructing the ways in which social oppositions have become sedimented there. Moreover, philosophical discourse recapitulates a class opposition, but in a deflected way; opposed to ordinary language, philosophy participates in a hierarchical set of oppositions that obscurely reenacts the very social oppositions sedimented in, and occluded by, ordinary language.

Bourdieu argues in favor of a theoretical reconstruction of this very split between ordinary and philosophical usage. In this sense, he opposes a hyper-intellectualism that fails to acknowledge the break from ordinary language that it performs, but he opposes as well an anti-intellectualism that fails to give a theoretical account of the split between the ordinary and the philosophical that he outlines.

Several kinds of views have been offered within recent American cultural politics to the effect that it makes sense to throw off the shackles of the censor and return to a more immediate and direct form of discourse. Within literary and cultural studies recently, we have witnessed not merely a turn to the personal voice, but a nearly compulsory production of exorbitant affect as the sign of proof that the forces of censorship are being actively and insistently countered. That these expressions quickly become generic and predictable suggests that a more insidious form of censorship operates at the site of their production, and that the failure to approximate a putatively rule-breaking emotionality is precisely a failure to conform to certain implicit rules, ones that govern the 'liberatory' possibilities of cultural life.

When anti-intellectualism becomes the counter to anti-censorship, and academic language seeks to dissolve itself in an effort to approximate the ordinary, the bodily, and the intimate, then the rituals of codification at work in such renderings become more insidious and less legible. The substitution of a notion of ordinary language, often romanticized and hypostacized, for an apparently evasive intellectual language becomes the alternative to censorship, fails to take account of the formative power of censorship, as well as its subversive effects. The 'break' with ordinary discourse that intellectual language performs does not have to be complete for a certain decontextualization and denaturalization of discourse to take place, one with potentially salutary consequences. The play between the ordinary and non-ordinary is crucial to the process of reelaborating and reworking the constraints that maintain the limits of speakability and, consequently, the viability of the subject.

The effects of catachresis in political discourse are possible only when terms that have traditionally signified in certain ways are misappropriated for other kinds of purposes. When, for instance, the term 'subject' appears to be too bound up with presumptions of sovereignty and epistemological transparency, arguments are made that such a term can no longer be used. And yet, it seems that the reuse of such a term in, say, a post-sovereign context, rattles the otherwise firm sense of context that such a term invokes. Derrida refers to this possibility as reinscription. The key terms of modernity are vulnerable to such reinscriptions as well, a paradox to which I will return toward the end of this chapter. Briefly, though, my point is this: precisely the capacity of such terms to acquire non-ordinary meanings constitutes their continuing political promise. Indeed, I would suggest that the insurrectionary potential of such invocations consists precisely in the break that they produce between an ordinary and an extraordinary sense. I propose to borrow and depart from Bourdieu's view of the speech act as a rite of institution to show that there are invocations of speech that are insurrectionary acts.

To account for such speech acts, however, one must understand language not as a static and closed system whose utterances are functionally secured in advance by the 'social positions' to which they are mimetically related. The force and meaning of an utterance are not exclusively determined by prior contexts or 'positions'; an utterance may gain its force precisely by virtue of the break with context that it performs. Such breaks with prior context or, indeed, with ordinary usage, are crucial to the political operation of the performative. Language takes on a non-ordinary meaning in order precisely to contest what has become sedimented in and as the ordinary.

Bourdieu insists that a certain intellectualism, taking place under the rubric of 'literary semiology' or 'linguistic formalism,' misconstrues its own theoretical construction as a valid description of social reality. Such an intellectual enterprise, according to Bourdieu, not only misunderstands the positions of social power that it occupies within the institutions of the legitimate academy, but it fails to discern the critical difference between the *linguistic* and *social* dimensions of the very textual practices it attends. Although Bourdieu does not elaborate on whose intellectual positions he is criticizing under the rubric of 'literary semiology,' he appears to be engaged in a tacit struggle with Jacques Derrida's reading in 'Signature, Event, Context' of Austin's theory of the performative.

Both Bourdieu and Derrida read Austin in order to delineate more clearly the 'force' of the performative utterance, of what gives a linguistic utterance the force to do what it says, or to facilitate a set of effects as a result of what it says. Austin makes clear that the illocutionary performative derives its forcefulness or efficacy through recourse to established conventions. Once a convention is set, and the performative participates in a conventional formula – and all the circumstances are appropriate – then the word becomes the deed: the baptism is performed, the alleged criminal arrested, the straight couple marries. For Austin, conventions appear to be stable, and that stability is mirrored in a stable social context in which those conventions have become sedimented over time. The thinness of this 'theory' of social context is criticized by Bourdieu precisely because it presumes without elaborating an account of the power of social institutions, including but not limited to language itself. In an effort to counter the incipient formalism of Austin's account, Bourdieu writes of 'the essence of the error which is expressed in its most accomplished form by Austin (and after him, Habermas)':

> he thinks that he has found in discourse itself – in the specifically linguistic substance of speech, as it were – the key to the efficacy of speech. By trying to understand the power of linguistic manifestations linguistically, by looking at language for the principle underlying the logic and effectiveness of the language of institutions, one forgets that authority comes to language from outside . . . Language at most *represents* this authority, manifests and symbolizes it.

For Bourdieu, then, the distinction between performatives that work and those that fail has everything to do with the social power of the one who speaks: the one who is invested with legitimate power makes language act; the one who is not invested may recite the same formula, but produces no effects. The former is legitimate, and the latter, an imposter.

But is there a sure way of distinguishing between the imposter and the real authority? And are there moments in which the utterance forces a blurring between the two, where the utterance calls into question the established grounds of legitimacy, where the utterance, in fact, performatively produces a shift in the terms of legitimacy as an *effect* of the utterance itself? Bourdieu offers the example of liturgical ritual, and offers several examples of the conditions of its utterance and the alterations in its formulae that render the liturgy false. His judgment, however, on what is a right and wrong ritual assumes that the legitimate forms of liturgical ritual have already been established, and that new forms of legitimate invocation will not come to transform and supplant the old. In fact, the ritual that performs an infringement of the liturgy may still be the liturgy, the liturgy in its futural form.

Bourdieu's example is significant because his theory fails to recognize that a certain performative force results from the rehearsal of the conventional formulae in non-conventional ways. The possibility of a resignification of that ritual is based on the prior possibility that a formula can break with its originary context, assuming meanings and functions for which it was never intended. In making social institutions static, Bourdieu fails to grasp the logic of iterability that governs the possibility of social transformation. By understanding the false or wrong invocations as *reiterations*, we see how the form of social institutions undergoes change and alteration and how an invocation that has no prior legitimacy can have the effect of challenging existing forms of legitimacy, breaking open the possibility of future forms. When Rosa Parks sat in the front of the bus, she had no prior right to do so guaranteed by any of the segregationist conventions of the South. And yet, in laying claim to the right for which she had no *prior* authorization, she endowed a certain authority on the act, and began the insurrectionary process of overthrowing those established codes of legitimacy.

Significantly, the very iterability of the performative that Bourdieu fails to see is what preoccupies the reading of Austin that Derrida provides. For Derrida, the force of the performative is derived precisely from its decontextualization, from its break with a prior context and its capacity to assume new contexts. Indeed, he argues that a performative, to the extent that it is conventional, must be repeated in order to work. And this repetition presupposes that the formula itself continues to work in successive contexts, that it is bound to no context in particular even as, I would add, it is always found in some context or another. The 'illimitability' of context simply means that any delineation of a context that one might perform is itself subject to a further contextualization, and that contexts are not given in unitary forms. This does not mean, and never meant, that one should cease any effort to delineate a context; it means only that any such delineation is subject to a potentially infinite revision.

If Bourdieu fails to theorize the particular force produced by the utterance as it breaks with prior context, enacting the logic of iterability, Derrida focuses on those ostensibly 'structural' features of the performative that persist quite apart from any and all social contexts, and all considerations of semantics. Performative utterances operate according to the same logic as written marks, according to Derrida, which, as signs, carry 'a force that breaks with its context ... the breaking force (*force de rupture*) is not an accidental predicate but the very structure of the written text ...' Later on that same page, Derrida links the force of rupture to spacing, or the problem of the interval that iterability introduces. The sign, as iterable, is a differential mark cut off from its putative production or origin. Whether the mark is 'cut off' from its origin, as Derrida contends, or loosely tethered to it raises the question of whether the function of the sign is essentially related to the sedimentation of its usages, or essentially free of its historicity.

Derrida's account tends to accentuate the relative autonomy of the structural operation of the sign, identifying the 'force' of the performative as a structural feature of any sign that must break with its prior contexts in order to sustain its iterability as a sign. The force of the performative is thus not inherited from prior usage, but issues forth precisely from its break with any and all prior usage. That break, that force of rupture, is the force of the performative, beyond all question of truth or meaning. Derrida opposes the structural dimension of language to the semantic and describes an autonomous operation of the structural apparently purified of social residue. In writing that a performative is 'repetitive or citational in its structure' he clearly opposes the Austinian account of repeatability as a function of language as social convention. For Derrida, the iterability proper to convention has a structural status that appears separable from any consideration of the social. That 'dissemination is irreducible to polysemy' means that the dissemination of the sign, as a graphematic mark, is not reducible to the sign's capacity to bear multiple meanings; the dissemination takes place at a structural rather than semantic level.

In response to Austin's claim that 'infelicity is an ill to which *all* acts are heir which have the general character of ritual or ceremonial, all *conventional* acts,' Derrida responds with the following reformulation of the performative (enacting the repetition of the formula with a difference):

> Austin, at this juncture, appears to consider solely the conventionality constituting the *circumstance* of the utterance (*énoncé*), its contextual surroundings, and not a certain conventionality intrinsic to what constitutes the speech act (*locution*) itself, all that might be summarized rapidly under the problematical rubric of 'the arbitrary nature of the sign,' which extends, aggravates, and radicalizes the difficulty. 'Ritual' is not a possible occurrence (*éventualité*), but rather, *as* iterability, a structural characteristic of every mark.

If iterability is a structural characteristic of every mark, then there is no mark without its own proper iterability; that is, for a mark to be a mark, it must be repeatable, and have that repeatability as a necessary and constitutive feature of itself. Earlier in this same essay, Derrida suggests that 'communicating, in the case of the performative ... would be tantamount to communicating a force through the impetus (*impulsion*) of a mark.' This force is associated with the break from context, the scene in which, through repetition, the formula establishes its structural independence from any of the specific contexts in which it appears. The 'force' is not derived from conditions that are outside of language, as Bourdieu suggests, but results from the iterability of the graphematic sign.

Noting that performative effects are linked with a force that is distinct from questions of meaning or truth, Derrida remarks that 'the semantic horizon that habitually governs the notion of communication is exceeded or split by the intervention of writing ...' He then adds the phrase that we considered briefly above: ' ... by a *dissemination* irreducible to *polysemy*.' In this formulation, the semantic and the structural appear to work always and only at cross-purposes. How is this 'always and only' to be defended? What guarantees the permanence of this crossed and vexed relation in which the structural exceeds and opposes the semantic, and the semantic is always crossed and defeated by the structural? Is there a structural necessity for that relationship of confounding, a structure that founds this structure or, perhaps, a semantics?

The question seems important if one takes seriously the demand to think through the logic of iterability as a social logic. Approaching the question of the performative from a variety of political scenes – hate speech, burning crosses, pornography, gay self-declaration – compels a reading of the speech act that does more than universalize its operation on the basis of its putatively formal structure. If the break from context that a performative can or, in Derridean terms, *must* perform is something that every 'mark' performs by virtue of its graphematic structure, then all marks and utterances are equally afflicted by such failure, and it makes no sense to ask how it is that certain utterances break from prior contexts with more ease than others or why certain utterances come to carry the force to wound that they do, whereas others fail to exercise such force at all. Whereas Bourdieu fails to take account of the way in which a performative can break with existing context and assume new contexts, refiguring the terms of legitimate utterance themselves, Derrida appears to install the break as a structurally necessary feature of every utterance and every codifiable written mark, thus paralyzing the social analysis of forceful utterance. We have yet to arrive at an account of the social iterability of the utterance.

When Austin wrote that all conventional acts are subject to infelicity and 'all conventional acts are exposed to failure,' he sought to isolate the conditions of failure, in part, as circumstantial. Derrida, however, argues that there is a conventionality and a risk of failure proper to the speech act itself – a failure that is the equivalent of the arbitrariness of the sign. The sense of convention in Austin, augmented by the terms 'ritual' and 'ceremonial' is fully transmuted into linguistic iterability in Derrida. The socially complex notion of ritual, which also appears in Althusser's definitions of ideology as a 'ritual,' is rendered void of all social meaning; its repetitive function is abstracted from its social operation and established as a inherent structural feature of any and all marks.

Bourdieu, on the other hand, will seek to expand the 'ritual' sense of 'convention' and exclude any consideration of the temporality or logic of performativity. Indeed, he will contextualize ritual within the social field of the 'market' in order more radically to exteriorize the source of linguistic power.

The Austinian 'infelicities' to which performatives are liable are thus conceived very differently: performatives fail either because, for Derrida, they must fail as a condition of their iterability or, for Bourdieu, they are not backed by the appropriate expressions of social power. Derrida claims that the failure of the performative is the condition of its possibility, 'the very force and law of its emergence.' That performative utterances can go wrong, be misapplied or misinvoked, is essential to their 'proper' functioning: such instances exemplify a more general citationality that can always go awry, and which is exploited by the 'imposture' performed by the mimetic arts. Indeed, all performativity rests on the credible production of 'authority' and is, thus, not only a repetition of its own prior instance and, hence, a loss of the originary instance, but its citationality assumes the form of a mimesis without end. The imposture of the performative is thus central to its 'legitimate' working: every credible production must be produced according to the norms of legitimacy and, hence, fail to be identical with those norms and remain at a distance from the norm itself. The performance of legitimacy is the credible production of the legitimate, the one that apparently closes the gap which makes it possible.

Bourdieu argues that every misfire or misapplication highlights the social conditions by which a performative operates, and gives us a way of articulating those conditions. Bourdieu charges Derrida under the rubric of 'literary semiology' with offering an excessively formal interpretation of the performative, and yet Bourdieu amplifies the social dimension of the performative at the expense of its transformability. In this way, paradoxically, Derrida's formulation offers a way to think performativity in relation to transformation, to the break with prior contexts, with the possibility of inaugurating contexts yet to come.

See also:

Miller (4.1)
Bowlby (6.4)
Duttmann (6.5)
Cornell (9.3)

'HOMOECONOPOESIS 1'

Fred Botting and Scott Wilson

We used to play until it was pitch dark: I dreamt of becoming a professional footballer

Jacques Derrida[1]

According to a recent video collection of the finest goals scored in World Cup football, 'the greatest goal of all time' was scored by Carlos Alberto playing for Brazil in the 1970 World Cup Final.[2] Late in the game, after a period of sustained midfield possession against Italian opposition, Rivelino releases Jairzinho on the left wing: he beats Facchetti at right back and plays a square ball to Pele who is patrolling the area outside the Italian eighteen yard box. Pele traps the ball and, at walking pace, rolls it into empty space towards the corner flag. Suddenly, the Brazillian right-back comes hurtling into view to connect with the ball which rockets into the back of the Italian net. Brazil 4, Italy 1.

Forget, for a moment, the strike on goal and, instead, savour the pass. On receiving the ball Pele seems disinterested, strolling lazily about in an imperious fashion. Brazil are already 3–1 up, they are into the last 10 minutes of the game, certain not to lose. Time is suspended before the release of the ball. Pele rolls the ball . . . to nowhere, into an empty space with no receiver in sight. But in slicing across empty space the pass anticipates and creates, from nothing and in nowhere, a move of exquisite precision: beyond the televisual frame, and out of position, a defensive player – who by his own admission did not (nor was he supposed to) score many goals for the national side – arrives to complete the move. Pele's pass, in the words of Eric Cantona, the celebrated and notorious

---

Source: Fred Botting and Scott Wilson, 'Homoeconopoesis 1'.

French poet-philosopher of the soccer field, was a 'poem'. The judgement recognised in Pele's play something more than the technical skill – the craft – of the world's greatest footballer: it glimpses the extra element of creativity and vision. The poem creates the poet. And, for Cantona, such an element of poetic genius exemplifies the qualities of the truly great footballer: 'to create the moment. To step out of time. To create space from nothing. To be truly spontaneous'. The footballer-poet is thus both 'surrealist and realist, a magician and a scientist'.[3] Cantona's critical evaluation of the poetic potentiality of football became an imperative that informed his own practice on the football field. In the ambiguous tribute attributed to his countryman Michel Platini, 'sometimes I think that if Eric cannot score a beautiful goal, then he would rather not', Cantona's imperative provides football with the paradoxical, aneconomic, poetic principle that sacralizes the game for so many spectators and television viewers around the world.

As such, Cantona's poetic principle coheres, broadly, with that of another philosopher-footballer Jacques Derrida. In an essay called 'Economimesis' on Kant's Third Critique, Derrida locates poetry in a paradoxical, heterogeneous place as the value of values, the value that exceeds all evaluation yet which provides the baseless base of all evaluative discourse. Poetry, and art, in its liberality and freedom, remains a form of production that 'must not enter into the economic circle of commerce'.[4] It is a gift 'capable of pure, that is non-exchangeable productivity', a 'pure productivity of the inexchangeable': it 'liberates a sort of immaculate commerce'.[5] Poetry is a gift presenting a divine 'plus-law' [un plus-de-loi] (underwritten by the plentiful financial called God):

> By breaking with the exchange of values, by giving more than is asked and more than it promises, poetic speech is both out of circulation, at least outside any finite commerce, without any determinate value, and yet of unfinite value. It is the origin of value. Everything is measured on a scale on which poetry occupies the absolutely highest level. It is the universal analogical equivalent, and the value of values. It is in poetry that the work of mourning, transforming hetero-affection into auto-affection, produces the maximum of disinterested pleasure.[6]

For Cantona, Pele's pass steps 'out of time', creating space from 'nothing', it produces within the competitive commerce of a football match, a moment of disinterested perfection; the priceless pleasure that precisely exceeds football and its whole rationale of winning. As such, however, this poem inaugurated a new cycle in football history. Pele's pass – enacting the PP of the poetic principle – symbolizes the poetic transformation of football associated with the Brazilian side of 1970: their flair, creativity, self-expression, spontaneity and skill constituted a visionary fashioning – a poesis – of the global game, a game whose 'globalization' increased throughout the 1970s partly as an effect of the expansion of the World Cup, the spread of television and the canonisation, institutionalization and endless re-playing of certain 'timeless' moments. After Brazil's success in securing the Jules Rimet trophy for the third and final time, football, in Pele's own words, was remade as 'the beautiful game'. Unlike the England World Cup victory of 1966, which marked the last belated triumph of empire, the 1970 event was transformed by 'the beautiful game' into a global spectacle exciting wonder through moments of sublimity. The physical expenditure of energy on the pitch magically transmuted into a display of solar brilliance in which creating beauty, beyond utility or results, seemed an end in itself. The global success of the game prompted Pele to predict – and hope – that by the year 2000 the World Cup would be won by a team from Africa displaying the same brilliance.

The magical transmutation of that physical energy has, of course, much to do with television which captures, records, transmits and multiplies its image beyond the particular time and locality of its expenditure, and therefore beyond its restricted function within the context of a particular game and the enjoyment of a set of interested supporters. The disinterestedness of the moment is heightened, expanded, stretched across the globe, to function as the auto-affective focus of a hundred million television viewers dreaming, perhaps, of one day being, or having been, a professional footballer. For these viewers, football's history quickly becomes analogous to a literary history of poetic and technical innovation. As Derrida argues, in 'That Strange Institution Called Literature', literature is

> this experience of writing [that is] 'subject' to an imperative: to give space for singular events, to invent something new in the form of acts of writing which no longer consist in a theoretical knowledge, in new constative statements, to give oneself to a poetico-literary performativity at least analogous to that of promises, orders, or acts of constitution or legislation which do not only change language, or which, in changing language, change more than language.[7]

The 'singular performativity' of literature consists, in football, in instances of flair or technical innovation (Pele's pass, Cruyff's turn) or even transgression (Maradona's 'hand of God') that transcend the immediate context of football and its history (as 'timeless moments') yet nevertheless (re-)define it and enable it to technically 'progress' and give it its history. These 'gifted' players give, in their own way, and no doubt often in spite of themselves, a different temporality and extension to football, offering up moments that exceed the temporal locality of the match, the tournament, the career. In the process, these moments redefine the language of football and its cultural and economic significance, function and 'performance' around the globe.

These poetic gifts have redefined football, then, and indeed the definition of footballing excellence, to the extent that the gift is not identified primarily by, or with, the player, but has become incorporated under the sign of the brand name. To Pele's chagrin, it is now Nike who shape Brazilian football: beauty is rewritten by an implacable imperative to 'Just Do It'. Controversy surrounded the 1998 World Cup where Pele's successor Ronaldo was allegedly required to 'just do it' while suffering from serious illness and injury, as a subdued Brazilian team succumbed 3–0 in the final. A further irony surrounded the victors who, as a team assembled largely from players originating from Africa and lead by an Algerian, Zinedine Zidane, it fulfilled Pele's prophecy. The irony consisted, of course, in the fact that they were playing for France. They vanquished a Brazilian side apparently traumatized by the off-field events surrounding their star player, Ronaldo, the World Footballer of the Year. No doubt, Ronaldo's simple presence on the pitch would have been adequate for Nike, rather than his poetry, because that poetry had already been produced, and repeatedly trans-mitted on prime time television everywhere, in their advertisements. The poetry of the Brazilian players (or 'Team Nike' as they became known by rival sup-porters) was simulated in the 'Airport Lounge' and 'Airport Runway' Ads. for the admiring gaze of an Eric Cantona whose acting career had just begun. To quote Deleuze and Guattari, 'the simulacrum has become the true concept; and the one who packages the product, commodity or work of art has become the philosopher, conceptual persona, or artist'.[8]

While football metaphors dominate corporate documents and management rhetoric with injunctions to perform at the peak of accountable excellence, corporate practices dominate football's exchanges on and off the field. This is not, however, to suggest that the realm of general economy, or poetry, creative gifts, reflective and aesthetic culture, has simply gone up in smoke, expelled by the drive of an all-too restricted and rationalized principle of productive efficiency, but that the always uncertain boundaries and general economies (in the terms of Geroges Bataille) have collapsed into something which may be described as a generalization of the restricted economy, a hypermodernisation, perhaps, overwriting the plays and pluralities of postmodern practices.

Another French theorist, Arsène Wenger, has summed up this apparently impossible generalization of a restricted economic principle with his formula that 'beauty is efficiency'.[9] In 1996 Wenger took over an Arsenal team famous throughout the 1980s and early 90s as the epitome of dour, even ugly efficiency, dedicated to the neutralization of the other team, winning through defensive, offside tactics, succeeding by the barest minimum. 1–0 to the Arsenal. Wenger took this dour, defensive efficiency and made it beautiful, winning in the 1997–98 season the FA League and Cup double, in the process transforming the nature of beauty *and* efficiency. The player often named as the metaphor for Wenger's transformation is Emmanuel Petit.[10] Once 'a left-back with attitude', Petit has taken midfield play to a new dimension, producing an efficiency that combines high aggression and intense work-rate with flair, innovation and beauty. Indeed, it was an 'Arsenal' goal – a pass by Patrick Vieira finished off with clinical precision by Petit – that applied the *coup de grace* to Brazil in the 1998 World Cup final, securing victory after two headed goals by Zidane. For Wenger, 'efficiency is scoring goals', or achieving goals in managerial discourse. Wenger is a manager, but a manager whose striving for excellence consists in an imperative for constant innovation, for a 'singular performativity' that creates space and moments of timeless beauty. As Jean-Joseph Goux writes,

> it is precisely at the moment when the entrepreneur must think himself into the model of the most advanced artistic genius, at the moment when the avant-gardist strategy of innovation at any price becomes the paradigm of dominant economic practice, that the artistic avant-garde necessarily loses its difference, its marginality, its deviance-value ... it becomes more difficult for the poet to distinguish himself from the grocer, more difficult for the surrealist to differentiate himself from the disheveled manager.[11]

And what could be more fantastic, more 'surreal' than this: Steve Bould, with a delicate turn of his instep, elegantly chips the ball from midfield over the Everton back three. The ball is met by Tony Adams in the inside left position, whose blistering pace takes him beyond the leaden footed Everton defenders. Within an instance, Adams is in range, and the hitherto 'one-legged donkey' of Arsenal's back four, rifles in an unstoppable left-foot shot.[12] 4–0 to the Arsenal 4–0! Arsenal have won the Premiership with two clear games to spare. In a week's time they add the FA Cup. For Pele and Carlos Alberto substitute Steve Bould and Tony Adams. This is the measure of Wenger's 'magic'. He instills 'unbelievable belief', as one of his players, Paul Merson, memorably claimed in a postmatch interview on *Match of the Day* shortly before he was sold to Middlesborough. With Wenger there is no difference between the manager and the surrealist poet.

Before he moved to Arsenal, Wenger coached in Japan. Perhaps it was there that he absorbed some Japanese principles of managerial practice. For example, the concept that is known, according to Shuichi Wada, as 'x-efficiency' seems appropriate to Wenger's method, at least in so far as it transforms that 'x' factor from paternalism to poesis.[13] The 'x' in 'x-efficiency' marks that aneconomic factor that enables the maximization of efficency over and above the purely allocative efficiency employed in the West, particularly in North American corporations. That is, the efficiency that is supposed to accrue when workforces are subjected to the full rigours of market forces and a 'flexible' labour force, when each worker is encouraged to maximize his or her own short term benefits, unconstrained by anything other than market economics. This purely allocative efficiency proves inefficient when compared to Japanese 'x-efficiency' which employs the rigours of market forces plus the particular Japanese mode of paternalist identification that provides the means by which corporations can extract 'everything plus x' from their workforce. For Japanese workers, according to Wada, paternal identification provides the 'x' factor that denotes the trust, faith, credit that is imaginarily given to the corporation by the workers in excess of all their time, an excess that guarantees maximum efficiency. In the West, where paternalism is greeted with an incredulity subversive of paternalistic and logocentric narratives in general, such an 'x-efficiency' may be located as an internalized principle driving a highly individuated desire. Pre-eminently, these internalized 'x-factors' are produced as a literary effect of the production of highly individuated narratives (imaginary autobiographies that accompany the portfolios of an individual's career) bound up with individual dreams informed by romantic and sporting, generic narratives ('Look for the hero inside yourself' as a recent car advertisement demanded). These narratives, dreams of a career in professional football, perhaps, provide the means by which the sporting metaphors of managerial discourse hook into workers' modes of auto-affection and maximize their performance. As Derrida writes of the narcissistic power of biography and autobiography, it is precisely that which 'fails to happen', the might-have-been, that provides the 'seal' and hidden secret of desire:

> So there was a movement of nostalgic, mournful lyricism to reserve, perhaps encode, in short to render both *accessible and inaccessible*. And deep down this is still my most naive desire. I don't dream of either a literary work, or a philosophical work, but that everything that occurs, happens to me or fails to, should be as it were *sealed* (placed in reserve, hidden so as to be kept, and in this very signature, really like a signature, in the very form of the seal, with all the paradoxes that traverse the structure of a seal). The discursive forms we have available to us, the resources in terms of objectivizing archivation, are so much poorer than what happens (or fails to happen, whence the excesses of hyper-totalization). This desire for *everything* + *n* – naturally I can analyze it, 'deconstruct' it, criticize it, but it is an experience I love, that I know and recognize.[14]

The point of identification, the point of 'recognition', for Derrida, and therefore the point of desire, motivation, fantasy, auto-affection, is this point of 'n' or 'x' that is located beyond the resources of 'objectivizing archivation', beyond the economizing accountability and speculation that ordinarily governs a life or career. Derrida's highly productive career, it seems, has been built upon the lost possibilities of, for example, professional football and a strange suspicion and love of literature. Speaking of his uninterest in literary narrative ('telling stories') Derrida acknowledges that 'I'm well aware that this involves an immense forbidden desire, an irrepressible need – but one forbidden, inhibited, repressed – to tell stories, to hear stories told, to invent (language and in language)'.[15] But how efficient would an already highly successful footballer become if he were persuaded that it was precisely his career as a successful footballer that 'failed to happen'. Yet this was the opinion of Tony Adams after Wenger took over as manager of Arsenal. Adams has speculated what might-have-been had Wenger taken charge earlier in his career rather than George Graham, and wonders how much more skillful, beautiful and efficient his play might have become. Wenger's 'x-efficiency' requires that one's very profession, skill, proficiency, become a point of lacuna, aporia, gap: what one is marks the mere trace of what one might be again, for the first time.

But what does it mean that 'beauty is efficiency'? Or that efficiency is beauty? For Jacques Lacan, following Kant, beauty arrests desire through producing a disinterested, priceless pleasure, a contemplative pleasure that protects us from desire even as it supports it:

> The true barrier that holds the subject back in front of the unspeakable field of radical desire that is the field of absolute destruction, of destruction beyond putrefaction ... is beauty – beauty in all its shining radiance, beauty that has been called the splendour of truth ... Beauty stops us, but also points us in the direction of the field of destruction.[16]

In a conventional, modernist sense, the goal of efficiency is beautiful because it is the expression of some 'human' end. Beauty is the product of a certain utopian idea of efficiency that aims at a unity of form and utility devoid of bourgeois kitsch and ornament. Efficiency that does not have an idea of human utility or beauty as its end unfolds in the field of pure destruction; it is a form of death-drive or radical desire in which desire is subsumed in or revealed as a purely machinic process that bears no relation to any human end whatever. For Wenger, however, beauty is not the end of efficiency, nor is beauty devoid of efficiency, beauty *is* efficiency. Beauty is incorporated in and as a hyperefficient process that takes the dazzling, aestheticised form of pure destruction. It is perhaps no accident that Wenger has not ceased, since his tenureship at Highbury began, to predict the destruction of domestic English football as it has been played and supported for the past century. The restricted economy of English football has been fully 'economized', that is, opened out on to a general economy denoted by an intrusive continental presence, corporate sponsorship, merchandising and global marketing, stock-market flotations, satellite broadcasting and so on, all effects of the gradual de-nationalization of the game. Naturally, that de-nationalization also implies an economic displacement of all of the nation's metonymies: city, town, region, local benefactor, paternal metaphor. Football has been thrown open to the unrestricted economy of the financial markets and the global economy. In the close season of 1999, for example, Manchester United plc, having long ago given up on the idea of locally based support, attempts to break into the 'Chinese Market', hoping to capitalize on the millions of potential Chinese Manchester United fans who will have dreamt, in their replica shirts, of playing at Old Trafford.

For Derrida, the '*a*' in différance maintains a non-oppositional place, the difference between restricted and general economy that is the différence différance makes:

> Here we are touching upon the point of greatest obscurity, on the very enigma of différance, on precisely that which divides its very concept by means of a strange cleavage. How are we to think *simultaneously*, on the one hand, différance as the economic detour which, in the element of the

same, always aims at coming back to the pleasure or the presence that have been deferred by (conscious or unconscious) calculation, and, on the other hand, différance as the relation to an impossible presence, as expenditure without reserve, as the irreparable loss of presence, the irreversable use of energy, that is, the death instinct, and the entirely other relationship that apparently interrupts every economy? It is evident – and this is the evident itself – that the economical and the noneconomical cannot be thought *together* . . . [Yet] . . . Elsewhere, in a reading of Bataille, I have attempted to indicate what might come of a rigorous . . . *relating* of the 'restricted economy' . . . to a general economy that *takes into account* the nonreserve . . . I am speaking of an investment and a différance that misses its profit, the *investiture* of a presence that is pure and without loss being here confused with absolute loss, with death.[17]

It is 'through such a relating of the restricted and general economy' that Derrida has sought to displace and reinscribe 'the very project of philosophy'.[18] It is through the means of différance that the phonocentrism, logocentrism and phallocentrism that holds in place the metaphysics of the subject of literature, philosophy, history, culture, nation and so on, is deconstructed and displaced and subjected to the play of a deregulated, generalized textuality. 'Subject' (in inverted commas) not just because that subject is subverted by the alternate play of différance but because that 'play' has, as we argue here, become a deregulated, generalized economic *process* whereby the internal division in différance, its 'strange cleavage', has, in the present economic circumstances, cleaved together to produce a death-driven, nonsubjective yet paradoxically speculative absolute expenditure that takes the form of the purest, most efficient (non)production. If the word 'deconstruction' were economic rather than architectural, it might describe the way in which football, and in particular English football, has been opened out to the very forces immanent to it. More self-aware than most, and always accompanied by a lament, an elegy for the demise of the form of English football that he professes to admire so much, and that he places at the heart of Arsenal's success, Wengermanagment nevertheless requires that the postmachinic poetics of Arsenal continue as a principle of pure becoming that exceeds any point or basis of tradition, home, nation, history. What it means to be and to support a football team is in the process of being 'deconstructed' as the very basis of one's sense of support and foundation, be it local, regional or national identification, is 'subject' to a multitude of extra factors, not least the econo-textual play of performance, consumer choice and commodification. 'There is' no more football in the sense that football is locatable geographically or ontologically as a simple game of two halves between two teams playing for the fierce enjoyment of a local rivalry.

The mode of enjoyment, consequently, becomes peculiarly 'deconstructive' in a way that ought to be more fully elaborated. Derrida writes, 'everytime there is "*jouissance*" (but the "there is" of this event is in itself extremely enigmatic), there is "deconstruction". Effective deconstruction. Deconstruction perhaps has the effect, if not the mission, of liberating forbidden *jouissance*'.[19] That Arsenal have already begun playing at Wembley Stadium may be related to the demise of the national stadium and the national team, but it has no bearing on the fate of Highbury, or wherever, which will always have been bound up with the spectacle that is Arsenal-on-screen. Arsenal-on-screen is simply the mimetic form of that beautiful hyperefficiency according to which the possibilities for postindustrial human existence, for those wired into the 'developed world', at least imaginarily, are played out. On the field of human dreams, Arsenal turn autoaffection into homoeconoaffection as an effect of the screen upon which flickers, in an endless movement, the maximum of disinterested jouissance beyond the pleasure and poetic principles.

There, where Overmars was, I will becoming.

NOTES

1. Geoffrey Bennington and Jacques Derrida, *Jacques Derrida* London: University of Chicago Press, 1993, p. 341.
2. *120 Greatest Goals of the World Cup 1954–1978*. Clear Vision. Transworld International © WPE 1994.
3. Eric Cantona, quoted in Blacker and Donaldson, *Eric Cantona* 1997, p. 155.
4. Jacques Derrida, 'Economimesis', *Diacritics* 11 (1981), pp. 3–25, 5.
5. Ibid., pp. 8–9.
6. Ibid., p. 18.
7. Jacques Derrida, *Acts of Literature* ed. Derek Attridge, London Routledge, 1997, p. 55.
8. Gilles Deleuze and Felix Guattari, *What is Philosophy* tr. Graham Burchill and Hugh Tomlinson. London: Verso, 1994, p. 10.
9. David Lacey, Interview with Arsène Wenger, *The Guardian* 23 November 23, 1996, p. 26.
10. See 'Emmanuel Petit, the New Cantona' *GQ* June, 1999, pp. 158–63.
11. Jean-Joseph Goux, 'General Economics and Postmodern Capitalism' in Fred Botting and Scott Wilson (eds.) *Bataille: A Critical Reader* Blackwell, 1997, pp. 206–7.
12. In an interview paying tribute to his manager, Adams recalls scoring the goal, but avows 'That wasn't me. I don't know who that was, but it wasn't me. It was one of the most beautiful moments in my life'. *Arsenal Wenger: A Year Through the Eyes of the Gunners' Boss* Arsenal FC Video © Chrysalis Sport Production.
13. Shuichi Wada, 'Paternalism as the Major Corporate Culture and Stratification Principle in Japanese Society' *Time and Value* April 1997. See also Shuichi Wada, 'The Status and Images of the Elderly in Japan: Understanding the Paternalist Ideology' in M. Featherstone and A. Wornick (eds.), *Images of Ageing: Cultural Representations of Later Life* London: Routledge, 1995.
14. Derrida, *Acts of Literature*, p. 35.
15. Ibid., p. 40.
16. Jacques Lacan, *The Ethics of Psychoanalysis* tr. Dennis Porter, London: Routledge, 1991, pp. 216–17.
17. Jacques Derrida, 'Différance' in *Margins of Philosophy* tr. Alan Bass, Brighton: Harvester Press, 1986, p. 19.

18. Ibid.
19. Derrida, *Acts of Literature*, p. 56.

See also:

Bataille (1.3)
Johnson (6.3)
Laclau (8.5)
Derrida (11.3)

PART 6
SEXUAL DIFFERENCE

6.1

'UNNECESSARY INTRODUCTIONS'

Diane Elam

INTRODUCTIONS

How do feminism and deconstruction go together, if at all? Does deconstruction need to be feminized? Or does feminism need to be deconstructed? In either case, it would be possible to be seduced by a narrative of initial mistrust and final reconciliation. However, I am not going to tell the kind of story in which feminism learns to love the hand that corrects the error of her ways, learns to appreciate proper theoretical rigor. Nor am I going to propose that what we need is either a kinder and gentler deconstruction or a deconstruction that can be put back in touch with real problems by the mediating action of women. Thus, rather than introducing feminism and deconstruction to each other or tracing the story of their partnership, I want to argue that there is an interest in setting these two ways of thinking (which do not make a pair) alongside each other, and that this interest does not simply reside in the question of what either one may usefully learn from a partnership with the other.

So, not 'how do they go together?' but 'how are they beside each other?'. Initially, the two seem to have little in common. Feminism seems to be a political project, whereas deconstruction appears more philosophical or literary. By this account, their mutual interests do not converge. Such an argument does indeed have some merit in so far as *convergence* is *not* the right way to characterize the interaction between feminism and deconstruction. Instead, I will argue that feminism and deconstruction are beside one another in that they share a parallel

Source: Diane Elam, *Feminism and Deconstruction: Ms. en abyme* (London: Routledge, 1998), pp. 1–11.

divergence from (or dislocation of) politics and philosophy. On the one hand, feminism shifts the ground of the political, interrogating the opposition between the public and the private spheres. On the other hand, deconstruction displaces our understanding of how theory relates to practice by rethinking the opposition of philosophical reflection to political action. To draw this distinction out a bit further, it would be fair to say that feminism necessarily upsets the way we think about politics because its activist political movement is inseparable from a critique of the history of representation. And it's inseparable because of a notion of solidarity. Deconstruction upsets the way we think about philosophy because its analysis of the philosophical tradition is inseparable from an attention to the performative effects of the discourse of analysis itself. This is what distinguishes deconstruction from ideology critique. In short, then, these double displacements undo the map of intellectual and social space inherited from the Enlightenment, and this book will argue that such untying is of crucial contemporary relevance.

The contemporary relevance of setting feminism and deconstruction beside one another may not, however, be immediately transparent. Feminism's academic success has been accompanied by an anti-feminist backlash in contemporary North America, and the high academism by which deconstruction is often characterized would hardly seem to be just what the doctor ordered. My sense that it is worthwhile to consider deconstruction and feminism together *now* takes issue with this view on two points. First, I am suspicious of dinstinctions between academic and practical feminism: in contemporary Western society, being a woman is just as much a philosophical as it is a practical problem. Secondly, I do not believe that deconstruction is as merely academic as it is often made out to be: deconstruction helps one to think about the schizophrenic complexity of contemporary experiences of time and representation.

DEFINITIONS

Given that supplying answers is not the only task of thinking and that there will be several ways to read this book, I want to turn to the problems which accompany the attempt to understand the terms of my discussion. The reader may be entitled to expect some answers, for example, to the questions 'what is feminism?' and 'what is deconstruction?' The answer to both these questions is the same: 'it is not, in any simple way, one thing.'

To understand why this is so, it is important to recall that definitions work on the basis of consensus, on general agreement as to what words or phrases mean. Limits must necessarily be imposed in order to fix the definition in either synchronic or diachronic terms. However necessary this process is for everyday communication, the danger of thinking you know it all is at no time greater than when it comes to grasping hold of definitions. Definitions threaten to function like final answers which erase the fact that there were ever any questions asked in the first place; their status becomes unshakable, almost natural, and rarely if ever interrogated.

Thus, I think it would be a mistake to offer up easy definitions of either feminism or deconstruction. In this regard, Alice Jardine seems to me to be on the right track when she hints that we will not solve our problems by reaching a consensus about what 'feminism' is or exactly who is or is not a 'feminist.' The same could be said of 'deconstruction' and 'deconstructionist.' In each instance, not only will 'we' fail to solve our problems, we may not even recognize that we have any in the first place if we spend too much time trying to find the right way down the lexicographical road. I would even go so far as to argue that not only is the search for a universally agreed upon definition of 'feminism' and 'deconstruction' a waste of time, it is also highly undesirable. For once you think you know what 'feminism' and 'deconstruction' are, then their political and ethical work is done. As I have already hinted, short hand definitions, while practical at times, can easily lead to caricature, dismissal, and unnecessary limits placed on thought and political action.

Still, the argument can be made that what I am doing here is simply taking a longer route to the same defining end. That is to say, the 'isness' (*Dasein*) of 'feminism' and 'deconstruction' will inevitably emerge over the course of the book, finally establishing limits which are unavoidable if not permanently necessary. I will concede that such is the problem of any writing, but however correct that may prove, I nonetheless want to postpone establishing my limits for as long as possible. This book, therefore, will neither begin with definitions nor openly establish them at any point; rather it will let such definitions emerge only as the limits of writing necessarily impose them after the fact. As much as possible, I want to keep the act of naming and defining as a site of contestation, for the question that should continually be posed is: who gets to name what?

As a way to postpone establishing unnecessary limits, as a way to keep open the question 'who names?' I want to deploy the terms of my argument in such a way as to embrace a plurality of changing definitions, encourage the thinking of feminisms and deconstructions in the plural. To put it simply, there is no single feminism or deconstruction to define, only feminisms and deconstructions. This is not to insist, however, that there need be a different feminism for every different deconstruction, or vice versa. I want to abandon an easy symmetry between the terms and concede that at times 'feminism' becomes dislodged from 'deconstruction.' One of the problems this book faces is taking into account the plurality within and between feminism and deconstruction, while at the same time acknowledging that these terms do determine realms, categories, or spaces with a certain coherence or rigor.

In putting it this way, I have, of course, raised the possibility that feminism and deconstruction are theories – although not exactly in the scientific or philosophical sense. Feminism and deconstruction would be theories insofar as they are said to describe observable practices and experiences from a meta-discursive position and, as such, proffer knowledge on the basis of which further practices can be elaborated. 'Theory' would also be appropriate in the sense that the term, in departments of literature, serves as a kind of catch-all category for certain interdisciplinary work. As Jonathan Culler describes it, 'theory' is a genre of works that 'exceed the disciplinary framework within which they would normally be evaluated and which would help to identify their solid contributions to knowledge.' Significantly, Culler also explains a popular objection to theory's disciplinary challenge:

> Works claimed by the genre [of theory] are studied outside the proper disciplinary matrix: students of theory read Freud without enquiring whether later psychological research may have disputed his formulations; they read Derrida without having mastered the philosophical tradition; they read Marx without studying alternative descriptions of political and economic situations.

In short, theory's skeptics see a sort of willed ignorance at work, a disregard for the knowledge derived from disciplinary contexts. Feminism, of course, provides a challenge – what is its original disciplinary context? What discipline is feminism removed from in the first place? These questions will form part of the focus for my discussion of crossdisciplinarity in 'Institutional Interruptions.' But without taking up these questions now, it would be possible to say much more simply that referring to deconstruction and feminism as theories possibly provides a way to acknowledge their plurality and connectedness, at the same time that it marks both feminism and deconstruction as excessive in the ways Culler maintains.

And yet another danger of thinking of feminism and deconstruction as theories is that of lapsing into a rigid distinction between theory and practice, the distinction in terms of which deconstructive theory has so often been opposed to feminist practice. For this reason, 'theory' is perhaps a bad name for the work Culler describes, an all too easy way to contain political practice. I will take up feminism's and deconstruction's joint engagement with the political in Chapter 3; at this point it is still worth mentioning that feminism and deconstruction are political practices that do not proceed from theories in any simple way. The threat of theory is that it allows us to forget the interaction with praxis. And in light of the seriousness of this memory lapse, I think it is worthwhile to pause and consider in more detail what happens when we begin to think of feminism and deconstruction as theories. In short, I want to point out what we would swallow if we were to take the theoretical bait.

THEORIES

Whether it is used in the name of academic innovation or political revolution, theory takes its toll. Understood as a set of interpretative generalizations which explain particular texts or justify political actions, theory can actually function as a methodology that contracts rather than expands the field of knowledge and the possibilities for political action. In the case of 'deconstruction turned theoretical method of literary analysis,' a sort of party game atmosphere takes over from serious intellectual work: undermine-the-binary-opposition replaces pin-the-tail-on-the-donkey as favorite pastime. Which is not to slight the value of the latter; sometimes it's hard to tell which, through sheer repetitive methodology, is the more ridiculous exercise. In a different light, or perhaps just at a more sophisticated party, deconstruction too often becomes 'deconstructionism' – yet another delicate reading of a poem or novel, yet another girls' and boys' club on the academic theoretical scene. In this instance, we're back to the problem Jardine posed, where too much time and energy is expended on trying to figure out who's in and who's out, who's allowed to wear the official badge 'deconstructor.'

To say this is not simply to bash deconstruction. There is altogether too much of that in the popular press and in academic essays whose authors rarely bother with a serious engagement with the issues. This is the danger when Derrida's insistence on deconstruction as neither a system nor a methodology has been ignored in favor of theoretical business as usual. The ethical obligations of which deconstruction should remind us are abandoned in favor of institutional recognizability.

Likewise, feminism verges on the possibility of turning into yet another form of thematic criticism appropriated by the academy. The most widespread form of this is an endless series of readings, whose theoretical operations could be described as: 1. find the women in the text; 2. women are oppressed in —; or 3. women find their voice in —. While there was certainly a great deal of political force behind the readings which first broached these topics so as to connect readings of representations of women to social and cultural positions of women, how many times must these readings be repeated? Is there another kind of injustice committed when all discussions must revolve around 'the problem of women' in history, science, literature, society, etc.? Feminism as thematic criticism (although I would not want to dismiss its legitimacy altogether) tends to forget the variety of inflections of feminism. For some, feminism means equal pay, abortion rights, and a partnership in a law firm. For others, feminism means a celebration of women as separate and distinct from men. To others still, feminism is a subversive ideology used to undermine authority and create alternative power structures. There is no thematic identity to 'woman' in these various arguments, which doesn't mean that feminism ought not to support them all in different contexts.

The problem with thematic criticism is that notions of 'women's issues,' 'women's interests,' and so on cannot help but imply that there is an identity to 'woman,' which would legitimate the determination of what the correct interests, attitudes, and concerns of any particular woman or of all women are. What this boils down to is a problem that feminism, especially in her academic gown, shares with deconstruction: the main concern becomes a question of: who's a good feminist and who's a bad daughter? What is correct feminist theory and political action? In this (dis)guise, feminism also threatens to become an old girls' (and sometimes boys') club, organized around the same power structure of the patriarchy that it set out to displace. That is to say, in the strongest version of this theoretical pitfall, feminism takes on the power structure in which hierarchical mothers make certain that their daughters remain dutiful in the name of feminism, or more precisely in the name of *the* theory of feminism.

Again, I think it's worth stating that my remarks about the restrictions potentially imposed in the name of feminism as a theory are not meant to join the chorus of backlash anti-feminists or 'post-feminists.' I neither simply oppose feminism nor write from a historical moment in which I believe that feminism is over, has done all the work she can do, or has been killed off by the patriarchy that she set out to fight. What I am trying to say is that when feminism fixes its theoretical gaze it is neither immune to appropriation designed to make it lose its political effectiveness nor exempt from committing the same kind of injustices it seeks to oppose.

Trinh Minh-ha compellingly articulates this serious predicament when she argues that:

> Theory no longer is theoretical when it loses sight of its own conditional nature, takes no risks in speculation, and circulates as a form of administrative inquisition. Theory oppresses, when it wills or perpetuates existing power relations, when it presents itself as a means to exert authority – the Voice of Knowledge.

Univocal theoretical methodology threatens to cripple any attempt by feminism and deconstruction to redefine the political or consider ethical obligations. However, it seems to me that salvation does not lie in purifying theory (keeping theory theoretical), as Trinh's remarks imply, but in the refusal of theoretical purity, the refusal to believe that action happens elsewhere. To illustrate this, I would like to return to the important nexus of theory/practice and thus imagine a critical space for feminism and deconstruction which is not simply a theoretical one.

MOVEMENTS

If feminism and deconstruction are neither terms available for definition, nor theories, we may perhaps consider them as 'movements.' The term already has considerable currency in the feminist context. While 'movement' does lend a sense of political coherence around which to negotiate, I would argue that it also can too readily associate itself with common cause identity politics, with political groups composed of leaders with identifiable followers (who 'identify' with one another). That a feminism and a deconstruction would want to challenge the foundationalism of identity politics is an important concern that I will take up in Chapter 3; the challenge actually could be said to begin earlier in Chapter 2 with the recognition that there is also no small problem with the deployment of the word 'women' – a problem exacerbated in this context by those who seek to oppose the women's movement with the deconstruction movement.

And yet for all these difficulties, 'movement' is still not without merit here, for it suggests that feminism and deconstruction, as political movements of sorts, have a historical development in a political context. There is a great deal of political strength to be gained from this description in the appeal to a kind of structural coherence which exerts a political force. In light of these remarks, if I were to describe the focus of this book as being on the feminist and deconstructive movements, such phrasing would suggest that I am tracing the development of their political effectiveness over time. And to a certain extent this book will do that, although it does not really need the term 'movement' to make its engagement with historical and political questions clear. In some instances, 'movement' even hinders more than it helps in highlighting the way in which this book is a historical project or feminism and deconstruction are political. For just as my argument hopes to challenge commonly held understandings of 'the political,' it also attempts to rethink its own will to historicity. The book will contain an interrogation of what it would mean to tell a historical story of the relationship between feminism and deconstruction, insofar as history, in the wake of feminism and deconstruction, does not remain the same – either in force or narrative structure. Deconstruction and feminism change what it means to understand the past, to recognize the force of and our obligation to past events. Thus, they cannot best be understood as movements, as the incarnation of modernist projects that seek to erase our obligation to the past in favor of our obligation to the future. The feminist movement has been condemned to a succession of generational tensions over the past eighty years or so, as each daughter claims to be a 'new woman,' the first to affirm her identity, and each mother complains that the daughter is ignoring an existing struggle – losing her identity, going too far. One important feature of the encounter between feminism and deconstruction is that it allows us to rethink the temporality of feminism's movement, perhaps as something closer to the dance than to Mao's long march.

PHILOSOPHIES

If 'movement' proves a less than satisfactory alternative for all occasions, other ready-to-hand choices certainly are available. Since philosophy has traditionally been charged with establishing the relations between disciplines, it would seem the most convenient and obvious choice of a disciplinary ground for the encounter of feminism and deconstruction. Nevertheless, philosophy does not supply an untroubled disciplinary ground upon which to judge the relationship between the two.

The fact that feminism and deconstruction have met at best with chilly receptions in most philosophy departments in the United States speaks to an initial difficulty: there is certainly some territory to be negotiated here. One of the problems is that some philosophers do not consider either feminism or deconstruction to be philosophy, properly speaking. Likewise, some feminists have sought to discard the Western philosophical tradition as irrevocably patriarchal. Deconstruction has evinced a similar uncertainty about its relation to philosophy. While Derrida insists that he has never done anything but philosophy, some epigones have identified deconstruction as the triumph of writing (or literature) over philosophy. Historically speaking, philosophy in the West has emphasized a notion of universal or absolute truth, of which deconstructors have been suspicious and of which women (among others) have been the victims.

But these are not the only problems in considering deconstruction and feminism both as philosophies. It would be unfair not to mention the increasing disciplinary divide between analytic or ordinary language philosophy, logic, and speculative philosophy – and each camp would certainly want to carve up feminism and deconstruction in their own ways, some dismissing them altogether from the realm of serious philosophy. If that is not enough, it would also be possible to say that there no longer is any such thing as philosophy in which deconstruction and feminism could participate. Such is the argument in Heidegger's late writing, where he claims that 'philosophy is ending in the present age' because 'it has found its place in the scientific attitude of socially active humanity.'

Leaving aside for the moment Heidegger's complaint and discarding an interest in whether philosophy has a disciplinary method of its own which would thus determine feminism's and deconstruction's status, I think the most significant obstacle or resistance to the wholesale appropriation of the term 'philosophy' is that feminism and deconstruction can be considered philosophies, can 'belong' to the discipline of philosophy, only if we rethink what it is we mean by 'philosophy' and what it might mean to belong to its discipline. The issue here is not one of 'add gender and stir,' or deconstructive party games invading the serious halls of wisdom. Rather, the double bind is that feminist philosophy turns into feminist readings of philosophy, deconstructive philosophy depends upon the deconstruction of philosophy. That is to say, there is no use in trying to fit feminism and deconstruction into the pre-existing disciplinary boundaries of 'philosophy' if those disciplinary borders cannot be renegotiated as deconstruction and feminism insist they must. While I will hold open the possibility that these borders can and have been renegotiated, that deconstruction and feminism are philosophy in a certain sense, I do not think that it is particularly useful to listen to the conversation between feminism and deconstruction solely positioned in the philosopher's seat. Although philosophy will have a certain status in my argument, it will not reign supreme throughout the entire book, not the least because there is always that rhetorical problem, as Derrida well understands, where 'philosophy, as a theory of metaphor, first will have been a metaphor of theory.'

See also:

Critchley (3.5)
Kamuf (4.6)
Butler (5.6)
Spivak (8.4)

6.2

'THE SAME DIFFERENCE'

Robert Young

Screen's Winter 1987 issue is entitled 'Deconstructing "Difference"'. What would it mean to deconstruct 'difference'? Given, that is, that deconstruction charts the operation of something called *différence* – which is already defined as deconstructed difference. Why does *Screen* need to do it all over again?

We soon discover, however, that neither 'deconstructing' nor 'difference' are being used in a technical deconstructive sense. In 'Difference and Its Discontents', the introduction to the issue, Mandy Merck makes it clear that by 'difference' is meant 'the theory of sexual difference'.[1] The theory of sexual difference, she suggests, requires deconstruction, in the name of sameness.

But is there such a thing as '*the* theory of sexual difference'?

Apparently so, for the complaint against 'the theory of sexual difference' is precisely that it is a homogenous theory. But, paradoxically, what is wrong with this homogeneous theory is that it always promotes heterogeneity. It neglects sameness in its desire for otherness: otherness always defined as 'the same difference' of heterosexuality.

Merck argues that what she calls 'the "difference" school' is 'largely unable to theorise homosexuality' (p 6). As proof she cites the lack of lesbian representation in the *Oxford Literary Review*'s 'Sexual Difference' conference, and the absence of homosexuality altogether in the exhibition *Difference: On Representation and Sexuality*.[2] While there is no doubt that homosexuality was under-represented in both cases, it does not necessarily follow that this was

Source: Robert Young, 'The same difference', *Screen*, 28 (3), 1987, pp. 4–11.

the result of a deficiency in theory. For it is not so much that the so-called difference school has been unable to theorise homosexuality as that its theorisation of homosexuality has produced certain theoretical problems. These in turn produce difficulties at the level of political strategy. However, Merck's own arguments demonstrate that such problems cannot be solved by attacking difference as such.

For difference has already been deconstructed[3], even if such deconstruction has been no less under-represented in the pages of *Screen* for the last twenty years than homosexuality itself. The awkward dilemma that arises is that in the first instance at least 'deconstructing "difference"' actually makes the representation of homosexuality more problematical. It is not necessarily a question of homosexuality being repressed but rather that difference theory makes categories such as homosexuality, no less than heterosexuality or bisexuality, more difficult to sustain. That was the reason why the *Oxford Literary Review*'s conference was called simply *Sexual Difference*. The point was that the instability or seeming dissolution of the terms through which sexual politics operate poses a political problem. It would be fair to add that this difficulty was not in the event adequately addressed by the conference, and more often simply produced expressions of anxiety, or even, disturbingly, of homophobia.

In this context it seems extraordinary that *Screen* still finds it necessary in 1987 to present a theoretical critique of sexual difference theory as a 'typology of dualism' (p 5). Has *Screen*, perhaps, had to revive it because a certain theorisation of homosexuality needs such a hypostatisation for its own self-definition, even if that self-definition presents itself in antithesis to it? Merck suggests that this curious theoretical timewarp is the result of the influence of Mulvey's 1975 essay, 'Visual Pleasure and Narrative Cinema' – despite the fact that many, including Mulvey herself, have since argued that it assumes too rigid a dualism of sexual division.[4] Of course it is possible to read both Freud and Lacan as implying a binary opposition masculine/feminine in a theory of sexuality organised around the terms phallus/castration. But, as Merck acknowledges, such a reading has also been disputed throughout the whole history of psychoanalysis, and especially since the '70s by critiques which either offer revisions of Freud and Lacan (Irigaray, Cixous, Montrelay, Heath, Kristeva) or re-readings of them so as to show the instability of such oppositions in their texts (Derrida, Rose).[5]

Merck goes on to suggest that despite the many critiques of sexuality as a binary opposition, from the perspective of lesbian and gay politics sexual difference still looks as if it is 'conceived within a dualism' (p 5). But does homosexuality in fact make trouble for 'the surprisingly stable opposites of "difference"' (p 9) as she claims? It is impossible to answer this question without asking another: what are the 'opposites of "difference"'? Does difference in fact have opposites at all – or are there only differences in difference? Here we encounter the real problem in Merck's argument, in as much as it repeats the very assumptions that she denounces: she complains that difference theory always presupposes the same difference (heterosexuality), but she in turn assumes difference theory to be always the same: 'the theory of sexual difference', 'sexual difference theory', 'difference theorists', 'the "difference" school', are all lumped together as one unchanging theory, one undifferentiated 'school'. This is, apparently, because from the perspective of gay and lesbian politics all difference theory seems to be predicated on a psychoanalytic account of difference that assumes a stable and untroubled masculine/feminine opposition. However not all difference theory is psychoanalytic – deconstruction, for instance.

In many areas of what Merck describes as 'difference theory' a distinction is made between differences and opposites. This is because such theories are predicated on Saussure's account of difference which denied that individual words possess intrinsic meaning, arguing instead that they only take on meaning by being distinguishable from other words 'in language there are only differences *without positive terms*', or, as Derrida puts it: 'difference inscribes itself without any decidable poles, without any independent, irreversible terms'.[6]

Although Merck follows Dugald Williamson in his Foucauldian critique of Lacan's stress on the function of language in psychoanalysis,[7] the rigid opposition masculine/feminine that she seeks to trouble can only be disturbed by showing that these terms are not in fact the positive terms of sexual identity. Lacan recognised that Freud's emphasis on the interchangeability of positionality in sexual fantasy shows that sexual difference operates in exactly the same way as linguistic difference: there are not just two poles masculine/feminine but an undecidable set of terms through which the subject circulates. As D N Rodowick points out in his analysis of 'A Child is being Beaten', the subject takes up multiple positions of identification, whether successively or simultaneously, 'in which transactions between the masculine and feminine positions are both variable and necessary', and beyond even that where:

> The very question of desire seems to require the transgression of the positionalities defined as 'masculine' and 'feminine' by constructing a sedimentary structure in which variable positions of identification and places of enunciation are overlayed.[8]

Thus sexuality, as both Freud and Lacan have argued, is not fixed but rather extremely mobile at the level of fantasy and only restricted or stabilised at all through social and cultural pressure with respect to object choice. But if there is no untroubled dualism of heterosexuality in psychoanalytic theory, the corollary follows that this also has to mean that there is no untroubled homosexuality either, indeed that there is no 'pure', stable or intrinsic homosexuality any more than there is 'pure', stable or intrinsic heterosexuality. No more than an unwavering masculine/feminine binary, there is no undisturbed heterosexual/homosexual binary.

Such a theory of undecidability means that, like language or the psyche itself, sexuality does not work by the rational logic of non-contradiction in which an entity cannot both be A and not A at the same time, a point which has escaped Williamson in his critique of Lacan. He demonstrates that the Lacanian theory of the Imaginary and Symbolic 'conflates two discontinuous ideas of difference' (p 18) and claims that this contradiction represents a major problem for Lacanian psychoanalysis. It certainly would if psychoanalysis operated, as Williamson does, according to the formal protocols of rational logic. Not using psychoanalytic concepts himself, Williamson forgets that the crucial innovation of psychoanalysis is that it offers a theory of unresolved conflict.

For Lacan, as for Freud, the psyche is constituted by antagonistic forces. There are no negatives or contradictions in the unconscious: the subject has to live its incompatible differences simultaneously, and that is why there is never accession to a full, self-present consciousness, nor, for that matter, assumption of a stable sexual identity. Subjectivity really is constituted by discontinuous differences: that is the whole problem – not for Lacanian psychoanalysis but for the psyche, and for us. The fact that according to Freud and Lacan the psyche operates according to the same structures as linguistic difference – double, contradictory, and undecidable – is either a measure of the primary role that language plays in psychic life or, as Derrida argues, demonstrates that the psyche itself is already an effect of linguistic difference. If the connection between subjectivity, language and sexuality were severed, however, as Williamson suggests it should be, then there would be no option but to return to the realm of a rational logic of non-contradiction and thus of fixed polarities in which difference means opposition – in which case there would be no incompatibility, no unconscious, no gap between representation and biology and nothing but an essentialist sexuality of a male/female dualism.

Merck's suspicion of the linguistic account of difference means that she finds it impossible to get out of the structure of the very oppositions which she criticises. She suggests that the heterosexual binary of masculine/feminine needs to be deconstructed – but it is open to question whether this so-called 'deconstruction' is likely to meet with any more success when all that happens is that Merck puts another binary, heterosexual/homosexual, in its place. Why challenge a binary opposition because it is restricted within a typology of dualism if you are only going to substitute another? Nor does Merck's 'deconstruction' of difference in the name of a sameness defined in opposition to otherness give any more promise of escaping the topology of binarisms.

For same and other, identity and difference, homosexuality and heterosexuality, homogeneity and heterogeneity, all are conceptual categories that work in the same way as the male/female dualism. It is true that culturally and politically the opposition will work as a hierarchy in which one term will be valorised over the other. But the simple reversal of this hierarchy only remains within its terms and does not challenge it – in fact it only perpetuates it. It is for this reason that Derrida makes the at first startling suggestion that 'phallocentrism and homosexuality can go, so to speak, hand in hand'.[9] If binary oppositions in effect depend on and reinforce each other then phallocentrism may indeed be a homosexual enterprise, both determined by and organised around the having or not having of the phallus. 'No genitally similar object can be legitimately eroticised' (p 6). Merck complains, clearly not too keen to advocate constructions of sexuality 'without pregiven "content"' (p 3).

But this contradiction, in which on the one hand she shows an inclination towards a theory of sexuality predicated on a biological genitality (whether it be the same or different) while on the other hand she criticises sexual difference theory for being too rigid in its dualisms suggests that a more interesting argument is being broached: sexual difference theory is too different but at the same time there are not enough differences. It is this apparent contradiction that unsettles the binary structure that Merck wishes to shift, both overturning it and at the same time displacing it.

This becomes clearest in the paragraph in which we are told that the counter-assertion to 'the same difference' of heterosexuality in the *Sexual Difference* conference and the *Difference: On Sexuality and Representation* exhibition took the form of an article and an exhibition both entitled – 'The Same Difference' (p 6). Is this second 'same difference' supposed to be the same difference or a different same difference to the first? Apparently it is impossible to tell: the 'same difference' is the term both of a complaint against heterosexuality and also the characterisation of what is being advocated against it. Merck writes that it 'can be read to criticise the hypostatisation of heterosexual difference in contemporary theory *or* [my emphasis] to claim an equivalent ratio of difference, and desire, for homosexuality' (p 6). It wants a difference, but then it also wants an equivalent difference (the same difference?). So 'the same difference' is not necessarily always 'the same old same' difference (p 9), even if it is the same difference. But if that is the case is it still the same difference – or is it really different?

Alternatively, perhaps the same differences really are the same, that is, the same difference of heterosexuality is the same as the same difference of homosexuality. But how can heterosexuality, that is sexuality for the other, be the same as homosexuality, sexuality for the same? Can the other be the same or the same be the other? They certainly need each other: after all, the same cannot be the same on its own, it has to be defined against the other in order to be the same. It is only the other that makes the same the same. But then the same cannot be the same except by being the other for the other, while, on the other hand, 'the other cannot be the other – of the same – except by being the same (as itself)'.[10] In order to be the same, the same must also be other; it must differ from itself.

If this suggests a problem for sameness at least Merck allows for a different option: it might be possible to revive Monique Plaza's attempt to separate sexual difference from identity. Identity is beset with the same problems as sameness, in that it cannot be thought except as differing from the different, and therefore difference is what enables identity to be itself.[11] But Plaza's attempt to separate sexual difference from such labyrinths does not succeed in evading them: she suggests that by detaching the hierarchy of male/not-male from the self/other distinction then woman could become '"other *than* not-male" rather than "other *and* not male"' (p 7). However, as the terms themselves indicate, this revision does not manage to avoid either the male/not-male or the self/other categories as such. What Plaza's argument suggests instead is a certain internal differentiation in the notion of the other, which can be either – and therefore both – not male and other than not-male. The other therefore differs from itself: just as for Merck's 'the same difference'. Perhaps it is not altogether by chance that both arguments end up by repeating nothing less than the structure of the unconscious itself; in Samuel Weber's description:

> If the unconscious means anything whatsoever, it is that the relation between self and others, inner and outer, cannot be grasped as an **interval between polar opposites** but rather as an irreducible dislocation of the subject in which the other inhabits the self as its condition of possibility.[12]

In view of this insistent logic of an internal difference in all attempts to define sexuality in terms of sameness or otherness it is intriguing that Merck approvingly cites Aimee Rankin's criticism that 'difference theory' 'displays more deference than difference' (p 9) – for the deconstruction of difference involves almost exactly that. In Derrida's words:

> The verb 'to differ' [**différer**] seems to differ from itself. On the one hand it indicates difference as distinction, inequality, or discernibility; on the other it expresses the interposition of delay, the interval of a **spacing** and **temporalizing** that puts off until 'later' what is presently denied, the possible that is presently impossible. Sometimes the **different** and sometimes the **deferred** correspond [in French] to the verb 'to differ.' This correlation, however, is not simply one between act and object, cause and effect, or primordial and secondary.
>
> In the one case 'to differ' signifies nonidentity; in the other case it signifies the order of the **same** ... We provisionally give the name **différence** to this **sameness** which is not **identical**: by the silent writing of its a, it has the desired advantage of referring to differing, **both** as spacing/temporalizing and as the movement that structures every dissociation.[13]

'*Différance* is the name for the spatio-temporal differed-and-deferred economy of this sameness which is not identical',[14] the very structure that Merck's own argument has led to. Derrida names it *différance* in order to bring attention to the way in which difference differs from itself: heard, *différence/différance* sound the same, but when written they are different from each other and no longer identical. *Différance* does not offer an alternative to the conceptuality of binary oppositions (for that would itself form another binary opposition) but instead both enables and confounds them:

The same, precisely, is **différance** (with an **a**) as the displaced and equi-vocal passage of one different thing to another, from one term of an opposition to another. Thus one could reconsider all the pairs of opposites on which philosophy is constructed and on which our discourse lives, not in order to see opposition erase itself but to see what indicates that each of the terms must appear as the **différance** of the other, as the other different and deferred in the economy of the same.[15]

Différance thus describes the operating conditions of the strange logic of binary oppositions in which they always exceed themselves, in which opposite terms will always be defined as different from each other, but by that very token as also the same: 'it is an operation that *both* sows confusion *between* opposites *and* stands *between* the opposites "at once"'.[16] The economy of *différance*, in short, produces the effects of undecidable difference between same and other, identity and difference, and all other binary oppositions that we have been charting.

As Derrida demonstrates, exactly the same structure can be found at work in the texts of Freud. At this point we may recall Freud's curious habit of making distinctions based on a male/female polarity that he then seems to disavow. Inevitably this has led to hotly contested arguments about whether Freud or Lacan's work is implicated in biologism or patriarchy or is set against them, and the argument could go on for ever as long as each side claims one kind of statement as Freud's authentic position – which can then be promptly denied by an appropriate citation supporting the other view. But to read Freud as either promulgating a fixed opposition, or attempting to redeem him by showing how elsewhere he disowns it is to miss the point. His texts argue both, simultaneously:

All the oppositions that furrow Freudian thought relate each of his concepts one to another as moments of a detour in the economy of **différance**. One is but the other different and deferred, one differing and deferring the other. One is the other in **différance**, one is the **différance** of the other. This is why every apparently rigorous and irreducible **opposition** (for example the opposition of the secondary to primary) comes to be qualified, at one moment or another, as a 'theoretical fiction'.[17]

Such a contradiction remains unthinkable according to the normal protocols of logic, but it is precisely the moves of such procedures that deconstruction, and indeed psychoanalysis, trace.

This structure may also account for the curious necessity remarked upon earlier for Merck to rerun the critique of sexuality as a dualism: the deconstruction of such an argument shows how it is constructed by means of certain ambivalent forms of inclusions and exclusions which have the effect of making it rely upon elements that it can neither fully assimilate nor control. For homosexuality to define itself it must begin by differentiating itself from what it is not, even though this means that it will never entirely succeed in separating itself from it: each term of the opposition appears as the *différance* of the other. In Weber's description this process enacts

> a movement of conflictual decomposition and recomposition in which that which is posited sets itself apart: that is, both demarcates itself from an other to which it is opposed; and **de-marks** itself by prescribing yet another, third term, which inexorably replaces and displaces the other two.[18]

This is the story of how sameness, in opposing itself to difference, becomes 'the same difference'.

From this perspective homosexuality can scarcely be regarded as a disavowal of difference, as Merck claims (pp 5–6), for 'the same, precisely, is *différance*': heterosexuality and homosexuality are distinguished as the same, but different, difference, each the supplementary double of the other. Homosexuality's cultural repression is perhaps a marker of just how close that difference is.[19] This account of the constitution of sexuality poses a political problem, however, for it seems to stand in antithesis to the general oppositional and self-defining strategies of gay politics. Yet the political problem is also that culturally and institutionally homosexuality and heterosexuality are marked as, simply, different. At this point gay politics comes up against the same difficulty as that of feminism, with which Merck concludes:

> in some cases the objectives of feminist politics go against sexual differences, in other cases they do not, and the problem is to find out which is which.[20]

The trick, however, is not to get caught within the binary terms of an either/or choice, of a bewildered 'which is which?'. The political strategy must be to assert sexual difference while simultaneously, paradoxically, showing that difference to be the same.

NOTES

1. Mandy Merck, 'Introduction – Difference and Its Discontents', *Screen* Winter 1987, vol 28 no 1, pp 2–9. Further references will be cited in the text.
2. See *Sexual Difference*, *Oxford Literary Review*, vol 8 nos 1–2, 1986, and *Difference: On Representation and Sexuality*, New York, The New Museum of Contemporary Art, 1985.
3. On January 27, 1968, to be precise. See Jacques Derrida, 'Différence', in *Speech and Phenomena and Other Essays on Husserl's Theory of Signs*, Evanston, Northwestn University Press, 1973, pp 129–60, also, in a slightly modified form, in *Margins of Philosophy*, Chicago, University of Chicago Press, 1982, pp 1–27.
4. Laura Mulvey, 'Visual Pleasure and Narrative Cinema', *Screen* Autumn 1975, vol 16 no 3, pp 6–18. The critiques of Mulvey's article are discussed by Merck, op cit, pp 4–5.
5. Luce Irigaray, *Speculum of the Other Woman*, Ithaca, Cornell University Press, 1985; Hélène Cixous, *The New Born Woman*, University of Minnesota, 1986; Michèle Montrelay, *L'Ombre et le nom: Sur la féminité*, Paris, Minuit, 1977; Stephen Heath, 'Difference', *Screen* Autumn 1978, vol 19, no 3, pp 51–112; Julia

Kristeva, *Powers of Horror: An Essay on Abjection*, New York, Columbia University Press, 1982; Jacques Derrida, 'The Purveyor of Truth', *Yale French Studies*, vol 52, 1975, pp 31–113; Jacqueline Rose, 'Introduction II' to Jacques Lacan and the école freudienne, *Feminine Sexuality*, London, Macmillan, 1982, pp. 27–57.

6. Ferdinand de Saussure, *Course in General Linguistics*, London, Fontana, 1974, p 120; Jacques Derrida, *Dissemination*, Chicago, University of Chicago Press, 1981, p 210.

7. Dugald Williamson, 'Language and Sexual Difference', *Screen* Winter 1987, vol 28 no 1, pp 10–25. Further references will be cited in the text.

8. D N Rodowick, 'The Difficulty of Difference', *Wide Angle*, vol 5 no 1, pp 11, 13.

9. Jacques Derrida and Christie V McDonald, 'Choreographies', *Diacritics*, vol 12 no 2, 1982, p 72.

10. Jacques Derrida, *Writing and Difference*, London, Routledge and Kegan Paul, 1978, p 128.

11. Mandy Merck, op cit, p 7, citing Monique Plaza, '"Phallomorphic Power" and the Psychology of "Woman"', *Ideology and Consciousness*, no 4, 1978, pp 4–36. For a succinct account of the complexities involved in the concepts of identity and difference, see Vincent Descombes, *Modern French Philosophy*, Cambridge, Cambridge University Press, 1980, pp 36–9.

12. Samuel Weber, *The Legend of Freud*, Minneapolis, University of Minnesota Press, 1982, pp 32–3.

13. Jacques Derrida, *Speech and Phenomena*, op cit, pp 129–30.

14. Jacques Derrida, *Margins of Philosophy*, op cit, p 9.

15. ibid, p 17.

16. Jacques Derrida, *Dissemination*, op cit, p 212.

17. Jacques Derrida, *Margins of Philosophy*, op cit, p 18.

18. Samuel Weber, op cit, p 31.

19. cf. Jonathan Dollimore, 'Homophobia and Sexual Difference', *Sexual Difference, Oxford Literary Review*, vol 8 nos 1–2, p 5.

20. Mandy Merck, op cit, p 9, citing Parveen Adams in '*m/f*: Interview 1984', *m/f*, nos 11–12, 1986, p 14.

See also:

Norris (3.1)
Benington (5.1)
Readings (8.3)
Bernasconi (9.2)

6.3

'GENDER THEORY AND THE YALE SCHOOL'

Barbara Johnson

As Harold Bloom puts it in the opening essay of the Yale School's non-manifesto, *Deconstruction and Criticism*: 'Reading well is not necessarily a polite process ... Only the capacity to wound gives a healing capacity the chance to endure, and so to be heard.'[1] I hope, therefore, that my hosts will understand the spirit in which I will use them as the starting point for the depiction of a much larger configuration, and that by the end of this paper I will not have bitten off more of the hand that feeds me than I can chew.

In January of this year, shortly after the death of Paul de Man, I received a call from Robert Con Davis inviting me to attempt the painful and obviously impossible task of replacing de Man in a conference in which Geoffrey Hartman, Hillis Miller, and Paul de Man had been asked to speak about genre theory in relation to their own work. I was invited to speak, however, not about *my* own work but about de Man's. The reasons for this are certainly understandable. I could easily sympathize with the conference organizers' impulse: there is nothing I could wish more than that de Man had not died. But the invitation to appear as de Man's *supplément* – supplemented in turn by a panel of my own choosing – gave me pause. For it falls all too neatly into patterns of female effacement already well established by the phenomenon of the Yale School – and indeed, with rare exceptions, by the phenomenon of the critical 'school' as such. Like others of its type, the Yale School has always been a Male School.

Source: Barbara Johnson, 'Gender theory and the Yale School', *Genre*, 17 (1–2), 1984, pp. 101–12.

Would it have been possible for there to have been a female presence in the Yale School? Interestingly, in Jonathan Culler's bibliography to *On Deconstruction* Shoshana Felman's book *La Folie et la chose littéraire* is described as 'a wide-ranging collection of essays by a member of the "école de Yale."'[2] Felman, in other words, *was* a member of the Yale School, but only in French. This question of the foreignness of the female language will return, but for now, suffice it to say that there was no reason other than gender why Felman's work – certainly closer to de Man's and Derrida's than the work of Harold Bloom – should not have been seen as an integral part of the Yale School.

At the time of the publication of *Deconstruction and Criticism*, several of us – Shoshana Felman, Gayatri Spivak, Margaret Ferguson, and I – discussed the possibility of writing a companion volume inscribing female deconstructive protest and affirmation centering not on Shelley's 'The Triumph of Life' (as the existing volume was originally slated to do) but on Mary Shelley's *Frankenstein*. That book might truly have illustrated the Girardian progression 'from mimetic desire to the monstrous double.' Unfortunately, this *Bride of Deconstruction and Criticism* never quite got off the ground, but it is surely no accident that the project was centered around monstrosity. As Derrida puts it in 'The Law of Genre' – which is also, of course, a law of gender – 'As soon as genre announces itself, one must respect a norm, one must not cross a line of demarcation, one must not risk impurity, anomaly, or monstrosity.'[3] After all, Aristotle, the founder of the law of gender as well as of the law of genre, considered the female as the first distortion of the genus 'man' en route to becoming a monster. But perhaps it was not *Frankenstein* but rather *The Last Man*, Mary Shelley's grim depiction of the gradual extinction of humanity altogether, that would have made a fit counterpart to 'The Triumph of Life.' Shelley is entombed in both, along with a certain male fantasy of Romantic universality. The only universality that remains in Mary Shelley's last novel is the plague.

It would be easy to accuse the male Yale School theorists of having avoided the issue of gender entirely. What I intend to do, however, is to demonstrate that they have had quite a lot to say about the issue, often without knowing it. Before moving on to a female version of the Yale School, therefore, I will begin by attempting to extract from the essays in *Deconstruction and Criticism* and related texts an implicit theory of the relations between gender and criticism. For the purposes of this paper, I will focus on the four members of the Yale School who actually teach full time at Yale. Since Derrida, the fifth participant in *Deconstruction and Criticism*, has in contrast consistently and explicitly foregrounded the question of gender, his work would demand far more extensive treatment than is possible here. I will confine myself to the more implicit treatments of the subject detectable in the writings of Bloom, Hartman, Miller, and de Man.

Geoffrey Hartman, ever the master of the throwaway line, has not failed to make some memorable remarks about the genderedness of the reading process. 'Much reading,' he writes in *The Fate of Reading*, 'is indeed, like girl-watching, a simple expense of spirit.'[4] And in *Beyond Formalism*, he claims: 'Interpretation is like a football game. You spot a hole and you go through. But first you may have to induce that opening.'[5]

In his essay in *Deconstruction and Criticism*, Hartman examines a poem in which Wordsworth, suddenly waylaid by a quotation, addresses his daughter Dora with a line from Milton's Samson that harks back to the figure of blind Oedipus being led by his daughter Antigone:

> A Little onward lend thy guiding hand
> To these dark steps, a little further on! (*DC* p. 215)

This is certainly a promising start for an investigation of gender relations. Yet Wordsworth and Hartman combine to curb the step of this budding Delilah and to subsume the daughter under the Wordsworthian category of 'child,' who, as everyone knows, is *Father* of the man. While the poem works out a power reversal between blind father and guiding daughter, restoring the father to his role of natural leader, the commentary works out its patterns of reversibility between Wordsworth and Milton. 'Let me, thy happy guide, now point thy way/And now precede thee …' When Wordsworth leads his daughter to the edge of the abyss, it is the abyss of intertextuality.

While brooding on the abyss in *The Fate of Reading*, Hartman looks back at his own precursor self and says:

> In *The Unmediated Vision* the tyranny of sight in the domain of sensory organization is acknowledged, and symbol making is understood as a kind of 'therapeutic alliance' between the eye and other senses through the medium of art. I remember how easy it was to put a woman in the landscape, into every eyescape rather; and it struck me that in works of art there were similar centers, depicted or inferred. (p. 6)

Yet the woman in Wordsworth's poemscape is precisely what Hartman does not see. And this may be just what Wordsworth intended. In the short paragraph in which Hartman acknowledges that there may be something Oedipal about this Oedipus figure, he describes the daughter as *barred* by the incest prohibition. The poem would then transmit a disguised desire for the daughter, repressed and deflected into literary structures. Yet might it not also be that Wordsworth so often used incest figures in his poetry as a way, precisely, of barring the reality of the woman as other, a way of keeping the woman in and *only* in the eyescape, making a nun out of a nymph? For the danger here is that the daughter will neither follow nor lead, but simply leave:

> the birds salute
> The cheerful dawn, brightening for me the east;
> For me, thy natural leader, once again
> Impatient to conduct thee, not as erst

> A tottering infant, with compliant stoop
> From flower to flower supported; but to curb
> Thy nymph-like step swift-bounding o'er the lawn,
> Along the loose rocks, or the slippery verge
> Of foaming torrents ...

The family romance takes a slightly different form in Hillis Miller's essay, 'The Critic as Host.' In that essay, Miller discusses Booth's and Abrams' image of deconstructive criticism as 'parasitical' on the 'obvious or univocal reading' of a text. Miller writes:

> 'Parasitical' – the word suggests the image of 'the obvious or univocal reading' as the mighty oak, rooted in the solid ground, endangered by the insidious twining around it of deconstructive ivy. That ivy is somehow feminine, secondary, defective, or dependent. It is a clinging vine, able to live in no other way but by drawing the life sap of its host, cutting off its light and air. I think of Hardy's *The Ivy-Wife* ...
>
> Such sad love stories of a domestic affection which introduces the parasitical into the closed economy of the home no doubt describe well enough the way some people feel about the relation of a 'deconstructive' interpretation to 'the obvious or univocal reading.' The parasite is destroying the host. The alien has invaded the house, perhaps to kill the father of the family in an act which does not look like parricide, but is. Is the 'obvious' reading, though, so 'obvious' or even so 'univocal'? May it not itself be the uncanny alien which is so close that it cannot be seen as strange? (*DC*, p. 218)

It is interesting to note how effortlessly the vegetal metaphor is sexualized in Miller's elaboration of it. If the parasite is the feminine, then the feminine must be recognized as that uncanny alien always already in the house – and in the host. What turns out, in Miller's etymological analysis, to be uncanny about the relation between host and parasite – and by extension between male and female – is that each is already inhabited by the other as a difference from itself. Miller then goes on to describe the parasite as invading virus in the following terms:

> The genetic pattern of the virus is so coded that it can enter a host cell and violently reprogram all the genetic material in that cell, turning the cell into a little factory for manufacturing copies of itself, so destroying it. This is *The Ivy-Wife* with a vengeance. (*DC*, p. 222)

Miller then goes on to ask, 'Is this an allegory, and if so, of what?' Perhaps of the gender codes of literature, or of criticism. But this image of cancerous femininity may be less a fear of takeover by women than an extreme version of the desire to deny difference. There is perhaps something reassuring about total annihilation as opposed to precarious survival. The desire to deny difference is in fact, in a euphoric rather than a nightmarish spirit, the central desire dramatized by the Shelley poems Miller analyzes. The obsessive cry for oneness, for sameness, always, however, meets the same fate: it cannot subsume and erase the trace of its own elaboration. The story told, again and again, by Shelley is the story of the failure of the attempt to abolish difference. As Miller points out, difference is rediscovered in the linguistic traces of that failure. But a failed erasure of difference is not the same as a recognition of difference. Unless, as Miller's analysis suggests, difference can only be recognized in the failure of its erasure.

If the parasite is both feminine and parricidal, then the parasite can only be a daughter. Miller does not follow up on the implications of a parricidal daughter, but Harold Bloom, whose critical system is itself a garden of parricidal delights, gives us a clue to what would be at stake for him in such an idea. In *The Map of Misreading* he writes:

> Nor are there Muses, nymphs who *know*, still available to tell us the secrets of continuity, for the nymphs certainly are now departing. I prophesy though that the first true break with literary continuity will be brought about in generations to come, if the burgeoning religion of Liberated Woman spreads from its clusters of enthusiasts to dominate the West. Homer will cease to be the inevitable precursor, and the rhetoric and forms of our literature then may break at last from tradition.[6]

In Bloom's prophetic vision of the breaking of tradition through the liberation of woman, it is as though the Yale School were in danger of becoming a Jael School.[7]

The dependence of Bloom's revisionary ratios upon a linear patriarchal filiation has been pointed out often enough – particularly in the groundbreaking work of Sandra Gilbert and Susan Gubar – that there is no need to belabor it here. I will therefore, instead, analyze the opening lines of Bloom's essay 'The Breaking of Form' as a strong misreading of the question of sexual difference. The essay begins:

> The word *meaning* goes back to a root that signifies 'opinion' or 'intention', and is closely related to the word *moaning*. A poem's meaning is a poem's complaint, its version of Keats' Belle Dame, who looked *as if* she loved, and made sweet moan. Poems instruct us in how they break form to bring about meaning, so as to utter a complaint, a moaning intended to be all their own. (*DC*, p. 1)

If the relation between the reader and the poem is analogous to the relation between the knight-at-arms and the Belle Dame, things are considerably more complicated than they appear. For the encounter between male and female in Keats' poem is a perfectly ambiguous disaster:

LA BELLE DAME SANS MERCI
A Ballad

I

O what can ail thee, knight-at-arms,
   Alone and palely loitering?
The sedge has withered from the lake,
   And no birds sing.

II

O what can ail thee, knight-at-arms,
   So haggard and so woebegone?
The squirrel's granary is full,
   And the harvest's done.

III

I see a lily on thy brow,
   With anguish moist and fever dew,
And on thy cheeks a fading rose
   Fast withereth too.

IV

I met a lady in the meads,
   Full beautiful – a fairy's child,
Her hair was long, her foot was light,
   And her eyes were wild.

V

I made a garland for her head,
   And bracelets too, and fragrant zone;
She looked at me as she did love,
   And made sweet moan.

VI

I set her on my pacing steed,
   And nothing else saw all day long,
For sidelong would she bend, and sing
   A fairy's song.

VII

She found me roots of relish sweet,
   And honey wild, and manna dew,
And sure in language strange she said –
   'I love thee true.'

VIII

She took me to her elfin grot,
    And there she wept, and sighed full sore,
And there I shut her wild wild eyes
    With kisses four.

IX

And there she lullèd me asleep,
    And there I dreamed – Ah! woe betide!
The latest dream I ever dreamed
    On the cold hillside.

X

I saw pale kings and princes too,
    Pale warriors, death-pale were they all;
They cried – 'La Belle Dame sans Merci
    Hath thee in thrall!'

XI

I saw their starved lips in the gloam,
    With horrid warning gapèd wide,
And I awoke and found me here,
    On the cold hill's side.

XII

And this is why I sojourn here,
    Alone and palely loitering,
Though the sedge has withered from the lake,
    And no birds sing.

Rather than a clear 'as if,' Keats writes: 'She looked at me *as* she did love,/And made sweet moan.' Suspicion of the woman is not planted quite so clearly, nor quite so early. In changing 'as' to 'as if,' Bloom has removed from the poem the possibility of reading this first mention of the woman's feelings as straight description. 'As she did love' would still be the knight's own interpretation, but it would be an interpretation that does not recognize itself as such. Perhaps Bloom is here demonstrating what he says elsewhere about the study of poetry being 'the study of what Stevens called "the intricate evasions of as."' By the end of the poem, it becomes impossible to know whether one has read a story of a knight enthralled by a witch or of a woman seduced and abandoned by a male hysteric. And the fine balance of that undecidability depends on the 'as.'

If the poem, like the woman, 'makes sweet moan,' then there is considerable doubt about the reader's capacity to read it. This becomes all the more explicit in the knight's second interpretive assessment of the woman's feelings: 'And sure in language strange she said – /"I love thee true."' The problem of under-standing the woman is here a problem of translation. Even her name can only be expressed in another tongue. The sexes stand in relation to each other not as two distinct entities but as two foreign languages. The drama of male hysteria is a drama of premature assurance of understanding followed by premature panic at the intimation of otherness. Is she mine, asks the knight, or am I hers? If these are the only two possibilities, the foreignness of the languages cannot be respected. What Bloom demonstrates, perhaps without knowing it, is that if reading is the gendered activity he paints it as, the reading process is less a love story than a story of failed translation.

That the question of gender is a question of language becomes even more explicit in an essay by Paul de Man entitled 'The Epistemology of Metaphor.'[8] Translation is at issue in that essay as well, in the very derivation of the word 'metaphor.' 'It is no mere play of words,' writes de Man, 'that "translate" is translated in German as "*übersetzen*" which itself translates the Greek "*meta phorein*" or metaphor.' (p. 17) In all three words, what is described is a motion from one place to another. As we shall see, the question of the relation between gender and figure will have a great deal to do with this notion of *place*.

De Man's essay begins as follows:

> Metaphors, tropes, and figural language in general have been a perennial problem and, at times, a recognized source of embarrassment for philo-sophical discourse and, by extension, for all discursive uses of language including historiography and literary analysis. It appears that philosophy either has to give up its own constitutive claim to rigor in order to come to terms with the figurality of its language or that it has to free itself from figuration altogether. And if the latter is considered impossible, philoso-phy could at least learn to control figuration by keeping it, so to speak, in its place, by delimiting the boundaries of its influence and thus restricting the epistemological damage that it may cause. (p. 13)

This opening paragraph echoes, in its own rhetoric, a passage which occurs later in the essay in which de Man is commenting on a long quotation from Locke. Locke concludes his discussion of the perils of figuration as follows:

> Eloquence, like the fair sex, has too prevailing beauties in it to suffer itself ever to be spoken against. And it is in vain to find fault with those arts of deceiving wherein men find pleasure to be deceived. (p. 15)

De Man glosses the Locke passage as follows:

> Nothing could be more eloquent than this denunciation of eloquence. It is clear that rhetoric is something one can decorously indulge in as long as one knows where it belongs. Like a woman, which it resembles ('like the fair sex'), it is a fine thing as long as it is kept in its proper place. Out of place, among the serious affairs of men ('if we would speak of things as

they are'), it is a disruptive scandal – like the appearance of a real woman in a gentleman's club where it would only be tolerated as a picture, preferably naked (like the image of Truth), framed and hung on the wall. (pp. 15–16)

Following this succinct tongue-in-cheek description of the philosphical tradition as a men's club, de Man goes on to claim that there is 'little epistemological risk in a flowery, witty passage about wit like this one,' that things only begin to get serious when the plumber must be called in, but the epistemological damage may already have been done. For the question of language in Locke quickly comes to be centered on the question, 'What essence is the proper of man?' This is no idle question, in fact, because what is at stake in the answer is what sort of monstrous births it is permissible to kill. Even in the discussion of Condillac and Kant, the question of sexual difference lurks, as when de Man describes Condillac's discussion of abstractions as bearing a close resemblance to a novel by Ann Radcliffe or Mary Shelley, or when Kant is said to think that rhetoric can be rehabilitated by some 'tidy critical housekeeping.' De Man's conclusion can be read as applying to the epistemological damage caused as much by gender as by figure:

> In each case, it turns out to be impossible to maintain a clear line of distinction between rhetoric, abstraction, symbol, and all other forms of language. In each case, the resulting undecidability is due to the asymmetry of the binary model that opposes the figural to the proper meaning of the figure. (p. 28)

The philosopher's place is always within, not outside, the asymmetrical structures of language and of gender, but that place can never, in the final analysis, be proper. It may be impossible to know whether it is the gender question that is determined by rhetoric or rhetoric by gender difference, but it does seem as though these are the terms in which it might be fruitful to pursue the question.

In order to end with a meditation on a possible female version of the Yale School, I would like now to turn to the work of a Yale daughter. For this purpose I have chosen to focus on *The Critical Difference* by Barbara Johnson.[9] What happens when one raises Mary Jacobus' question – 'Is there a woman in this text?' The answer is rather surprising. For no book produced by the Yale School seems to have excluded women as effectively as *The Critical Difference*. No women authors are studied. Almost no women critics are cited. And, what is even more surprising, there are almost no female characters in any of the stories analyzed. *Billy Budd*, however triangulated, is a tale of three *men* in a boat. Balzac's *Sarrasine* is the story of a woman who turns out to be a castrated man. And in Johnson's analysis of 'The Purloined Letter,' the story of Oedipal triangularity is transformed into an endlessly repeated chain of fraternal rivalries. In a book that announces itself as a study of difference, the place of the woman is constantly being erased.

This does not mean, however, that the question of sexual difference does not haunt the book from the beginning. In place of a dedication, *The Critical Difference* opens with a quotation from Paul de Man in which difference is dramatized as a scene of exasperated instruction between Archie Bunker and his wife:

> Asked by his wife whether he wants to have his bowling shoes laced over or laced under, Archie Bunker answers with a question: 'What's the difference?' Being a reader of sublime simplicity, his wife replies by patiently explaining the difference between lacing over and lacing under, whatever this may be, but provokes only ire. 'What's the difference?' did not ask for difference but means instead 'I don't give a damn what the difference is.' The same grammatical pattern engenders two meanings that are mutually exclusive: the literal meaning asks for the concept (difference) whose existence is denied by the figurative meaning. As long as we are talking about bowling shoes, the consequences are relatively trivial; Archie Bunker, who is a great believer in the authority of origins (as long, of course, as they are the right origins) muddles along in a world where literal and figurative meanings get in each other's way, though not without discomforts. But suppose that it is a *de*-bunker rather than a 'Bunker,' and a de-bunker of the arche (or origin), an archie Debunker such as Nietzsche or Jacques Derrida, for instance, who asks the question 'What is the Difference?' – and we cannot even tell from his grammar whether he 'really' wants to know 'what' difference is or is just telling us that we shouldn't even try to find out. Confronted with the question of the difference between grammar and rhetoric, grammar allows us to ask the question, but the sentence by means of which we ask it may deny the very possibility of asking. For what is the use of asking, I ask, when we cannot even authoritatively decide whether a question asks or doesn't ask?

Whatever the rhetorical twists of this magnificent passage, the fact that it is framed as an intersexual dialogue is not irrelevant.

Another essay in *The Critical Difference*, a study of Mallarmé's prose poem 'The White Waterlily,' offers an even more promising depiction of the rhetoric of sexual difference. The essay begins:

> If human beings were not divided into two biological sexes, there would probably be no need for literature. And if literature could truly say what the relations between the sexes are, we would doubtless not need much of it then, either. Somehow, however, it is not simply a question of literature's ability to say or not to say the truth of sexuality. For from the moment literature begins to try to set things straight on that score, literature itself becomes inextricable from the sexuality it seeks to comprehend. It is not the life of sexuality that literature cannot capture; it is literature that inhabits the very heart of what makes sexuality problematic

for us speaking animals. Literature is not only a thwarted investigator but also an incorrigible perpetrator of the problem of sexuality. (p. 13)

But the prose poem in question ends up dramatizing an inability to know whether the woman one is expecting to encounter has ever truly been present or not. It is as though *The Critical Difference* could describe only the escape of the difference it attempts to analyze. This is even more true of the essay subtitled 'What the Gypsy Knew.' With such a title, one would expect to encounter at last something about female knowledge. But the point of the analysis is precisely that the poem does not tell us what the gypsy knew. Her prophecy is lost in the ambiguities of Apollinaire's syntax.

There may, however, be something accurate about this repeated dramatization of woman as simulacrum, erasure, or silence. For it would not be easy to assert that the existence and knowledge of the female subject could simply be produced, without difficulty or epistemological damage, within the existing patterns of culture and language. *The Critical Difference* may here be unwittingly pointing to 'woman' as one of the things 'we do not know we do not know.' Johnson concludes her preface with some remarks about ignorance that apply ironically well to her book's own demonstration of an ignorance that pervades Western discourse as a whole:

> What literature often seems to tell us is the consequences of the way in which what is not known is not *seen* as unknown. It is not, in the final analysis, what you don't know that can or cannot hurt you. It is what you don't *know* you don't know that spins out and entangles 'that perpetual error we call life.' (p. xii)

It is not enough to be a woman writing in order to resist the naturalness of female effacement in the subtly male pseudo-genderlessness of language. It would be no easy task, however, to undertake the effort of re-inflection or translation required to retrieve the lost knowledge of the gypsy, or to learn to listen with re-trained ears to Edith Bunker's patient elaboration of an answer to the question, 'What *is* the difference?'

NOTES

1. 'The Breaking of Form,' in *Deconstruction and Criticism* (New York: The Seabury press, 1979), pp. 6, 5. Further references to this and other essays in the volume will be indicated in the text by the abbreviation *DC* followed by a page number.
2. Jonathan Culler, *On Deconstruction* (Ithaca, NY: Cornell University Press, 1982), p. 289.
3. *Glyph*, 7 (Baltimore: The Johns Hopkins University Press, 1980), pp. 203–04.
4. *The Fate of Reading* (Chicago: University of Chicago Press, 1975), p. 248.
5. *Beyond Formalism* (New Haven: Yale University Press, 1970), p. 351.
6. *A Map of Misreading* (New York: Oxford University Press, 1975), p. 33. I would like to thank Susan Suleiman for calling my attention to this quotation.
7. The story of Jael is found in Judges 4. Jael invites Sisera, the commander of the Canaanite army, into her tent, gives him a drink of milk, and then, when he has fallen asleep, drives a tent peg through his head and kills him. (I would like to thank Sima Godfrey for this pun.)

8. *Critical Inquiry*, 5 (1978).
9. Baltimore: The Johns Hopkins University Press, 1980.

See also:

Gasché (3.3)
Miller (4.1)
De Man (4.2)
Readings (8.3)

6.4

'DOMESTICATION'

Rachel Bowlby

In collections of essays on topics of current theoretical interest it's becoming quite common, if not yet a fully established part of the genre, to start off the piece with a little story about the final stages of its genesis. Such a story typically mentions the last-minute influence of a suggestion or critique by someone whose position, in terms of gender or race or sexual orientation, might give their opinion a legitimacy of a kind that the writer, by his or her own position, might be thought to lack. 'I was discussing this article over breakfast with a lesbian friend, and she said . . . ,' writes someone who will thereby be identifying herself or himself as either a man, or straight, or both.

This type of gesture serves a number of functions. It seems to apologize for writers' disqualifications to speak about what they are going to speak about, marking an awareness that what they say will be open to modification. And it also does the opposite, making up for the disqualifications through the medium of the qualified friend who puts things right, and supplying the text with a provisional certificate of political, or even general, correctness: with an input from every possible position, the chances are that you can add up all the elements into a complete account.

A third element is the setting of the little story, which is regularly given a context of domestic intimacy: this is the sort of friend I have breakfast with. This aspect contributes to the legitimation effect ('some of my best friends . . .'), but it also provides a bit of human interest and narrative enigma, by hinting,

Source: Diane Elam and Robyn Wiegman (eds), *Feminism besides itself* (London: Routledge, 1995), pp. 72–4.

through the provision of the homely detail, at the possibility of a personal story. In this instance, domestication functions in an odd kind of way: it supplements and disrupts the abstract theoretical scenario, taking us somewhere else. Yet it also harmonizes, calming down the possible disjunctions between the positions, theoretical and social, of the writer and his interrogator over the soothing influence of the shared bagels and cream cheese.

In these instances, an image of domestication serves as a hidden support to a theoretical argument which appears to be coming from somewhere else, from a would-be neutral, overview position which, for purposes of narrative and political plausibility, needs to be brought down to earth – into the kitchen. And this, it seems to me, is one of many diverse ways in which domestication, as a concept and as a theme, functions in relation to contemporary theoretical arguments, deconstructive and feminist in particular. In a minute, I will look at some of these, but first, let me just throw in one or two autobiographical nuggets of my own, which you can believe or not. They certainly have something to do with the writing of this paper, though I'm probably in no subject-position to say what.

In the summer of 1992, Gillian Beer asked me if I would like to give a lecture in a series that was being organized at Cambridge in the wake of a controversy over Derrida's election there to an honorary doctorate. I suggested the topic of domestication, and then noticed that this had happened in the week when I unexpectedly acquired a kitchen table, having always thought that the room wasn't big enough to take one. My pleasure at the transformation of this domestic space was both mitigated and reinforced by the events of the following two weeks, when I went to Paris – a place where I like to think I feel at home – and had my wallet snatched, twice within the space of one week. For the first time, I felt a strong sense of urban paranoia, if that's the phrase, huddling inside the cozy familiar interior of the place where I was staying, wondering how I was ever going to write this paper on, of all things, domestication.

The other story goes back a bit further, to earlier that year, when I woke up one morning to the sounds of two voices that turned out to be those of Gillian Beer and George Steiner, on the BBC Radio 4 *Today* programme, soundly and roundly in their different ways defending the importance of Derrida's work. As I drank my coffee and started to wake up, I reflected that, thanks to the Cambridge controversy, here was deconstruction apparently reaching, or being pushed, beyond the books and the seminar rooms, out onto the airwaves and the headlines and into the kitchens and bedrooms of the daily life of the supposed British nation. It was an ambivalent passage between hypothetical insides and outsides, crossing, erasing and reinforcing innumerable imaginary and symbolic borders. In some sense, it all seemed to suggest that Derrida was beginning to personify a particularly curious specimen of the proper noun: He was becoming what is called a 'household' name.

It seemed to me that this process was at the very least a strange and unpredictable one, aligning Derrida with a hitherto unfamiliar and probably unwelcome peer-group. Not so much Heidegger, Kant, Descartes and the rest, or, in another connection, not so much Lacan and Kristeva and Foucault. Instead, this new grouping would include, I suppose – if you are British – the likes of Brian Redhead, Domestos, Bruce Forsyth, Boot's, Fergie, Chanel no. 5, and Jeffrey Archer. On the other side of the Atlantic, perhaps this near-meaningless anglo-domestic list should be rewritten to something like David Letterman, Mr. Clean, Hilary Clinton, Chanel no. 5, Tylenol, and Judith Krantz. It can't be an easy or straightforward transition to find yourself sharing the household name status and facilities with such a heterogeneous community, one whose capacities for comfortable cohabitation, either with each other or with their new associate, might seem anything but assured.

And yet the notion of domestication is generally regarded as being the most obvious thing in the world – so obvious, in fact, that once someone or some idea is deemed to have been sent home in this public way, it is as if there is no more to be said. The front door closes definitively on a place removed and retired from the open air of its previous existence – and even though the movement implied is also one of extension, moving out. If a theory gets domesticated, that's the end of it. It becomes like everything else.

The term domestication is used in this way all the time in relation to deconstruction and to 'theory' in general, including feminist theory. But it does not usually feature the specificity or concreteness of any recognizably domestic location, 'Dunroamin' or wherever. Instead, 'domestication' is used to signal something unproblematically negative that happens to a theory, when – what? – well, when it loses its radical edge, gets tamed, is co-opted or institutionalized (these last two words are often used virtually as synonyms of domestication). The 'domestication' of deconstruction or other theories implies something that may include the kind of mediatization that occurred with the 'Cambridge and Derrida' story, but refers generally to processes of simplification, assimilation and distortion – any or all of these – to which the theory in question falls victim or which it is powerless to resist. It will already be clear that domestication, in this sense, involves a very undeconstructive story – of a wild and natural identity, a full presence, subsequently, and only subsequently, succumbing to forces that deprive it of an original wholeness.

Here's one particularly clear example of how the term is invoked, from Judith Butler's *Gender Trouble*, one of the most significant deployments of deconstruction in a feminist context:

> The complexity of gender requires an interdisciplinary and postdisciplinary set of discourses in order to resist the domestication of gender studies or women's studies within the academy and to radicalize the notion of feminist critique.

And later on, she says:

Parody by itself is not subversive, and there must be a way to understand what makes certain kinds of parodic repetitions effectively disruptive, truly troubling, and which repetitions become domesticated and recirculated as instruments of cultural hegemony.

What gets domesticated – in this case, a form of feminist theory – is something defined as being subversive of what will thereby attempt to take it over, settle it down, suppress its difference.

What interests me in this use of domestication in connection with theory as something radical and subversive is the way in which the word itself, and the implied narrative that it brings with it, can go unexamined within an argument that is deconstructively on the look-out all the time for the subtle simplifications and assumptions that discourses of every kind install and seek to maintain. In the opposition played out between radical critique and domesticating cultural hegemony, the qualifications of the two forces are not at issue: the first gets its value from the very fact that it is a challenge to the second, which is identified largely in terms of its superior force. In an inevitable movement, the latter then brings the former under its sway.

Butler's argument does not attribute anything inherently good or natural to the radical theory that succumbs to domestication: this is not a case of a hypothetical full presence or genuine content then becoming contaminated by something else. Rather, the narrative proceeds in terms of power, with the oppositional, positive force inevitably succumbing to the stronger, negative one that prompted its protesting existence in the first place. Implicitly, then, there are three stages to the story: initial homogeneity or harmony of the hegemonizing force, then the breakaway of the wild radical critique, to be followed by its reintegration or re-assimilation into the dominant culture, accompanied by the loss of its critical impetus.

At this point, we might take a first step back indoors to look at one of the stories implied by the word domestication in its more homely, extra-theoretical, everyday existence. Within the word itself, home does not appear as the first place or the natural place: It is a secondary development, *becoming* domestic. In one French usage, *domestiquer* means quite simply the subjugation of a tribe to a colonizing power. To 'domesticate' is to bring the foreign or primitive or alien into line with the 'domestic' civilization and power, just as a 'domesticated' animal is one that has been tamed into home life. Something wild, pre-civilized, and verging on the non-human gets brought into line with an existing order represented in this case as more complex and sophisticated, but also as less natural.

In anthropology, too, the concept of domestication has had an unexpectedly dynamic, if less imperialistic, existence. The word is used to mark a turning point that is supposed to represent not so much a takeover, a 'home' civilization taking in and thereby abolishing the difference of one that lies outside its domain, as a transition from what are thereby recognizable as two distinct states of culture. 'The domestication of the savage mind,' in Jack Goody's recapitulation of a categorization adopted by Lévi-Strauss in *The Savage Mind*, links together a whole series of two-term oppositions that are deployed in accounts of the history of humanity in general, and also in relation to the changes affecting what are now called 'developing' countries in this century. Domestication in these connections is associated with a move from oral to literate culture; from collective life to individualism and private families; from myth to history; and from concrete to abstract thinking.

The reliance on the two-term division and the set order of events – or rather the set position of the one event, which can somehow only be pointed to retrospectively as a boundary that a collectivity is seen to have passed – is of a type that deconstruction, even garden-variety or kitchen-variety deconstruction, would be quick to point out. Goody implicitly answers in another way: Yes, there are narratable changes, but historically and culturally they by no means fall into these easily superimposable parallels. This line is different from, but not I think necessarily incompatible with deconstruction, despite what kitsch deconstruction might think or be thought to think. To say that this is a pre-deconstructive mode of argument would be to restore just that narrative logic of identifiable progressions and demarcations that deconstruction seeks to make problematic: to operate, in fact, with an already 'domesticated' version of deconstruction that would assert its own logics as superior to and clearly distinguishable from the others.

But there is still a further layer to this, which is indicated by the concentration on domestication as a process of civilization or taming. For insofar as domestication has to do with home, it would seem to elide the starting point. Home is the place of origin, the place that has always been left; domestication, then, would be a return to or reinvention of the home that you left or lost. This three – part story has its standard modern forms in relation both to daily life – wake up, go to work, return – and to the process of growing up: from home, out into the world, and then on or back to some form of domestic 'settling down.' In this narrative of nostalgia, home is imagined as a place of peace, stability and satisfaction that has subsequently ceased to be; but also as a withdrawal or seclusion from a 'real' world envisaged as a source of the energy or the troubles or the mobility that are absent from the home.

It is in the context of this other kind of story that domesticity is imagined as a first place of wholeness and rest, but a place from which – and in order for it to be retrospectively seen as such – a separation has always taken place. Two books from the late fifties, one English, one French, illustrate this in very different ways. Richard Hoggart's *The Uses of Literacy* gives a nostalgic portrait of a working-class culture described in terms of concreteness, locality, and oral expression, and in the process of being subsumed by a materialistic American print culture. In numerous vignettes, the home is represented as the focus and epitome of this all-but-lost world, which is seen as at once authentic and claustrophobic: It is not so much that it should not give way or give place to some other mode, but that it is being taken over by the wrong kinds of force. In place of the false commercial culture, endlessly secondarized through images of superficiality – tinsel, glitter, tawdriness, show – Hoggart would substitute something else, the abstract and general thinking of which his own argument, by implication, is meant to serve as an example. So the sequence here is not unlike the anthropological schema deployed by Goody, from oral to intellectual and from local to generalized; but here the terms are reversed, so that the domestic figures are the first, and in this case limited, devalorized state, prior and vulnerable to a mutation that may be negatively or positively viewed, in the direction of commercial fake, or in the direction of intellectual generality.

In a different genre, Gaston Bachelard's *The Poetics of Space* lyrically evokes the peace and dreaminess of the home as a place of corners and nests, with its secret and private spaces. Houses are associated with primitiveness and child-hood, and thence with a capacity for maintaining throughout life the qualities of stability, habit and restfulness in which it begins. There is a lovely section on chests of drawers, which Bachelard sees as full of imaginative possibilities of a kind that are lost when philosophers like Bergson use them as no more than a polemical metaphor against tidy separation or compartmentalization of con-cepts, as though into drawers. Bachelard, for his part, wants to bring out the full poetic suggestiveness of such seemingly insignificant domestic things: When Bergson speaks of a drawer, what disdain!'

Nestlingly benign as Bachelard's enclosure is, it maintains itself nonetheless partly in its firm distance from two other, related schools or homes of thought. First, there are the twentieth-century philosophers with their hyphen-crazy abstractions: a being-in-the-world that is always already split up. And second, there is the psychoanalysis of negativity, refusing a primary sense of oneness and always finding evidence of a threatening sexuality.

Bachelard's distinction from Freudian psychoanalysis appears most clearly in his tranquil hymn to homeliness as a source of poetic inspiration:

> In its freshness, in its specific activity, the imagination makes of the familiar something strange [*avec du familier fait de l'étrange*]. With a poetic detail, the imagination places us before a new world.

This version of strange or anxiety-provoking familiarity is a far cry from the covertly menacing reversibility of Freud's analysis of the uncanny, the homely *heimlich* which is also, within the same word, the unhomely, marking that unwelcome presence within what is most apparently reassuring in its famil-iarity and familiality. The house of Freudian psychoanalysis is irredeemably riven by the presence of ghosts, its comforting appearance of womblike unity doubled from the start by intruding forces, such that human life can never securely make a return to a place untroubled by the untimely and dislocating hauntings of other times and places, and other presences that interfere with the imagined separateness and identifiability of places and people who are known and loved.

I don't want to dwell – if that is the word – too long on Freud's uncanny. But it is obvious that in psychoanalysis, the home is no place of harmony – and all the less for functioning so forcefully as the embodiment of a harmony that has always been lost. The home is where the muddle begins and continues; here domestication is not a smoothly operating process of adjustment or progress. And Freud, in fact, is rather specific about possible domestic disturbances, pointing out in *The Interpretation of Dreams* that 'The ugliest as well as the most intimate details of sexual life may be thought and dreamt of in seemingly innocent allusions to activities in the kitchen.' This is, after all, the world of 'kettle logic'; and along such murky paths of connection, we might reflect that if you hear, rather than write, the word 'domestication' – if you return to that famous pre-civilized primitiveness of an oral culture – what you get, none too neatly tidied away into this capaciously polysyllabic word, is 'mess' and 'stickiness' – an Anglo-Saxon sprawl screeching for attention out of the nicely abstracted Latinate term. As every housewife knows.

See also:

Marx (1.1)
Gasché (3.3)
Tschumi (5.3)
Beardsworth (5.4)

6.5

'RECOGNISING THE VIRUS'

Alexander Duttmann

AIDS is always already inscribed in the program, is always already programmed and is always already on the program, that is, on the agenda. Another thinking resonates with these formulations, a thinking associated with the name Derrida. Along with Nancy, Jacques Derrida is probably one of the few philosophers or thinkers to inquire into the meaning of AIDS and remind us of the urgency of this question. He does so in an interview entitled 'The Rhetoric of Drugs.' In a different interview, responding to Nancy's question 'Who comes after the subject?,' Derrida expresses his wish to talk about AIDS and immediately adds that for him the emergence and spread of the virus represents an event [*Eregnis*]: 'an event that one could call *historical* in the *epoch* of *subjectivity*, if we still gave credence to *historicality*, to *epochality*, and to *subjectivity*'. What does this curious statement tell us? On the one hand, we no longer give credence to the concepts Derrida enumerates; we no longer consider them creditworthy; we distrust them; we are not willing to support them and to be supported by them. On the other hand, we continue to credit them; their value still remains high enough; we believe that, despite their loss of credit, they might contribute to clarification of what AIDS challenges us to think. The emergence and spread of AIDS, then, is not an event. Or rather, it is an event because it is not a *pure* event. If we can think about AIDS by relying, even with the greatest mistrust, on subjectivity (and Derrida has demonstrated that the concepts of historicity and epochality derive from the concept of subjectivity, from the concept itself), it is

Source: Alexander Duttmann, *At Odds with Aids: Thinking and Talking about a Virus*, tr. Peter Gilgen and Conrad Scott-Curtis (Stanford: Stanford University Press, 1996), pp. 70–101.

only because the virus weakens the subjective recuperation of the event, because it loosens and unhinges the 'stabilizing arrest' [*arrêt stabilisateur*], which one calls 'the subject.' We give credence to the subject, we credit it, only after having denied it credit. AIDS not only receives credit through the confession, as Guibert maintains. It decides on creditworthiness itself. However, is not the emergence and epidemic spread of AIDS exactly that event which poses the challenge to think its own im-pertinence? This im-pertinence consists in the impossibility, for the event, of appropriating itself and of belonging to itself. This does not mean, however, that it therefore simply belongs to that which is not event-like. A thinking that concerns itself with AIDS, with the event of its emergence and spread, with contamination and the relation between event and contamination, seems unable to prevent its own contamination, to prevent AIDS.

'The virus (which belongs neither to life nor to death) may *always already* have afflicted and broken into any "intersubjective" trajectory,' Derrida insists in the interview 'The Rhetoric of Drugs.' At this point in the interview, conducted in the same year as the interview on the subject, Derrida calls AIDS a hitherto 'completely unknown' and now 'indelible given' [*donnée absolument originale et ineffaçable*], which marks 'our time.' How should one think the specificity, the originality, the novelty, the event-like dimension of *this* event, if the emergence of AIDS is determined by the fact that it refers back to something that *always already* may have happened, that *always already* has happened, that *always already* has broken into thinking, that always already has been said or spoken by the thinking of this '*always-already*'? Is the emergence of AIDS *the event of the event* and thus that which only happens by giving way to a sort of 'retreat into the event' [*Einkehr in das Ereignis*]? What is at stake in the time of this event – of the – event – what is at stake in 'our time'? Derrida says, 'And given its spatial and temporal dimensions, its structure of relays and delays, no human being is ever safe from AIDS. This possibility is thus installed at the heart of the social bond as intersubjectivity. And at the heart of that which would preserve itself as a dual intersubjectivity it inscribes the mortal and indelible trace of the third party – not the third term as the condition of the symbolic and the law, but the third as destructuring structuration of the social bond, as social disconnection (*délaison*) and even as the disconnection of the interruption, of the "without relation" that can constitute a relation to the other in its alleged normality. The third itself is no longer a third, and the history of this normality more clearly displays its simulacra, almost as if AIDS painted a picture of its exposed anatomy. You may say this is how it's always been, and I believe it. But now, exactly as if it were a painting or a giant movie screen, AIDS provides an available, daily, massive *readability* to that which the canonical discourses . . . had to deny, which in truth they are destined to deny, founded as they are by this very denial'. To the degree to which it concerns itself with AIDS, with the emergence and spread of the virus, the thinking of deconstruction, which is a thinking of contagion or of contamination, must approach two questions.

1. If deconstruction still gives credence to historicity, if it trusts in historicity up to a certain point and under certain circumstances – what then does it share with Heidegger, what does it still have in common with Heidegger?

2. If deconstruction recognizes (itself in) AIDS, if AIDS recognizes itself in deconstruction, if deconstruction and AIDS recognize one another – what does such a recognition mean, what does it mean that both deconstruction and AIDS acknowledge each other's existence, that they acknowledge their own existence in the existence of the other?

Ad 1 – Deconstruction, Historicity, AIDS. Whoever understands the emergence and epidemic spread of AIDS as a 'historical' event – and at the same time emphasizes the impossibility of a discourse based on such an understanding – directs attention to those passages in Heidegger that deal with sickness. What place does the sickness have in the analysis of history and historicity? To begin with, it may be sufficient to point to two paragraphs in which Heidegger mentions and even develops the motif or theme of sickness.

The paragraph in *Being and Time* that delimits the existential analysis of death in order to distinguish it from all other interpretations that have death as their object refers to the phenomenon of being sick and does so in a way entirely in accord with the project of a fundamental ontology. Heidegger actually suggests (Is it a matter of a mere hypothesis?) that we think sickness as existential phenomenon. He mentions sickness at the point he mentions death and adds that the existential understanding of these two phenomena also affects medicine. He does not merely want to claim, however, that physicians who would comprehend the essential and decisive features of the science they practice must obtain an ontological understanding of Dasein and the relationship among Dasein, death, and sickness *in retrospect*. Heidegger's gesture is much more radical, not at all satisfied with a distribution that concedes a certain autonomy to positivist science if only it eventually followed the directives of fundamental ontology: 'Medical and biological investigation into "demising" [into the "intermediate phenomenon," which is supposed to be neither a perishing nor a dying – author's note] can obtain results which may even become significant ontologically if the basic orientation for an existential interpretation of death has been made secure. Or must sickness and death in general – even from a medical point of view – be primarily conceived as existential phenomena?' From whatever viewpoint one considers its symptoms, in the final analysis sickness remains an existential phenomenon, as does death. Perhaps it is important at this point to understand sickness as something that affects Dasein itself, Dasein in its entirety or as a whole; perhaps it is necessary to understand that one cannot think the possibility of a 'potentiality for Being-a-whole' [*Ganzseinkönnen*], which is supposed to characterize Dasein, without thinking sickness and 'understanding [it] as primarily existential.'

In order to attain the primordiality or originality of an ontological ground, on which every possible interpretation of existence is based, the existential analytic must analyze the potentiality-for-Being-a-whole of that being [*Seiendes*] which alone has an understanding of Being [*Sein*]. Heidegger begins by outlining the boundaries that constitute this Being-a-whole and that bestow on it a distinguishable shape (the shape of the incomplete and of that which is yet outstanding) without being able to bestow this shape on it completely. For as soon as the boundaries draw the outlines of this shape, they open it up to a shapeless outside or a shapeless incompleteness; they open it to something that is shapeless because it is still outstanding. Heidegger writes, 'As long as Dasein is, there is in every case something still outstanding, which Dasein can be and will be'. The end of 'Being-in-the-world,' 'Dasein's Being-at-an-end in death,' is pertinent because it 'belongs to existence,' to that existence which is something outstanding, a potentiality-for-Being. Of course, the interpretation of Dasein as something that relates to death as outstanding turns it into something present-at-hand, and Heidegger therefore says that death rather stands before our existence. Death belongs to Dasein, to which, however, it cannot be in a simple relationship of 'belonging': it 'limits and determines in every case whatever totality is possible for Dasein.' The phenomenal and ontological understanding of potentiality-for-Being-a-whole thus depends on an existential notion of death. The 'existential structure of Being-toward-death' is nothing other than 'the ontologically constitutive state of Dasein's potentiality-for-Being-a-whole.' If now temporality is 'the primordial ontological ground for Dasein's existentiality,' if on the basis of a non-vulgar conception of time we can understand why Dasein is fundamentally historical, it becomes clear that the phenomenon of sickness, which Heidegger relates immediately to the phenomenon of death, cannot be understood as long as it is not thought in its connection with the potentiality-for-Being-a-whole of historical Dasein.

In a passage of the transcription of the lecture course that he dedicated to Schelling in 1936, Heidegger again takes up the motif or theme of sickness, barely touched upon in *Being and Time* and only mentioned in the sentence quoted above. Heidegger establishes an essential relationship between disease and existence as a whole, between the dissolution of the totality in disease and the overall state or condition of existence, and he does so explicitly. But as is so often the case in reading the comprehensive, reconstructive interpretations by means of which Heidegger approaches thinkers and poets, it is not easy to decide what meaning to ascribe to this explicit linking of the two. Do we have here a discussion or explication that concerns only the text to which it refers? Or does Heidegger also speak in his own name? Maybe the first hypothesis does not exclude the second one: 'By way of clarifying malice Schelling mentions disease. Disease makes itself felt to "feeling" as something very real, not just as a mere absence of something. When a man is sick, we do say that he "is not quite all right" [*daß ihm etwas "fehle"*] and thus express the sickness merely negatively as a lack. But this: "Why is he not quite right?" ["*Wo fehlt es?*"] really means "What is the matter with him? Something has, so to speak, gotten loose from the harmony of being healthy and, being on the loose, wants to take over all of existence and dominate it." In the case of sickness, there is not just something lacking, but something wrong [*falsch*]. "Wrong" not in the sense of something only incorrect, but in the genuine sense of falsification, distortion, and reversal. This falsification is at the same time false in the sense of what is sly. We speak of malignant disease. Disease is not only a disruption, but a reversal of the *whole existence* which takes over the *total condition* and dominates it' (my emphasis). An attentive reading of this passage should begin by relating it to the entire lecture course and would have to situate its statements within that context. When Heidegger says that disease is not merely a negative phenomenon, he is in accord with Schelling, that is, with one of the decisive points in the *Treatise on the Essence of Human Freedom*, namely, with the thought that evil cannot be considered mere negativity. On several occasions, Heidegger returns to the point that evil is nothing negative in Schelling's treatise, that its ground is positive. At the same time, an interpretive reading, concerned with details and aimed at a comprehensive reconstruction, would have to mark the relation between the mystical-romantic tradition of the German philosophy of nature and the interpretation of disease that Heidegger elucidates *and* proposes himself. Furthermore, such a reading would have to pay attention to the differences that differentiate Heidegger's use of privative concepts elsewhere. But first and foremost it would have to compare the statements about the falsity of disease with the writings on the question concerning truth. In his lecture course on Parmenides, for example, held in the winter semester of 1942–43, Heidegger examines the etymology of the German word *falsch* [wrong] and enters it into the Greco-Latin-English history of translation, which both reveals and conceals the essence of truth. The series in question consists of the expressions *pseudos, falsum*, and *trick Pseudos* is a Greek word that, according to Heidegger, belongs to the essential field of *aletheia*. *Falsum* is a Latin translation that inverts the meaning of *pseudos* by incorporating it into the imperial space of craftiness and cunning, of bringing-to-a-fall. In German, *trick* is a foreign word of Anglo-Saxon descent, a descent that Heidegger points out must not be evaluated as contingent.

Immediately after the passage just quoted, the lecture course on Schelling points to the bond that links sickness and truth. Heidegger attempts to find an explanation for this confusion that interferes with our understanding sickness. Why do we misunderstand the *wrong* to which sickness points as 'disruption,' as a simple, that is a temporary or partial change, as aberration effected from outside, as interference in the mechanism? If we let ourselves be deceived in thinking about *wrongness*, if we falsify or invert *wrongness* (this is a sort of sickness of the wrong), it is because we persist in representing wrongness according to the logical model of the *negative* proposition. Negation, which 'revolts as reversal in evil' and in disease, which manifests itself in both evil and disease as wrongness or reversal, resists comprehension as long as propositions follow this model and remain 'simple sentence[s] about a real state of things [*dinglichen Sachverhalt*]'. The expression 'a real state of things' implicitly points the reader to Heidegger's lecture *On the Essence of Truth*, which opens with a discussion of the relationship between propositional statement and thing. In order to avoid the confusion that limits us to a merely negative thinking of disease, we must think the disharmony and discord that can be felt in being sick from the point of view of consonance and accord or harmony. That is, there is an originary affirmation and assent without which we have no access to the negation, falsification, and inversion of sickness and of evil: 'What replaces the place of harmony and attunement is disharmony, the wrong tone which *enters the whole*. Primordially conceived, affirmation is not just the recognition coming afterward from without of something already existing; it is an assent, a yes harmonizing everything, penetrating and putting it in tune with itself; similarly the no' (ibid.; my emphasis). This similarity, which Heidegger does not describe, is, however, asymmetrical. If 'negation is not just rejection of what is objectively present,' the reason for this is that 'no-saying' is supposed 'to place itself in the position of the yes' (ibid.), and by doing so turn the position of the whole that has been understood 'primordially enough' (the position of the whole existence, the position of its total condition) into a position that is dissonant and out of tune. Here sickness is perceived as the falsifying, distracting exposure of accord and harmony, as a multiplication of voices to the point of discord and disharmony, as (de-)positing and dismaying dissonance, which destroys 'the essential unity of a being as a whole,' detaches the 'with-and-in-itself' from the 'in-tune-with-and-in-itself' and engenders a 'reversed unity' – but still a unity, since Heidegger still comprehends negation as position. However, the perverting negation, negation as sickness, is possible only where what is ordered and joined in the 'yes' that harmonizes everything is traversed by a difference; it is possible only where the 'yes' itself displays an opening, a latitude, a minimal distance, a certain freedom. This latitude, this freedom always already exposes Being-with-and-in-itself to an outside and can neither be reduced to originary affirmation nor to true negation, neither to consonance nor to dissonance, neither to the *unity* of what holds together nor to the *unity* of what turns against it. Rather, this latitude and freedom must be thought as a dis-united 'yes/no,' which permits the production of both unities; they must be thought as originary Being-not-one or as originary im-pertinence – which necessarily elude the recognition of the 'yes' in the 'no' of the attuned totality in its inversion, of disease. It is precisely this structure, that is, the unstable structure of primordial Being-not-one, of pre-primordiality in the primordial, that Heidegger points out after discussing originary affirmation and true negation, at the very moment he returns to Schelling's thoughts about evil and freedom and to the relation of ground to existence. Heidegger underlines the instability that contaminates the origin and makes it possible. Is such thinking still a 'philosophy of origin'? 'Negation as reversal is thus only and truly possible when ground and existence (both are in themselves ordered in such a way that they relate to each other) become free to move and thus make it possible for the unity to be reversed' (ibid.). Heidegger leaves no doubt that the reversal never touches the unity itself. But perhaps there is not even a unity that could posit itself as unity, since all unity seems to depend on a primordial Being-not-one.

Precisely because of the caution necessary here, we must not reductively label Heidegger's 'holistic' understanding of disease as 'anti-scientific' or as a strategy of 'counterenlightenment.' In light of this understanding, how can we respond to the peculiar credence Derrida seems to give the concepts of fundamental ontology and of the thinking of Being? If we want to pave a connection between Heidegger's reflections on sickness and Derrida's remarks about AIDS in order to formalize the feature common to these discourses and transform it into a kind of axiom, perhaps we must venture the following claim: sickness can *become significant* for thought, it can *have a signification*; but it *has a signification*, it *becomes significant* for thought only at the moment it is and must be thought as that which delimits, determines, constitutes, inverts, destructures, deconstructs, a whole or a unity. The sickness of thinking threatens the whole and by no means remains 'external' to it. Every time, it is a lethal and consequently historical – or almost historical – sickness. Must we not resort to this axiom to clarify the relation between confession and sickness or disease?

However, is AIDS (still) a disease? And if it is (still) a disease, is it an ancient disease that has been around for a long time, or is it novel, even a novel type of, disease? Since the discovery of the HIV-retrovirus, which has provoked and continues to provoke scientific, legal, institutional, international, disputes, the etiological definition of AIDS has changed: it no longer corresponds to the definition of a syndrome. AIDS is now defined as a 'retroviral infectious disease'. As to whether the pandemic infection caused by the virus can be described as a new type of disease, Grmek answers: 'It is not a disease in the old sense of the word, inasmuch as the virus is immunopathogenic, that is, it affects the immune system and produces symptoms only through the expedient of opportunistic infection or malignancy. However, AIDS can be partially conceived as a disease in the classical sense inasmuch as the virus can also exert a direct cytopathogenic action, that is, it can directly affect, impede, or destroy certain cells'. On the other hand, 'AIDS is definitely new in its present epidemiological dimension. In the past, biological and social conditions prevented a major outbreak of a retroviral infection transmitted in such a special manner, and especially one that so ruthlessly attacks the immune system. A disastrous epidemic of this type could not have occurred before the mingling of peoples, the liberalization of sexual and social mores, and, above all, before progress in modern medicine had accomplished the control of the majority of serious infectious diseases and introduced intravenous injections and blood transfusion. All this does not necessarily imply that the virus in question is a newborn in the absolute sense, a mutant whose ancestors were never pathogenic'.

Ad 2–AIDS, Deconstruction, Re-cognition. The emergence and spread of AIDS, Derrida emphasizes repeatedly, is an event that leaves indelible traces and has irreversible effects, and that always holds something of itself in reserve. That we might someday develop a vaccine to control AIDS changes nothing here. The 'indestructibility' of that which belongs to the order of events is due precisely to its own destructive force and is not simply opposed to destruction: a singularity or uniqueness (of the event) that is all the more unique because it exposes the singular or unique to contamination, to infection, to generalized immune deficiency. Derrida states, 'If I spoke a moment ago of an event and of indestructibility, it is because already, at the dawn of this very new and ever so ancient thing, we know that, even should humanity someday come to control the virus (it will take at least a generation), still, even in the most unconscious symbolic zones, the traumatism has irreversibly affected our experience of desire and of what we blithely call intersubjectivity, the relation to the alter ego, and so forth'. A traumatic experience, whose effects one assumes are irreversible, is an experience that precedes any form of memory or recollection. If we reconstruct the 'logic' of Derrida's remarks, we will have to say that the emergence and epidemic spread of AIDS destructure a certain organization of society, because they are the cause of a trauma at once novel and immemorial. Time is always the time of AIDS, AIDS time. But this assertion does not preclude the worldwide spread of the virus from being 'a historic (historial!) knot or dénouement which is no doubt original'.

To be sure, the fact that an effective medical strategy to fight AIDS has not (yet) been found should not lead us to recognize in the disease the 'economy of death,' of which Derrida writes in other contexts, an economy that describes the spacing of writing (see *Of Grammatology*), and that produces itself as or in *différance* (*Différance*). But perhaps it is easier to understand why in Derrida's texts the HIV infection is assigned such prominence if we take into consideration its specificity. The 'classic model of infection,' as Grmek explains, 'places the invading microbe in frank opposition to the cell.' But HIV, this retrovirus, acts as a parasite that just inscribes itself in 'the very heart of the host's control center,' which defines the cell, *without opposing it.* 'Integrated like this into the cell genome, the virus temporarily loses its individuality and can remain latent for a number of years. During this period, the cell appears to be normal and the virus seems to disappear. Its essential part is hidden in the form of a so-called provirus, a piece of viral DNA attached to the host DNA. In this state, the virus is invulnerable to drugs; it can be destroyed only by killing the cell. The proviral DNA *may be silent*, but it is still 'alive' because it is transmitted to every daughter cell after each cellular division'. The transition to a state that is called HIV-positive – and bears the French name *séroconversion*: transformation, inversion, conversion of the blood – happens only later, when another infection activates the lymphocyte infected with HIV. 'The provirus can "wake up." It takes over the enzymes and ribosomes of the host cell, inducing them to make viruses'. Is not deconstruction also a kind of virus that one day 'wakes up'? If no system, no concept, no thought, no culture, no nature, is exempt from decon-struction, if there is always already deconstruction, then the intervention of a deconstruction that can be called by its ('im-proper') name is no less an event. As an event that receives a name, deconstruction happens at a specific point in time, *today*; hence the semblance of stability offered, for a longer or shorter period of time, by that which is untouched and simultaneously infected. Does deconstruc-tion, then, recognize itself in the (mirror) image that the wide screen of AIDS holds up to it? Does it decipher itself as the image projected on this 'mirroring screen'? A peculiar and confusing speculation, a non-speculative speculation: the recognition implied by the 'massive legibility' allegedly produced by the emergence and spread of AIDS cannot be a *recognizing oneself that produces an identity*, but is recognizable enough to permit us to speak of a *recognition of deconstruction*. It is as if deconstruction would recognize and acknowledge AIDS because it recognizes itself in it. The time of AIDS, AIDS time, is a caesura in time. It is the untimely moment when deconstruction continues deconstruct-ing *and* interrupts 'itself.'

Because deconstructive 'work' is not the work or the labor of the concept, the recognition of deconstruction differs from self-recognition, from a recognition that produces an identity. Deconstruction cannot relate to itself as a subject does. But after reading the interview 'The Rhetoric of Drugs,' after reading what is said there about the event 'of our time,' one is undoubtedly inclined to assume that Derrida says nothing about AIDS he would not have said about deconstruc-tion. Admittedly, it would probably be facile to suspect the gesture of recogni-tion of being nothing more than a gesture of appropriation – gesture of appropriating that which is recognized or recognizes itself. Nevertheless, such a suspicion would not be groundless. Why? This question allows us, perhaps, to touch on the paradox of a thought that does not recollect or assemble itself in an identity of the identical and the non-identical. For if thought always has the task of thinking that which cannot be reduced to itself, if we think only when we pursue this task, then there is no thinking that does not distinguish itself as something excessive and that does not turn out to be essentially im-pertinent. When Adorno, for example, declares that the truth of psychoanalysis depends on its exaggerations, when he defines philosophy as the thinking of that which thought itself is not, he clearly points to this constitutive excess of all thinking. For a thinking that cannot absorb its own excess and thus make it commensur-able, for a thinking that does not sublate its im-pertinence, recognition cannot designate a point at which the subject relates itself to itself, defining itself as subject and appropriating all its elements with no excess outstanding. But the reason recognition always exposes itself to the suspicion of being a (re)appro-priation is that it inescapably implies a certain *self*-recognition, a certain recog-nizing *oneself*. Thus it could almost be said that a thinking not-at-one with AIDS, that wishes to fight AIDS, requires a supplement of im-pertinence. But in what does the im-pertinence of thought consist when it strives to think AIDS and its consequences, when it is required in the process to *recognize itself in a*

Being-not-one that is its 'own' Being-not-one? That is the question of deconstruction, and of any thinking that measures up to it in the time of AIDS, in AIDS time.

See also:

Critchley (3.5)
Beardsworth (5.4)
Ronnell (5.5)
Butler (5.6)

6.6

'WHAT IS IT O'CLOCK? OR THE DOOR (WE NEVER ENTER)'

Hélène Cixous

The first time I saw Jacques Derrida (it must have been in 1962) he was walking fast and sure along a mountain's crest, from left to right, I was at Arcachon, I was reading (it must have been *Force et signification*), from where I was I could see him clearly advancing black on the clear sky, feet on a tightrope, the crest was terribly sharp, he was walking along the peak, from far away I saw it, his hike along the line between mountain and sky which were melting into each other, he had to travel a path no wider than a pencil stroke.

He wasn't running, fast, he was *making* his way, *all* the way along the crests. Going from left to right, according to the (incarnate) pace of writing. Landscape without any border other than, at each instant, displacing him from his pace. Before him, nothing but the great standing air. I had never seen someone from our century write like this, on the world's cutting edge, the air had the air of a transparent door, so entirely open one had to search for the stiles – later I would call this tableau:

– Circumcision of the world –

'*Alone*, very alone on a line – a line of poetry,' as it says on page 107 of *Schibboleth*.

Drawing the inner margin of the universe, thus the universe, nobody in person, the ultimate surveyor of ultimity.

Source: Hélène Cixous, *Stigmata: Escaping Texts* (London: Routledge, 1998), pp. 57–84.
'Quelle heure est-il ou La porte (celle qu'on ne passe pas)' was first published, in a slightly different version, in *Le passage des frontières* (Galilée, 1994): 83–98.

'To see oneself always placed *at the head*, if one may say so,' this is how we recognize him, placed at the head, on the crest, at the peak. Alone without solitude not yet followed or pursued, alone (I tell myself) like a Jew amongst Jews, and amongst Jews and non-Jews, alone like a 'J' trying to slip his crazy *signifiance* out of the game of fatal definitions, spinning his path beyond the points (of departure), and, for this, attempting to be de-born, without denying the being born that aims beyond the border, the bound.

Alone, not less alone than a poem

not less strong on air than a ship that travels the sea, which opens and closes, without slicing it.

What was separated by his step was the on high and the most high (the up above).

First vision, which acted then, for me, without my knowledge, like the revelation of a door. There is a door. In the world, there are doors.

Happily there isn't only the world. Beyond the world is the Other side. One can pass over, it's open or it opens. Happily one can go there. Where? There.

(How? We need a door.)

Who invented doors? I dedicate what follows to the inventors of doors, and of nexts, to the angels, to the peoples of Apocalypses, to the secret angels, to secrets –

> Next I had a vision. Behold, a door had opened in the sky, and the first voice that had spoken to me, like a trumpet, said to me: come up here, that I may show you what must come next.
>
> (4:1)

said the angel of the *Apocalypse*, apostrophizing to his John like his voice apostrophizes to J. D. in *Circonfession*.

No revelation without a door. But which door? A non-door, a door that stands aside so as to let pass: (The door is not a shibboleth). A smile perhaps, or the sensation of a smile. A door so as to better open. Smile.

'The door opens' – one never knows who opens it, from which side he or she enters or leaves.

The door opens.

Enter – the Hour.

The Hour is my story's main character.

'The door opens,' says the language that doesn't say 'someone opens the door.' Is it mother, is it cat, is it wolf, is it you?

The door opens, says the poem – that knows that all doors are magic spirits, and all poems are doors, and, in the same way Time opens and closes, according to its strange magic, Time, which is the very matter of our soul, our very substance, strange and dreaded.

What time is it? That is the question.

In the wee hours, when I'm no longer sleeping but still dreaming and I'm in the midst of waking, it comes, the question, to spur me on, and in the same way in the middle of the day, it comes to rouse me. What time is it, do you know what time it is? As soon as I wonder what time it is, I'm lost.

What time is it, I mean to say where am I, I mean to say where have I gone – I don't know anymore, in this instant when I call out to myself, where I'm passing or where I'm going.

When do we wonder this? So often. We grope our way along in time, worried, distracted. And blindly we forefeel.

What time is it? is the best-known fateful question, the one we repeat ten times an hour with automaton lips, and time doesn't pass, the one we listen to with the tips of our ears, the gravest question in its familiar appearances, the question that admits our anxiety without our knowledge, the most wily, the least recognizable, the one that announces. Something is going to happen. And we don't know if it isn't already, the thing, the hour, already on the way to happening, already there, a little to the left, we find ourselves on a terrestrial platform, held back, there to the left in the sky, this isn't the moon, it's the all-white face of a handless clock, and we too we have an all-white, uncertain face.

I've always loved *Julius Caesar*, the one from the Shakespeare play, this play bathed in the light of a handless clock.

First I loved the love, by which Julius Caesar and Brutus were mortally bound. Two beings who loved each other equally, as much as mother, as much as child, elected son chosen father, two beings bound by the same possibility of giving each other death, each one life for the other, therefore mortality.

Caesar can fear blows from no one, if not from Brutus. This is why Caesar is fearless. This is why Caesar is mortal. Brutus can fear betrayal from no one, if not from Caesar, the one he loves so much. This is why he doesn't fear Caesar, this is why he fears him: if there is betrayal, it can only come from the one who can't betray. Caesar alone is to be feared, if there were something to fear. If the hour to fear were to arrive.

It was then, while I was loving them, Caesar and Brutus, that I discovered, trembling: so there is a time to fear. It was the story of a dangerous hour. If the hour doesn't come this year, Caesar and Brutus will live to the age of ninety-two.

O this sentence disguised as cliché, 'what time is it?' – see how it sounds ceaselessly as soon as the play begins, each goes around asking the other what time it is (What is it o'clock?) As though one knew! What are they all up to, even the smallest roles, the walk-ons, looking at their watches all the time? How does Shakespeare tell what time is it? In a hundred ways: What is it o'clock.

> *Brutus*:   What, Lucius, ho!
> I cannot by the progress of the stars
> Give guess how near to day. Lucius, I say!
> I would it were my fault to sleep so soundly.
> When, Lucius, when? Awake, I say! What, Lucius!
>
> . . .

Brutus:	Get you to bed again, it is not day.
	Is not to-morrow, boy, the Ides of March?
Lucius:	I know not, sir.
Brutus:	Look in the calendar, and bring me word.
Lucius:	I will, sir.

. . .

Lucius:	Sir, March is wasted fifteen days.

(Knock within.)

Brutus:	'T'is good. Go to the gate; somebody knocks.

. . .

Decius:	Here lies the east: doth not the day break here?
Casca:	No.
Cinna:	O, pardon, sir, it doth; and yon gray lines
	That fret the clouds are messengers of day.
Casca:	You shall confess that you are both deceived.
	Here, as I point my sword, the sun arises;
	Which is a great way growing on the south,
	Weighing the youthful season of the year.
	Some two months hence, up higher toward the north
	He first presents his fire; and then the high east
	Stands, as the Capitol, directly here.

. . .

(Clock strikes.)

Brutus:	Peace! count the clock.
Cassius:	The clock hath stricken three.
Trebonius:	'Tis time to part.

. . .

Cassius:	Nay, we will all of us be there to fetch him.
Brutus:	By the eighth hour: is that the uttermost?
Cinna:	Be that the uttermost; and fail not then.

(II, 1)

Publius:	Good morrow, Caesar.
Caesar:	Welcome Publius.
	What Brutus, are you stirr'd so early too?
	Good morrow, Casca. Caius Ligarius,
	Caesar was ne'er so much your enemy
	As that same ague which hath made you lean.
	What is't o'clock.

Brutus:	Caesar, 'tis stricken eight.
Caesar:	I thank you for your pains and courtesy.

(II, 2)

(Enter the SOOTHSAYER)

Portia:	Come hither, fellow: which way have you been?
Soothsayer:	At mine own house, good lady.
Portia:	What is't o'clock?
Soothsayer:	About the ninth hour, lady.
Portia:	Is Caesar yet gone to the Capitol?

(II, 4)

Caesar:	The Ides of March are come.
Soothsayer:	Ay, Caesar, but not gone.
Artemidorus:	

Hail, Caesar! read this schedule

(III, 1)

The sulfurous odor of imminence goes to our heads.

It smells like time, as is always the case in a love story. As soon as we enter a 'love story,' what is imperceptible, colorless and odorless in ordinary life becomes extraordinarily insistent. The time-of-life substance begins to beat endlessly, reminding us of the High Fear of Love. Time is the Other's odor. The clock rises. The door opens, enter the outdoors. We fall outside ourselves. The clock strikes. Fire. We fall. In love. Headfirst. Arms open, torso open. The stranger enters our body, nervous, opens the avid mouths in the heart, in the belly, the mouths fill up with famine, it burns it bites in the breast, painful signs, nameless, very powerful phenomena,

finally all this inconvenient, invincible pain, this aggression, this displeasure that twists its great vital nerve, this martyrdom without malady, this voracity for meat, with hesitation we call it love. The odor of fire, the taste of blood, life enriched by wounds, enhanced by murders – love.

The day breaks: the day breaks, with the night, with the day.

The hour is unknown. The hour that I don't recognize when I don't recognize myself – this hour troubles me. The hour is near. We don't know if it is coming upon us or if we're going towards it, and with what step.

The hour is foreign. Will it resemble us? Us who? We fear it, we hope for it. This precise hour we're thinking of.

It takes its time. It can take a long time, this *arrivance*. Afterwards, nothing more will be as before.

The hour is always not-yet and imminent. Waiting for it we are in a Night. The interval is dark. In this night we prick up our ears. We roam outside ourselves, before us Brutus worries about the time – hold me, give me your hand, Lucius, give me my name – the not-yet is on the verge of tears, it resembles so much already the nevermore. And if Brutus clings to Lucius like to the last light of the known day, it is because he is not in his time, but in the other, the terrible time, the hour that is going to make of Brutus a stranger. We're afraid of this hour.

– Time, are you there? – I'm putting my socks on, time grumbles. – Another minute, and I ask again, trembling: Time, are you there? – I'm putting my shoes on.

The hour frightens me. I'm afraid it may be the last one. The hour I call upon is always the last one, the last hour of this time, or perhaps the first hour of the next world.

'The sisterless hour.' The time towards which we are turned, obscure in the obscurity, is always sisterless.

I'm afraid of it, yes, and yet I hold myself in its power, I hold myself at the ready to flee in full flight from it, I make light of it, yes, and yet it keeps me in ecstasy ... With delight we ask the wolf if he's there, if he's done, now it's time for the trousers, now it's time for the shoes, and now, we shout, what time is it Mr Wolf? It's time to eat you!

That's what we were waiting for! Now we must flee on both feet or be devoured. It's comedy – or it's tragedy.

We wouldn't miss this hour before the mouth and the teeth for anything.

But then, when it's time, at the last minute we run away and we lose it – at least when we were little. We did nothing else but: prepare to escape. What is poignant in the case of *Julius Caesar* is that when it's time, no one runs away. We go all the way to the altar, to the butcher's, we can't help ourselves, we go all the way to where we don't want to go, it's irresistible. Pushed by desire and terror mixed.

The hour we ask of the wolf is the only one that impassions us. Because it makes of our body an earth convulsed. One must almost die in order to take pleasure in being made of flesh, we've always known this. What time is it? Time to be eaten. Passion.

Ah if we could go over to die, taste, be tasted, and then return to this side. Ah if we could go all the way to the instant when what disgusts us intoxicates us,

The dream would be to be there, at that hour, this is the poet's dream – and getting there has always been the poem's hope. And the poem or poet is the hope for this meeting with ourselves at the hour of our most intimate foreignness, at our last minute. And then? – Then.

Ah if we could go out, and, once outside, turning around, see with our own eyes the face of our own door.

Have once on ourselves the other's point of view. Taste our taste.

Ah if we could catch ourselves at it.

Travel around ourselves perhaps.

To see, our limit, to have seen, with other eyes, other eyes. Be present at the marriage of nothingness and nascentness, of our life and our death.

Sometimes, trying to circumscribe ourselves, we graze our door. This occurs in certain circumstances, usually around a birthday, for it's then that the mother returns to us, and with her comes the aid of an other regard, the only one that 'remembers' us since our first second.

Or else around a fateful event, the death of a parent or a child, the disappearance of someone close to us by blood, who awakens in us the always forgotten source (blood). Alive I die piece by piece, I die several deaths before my own death, I know it but this is what I've forgotten. For this is the mystery of my body that stretches out beyond my body, my body at the mercy of your body.

Give your name, your age, your address, the judge enjoins. I say my name. *My age?* How to say? We aren't an age, and it isn't us. We're never of age for the judge. That one we never manage to be. Something makes it precede us, like a mobile border. 'You know I was, I am, I just turned sixty?' a friend tells me who can't believe it at all and neither can I. We announce it to each other, we denounce it, I took, I caught, we're hit, defamed, marked, amazed. We would never have believed, and we don't believe. If it wasn't for our mother, the one we love. My mother, the dawn of the anniversary of her giving birth to me, asking me, when was it, do you remember?

fifty years ago? More. Is it possible, I can't believe it, my mother says, taking me as a witness.

Alles ist näher, als
es ist, Alles ist weniger
And it's true: seeing my mother . . .
Jahre.
Jahre. Jahre.[9] Years. That's all. Years. It doesn't add up. Only years. It *makes* time, without taking any off.

No, we are not these little scraps, tiny finished scraps of an infinite Time. We are not the fingernail clippings of God. We are books, we are wholes, we are ourselves the subject of our books, Celan is right to ask *when when.*

> *Wann,*
> *wann blühen, wann*
> *wann blühen . . . ja sie, die September –*
> *rosen?*[4]

> When do they flower, when
>   yes they, the Septembers
>   the Seven ambers
> Roses, when when

The September Roses – when – at what time will it be time, my time?

'Our age,' 'if it counts,' is for our mother, it's our mother who is it, it's she who keeps count. We, we are always interiorly our secret age, our strong-age, our preferred age, we are five years old, ten years old, the age when we were for the first time the historians or the authors of our own lives, when we left a trace, when we were for the first time marked, struck, imprinted, we bled and signed, memory started, when we manifested ourselves as chief or queen of our own state, when we took up our own power, or else we are twenty years old or thirty-five, and on the point of surprising the universe.

The other age, the one which our mother authenticates, remains for ever foreign to us, and yet, bound to the mother, it is sacred to us.

Sometimes we write a book so as to name an age, the one that comes to us from our mother, sometimes to celebrate the natal event and the author of the event, the mother. We keep count, humbly: *Circonfession*: 59 periods, the book due to the mother. This is where you've led me, you, mysterious and innocent accomplice, co-author and co-mother of my mystery, see where I how stand, what I owe you, how much, with what love you have wounded me once and for all times, wounded and dated. Apparently, we are in 1992 after J. C., but Circonfession comes to pass in 59 after the birth of J. D., since it writes itself *from the invisible inside* (second period)

writes itself, setting off for the outside, writes itself all alone, masculine or feminine, with J. D. aboard, flowing from the first notch,

extracting from the inside of his life small volumes of blood that he, the forever-child, still looks at with the same surprise, today still a child before the blood feels the same surprise, the child remains, the blood remains, time passes without the blood changing, without the child passing, the limitless child (Period 2), without the child knowing what blood is, this inside that exits, and which, one says, has a voice, the same voice for you and for me, the voice of blood.

He himself wasn't there at his own circumcision, but afterwards what jealous curiosity for his own inside! At the beginning of this whole book, to begin, there will have been this moment of separation within me, the instant of opening what must remain closed, and then, the dazzling effusion of blood, frightening, sudden appearance of what can only be interior – at the beginning of every book, there is this: the 'unexpected discovery': I see my blood gush forth, I see the inside come out, and that there is an inside. With my own eyes I see the stranger who lives inside me, the inside who doesn't obey me, and who has my numbers and my keys, I saw my blood, my unconscious, my kinship. I see my invisible. I see the age, the blood, the one that is and isn't there; through a tear, I see my marrow my secret; and if I quiver it's because I feel what I do not know: behold my death which I will never see. *Our* death, ours, the instant of our life which we cannot appropriate. Our death which strips us of our death. We have the experience we have not to have, of not having. The thing that will come from us to us so as to escape us. Like blood. Once the wound closes up we speak of it no longer, but we never forget it.

See also:

Jabes (1.6)
Blanchot (1.8)
Belsey (4.5)
Caputo (9.6)

PART 7
PSYCHOANALYSIS

7.1

'PSYCHOANALYSIS:
THE FRENCH CONNECTION'

Geoffrey Hartman

To be stripped of every fiction save one
The fiction of an absolute

Wallace Stevens

The language of Lacan and Derrida is shaped by a Heideggerian detour. Both writers see Western philosophy as reflecting through its grammar, its categories, and its now inbuilt manner of discourse a desire for reality-mastery as aggressive and fatal as Freud's death instinct. Their critique of metaphysics seems to blend with the findings of Freudian metapsychology. The Western thinker gloats over reality like Shakespeare's Achilles over the living body of Hector. Achilles, in a jocose and terrible taunt, inspects Hector as if he were infinitely vulnerable:

> Tell me you heav'ns, in which part of his body
> Shall I destroy him? whether there, or there, or there,
> That I may give the local wound a name;
> And make distinct the very breach, whereout
> *Hector*'s great spirit flew.
>
> (*Troilus and Cressida* IV.ix.)

This fearful power of pointing out, or pointing at, expresses what Lacan describes as the phantasm of morcellation, or of the 'corps morcelé' – a phantasm that the psyche is always seeking to allay. If we remember that Achilles is

Source: Geoffrey Hartman, *Saving the Text: Literature/Derrida/Philosophy* (Baltimore: Johns Hopkins University Press, 1981), pp. 96–118.

almost immortal, that in theory he can only be wounded through a heel left untouched by his immersion in the Styx, then we see the connection between this taunt and a deeply human anxiety. In ordinary mortals the Achilles heel is everywhere; psychic development is therefore a balance between the hope of immortality and the continuous fear of mortal exposure.

Directness – the 'fingering' or 'prenominating' mode of Achilles – has its shadow side, which is part of the very subject of French investigations linking language and the psyche. Yet to say we are crucified, or morcellated, by language is as pathetic and exaggerated as to claim we are potentially redeemed by it. The fundamental concern of Lacan and Derrida is with directness, or *intellectual* passion: that rigorous striving for truth, exposure, mastery, self-identification – in short, science and metaphysics – which at once defines and ravages the human actor.

Against this rigor, and often from within it, various doctors, including those of the Church, have sought to defend us; poetry, too, has been considered a *remedium intellectus* and the poet-humanist a 'physician to all men.' It is not surprising, then, that Derrida should open his tortuous and capital work, *Glas*, with reflections on Hegel's 'absolute knowledge' – that immediacy of person to truth which is the exact obverse of the naïve immediacy Hegel calls 'abstract' and which the absolute thinker sees filled or made concrete by historical experience in its very negativity, its morcellating if also self-healing movement.

Speaking of passion we evoke necessarily a family of words: *patience, patient, passio gloriosa*, even *crime passionel*. In the column opposite the one that opens with an allusion to Hegel's absolute thinker, Derrida quotes from Genet what seems to be a fit of passion or else a gratuitous act: the tearing to pieces of an essay manuscript on Rembrandt, rendered as if a picture itself, or the very name Rembrandt, had been defaced. 'Ce qui est resté d'un Rembrandt déchiré en petits carrés réguliers et foutu aux chiottes' (*Glas*, 7b). This strange, onomatoclastic act is directed against what I will call 'l'imago du nom propre' (the imago of the proper name) and it again evokes the fantasy of the 'corps morcelé.' We are made to realize how easily the psyche is punctured by image, photo, phantasm, or phrase. The terrible rigor of psychic, like logicistic, process sets this human vulnerability in a perversely radiant frame, one that may extend toward infinity like the Chinese torture of 'a hundred pieces.' Psychoanalysis, in this light, reveals once more the unresolvable ambivalence of passion as both suffering and ecstasy: as a *geometry* of beatitude achieved by submitting again and again to the wounding power of some ultimate penetration, or the illusion of coming 'face to face' with life or death or truth or reality.

'I am half sick of shadows,' says Tennyson's Lady of Shalott, before she turns to what she thinks is reality and dies. The wish to put ourselves in an unmediated relation to whatever 'really' is, to know something absolutely, means a desire to be defined totally: marked or named once and for all, fixed in or by a word, and so – paradoxically – made indifferent. 'He (She) desired to be without desire' is the underlying clue in the psychodrama of many Lacanian patients. The story of I (for identity) begins to cheapen into the Story of O, and can be more dehumanizing even in the noble form of Descartes's 'cogito ergo sum' than the dangers of the Id. Pornosophy, so at home in France, so alien to English and American literature, depicts prophylactically the Ego's demanding a 'divine' violation into thinghood or invulnerability. The indeterminacy principle, however, that Lacan and Derrida develop from dream logic and literary language begins with the Id rather than with the Ego: or minimally with the *id est*, which, like the *à savoir* ('namely'), defers absolute knowledge and definitive naming in the very act of exemplary instancing. 'Id est, ergo id non est.' Exemplification is always serial, subversive, plural.

We return by this route to the subtle links between psyche and language. For one wonders, in reading Lacan, whether philosophical discussions concerning the *stigme*, or 'here and now,' are so removed, after all, from psychoanalytic speculations on the divine or hysterical stigmata, and the whole issue of ecstasy, identification, incorporation, conversion. Did Freud really succeed in ushering in an era of 'deconversion' or of purely 'psychological man'? With Lacan in particular, the project of psychoanalysis is not only involved in what the relation of analyst and analysand may mean for the 'order of discourse' each embodies – just as Derrida, in *Glas*, explores simultaneously the question of a relation between the paternal discourse of a magister ludi called Hegel and the thievish, maternal 'calculus' revealed by Genet. Lacan's project is not only this sensitive exploration of the power relations between codes or idioms within language; it is also an attempt to restructure them, in order to build a new communitarian model on the basis of psychiatric experience, Though we have entered the age of Freud we remain in the age of Saint-Simon.

Lacan exposes the self-protective devices and rules so important to Freudian psychiatry, and demands of the clinician that he listen to the 'Other' who is as much in himself as in the patient. This Other solicits the labor of recognition that must keep analyst and analysand apart despite transference and counter-transference. The 'pathos' of the analytic situation is linked to its representational character: something is acted out here-and-now to cure the here-and-now by a respect for there-and-then; for difference, otherness, change, mortality. The patient is to become patient rather than fitful-passionate, and the analyst must be patient too in order to *hear* what is going on, to decipher or even redeem from the *res* the *rebus* presented to him.

> Hieroglyphics of hysteria, blazons of phobia, labyrinths of the *Zwangs-neurose* – charms of impotence, enigmas of inhibition, oracles of anxiety, talking arms of character, seals of self-punishment, disguises of perversion – these are the hermetic elements that our exegesis resolves, the equivocations that our invocation dissolves, the artifices that our dialectic absolves.

Yet the analyst is attracted to and therefore protects himself from the ecstatic message, the heart of darkness in the patient, that is, in himself. He hunts that wounded hart as in some spiritual chase, but only to build on it (strange rock that weeps) an acknowledgment of a purely human crucifixion, of a secular, self-inflicted stigmatics.

Freud, according to Lacan, founded psychoanalysis on this attraction to the hysterical patient, usually a woman; and inattention to that origin means that theory must 'cherchez la femme' once again, or take 'le discours de la femme' (the woman's word) again into the method. A quasi-sacred detective story unfolds as Lacan follows the traces, semiobliterated, of Freud. He begins his own career with a thesis of 1932 that reflects on what is practically a literary theme: the self-inflicted wound of a woman he calls Aimée. The question elaborated since 1932 is that of the *Eigentlichkeit*, or 'propriety,' of this wound, one that is contagious in the sense that it cannot be localized, much less contained. Lacan's thesis is that the erotomanic woman who knifed an actress was really attacking her own person: the mystery is that the wound had to go through that detour.

In much of his work Lacan interprets a *blessure* (wound) that is so ambiva-lently a 'blessing' as the *symptom* that acts out whatever is human in us. He names the wound, or makes 'distinct the very breach' that renders the psyche visible. It is a movement of desire that cannot define itself except as a desire of, and belonging to, an other: a desire that may not be appropriated by the self, and so cannot build up (as ego psychology would have it) a stable self. In terms of sexual differentiation the breach is related to the (absent) phallus and in terms of noncarnal conversation it is related to a language where the signifier cannot be completed by the signified. The phallus as signifier is not circumscribed by its function of procreation but serves to open the wound, and womb, of significa-tion. If the psyche is said to be structured like language it is because the symptom is always like a displaced or forgotten word, a repressed signifier that pretends to be *the* signified and a terminus to desire. The analyst recovers the signifier and with that not only the meaning of symptoms but a blocked mode or force of speech. Hence, all psychoanalysis draws others into its contagious orbit and stimulates an epidemic of soul-(un)making. The history of religion is full of such epidemics, of course; and Lacan's project, however self-aware, remains under that shadow.

I am consciously reading Lacan (and also Derrida) in the light of what Sartre called 'la grande affaire' – the scandal of theological survivals in even the most secular thinkers. This survival may simply mean that the concept of seculariza-tion as presently understood is premature or crude. It is clear, however, that French thought in the area of psychoanalysis has removed language from the hope of being purified through a curative metalanguage. A language that is authentic, that lies beyond the eloquence of wounds or religious pathos or the desire for reality-mastery, is not to be found. Lacan, in this, must sometimes be distinguished from his followers, whose belief in the truth of words is more directly thaumaturgic and whose case histories can be more transparent and frightening in their reductionist clarity than those of the early Freud. At best both Lacan and Derrida remind us that language, like sexual difference or passion in general, is that in which we live and breathe and have our being. It cannot be subdued but remains part of the subtle knot that perplexes even as it binds together man and woman in the 'scène familiale.'

> Que tu brilles enfin, terme pur de ma course.
>> Valéry, 'Fragments du Narcisse'

In a glass darkly. Lacan discovers a 'stade du miroir' (mirror phase) in the early development of what is to be the child's ego. By the complaisance of the mirror the child sees itself for the first time as a coordinated being and, triumphantly, jubilantly, assumes that image. But what is found by means of this play ('je-jeu') with the mirror is really a double rather than a differentiated other. The myth of Narcissus is given clinical verisimilitude. The other (Rimbaud: 'Je est un autre') is necessary for self-definition, but in the mirror is simply an illusory unification. The 'corps morcelé,' moreover, the fragmented or uncoordinated body image prior to the mirror phase, is only suspended. It remains active in the domain that Lacan names the verbal or symbolic in contrast to the nonverbal or imaginary.

Beyond these observations lies a difficult psychopathology that we need not oversimplify except to say that the concept of a 'corps morcelé' (cf. *Glas*, 'un Rembrandt déchiré') is connected with Lacan's understanding of the castration complex, or how the phallus or the body part that 'represents' the sexual foundation of otherness is enmeshed in an extraordinary developmental series of differential yet substitutive (compensatory) mechanisms. Acceptance of the (absent) phallus, or of the (absent) father, or, basically, of the mediacy of words, allows a genuine recognition of difference.

Since the mirror phase, although using gestaltist and biological evidence, is not securely based on experimental data (especially when compared to the painstaking work of Piaget) it might be better to call it the *Marienbad complex*. Not only is Marienbad where the hypothesis was first made public, but also Resnais's film *Last Year at Marienbad* expresses Lacan's mirror domain as a fact of the imagination: the image or heroine in that film's mobile mirror seems to quest for a specular yet totally elusive identity, for some unique reduction to one place, one time, one bed, one fixative spectral event.

The mirror phase, then, deals with images, with thing rather than word representation. (In *Last Year at Marienbad*, the sound track is dissociated from the life of the images, running nonparallel with it, an arbitrary or contrapuntal yet related experience. It is exactly like the somewhat mysterious juxtaposition, in Lacan, of symbolic and imaginary spheres.) The notion of a 'corps morcelé' does, however, connect with the differential system of a psycholinguistics. The question therefore arises: Is there anything comparable to the mirror stage on the level of language?

Lacan's emphasis on the birth of language out of a 'symbolic' rather than 'imaginary' sphere seems to moot this line of inquiry. He suggests that the specular image, as the base of other imagery that serves an integrative or unifying function, is an illusory modification of a deeper or prior system, inherently differential. Thus, the question of what corresponds to the mirror phase on the level of language (to its unifying if illusory effect) may seem unanswerable in terms of Lacanian psychiatry.

Yet there is the well-known magical or religious ambition to possess *the* word. Does not the concept of Word or Logos in religion, or in such artists as Hölderlin, provide a clue? And is not the Lacanian psychopompos, who recovers an interior signifier, of that tradition? We are looking for a correlative in language to the specular image. The logos understood as that in whose 'image' whatever it is signifying seems to motivate a logocentric phase of development – the very thing Derrida is seeking to expose.

Or consider the importance of the proper name in Shakespeare. 'Had I it written, I would tear the word,' Romeo says to Juliet, referring to his family name. The wounding of a name is too much like the wounding of the body not to be significant. We don't know why Genet tore 'Rembrandt,' but the effacing or defacing of the proper name suggests that there may be such a thing as a specular name or 'imago du nom propre' in the fantasy development of the individual, a name more genuinely one's own than a signature or proper name. Signatures can always be faked. Is there something that cannot be faked? 'The signature is a wound, and there is no other origin to the work of art' (*Glas*, 207b). Is it possible to discern a specular word, logos phase, or imago of the proper name in the development of the individual?

Derrida's reflections on Hegel, in *Glas*, open with a play on the idea of 'naming' or 'nomination,' a theme fully elaborated in his juxtaposed column on Genet. He implies, without calling it so, an imago of the proper name on the basis of what we know of the haunting, fixative, unifying effect of 'being named.' Just as the specular image produces a jubilant awareness tested and affirmed by the child's mirror mimicry, so the specular name can produce a hallelujah and magnifying language that mimics a sublimity associated with the divine logos. This is so even if the identifying name, the *nom unique* or *nom propre*, is accusatory. Indeed the *scene of nomination* (my own phrase) is bound to be accusative as well as nominative, or to include within it a reflexive, intense response to the act of vocative designation. 'You are a thief,' that commonplace accusation, that merest insult addressed to Genet as a child, strikes inward as a divine apostrophe and perhaps founds the perverse high ritualism of his style.

In such a scene of nomination, then, the mirror speaks. We suspect, of course, that our primary narcissism has already spoken to it, like the queen in *Snow White*. But whatever question has been put remains obscure: only the mirror's response is clear, indeed so clear that it obliges us to assume its answer as an identity, to construct or reconstruct some feature in us clarified by this defining response. At the same time, the specular name or identity phrase – our true rather than merely proper name – is reaffirmed *in time* by a textual mimicry, joyful, parodistic, or derisory, of the original 'magnification.' The repetition of the specular name gives rise to texts that seem to be anagrammatic or to conceal an unknown-unknowable key, a 'pure' signifier. These texts are called literature.

Can we assert that the specular name 'exists'? Derrida knows that such words as *exist* and *is* point to a static order of things, and he tries to avoid the trap of this inbuilt language-metaphysic. He suggests, instead, that if there is a Hegelian *Sa* ('*savoir absolu*') it may be incompatible with the *Sa* (*signifiant*) we call a signature: the proper name (Hegel) affixed to a text as its authenticating seal.

A similar counterpointing of proper and specular name is suggested in Genet's case. The 'antherection' of his name in a given passage (that is, the flowery style that alludes to his flower name, 'genêt') makes a tomb of it: as in Saussure's anagrams, the text generated by the name is bound to enlace and so to bury it. Like a child who will not believe his parents are his real parents but engages imaginatively in a 'family romance,' so the proper name, or signature, is always being 'torn up' in favor of a specular name, whether or not it can be found:

> The grand stakes of discourse (I mean *discourse*) that is literary: the patient, tricky, quasi animalistic or vegetative transformation, unwearying, monumental, derisive also, but turning derision rather against itself – the transformation of the proper name, *rebus*, into things, into the name of things [*Glas*, 11b].

More radically still: writing is coterminous with that canceling movement, 'la nécessité du passage par la détermination biffée, la nécessité de *ce tour d'écriture*.' Every return, then, as in Genet, to a scene of nomination, must be unmasked as a figure. It introduces a factitious present or fictitious point of origin that may not be taken literally ('livré à la police') unless we are in search of an 'ordinateur secret' leading back to baptism or birth.

> A text only exists, resists, consists, represses, lets itself be read or written if it is elaborated [*travaillé*] by the unreadability [*illisibilité*] of a proper name. I have not said – not yet – that such a proper name exists and that it becomes unreadable when it falls [or is entombed, *tombe*] into the signature. The proper name does not ring forth [*résonne*], lost at once, save at the instant of its *débris*, when it breaks – embroils – checks itself on touching the signature [*seing*] (*Glas*, 41b).

Glas ends, therefore, with the words 'le débris de' [Derrida] – that is, it touches, without actually stating, the 'seing.' The proper name seems to have been 'disseminated': *Glas* has told (tolled) its demise. This concept of dissemination moves to the fore in Derrida's writings after the *Grammatology*. It is essential for his critique of Lacan or Sartre or any hermeneutic that relapses into a thematics (even a polythematics) by its insistence on an explanatory 'key.' In his grimly funny way, Derrida compares this procedure of 'slipping the universal passkey into all lacunae of signification' to a police action. 'It would mean arresting once again, in the name of the law, of veracity, of the symbolic order, the free movement [*marche*] of an unknown person' (*Glas*, 36b).

The signature, which denotes propriety through the proper name, is the *cas limite* of this arrest. Only courts of justice should insist on it, with their cumbersome machinery of registration, verification, ceremonial gravity, etc. Dissemination is, strangely enough, a pastoral though totally uninnocent protest against such restrictive or paralegal types of hermeneutic. It is the obverse, in fact, of classification. 'What makes us write is also what scatters the semes, disperses *signacoupure* and *signacouture*' (*Glas*, 192b).

The passage from cl (for *class*, *clé*, *clue*) to gl (for *glas* or *glu*) analogizes these contraries: classification and dissemination. 'At the very moment,' Derrida continues,

> we try to seize, in a particular text, the workings of an idiom, linked to a chain of proper nouns and actual denotative configurations, *glas* also names *classification*, that is, their inscription in networks of generalities infinitely articulated, or in the genealogies of a structure whose cross-weaving, coupling, switching, detouring, branching can never be derived merely from a semantic or a formal rule. There is no absolute idiom or signature ... The bell tolls always for the idiom or the signature. For the absolute precursor [*aïeul absolu*: perhaps 'primal father'] (*Glas*, 169b).

Thus, we enter a chain of secondary elaborations stretching to infinity. There is no way of tracing them to an origin, to a logos that may have been 'In the Beginning.' When, in a quasi-heraldic moment – talking arms of character, Lacan might say – Nerval's *Desdichado* recites, 'Je suis le ténébreux, le veuf, l'inconsolé,' we know that the family name 'Labrunie' has been cast out in favor of a specular identity that is the widowed logos itself: the babel of 'à la tour abolie.' The appropriate hermeneutic, therefore, is like the interminable work of mourning, like an endless affectional detachment from the identity theme as such, whether that is linked to the (absent) logos or to a maternal and sexual presence distanced by the logos into the idea of an Immaculate Conception.

Perhaps the most persistent – obsessive – theme in *Glas* is the Immaculate Conception. It surges into the opening page before its time. No sooner has the author said, in the margin, '*Sa* will henceforth be the mark [*sigle*] of absolute knowledge,' than he adds, 'And IC, let us note it already, because the two portals [i.e., columns on the page] represent each other mutually, the mark of the Immaculate Conception.' The notion of *sigle* (of words represented by their first letter) enters a series including 'signature' and 'seing' (seal or mark at the end of a text, representing the signatory, with a possible interlingual pun on *seing/sein/Sein*: seal/breast/Being). This tripling could be explained by the special function assigned each term, but Derrida is more concerned with how language moves by marginal differentiation through a signifying series that can never quite circumscribe, or comprise, a body (corpus).

This term *Sa*, therefore, which he institutes but which is homophonic with Saussure's abbreviation for signifier (*signifiant*), although made of first and last (of *initial* letters that denote an *end* state) is neither a first or last term, for it enters an indefinite sequence that includes other words already mentioned, as well as *signe, ensigner, enseigner*. Writing *Glas* in two columns, or beginning with two Hegel passages, reinforces our awareness that the 'scene of writing' never takes place in one place: its locus (corpus) is always also 'ein anderer Schauplatz,' as Freud put it: displaced from right to left, to a supplementary comment or even into a physical symptom, which Lacan rightly analogizes to a 'truth' already written down elsewhere and therefore in part missing from present discourse. There is, in short, no absolute or transcendental *Sa* (signifier) any more than an absolute or certain *Sa* (knowledge of what is signified). We cannot say, like Christ, 'This is my body' without being already dead: pre-monumentalized.

From the start of *Glas*, then, we are presented with two illusory moments of ecstatic identification some eighteen hundred years apart: absolute knowledge, or Hegel's vision of an end to dialectic and alienation in the thought process of the philosopher who has internalized history; and the phantasm of the Immaculate Conception. Why the latter? What bearing has it, as developed in the column on Genet, on the Hegelian 'legend' unfolded opposite? And why emphasize, of all literary writers, Genet? Among Anglo-American readers the juxtaposition will cause a resistance that even the brilliance of the result may not remove.

See also:

Miller (4.1)
De Man (4.2)
Johnson (6.3)

FROM *THE WOLF MAN'S MAGIC WORD*

Nicholas Abrahams and Maria Torok

The Wolf Man's drama remains incomplete for its hero. But once set in motion, its action cannot be stopped; it must proceed in us inevitably to its final outcome. And here our dissatisfaction, spurred on by a providential *deus ex machina*, expounds, imagines, dreams. An irresistible force pulls us: to save the analysis of the Wolf-Man, to save ourselves. With time the fourth act opens within us, stretches before us, and in us comes to fulfillment, bringing salvation.

1. An Impromptu Walk Through a Verbarium: Cryptonyms and What They Hide

The authors arrived at this very juncture in the process of their writing, and planned to take up Freud's text again with their point of view – incorporation – in mind, when it occurred to them to consult a Russian dictionary. This gesture, performed out of conscientiousness, brought an extra load of unforeseen work, but also a host of altogether unexpected insights. First, it enabled the authors to refine their hypotheses about the genesis and working of incorporation in general and about the specific incorporation of which the Wolf Man was both actor and victim. But even more, it brought home the fact that someone could be driven to take on the same attitude toward words as toward things, namely, objects of love, and that such word-objects could upset a topography to the point where incorporation would seem a self-therapeutic measure.

Source: Nicholas Abrahams and Maria Torok, *The Wolf Man's Magic Word*, tr. Richard Rand (Minneapolis: University of Minnesota Press, 1986).

Initially, the authors had wanted to be certain there was no hidden ambiguity behind the repeated retraction of the number that first appeared in the principal dream. The original number given is six, immediately corrected to seven, whereas on the well-known drawing the number is reduced to five. Six in Russian, SHIEST, also means perch, mast, and probably genitals, at least symbolically. This could have satisfied an ill-formed psychoanalytic mind. Fortunately, the authors' eyes fell on the neighboring words: SHIESTIERO and SHIESTORKA, meaning six or a lot of six people. Contaminated by the German *Schwester* (sister), they could not help checking the word sister as well, and there they discovered, to their amusement and confirming their suspicion, the words SIESTRA and its diminutive SIESTORKA. It became clear that the 'pack of six wolves' did not contain the idea of multiplicity, but of the sister instead. Were we not justified from then on to look for the same association of ideas elsewhere? It was likely, in fact, that in the nightmares and the Wolf Man's phobic moments, wolf and sister would occur together. We simply had to survey the Russian vocabulary of the dreams and phobias and, where needed, fill in the gaps with his second language, German.

Here is a brief review of what we found. The nightmare about the 'wolves' analyzed in the preceding chapter enabled us to establish rather easily that the 'pack of wolves' crowding behind the door in the wall corresponded, insofar as it was a 'pack,' to a 'pack of six,' to a 'sixter' of wolves so to speak, though the number is not stated this time. We nevertheless potentially have SIESTORKA-BUKA (siswolf). In the dream of the celestial bodies we find ZVIEZDA-LUNA (star moon), the same arrangement of vowels with a slight phonetic distortion. The nightmare of the skyscraper gave us more trouble. NIEBOSKREB (skyscraper in Russian) did not seem to have anything to do with either wolf or sister. Conversely, the German word for skyscraper (*Wolkenkratzer*) – we had to think of it – does indeed contain the 'wolf' we were seeking; the other Russian name for wolf, BUKA, being precisely VOLK. As for the 'sister,' we could only find disagreeable words in the places we had expected her: SKREB, the root of SKREBOK = scraper; SKROÏT = to sharpen; SKRIP = scraping sound, and here we came close to giving up Russian altogether. But by tinkering with these words, we gained some new terms for our vocabulary: scrape, scratch, cut, bruise, scar, and, through German, cancer (*skreb* = *Krebs*) – all meanings we will encounter again, under various guises, in the clinical material.

Then we ventured a final hypothesis, and this turned out to be our lifesaver. If all these words – we advanced – in some way allude to the sister, this time they do so otherwise than through a veiled evocation of the word: sister. Why restrict our attention to the nightmares and phobias when the hypochondriac fears concerning the nose speak explicitly about scratch, scar, and cancer? Obviously, behind this was lurking the association, undoubtedly left nonverbalized, of a *lupus*, namely a *lupus seborrheus*. The hypochondriac ideas would appear to rest on the same verbal support as the nightmare of the 'skyscraper.' The same support, no doubt, but what on earth was it? We pursued our inquiry. What was striking – we used to tell each other – was a certain unity of meaning among all these rather different-sounding words whose list could be lengthened at will by a whole series of analogies. This profusion of terms, carrying the idea of *wound* and stated in such diverse forms, did it really refer to the idea of castration? On the basis of the two word couples just reconstituted, *siestorka-buka* and *zviezda-luna*, we had no reason to stick with such a hypothesis. Why deviate here from our initial line of thought and not admit – even at the cost of extrapolation – that all these locutions simply cover up another word, this one signaling sexual pleasure and alluding to the so-called seduction scene? Given the abundance of synonyms, we also understood that there was no mere phonetic or paronymic displacement at work here as in *zviezda-luna*, but that, in order to reach the sought-after key word, we had to move across the signifieds and search for semantic displacements. The key word, no doubt unutterable for some reason, and unknown for the moment, would have to be polysemic, expressing multiple meanings through a single phonetic structure. One of these would remain shrouded, but the other, or several other meanings now equivalent, would be stated through distinct phonetic structures, that is, through synonyms. To make our conversations about this easier, we would call them *cryptonyms* (words that hide) because of their allusion to a foreign and arcane meaning. We also wanted to set them apart from simple metonymic displacement.

Spurred on by these considerations, we turned to the privileged libidinal moment, Grusha, the floor scrubber with her bucket and broom. A rather problematic scene as to its historical truth but nonetheless significant – we thought – for its erogenous value. How to link it to the seduction by the sister? Would she have touched him in a way that the child could have called 'polish' as one also says 'polish' a wooden floor? What an incongruous idea! Let's check it out anyway'. The French-Russian dictionary gives TIERET, NATIERET. Let's go to the Russian–French dictionary; it will tell us whether the meaning 'polish' coexists with others like scratch, scrape, and so forth, a necessary condition for the cryptonymic displacement just conjectured. Conscious of our duty, but not very hopeful, we then turned to the word *tieret* and read: (1) to rub; (2) to grind, to crunch; (3) to wound; (4) to polish. The second word *natieret*, of the same root, did not disappoint us either. It exhibits a comparable semantic variety, going from (1) to rub down, rub; through (2) to rub, scrub, wax; to finally (3) to scrape or wound oneself. We could not have asked for more! Finally we understood the rebus of the skyscraper! With all the necessary substitutions, the solution is simple: It concerns the association of the wolf with sexual pleasure obtained by rubbing.

By the same token, a whole area of the Wolf Man's enigmatic material was opened to our understanding. Lingering for the moment on the nose symptom, it became precise and concrete. The symptom had been produced, it was clear now, through the association of two words: one omitted and the other transformed into a cryptonym. The first pointed to the object of the hypochondriac fear, *lupus* (wolf); the second, scar, referred to the name of the action through which the dreaded pleasure would be accomplished: *tieret, natieret*. The hypochondriac *lupus*, coupled with the cryptonym 'scar', did nothing more than show/hide the desire of a pleasurable rubbing applied to the 'wolf' in order to make it stand up. 'Sis, come and rub my penis.' This was the key sentence. These were the unsayable words that he posted in the form of a rebus, making sure to add at the bottom: 'You will never guess.' It became obvious that this hidden sentence would be found everywhere in the Wolf Man's material.

We could fill pages and pages drawing up the catalog of its various guises. We could also, in light of this new approach, take up again, point by point, our earlier psychodramatic reinterpretation of Brunswick's text. In many places we could simplify or even rectify it. If we have left this up to our readers, by printing our initial version intact, we did so wanting to include them all the more in our fumbling around. They will much better appreciate the ground covered.

Among the applications of our discovery concerning the use of cryptonyms, we found most striking our realization that certain words suffered an extra-ordinary exclusion and that this same exclusion seemed to confer on them a genuinely magic power. The verbs *tieret* and *natieret* had to be entirely banished from the active vocabulary and not only in the sense of rubbing, but also in the sense of waxing or scraping. What if these parallel meanings, these allosemes, had to be stated? Each time they were, by means of synonyms, they obviously implied a constant reference, even if a negative one, to the *taboo word*. It was, we thought, because a given word was unutterable that the obligation arose to introduce synonyms even for its lateral meanings, and that the synonyms acquired the status of substitutes. Thus they became *crypto-nyms*, apparently not having any phonetic or semantic relationship to the prohibited word. *tzarapat* (scratch, scrape) bears no apparent relation to *tieret* (to rub). In sum, no simple metonymic displacement is at work here, referring to one element of a concrete situation instead of another element actually intended (as when we say pen to mean style or writer), but a displacement on a second level: The word itself as a lexical entity constitutes the global situation from which one particular meaning is sectioned out of the sum total of meanings. This characteristic could be expressed by saying that what is at stake here is not a *metonymy of things* but a *metonymy of words*. The contiguity that presides over this procedure is by nature not a representation of things, not even a representation of words, but arises from the lexical contiguity of the various meanings of the same words, that is, from the *allosemes*, as they are catalogued in a dictionary. For TZARAPINA (scar), to evoke *tieret* (to rub), a form of lexical contiguity has to be inserted. Having understood the real originality of this procedure, which lies in replacing a word by the synonym of its alloseme, we felt the need of applying to it a distinctive name, *cryptonymy*.

2. BEHIND THE SCENES: INTERNAL HYSTERIA – SETTING UP AND WORKING A MACHINERY

With this added clarification and the necessary verification done in the material, the question emerged of how one is led to invent such a procedure considering that it does not provide, either phonetically or semantically, the hallucinatory satisfaction we might reasonably expect. The only pertinent answer seemed as follows: It is not a situation *including* words that becomes repressed; the words are not dragged into repression by a situation. Rather, *the words themselves, expressing desire, are deemed to be generators of a situation that must be avoided and voided retroactively.* In this case, and only in this case, can we understand that repression may be carried out on the word, as if it were the representation of a thing, and that the return of the repressed cannot have at its disposal even the tortuous paths of metonymic displacement. For this to occur, a catastrophic situation must have been created precisely by words. We understand then why they would be excluded, responsible as they are for a situation; why they would be repressed from the Preconscious, dragging with them their lateral and allosemic meanings. In short: It is the idea that words can be excluded from the Preconscious – thus also from the dream texts – and replaced, in the name and capacity of the return of the repressed, by cryptonyms or their visual representation that is required for a general preliminary conclusion to our inquiry.

Let us now try to fill this formal frame with more concrete content. For such a construction, two elements have to be taken into account: First, the words in question must signify an erotic pleasure received from the sister; and second, they are responsible, because stated inauspiciously, for the castration, that is, the demolition of the father. Based on this double hypothesis, various possibilities can be imagined, and among them we settled on the idea that the traumatic catastrophy could not have taken place at one definite moment, but would have unfolded in four stages.

1. *The 'seduction' of the younger brother by the older sister.* The term 'seduction' might seem somewhat excessive to describe, as Freud did, sexual play among little children. For such games to take on the magnitude we know they can, an adult must be implicated. That is why we have suggested from the very beginning a stage –

2. *The alleged seduction of the daughter by the father.* The sister would have boasted about the privilege she had over her little brother, and in the process would have threatened him with castration at the moment of pleasure. Now, in light of the cryptonymic procedure, we abandon the idea stated at the beginning of this work of such a threat of castration. We now in fact know that the terms that in the material seemed to evoke castration are simply the cryptonyms of repressed pleasure-words. Nevertheless, the hypothesis of two further stages forces itself on us, stage –

3. *The boy's verification with adults of the allegations made by his sister*, at first perhaps with Nania or the English governess, then with his mother back from a trip, finally with his father – then stage
4. *The outbreak of a scandal*, with an investigation as regards the meaning of the words *tieret, natieret* indicting the father.

This fourth stage is postulated as having the mark of a real experience and can in no way be merged with fantasy. This is what explains, to our mind, the uniqueness of the Wolf Man's case: the radical exclusion of the words of desire. The excluded *words* work as if they were representations of repressed *things*. They seem to have migrated from the Preconscious to the Unconscious. They have taken with them the very possibility of remembering the trauma. Their absence in the Preconscious signifies: The trauma never took place. What distinguishes a verbal exclusion of this kind from neurotic repression is precisely the fact that it renders verbalization impossible. The return of the deeply repressed, if it happens at all, cannot come about within a relation, in the form of symptoms or symbols. It will occur within the psychic apparatus through a kind of *internal hysteria* and will be directed toward the internal. Objects incorporated for this purpose. Settled within the Ego with their complete topography – as it had been experienced at zero hour – these Objects remain the invisible yet omnipresent partners of the excluded desire concerning them. They will be oppressed by their own Superegos as in melancholy, or they will be satisfied by fulfilling *their* unconscious desire as in mania. The Ego proper, whose function is to be Hand for the Libido, Hand for Sex, will have become Sex for *another* Hand, Hand for *another* Sex. Its own activity will consist in satisfying or counteracting the desires lent to its Guests, or to their respective Ego Ideals, and of thus maintaining them within itself. The return of the deeply repressed can come about only in relation to this internal world. On the outside, it will merely appear in the form of failure, somatization, or delirium. The *incorporated* guests – hence the term – lodge in the *corporeal* Ego. The internal hysteria of the Ego proper reaches them there. The crypto-nymic procedure manages somehow to pass over their heads and address external Objects. The work of the only authentic area remaining in an alienated Ego, it deserves, its strangeness notwithstanding, the respect due any attempt at *being* in spite of everything.

For the Wolf-Man – we understand why – a return of the repressed in the waking state through symbolization, for example, is out of the question. The single exception concerns the expression of *the very act of the retention of telling*, well expressed hysterically by tenacious constipation. But whatever might be the *object* of telling is so deeply buried behind words never to be uttered that its emergence, when it does take place, occurs not in the form of a symbol or a symptom but of a delirium such as that of the nose or later of the cut finger, and finally of the erogenous fantasy itself. In this last instance, the appearances seem safe: What would be delirious about imagining a coitus performed a tergo and the suitable position of the partners (a tiergo the analyst would say with well-taken mischief). Apparently nothing, were it not for its incredible verbal origin: *tieret* visualized into a floor scrubber. We see here a genuine dream process in full wakefulness. In order to tell himself his desire, he has to have recourse to dream distortion. The erogenous fantasy, Grusha the floor scrubber, the washerwoman at the fountain as well as the parents' supposed coitus a tergo, were nothing but a word, translated into an image. The face, the person of the woman are of no importance, provided she illustrates, she embodies the taboo word. It is in this sense that we are going to call this erogenous image, this good-luck-charm fantasy, this magical taboo dodger: *a fetish*. Beneath the fetish, the occult love for a word-object remains concealed, beneath this love, the taboo-forming experience of a catastrophe, and finally beneath the catastrophe, the perennial memory of a hoarded pleasure with the ineducable wish that one day it shall return.

The Wolf Man's hope was deposited in the word whose secret lover he was. This word, his Object, he kept in his possession for an entire lifetime. Initially and by vocation, the word was addressed to someone. As an Object of love, it had to be removed from everyone's reach so that it would not be lost. Saying it without saying it. To show/hide. Walk around with a rebus and pretend it is undecipherable. Repeat tirelessly to one and all, especially to his analyst: 'Here is nothing, hold it tight.' Inaccessible, wending his way alongside the unattainable. To love without knowing, to love desperately, to love loving the analyst endlessly.

3. THE FOURTH ACT: ON FREUD'S COUCH – THE WOLF MAN AS UNTO HIMSELF

It was – we now know – for never having been able to utter certain words that, sixteen years earlier, the Wolf Man went to consult the famous Professor Freud. Following a bout of gonorrhea (curbed, however, by rather drastic means five years earlier), he remained in a state of near-total impotence. He dragged himself from doctors to health care centers without finding a remedy for what ailed him. The Professor was his last resort. Freud did not consider him a 'maniac' for his loves at first sight as psychiatrists had done. He listened, he tried to understand, he requested his collaboration. Together they would find the cause of so much suffering. The Professor inspired confidence in particular by his subdued style of dressing, and the furniture of his office suggested praiseworthy occupations. The austere and sympathetic man of science was perfectly suitable. S. P. was more than reassured. What got into him then when, hardly having lowered himself on to the couch, he requested from his respectable therapist the favor of performing anal coitus and invited him to defecate while standing on his head? Had he been the Tierka he knew at four years of age, he could not have done better. Without a doubt, his 'wolf' was surfacing. The same one that had been so cruelly treated at the time of his gonorrhea. Since then, almost five years earlier, his depression had not left him. This was evidence that one does not make 'wolf' without risking one's tail, even if it was only a father's tail. Could he ever recover his *buka* standing up, could he finally protect it from danger? He placed all his hopes in the Professor. He would tell him everything. Everything, yes, except ... one thing: the unsayable. They would launch their investigation together, they would study the facts, their chronology. Together they would draw conclusions about the causes and the consequences. He could sleep with peace of mind, nothing will escape the sagacity of the Professor. Yet, hardly reclined on the couch, this strange thing happens. What a *coup de théâtre* for the analyst! And for him! Has anyone seen a well-bred young man, not suspected of homosexuality, make such a request of an eminent specialist of fifty? No, really, he was no longer himself.

But who, in fact, was he? Before and now? Freud in truth could never establish it. Are we, at the end of this study, in a position to put forth a hypothesis on this score? It seems fairly certain that no affective recollection took place during the transference and that nothing occurred that could have identified him: 'Yes, here he is, this is definitely S. P., seduced at three years of age by his sister, desiring his father at five, his mother at eight.' S. P. in person was not present. His official identity only served to cover up the other characters he clandestinely sheltered within himself: his father, his sister. A depressed and castrated father for having rubbed up against Tierka, Matrona, that is who he was during his depression. But once on the couch everything changed: The man in the chair was now named Father and the man on the couch automatically took on the complementary role, Tierka's role. This was the unexpected but inescapable effect of the analytic situation. His depression vanished, and with his extravagant request began a flirtation between Father and Sister that was to last four and a half years. This unusual first session was simply Tierka dallying with Papa. As the years went by, the coquetry took on forms more suited to the norms of the analytic dialogue and to the widely publicized desiderata of the father of psychoanalysis. Throughout more than one thousand sessions, Tierka unflinchingly recounted Stanko's memories, dreams, nightmares. She added some of her own invention. Father and Daughter could live happily.

As for Freud, he must have been thrilled and disconcerted all at the same time. Soon he thought he could identify the 'wolf' in the nightmare, the 'wolf' in the infantile phobia: It represented some terrifying image in relation to the father. It must have been the father himself. He still needed to understand how this kind and loving father could have instilled fright in the child when all the memories of 'castration' were linked to female images. Should one incriminate a phrase such as the unfortunate one used to tease children: 'I'm going to eat you,' or should one appeal to the phylogenetic fear of being castrated by the father? Such answers hardly convinced anyone, including their author. Freud was just as baffled when faced with the allegation of a Primal Scene supposedly observed at the age of eighteen months. Still, the parents' coitus a tergo seen at this tender age could – theoretically – have caused a neurosis and subsequent sexual behavior. The case seemed too good not to be used in the polemic against Jung. Let us admit though that, removed from its context of heated controversy, such an example was altogether untenable. Moreover, Freud needed no such arguments to defend his ideas. In any case, this matter remains a prime example of theoretical and clinical errors occasioned by a heated controversy.

The Wolf Man himself felt reassured. Tierka and Father united, they spoke of Stanko, and for all of them everything turned out for the best. Of course the 'wolf' was Father, of course Father had to castrate Stanko, of course Stanko feared him with good reason. So long as Father is not castrated again, never ever, through inopportune words, through the explosion of outraged anger. To void what had taken place once upon a time, the catastrophic words had to be contained at all costs: Squeeze the sphincter tighter and tighter! Constipate the fatal word! And above all, the 'window' must never open by itself! Otherwise there would be the horrifying nightmare of the wolves of long ago: a fossilized phrase in a fossilized picture. '*Siestorka* makes *buka* to Father.' 'Sis, come and make Stanko's "wolf" stand up.' No! Such words will forever remain in his throat. Let the two of them be happy and S. P. can live!

Yes, S. P. is entirely a gift of himself in the strictest sense. Did he keep to himself some desire that he had not offered? This will remain unknown to all including himself. No one on earth must know who he is. No one on earth must know that one day he *became* his father or that he carried him within himself along with his castrated desire. This father has to be restored, such is his most fervent desire; otherwise he, Stanko, could never pronounce, in his own name, the sentence of his own desire, say it to Tierka without disaster: 'Come Sis, rub me, do Buka to me!' Alas, these words, these diabolical words, he will never give voice to them, for they – yes, we have to admit it – castrated the father, castrated the son. They are the ones that threw the mother into despondency. They are the ones that, through their belated effects, led to the sister's suicide, to the father's premature death. A few innocent words, and all of a sudden the whole family is destroyed.

This sentence, however, always the same one, the Wolf Man will never tire of repeating in riddles. Tieret, to rub, wax, wash. Sissy, 'get on all fours' to 'brush,' Grusha, to 'wax,' Matrona, yes, do *tronut*, do touch, touch me! I'll go crazy ('become touched'). Oh, Matrona! Matrona, a cherished word: Russian doll, you hold my Jack-in-the-box, *vanka*, *vstanka*, let's put it on its head, you'll see how it *makes out*! It was enough for me to *act* a word: 'scrape,' 'cut' into a tree and I was already in heaven, I had my little finger 'cut.' Come, Professor, do these words to me. 'Cut,' oh! 'cut me,' 'pull me,' 'rip me,' oh, confounded words, unsayable words, oh! yes, rub, rub my genitals for me so they stand up on two paws like a wolf disguised as a grandmother with a white bonnet on its head. Oh, yes 'rip off (*tierebit*) the wings of this wasp, of this S. P.' (*Wespe*), rub, rub it for he cannot stand it – but . . .

All this, S. P. does not say clearly. But fast, very fast, in hardly three months, since that was the nonnegotiable deadline Freud had set in order to finish it off, he laid it out in cryptonyms and cryptomyths.

And with his time up, the Wolf Man left, relieved, for his native Russia. He felt relieved since he had spoken and invented disguises for his desire. Relieved also not to have to speak it in disaster words, relieved finally, since he could take back the memory of a new kind of father, of a father whose seductive practices were restricted to harmless words, rather amusing by the way, like the word 'castration,' so often on the lips of the Professor, and which happily joined the list of cryptonyms.

And in all likelihood everything would have been fine for him after that had the incidents of the Revolution not forced him into exile five years later. In 1919, upon his arrival in Vienna, Freud's famous case study had just been published. He was so happy reading it! The illustrious father had become involved with his case, and more than that, he released his appreciative judgment to the public: '... pleasant and likeable personality'; he had spoken of his 'sharp intelligence' and of 'his refinement of thought.'

Yet, deep down in the Wolf Man, there was disappointment and revolt. He went to see the Master once more. He let him know that he had not been cured, and especially not of this constipation that Freud so proudly claimed to have alleviated. Moreover, being financially ruined as he was, he could not afford another analysis. That should not stand in the way! the Professor said with sympathy. And then came free analysis, donations. Wages for not being himself. For the Wolf Man, the apparently happy situation revived a latent despair: Stanko misunderstood, castrated, disposed of. Father giving money to Tierka... When in October 1923, the seriousness of Freud's illness became common knowledge, the horizon blackened even more. If Father disappeared, who would ever free S. P.'s desire? We know the rest.

> Forever he will keep his love in his own possession, his Objects which are words. Unable to convert these word-objects into words for the object, his life remains, for himself and for us all, an enigma. Yet, in all this life, unfurling the flag of enigma, the Wolf Man has never left us. He remains with us analysts, to quicken our desire to know. Whether he appears to us as a living support for our projections and resistances or as an ever-renewing source of inspiration, we owe him a character: The Wolf Man, an intuition: Mourning and Melancholia, an anthropology: the second topography. Ever bent on offering a new element in order to clear up his mystery, he further obscures it. Our companion of misfortune in no-knowledge, he has become the symbol of a mirage – haunting every analyst – the mirage of understanding. After so many others, we too have succumbed to it.
>
> Let him be thanked for it!
> And let us be forgiven for it!
>
> September 27, 1970

Postscript. It should be clear that the preceding considerations relate to the Wolf Man only as a mythical person. Their wholly fictitious – though not gratuitous – nature illustrates an approach that can be of clinical use. What we termed *internal hysteria*, and considered as the consequence of *incorporation*, often implies unconscious procedures motivated by a particular topographical structure involving the *cryptonymic displacement of a taboo word*. Rightly or wrongly, we discovered such a taboo word in the Wolf Man: *tieret* and its derivatives. The reader may be interested in some additional information that has come to us through the kind generosity of Muriel Gardiner. We refer here to the Wolf Man's *Memoirs*, which began appearing in serial form in 1961 in the *Bulletin of the Philadelphia Association for Psycho-analysis*. These memoirs are of great psychoanalytic interest and deserve an extended study. We mention only two details because they relate directly to our findings. The first is this: Following the suicide of his sister Anna (this was her real name), who ingested a bottle of mercury during a trip to the Caucasus, the Wolf Man went on a trip to these same mountains, without realizing, however, that there might be a geographic connection between these facts. On close reading of his recollections it becomes apparent that the unconscious goal of this trip was to climb to the head of a mountain stream named Tierek. Upon arriving after a long and anxious ascent, he could not keep from taking out his paintbox and brushes to 'paint' (*tieret*) a view of the landscape. He also recalls that he was served *trout* caught in the *Tierek* River. The second point we want to make concerns the love at first sight he conceived for his future wife, a pretty nurse in a Kraepelin clinic (in Munich) where he had come to stay in the throes of a depression. He did not exchange a word with her, but an elderly Russian lady, also a resident there, furnished, with the appropriate Russian accent no doubt, one crucial piece of information: the name of the young woman. Her name was Sister Theresa (homophone of the Russian verb TIRETSIA, to rub oneself) and the diminutive was Terka, pronounced in Russian fashion: Tierka. We might have guessed it. In any case, our choice of the same name to designate the incorporated sister predates this information and – though inspired by the verb *tieret* – must be considered the work of some lucky coincidence.

See also:

Freud (1.2)
Royle (4.4)
Attridge (4.3)
Laclau (8.5)

7.3

'THE SIDESHOW, OR: REMARKS ON A CANNY MOMENT'

Samuel Weber

The first text I propose to investigate is Freud's essay on the uncanny. A relatively exhaustive and satisfactory reading of this seminal (or perhaps 'disseminal') paper cannot be attempted here. Such a reading would have to explore a wide range of problems, beginning with that of situating the essay, both within the development of Freud's thought in general, and in particular with regard to the particular perspectives opened by Freud's move 'Beyond the Pleasure-Principle,' a text written at the same time as the Uncanny and related to it in various fundamental respects. Jacques Derrida has already indicated certain of the main lines which such an investigation would have to take, placing particular emphasis upon the significance of the *Todestrieb* (Death-drive) and the *Wiederholungszwang* (Repetition-Compulsion) for Freud's approach to art and literature.[1] This line of inquiry has been pursued by Hélène Cixous in a recent article, 'La fiction et ses fantômes,'[2] which represents one of the first attempts to read Freud's text not simply in terms of its conceptual content but also with regard to its rhetorical and stylistic movement. Whether or not one accepts the major premise of Hélène Cixous' reading: that Freud's text is to be regarded as itself an example of the uncanny: 'moins comme un discours que comme un étrange roman théorique'[3] the alert reader will hardly remain insensitive to the peculiar merging of subject-matter and discourse in Freud's essay. Yet this merging does not simply fulfill the exigencies of theoretical discourse, the adaequatio intellectus et rei, since here the 'adequacy'

Source: Samuel Weber, 'The sideshow, or: Remarks on a canny moment', *Modern Language Notes*, 88, 1973, pp. 1103–33.

of discourse and object tends as much to dislocate the discourse as to locate the object.

But unfortunately such decisive questions can only be touched upon here: instead of pursuing them in a direct and systematic manner, I shall proceed in a more naive but perhaps more accessible fashion, treating the uncanny as one theme or subject among others, forgetting – at least for the moment – its peculiar locality, *abseits*. Instead I shall begin by repeating Freud, in a certain manner, by treating his own text as it itself treats the uncanny, attempting to penetrate to its conceptual nucleus by mustering up its manifold manifestations.

Freud divides his paper into three sections: the first is devoted to a lexical and etymological investigation of the words 'heimlich' and 'unheimlich' and arrives in short time at what is to be Freud's major hypothesis: 'Das Unheimliche sei jene Art des Schreckhaften, welche auf das Altbekannte, Längstvertraute zurückgeht.'[4] (The uncanny is that class of the terrifying which leads back to something long known to us, once very familiar) Freud's point of departure – or is it arrival? – is thus that the words 'heimlich' and 'unheimlich' are not simply opposites, but that heimlich itself is the repository of ambivalent meanings, signifying on the one hand, the familiar and domestic, on the other and simultaneously the concealed and the hidden. In this connection Freud quotes Schelling's description of the uncanny as anything which 'im Geheimnis, im Verborgenen (...) bleiben sollte und hervorgetreten ist' (which ought to have remained secret and concealed, but which has come to light).[5] This lexical investigation thus leads Freud to a conclusion which is no less important for being negative: the uncanny is not, as might be supposed, something entirely unknown or unfamiliar but rather 'irgendwie eine Art von heimlich' (in some way or other a sub-species of the canny, of heimlich).[6]

The second and major part of the essay consists of a *Musterung*: a mustering of those 'Personen und Dinge, Eindrücke, Vorgänge und Situationen' which embody, with particular clarity and force, the uncanny; yet the German word, *Musterung* – like its English counterpart – suggests not simply the peaceful assemblage, display and review of exemplary phenomena, but equally the marshalling of forces, conscription, constraint and conflict. We shall see that this connotation is not entirely arbitary.

The *Musterung* begins – necessarily – with the choice of a good example (*Muster*): Hoffmann's story, *The Sand Man*, leads Freud to the conclusion that the uncanny effect of the tale resides in the dread of losing one's eyes, which in turn is for Freud nothing but a substitute manifestation of castration-anxiety. But castration reveals itself here to be only one theme among the many which Freud musters up and which include, as second major thematic complex, that of the *Doppelgänger*, the Double, be it as duplication, ego-splitting, revenant, or the recurrence of traits, characters, destinies. Behind the motif of the Double Freud sees the *solid ground* of what he calls 'primary narcissism': 'Diese Vorstellungen sind auf dem Boden der uneingeschränkten Selbstliebe entstanden, des primären Narzißmus, welcher das Seelenleben des Kindes wie des

Primitiven beherrscht ...' (Such notions developed out of a basis of unlimited self-love, from primary narcissism, which dominated the psychic life of the child no less than that of primitive peoples ...)

The *Musterung* continues. Upon the heels of the *Doppelgänger* follows a motif which is in a sense itself a double, since it doubles the *Doppelgänger*: the motif of repetition (*Wiederholung des Gleichartigen*), which Freud links to the repetition-compulsion (*Wiederholungszwang*), 'der wahrscheinlich von der innersten Natur der Triebe selbst abhängt'[7] (which probably derives from the innermost nature of the drives themselves). At this point the uncanny converges with the death-drive (*Todestrieb*), but instead of dwelling on this relation Freud hurries on, intent upon bringing about a 'final decision concerning the validity of our supposition.' Yet before reaching that 'endgültige Entscheidung,' he introduces a fourth major thematic complex, which he terms 'the omnipotence of thought' (*Allmacht der Gedanken*) and which, as with the Double, he traces back to archaic narcissism, this time however not of the individual but of primitive cultures and their animistic world-view.

Here once again Freud suddenly stops short, this time, however, to reveal the 'wesentlichen Inhalt dieser kleinen Untersuchung'[8] (the essential substance of this small study), couched – curiously enough – in two remarks (*Bemerkungen*): first, since the uncanny is a form of anxiety, and since anxiety in general is produced by the mechanism of repression, the uncanny must involve some form of the return of the repressed. Second, this explains why the word *hiemlich* includes its opposite, *unheimlich*, since the latter is nothing new but only something originally familiar, which has been repressed.

The remainder of this section of the essay, writes Freud, can not consist merely in the *testing* (erproben) of this basic *insigh* (Einsicht). What follows, however, is a most remarkable proliferation of examples; the mustering grows to monstrous proportions as Freud amasses motif upon motif, many of which seem to repeat previous thematic complexes, such as the 'relation to death,' and the return of the dead, whereas others are of a very heterogeneous character and much more difficult to situate, such as the confusion of fantasy and reality or of symbol and symbolized. An even remotely adequate reading of Freud's essay would have to dwell here not merely on the conceptual conclusion of this remarkable proliferation of *Muster*, but on the *parade* itself, on the rhetorical structure and strategy of this curious *Musterung* and the constraints and desires to which it responds. Here I can only touch one of these: it is the struggle against *doubt*, a struggle that Freud conducts in various ways and at various levels, all of which are highly significant. Doubt – *Zweifel* – is the *malin génie* of the Unheimliche, and its shadow looms ever larger as the *Musterung* proceeds: for each doubt banned, two return in its place. Yet the doubts which remain, after Freud has marshalled all the forces at his command, are so fundamental that they require a third and final section of the essay in order to be discussed. These doubts call into question not only the theoretical thesis, involving the role of repression in producing the uncanny, but the status of the thematic examples as well. To begin with the latter: a severed hand, or any of the other motifs cited by Freud as uncanny, *can* produce such an effect but need not do so. Similarly for the mechanism of repression: the return of the repressed can be uncanny but is not necessarily so. That 'conceptual nucleus,' which Freud sought to disengage, has eluded his grasp, at least so far. The 'material conditions' (*stoffliche Bedingungen*)[9] isolated by Freud reveal themselves to be inadequate in determining the specific difference of the uncanny. Here, Freud observes, we seem to reach the limits of a purely psychological investigation and enter the realm of aesthetics. Yet to halt here would be to open the way to doubt – '*dem Zweifel das Tor öffnen*'[10] and this might well call into question Freud's entire analysis of the question. Freud is therefore constrained to muster up once more: this time, however, not examples (*Muster*), whose exemplary status might again be subject to doubt, but rather other *divisions*, namely two, a double division: first, between the uncanny of *immediate experience* (*des Erlebens*) and that of *fiction*; and second, das Unheimliche deriving from *repression* (*Verdrängung*) or from *surmounting* or *over-coming* (*Überwundensein*). The uncanny of experience presupposes in general the only partial surmounting of archaic modes of thought – above all, animism; to a lesser extent it derives from the repression of infantile complexes. Yet the double division complicates the initial distinction, inasmuch as overcoming relates ultimately to 'material reality,' to 'reality-testing,' whereas the formal condition of fiction is precisely the exclusion of such testing. This perhaps explains why Freud argues that the resources of fiction in regard to the uncanny include all those of reality and many more – although, on the other hand, much of that which would seem uncanny in reality does not produce this effect in fiction. Moreover Freud himself limits the distinction between repression and surmounting, inasmuch as 'die primitiven Überzeugungen auf das innigste mit den infantilen Komplexen zusammenhängen und eigentlich in ihnen wurzeln' (primitive convictions are not simply profoundly connected with infantile complexes but indeed derive from them), and, he concludes, we need not be surprised if these distinctions are somewhat blurred ('wird man sich über diese Verwischung der Abgrenzungen nicht viel verwundern').[11]

After a brief discussion of some non-thematic elements involved in the uncanny quality of literary texts – the relation of the reader to the characters, the kind of 'reality' selected by the 'author,' the certainty or uncertainty surrounding this reality, etc. – Freud abruptly breaks off this line of thought with a gesture that strangely supplements the broad sweep of the *Musterung* of Part Two, where the parade of examples seemed endless, as though – in accordance with a tendency of dream-articulation[12] – the proliferation of *Muster* served to conceal (and to represent) something quite different and more elusive. Here, at the point in his investigation where he is led beyond a strictly thematic-motivic treatment of the *Unheimliche*, where contextual factors begin to emerge, or at least their necessity, Freud draws back, invoking the academic division of labor which he elsewhere shows little scruple in violating when necessary: 'Wir sind auf dieses Gebiet der Forschung ohne rechte Absicht geführt worden, indem wir der Versuchung nachgaben, den Widerspruch gewisser Beispiele gegen unsere Ableitung des Unheimlichen aufzuklären'[13] (We have been led into this field of research without really intending it, by succumbing to the temptation of explaining the contradiction of certain of our examples to our derivation of the uncanny). At the conclusion of this essay, Freud has in a sense been led back to his starting point, by a strange *temptation*, without really intending it, except that this time it is not merely the Uncanny which is off-beat, off-side and far-out, *abseits*; for Freud himself has been led astray. The reasons for this pertain surely no less to the nature of the uncanny, to its position *abseits*, than to any peculiarities of Freud, or weaknesses in his argument. These are, as I have indicated, and as Freud himself admits, undeniable: the central thesis, involving repression (and then surmounting) is too abstract and too formal, and the particular relation between repression, anxiety and the Unheimliche is left open: however interrelated these three are, they are not simply identical. Secondly, the status of Freud's 'evidence' remains open to question: how exemplary are the examples, if the elements they comprise are not necessarily uncanny? Furthermore, the examples which he cites, or musters up, are often of a very heterogeneous nature: the confusion of fantasy and reality, or of symbol and symbolized, is obviously not necessarily a thematic question but can pertain to the form of a text (or of an experience).

Summarizing these objections – which are by no means exhaustive – it can be said that the relation of formal, thematic and causal factors is not adequately worked out by Freud in his essay. And as is generally the case when Freud is confronted with the necessity of affirming the interdependency of these moments without having sufficiently developed their constitutive connections, he resorts to a genetic-empiricist derivation, which explains less than it obscures. The following 'example' can be risked as being exemplary: the fact that castration-anxiety plays an 'enormous role' (eine großartige Rolle[14]) in the child's development, and that children often display the fear of losing their eyes, suffices – for Freud – establish a causal relation between the two: ocular anxiety becomes the effect of and substitute for castration-anxiety.

In place of this pseudo-explanation I shall naively endeavor to develop an alternative argument, which is no longer genetic or empiricist, but which, for want of a better term, I shall call 'structural'; this argument adopts certain elements of Lacan's reading of Freud but it begins with Freud's theory of anxiety, which, as we have seen, remains one of the unsolved problems in his paper on the Unheimliche.

However, there are *two* Freudian theories of anxiety, and as their difference is germane to the problem, I shall have to recapitulate, very briefly, both. The first theory, which Freud still held in 1919, while writing *Das Unheimliche*, affirmed that anxiety is the result of repression, which separates the affective cathexis (Triebbesetzung) from the representation (Vorstellungsinhalt) to which it was previously bound, and which alone forms the object of repression. This affective energy is thus cut off from the representation, becomes free-floating and is thus transformed into anxiety, which Freud regarded as unbound psychic energy. This entire process Freud regarded as functioning entirely independently of the particular representation involved and no less so of the nature of the affect originally connected to the representation. This 'first' anxiety theory thus included the decisive and radical insight, that the particular ideational content (Vorstellungsinhalt), which alone was the object of repression, was not in itself – that is in its intrinsic, qualitative content – sufficient to explain the genesis of anxiety, implying that it was only as the element of a broader context, that individual representations become psychically relevant. Yet the weakness of this early theory, which Freud later qualified as being 'descriptive,' is that it leaves both the basic cause of repression obscure, as well as the specific mechanism by which repression produces anxiety.

From 1926 on – the year Freud wrote his paper on *Inhibition, Symptom and Anxiety* (*Hemmung, Symptom und Angst*) – this first theory of anxiety was not only altered: it was reversed. Freud came to the conclusion that it was not 'repression (. . .) which produces anxiety,'[15] but anxiety which produces repression. This position thus compelled Freud to examine more closely the nature of anxiety, which could no longer be explained simply as the result of repression. Without going here into the typology of anxieties that Freud developed, one point can and should be retained: the particular anxiety which now became paradigmatic for the structure of anxiety itself was *castration-anxiety*.[16]

The implications of this second theory of anxiety for the problem of the uncanny are nothing less than decisive: it implies that it is not the return of the repressed as such which produces das Unheimliche, thus relegating castration to the level of one thematic-material element among others; on the contrary, the castration-complex now appears as the *nucleus* of the Freudian theory of the uncanny, permitting this theory to bring its otherwise disparate elements into a coherent connection. On one condition, however: that the *complexity* of the castration-*complex* not be overlooked, either by reducing castration to a 'real' event or by equating it with an imaginary or arbitrary fantasy.

Yet if it is neither simply real nor simply imaginary, what *is* castration? The only adequate response to this question, however disappointing it may seem, is that castration is *almost nothing, but not quite*. The Freudian theory of castration, as developed by Jacques Lacan, marks the *moment* – in a genetic, but also in a structural sense – of discovery when the subject is confronted with the object of its desire as being almost nothing, but not quite. The discovery of the penislessness of the mother by the child demolishes – or at least severely disrupts – the 'infantile sexual theory' which postulates that all living human beings, regardless of sex, are equipped with the male organ. Yet the effects of the castration complex extend far beyond the blow that it thus metes out to the narcissism of the child; its implications and consequences can neither be interpreted in a strictly genetical nor in a simply psychological sense. For castration involves a structuring of experience that far transcends the realm of the individual psyche; and what it dislocates by its violent movement is the primacy of what Freud termed the 'System Perception-Consciousness,' which dominates both everyday experience and the tradition of western thought as a whole. For what the child 'discovers' – that is, interprets – as 'castration' is neither nothing nor simply something, at least in the sense in which the child expects and desires it to be: what is 'discovered' is the absence of the maternal phallus, a kind of negative perception, whose object or referent – perceptum – is ultimately nothing but a difference, although no simple one, since it does not refer to anything, least of all to itself, but instead *refers itself indefinitely*. To use a language made popular by Lacan: castration inscribes the phallus in a chain of signifiers, signifying the sexual difference, but also as the difference (and prohibition) which necessarily separates desire – in the Freudian theory at least – from its 'object.'[17] Castration thus structures the future identity and experience of the subject, by confronting it with its unconscious desire as a violent and yet constitutive difference, preventing the subject from ever being fully present to itself, or fully self-conscious.

This summary allusion to the enormously complex Freudian-Lacanian theory of castration will probably confuse as much as it helps. An adequate exposition of the theory would obviously require a protracted discussion that cannot be attempted here. Instead what I shall try to do is to describe some of the consequences of this theory for the problem of the uncanny, in order then to propose this interpretation of castration as a working hypothesis in the reading of certain texts. Whatever the purely theoretical merits or difficulties of the theory of castration, I hope thus to be able to demonstrate its hermeneutical relevance. The determination of castration not as an event or mere fantasy but as a structure bears implications both for the articulation of the subject and for its access to reality. These implications can perhaps best be demonstrated in regard to the relation of castration and ocular anxiety. Whereas Freud, as we have indicated, could only equate concomitance with causality, it is now possible to discern a more stringent necessity linking castration to the eyes, inasmuch as they play a decisive role in the peculiar *non-discovery* of castration. Not merely do the eyes present the subject with the shocking 'evidence' of a negative perception – the absence of the maternal phallus – but they also have to bear the brunt of the new state of affairs, which confronts the subject with the fact that it will never again be able to believe its eyes, since what they have seen is neither simply visible nor wholly invisible. The particular relation of castration to the eyes is thus not primarily based on a genetic fact or experience, the actual moment of non-perception, however important this may be; instead what is involved here is a restructuring of experience, including the relation of perception, desire and consciousness, in which the narcissistic categories of identity and presence are riven by a difference they can no longer subdue or command. The peculiar evidence of castration is peculiar because it is both too evident and never evident enough. It robs the eyes of the desired phenomena and thus alters the structure of perception; yet even more important, it carries a threat of enormous violence directed at the body and its self-image, narcissistic basis of the subject, since the perception of the 'incompleteness' of the maternal body includes and implies a threat to the child's notion of the totality of its own body. This explains why Freud, in his *Introduction to Narcissism*, could describe castration as 'the most important (...) disturbance of the original narcissism of the child,'[18] since narcissism is both the precondition of and in part the reaction to the castration-complex.

These remarks enable us to situate more precisely the relation between castration and narcissism in regard to the uncanny, a relation which Freud describes but does not analyze. In his essay, Freud noted the importance of recurrent, repressed or (half-) overcome narcissism in explaining the uncanny nature of the motifs of the double and of the omnipotence of thought; The Doppelgänger for instance, Freud argued – following Rank's interpretation – has an ambivalent, narcissistic significance. On the one hand, it originally represented the attempt to protect the self against death by duplication (involving probably, although Freud does not discuss this, identification with the other). On the other hand, the double has come to be a portent of death once the second self is no longer protected by primary narcissism: duplication, the multiplication of selves, becomes the splitting of the self, no longer overcoming but rather confirming its non-identity and mortality. Freud himself indicated, but did not develop, the relation between this kind of narcissistic redoubling and castration by comparing the double to the representation of castration in dreams through the multiplication of genital symbols.[19] Repetition, duplication, recurrence are inherently ambiguous, even ambivalent processes: they seem to confirm, even to *increase* the 'original' identity, and yet even more they *crease* it as its problematical and paradoxical precondition.[20] Castration marks this crease as repetition, or more precisely, as the shift from a form of repetition based on identity – the repetition of narcissism, the 'infantile sexual theory' that repeats the penis by universalizing it – to another repetition, the articulation of difference, which is equally a dis-articulation, dis-locating and even dis-membering the subject – rather as the Sand Man treats and mistreats poor Nathanael in E. T. A. Hoffmann's tale, which Freud invokes as that 'happy first example' and to which I shall now turn, or return.

The question of the historical status of the Unheimliche, its relation to socially determined objective structures which themselves involve something like that crisis of perception and representation active in the uncanny, is problematic. Without being able to do more than indicate a possible line of research here, I would like to call attention to Marx's description of the circulation and production of commodities, which themselves appear as 'sensuous-supersensuous entities,' as 'phantasmagorias,' which represent both the objectified labor-power of society and an ambivalent, antagonistic social relationship. This antagonism can be articulated in various ways: the commodity is both necessary to the reproduction of the producers (under a particular social system:

capitalism), and at the same time absorbs and consumes their physical energies, and thus embodies a permanent threat to their physical existence. And capital is also described by Marx in terms of the return of 'dead labor' of the past, which 'lives like a vampire sucking up living labor, and which thrives all the more, the more it devours' ('verstorbene Arbeit, die sich nur vampyrmäßig belebt durch Einsaugung lebendiger Arbeit, und umsomehr lebt, je mehr sie davon ein-saugt.'[21] Whatever the methodological difficulties posed by such questions, it would be precipitate to ontologize 'castration' before having clarified its relation to such historical factors. Their influence on the uncanny is scarcely to be ignored and they doubtless have contributed to the fact that this 'off-side' region has lost little of its actuality since the days of Hoffmann, Villiers, and Freud. But that is a long story which we have only begun to recount.

NOTES

1. Jacques Derrida, *La Dissémination*, Paris, 1972, pp. 279, 300.
2. *Poétique* III (1972), 199–216.
3. *Ibid.*, 199. In addition to Derrida and Cixous, I am indebted tc Hans-Thiess Lehmann's unpublished paper, 'Zu Freuds Theorie des Unheimlichen' (Berlin, Jan./1972), especially concerning Freud's reading of Hoffmann's *Sandmann*.
4. S. Freud, 'Das Unheimliche,' GW XII, 231. Collected Papers 4, 396–70.
5. *Ibid.*, S. 235–36; p. 376.
6. *Ibid.*, S. 237; p. 377.
7. *Ibid.*, S. 247.
8. *Ibid.*, S. 251.
9. *Ibid.*, S. 254.
10. *Ibid.*, S. 261.
11. *Ibid.*, S. 264.
12. Freud describes this symbolic representation in connection with the Double: 'Die Schöpfung einer solchen Verdopplung zur Abwehr gegen die Vernichtung hat ihr Gegenstück in einer Darstellung der Traumsprache, welche die Kastration durch Verdopplung oder Vervielfätigung des Genitalsymbols auszudrücken liebt (...),' S. 247. See also *Die Traumdeutung*, GW II/III, S. 362.
13. 'Das Unheimliche,' GW XII, 267. Collected Papers, p. 406 (translation altered – S. W.).
14. *Ibid.*, 243.
15. This formulation is to be found not in *Hemmung, Symptom und Angst*, where Freud first worked out the 'second' theory of anxiety, but in the *Neue Folge der Vorlesungen zur Einführung in die Psychoanalyse*, Lecture 32, 'Angst und Trie-bleben,' Sigmund Freud Studienausgabe, Bd. I, S. Fischer, Frankfurt am Main, 1969, S. 521: 'Nicht die Verdrängung schafft die Angst, sondern die Angst ist früher da, die Angst macht die Verdrängung!' See also *Hemmung, Symptom und Angst*, GW XIV, S. 138 et passim.
16. 'Die Angst ist die Reaktion auf die Gefahrsituation (...) Diese Gefahr war aber in den bisher betrachteten Fällen die Kastration oder etwas von ihr Abgeleitetes.' *Hemmung, Symptom und Angst*, S. 159. After developing the decisive function of castration-anxiety, Freud warns against the tendency to absolutize it, to regard it as 'den einzigen Motor der zur Neurose führenden Abwehrvorgänge' (173). Freud introduces the notions of *separation (Trennung)* and object-loss *(Objektverlust)*, under which he seems to subsume that of castration. This only holds, however, for a *restricted* conception of castration, a conception which the Lacanian theory is designed to criticize and to supplant. That this theory itself runs the risk of

hypostasizing castration as an ontological structure is what I have endeavored to suggest in an unpublished study of Lacan, chapter 9: 'Die Bedeutung des Phallus, oder: Was der Fall ist.' For a critical reading of Lacan – in particular of his essay on the *Lettre volée* – see the excellent study of Jean-Luc Nancy & Philippe Lecoue-Labarthe, *Le titre de la lettre*, in which the Lacanian hypostasis is interpreted as a negative ontology, with castration (implicitly) at its center: 'Il s'agit, certes, d'une ontologie *négative*. C'est un trou qui en désigne le centre – et en ordonne la circonférence, se trou en face duquel il faut "avoir les yeux."' (Éditions Galilée, 1973, p. 131). See also Jacques Derrida, in *Positions* (Paris, 1972): '... car il peut aussi y avoir un signifiant transcendental, par exemple le phallus comme corrélat d'un signifié premier, la castration et le désir de la mère ...' (p. 120).

17. See J. Lacan, 'La signification du phallus,' in *Ecrits* (Paris, 1966) et passim.
18. *Zur Einführung des Narzißmus*, GW X, 158.
19. 'Das Unheimliche,' GW XII, 247.
20. The problem of repetition in the texts of Freud remains to be worked out. For the general lines along which such an elaboration will probably have to proceed, see the probing reading of Husserl by Derrida, *La voix et le phénomène*, Paris, 1967, in particular the chapter entitled 'Le vouloir-dire et la représentation.'
21. Karl Marx, *Das Kapital I*, Dietz Verlag, Berlin-Ost, 1961, 241.

See also:

Marx (1.1)
Attrdge (4.3)
Royle (4.4)
Maley (8.2)

7.4

'THE REMAINS OF PSYCHOANALYSIS (I): TELEPATHY'

Nicholas Royle

> The gift is always a strike of force, an irruption.
>
> WB, 199

In the interview with Derek Attridge published in *Acts of Literature* (1992), Derrida talks about his time at school, in the 1940s, and his bewilderment when 'beginning to discover this strange institution called literature' (TSICL, 36). He states:

> Bewilderment, then, faced with this institution or type of object which allows one to say everything. What is it? What 'remains' when desire has just inscribed something which 'remains' there, like an object at the disposal of others, one that can be repeated? What does 'remaining' mean? (TSICL, 36–7)

All of Derrida's work can be read as an attempt to respond to this question of 'remains' – especially, but not only, to the question of 'remains as a written thing' (TSICL, 37). This is evident from the consistent deployment of a number of terms across his oeuvre, including the trace, remainder (*restance*), remains (*reste*), cinders (*cendre*), ruins and ghosts. While these terms remain singular and heterogeneous, to the extent that they arise in different contexts and pertain to different expositions, they all serve to highlight Derrida's more general argument that remains are never simple and indeed that the notion of remains calls to be thought in terms of what was never present. Thus the challenge of

Source: Nicholas Royle, *After Derrida* (Manchester: Manchester University Press, 1995), pp. 61–72.

Derrida's work as a whole comprises the difficulty of thinking remains *other than on the basis of what was once present*. The trace, for example, is not the remains of something that was once present and might be rendered present once again: rather it is that which prevents any present, and any experience of presence, from being completely itself, from ever coinciding with itself. In the final analysis, then, remains are always and only the remains of remains, just as there are always and only traces of traces. There is no trace-in-itself, no remains-in-themselves. 'Nothing beside remains', to recall the words of that revenant from an antique land in Shelley's 'Ozymandias'. But Derrida's work suggests that remains, like ruins, are not negative: the cryptic structure they (impossibly) figure is, for him, linked to the most affirmative, even the only affirmative kind of thinking, affirmation itself.

What, then, of the remains of psychoanalysis?

It is part of the affirmative character of Derrida's thought that nothing is apparently repudiated, written off, dismissed: thus, in the Attridge interview, he stresses that he has 'no desire to abandon ... the memory of literature and philosophy', even though he is concerned above all with 'the dream of another institution', with a kind of writing, for example, that would be 'neither philosophy nor literature' (TSICL, 73). A similar point can be made with regard to the relationship between his work and psychoanalysis. The imperative of keeping the memory of psychoanalysis is clearly expressed in a short text entitled 'Let Us Not Forget – Psychoanalysis'. Here Derrida's passionate, psychoanalytically-informed engagement with the notion of a new enlightenment is articulated in contradistinction to those aspects of contemporary intellectual and culturo-political life that evidently embody a desire precisely to forget psychoanalysis. Outside 'Circumfession' (*JD ii*) what follows has to be one of the longest sentences in Derrida's work and this is not even the complete version. I cite, commencing with an ellipsis:

> ... people are starting to behave as though it was nothing at all, as though nothing had happened, as though taking into account the event of psychoanalysis, a logic of the unconscious, of 'unconscious concepts', even, were no longer *de rigueur*, no longer even had a place in something like the history of reason: as if one could calmly continue the good old discourse of the Enlightenment, return to Kant, call us back to the ethical or juridical or political responsibility of the subject by restoring the authority of consciousness, of the ego, of the reflexive cogito, of an 'I think' without pain or paradox; as if, in this moment of philosophical restoration that is in the air – for what is on the agenda, the agenda's moral agenda, is a sort of shameful, botched restoration – as if it were a matter of flattening the supposed demands of reason into a discourse that is purely communicative, informational, smooth; as though, finally, it were again legitimate to accuse of obscurity or irrationalism anyone who complicates things a little by wondering about the reason of reason, about the history of the

principle of reason or about the event – perhaps a traumatic one – constituted by something like psychoanalysis in reason's relation to itself. (LUNFP, 4)

Derrida has written numerous essays on the work of Freud, Lacan, and Abraham and Torok, and everything he has said, for example, about memory, desire, mourning, crypts and ghosts, demands to be read within the context of psychoanalytic concepts and their possible translations and transformations.

This chapter and the one that follows are focused on 'the remains of psycho-analysis' in quite narrowly-defined terms. In particular I wish to consider the role and significance of two kinds of 'remains' or 'remainders' in Freud's thought. The first is the question of telepathy, the second is the so-called Bacon – Shakespeare controversy. These two concerns may appear marginal to Freud's work and thus to the foundations of psychoanalysis. I would like to suggest, however, that they can be seen as quite central – or, at least, as irremediably interfering with the borders, the relations between what is proper and what is not proper, what belongs and does not belong, what is the inside and outside of psychoanalysis, giving us a quite different archaeology of psychoanalysis and the promise of another kind of thinking and writing. These 'remains of psycho-analysis' – which would not constitute presences, rather the opposite – perhaps have as much to do with the future of psychoanalysis as with its ostensive history.

THE COMIC WRITINGS OF JACQUES DERRIDA

Jacques Derrida can be so funny. It's no wonder people refer to his 'superb comic prose' and talk about him as 'a great comic writer'. Yet this aspect of Derrida's work *remains*, to date at least, comparatively unexamined. It may seem slightly surprising to want to approach 'the remains of psychoanalysis' from this perspective, but in what follows I shall attempt to justify it and to move towards some sort of clarification of an observation and a question (or double-question) which Derrida articulates in the course of what is, along with 'Limited Inc' (LI), perhaps his most celebrated comic essay to date, that is to say 'Ulysses Gramophone: Hear Say Yes in Joyce' (1984). Here he writes: 'It remains perhaps to think of laughter, as, precisely, a remains. What does laughter want to say? What does laughter want? [*Qu'est-ce que ça veut dire, le rire? Qu'est-ce que ça veut rire?*]' (UG, 291).

My main focus here is another Derrida text, entitled 'Telepathy', published in 1981. As well as being weird and (I can confirm from so-called personal experience) more than usually untranslatable, 'Telepathy' is also one of Derri-da's funniest works. In this essay or experiment – comprising, like *The Post Card*, fragments of postcards, intermittent envois without a nominally identi-fied addressee – he considers one of the two 'remains of psychoanalysis', that theme which, together with the Bacon-Shakespeare controversy, 'always per-plexed [Freud] to the point of distraction [*bringen mich immer aus der Fassung*]'. This is the occult or, more specifically, the question of telepathy.

As Derrida's essay suggests, telepathy is a topic, a concept or phenomenon, which is closely bound up with psychoanalysis but with which psychoanalysis cannot come to terms. Freud wrote a number of lectures and shorter papers on telepathy and occultism, of which Derrida declares: 'Until recently I imagined, through ignorance and forgetfulness, that "telepathic" anxiety was contained in small pockets of Freud – in short, what he says about it in two or three articles regarded as minor' (T, 14). Derrida's 'Telepathy' could be described as deconstructively exemplary in the sense not just that it is focused on some putatively 'minor' or marginal texts, on the 'small pockets' of another writer, but also that it is in turn presented as a minor or marginal work, in relation to its author's other, ostensibly more central and substantial texts. One could say that this work entitled 'Telepathy' was remaindered before it was even published. At any rate, it is from the outset offered as a remains or remainder, as Derrida testifies in a footnote: 'Such a remainder [*restant*], I am no doubt publishing it in order to come closer to what remains inexplicable for me even to this day . . . [It] should have appeared, as fragments and in accordance with the plan [*dispositif*] adopted at that time, in "Envois" (Section One of *La carte postale* [Paris: Flammarion, 1980])' (T, 38–9, n. 1). In spite or perhaps because of its fragmentary character, however, 'Telepathy' makes persuasive and important claims about the place of telepathy in relation to psychoanalysis. Derrida shows how the question of telepathy disturbs psychoanalytic theory at its very core. It is, he suggests, 'Difficult to imagine a theory of what they still call the unconscious without a theory of telepathy. They can be neither confused nor dissociated' (14). What is implied by this proposition that a theory of telepathy and a theory of the unconscious 'can be neither confused nor dissociated' is a logic of the crypt or parasite, a logic according to which 'telepathy' becomes a kind of foreign body within psychoanalysis.

Derrida traces the history of this foreign body within the chronology of Freud's writings and within the development of the psychoanalytic movement. Freud has a lifelong obsession with the question of telepathy but it is only in 1926 that he announces his 'conversion'. But even then it is not a public matter, according to Freud, this 'sin' of believing in telepathy. As he tells Ernest Jones, in a letter dated 7 March 1926: 'When anyone adduces my fall into sin, just answer him calmly that conversion to telepathy is my private affair like my Jewishness, my passion for smoking and many other things, and that the theme of telepathy is in essence alien to psychoanalysis'. As Derrida points out, 'this letter is contradictory from start to finish' (T, 35). Not only, for example, is it impossible rigorously to separate the public from the private here, to distinguish between on the one hand what the founder of psychoanalysis subjectively and privately believes and, on the other, what he objectively and publicly proclaims in his writings; but it is also the case that Freud did after all write a number of essays on the topic and indeed that the concept of telepathy is significantly invoked in numerous other of his writings including, for example, 'The "Uncanny"' (PFL, 12: 335–76), 'The Theme of the Three Caskets' PFL, 12: 233–47) and *Totem and Taboo* (PFL, 13: 43–224). In other words, Freud's claim that 'the theme of telepathy is in essence alien to psychoanalysis' is both right and wrong at the same time: the theme of telepathy is like a foreign body. From Freud's point of view, says Derrida, it is a question 'of admitting a foreign body into one's head, into the ego of psychoanalysis. Me psychoanalysis, I have a foreign body in my head ...' (T, 35).

It is integral to the strangeness and power of a foreign body, in this context, that it has to do with both assimilation and vomit. This is how Derrida's essay concludes: 'So psychoanalysis ... resembles an adventure of modern rationality set on swallowing *and* simultaneously rejecting the foreign body named Telepathy, on assimilating it and vomiting it without being able to make up its mind to do one or the other' (38, tr. mod.). If, as Derrida suggests, psychoanalysis disturbs and even traumatises 'reason's relation to itself' (LUNFP, 4), this 'adventure of modern rationality' is in turn traumatologised or traumaturged. Freud's 'conversion' in this respect is neither 'a resolution nor a solution, it is still the speaking scar of the foreign body' (38). Freud pussyfoots or, as Derrida puts it, practises the hesitation-waltz (*la valse-hesitation*) (15) around the question of telepathy, but even after his 'conversion', for instance in the lecture 'Dreams and Occultism' (*PFL*, 2:60–87), we continue to hear 'the speaking scar of the foreign body'. A strange kind of hearing, to be sure, since the lecture entitled 'Dreams and Occultism' is, as Derrida observes, not really a lecture at all but rather a 'fake lecture' (see T, 18): although written as a lecture ('Ladies and Gentlemen [*Meine Damen und Herren!*]', it begins), it was never given. Indeed it is part of the foreign body nature of this affair that none of Freud's various so-called lectures on telepathy was ever delivered: 'Psychoanalysis and Telepathy' (1921) and 'Dreams and Telepathy' (1922) were likewise 'fake lectures' (see T, 18).

What is so funny about Derrida's 'Telepathy' has to do, at least in part, with the ways in which it mimics and upsets the tone of Freud's 'fake lectures' and with the ways in which it unsettles, dislocates and transforms distinctions between a public and private discourse, between science and belief, between the frivolity of a postcard and the sobriety of a scientific paper, between – last but not least – 'Freud' and 'Derrida' themselves. Permit me to extract and cite, for example, as follows:

> What a strategy, don't you admire it? I neutralise all the risks in advance. Even if the existence of telepathy (about which I know nothing and about which you will know nothing, especially not whether I believe in it and whether I want to know anything about it), were attested with all its requirements, even if it were assured, *sichergestellt*, there would be no need to change anything in my theory of the dream and my dream would be safe. (T, 23)

Or, a bit later on: 'In my new fake lectures, I insist as always on reestablishing the legitimate order: only psychoanalysis can teach something about telepathic phenomena and not vice-versa' (29). In each case Derrida's text is making a perfectly serious point – that Freud is clearly resistant even to entertaining the idea that telepathy might fundamentally call into question some of the basic tenets of psychoanalysis (dreams as wish-fulfilments, the concepts of the ego, the unconscious, and so on) – but this perfectly serious insight is being offered in a very bizarre fashion. Insight, in effect, ceases to be out of sight. Derrida's text takes on the first person singular of Freud's voice and says what Freud may in some sense have thought – whether consciously or unconsciously (that distinction is precisely what is being dismantled here) – but never said.

Telepathy here would seem to be, at least from one perspective, an apocalypse or uncovering comparable to that dramatised in George Eliot's *The Lifted Veil*: Derrida's text is reading Freud's thoughts and, in a manner that also corresponds in remarkable ways with Eliot's work, these thoughts are intensely egocentric. Just as George Eliot presents her protagonist's 'participation in other people's consciousness' as an intolerable revelation of 'all the suppressed egoism . . . from which human words and deeds emerge like leaflets covering a fermenting heap', so Derrida presents a markedly ego-centred rendition of what is going on in Freud's mind. Derrida's miming of Freud's thoughts as 'Totally autobiographical' (24), as relentlessly egotistical – preoccupied with personal ambition ('My theory of the dream', 23) and so-called private sexual fantasy (if only she could be 'my second wife' (see T, 30–1)) – is at once a kind of conservatism in Derrida and a source of fine comedy. Egoic discourse is conserved, at the same time as being ridiculed. To adumbrate a point I will be trying to develop further in various ways in the *remains* of the present study, I would like simply to remark that there is, by comparison, strikingly little sense in this Derridamime of the kind of post-egoic or 'psychotic raving' about which Leo Bersani has written in relation to the discourse of characters in the writings of Samuel Beckett.

To get in touch with telepathy is 'to lose one's head, no more no less' (T, 20). But if this Derrida essay is about losing one's head it is also, and at the same time, about maintaining a balance. Derrida proceeds, as he puts it, 'like the trapeze artist I have always been' (7). Even more perhaps than the postcards of 'Envois' (E), 'Telepathy' suggests a deconstructive sense of confiding. If Freud's articles on telepathy are 'fake lectures because he confides in them so much, poor man' (T, 18), it would also be possible to characterise Derrida's own essay in this fashion – in particular to the extent that we may feel inclined to read it as fake postcards. In this respect every thought can seem undecidably fake, undecidably programmed: the conflations and fragmentations of identity in Derrida's text disturb the very *fides* of confiding and confidence.

Derrida writes as Freud. He writes *after* Freud no doubt, but he also inhabits, mimes, interpolates the prose, the tone and manner of Freud in ways that undermine confidence in general – the sense of Freud's confidence in himself and in his theories, the sense of Derrida's confidence as writer and of our own confidence as readers, the notion of confiding something to someone and especially of confiding something to oneself. What is meant by *confiding*? *Who* is confiding, in whom, and how? It is a distinctive feature of Derrida's work that it takes the text of another writer (Rousseau, Kant, Nietzsche, Ponge) in an unusually intimate embrace, citing, paraphrasing, rendering it in such a way that it is no longer straightforwardly possible to say that 'that is what the "earlier" writer is saying whereas Derrida on the other hand is saying this'. Such writing can itself be described in terms of a telepathic relation (is such and such a moment in 'Parergon', for example, a presentation of 'Kant's thought' or is it not rather some sort of transference and effacement of the singularity of 'thought' within or across texts?). But this kind of critical telepathy finds its apogee in the essay 'Telepathy', for here Derrida goes beyond the grammatical, proprietorial boundaries of the 'I' which conventionally govern discourse, including his own. Freud is no longer 'he' but 'I' as well. If the strategies of Derrida's writing and reading are especially well-demonstrated in this essay, they are also *other* – no longer Derrida's, no more Derrida, bye now

REPRESENTATIONS OF TELEPATHY

Up to this point it may appear that we have proceeded as if it were obvious what the word 'telepathy' means. There is a correspondence here, perhaps, with how Derrida writes about the term 'representation' in the essay entitled 'Sending: On Representation':

> If I read, if I hear on the radio that the diplomatic or parliamentary representatives (*la représentation diplomatique ou parliamentaire*) of some country have been received by the Chief of State, that representatives (*représentants*) of striking workers or the parents of schoolchildren have gone to the Ministry in a delegation, if I read in the paper that this evening there will be a representation of some play, or that such and such a painting represents this or that, etc., I understand without the least equivocation and I do not put my head into my hands to take in what it means. (SOR, 319)

Comic prose on a comic pose, perhaps; but it is also the case that such conceptual breakthroughs as may be ascribed to Derrida's work pertain precisely to an unsettling of the accepted relationship between a given word and concept. As he asserts, without the least equivocation, in his thesis-defence, 'The Time of a Thesis: Punctuations' (TTP): 'Every conceptual breakthrough amounts to transforming, that is to deforming, an accredited, authorised relationship between a word and a concept, between a trope and what one had every Interest to consider to be an unshiftable primary sense, a proper, literal or current usage' (TTP, 40–1).

Derrida's 'Telepathy', along with other recent work done in this area, promotes nothing less than a deformation and transformation of what may once have been supposed to happen under the aegis of this word 'telepathy'. The linkage between psychoanalysis and telepathy is historically specific: as is well known, the rise of spiritualism and the emergence of modern psychology in the second half of the nineteenth century belong together. The word 'telepathy' was invented and first used by Frederic Myers in 1882; psychoanalysis came into being a few years later and it can be seen to have done so by marking itself off, not only in relation to other more or less medically and scientifically respectable forms of psychology, but also in relation to the occult. In its original formulation, Myers tells his colleagues at the Society for Psychical Research in London, in December 1882: 'we venture to introduce the words *Telesthesia* and *Telepathy* to cover all cases of impression received at a distance without the normal operation of the recognised sense organs.' Freud's definition, which involves bringing together the concepts of telepathy and thought-transference (this is part of his 'pussy-footing': they can, he says, 'without much violence be regarded as the same thing' (*PFL*, 2: 69)) is very close to Myers's: telepathy and thought-transference, says Freud, concern the idea 'that mental processes in one person – ideas, emotional states, conative impulses – can be transferred to another person through empty space without employing the familiar methods of communication by means of words and signs' (69). We might underline, in these definitions, the importance of the *normal*, of what is *recognised* and of what is *familiar* ('the normal operation of the recognised sense organs', says Myers; 'the familiar methods of communication', says Freud).

It is also clear, however, that in historical terms the word 'telepathy' is part of an explosion of forms of communication and possibilities of representation. Telepathy (like 'telesthesia') is indissociably bound up with other forms of tele-media and teleculture whose emergence also belongs to the nineteenth century: telegraphy (*OED* first recorded usage: 1795), photography (1839), the telephone (1835), the phonograph (1877) and gramophone (1888), and so on. The emergence of the term 'telepathy' is moreover closely linked to the so-called decline of Christianity in European and North American culture: a belief in telepathy, in the late nineteenth century, often (though by no means always) appears to have provided a kind of substitute for a belief in God. Finally, it is possible to regard the emergence of the concept of telepathy as, in effect, epistemologically programmed within the Romantic concept of sympathy. Telepathy embodies both the hyperbolisation or extreme limit of sympathy and *at the same time* its opposite, that is to say a loosening or fragmenting, a dispersion and dissemination of the conceptual grounds of sympathy. This dissemination is in part the challenge presented by Derrida's work on telepathy.

The effect of this work has been to shake up and transform the very criteria by which the 'normal' and 'familiar' are understood. As Claudette Sartiliot suggests, in an essay on 'Telepathy and Writing in Jacques Derrida's *Glas*', Derrida starts by drawing on what is, in some respects, the most 'familiar' because 'oldest' or most 'archaic' sense of 'telepathy' – that is to say, Derrida's essay goes back to the Greek *tele-pathein* which 'implies both the idea of distance (*tele*) and that of suffering, feeling, being touched (*pathein*) in its physical, emotional and aesthetic sense'. What is distant feeling, feeling in the distance? What if all analysis, including psychoanalysis, is tele-analysis? How are thinking, pleasure, beauty, love *affected* at a distance, *as* distance? But Derrida's reading is not a nostalgic or quasi-Heideggerian etymologism (as Sartillot's account might here suggest): it is not a question of getting home, of going back to some original meaning, the comforting womb or matrix of sense. As Derrida points out: 'The ultimate naivety would be to allow oneself to think that Telepathy guarantees a destination which "posts and telecommunications" fail to provide' (16). The interest of his account consists rather in the fact that, as Sartiliot puts it, 'telepathy breaches the discreteness and unity of the subject, as well as the systems of thought derived from it'. Far from reinstating or retracing a purportedly original or proper meaning of 'telepathy', Derrida's essay opens up spaces of thought which dissolve all 'familiar' assurances of the sense of that word. In question, and under threat, here is what Derrida calls 'the truth': thus he speaks of 'the truth, what I always have difficulty getting used to: that non-telepathy may be possible' (13, tr. mod.).

'Outside the subject' (32). Derrida picks up this phrase and throws it off, in passing, as a definition of 'telepathy', a definition which Freud must at once appreciate and disavow: 'telepathy', says Derrida, 'that's what it is, the outside-the-subject, [Freud] knows the score' (32). Derrida's 'Telepathy' challenges us among other things to think telepathy (and indeed sympathy) no longer in terms of a relation between two or more subjects whose identity is already constituted and assured. Rather than conceiving telepathy as something supplementary, something added on to the experience of a subject, Derrida situates it in accordance with the logic of a foreign body, as being at once outside-the-subject and at the very heart of the subject.

ABBREVIATIONS

TSICL	'This strange institution called literature', in Attridge (ed.), *Acts of Literature*
JD	Geoffrey Bennington and Jacques Derrida, *Jacques Derrida*
LUNFP	'Let us not forget – psychoanalysis' (1990)

See also:

Freud (1.2)
Royle (4.4)
Ronnell (5.5)
Derrida (11.2)

7.5

FROM *PROSTHESIS*

David Wills

To hear Ernest Jones tell it:

> The huge prosthesis, a sort of magnified denture or obturator, designed to shut off the mouth from the nasal cavity, was a horror; it was labeled 'the monster.' In the first place it was very difficult to take out or replace because it was impossible for him to open his mouth at all widely. On one occasion, for instance, the combined efforts of Freud and his daughter failed to insert it after struggling for half an hour, and the surgeon had to be fetched for the purpose. Then for the instrument to fulfill its purpose of shutting off the yawning cavity above, and so make speaking and eating possible, it had to fit fairly tightly. This, however, produced constant irritation and sore places until its presence was unbearable. But if it were left out for more than a few hours the tissues would shrink, and the denture could no longer be replaced without being altered.[1]

By all reports Freud was more fortunate than Louis XIV, who lost large chunks of the roof of his mouth through bad dentistry and expelled as much food through his nose as he swallowed in the last years of his life. 'We are astonished to learn of the objectionable smell which emanated from the *Roi Soleil*,' Freud wrote.[2] He was lucky to have the advantage of a prosthesis, even if it had to be replaced many times after the diagnosis of and first major surgery for throat cancer in 1923, about the time of *The Ego and the Id* (*SE* XIX). He returned to

---

Source: David Wills, *Prosthesis* (Stanford: Stanford University Press, 1995).

Berlin for yet another replacement in 1929, after finishing *Civilization and Its Discontents*. That text was completed at Schneewinkl, near Berchtesgaden, on July 28, 1929, as Freud recounted to Lou Andreas-Salomé:

> You will with your usual acuteness have guessed why I have been so long in answering your letter. Anna has already told you that I am writing something, and today I have written the last sentence, which – so far as it is possible here without a library – finishes the work. It deals with civilization, consciousness of guilt, happiness and similar lofty matters, and it strikes me, without doubt rightly so, as very superfluous, in contradistinction from earlier works, in which there was always a creative impulse. But what else should I do? I can't spend the whole day in smoking and playing cards, I can no longer walk far, and the most of what there is to read does not interest me any more. So I wrote, and the time passed that way quite pleasantly. In writing this work I have discovered afresh the most banal truths.[3]

In that book, presented here as something of a work of dotage, of the psychoanalyst turned dilettante, Freud nevertheless presents ideas very dear to his heart concerning the superego, the death drive, and their relations to religious belief. One might well wonder, therefore, to what extent the superfluity of *Civilization and Its Discontents* reaches back to affect or infect *The Future of an Illusion* (SE XXI), published shortly before and in a similar vein, and indeed back through all the works of that decade, especially *The Ego and the Id* and *Beyond the Pleasure Principle* (SE XVIII). To what extent are those works banal, less than creative, and presumably less valued by their author than those preceding them? Granted, Freud does not specify what earlier works he considers to be in contradistinction to *Civilization and Its Discontents*, and he may in fact be referring to the important modifications his theory underwent with those two essays of the earlier part of the 1920's. On the other hand, if we follow the logic of what I have just said, then the question that continues to be posed even as far back as *Beyond the Pleasure Principle* cannot be seen to stop there, given the pivotal nature of that work with respect to everything that preceded it, and indeed with respect to the whole armature of Freudian theory.[4] If there is a hypothesis to be advanced at this juncture, it would be that the armature put in place in the works of 1919–29, has something of the prosthetic about it, something precisely of the monster that became an unavoidable part of Freud's body and existence. But this is no psychobiocriticism I am advancing, and the hypothesis no more relies on the fitting of a prosthesis in 1923 than does the death drive on the death of Sophie in 1920. It is quite the opposite of psychobiocriticism. It is rather the figure for certain aspects of Freudian theory, and perhaps for a certain type of theorizing in general, which lends something of an inevitability to Freud's affliction, as if a theory informed by prosthesis and all that it involves could not but find some sort of fulfillment of its own prophecy in its author's health problems beyond a simple relation of cause and effect. For what Freudian theory brings about more than anything else – and we will likely be still dealing with its consequences for a long time to come – is an upsetting of the order of supposedly straightforward relations, those of time and consecution, of cause and effect, and so on.

There is on the one hand a very straightforward and logical idea at work here, namely that theorizing – Freudian theory in particular – and perhaps knowledge in general advances by means of successive accommodations, molding itself to a better and better fit with the data it is placed over. That seems very obviously to be the story of Freudian theory, Freud's prosthesis, and prostheses in general. On the other hand, a contrary logic threatens at the same time to ruin everything straightforward and obvious about that. It finds that the major tenets of Freudian theory, from childhood sexuality to the uncanny and the death drive, turn the obvious on its head, set things back to front, and finally do the same for those tenets that bring about the very operation of reversal. It is such effects that will go, here also, by the name of prosthesis.

My hypothesis is developed in the space between the pro*positions* that constitute Freudian theory and an ill-defined series of pro*jections* that can easily be seen to grow out of it, indeed that still identify themselves as belonging to it. It is the space of a prosthetic supplement, falling between or upon what is posed in the quiet confidence of the apposite, the here and now of the current state of research, and what shocks as the banal and commonplace within the rarefaction of scientific inquiry; or, on the other hand, between the apposite and what is thrown up as that inquiry's outer possibility; in either case continually broaching and breaching the threshold of the opposite or of contradiction. It is those latter tendencies that seem to characterize more and more the works of the 1920s. By his own avowals, the author values as little more than conjecture what he propounds in works ranging from *Beyond the Pleasure Principle* – 'What follows is speculation, often far-fetched speculation … It is further an attempt to follow out an idea consistently, out of curiosity to see where it will lead' (*SE* XVIII: 24) – to *Civilization and Its Discontents* – 'In none of my previous writings have I had so strong a feeling as now that what I am describing is common knowledge and that I am using up paper and ink and, in due course, the compositor's and printer's work and material in order to expound things which are, in fact, self-evident' (*SE* XXI; 117).

However, the importance for science and for theory of such speculation or conjecture, or of such everyday musing, was something psychoanalysis made explicit from the very beginning, once it set out to elaborate a theory that could not but draw the scorn of official science. Analysts, Freud wrote in 1921 in a piece that he declined to publish (about which more later), 'cannot repudiate their descent from exact science,' but 'they are ready, for the sake of attaining some fragment of objective certainty, to sacrifice everything … They are content with fragmentary pieces of knowledge and with basic hypotheses lacking preciseness and ever open to revision' ('Psycho-analysis and Telepathy,' *SE* XVIII: 178–79).

Freudian theory will therefore have more than a little of the *bricolé* or ad hoc about it. It will be constantly adjusting itself to accommodate whatever its musings and speculations bring to bear upon it. It will be prepared when necessary to throw out the whole apparatus of its tenets and replace it with another that better fits, one that can be more easily swallowed, sticks less in the throat. It will be determined to make do as best it can, to prop itself up by whatever means are at hand. For example: 'Of all the slowly developed parts of analytic theory, the theory of the instincts is the one that has felt its way the most painfully forward. And yet the theory was so indispensable to the whole structure that something had to be put in its place' (*SE* XXI: 117). Given that, one cannot help but ask to what extent the theory thereby distinguishes itself from superstition on the one hand and philosophy or pure science on the other. Such a question lies beyond the scope of the present discussion even though it is automatically posed by it. That is to say the answer to such a question can only, in the present context and perhaps anywhere, take the form of speculations of our own. But whence and on what basis does psychoanalysis derive its exact dose of rigor – indeed how can we measure the exact dose – and why the recourse to scientific principle at the same time as a suspicion of official science? How precisely does its skepticism articulate with its scientificity? Because of, and indeed in spite of, such questions Freudian theory, with its musing and propositions, projections and conjectures, will attach to itself a series of differences that, while perhaps molding themselves to its fit, nevertheless distinguish themselves as irrevocably other, as opposite in nature, as opposite as is the artificial or prosthetic to nature itself.

'Projection' is of course a psychoanalytic term. As Freud reminds us in *Beyond the Pleasure Principle*: 'a particular way is adopted of dealing with any internal excitations which produce too great an increase of unpleasure: there is a tendency to treat them as though they were acting, not from the inside, but from the outside . . . This is the origin of *projection*' (*SE* XVIII: 29). It is not that precise mechanism that I am imputing to Freudian theory in general, but there is one aspect of it made explicit here that I wish to reinforce, namely the fact of a change in direction, the psychic fact of looking in the wrong direction. When things don't fit they are felt to be back to front, inside out. The idea of a change in direction, an adestination on the part of the psyche, presented in the guise of a decision of convenience, can be seen to underscore the whole of the Freudian opus. It is there from the beginning, in the line from Virgil's *Aeneid* that *The Interpretation of Dreams* takes as its epigraph: *Flectere si nequeo superos, Acheronta movebo* – 'If I cannot bend the higher powers, I will move to infernal regions' (*SE* IV: IX). Changes in direction, or reversals, occur time and time again, with narcissism, with masochism, with projection, with the instincts or drives. The unconscious, and psychoanalysis, might be said to be defined more by the possibility of directional change or teleological contradiction than by anything else. By virtue of being internally excited, in a state of change, reexamination, revision, speculation, and so on, psychoanalysis permanently projects. How far out its projections reach, to what extent they lie beyond the reach of recovery, in what precise direction they might be seen to be leading, these are some of the questions that underlie this discussion.

However, what I have just described as the prosthetic structure of Freudian thinking is, as I have also suggested, not necessarily specific to his theory as distinct from theory in general. Nor is it absent from this set of musings and speculations on the basis of that theory; and by no means is it reducible to a relation between a theory and a Freud suffering from throat cancer. Rather, what I am calling here the figure of prosthesis appears, in striking profile, through a discussion of some of Freudian theory's liminal relations, through examination of what it approaches when it acknowledges – and it does so particularly explicitly – its own fringe.

Take for instance – what will develop for me as *the* instance – the not infrequent reference to the occult as it relates to the wider question of religious belief in general. Given the possible objections to such belief, one might reasonably expect it to display a prosthetic structure parallel to that just described for Freudian theory: a sort of overreaching and compensating attempts at accommodation, a structural crisis and a contrived solution. Instead of speculation, a suspension of rational standards of examination in favor of faith; instead of scientific rigor, a certain doctrinal consistency that tends in many cases to be applied in the extreme; but the two currents coexisting and producing their own tensions and contradictions. Now, on one level the two types of belief – religion and the occult – are, for Freud, distinct, the latter being characterized by a particularly superstitious form of credulity and the former more by its propensity to moral and behavioral injunction, how it regulates relations between the individual and society. In his view, religion is less a question of ideas than of behavior; it is a function of and a question of civilization, occurring at the interface between psyche and *socius*. The occult is regarded as more of an individual psychic phenomenon, reduced finally to the questions of telepathy and thought transference.

But from another point of view it is clear that the occult connects with a 'general tendency of mankind to credulity and a belief in the miraculous.' Given that 'a resistance stirs within us against the relentlessness and monotony of the laws of thought and against the demands of reality-testing,' one must accept that 'the interest in occultism is in fact a religious one' ('Dreams and Occultism,' *SE* XXII: 33, 34). And religion, occultism, and psychoanalysis alike give rise to similar objections: 'It does not follow as a matter of course that an intensified interest in occultism must involve a danger to psychoanalysis. We should, on the contrary, be prepared to find reciprocal sympathy between them. They have both experienced the same contemptuous and arrogant treatment by official science. To this day psychoanalysis is regarded as savouring of mysticism' (*SE* XVIII: 178). Thus when Freud talks about his growing interest in telepathy it becomes, however tongue in cheek, both a conversion and a fall into sin: 'When anyone adduces my fall into sin, just answer him calmly that conversion to telepathy is my private affair like my Jewishness, my passion for smoking and many other things.'[5] It is doubtful, therefore, that one can talk about the occult outside the context of religious belief in general, and it is just as doubtful that one can talk about psychoanalysis outside the same. When the discussion begins, when it comes to the interpretation of dreams, it has to be acknowledged that some of the best-known examples in the literature are the prophetic dreams of the Jewish tradition, such as the hand writing its portentous *mene mene tekel upharsin* upon the walls of Babylon. Freud doesn't refer to that famous case but quotes the Greek tradition of two types of dream, those that refer to the past and those that foresee the future (see *SE* IV: 3).

The question of religion becomes most explicit in the two texts of the late 1920s, *The Future of an Illusion* (1927) and *Civilization and Its Discontents* (1930). The fact of their being, by the author's own admission, banal, saying 'nothing which other and better men have not said before me in a much more complete, forcible and impressive manner' (*SE* XXI: 35), perhaps obscures a greater failing, namely that they are singularly unprophetic in their positioning with respect to an approaching catastrophe. In a final sentence added to *Civilization and Its Discontents* in 1931, added to a paragraph that raises the specter of the 'current unrest,' unhappiness,' and 'mood of anxiety' and the hope of a resurgence of Eros to counteract the instincts of aggression and self-destruction, the question is asked: 'But who can foresee with what success and with what result?' (*SE* XXI: 145). However, we may be reading precipitately if we do not find anything prophetic about Freud in these or other texts. For the gist of my whole argument is that Freudian theory projects more than it knows, even to the point of contradiction. But to read in that sense of prophecy a vision of the apocalypse (is there any other sense of prophecy?), we will have to read even more in opposition to what seems to be the impetus and direction of the theory itself.

In *Civilization and Its Discontents* religion is posited first of all in terms of the reconciliation it offers between psyche and *socius*, as the experience of the 'oceanic feeling.' But that reconciliation, the coming together of what has been held apart, is also read as a reversion to an ideal prior state, before the emergence of the ego; or at least the sign of the persistence, or survival, of a 'primary ego-feeling' (*SE* XXI: 68). From that basis Freud goes on to trace the relations between the ego and the threats presented by the external world, the antagonism between the desires of the individual and those of the community, or more generally of civilization.[6] By means of the 'oceanic feeling' the religious experience comes closest to whatever might be represented in vague or specific circumstances by the occult. Yet Freud devotes only his first chapter to the idea, conceding that it exists in many people, but reducing it to 'something like the restoration of limitless narcissism' traceable 'back to an early phase of ego-feeling' (72). In subsequent chapters the discussion follows through the matter of the quest for happiness, the extent to which civilization stands in the path of that happiness, the sacrifices it demands of the sexual and aggressive-destructive drives, and the imposition of the superego.

Now, an important question can be raised with respect to the idea of religion as regression to an early phase of ego-feeling. In terms of the developmental progression from the subject's failure to differentiate between itself and the world to the varying positions of compromise it adopts between the principles of pleasure and reality, there is no binding logical obligation to read the oceanic feeling as a regression rather than a progression. There may be good ideological reasons for that, a resistance to idealism and so on, but the idea of reconciliation is in fact held out as a *future* promise for the psychic system when it comes to the schism between the libido and the death drive. That is certainly how I read the final words of *Civilization and Its Discontents*, where it is 'expected' that Eros 'will make an effort to assert himself in the struggle with his equally immortal adversary' (145), Thanatos. Again, it is no oceanic reconciliation that is promised, although in hindsight the prophecy seems fraught with its own version of quietism. Why then would a similarly *prospective* reconciliation be refused for the ego and treated instead as reversion? Why this change in direction? Does the theory know its back from its front?

NOTES

1. Jones, *Life and Work of Freud*, 3: 95.
2. S. Freud, *Civilization and Its Discontents*, in his *Standard Edition*, xxi: 93. Further references to the *Standard Edition* will hereafter be cited in text by the abbreviation *SE*, followed by a volume number in Roman numerals.
3. E. Freud, *Letters of Sigmund Freud*, 389–90.
4. The logic of such a question is already made explicit in 'To Speculate – on "Freud,"' in Derrida, *Post Card*. The present formulations draw much from that discussion.
5. Quoted in Jones, *Life and Work of Freud*, 3: 395–96.
6. It is worth bearing in mind, as the German title of this essay indicates – *Das Unbehagen in der Kultur* – that it is 'culture' that is most often translated in the *Standard Edition* as 'civilization.'

See also:

Freud (1.2)
Royle (4.4)
Beardsworth (5.4)
Caputo (9.6)

PART 8
POLITICS

8.1

'MARX AND DERRIDA'

Michael Ryan

Derrida admits his work occupies a marginal cultural sphere. Collections of
love letters and autobiographical reviews of Parisian art displays have little
perceivable immediate pertinence to such questions as the proletarianization of
peasants or the poisoning of the world by transnationals. Nevertheless, capitalism is not merely political and economic, but also cultural and social, not
merely economically exploitative, but also patriarchal and racist. Indeed, to
succeed as political-economic domination, capital requires power in these other
spheres. Writing critiques of bourgeois models of communication and representation, philosophizing, and so on may not be the best way to seize state
power, but unless they pretend to be a substitute for other forms of struggle (i.e.,
the Frankfurt School), they can have an important place. In fact, I would argue
that a narrow focus on questions of political-economic power, at the exclusion
of other plural, multisectoral critiques and reconstructions, can be as self-
defeating as a narrow focus on cultural concerns. It is not accidental, after all,
that Lenin's crude philosophic objectivism accompanied an equally crude vision
of socialism. Without further apologies, then, I will try to show that the critical
methods of Marx and Derrida can be compared and that deconstruction can be
articulated with critical marxism. There are four reasons why this comparison is
possible: first, because Derrida follows Marx as a critic of metaphysics; second,
because the deconstructive rewriting of the classical dialectic removes the
justification for the conservative marxist model of a linearly evolutionary

Source: Michael Ryan, *Marxism and Deconstruction: A Critical Articulation* (Baltimore: Johns
Hopkins University Press, 1982), pp. 43–6.

and finalistically resolutive progress to socialism, while implicitly furthering a politics predicated upon a more realistic assessment of the antagonistic forces and irreducible differences that characterize capitalist social and productive relations; third, because deconstruction can provide the principles necessary for a radical critique of capitalist-patriarchal institutions that is not merely oppositional but undermines from within the legitimating grounds for those institutions and fourth, because deconstruction can supply conceptual models for the economic and political institutions required in egalitarian and nonhierarchic socialist construction.

Here, I will deal with the first point, the critique of metaphysics in Marx and Derrida, and I will be concerned primarily with questions of method of analysis and of the critique of knowledge. I will begin with a comparison of the concepts of relation, difference, and antagonism in Marx and Derrida. Then, I will work out the similarities and differences between their critiques of positivism, idealism, naturalism, and objectivism.

Derrida has not always been willing to consider himself a marxist. In early texts, he suggests that marxism itself is subject to deconstruction, that it belongs to the metaphysics of presence. He pitches together the materialist dialectic with the speculative idealist dialectic and accuses both of being metaphysical, that is, of adhering to the horizon of presence and of self-identity, of positing a resolutive telos of noncontradiction and indifference, and of reducing the infinite displacement of the trace (the inscription of alterity in what seems selfsame) to stable, homogeneous structures of meaning and of being: 'I don't believe there is a "fact" which permits us to say: in *the* marxist corpus, *the* notion of contradiction and *the* notion of dialectics escapes *the* domination of metaphysics ... I don't believe one can speak, even from a marxist perspective, of a homogeneous marxist text which would instantaneously liberate the concept of contradiction from its speculative, teleological, and eschatological horizon.' The interview quoted here occurred in 1971. In a later text (1972), he reverses himself and suggests that Marx's postscript to Hegel escapes the metaphysical urge for logocentric closure and sublative resolution through the speculative dialectic. In 'Hors Livre' he describes Marx's difference from Hegel by considering the status of the 'preface' in their texts. In attempting, like Hegel, to avoid 'formal anticipation,' Marx, unlike Hegel, did not seek a result that would be a 'pure determination of the concept, even less a "foundation."' Derrida then cites one of Marx's prefaces, saying that it exhibits a 'quantitative and qualitative heterogeneity of developments, and the whole historical scene in which it is inscribed.' He concludes: 'Thus, the asymmetrical space of a post-script to the greater Logic is sketched out. An infinitely differentiated general space ... a force of historical non-return, resisting every circular re-comprehension in the reflexive domesticity (*Erinnerung*) of the Logos, recovering and proclaiming truth in its full speech' (*Dissemination* 41). Perhaps Derrida gave the question more thought between 1971 and 1972. Certainly, in earlier texts, his condemnation of all forms of the dialectic is unremitting. I quote from *Of Grammatology*, published in French in 1968: 'All dualisms, all theories of the immortality of the soul or of the spirit, as well as all, monisms, spiritualist or materialist, dialectical or vulgar, are the unique theme of a metaphysics whose entire history was compelled to strive toward the reduction of the trace. The subordination of the trace to the full presence summed up in the logos [is] an onto-theology determining the archeological and eschatological meaning of being as presence, as parousia, as life without differance' (*Gram*, 71). By 1972, Derrida markedly changed his tune. In between 1968 and 1972 stands the 1971 interview with Jean Louis Houdebine and Guy Scarpetta during which he was first publicly (in writing) taken to task on the question of marxism.

After 1972, such pieces of Marx's vocabulary appear in Derrida's work as capitalization and surplus value. In 1976, during an interview, Derrida redefined the relationship of deconstruction to 'marxism.' The deconstructive question, he said, concerns 'the philosophical project inasmuch as it calls for a foundation and an architechtonics, systematics, and therefore as well the onto-encyclopedic *universitas* ... Does marxism (inasmuch as it contains a system named dialectical materialism) present itself as a philosophy, elaborated or to be elaborated, as a *founded* philosophical practice, as a "construction" ... I don't know a marxist discourse – considering or calling itself such – which would respond negatively to that question. Nor, I would add, which poses it or even recognizes it.' Derrida wisely limits his reservation to marxist philosophy and to dialectical materialism, but he mistakenly equates marxism with a philosophical system. Once that is done, marxism can be reduced to althusserianism or Communist party diamat, both of which are indeed subject to the deconstructive question, because both apply founded systematic constructions to the world. Each in its own way is more concerned with the scientific or philosophic purity of the conceptual edifice or construct than with practice carried out in a problematic historical arena whose heterogeneity makes complete systematic formality questionable. It is not surprising that both philosophies have been accused of effacing class struggle, that practical war of forces which makes the construction of 'marxist' philosophical *systems* seem irrelevant.

In the same interview Derrida spoke of the necessity of the marxist problematic of ideology, and he suggested ways deconstruction might engage the question by considering such oppositions as science/ideology and ideology/ philosophy. He said marxists would do well to address the texts of Nietzsche and Heidegger in terms of ideology. And, while criticizing 'dogmatic' marxism, he nonetheless expressed distaste for the 'derisory and reactive' French 'postmarxists.' He did the same in the 1979 interview from which I have already quoted and in which, for the first time in print, he speaks of himself as a marxist. There also he provides a sympathetic description of marxism: 'Marxism presents itself, has presented itself from the very beginning with Marx, as an open theory which was continually to transform itself and not become fixed in dogma, in stereotypes.'

Derrida, then, is a critical philosopher who undertook a deconstruction of bourgeois philosophy in its most powerful incarnations, from Rousseau to Hegel to Husserl to Heidegger to Searle, who made the uninformed mistake early on of lumping Marx's materialist with Hegel's speculative dialectics, who, after reading Marx, corrected the misattribution and acknowledged the parallel nature of Marx's undertaking to his own (inasmuch as Marx's was methodological or philosophical), and who still maintains a critical distance in regard to Soviet diamat and to dogmatic, precritical marxist 'philosophy.'

I am convinced that if marxists were to cease pretending to be'philosophers' and to stop mistaking the construction of 'marxist' philosophical systems for a political practice that calls itself marxist and also to cease mulling over such conceptual abstractions as 'mode of production' or 'determination in the last instance' or 'relative autonomy,' and instead to carry the critique of capitalism and of bourgeois culture into the home turf of bourgeois philosophy and thought, the result would be something *like* a politicized version of deconstruction. Not exactly the same, because an analysis of the circuit that leads from John Searle's reactionary philosophic study to David Rockefeller's bank office, to the torture chambers of Santiago de Chile, requires supplementing Derrida's fine micrological critique of the structural principles and operations of the institutions of power and domination in philosophy with a more macrological and social mode of analysis.

See also:

Marx (1.1)
Royle (4.4)
Attridge (4.3)
Weber (7.3)

8.2

'SPECTRES OF ENGELS'

Willy Maley

The specters of Marx. Why this plural? Would there be more than one of them?

BETTER DEAD THAN FRED

Friedrich Engels died in 1895. On the centenary of his death in 1995 it might have been appropriate, if anachronistic, to consider his legacy, especially in the wake of the publication of Jacques Derrida's fullest, but by no means first, engagement with Marx. It may take a hundred years for the impact of *Specters of Marx* to be felt and its implications thought through, but one thing that disappointed me was the low visibility of Engels. It seems that Derrida finds it as hard as anyone else to keep Engels in mind, or in sight, when dealing with Marxism. One could count on the fingers of two hands the references to Engels, including one hyphenated allusion to a body called 'Marx-Engels'.

This was especially disheartening for me, because deconstruction is precisely that form of textual practice that one would expect to be most sensitive to the question of co-authorship. What happens between two authors? Co-authorship – itself a kind of ghost-writing, like all writing – is an unavoidable reality for all of us, yet we continue to experience difficulty in dealing with Marx's other half. Indeed, paraphrasing Derrida, one might venture the following proposition: 'There is nothing outside of co-authorship, no discourse that is not haunted by the other.' So much of Derrida's writing depends upon multiple reading heads, and although he has not, on the face of it, engaged in co-authorship, narrowly

Source: Peter Buse and Andrew Stott (eds), *Ghosts: Deconstruction, Psychoanalysis, History* (London: Macmillan, 1999), pp. 23–50.

conceived, if we think in broader terms, in terms of interviews, dialogues, translations, examples, citations, iterability, double bands like those in *Glas*, or 'Living On/Borderlines', the heat-seeking missives of *The Post Card*, or simply in terms of the medley of styles that he adopts, not to mention his constant openness to the other, then we could say that Derrida only ever co-authors. He has only ever ghost-written. Yet the signature remains singular. Thus we have Marx and Engels, Macherey and Balibar, Deleuze and Guattari, JanMohamed and Lloyd, Dollimore and Sinfield, Derrida and . . . Derrida?

Still, the question of co-authorship, central to the study of Marx and Engels, seems conspicuous by its absence in *Specters of Marx*. This omission is glaring in so far as Engels is one of the most awesome spectres of Marx, one of the few who were in at the death of Marx. In his 'Speech at the Graveside of Karl Marx', delivered on 17 March 1883, Engels, coming not to bury but to praise, said: 'On the 14th of March, at a quarter to three in the afternoon, the greatest living thinker ceased to think. He had been left alone for scarcely two minutes, and when we came back we found him in his armchair, peacefully gone to sleep – but for ever'. The greatest living thinker had also ceased to live. But Engels lived on. In a letter to Sorge written the day after Marx's death, Engels had quoted Marx quoting Epicurus: 'Death is not a misfortune for him who dies, but for him who survives.'

There is a part of Marxism that is forever Engels. Engels survives, but in Derrida's *Specters of Marx* he is haunted by the *funereality* of his more famous collaborator. A ghost, Stephen Dedalus remarks in *Ulysses*, is someone who isn't there. Engels simply isn't there in so much speculation on Marx. This is understandable, and for a number of reasons. On the one hand, 'Marx', the proper name of Marx, has attached itself to, and has absorbed, other names and texts apparently independent of Marx 'himself'. On the other hand, Engels, self-effacing in the extreme, gave all tribute to Karl, so that even in the collaborative works – *The Holy Family*, *The German Ideology*, *The Manifesto of the Communist Party* – Marx apparently has the upper hand, with Engels acting as cipher, sounding-board, medium.

In 1911, the German Hegelian Johann Plenge wrote: 'Hegel continues to live in Marxism.' Engels continues to live there too. Marxism is the home of the homeless. Derrida cites homelessness as one of the ten plagues in *Specters of Marx*, but home is where democracy is, as Cixous once remarked, which is to say nowhere, and indeed Derrida wants to retain Marx as the unaccommodated man, of no fixed abode, address unknown:

> Marx has not yet been received. The subtitle of this address could thus have been: 'Marx – *das Unheimliche*.' Marx remains an immigrant *chez nous*, a glorious, sacred, accursed but still a clandestine immigrant as he was all his life. He belongs to a time of disjunction, to that 'time out of joint' in which is inaugurated, laboriously, painfully, tragically, a new thinking of borders, a new experience of the house, the home, and the

economy. Between earth and sky. One should not rush to make of the clandestine immigrant an illegal alien or, what always risks coming down to the same thing, to domesticate him. To neutralize him through natur-alization. To assimilate him so as to stop frightening oneself (making oneself fear) with him. He is not part of the family, but one should not send him back, once again, him too, to the border.

And, one might add, the same goes for Engels.

There'll always be an Engels. Engels is, after all, Marx's ghostly double, the vulgar, scientific, custodian of the crypt. Primary medium of the spirit of Marx. Second guardian of the ghost of Marx, after Marx himself. Freddy's nightmare weighs heavily on the brains of the living, and the mysterious disappearance of Engels – engineered by himself in the twelve years after Marx's death – is a phenomenon that has to be charted. Long before Derrida's book appeared, Terrell Carver, in the volume on Engels in the Fontana Past Masters series, wrote: 'What is lacking in the literature on Engels is a treatment of his intel-lectual life that is not always haunted by the spectre of Marx.' That haunting continues unabated.

There is of course the long tradition of seeing Engels as just another malignant growth on the dark underside of Marxism, less harmful perhaps than Lenin or Stalin – one thinks of Engels playing Dr Watson to Marx's Sherlock Holmes – but nonetheless a figure that remains to be exorcized in order to preserve the integrity of Marx. Struggling to define Marxism, Henri Lefebvre rehearses the available options – late and early, philosophical and political (all distinctions that Derrida rejects in *Specters of Marx*, incidentally), then remarks:

> which Marx? For others, Marxism is defined through the works of Marx *and* Engels. But between Marx and Engels there are notable differences, especially concerning the philosophy of nature, which was an essential consideration for Engels yet had only a subordinate importance for Marx. Thus, if one argues that Marx *and* Engels constitute Marxism, one is still left to decide which one is primary and which are the fundamental texts?

The hierarchy and the canon. These have to be decided. Invariably, Engels loses out. Even when the co-authored works are the subject of discussion, it is Marx's name that is used as a synecdoche for both.

IMAGINE NO RELIGION

Fredric Jameson argues in a recent response to *Specters of Marx* that 'religion is once again very much on the agenda of any serious attempt to come to terms with the specificity of our own time'. This feeds into Derrida's contention that: 'Religion ... was never one ideology among others for Marx. What, Marx seems to say, the genius of a great poet [i.e. Shakespeare] – and the spirit of a great father – will have uttered in a poetic flash, with one blow going faster and farther than our little bourgeois colleagues in economic theory, is the becoming-god of gold, which is at once ghost and idol, a god apprehended by the senses.' Curiously, Engels, in an aside, once remarked: 'By the way, there exists a very close connection between alchemy and religion. The philosopher's stone has many godlike properties and the Egyptian-Greek alchemists of the first two centuries of our era had a hand in the development of Christian doctrines.' Engels is disinclined, unlike Derrida, to develop what is more than an analogy.

Religion and ideology, a crucial conjunction, that is the crux of the matter. Derrida is convinced that *The German Ideology* remains haunted by the spectre of religion:

> The treatment of the phantomatic in *The German Ideology* announces or confirms the absolute privilege that Marx always grants to religion, to ideology as religion, mysticism, or theology, in his analysis of ideology in general. If the ghost gives its form, that is to say, its body, to the ideologem, then it is the essential feature [*le propre*], so to speak, of the religious, according to Marx, that is missed when one effaces the semantics or the lexicon of the specter, as translations often do, with values deemed to be more or less equivalent (fantasmagorical, hallucinatory, fantastic, imaginary, and so on). The mystical character of the fetish, in the mark it leaves on the experience of the religious, is first of all a ghostly character.

Later, Derrida emphasizes that for him 'at stake is doubtless everything which *today* links Religion and Technics in a singular configuration'.

Marx and Engels may have abandoned their voluminous text 'to the gnawing criticism of the mice', as Marx put it, but the corpus as a whole remains caught up in professions of faith. In *Specters of Marx*, Derrida actually takes on board the charge that Marxism is religious and argues for a messianism without a messiah, something that has disturbed some Marxist critics. Religion remains central to any discourse on Marx and Engels, whether as the great ghost with which they must struggle into the night, or as that which they are accused of creating – another doxa, another utopia, another attempt to go 'beyond the text'.

Engels had, from an early age, and in advance of his encounter with, or haunting by, Marx, a keen interest in religion, spiritualism and the supernatural. In 1839, Engels confessed that his strict religious upbringing had contributed to his protest against and eventual rejection of spiritualism. Writing to a schoolfriend, Wilhelm Graeber, Engels declared:

> If I had not been brought up in the most extreme orthodoxy and piety, if I had not had drummed into me in church, Sunday School and at home the most direct, unconditional belief in the Bible with that of the church, indeed, with the special teaching of every minister, perhaps I would have remained stuck in some sort of liberal supranaturalism for a long time.

Engels's progress towards atheism was slow and painful. Earlier the same year he had written:

> Well, I have never been a pietist. I have been a mystic for a while, but those are *tempi passati*. I am now an honest, and in comparison with others, very liberal, supernaturalist. How long I shall remain such I don't know, but I hope to remain one, even though inclining now more, now less towards rationalism.

Tempi passati. But spectres are anachronistic – they come back. Three months later, Engels's supernaturalism was showing signs of wear and tear. He no longer believed that 'rationalism purified and strengthened the religious feeling':

> I pray daily, indeed nearly the whole day, for truth, I have done so ever since I began to have doubts, but I still cannot return to your faith. And yet it is written: 'Ask, and it shall be given you' ... Tears come into my eyes as I write this. I am moved to the core, but I feel I shall not be lost; I shall come to God, for whom my whole heart yearns.

I want to turn now to a text written forty years after those tears, but written, I shall argue, through those tears, as indeed the best texts are, whether in laughter or sorrow.

In 1886, Engels, in his critique of Feuerbach, would write:

> Religion is derived from *religare* and meant originally a bond. Therefore every bond between two people is a religion. Such etymological tricks are the last resort of idealist philosophy. Not what the word means according to the historical development of its actual use, but what it ought to mean according to its derivation is what counts. And so sex, love and the intercourse between the sexes is apotheosised to a *religion*, merely in order that the word religion, which is so dear to idealistic memories, may not disappear from the language. The Parisian reformers of the Louis Blanc trend used to speak in precisely the same way in the forties. They likewise could conceive of a man without religion only as a monster, and used to say to us: '*Donc, l'atheisme c'est votre religion!*'

Engels's impatience with Feuerbach's etymology recalls Derrida's famous footnote in *Margins of Philosophy* on the vexation caused to Marx and Engels by Stirner's etymologism in *The German Ideology*. Religare – to bind. Do we stick to the letter or the spirit of the bond? What binds Engels to Marx, and why has the latter been relegated? Why must Engels play second fiddle while Marxism burns?

See also:

Marx (1.1)
Royle (4.4)
Botting and Wilson (5.7)
Weber (7.3)

8.3

'THE DECONSTRUCTION OF POLITICS'

Bill Readings

> What importance, for example, had the power, merely formal up till now, which Klamm exercised over K.'s services, compared with the very real power which Klamm possessed in K.'s bedroom? So it came about that while a light and frivolous bearing, a certain deliberate carelessness was sufficient when one came in direct contact with the authorities, one needed in everything else the greatest caution, and had to look round on every side before one made a single step.
>
> – Kafka, *The Castle*

At the Oklahoma Conference on Contemporary Genre Theory in 1984, Barbara Johnson, at the opening of a symposium with J. Hillis Miller and Louis Mackey, called for a dialogue between Marxism and deconstruction that would take the form of an interchange between the realm of 'discourse' and the 'realm of historical and political action':

> Deconstruction ... has within it the creation of a feeling of imperative ... a feeling that if deconstruction can take you this far in the critique of power structures in discourse, then why not go further? Why not actually translate what deconstruction has done on texts into the realm of historical and political action?[1]

This then, would be the manifesto of the encounter between textual deconstruction and active politics. Its description of a possible relationship is shared both by those like Barbara Johnson who are identified as deconstructive critics,

Source: Lindsay Waters and Wlad Godzich (eds), *Reading de Man Reading* (Minneapolis: University of Minnesota Press, 1989), pp. 223–44.

and by those like Said and Eagleton who attack deconstruction for having failed to effect such a shift from textual subversion to the subversion of power in the world of action, and who argue that deconstruction cannot perform such a shift.[2] I want to argue first of all that Said and Eagleton are correct in saying that deconstruction cannot provide a program of coherent action in a political sphere conceived as distinct from the textual sphere in which they think that deconstruction takes place, yet that, like Barbara Johnson, they are seriously in error in phrasing the question in these terms, in asking the question of deconstruction *and* politics. I shall consider what is at stake in the deconstruction *of* politics with regard to the three main charges laid against deconstruction: (1) that it preaches a pantextualism that infinitely regresses from the possibility of political action; (2) that deconstructive indeterminacy offers no criteria for political judgment; (3) that deconstruction's assault on traditional conceptions of subjectivity erases the possibility of a potent agent of political action.

Edward Said has joined Terry Eagleton in what has now become a standard attack on deconstruction as the privileging of textuality at the expense of the real world and its political imperatives, as the concentration on language to the exclusion of its referent, as the paying of attention to rhetoric so as to elide the literal, which is considered by them as the sphere of political action.[3]

Perhaps we should ask ourselves what the project of translating deconstruction into politics in the manner suggested by Johnson might resemble. Bluntly, it would not be deconstruction at all, because in the first instance, deconstruction would have to be reduced to a theory and its working to a process of *demystification*, a powerful mechanism of assault on texts, which could show the rhetorical (false) at work in phrases purporting to be literal (true), to describe the real world. Political action would thus be the insistence on pure literality, the annulment of the oppressive function of rhetoric when taken as literal. Johnson's political deconstruction would thus counter effects of power such as the metaphysical erection of property into the very ground of being itself, but in the name of an undifferentiated being, prior to any act of appropriation. In other words, deconstruction would be a souped-up version of the practice of Roland Barthes in his early work, with its distinction between denotative and connotative signifying practices, more sophisticated in that deconstruction extends the analysis to the subject as well as to the representation of which he or she is, for Barthes, the vanishing point.[4] Deconstruction according to Johnson's model would thus *preserve* the distinction and hierarchization of the literal over the rhetorical at the price of the infinite regression of the literal in the analysis of signifying practice, in its peeling away of the onion-skin layers of rhetoric. This would permit the belief in the political 'application' of critical insight, and with it the grounding of critical insight as pure *knowledge*. The desire for a political *application* of deconstruction masks the desire to preserve deconstruction as a critical method *before* politics, and thus to guarantee its status as a critical method, to ground in some sense the insights that it offers as 'real.' Any attempt to get out of the problems of this model of deconstruction, to preserve a possibility of literal action through deconstruction by invoking the 'strategic' rather than the homeomorphic as the groundless ground of agency, is redundant insofar as we continue to think strategy within the literal, as having a literal function, and hence a *literal telos*, which deconstruction must interrogate or refuse.

The attempt to lend deconstruction the status of demystification and then to seek to empower it for social change in a literal sphere of agency is futile.[5] This process becomes either nihilistic or quietistically utopian, leading either to the complete negation of the possibility of political agency in the sphere of the literal (because of the impossibility of access to the literal except in a language conceived as secondary and as always already figural),[6] or to the renunciation of any contingent agency in attendance upon the point at which capitalism (the power structure governing historical and political action in the era of deconstruction) will be forced to face its own contradictions. Capitalism will then be forced to have recourse to the literal (and thus to know itself as terror) in order to reorder a paradigm of self-representation (capitalism's 'image,' if you will) that has become nonfunctional because of the deconstructive explosion of its rhetorical or superstructural contradictions. Deconstruction can produce no simple model for political action, as Spivak has recognized.[7] However, neither can it produce any possibility of political agency at all, either fully instrumental or contingent (strategic), within a sphere of political action conceived as literal, as functioning literally, as in any sense finally detached from the rhetorical sphere of signifying practice. Therefore, deconstruction cannot be translated into the literal, either as model or as strategy. As I shall argue, the force of deconstruction is the extent to which it forces a rethinking of the terms of the political.

The interrogation by the Left of deconstruction in terms of its political implications seems to me to be the product of a strange refusal to extend the operation of deconstruction to the manner in which the sphere of the political is conventionally thought (to risk using the term 'thought' as a misnomer). This will not have been an analysis of deconstruction *and* politics, but the deconstruction *of* politics, or rather of the opposition of politics to textuality, an opposition traditionally conceived in terms of that of action to language, of the rhetorical to the literal.

To speak of deconstruction and politics would be to submit deconstruction to the law of analogy in its most undeconstructed form, to presume that a practice reserved to an isolated sphere of textuality might be lifted across, transported into, an isolated sphere of political action, so that we might practice our politics as if we were reading 'texts,' and vice versa. As Barbara Johnson put it, with a disregard for all the work deconstruction has done on the status of 'translation' as a metaphor, as the metaphor of metaphor (metaphor may be 'translated' by *translatio*), which is surprising in so fine a critic, 'Why not actually translate what deconstruction has done on texts into the realm of historical and political action?'[8]

First, the division of the textual from the political is founded in an *undeconstructed notion of textuality*, a notion that has admittedly functioned in some of the manifestations of liberal pluralism that have been named under the name of deconstruction in the United States. Second, Johnson ascribes a neutral status to that act of transportation, as if the law of analogy, of the *as if*, were not itself a metaphor, which might in turn be deconstructed.[9] This implies a vision of politics as a pure metalanguage into which all theoretical dialects could be translated. Politics would be the horizon of action in terms of which competing theories could be judged, which is to lend metaphysical status to political action.

There are three common levels to the undeconstructed opposition of the textual to the world of action. Most simply, a real world of action is counterposed to a fictional world of books. The function of criticism is to judge those books insofar as they escape fiction to present as content the described world and thus the imperatives of the world of politics. The struggle of criticism is to produce practice by demystifying and reducing the ideological function of the literary. Political action is conceived as the escape from literary ideology. Second, if the Marxist insistence on the ideological functioning of the superstructure is admitted, a division is made *within* texts between the literal sphere of political activity and their rhetorical form. Literature itself becomes a field of ideological struggle as content. The function of criticism becomes itself an element of class struggle and criticism struggles to produce a revolutionary literature, a way of writing that will most literally communicate the political imperative of practice. The literary sphere is itself conceived as an instance of the political. Third, if literary form itself is admitted to have a political function, a division is made between rhetorical forms as politically acceptable or not, conceived in terms of the functioning of rhetorical form as *literal content* in the political sphere. The work of Eagleton or Said reaches this level, at which the rhetorical or formal aspects of literature are translated into the political sphere as the literal political content of literature: thus, formal or rhetorical analysis is proper to the criticism of Brecht, for example, insofar as it can describe a literary form that is its own (political) content.

This sketchy description of the development of the political criticism of literature – from philistine opposition to the bourgeois institution of literature, through the struggle to enlist literature for political practices, to the recognition of the ideological specificity of literary form – reveals the whole project of classical 'political' criticism of literature as organized through an abiding opposition between the literal or contentual (the political) and the rhetorical or formal (the textual). Even the most sophisticated form of analysis, insofar as it continues to conceive the question as that of the relation between the political *and* the textual, performs the analysis of literary form solely in terms of its becoming-literal in the sphere of the political. The textual is implicated in the political only at the expense of its relinquishing the rhetorical for the literal: even if it may adopt or employ rhetorical forms, in the final (Althusserian) analysis political discourse or political action seeks to authenticate itself by appeal to the literal, gesturing to its concern with 'real people' or 'real struggles.'[10] The conventional description of the political is always governed by the binary split of text from world. To put it bluntly, literature is political only to the extent that the political is in some sense the *referent* of the text, a referent that is conceived literally, as something exterior to the text. Nor is this attitude confined to Marxists: they share it with conservatives who attack the humanities as having nothing to do with the real world, or with deconstructors like Barbara Johnson who request a translation of deconstructive moves into the political sphere.

In seeking to provide a deconstruction of this classical opposition of the textual to the political, of the rhetorical or formal to the literal or referential, three moves are necessary. First, we shall consider the deconstruction of the relation of the political to the textual, following the hints thrown out by Derrida in his interview 'Deconstruction in America.' Second, we shall perform a reading of the law of analogy, of the representationality of law as analogy, the structuration of prescriptives by analogy with descriptives. A third move will sketch how a deconstruction of the opposition of action to texts would alter the conceptual structure governing the way in which the political is thought.[11] It will suggest that politics is always textual because the literal political referent is to be found only within the text, as a rhetorical form of textuality.

TEXTUAL POLITICS

Consider the reaction of Derrida to Said's criticism that deconstruction represents a limitless 'discursivization' of the political, to the extent that any concrete political referent, and hence any possibility of political action, is lost. In 'Deconstruction in America,' Derrida resists the implication that deconstruction is an 'enclosure in "the prison house of language"' by saying:

> It is incumbent on you to try to see *why* it seemed strategically useful at a given moment to say, for example, 'a body is text, the table is text, the market – Wall Street, etc. – is text.' Or else 'nuclear arms are text.' That seemed strategically useful at a given moment. And I believe that it has in fact been useful. So, it's everything but a textualization in the sense that Foucault and Said want to represent it ... To say for example, 'deconstruction suspends reference,' that deconstruction is a way of enclosing oneself in the sign, in the 'signifier,' is an enormous naiveté stated in that form ... Not only is there reference for a text, but never was it proposed that we erase effects of reference or of referents. Merely that we re-think these effects of reference. I would indeed say that the referent is textual. The referent is in the text. Yet that does not exempt us from having to describe very rigorously the necessity of those referents.[12]

Derrida's point is that to say that everything is text is not to say that everything happens in books, merely that there is no referent that is exterior to effects of textuality.[13] Deconstruction does not assert the primacy of the signifier, does not say that there is no escape from the prison house of language to the real world, but that the 'real world' is itself a textual effect, rather than something outside textuality toward which we might be able or unable to move.

The deconstruction of politics would be the consideration of the politics of this move outside the text into 'politics,' outside the rhetorical into the literal, a project that the work of Paul de Man mapped out in the most rigorous fashion, the more rigorous in its studious avoidance of any recuperative claims to 'strategy.' De Man's work articulates most fully the deconstruction of politics in its scrupulous refusal to invoke the suggestion either of subjective generalship or the literal finality of 'political ends' underpinning his rhetorical politics. *Allegories of Reading* AR enforces a reading of the politics of reference that avoids any easy deferral of the question of politics by the invocation of strategic claims that always tend toward transcendence. To pay attention rigorously to effects of reference is to think reference within the text, which deconstruction does by undermining the distinction of literal (reference-oriented) language from referential or figural language (see esp. AR, 103–18). Literary criticism draws the conventional formula of this description from a tradition at least as old as Rousseau, by which the rhetorical trope is seen as a detour in the field of meaning that is governed by literal reference, by reference either to the gaze of a conscious subject intending objects or to the prelinguistic presence of objects themselves.[14] Therefore rhetoric is anchored to intention or to expression, to a prelinguistic content ('what is, to be said') that finds itself outside itself in the literal. The literal is conventionally that which most properly respects the properties of things, of events conceived as either mental (intentions) or physical (the being of things), that which speaks them most properly, most cleanly.[15] Figuration is a secondary or mediating function ('how it is said, what is'), a detour within language, which departs from the literal in language in order to reveal what is most proper, most literal, in the proper. The conventional literary analysis of rhetoric is thus more literal than the literal in that it allows us to apprehend the hidden properties of things in themselves prior to their transportation into the purely denotative, closed order of a literal language. Thus literary critics can read menstruation, that for which the literal code of nineteenth-century narrative realism had no word, in George Eliot's metaphorical insistence on flooding.

Rhetoric, conventionally, considered, is the means by which the literality of being or of thought, the elementary being-literal of meaning itself, is preserved against the risk of the insufficiency of literal, denotative language, be it an insufficiency of content (the literal code has no word for it, as in the case of 'menstruation' in the nineteenth-century novel) or of form (meaning has an organic vivacity that would be lost in the systematic functioning of the code, meaning has a latency that would be betrayed by pure denotation, etc., etc.). Thus the literal governs the figural in that, even if language may be rhetorical, may turn away from the literal, meaning itself, prior to language, must always be literal. Prelinguistic meaning is governed, even before it comes to language, by a linguistic metaphor of literality. The referent's standing outside language, and the concomitant possibility of a purely literal use of language, is only guaranteed by a *linguistic figure*. The nonlinguistic meaning, the sense to which language refers, can only be in-itself before language as *prepared for literal speech*.

The referent is in the text in the sense that reference is a figural necessity of the fiction that language is the vehicle of a communication or an expression, a vehicle that can *transport*, can move outside itself to the properties of things (whether present to subjective consciousness in communication or present as objects in expression), can function *literally*. The name of the figure of the referent is the literal, and this figure is the trope of a language that can erase its own metaphoricity. Yet the referent is in the text in an even stronger sense, in that this sublime dream, this transport (metaphor), which is at the same time the carrying off of language itself, is itself, as a transportation, a metaphor, a formal and 'secondary' operation of language. The literal, in its most rigorous sense, is a metaphor, and in that branch of Western philosophy named positivism, it has become the metaphor of metaphors. The literal is thus a trope among tropes, which is not to erase literality but to insist that the literal be rhetorically rather than literally described: that is, that the literal cannot ground itself outside rhetoric, in a referential real abstracted from the figural. Furthermore, the distinction between the figural and the literal must be read as a tropaic distinction in an order of rhetoric, rather than as a literal one in an order of meaning. At this point we must signal a point of differentiation from the de Manian project, in *Allegories of Reading*, of reading the distinction of the figural from the literal, or the 'grammatical' from the 'rhetorical.' De Man's failure lies in the fact that he continues to distinguish the literal from the rhetorical on grounds of a difference in semantic meaning (content) rather than trope (form): as he puts it, 'Our recurrent question is whether this transformation is semanti-cally controlled along grammatical or along rhetorical lines' (AR, 13). Even within a reading that refuses to subordinate the figural potentiality of language to grammatical literality, which questions 'the reduction of figure to grammar' (AR, 7), the distinction between tropes (catachresis, literality) is illegitimately fixed as a *semantic* one, as a difference of content, rather than of form, if you like. That is, it is not enough simply to refuse to say which came first, the chicken or the coward, to refuse to apportion priority to either the literal meaning or the rhetorical swerve; one must, furthermore, refuse to think the rhetorical solely as a swerve away from literal meaning. The question of the separation of the rhetorical from the literal illustrates the point that it is not simply the hier-archization of literal and rhetorical but the descriptive order of the distinction between them that must be challenged: we must investigate what the politics of a literal distinction of figural from literal might be. The distinction of figural from literal must not be read as a difference *in the order of literal* meaning.

The referent is in the text in the same way as we have seen that the literal is a trope within rhetoric, rhetoric's trope of the absence of rhetoric. The referent is the text's fiction of the absence of text, the text's fiction of its own outside. This fiction of an outside is, of course, produced from the inside of the text. There is no pure exteriority, no referent outside the text. Nor, however, is there a pure interiority: the referent is not just a verbal fiction, it is not simply the case that everything happens in books, because the fiction of the real is a necessary or determining one. The fiction of the outside is a structural necessity of the inside. Deconstruction of the text/referent opposition does not replace the conventional primacy of the real over the text with a new primacy of the text over the real, or of signifier over signified, but reveals their interdependence and mutual contamination.

The possibility of a translation from deconstructive textuality to politics, from the figural to the literal, from the textual to the real, is founded upon this misrecognition of the figural status of the literal, and the correlative positing of an empirical real outside the text. The condition of the operation of power in Western society (the condition by which domination effects are invisible in the representation of democratic participation) is to think politics as empirical, as that which is self-evident, which makes its place as it takes it. That is, domination works by denying its politics, by establishing its particular politics as an empirical or prepolitical real, so that domination is invisible in that it takes place before what is named as the political. The operation of domination is in defining the political, so that power appears to operate in a political vacuum (that is, in no place, nowhere), a vacuum guaranteed by the notion of representation as transparency. Thus, what is at stake in the deconstruction of the opposition of the textual to the political, is the refiguration of the literal, is precisely politics itself, the terror of the real that governs the government and the argument (so that argument is limited to government) of Western politics in democracy or in its most extended form in totalitarianism, a terror that operates by grounding its prescriptive judgments as the descriptions of an empirical reality outside signifying practice.

NOTES

1. Barbara Johnson, symposium transcript in Robert C. Davis and Ronald Schliefer (eds.), *Rhetoric and Form: Deconstruction at Yale* (Norman: University of Oklahoma Press, 1985), 78.
2. Said attacks deconstruction because its 'oppositional manner ... does not accurately represent its ideas and practice, which, after all is said and done, further solidify and guarantee the social structure and the culture that produced them' (Edward Said, *The World, The Text, and The Critic* [Cambridge, Mass.: Harvard University Press, 1984], 159). His reflex use of the idiom 'when all is said and done' betrays the desire of his argument for an escape from language into a pure realm of understanding, a detextualized sphere of knowledge the impossibility of which it is the purpose of this essay to mark. Eagleton characterizes deconstruction as a subversive textual practice that, for reasons he does not analyze, functions 'in ways that objectively legitimate bourgeois hegemony' (Terry Eagleton, *Walter Benjamin or Towards a Revolutionary Criticism* [London: Verso, 1981] 140). The strict division of theory from practice in this model of argument is a little strange in one concerned to defend a version of Marxism in the face of Stalinist manifestations.

3. Said (*World, Text, and Critic*, 292) attacks Derrida for an undifferentiated pan-textualism, an argument that is concisely summarized in his conclusion, 'Folding back upon itself, criticism has therefore refused to see its affiliations with the political world it serves, perhaps unwittingly, perhaps not.'

4. See Roland Barthes, *Mythologies*, ed. and trans. Annette Lavers (London: Granada, 1973).

5. The only demystification that deconstruction can perform is the demystification of the literal as itself a figure among figures, which is to demystify the notion of demystification as a returning of things to their literal being.

6. This position is otherwise known as unreconstructed Lacanianism.

7. See Gayatri Spivak, 'Revolutions That As Yet Have No Model,' *Diacritics*, 10 (1980): 24–49.

8. Barbara Johnson in Davis and Schliefer (eds.), *Rhetoric and Form*, 78. In Johnson's defense, one should adduce the point made in 'Apostrophe, Animation, and Abortion' (in Barbara Johnson, *A World of Difference* [Baltimore: Johns Hopkins University Press, 1987], 184–99) that 'the undecidable *is* the political. There is politics because there is undecidability.' Owing to the lack of theoretical elaboration in that essay, this interesting formulation unfortunately ends up sounding uncomfortably like a proverbial observation on the fact that some people will never agree, when much more could be made of it.

9. As Jean-Luc Nancy has pointed out, the *as if* is merely an inverted form of ontological realism. See Jean-Luc Nancy, 'Dies Irae,' in Jean-François Lyotard (ed.), *La Faculté de Juger* (Paris: Minuit, 1985). 14.

10. 'The liberal humanists are right to see that there is a *point* in studying literature, and that this point is not itself, in the end, a literary one' (Terry Eagleton, *Literary Theory: An Introduction* [Minneapolis: University of Minnesota Press, 1983], 208). The point is, of course, a political one, a political point conceived as lying, in the last analysis, firmly outside the sphere of the textual or literary.

11. The nature of the preceding two moves in the strategy will, of course, render it impossible that this resemble a program of political action, conventionally considered.

12. Jacques Derrida, 'Deconstruction in America' (interview with James Creech, Peggy Kamuf, and Jane Todd), in *Critical Exchange*. no. 17 (1985): 15–19.

13. As he has recently pointed out, '*Text*, as I use the word, is not the book … It is precisely for strategic reasons … that I found it necessary to recast the concept of text by generalizing it almost without limit, in any case without present or perceptible limit, without any limit that *is*' ('But, beyond … ,' *Critical Inquiry*, 13 (1986): 167).

14. J.-J. Rousseau, 'Essay on the Origin of Languages,' in J.-J. Rousseau and J. G. Herder, *On the Origin of Language*, ed. and trans. J. H. Moran and A. Gode (Chicago: University of Chicago Press, 1986). Rousseau posits that figural language preceded literal language in its chronological development, but asserts that the literal is the true or proper form of language, the condition of meaning itself: 'Figurative language was the first to be born. Proper meaning was discovered last' (12).

15. The literal is the *sens propre*, the clean or proper sense, that which presents the property of the referent cleanly.

See also:

Lyotard (3.6)
De Man (4.2)
Young (6.2)
Derrida (11.3)

8.4

'PRACTICAL POLITICS OF THE OPEN END'

Gayatri Spivak

HARASYM   What political interventional force could or does deconstruction have in the political rewriting of the ethico-political, socio-historical text and its destination?

SPIVAK   Deconstruction cannot found a political program of any kind. Deconstruction points out that in constructing any kind of an argument we must move from implied premises, that must necessarily obliterate or finesse certain possibilities that question the availability of these premises in an absolutely justifiable way. Deconstruction teaches us to look at these limits and questions. It is a corrective and a critical movement. It seems to me, also, that because of this, deconstruction suggests that there is no absolute justification of *any* position. Now, this is not the final say about the position. Deconstruction, also insistently claims that there cannot be a fully practicing deconstructor. For, the subject is always centered as a subject. You cannot *decide* to *be* decentered and inaugurate a politically correct deconstructive politics. What deconstruction looks at is the limits of this centering, and points at the fact that these boundaries of the centering of the subject are indeterminate and that the subject (being always centered) is obliged to describe them as determinate. Politically, all this does is not allow for fundamentalisms and totalitarianisms of various kinds, however seemingly benevolent. *But it cannot be foundational.* If one wanted to *found* a political project on deconstruction, it would be something

Source: Gayatri Spivak, 'Practical politics of the open end', *Canadian Journal of Political and Social Theory/Revue canadienne de théorie politique et sociale*, 12 (1–2), 1988, pp. 104–11.

like wishy-washy pluralism on the one hand, or a kind of irresponsible hedonism on the other. That's what would happen if you changed that morphology into a narrative. Yet in its suggestion that masterwords like 'the worker', or 'the woman' have no literal referents deconstruction is again a political safeguard.

For, when you are *succeeding* in political mobilizations based on the sanctity of those masterwords, then it begins to seem as if these narratives, these characteristics, really existed. That's when all kinds of guilt tripping, card-naming, arrogance, self-aggrandizement and so on, begin to spell the beginning of an end.

A deconstructive awareness would insistently be aware that the masterwords are catachreses . . . that there are no literal referents, there are no 'true' examples of the 'true worker,' the 'true' examples of the 'true worker,' the 'true woman,' the 'true proletarian' who would actually stand for the ideals in terms of which you've mobilized. The disenfranchised are quite often extremely irritated with that gesture of the benevolent towards them which involves a transformation through definition. They themselves do not like to fit into a category like the 'true worker,' 'the true woman,' etc. I often cite a story by Toni Cade Bambara, 'My Man Bovanne,' a story in which she actually deals with this phenomenon very beautifully. In national liberation movements, for example, there is a critical moment when a deconstructive vigilance would not allow a movement toward orthodox nationalism.

HARASYM   How is this political interventional force related to what you describe in the final footnote of 'Scattered Speculations on the Question of Values' as a practical politics of the open end?

SPIVAK   You will remember that I am talking there of Derrida's essay 'Of an Apocalyptic Tone.' I made those remarks with reference to a piece that is very abstruse, very beautiful, but extremely difficult, and I'm going to answer you here in as easy a way as I can find. So when you ask me to refer specifically to the last footnote, there will be this gap. I think that a practical politics of the open end can be understood through this analogy. For example, when we actually brush our teeth, or clean ourselves everyday, or take exercise, or whatever, we don't think we are fighting a losing battle against mortality, but, in fact, all of these efforts are doomed to failure because we are going to die. On the other hand, we really think of it much more as upkeep and as maintenance rather than as an irreducibly doomed repeated effort. This kind of activity cannot be replaced by an operation. We can't have a surgical operation which takes care of the daily maintenance of a body doomed to die. That operation would be identical with death. This analogy, like all analogies, is not perfect. It applies to the individual, and if one applied it directly to historical collectivities, one might be obliged to suggest that there are Spenglarian cycles to civilizations. This analogy, itself catechretical, can help us understand the practical politics of the open end. It is not like some kind of massive ideological act (the surgical operation) which brings about a drastic change. Now, in all my thinking about practical politics I have always emphasized that there has to be both these two kinds of things, each – anticipate something we are going to talk about later – each bringing the other to crisis. Because quite often this tooth-brushing style of daily-maintenance politics seems to require acting out of line. On the other hand, the massive kind of surgery, surgical-operation-type politics which can go according to morphology, seems to deny the everyday maintenance of practical politics. When each brings the other to productive crisis, then it seems to me you have a practical politics of the open end: neither is privileged. In fact, the relationship between feminism and Marxism, the fights that arise, even with people such as Sheila Rowbotham, quite often are based in a misunderstanding of this. So that feminism sees itself as one kind of practical politics wanting, also, to be the other kind. That's just divisiveness, and, just as the disenfranchised 'know' that the labels that describe them are catachretical; this kind of practical politics of the open-end, too, is something quite familiar. That's one of the beautiful things about deconstruction: that it really, actually, points at the theoretical implications of the familiar. And so, we in fact know this, but it is always considered an aberration: it is strategically excluded when one is talking theory.

HARASYM   When you were lecturing in Alberta (1986) you gave a very interesting reading of the 'living feminine' and the problem of determination in Derrida's text, *The Ear of the Other*. What place does the 'living feminine' occupy in this text? Is it structurally similar to the position of the feminine in Derrida's other texts? What is useful in this text to your own work?

SPIVAK   In *The Ear of the Other*, the living feminine seems to me to occupy a place with many other articulations in Derrida's other texts. I think that woman, or the feminine, is a kind of *mame* for something in Derrida. It is, as he has insisted elsewhere, neither a figure nor a kind of empirical reality, and the best I have been able to do with my careful reading of his texts is that it is a kind of *name* for something in Derrida. It is, as he has insisted elsewhere, neither a figure nor a kind of empirical reality, and the best I have been able to do with my careful reading of his texts is that it is a kind of name. Just as Foucault in his most interesting texts suggests that power is a name for a certain complex. In the paper that's going to be in the Brennan anthology, I have tried to discuss some of the problems and some of the positive and the useful elements in Derrida's use of the name 'woman' for a whole *ensemble* in his morphology: I think the place occupied by the 'living femimine' in *The Ear of the Other* is simply the place that stands over against the pact between autobiography and death. The possibility of autobiography is related to death through the fact that autobiography is not life, even biography is not life, and the autobiographer grasps at a name, a name which is bequeathed by the father. What is over against it is the 'living feminine, which subtends the nameable, the father's part'. O.K. But, if one really wanted to pull out the logic of the concept-metaphor one would see that the 'living feminine' once it is named the mother, already has within it a certain kind of repetitive structure. And perhaps, Derrida is looking at *that* when he looks at the contradictions in Nietzsche's texts around the 'living feminine.' I'm not quite sure of it. I'll have to look at the text again to tell you what I think. It seems to me, also, that in the earlier, much earlier pieces like 'Speech and Phenomena,' one of the most interesting things that he shows us is that any conception of a 'living present' for the human subject has to assume the subject's death, for this 'living present' must have existed before the subject and will exist after the subject. And to an extent, I would feel happier if that kind of thing already encroached into the 'living feminine.' Otherwise, the 'living feminine' becomes a sort of a methodological supposition which is given a name. Now this play between history, the historical place of the name of the mother, as it were, and morphology, the feminine on the other side of difference, etc. – this is what I'm trying to attack in that piece for Teresa Brennan.

What is useful to my own work? I like this text a great deal. What is supremely useful is Derrida's articulation of the new politics of reading: that you do not excuse a text for its historical aberrations, you admit that there is something in the text which can produce these readings. That is extremely useful. But then making the protocols of the text your own, you tease out the critical moments in the text and work at useful readings – readings that are scrupulous re-writings. I have repeated this to students and in talks many times, and I don't want it to become a formula. That's the problem, you know, these wonderful things become formulas, and then people just kind of – it's like a dance step. But, nonetheless, trying to teach Marx this semester, remembering the history of Marxism, remembering the problems, not trying to excuse Marx or on the other hand, trying to simply turn my back on him, has been a very, very useful, a very productive exercise. I remind myself of this essay as I go on.

HARASYM   In 'Imperialism and Sexual Difference' you both borrow and show the limits of borrowing uncritically a strategy of reading articulated by Paul de Man. Please correct me if I am wrong. But, whereas Paul de Man's readings *tend* to stop at various aporias, your readings – here, I am thinking in particular of your work on cultural self-representation – your readings stress the necessity of thinking beyond the aporia as they focus on the situational specific forces of the opposition in order to find a place of practice. What are your thoughts on this reading?

SPIVAK   I think I would partially agree with what you're saying. However, in De Man, the later suggestion: that in order to act you have to literalize the metaphor is important because it takes one beyond the perception of De Man as attempting to reside in an aporia. People like us learned the predicament of discovering in aporia in a text, and then moved in other directions with the aporetic structure. Whereas, since he was articulating it, it took him a long time simply establishing it in text after text, and, in deed, I think it is not to undermine his excellence to say that in the texts of the period of *Allegories of Reading*, one might feel that that's all he is doing. But, I think, again, to read him with a new politics of reading, not to excuse the fact that it can lead in people who are blind followers, into a celebration of what Wlad Godzich, I think incorrectly, although normally I think he is a very astute reader, what he's called 'cancelling out' in De Man. I think one can get to a position like that, but, on the other hand, it's also possible to see that in every text there is a signal that aporias are never fully balanced. So that you know that even in the *Allegories of Reading*, the text on Proust, 'Reading,' when he's discussing metaphor and narrative, you can see that, in fact, in the way he's talking the metaphor is privileged, so that one cannot have a full aporia. De Man always marks the moments of asymmetry in *Allegories of Reading*. But, then, in the later text, 'Promises,' where he suggests that in order to act you turn the metaphor, you literalize the metaphor, then he's out of simply articulating aporias. This is the work he was on when he died: the work of moving from the description of tropological and performative deconstruction to a definition of the act.

I think you're right when you describe my stuff as you do. Given what I think my usefulness is, I tend to emphasize the asymmetry in terms of the opposition. That's just *my* political style as opposed to theirs. I think without learning from them, this political style would be less, would begin to resemble more and more a kind of old-fashioned understanding of dialectics.

HARASYM   In 'Can the Subaltern Speak?' you argue that if the critique of the ideological subject constitution within state formation and systems of the 'political economy' and if the 'affirmative practice of the transformation of consciousness' are to be taken up, the shifting distinctions between representation as *Vertretung* (political representation) and as *Darstellung* must not be effaced. Could you elaborate on this distinction and indicate what place the double session of representation occupies within your work on the gendered subject?

SPIVAK   First, about *Vertretung*, stepping in someone's place, really. *Tritt* (from *treten*, the second half of *vertretung*) has the English cognate *tread*. So that it might make it easier to look at this word as a word. *Vertretung*, to tread in someone's shoes, represents that way. Your congressional person, if you are talking about the United States, actually puts on your shoes when he or she represents you. Treading in your shoes, wearing your shoes, that's *Vertretung*. Representation in that sense: political representation. *Darstellung – Dar*, there, same cognate. *Stellen*, is to place, so 'placing there.' *Representing*: proxy and portrait, as I said, these are two ways of representing. Now, the thing to remember is that in the act of representing politically, you actually represent yourself and your constituency in the portrait sense, as well. You have to think of your constituency as working class, or the black minority, the rainbow coalition, or yet the military-industrial complex and so on. That is representation in the sense of *Darstellung*. So that you do not ever 'simply' *vertreten* anyone, in fact, not just politically in the sense of true parliamentary forms, but even in political practices outside of parliamentary forms. When I speak as a feminist, I'm representing, in the sense of *Darstellung*, myself because we all know the problems attendant even upon defining the subject as a sovereign deliberative consciousness. But then if you take the sovereign deliberate consciousness and give it an adjective like feminist, that is, in fact, a rather narrow sense of self-representation, which you cannot avoid. But, what I'm saying is that this shifting line between treading in, the shoes of all the disenfranchised women in my corner, and if I were very hubristic I would say, in the world. That way of representing: I speak for them and represent them. *Darstelling* them, portraying them as constituencies of feminism, myself as a feminist. Unless the complicity between these two things is kept in mind, there can be a great deal of political harm. The debate between essentialism and anti-essentialism is really not the crucial debate. It is not possible to be non-essentialist, as I said; the subject is always centered. The real debate is between these two ways of representing. Even. non-fundamentalist philosophies must represent themselves as non-foundationalist philosophies. For example, you represent yourself when you speak *as* a deconstructor. There's the play between these two kinds of representations. And that's a much more interesting thing to keep in mind than always to say, 'I will not be an essentialist.'

I heard when I went to Alabama to listen to Derrida talking on Kant, that apparently in the morning – and I was unable to be present at the session in the morning – the speaker had referred to an expression of mine in that *Thesis Eleven* interview, 'strategic use of essentialism.' Hillis Miller actually told me this, and he said, 'Well, you know people talked about you and it was stressed that Stephen Heath had actually said this before you and that you had learned it from Stephen Heath.' I said, 'Well, I might have but not through reading the text. I don't know how then. I thought that I was thinking about this myself but who knows.' Then he said that the point was made that you had said that feminists have to be strategic essentialists. I said, 'Well, since I wasn't there, I don't know what was actually said. But I, myself, had thought I was saying that since it is not possible not to be an essentialist, one can self-consciously use this irreducible moment of essentialism as part of one's strategy. This can be used as part of a 'good' strategy as well as a 'bad' strategy and this can be used self-consciously as well as unself-consciously, and neither self-consciousness nor unself-consciousness can be valorized in my book. As for Stephen Heath, I don't know. The relationship between the two kinds of representation brings in, also, the use of essentialism because no representation can take place – no *Vertretung*, representation – can take place without essentialism. What it has to take into account is that the 'essence' that is being represented is a representation of the other kind, *Darstellung*. So that's the format, right, and I think I've already said enough about the format to show how this would apply to representing the gendered subject also.

One last word. The reason why I am so devoted to the fiction of Mahasweta Devi is because she is very careful about – and now since we are talking about literary technique, our terms take on a slightly different meaning – she is very careful about representing the gendered, subaltern as she represents her. So that single-issue bourgeois feminists, who want to represent themselves as *the* people – I'm now quoting Marx on the typical gesture of the petit bourgeoisie when they want themselves to be understood as *the* people, so that the 'real' people can take short shrift; they are very irritated about the fact that Mahasweta Devi doesn't do this herself, and speak *as* the gendered subaltern *herself*. But the strength of her texts is that this shifting play between the two kinds of representation is always intact there in various ways. That is what gives them their difficulty and that's what gives them their power.

HARASYM   When you were lecturing in Alberta you argued that Marxism, feminism and deconstruction must critically interrupt each other. Could you comment on this program?

SPIVAK   O.K., my notion of interruption. I kind of locate myself in that idea as a place of the reinscription of the dialectic into deconstruction. It's already there – interruption. My example is, always, Marx's discussion of industrial capitalism in *Capital*, Vol. 2, when he talks about the three moments of industrial capitalism interrupting each other, but, thus, providing a single circuit. He is using – it so happens that the example he is using is ambiguous. Industrial capitalism is not an unquestioned good in Marx, to say the least. But, on the other hand, if one reads Marx carefully, there is also the relationship between what Marx called *Vergesellschaftet* labor, which is translated as 'associated labor' in English, but it's not a very happy translation because *Vergesellschaftet* is a very awkward and clumsy word; whereas, associated labor is a common word which makes us think about various workers' associations and so on. But anyway, what Marx calls *Vergellschaftet* labor in his work learns a lot morphologically from what happens in the moment of industrial capitalism. This, unfortunately, has been narrativized into 'One must pass through advanced capitalism in order to get to socialism.' I can't talk about that in the interview because we are focusing on something else. But, to go back to industrial capitalism, its place is dubious. But, nonetheless, this morphological articulation of a necessary interruption which allows something to function is very interesting, and, just as I said in terms of the politics of the open end and the great-narrative politics in the same way, it seems to me, that Marxism which focuses and must focus in order to be useful (a) on labor that is productive of self-valorizing value and the problems of disguising that situation, and how, to use Marx's own words, how to read the proper signification of that scenario through the language of commodities, *Warensprache*, on the other hand, and feminism, on the other, is one of interruption. Feminism, must think of the human being predicated as work in senses other than this definition of the work that produces self-valorizing value. Feminism is involved with both anti-sexist work and transformation of consciousness outside of the Marxist project, which is to make the worker his (or her) unwitting production of capitalism. And deconstruction which is the critical moment, the reminder of catachresis, the reminder of the politics of the open end, or of the politics of great-narrative, depending on what the moment asks for, the reminder of the fact that any really 'loving' political practice must fall a prey to its own critique. This reminder is, also, and necessarily, an interruption of both of these projects.

Unless there is this understanding, there will be divisiveness in the radical camp. Crisis management in the global economy will, in fact, act according to these productive interruptions, and we, on the other side, like stupid fools will take the interruptions as divisive positions so we are at each other's throats.

And, of course, the historian and the teacher of literature is a small example, a small case, if you like, of what happens when disciplinary privileging makes us forget that we can pull together even if we bring each other in crisis. One of the great cases was E. P. Thompson and Althusser, in *The Poverty of Philosophy*. Another case now is Habermas' completely useless task of deriding Derrida. Habermas makes a lot of sense in the history of the West German political context. He makes a mistake by universalizing it. He also makes a mistake by confronting Derrida, whose project is quite discontinuous with his. How does he do it? By trivializing and canonizing a kind of disciplinary subdivision of labor, in his latest essay, *The Philosophical Discourse of Modernism*, where he chides Derrida because Derrida is not honoring the disciplinary prerogatives of philosophy and literature as they have developed in the European academy since the eighteenth century. And Habermas gives to rhetoric a completely trivializing definition as literary style, as it were, and in the interest of this kind of honoring of disciplinary subdivision of labor, which is quite useful up to a point, he throws away anything which might be useful in deconstruction. Just as I said, it's not a matter of throwing away one and keeping the other but bringing the two to productive crisis. You see these examples where one is privileged so that all you have is division – people can't work together anyway; whereas, on the other side, what wins is precisely people pulling together. That's my last word. Thank you.

HARASYM   Thank you.

See also:

Critchley (3.5)
Royle (4.4)
Elam (6.1)
Nancy (9.5)

8.5

'WHY DO EMPTY SIGNIFIERS MATTER IN POLITICS?'

Ernesto Laclau

THE SOCIAL PRODUCTION OF 'EMPTY SIGNIFIERS'

An empty signifier is, strictly speaking, a signifier without a signified. This definition is also, however, the enunciation of a problem. For how would it be possible that a signifier is not attached to any signified and remains, nevertheless, an integral part of a system of signification? An empty signifier would be a sequence of sounds, and if the latter are deprived of any signifying function the term 'signifier' itself would become excessive. The only possibility for a stream of sounds being detached from any particular signified while still remaining a signifier is if, through the subversion of the sign which the possibility of an empty signifier involves, something is achieved which is internal to significations as such. What is this possibility?

Some pseudo answers can be discarded quite quickly. One would be to argue that the same signifier can be attached to different signifieds in different contexts (as a result of the arbitrariness of the sign). But it is clear that, in that case, the signifier would not be *empty* but *equivocal*: the function of signification in each context would be fully realised. A second possibility is that the signifier is not *equivocal* but *ambiguous*: that either an overdetermination or an underdetermination of signifieds prevents it from being fully fixed. Yet this floating of the signifier still does not make it an empty one. Although the floating takes us one step towards the proper answer to our problem, the terms of the

Source: Ernesto Laclau, *Emancipations* (London: Verso, 1996), pp. 36–46.

latter are still avoided. We do not have to deal with an excess or deficiency of signification, but with the precise theoretical possibility of something which points, from within the process of signification, to the discursive presence of its own limits.

An empty signifier can, consequently, only emerge if there is a structural impossibility in signification as such, and only if this impossibility can signify itself as an interruption (subversion, distortion, etcetera) of the structure of the sign. That is, the limits of signification can only announce themselves as the impossibility of realizing what is within those limits – if the limits could be signified in a direct way, they would be internal to signification and, *ergo*, would not be limits at all.

An initial and purely formal consideration can help to clarify the point. We know, from Saussure, that language (and by extension, all signifying systems) is a system of differences, that linguistic identities – values – are purely relational and that, as a result, the totality of language is involved in each single act of signification. Now, in that case, it is clear that the totality is essentially required – if the differences did not constitute a system, no signification at all would be possible. The problem, however, is that the very possibility of signification is the system, and the very possibility of the system is the possibility of its limits. We can say, with Hegel, that to think of the limits of something is the same as thinking of what is beyond those limits. But if what we are talking about are the limits of a *signifying system*, it is clear that those limits cannot be themselves signified, but have to *show* themselves as the *interruption* or *breakdown* of the process of signification. Thus, we are left with the paradoxical situation that what constitutes the condition of possibility of a signifying system – its limits – is also what constitutes its condition of impossibility – a blockage of the continuous expansion of the process of signification.

A first and capital consequence of this is that true limits can never be neutral limits but presuppose an exclusion. A neutral limit would be one which is essentially continuous with what is at its two sides, and the two sides are simply different from each other. As a signifying totality is, however, precisely a system of differences, this means that both are part of the same system and that the limits between the two cannot be the limits of the system. In the case of an exclusion we have, instead, authentic limits because the actualization of what is beyond the limit of exclusion would involve the impossibility of what is this side of the limit. True limits are always antagonistic. But the operation of the logic of exclusionary limits has a series of necessary effects which spread to both sides of the limits and which will lead us straight into the emergence of empty signifiers:

1. A first effect of the exclusionary limit is that it introduces an essential ambivalence within the system of differences constituted by those limits. On the one hand, each element of the system has an identity only so far as it is different from the others: difference = identity. On the other hand, however, all these differences are equivalent to each other inasmuch as all of them

belong to this side of the frontier of exclusion. But, in that case, the identity of each element is constitutively split: on the one hand, each difference expresses itself *as*-difference; on the other hand, each of them *cancels* itself as such by entering into a relation of equivalence with all the other differences of the system. And, given that there is only system as long as there is radical exclusion, this split or ambivalence is constitutive of all systemic identity. It is only in so far as there is a radical impossibility of a system as pure presence, beyond all exclusions, that actual *systems* (in the plural) can exist. Now, if the systematicity of the system is a direct result of the exclusionary limit, it is only that exclusion that grounds the system as such. This point is essential because it results from it that the system cannot have a positive ground and that, as a result, it cannot signify itself in terms of any positive signified. Let us suppose for a moment that the systematic ensemble was the result of all its elements sharing a positive feature (for example that they all belonged to a regional category). In that case, that positive feature would be different from other differential positive features, and they would all appeal to a deeper systematic ensemble within which their differences would be thought of as differences. But a system constituted through radical exclusion interrupts this play of the differential logic: what is excluded from the system, far from being something positive, is the simple principle of positivity – pure being. This already announces the possibility of an empty signifier – that is a signifier of the pure cancellation of all difference.

2. The condition, of course, for this operation to be possible is that what is beyond the frontier of exclusion is reduced to pure negativity – that is to the pure threat that what is beyond poses to the system (constituting it that way). If the exclusionary dimension was eliminated, or even weakened, what would happen is that the differential character of the 'beyond' would impose itself and, as a result, the limits of the system would be blurred. Only if the beyond becomes the signifier of pure threat, of pure negativity, of the simply excluded, can there be limits and system (that is an objective order). But in order to be the signifiers of the excluded (or, simply of exclusion), the various excluded categories have to cancel their differences through the formation of a chain of equivalences to that which the system demonizes in order to signify itself. Again, we see here the possibility of an empty signifier announcing itself through this logic in which differences collapse into equivalential chains.

3. But, we could ask ourselves, why does this pure being or systematicity of the system, or – its reverse – the pure negativity of the excluded, require the production of empty signifiers in order to signify itself? The answer is that we are trying to signify the limits of signification – the real, if you want, in the Lacanian sense – and there is no direct way of doing so except through the subversion of the process of signification itself. We know, through psychoanalysis, how what is not directly representable – the unconscious – can only find as a means of representation the subversion of the signifying

process. Each signifier constitutes a sign by attaching itself to a particular signified, inscribing itself as a difference within the signifying process. But if what we are trying to signify is not a difference but, on the contrary, a radical exclusion which is the ground and condition of all differences, in that case, no production of *one more* difference can do the trick. As, however, all the means of representation are differential in nature, it is only if the differential nature of the signifying units is subverted, only if the signifiers empty themselves of their attachment to particular signifieds and assume the role of representing the pure being of the system – or, rather, the system as pure Being – that such a signification is possible. What is the ontological ground of such subversion, what makes it possible? The answer is: the split of each unit of signification that the system has to construct as the undecidable locus in which both the logic of difference and the logic of equivalence operate. It is only by privileging the dimension of equivalence to the point that its differential nature is almost entirely obliterated – that is emptying it of its differential nature – that the system can signify itself as a totality.

Two points have to be stressed here. The first is that the being or systematicity of the system which is represented through the empty signifiers is not a being which has not been *actually* realized, but one which is constitutively unreachable, for whatever systematic effects that would exist will be the result, as we have seen, of the unstable compromise between equivalence and difference. That is, we are faced with a constitutive lack, with an impossible object which, as in Kant, shows itself through the impossibility of its adequate representation. Here, we can give a full answer to our initial question: there can be empty signifiers within the field of signification because any system of signification is structured around an empty place resulting from the impossibility of producing an object which, none the less, is required by the systematicity of the system. So, we are not dealing with an impossibility without location, as in the case of a logical contradiction, but with a *positive* impossibility, with a *real* one to which the x of the empty signifier points.

However, if this impossible object lacks the means of its adequate or direct representation, this can only mean that the signifier which is emptied in order to assume the representing function will always be constitutively inadequate. What, in that case, does determine that one signifier rather than another assumes in different circumstances that signifying function? Here, we have to move to the main theme of this essay: the relation between empty signifiers and politics.

HEGEMONY

Let me go back to an example that we discussed in detail in *Hegemony and Socialist Strategy*:[1] the constitution, according to Rosa Luxemburg, of the unity of the working class through an overdetermination of partial struggles over a long period of time. Her basic argument is that the unity of the class is not determined by an a priori consideration about the priority of either the political struggle or the economic struggle, but by the accumulated effects of the internal split of all partial mobilizations. In relation to our subject, her argument amounts to approximately the following: in a climate of extreme repression any mobilization for a partial objective will be perceived not only as related to the concrete demand or objectives of that struggle, but also as an act of opposition against the system. This last fact is what establishes the link between a variety of concrete or partial struggles and mobilizations – all of them are seen as related to each other, not because their concrete objectives are intrinsically related but because they are all seen as equivalent in confrontation with the repressive regime. It is not, consequently, something positive that all of them share which establishes their unity, but something negative: their opposition to a common enemy. Luxemburg's argument is that a revolutionary mass identity is established through the overdetermination, over a whole historical period, of a plurality of separate struggles. These traditions fused, at the revolutionary moment, in a ruptural point.

Let us try to apply our previous categories to this sequence. The meaning (the signified) of all concrete struggles appears, right from the beginning, internally divided. The concrete aim of the struggle is not only that aim in its concreteness; it also signifies opposition to the system. The first signified establishes the differential character of that demand or mobilization *vis-à-vis* all other demands or mobilizations. The second signified establishes the equivalence of all these demands in their common opposition to the system. As we can see, any concrete struggle is dominated by this contradictory movement that simultaneously asserts and abolishes its own singularity. The function of representing the system as a totality depends, consequently, on the possibility of the equivalential function neatly prevailing over the differential one; but this possibility is simply the result of every single struggle always being already, originally, penetrated by this constitutive ambiguity.

It is important to observe that, as we have already established, if the function of the differential signifiers is to renounce their differential identity in order to represent the purely equivalential identity of a communitarian space as such, they cannot construct this equivalential identity as something belonging to a differential order. For instance: we can represent the Tzarist regime as a repressive order by enumerating the differential kinds of oppression that it imposed on various sections of the population as much as we want; but such enumeration will not give us the specificity of the repressive moment, that which constitutes – in its negation – what is peculiar to a repressive relation between entities. Because in such a relation each instance of the repressive power counts as pure bearer of the negation of the identity of the repressed sector. Now, if the differential identity of the repressive action is in that way 'distanced' from itself by having itself transformed into the mere incarnating body of the negation of the being of another entity, it is clear that between this negation and the body through which it expresses itself there is no necessary relation – nothing predetermines that one particular body should be the one predestined to incarnate negation as such.

It is precisely this which makes the relation of equivalence possible: different particular struggles are so many bodies which can indifferently incarnate the opposition of all of them to the repressive power. This involves a double movement. On the one hand, the more the chain of equivalences is extended, the less each concrete struggle will be able to remain closed in a differential self – in something which separates it from all other differential identities through a difference which is exclusively its own. On the contrary, as the equivalent relation shows that these differential identities are simply indifferent bodies incarnating something equally present in all of them, the longer the chain of equivalences is, the less concrete this 'something equally present' will be. At the limit it will be pure communitarian being independent of all concrete manifestation. And, on the other hand, that which is beyond the exclusion delimiting the communitarian space – the repressive power – will count less as the instrument of particular differential repressions and will express pure anti-community, pure evil and negation. The community created by this equivalential expansion will be, thus, the pure idea of a communitarian fullness which is absent – as a result of the presence of the repressive power.

But, at this point, the second movement starts. This pure equivalential function representing an absent fullness which shows itself through the collapse of all differential identities is something which cannot have a signifier of its own – for in that case, the 'beyond all differences' would be one more difference and not the result of the equivalential collapse of all differential identities. Precisely because the community as such is not a purely differential space of an objective identity but an absent fullness, it cannot have any form of representation of its own, and has to borrow the latter from some entity constituted within the equivalential space – in the same way as gold is a particular use value which assumes, as well, the function of representing value in general. This emptying of a particular signifier of its particular, differential signified is, as we saw, what makes possible the emergence of 'empty' signifiers as the signifiers of a lack, of an absent totality. But this leads us straight into the question with which we closed the previous section: if all differential struggles – in our example – are equally capable of expressing, beyond their differential identity, the absent fullness of the community; if the equivalential function makes all differential positions similarly indifferent to this equivalential representation; if none is predetermined *per se* to fulfil this role; what does determine that one of them rather than another incarnates, at particular periods of time, this universal function?

The answer is: the unevenness of the social. For if the equivalential logic tends to do away with the relevance of all differential location, this is only a tendential movement that is always resisted by the logic of difference which is essentially non-equalitarian. (It comes as no surprise that Hobbes's model of a state of nature, which tries to depict a realm in which the full operation of the logic of equivalence makes the community impossible, has to presuppose an original and essential equality between men.) Not any position in society, not any struggle is equally capable of transforming its own contents in a nodal point that becomes an empty signifier. Now, is this not to return to a rather traditional conception of the historical effectivity of social forces, one which asserts that the unevenness of structural locations determines which one of them is going to be the source of totalizing effects? No, it is not, because these uneven structural locations, some of which represent points of high concentration of power, are themselves the result of processes in which logics of difference and logics of equivalence overdetermine each other. It is not a question of denying the historical effectivity of the logic of differential structural locations but, rather, of denying to them, as a whole, the character of an infrastructure which would determine, out of itself, the laws of movement of society.

If this is correct, it is impossible to determine at the level of the mere analysis of the *form* difference/equivalence which particular difference is going to become the locus of equivalential effects – this requires the study of a particular conjuncture, precisely because the presence of equivalential effects is always necessary, but the relation equivalence/difference is not intrinsically linked to any particular differential content. This relation by which a particular content becomes the signifier of the absent communitarian fullness is exactly what we call a *hegemonic relationship*. The presence of empty signifiers – in the sense that we have defined them – is the very condition of hegemony. This can be easily seen if we address a very well known difficulty which forms a recurring stumbling block in most theorizations of hegemony – Gramsci's included. A class or group is considered to be hegemonic when it is not closed in a narrow corporatist perspective, but presents itself as realizing the broader aims either of emancipating or ensuring order for wider masses of the population. But this faces us with a difficulty if we do not determine precisely what these terms '*broader* aims', '*wider* masses' refer to. There are two possibilities: first, that society is an addition of discrete groups, each tending to their particular aims and in constant collision with each other. In that case, 'broader' and 'wider' could only mean the precarious equilibrium of a negotiated agreement between groups, all of which would retain their conflicting aims and identity. But 'hegemony' clearly refers to a stronger type of communitarian unity than such an agreement evokes. Second, that society has some kind of pre-established essence, so that the 'broader' and 'wider' has a content of its own, independent of the will of the particular groups, and that 'hegemony' would mean the realization of such an essence. But this would not only do away with the dimension of contingency which has always been associated with the hegemonic operation, but would also be incompatible with the consensual character of 'hegemony': the hegemonic order would be the *imposition* of a pre-given organizational principle and not something emerging from the political interaction between groups. Now, if we consider the matter from the point of view of the social production of empty signifiers, this problem vanishes. For in that case, the hegemonic operations would be the presentation of the particularity of a group as the incarnation of that empty signifier which refers to the communitarian order as an absence, an unfulfilled reality.

How does this mechanism operate? Let us consider the extreme situation of a radical disorganization of the social fabric. In such conditions – which are not far away from Hobbes's state of nature – people need *an* order, and the actual content of it becomes a secondary consideration. 'Order' as such has no content, because it only exists in the various forms in which it is actually realized, but in a situation of radical disorder 'order' is present as that which is absent; it becomes an empty signifier, as the signifier of that absence. In this sense, various political forces can compete in their efforts to present their particular objectives as those which carry out the filling of that lack. To hegemonize something is exactly to carry out this filling function. (We have spoken about 'order', but obviously 'unity', 'liberation', 'revolution', etcetera belong to the same order of things. Any term which, in a certain political context becomes the signifier of the lack, plays the same role. Politics is possible because the constitutive impossibility of society can only represent itself through the production of empty signifiers.)

This explains also why any hegemony is always unstable and penetrated by a constitutive ambiguity. Let us suppose that a workers' mobilization succeeds in presenting its own objectives as a signifier of 'liberation' in general. (This, as we have seen, is possible because the workers' mobilization, taking place under a repressive regime, is also seen as an anti-system struggle.) In one sense this is a hegemonic victory, because the objectives of a particular group are identified with society at large. But, in another sense, this is a dangerous victory. If 'workers' struggle' becomes the signifier of liberation as such, it also becomes the surface of inscription through which *all* liberating struggles will be expressed, so that the chain of equivalences which are unified around this signifier tend to empty it, and to blur its connection with the actual content with which it was originally associated. Thus, as a result of its very success, the hegemonic operation tends to break its links with the force which was its original promoter and beneficiary.

HEGEMONY AND DEMOCRACY

Let us conclude with some reflections on the relation between empty signifiers, hegemony and democracy.

Consider for a moment the role of social signifiers in the emergence of modern political thought – I am essentially thinking of the work of Hobbes. Hobbes, as we have seen, presented the state of nature as the radically opposite of an ordered society, as a situation only defined in negative terms. But, as a result of that description, the order of the ruler has to be accepted not because of any intrinsic virtue that it can have, but just because it is *an* order, and the only alternative is radical disorder. The condition, however, of the coherence of this scheme is the postulate of the equality of the power of individuals in the state of nature – if the individuals were uneven in terms of power, order could be guaranteed through sheer domination. So, power is eliminated twice: in the state of nature, as all individuals equally share in it, and in the commonwealth, as it is entirely concentrated in the hands of the ruler. (A power which is total or a power which is equally distributed among all members of the community is no power at all.) So, while Hobbes implicitly perceives the split between the empty signifier 'order as such' and the actual order imposed by the ruler, as he reduces – through the covenant – the first to the second, he cannot think of any kind of dialectical or hegemonic game between the two.

What happens if, on the contrary, we reintroduce power within the picture – that is if we accept the unevenness of power in social relations? In that case, civil society will be partially structured and partially unstructured and, as a result, the total concentration of power in the hands of the ruler ceases to be a logical requirement. But in that case, the credentials of the ruler to claim total power are much less obvious. If partial order exists in society, the legitimacy of the identification of the empty signifier of order with the will of the ruler will have the further requirement that the content of this will does not clash with something the society *already* is. As society changes over time this process of identification will be always precarious and reversible and, as the identification is no longer automatic, different projects or wills will try to hegemonize the empty signifiers of the absent community. The recognition of the constitutive nature of this gap and its political institutionalization is the starting point of modern democracy.

NOTE

1. Ernesto Laclau and Chantal Mouffe, *Hegemony and Socialist Strategy*, London, Verso 1985.

See also:

Marx (1.1)
Benjamin (1.4)
Lyotard (3.6)
Butler (5.6)

8.6

'OF MIMICRY AND MAN: THE AMBIVALENCE OF COLONIAL DISCOURSE'

Homi K. Bhabha

Mimicry reveals something in so far as it is distinct from what might be called an itself that is behind. The effect of mimicry is camouflage . . . It is not a question of harmonizing with the background, but against a mottled background, of becoming mottled – exactly like the technique of camouflage practised in human warfare.

Jacques Lacan, 'The line and light', Of the Gaze.

It is out of season to question at this time of day, the original policy of a conferring on every colony of the British Empire a mimic representation of the British Constitution. But if the creature so endowed has sometimes forgotten its real significance and under the fancied importance of speakers and maces, and all the paraphernalia and ceremonies of the imperial legislature, has dared to defy the mother country, she has to thank herself for the folly of conferring such privileges on a condition of society that has no earthly claim to so exalted a position. A fundamental principle appears to have been forgotten or overlooked in our system of colonial policy – that of colonial dependence. To give to a colony the forms of independence is a mockery; she would not be a colony for a single hour if she could maintain an independent station.

Sir Edward Cust, 'Reflections on West African affairs . . .
addressed to the Colonial Office', Hatchard, London 1839.

The discourse of post-Enlightenment English colonialism often speaks in a tongue that is forked, not false. If colonialism takes power in the name of history, it repeatedly exercises its authority through the figures of farce. For the

Source: Homi K. Bhabha, *The Location of Culture* (London: Routledge, 1994), pp. 85–92.

epic intention of the civilizing mission, 'human and not wholly human' in the famous words of Lord Rosebery, 'writ by the finger of the Divine' often produces a text rich in the traditions of *trompe-l'oeil*, irony, mimicry and repetition. In this comic turn from the high ideals of the colonial imagination to its low mimetic literary effects mimicry emerges as one of the most elusive and effective strategies of colonial power and knowledge.

Within that conflictual economy of colonial discourse which Edward Said describes as the tension between the synchronic panoptical vision of domination – the demand for identity, stasis – and the counter-pressure of the diachrony of history – change, difference – mimicry represents an *ironic* compromise. If I may adapt Samuel Weber's formulation of the marginalizing vision of castration then colonial mimicry is the desire for a reformed, recognizable Other, *as a subject of a difference that is almost the same, but not quite*. Which is to say, that the discourse of mimicry is constructed around an *ambivalence*; in order to be effective, mimicry must continually produce its slippage, its excess, its difference. The authority of that mode of colonial discourse that I have called mimicry is therefore stricken by an indeterminacy: mimicry emerges as the representation of a difference that is itself a process of disavowal. Mimicry is, thus the sign of a double articulation; a complex strategy of reform, regulation and discipline, which 'appropriates' the Other as it visualizes power. Mimicry is also the sign of the inappropriate, however, a difference or recalcitrance which coheres the dominant strategic function of colonial power, intensifies surveillance, and poses an immanent threat to both 'normalized' knowledges and disciplinary powers.

The effect of mimicry on the authority of colonial discourse is profound and disturbing. For in 'normalizing' the colonial state or subject, the dream of post-Enlightenment civility alienates its own language of liberty and produces another knowledge of its norms. The ambivalence which thus informs this strategy is discernible, for example, in Locke's Second Treatise which *splits* to reveal the limitations of liberty in his double use of the word 'slave': first simply, descriptively as the locus of a legitimate form of ownership, then as the trope for an intolerable, illegitimate exercise of power. What is articulated in that distance between the two uses is the absolute, imagined difference between the 'Colonial' State of Carolina and the Original State of Nature.

It is from this area between mimicry and mockery, where the reforming, civilizing mission is threatened by the displacing gaze of its disciplinary double, that my instances of colonial imitation come. What they all share is a discursive process by which the excess or slippage produced by the *ambivalence* of mimicry (almost the same, *but not quite*) does not merely 'rupture' the discourse, but becomes transformed into an uncertainty which fixes the colonial subject as a 'partial' presence. By 'partial' I mean both 'incomplete' and 'virtual'. It is as if the very emergence of the 'colonial' is dependent for its representation upon some strategic limitation or prohibition *within* the authoritative discourse itself. The success of colonial appropriation depends on a proliferation of inappropriate objects that ensure its strategic failure, so that mimicry is at once resemblance and menace.

A classic text of such partiality is Charles Grant's 'Observations on the state of society among the Asiatic subjects of Great Britain' (1792) which was only superseded by James Mills's *History of India* as the most influential early nineteenth-century account of Indian manners and morals. Grant's dream of an evangelical system of mission education conducted uncompromisingly in the English language, was partly a belief in political reform along Christian lines and partly an awareness that the expansion of company rule in India required a system of subject formation – a reform of manners, as Grant put it – that would provide the colonial with 'a sense of personal identity as we know it'. Caught between the desire for religious reform and the fear that the Indians might become turbulent for liberty, Grant paradoxically implies that it is the 'partial' diffusion of Christianity, and the 'partial' influence of moral improvements which will construct a particularly appropriate form of colonial subjectivity. What is suggested is a process of reform through which Christian doctrines might collude with divisive caste practices to prevent dangerous political alliances. Inadvertently, Grant produces a knowledge of Christianity as a form of social control which conflicts with the enunciatory assumptions that authorize his discourse. In suggesting, finally, that 'partial reform' will produce an empty form of 'the *imitation* [my emphasis] of English manners which will induce them [the colonial subjects] to remain under our protection'. Grant mocks his moral project and violates the Evidence of Christianity – a central missionary tenet – which forbade any tolerance of heathen faiths.

The absurd extravagance of Macaulay's 'Minute' (1835) – deeply influenced by Charles Grant's 'Observations' – makes a mockery of Oriental learning until faced with the challenge of conceiving of a 'reformed' colonial subject. Then, the great tradition of European humanism seems capable only of ironizing itself. At the intersection of European learning and colonial power, Macaulay can conceive of nothing other than 'a class of interpreters between us and the millions whom we govern – a class of persons Indian in blood and colour, but English in tastes, in opinions, in morals and in intellect' – in other words a mimic man raised 'through our English School', as a missionary educationist wrote in 1819, 'to form a corps of translators and be employed in different departments of Labour'. The line of descent of the mimic man can be traced through the works of Kipling, Forster, Orwell, Naipaul, and to his emergence, most recently, in Benedict Anderson's excellent work on nationalism, as the anomalous Bipin Chandra Pal. He is the effect of a flawed colonial mimesis, in which to be Anglicized is *emphatically* not to be English.

The figure of mimicry is locatable within what Anderson describes as 'the inner compatibility of empire and nation'. It problematizes the signs of racial and cultural priority, so that the 'national' is no longer naturalizable. What emerges between mimesis and mimicry is a *writing*, a mode of representation, that marginalizes the monumentality of history, quite simply mocks its power to be a model, that power which supposedly makes it imitable. Mimicry *repeats* rather than *re-presents* and in that diminishing perspective emerges Decoud's displaced European vision of Sulaco in Conrad's *Nostromo* as:

> the endlessness of civil strife where folly seemed even harder to bear than its ignominy ... the lawlessness of a populace of all colours and races, barbarism, irremediable tyranny ... America is ungovernable.

Or Ralph Singh's apostasy in Naipaul's *The Mimic Men*:

> We pretended to be real, to be learning, to be preparing ourselves for life, we mimic men of the New World, one unknown corner of it, with all its reminders of the corruption that came so quickly to the new.

Both Decoud and Singh, and in their different ways Grant and Macaulay, are the parodists of history. Despite their intentions and invocations they inscribe the colonial text erratically, eccentrically across a body politic that refuses to be representative, in a narrative that refuses to be representational. The desire to emerge as 'authentic' through mimicry – through a process of writing and repetition – is the final irony of partial representation.

What I have called mimicry is not the familiar exercise of *dependent* colonial relations through narcissistic identification so that, as Fanon has observed, the black man stops being an actional person for only the white man can represent his self-esteem. Mimicry conceals no presence or identity behind its mask: it is not what Césaire describes as 'colonization-thingification' behind which there stands the essence of the *présence Africaine*. The *menace* of mimicry is its *double* vision which in disclosing the ambivalence of colonial discourse also disrupts its authority. And it is a double vision that is a result of what I've described as the partial representation/recognition of the colonial object. Grant's colonial as partial imitator, Macaulay's translator, Naipaul's colonial politician as play-actor, Decoud as the scene setter of the *opéra bouffe* of the New World, these are the appropriate objects of a colonialist chain of command, authorized versions of otherness. But they are also, as I have shown, the figures of a doubling, the part-objects of a metonymy of colonial desire which alienates the modality and normality, of those dominant discourses in which they emerge as 'inappropriate' colonial subjects. A desire that, through the repetition of *partial presence*, which is the basis of mimicry, articulates those disturbances of cultural, racial and historical difference that menace the narcissistic demand of colonial authority. It is a desire that reverses 'in part' the colonial appropriation by now producing a partial vision of the colonizer's presence; a gaze of otherness, that shares the acuity of the genealogical gaze which, as Foucault describes it, liberates marginal elements and shatters the unity of man's being through which he extends his sovereignty.

I want to turn to this process by which the look of surveillance returns as the displacing gaze of the disciplined, where the observer becomes the observed and 'partial' representation rearticulates the whole notion of *identity* and alienates it from essence. But not before observing that even an exemplary history like Eric Stokes's *The English Utilitarians and India* acknowledges the anomalous gaze of otherness but finally disavows it in a contradictory utterance:

> Certainly India played *no* central part in fashioning the distinctive qualities of English civilisation. In many ways it acted as a disturbing force, a magnetic power placed at the periphery tending to distort the natural development of Britain's character. (My emphasis)

What is the nature of the hidden threat of the partial gaze? How does mimicry emerge as the subject of the scopic drive and the object of colonial surveillance? How is desire disciplined, authority displaced?

If we turn to a Freudian figure to address these issues of colonial textuality, that form of difference that is mimicry – *almost the same but not quite* – will become clear. Writing of the partial nature of fantasy, caught *inappropriately*, between the unconscious and the preconscious, making problematic, like mimicry, the very notion of 'origins', Freud has this to say:

> Their mixed and split origin is what decides their fate. We may compare them with individuals of mixed race who taken all round resemble white men but who betray their coloured descent by some striking feature or other and on that account are excluded from society and enjoy none of the privileges.

Almost the same but not white: the visibility of mimicry is always produced at the site of interdiction. It is a form of colonial discourse that is uttered *inter dicta*: a discourse at the crossroads of what is known and permissible and that which though known must be kept concealed; a discourse uttered between the lines and as such both against the rules and within them. The question of the representation of difference is therefore always also a problem of authority. The 'desire' of mimicry, which is Freud's 'striking feature' that reveals so little but makes such a big difference, is not merely that impossibility of the Other which repeatedly resists signification. The desire of colonial mimicry – an interdictory desire – may not have an object, but it has strategic objectives which I shall call the *metonymy of presence*.

Those inappropriate signifiers of colonial discourse – the difference between being English and being Anglicized; the identity between stereotypes which, through repetition, also become different; the discriminatory identities constructed across traditional cultural norms and classifications, the Simian Black, the Lying Asiatic – all these are *metonymies* of presence. They are strategies of desire in discourse that make the anomalous representation of the colonized something other than a process of 'the return of the repressed', what Fanon unsatisfactorily characterized as collective catharsis. These instances of metonymy are the non-repressive productions of contradictory and multiple belief.

They cross the boundaries of the culture of enunciation through a strategic confusion of the metaphoric and metonymic axes of the cultural production of meaning.

In mimicry, the representation of identity and meaning is rearticulated along the axis of metonymy. As Lacan reminds us, mimicry is like camouflage, not a harmonization of repression of difference, but a form of resemblance, that differs from or defends presence by displaying it in part, metonymically. Its threat, I would add, comes from the prodigious and strategic production of conflictual, fantastic, discriminatory 'identity effects' in the play of a power that is elusive because it hides no essence, no 'itself'. And that form of *resemblance* is the most terrifying thing to behold, as Edward Long testifies in his *History of Jamaica* (1774). At the end of a tortured, negrophobic passage, that shifts anxiously between piety, prevarication and perversion, the text finally confronts its fear; nothing other than the repetition of its resemblance 'in part': '[Negroes] are represented by all authors as the vilest of human kind, to which they have little more pretension of resemblance *than what arises from their exterior forms*' (my emphasis).

From such a colonial encounter between the white presence and its black semblance, there emerges the question of the ambivalence of mimicry as a problematic of colonial subjection. For if Sade's scandalous theatricalization of language repeatedly reminds us that discourse can claim 'no priority', then the work of Edward Said will not let us forget that the 'ethnocentric and erratic will to power from which texts can spring' is itself a theatre of war. Mimicry, as the metonymy of presence is, indeed, such an erratic, eccentric strategy of authority in colonial discourse. Mimicry does not merely destroy narcissistic authority through the repetitious slippage of difference and desire. It is the process of the *fixation* of the colonial as a form of cross-classificatory, discriminatory knowledge within an interdictory discourse, and therefore necessarily raises the question of the *authorization* of colonial representations; a question of authority that goes beyond the subject's lack of priority (castration) to a historical crisis in the conceptuality of colonial man as an *object* of regulatory power, as the subject of racial, cultural, national representation.

'This culture ... fixed in its colonial status', Fanon suggests, '[is] both present and mummified, it testified against its members. It defines them in fact without appeal.' The ambivalence of mimicry – almost but not quite – suggests that the fetishized colonial culture is potentially and strategically an insurgent counter-appeal. What I have called its 'identity-effects' are always crucially *split*. Under cover of camouflage, mimicry, like the fetish, is a part-object that radically revalues the normative knowledges of the priority of race, writing, history. For the fetish mimes the forms of authority at the point at which it deauthorizes them. Similarly, mimicry rearticulates presence in terms of its 'otherness', that which it disavows. There is a crucial difference between this *colonial* articulation of man and his doubles and that which Foucault describes as 'thinking the unthought' which, for nineteenth-century Europe, is the ending of man's alienation by reconciling him with his essence. The colonial discourse that articulates an *interdictory* otherness is precisely the 'other scene' of this nineteenth-century European desire for an authentic historical consciousness.

The 'unthought' across which colonial man is articulated is that process of classificatory confusion that I have described as the metonymy of the substitutive chain of ethical and cultural discourse. This results in the *splitting* of colonial discourse so that two attitudes towards external reality persist; one takes reality into consideration while the other disavows it and replaces it by a product of desire that repeats, rearticulates 'reality' as mimicry.

So Edward Long can say with authority, quoting variously Hume, Eastwick and Bishop Warburton in his support, that: 'Ludicrous as the opinion may seem I do not think that an orangutang husband would be any dishonour to a Hottentot female.'

Such contradictory articulations of reality and desire – seen in racist stereotypes, statements, jokes, myths – are not caught in the doubtful circle of the return of the repressed. They are the effects of a disavowal that denies the differences of the other but produces in its stead forms of authority and multiple belief that alienate the assumptions of 'civil' discourse. If, for a while, the ruse of desire is calculable for the uses of discipline soon the repetition of guilt, justification, pseudo-scientific theories, superstition, spurious authorities, and classifications can be seen as the desperate effort to 'normalize' *formally* the disturbance of a discourse of splitting that violates the rational, enlightened claims of its enunciatory modality. The ambivalence of colonial authority repeatedly turns from *mimicry* – a difference that is almost nothing but not quite – to *menace* – a difference that is almost total but not quite. And in that other scene of colonial power, where history turns to farce and presence to 'a part' can be seen the twin figures of narcissism and paranoia that repeat furiously, uncontrollably.

In the ambivalent world of the 'not quite/not white', on the margins of metropolitan desire, the *founding objects* of the Western world become the erratic, eccentric, accidental *objets trouvés* of the colonial discourse – the part-objects of presence. It is then that the body and the book lose their part-objects of presence. It is then that the body and the book lose their representational authority. Black skin splits under the racist gaze, displaced into signs of bestiality, genitalia, grotesquerie, which reveal the phobic myth of the undifferentiated whole white body. And the holiest of books – the Bible – bearing both the standard of the cross and the standard of empire finds itself strangely dismembered. In May 1817 a missionary wrote from Bengal:

> Still everyone would gladly receive a Bible. And why? – that he may lay it
> up as a curiosity for a few pice; or use it for waste paper. Such it is well

known has been the common fate of these copies of the Bible ... Some have been bartered in the markets, others have been thrown in snuff shops and used as wrapping paper.

See also:

Critchley (3.5)
Young (6.2)
Cornell (9.3)
Lacoue-Labarthe (9.4)

PART 9
ETHICS

9.1

'JACQUES DERRIDA: WHOLLY OTHERWISE'

Emmanuel Levinas

TODAY IS TOMORROW

Does Derrida's work constitute a line of demarcation running through the development of Western thought in a manner analogous to Kantianism, which separated dogmatic from critical philosophy? Are we once again at the end of a naivety, an unsuspected dogmatism that slumbered in the depths of what we took to be the critical spirit? We may well ask ourselves that question. The Idea, as the end of a series that begins in intuition but is unable to reach its end within it – the Idea 'in the Kantian sense of the term' as it is called – is, according to Derrida, operative at the heart of intuition itself. A transcendental semblance, engendering a metaphysics, produces an illusion at the heart of presence itself, which is incessantly lacking to itself. Is this a new break in the history of philosophy? It would also show its continuity. The history of philosophy is probably nothing but a growing awareness of the difficulty of thinking.

In the meantime, we tread a *no-man's land*, an in-between that is uncertain even of the uncertainties that flicker everywhere. Suspension of truths! Unusual times! We all feel this as we write, perhaps to the degree that we catch ourselves using familiar ideas with excessive caution, while the new critique would question both the sense of risk and the virtue of prudence. We become aware of a new style of thought as we read these exceptionally precise, yet very strange texts. In *Speech and Phenomena*, which overthrows logocentric discourse, there

---

Source: Emmanuel Levinas, *Proper Names* (Stanford: Stanford University Press, 1997), pp. 55–62.

is not a haphazard phrase. A marvelous rigor, learned at the school of pheno-menology, by devoting extreme attention to Husserl's discrete moves and Heidegger's more sweeping ones, but applied with consistency and consum-mate skill: an inversion of the limiting concept into precondition, of defect into source, of abyss into condition, of discourse into locus [*lieu*], and the inversion of these very inversions into destiny: the concepts having been stripped of their ontic resonance, freed from the alternative of true or false. At the outset, everything is in place; after a few pages or paragraphs of formidable calling into question, nothing is left inhabitable for thought. This is, all philosophical significance aside, a purely literary effect, a new *frisson*, Derrida's poetry. In reading him, I always see the 1940 exodus again. The retreating military unit reaches an area that still doesn't know what is happening. The cafés are open, the ladies are at the 'Ladies' Latest' stores, barbers are cutting hair, bakers are baking, viscounts meeting and telling one another viscount stories. An hour later, everything is torn down [*déconstruit*] and left desolate: the houses closed up, or abandoned with their doors open, are emptied of their inhabitants, who are caught up in a stream of cars and pedestrians through the streets, which have reverted to their 'deep past' ['*profond jadis*'] of routes, traced out in an immemorial past by the great migrations. In those days of a time between times, there occurred the following symbolic episode. Somewhere between Paris and Alençon, a half-drunk barber invited the soldiers who were passing by on the road (the 'boys,' [les '*petits gars*'] as he called them, in a patriotic language gliding above the waters, or keeping afloat in the chaos) to come into his little shop for a free shave. He, along with his two co-workers, shaved them for free and suddenly it was today. The essential procrastination – the future *différence* – was reabsorbed into the present. Time was reaching its end with the end, or the interim, of France. Or was the barber as delirious as the fourth form of delirium in the *Phaedrus*, a delirium in which, since Plato, the discourse of Western metaphysics is conducted?

THE PASS-TIME

Philosophy as defeat, desertion of an impossible presence. Western metaphy-sics, and probably our entire history in Europe, may turn out to have been, through a conceptual apparatus that Derrida dismantles or deconstructs, the edification and preservation of that presence: the founding of the very idea of foundation, the founding of all the relations that become experience, i.e. the manifestation of beings architectonically arranged on a basis that supports them, the manifestation of a world that is capable of being constructed, or, as the expression goes, of constituting itself for a transcendental apperception. Presence of the present, gathering, synchrony. Leave nothing lying about! Don't lose anything! Keep everything that is yours! The security of the peoples of Europe behind their borders and the walls of their houses, assured of their property (*Eigenheit* that becomes *Eigentum*), is not the sociological condition of metaphysical thought, but the very project of such thought. A project impossible of accomplishment, ever deferred, a *messianic future* as that missing present. *Speech and Phenomena* denounces this metaphysical simulacrum of presence, which is sustained by the voice that listens to itself: presence and possession united in self-consciousness. A simulacrum or an illusion, but prior to ontic illusion and appearance, prior to the distinction between reality and fantasy. All materialism is marked by this, as is all idealism.

The desertion of presence, carried out to the point of desertion of the true, to the point of meanings that are no longer held to respond to the summons of Knowledge. Truth is no longer at the level of eternal or omnitemporal truth – but this is a relativism beyond historicism's wildest dreams. An exile or casting adrift of Knowledge beyond skepticism, which remained enamored of truth, even if it did not feel itself capable of embracing it. Henceforth meanings do not converge on truth. Truth is not the main thing! Being does not succeed in being all the way: its bankrupt way of life needs more time to pay, recourse to signs, amidst a presence that eludes itself; but in the signified of these signs nothing but signs are produced. Husserl's notion of infinite iteration, which he understood by means of the 'idea in the Kantian sense,' endlessly postpones the contemporaneousness of the signified with a presence. The latter, always pointed toward, escapes prehension. Hence the wearing away of the signified, releasing a system of signs, of signifiers without signifieds, of a language that no full meaning guides. Thus is expressed, in the guise of dissemination, the *différence* in which presence is deconstructed, a postponement without due date to be met, which time is, or, more precisely, which the pass-time itself is. Play within the interstices of being, in which the centers of gravity are not the same as in the world. But are there centers? Is there gravity? Is there there is [*Y a-t-il*]? All is otherwise, if one can still speak of being.

What remains constructed after deconstruction is, to be sure, the stern architecture of the discourse that deconstructs and uses the verb 'to be' in the present tense in predicative statements. A discourse in the course of which, amidst the quaking of truth's underpinnings and in opposition to the self-evidence of the lived presence, which seems to offer presence a last refuge, Derrida still has the strength to utter: 'Is this certain?' As if anything could be certain at that point, and as if certainty or uncertainty should still matter.

One might be tempted to draw an argument from this recourse to logocentric language in opposing that very language, in order to question the validity of the deconstruction thus produced. That is a course that has frequently been followed in refuting skepticism; but the latter, thrown to the ground and trampled on at first, would right itself and return as philosophy's legitimate child. It is a course Derrida himself, perhaps, has not always disdained to follow in his polemics.

But in pursuing that course, we would risk missing the significance of that very inconsistency. We would miss the incompressible non-simultaneity of the Said and the Saying, the discrepancy in their correlation: a very slight discrepancy, but wide enough for the discourse of skepticism to creep into it without being choked off by the contradiction between what its *said* means and the meaning of the very fact of uttering a *said*. It is as if the two meanings lacked the simultaneity that would be required for contradiction to sunder their connection. It is as if the correlation of the *Saying* and the *Said* were a diachrony of the unassemblable; and as if the situation of the Saying were already, for the Said, a 'retention memory,' but without the lapse of the instants of the Saying letting themselves be recovered in this memory.

The truth of truths, then, cannot be gathered into an instant, nor into a synthesis in which the so-called movement of the dialectic would stop. It [the truth of truths] is in the Said and the Un-Said [*le Dédit*] and the Said Otherwise – return, reiteration, reduction: the history of philosophy, or its preliminary. Is that what Blanchot suggests in *L'attente L'oubli*, giving the subject of the statement a predicate that is successively in the affirmative and the negative? The truth of truths may not have the style of verbal dissemination; but it is of the same non-world, the end of the 'eternal truths,' whose death-throes and figures of convulsion are unsuspected by both empiricism and historical relativism. It is therefore not absurd that a rigorous reflection should vouchsafe us a glimpse of these interstices of being, in which that very reflection unsays itself. Nothing can be seen without thematization, or without the oblique rays reflected by it, even in the case of the non-thematizable.

The path leading toward these pathless 'places,' the subsoil of our empirical places, does not, in any case, open out upon the dizziness caused by those who – frightfully well informed and prodigiously intelligent and more Derridian than Derrida – interpret the latter's extraordinary work with the help of all the key words at once, though neither having, nor leaving to their readers, the time to return to the thinking that was contemporary with those words.

THE CHIASMUS

Derrida's critique – which frees time from its subordination to the present, which no longer takes the past and the future as modes, modifications, or modulations of presence, which arrests a thinking that reasons upon signs as if upon signifieds – thinks through to the end Bergson's critique of being and Kant's critique of metaphysics. Through that deconstruction of presence, the testimony of consciousness to itself loses its Cartesian privilege. Must we excuse ourselves for quoting these old authors? It doesn't prevent this doggedly rectilinear thinking ['*jusqu'au boutisme*'] from leading us into the strange non-order of the excluded middle, in which the disjunction of the yes and no, the imperious alternative, thanks to which computers decide about the universe, is challenged.

It will be less readily recognized – Derrida would probably refuse to do so – that this critique of being in its eternal presence of ideality allows us, for the first time in the history of the West, to conceive of *the being of the creature* without resorting to the ontic narrative of a divine operation – without treating the 'being' ['*être*'] of the creature as *a* being [*un étant*] from the outset, without bringing to bear negative and empirical concepts, such as contingency or 'generation and corruption' – concepts as ontic as the incorruptibility of the Whole. For the first time, the 'less being,' which is that of the creature, is shown in its verbality of verb. It is true that, in order to avoid the return of the metaphysics of presence in that thought, Derrida would have the reader seek, for the operative concept of the sign of a failed presence, a reference other than the failure of that presence, and a place [*lieu*] other than the Said of language (oral or written) – a place other than a language, which, completely at the disposal of the speaker, itself feigns synchrony, the pre-eminent presence of a system of signs that is already presupposed by any empirical simultaneity. But would not any attempt to express this lack of presence positively be still one more way of returning to presence, with which positivity converges? To say that this lack is still being is to turn in the circle of being and nothingness (which are ultimate concepts, but of the same degree) and retain nothing of being but a taste for unhappiness. It is no doubt surer than the hoped-for happiness, which, beyond the pleasures and intoxications, is the impossible fullness of presence. But is there no way out of ontology?

The fact that language is grafted upon time's most invisible difference, that its saying is dislocated from its said, and that the correlation is not rigorous (already rupturing the unity of apperception, and, consequently, the possibilities of experience) – certainly sets language apart from everything empirical, which is exhausted in presence and lack of presence. Indeed, it would be necessary one day to find, setting out from Saying and its own meaning, Saying's correlation with the Said – and this is not impossible. But the Saying is not exhausted in this *Said*, and the sign did not spring from the soil of the ontology of the Said, to receive from it its paradoxical structure of relation (which astonished Plato to the point of pushing him to parricide) and make up for a self-eluding presence. The sign, like the Saying, is the extra-ordinary event (running counter to presence) of exposure to others, of subjection to others; i.e. the event of subjectivity. It is the one-for-the-other. It is meaning that is not exhausted in a simple absence of intuition and of presence. I enquire: Whence the sign from which the presence that is lacking to itself is made, or the inassemblable diachrony from which creatureliness is made? It does not begin (if it does begin, if it is not anarchy through and through) as a Said. Is not substitution, replacement, the one-for-the-other – in its decisive suspension of the *for itself* – the for-the-other of my responsibility for others? The difference between the Same and the Other is the non-indifference for the other of fraternity. What appears truly in deconstructive analysis as a lacking to self is not *the surplus* (which would be yet another promise of happiness and a residuum of ontology) but the *better* of proximity, an excellence, an elevation, the ethics of before being or the Good beyond Being, again to quote an ancient author. The presence of the present that Descartes discovered in the *cogito*, without suspecting the unconscious that undermined it, immediately burst apart with the idea of God that it could not contain.

I shall not prolong the trajectory of a thought in the opposite direction from the one toward which its verb disseminates itself. The ridiculous ambition of 'improving' a true philosopher is assuredly not my intent. Our crossing of paths is already very good, and it is probably the very modality of the philosophical encounter. In emphasizing the primordial importance of the questions raised by Derrida, I have desired to express the pleasure of a contact at the heart of a chiasmus.

See also:

Critchley (3.5)
Lyotard (3.6)
Cixous (6.6)
Derrida (10.3)

9.2

'THE TRACE OF LEVINAS IN DERRIDA'

Robert Bernasconi

The lecture 'La différance' was delivered to the Société Française de philosophie in 1968. In a summary provided on that occasion, Derrida records how the nonword or nonconcept *différance* assembles 'the juncture of what has been most decisively inscribed in the thought of what we conveniently call our "epoch."' He names in this regard five thinkers and certain fundamental ideas associated with them: 'the difference of forces in Nietzsche, Saussure's principle of semiological difference, differing as the possibility of facilitation, impression and delayed effect in Freud, difference as the irreducibility of the trace of the other in Levinas, and the ontic-ontological difference in Heidegger.'[1] The emphasis in the summary is on difference, but the notion of trace could have served to unite the theme of the lecture almost as well. The trace provides the focus for Derrida's discussion of Saussure, Freud, and Heidegger at least as much as the notion of difference does. And although it could be said that no discussion of Nietzsche and the trace is offered, it could equally well be observed that, in the short paragraph devoted to Levinas, it is the trace and not difference which is specified: 'A past that has never been present: with this formula Emmanuel Levinas designates (in ways that are, to be sure, not those of psychoanalysis) the trace and the enigma of absolute alterity, that is, the Other. At least within these limits, and from this point of view, the thought of *différance* implies the whole critique of classical ontology undertaken by Levinas' (M [*Marges – de la philosophie* (1972)] 22/21; SP [*Speech and Phenomena*] 152).[2]

Source: Robert Bernasconi and David Wood (eds), *Derrida and Différance* (Evanston, IL: Northwestern University Press, 1988), pp. 13–29.

Most of Derrida's writings up to this time had been readings of texts. His writing had been interwoven into the text or texts of another – as a supplement. And yet in 'La différance' only the discussion of Heidegger is actually a reading of this kind. For the rest, Derrida's lecture is still parasitic, but not directly parasitic on the texts of another so much as on his own texts, his own previous readings. The discussion of Freud in 'La différance' draws on the essay 'Freud and the Scene of Writing,' as the discussion of Saussure draws on material contained in the chapter 'Linguistics and Grammatology' in *Of Grammatology*. And Derrida's long essay of 1964, 'Violence and Metaphysics,' provides the justification for the place accorded to Levinas in 'La différance' as well as making good the lack of any discussion there of difference in Levinas; if we return to 'Violence and Metaphysics,' we find discussions both of the difference between the same and other and of the difference between totality and infinity, which difference Derrida identifies as history (*ED L'écriture et la différance* 170/116, 180/123). So, as befitted the occasion, 'La différance' has all the appearance of being a summary of what Derrida had accomplished elsewhere.

Yet, by offering this distillation of the thinking of our epoch, Derrida does more than simply repeat himself; the resulting montage – this 'assemblage' – amounts to more than a summary (*M* 3–4; *SP* 131–32). In this essay I shall be concerned with whether the inclusion of Levinas among the five thinkers necessitated a rewriting of the conclusions of 'Violence and Metaphysics.' For in 'Violence and Metaphysics' Derrida seems to reject the notion of the trace. We read, 'The notion of a past whose meaning could not be thought in the form of a (past) present marks the *impossible-unthinkable-unsayable* not only for philosophy in general but even for a thought of being which would seek to take a step outside philosophy.'[3] How then does Derrida come to reintroduce the Levinasian trace into 'La différance' with apparent approval?

The question arises not only in relation to 'La différance.' Already in January 1966, in a discussion of Saussure, Derrida appealed to the 'concept of trace which is at the center of the latest writings of Levinas.'[4] And the appeal was made without mention of the trace as it appears in Freud or Heidegger, references which were added only subsequently when the essay was revised to form the basis for the chapter 'Linguistics and Grammatology' in *Of Grammatology*. But in 1966 Derrida brought to Levinas's notion of the trace, not as in 'La différance' Heidegger's usage of a similar term with which it could be conjoined, but 'a Heideggerian intention.' This serves to remind us that Derrida had at this time done very little to distance himself from Heidegger. Derrida wrote of his adoption of the trace that 'reconciled here to a Heideggerian intention – as it is not in Levinas's thought – this notion signifies the undermining of an ontology which, in its innermost course, has determined the meaning of being as presence and the meaning of language as the full continuity of speech' (*G* [*Of Grammatology*] 103/70).[5] What accounts for Derrida's apparent rejection of Levinas's trace on his first exposure to it and his subsequent acceptance of it? Does Derrida adopt the trace to have it do precisely what it seemed he would not allow it to do when he rejected it in 1964?

'Violence and Metaphysics' first appeared as a two-part essay in the *Revue de métaphysique et de morale*. It was revised before being included in Derrida's 1967 collection of essays *Writing and Difference*. An examination of these revisions will be important for gauging the meaning of Derrida's response to the Levinasian trace. It should not be forgotten that Levinas first introduced the trace in the two essays 'The Trace of the Other,' published late in 1963, and 'Signification and Meaning,' which was published early in 1964.[6] In the notes to the 1964 version of 'Violence and Metaphysics,' Derrida explained that it was only when the essay was *à l'impression* – in press – that he first became aware of these two important texts and that in consequence there could only be brief allusions to them, added when the proofs were being corrected.[7] In fact it seems that Derrida had had an earlier encounter with the Levinasian trace in 1963, when Levinas presented a version of 'Signification and Meaning' in a lecture at the Collège Philosophique.[8] But whenever Derrida first heard or first read of the trace, references to these publications are confined to the notes of 'Violence and Metaphysics,' added presumably at the proof stage; the passage on the trace as 'impossible-unthinkable-unsayable' first appeared as a footnote and is a clear case of an addition of this kind. When 'Violence and Metaphysics' came to be republished in *Writing and Difference* many of the additional footnotes were moved up into the main body of the text, so the supplementary nature of Derrida's first reading of Levinas's essays on the trace was no longer apparent from the subordinate typographical position of these footnotes.[9] The main body of the 1964 text and the additional footnotes thus represent two different stages in Derrida's encounter with Levinas's notion of the trace. The 1967 version of the essay erases that difference, and it makes some new additions. But, significantly, these additions do not seem to reflect the more positive attitude to the trace revealed in other contemporary essays by Derrida.

In *Totality and Infinity* Levinas had sought in the name of ethics to challenge the predominance accorded by the tradition to ontology. His aim, announced in 1947, to break with Parmenides appears to have been fulfilled to his own satisfaction by 1961: 'We thus leave the philosophy of Parmenidean being' (*TI* 247/269).[10] In this context, Parmenides represents the philosophy of the unity of being which suppresses what Levinas variously calls 'the good,' the 'beyond Being,' and 'infinity.' The general thrust of 'Violence and Metaphysics' is to insist on Levinas's dependence on Western ontology, even (perhaps especially) in his attempt to break with it.[11] For example, Derrida sought to expose how the other 'must be other than myself,' and therefore cannot be infinitely, absolutely other (*ED* 185/126). Levinas attempts to think the Other not by negation but as a positive plenitude; and yet, Derrida observes, he is nevertheless obliged to use the negative word – 'infinity' – to do it. The term 'infinite' is, according to Derrida, in an argument which in certain respects recalls Hegel's *Faith and*

Knowledge, relative to the finite. It thus bears the mark of the finite within it. If we let the finite stand for the totalizing thought of the tradition of Western ontology, as the infinite stands for the attempt to surpass it, it is at once apparent how this argument draws the thought of the infinite back within the sphere of philosophy. Levinas attempts to go beyond philosophical discourse without acknowledging the limitations imposed by the fact that it can only be done in a language inherited from the tradition he seeks to surpass.

But there is another strand to Derrida's reading of Levinas, perhaps more pronounced in the footnotes to the 1964 text but not entirely absent from the main body of the text. In this other reading attention is drawn to how Levinas seems to embrace the unthinkable. So in a passage which echoes that on the trace quoted earlier, and which like it first appears in a footnote to the 1964 article, Derrida takes up the question of the infinite in these terms: 'As soon as one attempts to think Infinity as a positive plenitude ... the other becomes unthinkable, impossible, unsayable. Perhaps Levinas calls us toward this unthinkable-impossible-unsayable beyond Being and the Logos (of tradition). But it *must not be possible either to think or to say* this call (*ED* 168/114).'[12] Derrida's emphasis on the 'unthinkable,' the 'impossible,' and the 'incomprehensible' in Levinas is by no means confined to the footnotes of the 1964 essay. Individually these words can already be found as a central component of the main body of the 1964 version of 'Violence and Metaphysics.' But with the publication of Levinas's two essays on the trace, Derrida came to give greater emphasis to this aspect. In using these terms Derrida was not saying anything of which Levinas was himself unaware. Indeed Levinas had in 'The Trace of the Other' introduced the trace as 'unthinkable.' His question, 'must it be that, up against the primarily unthinkable, against transcendence and otherness, we give up philosophizing?' (T 190/37), is the same that Derrida is addressing.

How then are we to understand Derrida's charge that the trace is 'unthinkable-impossible-unsayable'? Once it is recognized that this point had been conceded in advance by Levinas, does it not alter the way in which we hear Derrida's insistence upon it? The two 'arguments' of Derrida's essay – the one situating Levinas within the limits of metaphysical discourse, the other placing him outside – may be seen as part of a single attempt to restrict Levinas's efforts to go beyond the tradition and confine him within it. Then the claim would be that whether Levinas depends too heavily on the language of classical ontology and is in consequence unsuccessful in his attempt to transcend it, or whether he is too bold in his attempt to go beyond the tradition and, in ceasing to rely upon it, ceases to make any sense, the upshot is the same: Levinas is held to the tradition he seeks to escape. But Derrida's essay can also be read so that it ceases to have the appearance of either an internal critique or a critique from a standpoint situated outside the essay and instead already exhibits the double strategy of a deconstruction.

Although not explicitly required by the essay, it is possible to read 'Violence and Metaphysics' as participating in the double strategy announced at the end of the 1968 lecture 'The Ends of Man.' The double strategy was to weave and interlace two responses to the tradition, one of which was 'to attempt an exit and a deconstruction without changing ground,' while the other was 'to decide to change ground in a discontinuous and irruptive fashion.' The result was that one would be speaking several languages and producing several texts at once (*M* 163/135). Cannot this strategy already be found in Derrida's essay on Levinas, particularly in his response to the provocative notion of the trace? When Derrida insists that Levinas retains his dependence on the tradition in his very attempt to put it into question, this is to show Levinas attempting the exit from within. And when Derrida emphasizes that the trace is 'impossible-unthinkable-unsayable' the point is not to make an objection, but to show Levinas attempting to change ground in an irruptive manner. The second of these strategies is the one that predominates in Levinas, and it is the one that Derrida had said in 'The Ends of Man' was mostly dominant in France at that time, as the first was said to be more characteristic of Heidegger. But it is crucial to Derrida that both be found to be at work together, and one might say that it was in his insistence on this that the force of his reading of Levinas lay.

Of course, to the extent that the second strategy predominates in Levinas, Derrida must provide, as his own contribution, the other strategy to balance it. This is what is happening when he declares that 'as soon as *he speaks* against Hegel, Levinas can only confirm Hegel' (*ED* 176/120) and that 'Levinas's metaphysics in a sense presupposes – at least we have attempted to show this – the transcendental phenomenology that it seeks to put in question' (*ED* 195/133). Above all it is conveyed by his insistence on 'the necessity of lodging oneself within traditional conceptuality in order to destroy it' (*ED* 164–65/111). And yet, in consequence, it is precisely by insisting upon the second strategy as it operates in Levinas, that is to say, it is by maintaining the emphasis on the way in which the trace and the infinite are unthinkable according to the manner of thinking of Western ontology, that Derrida allows the first strategy to become, not the basis of a critique of Levinas that he has manufactured, but a strand in a double reading.

That the discussion of the trace in 'Violence and Metaphysics' was not a critique but part of a double strategy explains why Derrida found no need to revise that part of the essay for its inclusion in *Writing and Difference*. Undoubtedly the most important addition made at this time was the passage that includes these lines:

> And, if you will, the attempt to achieve an opening toward the beyond of philosophical discourse, by means of philosophical discourse, which can never be shaken off completely, cannot possibly succeed *within language* – and Levinas recognizes that there is no thought before language and outside of it – except by *formally* and *thematically* posing *the question of the relations between belonging and the opening*, the *question of closure*. (*ED* 163/110)

435

When we read the essay today these additional, supplementary lines are liable to form the starting point of our reading. It is, after all, these lines which more than any other seem to make the essay 'Derridean' and form the starting point for understanding it as a deconstruction of Levinas. Not that they were unanticipated in 1964. By prefacing the essay with the question of the death of philosophy and by appealing in this regard to the discourses of Hegel, Marx, Nietzsche, and Heidegger, Derrida had placed Levinas within the context of an assemblage – like that of 'La différance' – which ruled out choosing 'between the opening and the totality' (*ED* 125/84), between passing beyond and remaining within.

Certainly Levinas, in Derrida's view, seems sometimes to write as if it were simply a question of stepping out beyond metaphysics. Derrida presents Levinas as unprepared for certain difficulties that can be brought to his work and that arise from a reflection on the historical nature of language and its dependence on what has passed before. Is not the failure to raise these considerations itself to remain within metaphysics? Derrida judges such questions to be not second-order but fundamental for the thinkers of our epoch, so that the only way to enter into the epoch, the time of the closure (which is neither a belonging to metaphysics nor a straightforward passing beyond it), is to raise 'formally and thematically' the question of the closure itself. Then one might even say that what allows Derrida to retain in 1967 the statement that the trace is 'unthinkable-impossible-unsayable not only for philosophy in general but even for a thought of being which would seek to take a step outside philosophy' is that he had come to consider his own thinking as being neither within philosphy nor outside it, but at the closure. The terms of the alternative – 'inside' or 'outside' philosophy – were no longer regarded by Derrida as mutually exclusive.[13] Does this differentiation of Levinas from Derrida ultimately form the basis of a criticism, as if Levinas's failure was not to have raised the question of the closure 'formally and thematically'? Or would Derrida concede that to have announced the break with Parmenides amounts to having raised the question of the closure?[14] Is not Derrida in this additional passage attempting rather to clarify the conditions underlying the double reading that characterizes deconstruction?

Commentators on Levinas tend to talk of 'Derrida's critique of Levinas' as if they were unaware of what the name Derrida stands for in contemporary thinking or as if they did not recognize the difference between critique and deconstruction.[15] The difference is a matter of two very different ways of reading the essay. If 'Violence and Metaphysics' is a deconstruction, then one can no longer talk about 'arguments against Levinas.' We would have to take up instead the distinction between Levinas's 'intentions' and his 'philosophical discourse' (*ED* 224/151), which would operate like, for example, the distinction in *Of Grammatology* (*G* 321/218) between Rousseau's declarations (his declared intentions) and his descriptions. Levinas's intention is to pass beyond the discourse of Western philosophy; he summons us to a dislocation of the Greek logos (*ED* 122/82). But the only means at his disposal are those of philosophical discourse itself. Derrida interweaves a reading of Levinas in terms of his intentions with another reading in which the emphasis is placed on the limitations imposed by his inability to evade philosophical discourse. Taken in isolation, an extract from 'a deconstruction' will often look like critique.

Yet in 'Violence and Metaphysics' Derrida warns us more than once against understanding his reading of Levinas as a critique. 'We are not denouncing, here, can incoherence of language or a contradiction in the system. We are wondering about the meaning of a necessity: the necessity of lodging oneself within traditional conceptuality in order to destroy it.' (*ED* 164–65/111). Undoubtedly Derrida already anticipates here his later understanding of deconstruction, and if he nowhere speaks of 'deconstruction' in this essay, it is because in 1964 he was still content to use Heldegger's word 'destruction.' Furthermore, Derrida understood Levinas's writings to be a destruction also (*ED* 161n/315 n. 40) and, it seems, in the same sense of the word. Levinas's respect for 'the zone or layer of traditional truth' (*ED* 132/88) serves as that recognition of the necessity of 'lodging oneself within traditional conceptuality' upon which Derrida insists. And just as we have found Derrida careful not to present his account of Levinas as a critique, so he says of Levinas that 'the philosophies whose presuppositions he describes are in general neither refuted nor criticized' (*ED* 132/88). Yet alongside such passages that would give us to understand that Derrida recognizes a community of practice between his own procedures and those of Levinas, we could find others that would make us hesitate. Is the double strategy brought to Levinas or is it already to be found there? Would Derrida not insist that we cannot now distinguish between these two possibilities? Would the ability to make that distinction in a specific case not be a mark – perhaps the only mark – of a bad reading, a sign that the seam had not held? And yet precisely at the point when Derrida is wondering about the meaning of 'the necessity of lodging oneself within traditional conceptuality in order to destroy it,' he goes one step further and reminds us of the 'indestructible' nature of the Greek logos (*ED* 164–65/111). Is it perhaps this recognition that the destruction is a destruction of the indestructible which, in Derrida's view, is lacking in Levinas?

Derrida's explication of the trace in Levinas does not follow Levinas exactly but already belongs to his attempt to reconcile Levinas's manner of breaking with the tradition with a 'Heideggerian intention.' What Levinas writes is that 'the trace is the presence of whoever, strictly speaking, has never been there [*été là*]; of someone who is always past' (*HH* 62; T 201/45). What Derrida reads and what he records when he attempts to paraphrase Levinas – both in 'Violence and Metaphysics' and in 'La Différance' – 'a past that has never been present.'[16] The significance of the difference between the two formulations is that Derrida's version seems to have been phrased with an eye to the Heideggerian determination of the history of Western ontology as a history of presence, a determination Derrida always observes. Derrida seems more concerned here to direct Levinas against the philosophy of presence that to do justice to Levinas's attack on the neutrality of philosophy. In *Totality and Infinity* Levinas is not always so cautious in his discussions of presence as one would have expected had his target been Western ontology as the philosophy of presence specifically. Hence the need for Derrida's insistence in 'violence and Metaphysics' that presence in *Totality and Infinity* is 'present not as a total presence but as the trace' (*ED* 142/95).

And yet Derrida's reading here can be defended. Levinas had often insisted on the simultaneity of presence and absence, not only in *Totality and Infinity*, but even in the 1947 lectures *Time and the Other*. The essays on the trace continue this theme when the presence of the face is said to be inseparable from absence; but it is in terms of the infinity of the absolutely other that Levinas seeks to explain how this is to escape from ontology (*HH* 60; T 199/44). Certainly, after the mid-sixties Levinas's concern for presence becomes more marked.[17] In the studies that culminate in *Otherwise than Being* he explicates the trace in phrases that seem not only to qualify the form of presencing of the Other in the trace, but also to direct the trace against presence as such. So in *Otherwise than Being* we read that 'the trace of the past in a face is not the absence of a yet non-revealed, but the anarchy of what has never been present . . .' (*AO* 123–24/97). And in 'God and Philosophy' it is explicated as the 'trace of a past which will never be present, but this absence still disturbs' (DP 117 n. 3/145 n. 19). It seems that Levinas came, following Derrida's essay, to invest the trace with the 'Heideggerian intention' of addressing the philosophy of presence, even if he would maintain his distance from Heidegger as strenuously as before.

The trace was not introduced to address the philosophy of presence, pre-supposing – as Derrida would do – Heidegger's account of the history of Being. Levinas's deep indebtedness to Heidegger was of another sort, and the Levinasian rupture with the tradition had another basis. When Levinas introduced the trace in the two essays 'The Trace of the Other' and 'Signification and Meaning,' the discussion of the trace in both was exactly the same. What distinguished the two essays was only the preparatory discussion. 'The Trace of the Other' begins with a discussion of identity, work, desire, and responsibility, but the guiding thread of the analyses is a confrontation with Heidegger, and in particular sections 9 to 18 of *Being and Time*. In 'Signification and Meaning' the themes are very similar; the focus is more directly on Merleau-Ponty, but Heidegger is never far absent. If, as is so often the case with Levinas, the details of his polemic against Heidegger had their basis in a questionable reading, it is more important here to look to the broader issues of Levinas's relation to Heidegger.

When Levinas writes that the trace is the presence of someone who has never been there, his aim is to call into question Heidegger's determination of human being as *Dasein* – Being-there, in French *être là*. It is because Levinas is calling *Dasein* into question that he begins 'The Trace of the Other' with a discussion of a kind of work that arises from generosity, goes out toward the Other, and demands ingratitude from the Other: 'Gratitude would be precisely the return of the movement to its origin' (T 191/37). This 'movement without return' disrupts the circularity of selfhood as it is presented in Heidegger; it disrupts the worldhood of the world. In this way, by opposing to the myth of the return of Ulysses the story of Abraham leaving his fatherland for an unknown land, Levinas insists on the Good beyond Being. Fundamentally the essay 'Signification and Meaning' is no different: the point of focus is simply another of the attempts on the part of modern philosophy to overcome the subject-object distinction, attempts whose limitations Levinas has sought to expose ever since *Existence and Existents* in 1947 on the grounds that they remain within the totalizing tendencies of Western philosophy.

The trace in Levinas develops out of the discussion of dwelling in *Totality and Infinity* and particularly the notion of the 'anterior posterior,' a notion introduced as part of the discussion of the Heideggerian analyses of the world (*TI* 144/170). It is not raised specifically to challenge those analyses, but to explore their structure – a structure Levinas will develop in his own way. The starting point is Heidegger's discussion of *Geworfenheit*. Briefly, Levinas regards 'the idealist subject' in these terms: 'The idealist subject which constitutes a priori its object and even the site at which it is found does not strictly speaking constitute them a priori but precisely *after the event*, after having dwelt in them as a concrete being' (*TI* 126/153). To a certain extent Levinas thinks of even Heidegger's *Dasein* as an idealist subject insofar as it is 'In view of itself' and not in view of the Other. The important point here is not Levinas's interpretation of Heidegger, but the insight into the structure of the a priori that he has learned from him. The constitution of the world is an a priori constitution, but insofar as the subject who constitutes presupposes a world, the constitution is a posteriori. What is both anterior and posterior? The answer is an anteriority that is '"older" than the a priori' – the trace (*AO* 127/101).

In hindsight it can be recognized, therefore, that the trace was already operative in *Totality and Infinity*, and nowhere more so than in the discussion on the origin of language. The Other whose first words are the first words ever spoken – 'You shall not commit murder' – never existed, was never there. But nevertheless he is always past insofar as all language presupposes those words. Equally far-reaching is the claim that the Other is always 'the first one on the scene' (*AO* 109/86), that I always find myself responsible to him, and that in that sense he is 'always past.' There are clear parallels between Levinas's discussion of the origin of language and Derrida's treatment of the same theme in Rousseau. Derrida shows how the natural, the state of nature, though anterior to language, acts within language after the fact (*après coup*). Futhermore, the state of nature in Derrida's reading of Rousseau amounts, one might almost say, to 'a past that has never been present,' a suggestion that harmonizes with Rousseau's own presentation of the state of nature as hypothetical.[18] It is as if Derrida in *Of Grammatology* had simply set himself the task of being faithful to this instruction. But these similarities between the texts of Rousseau and those of Levinas raise a question. Is there no fundamental difference in kind between these two sets of text, a difference based on Levinas's position as a thinker at the juncture of 'what we conveniently call our epoch,' the epoch of the closure? How does deconstructive practice recognize that difference? And in what sense would Derrida allow the closure to serve as the mark of an epoch?

NOTES

Works of Emmanuel Levinas cited in this article:

AQ   *Autrement qu'être ou au-delà de l'essence* (The Hague: Nijhoff, 1974); trans. Alphonso Lingis, *Otherwise than Being or beyond Essence* (The Hague: Nijhoff, 1981).

DP   'Dieu et la philosophie,' *Le nouveau commerce* 30–1 (1975): 97–128; trans. Richard Cohen, 'God and Philosophy,' *Philosophy Today* 22 (1978): 127–47.

HH   *Humanisme de l'autre homme* (Montpellier: Fata Morgana, 1972).

T   'La trace de l'autre,' *En découvrant l'existence avec Husserl et Heidegger* (Paris: Vrin, 1967), pp. 187–202; trans. Daniel Hoy, 'On the Trail of the Other,' *Philosophy Today* 10 (1966): 34–45.

TI   *Totalité et infini* (The Hague: Nijhoff, 1961), trans. Alphonso Lingis (Pittsburgh: Duquesne Univ. Press, 1969).

1. *Bulletin de la Société Française de Philosophie* 63 (1968): 7; trans. David Allison, *Speech and Phenomena*, p. 130. The passage was not included when the essay was reprinted for inclusion in *Marges* and the collection *Théorie d'ensemble* (Paris: Seuil, 1968).
2. References are given in the main body of the text to the French edition followed by the English translation, using the abbreviations given above and in the Abbreviations. I have usually followed David Allison's translation of 'La différance' as the most familiar.
3. *RMM* 449n. *ED* 194/132. References to the first publication of the essay in the *Revue de métaphysique et de morale* will be given only when it differs from the subsequent presentation in *L'écriture et la différence*.
4. 'De la grammatologie (II),' *Critique* 22 (1966): 37 n. 13.
5. In 1967, on its republication in *Of Grammatology*, the phrase 'sometimes beyond Heideggerian discourse' was added after the word 'signifies.'
6. 'La trace de l'autre' was first published in the *Tijdschrift voor filosofie* (1963) and reprinted in *En découvrant l'existence avec Husserl et Heidegger* (1967). 'La signification et le sens' was first published in *Revue de métaphysique et de morale* (1964), and reprinted in *Humanisme de l'autre homme* (1972). The word *trace* occasionally appears in Levinas before these two essays, but not in the sense it subsequently acquired.
7. *RMM* 322 n. 1. In 1967 that was altered to say that 'this essay was already written' when the two essays appeared (*ED* 117 n./311 n. 1). The phrase saying that 'the Trace of the Other' was 'read at the time when the proofs of this study were being corrected' (*RMM* 341 n. 1) was omitted in 1967.
8. *RMM* 347. Elsewhere Derrida refers to the *conférence* (pp. 350, 427), a word that subsequently becomes *méditation*. He also quotes Levinas from memory (p. 353). Levinas details the history of his text at *HH* 105.
9. In making his revisions Derrida deleted most of the page references and raised many of the footnotes into the main body of the text. He also made some important additions to the texts to which I shall refer later, but there was no attempt either to take account of the additions to the Levinasian corpus, or even to expand on the brief allusions to the essays on the trace. The different versions of Derrida's essay belong as much to what Derrida would call the history of a text as do its subsequent readings.

10. The 1947 phrase occurs in *Le temps et l'autre* (Paris: Arthaud), p. 130; reprinted 1979 (Montpellier: Fata Morgana), p. 20.

11. *RMM* 430 n. 1; *ED* 168/114. Unfortunately Derrida does not address Levinas's reading of Descartes's Third Meditation. Levinas understands Descartes to have found God in the fact that the infinite is unthinkable or, as he puts it, 'the thought of infinity is not a thought' (*TI* 186/211).

12. A similar point, again added in a footnote, is made by Derrida when he says that even when Levinas is most free from traditional conceptuality, his descriptions depend upon a conceptual matrix that ceaselessly regenerates the same problems (*RMM* 354 n.) – the problems that arise essentially out of his attempt to be free of traditional conceptuality.

13. The phrase 'for a thought of being which would seek to take a step outside philosophy' seems to be a clear reference to Heidegger. It does not refer to Levinas, who had always made it clear – and Derrida was well aware of it (*ED* 122/82) – that his own thinking was a thinking beyond being. But the question how Derrida stands in reference to this designation is highly equivocal. It seems most likely that in 1964 it was a phrase he might have endorsed as a description of his own thinking whereas by 1967 he would have been most hesitant to do so; indeed in *Of Grammatology* he says of 'the thought of being' that it 'speaks *nothing other than* metaphysics, even if it exceeds it and thinks it as what it is within its closure' (*G* 206/143) – a remark with which Heidegger in the 1960s would not have disagreed. We might speculate on what allowed Derrida to retain the phrase unchanged when he was making a host of other changes. Perhaps the most satisfactory answer lies away from a strictly 'developmental approach,' which of itself does not illuminate the thinking at issue, and instead might be found in the equivocation that lies at the heart of a double reading and to which the name 'undecidable' may also be given.

14. Although Derrida does sometimes differentiate 'closure' and the 'end' of philosophy (e.g., *G* 14/4; *SP* 115/102), it seems to be a mistake to accord the distinction undue significance. That the closure is not supposed to provide the basis of a criticism against Levinas but, on the contrary, that Levinas (along with Nietzsche, Freud, and especially Heidegger) helps pose the question of the closure is indicated at *M* 24/23, *SP* 154–55.

15. For a recent example of Derrida's remarks, some of which are undoubtedly critical, being confused with a critique see John Patrick Burke, 'The Ethical Significance of the Face,' *Proceedings of the American Philosophical Association* 56 (1982): 200.

16. *M* 22/21; *SP* 152. This is also how Derrida records it in 'Violence and Metaphysics' (*ED* 194/132). Already in 1963 in 'Force and Signification' Derrida had written that the 'history of the work is not only its *past* ... but is also the impossibility of its ever being present,' (*Critique*, nos. 193–94, p. 498; reprinted *ED* 26/14). The phrase 'a past that has never been present' can also be found in Merleau-Ponty's *Phénomenologie de la perception* (Paris: Gallimard, 1945) p. 280; trans. C. Smith, *Phénomenology of Perception* (London: Routledge & Kegan Paul, 1970), p. 242.

17. And yet a good indication that Levinas does not in the early 1960s exhibit Derrida's sensitivity to the metaphysical dominance of presence is that it is not until ten years later that he accepts Derrida's contention (e.g., *ED* 225/152) that the term, *experience* is determined by the metaphysics of presence and accordingly, as in 'God and Philosophy' (*DP* 107/132), refers it back to the *cogito* – overhastily in my view.

18. Derrida, in fact, calls it a non-place (*non-lieu*). In doing so he was simply being faithful to Rousseau's own description of the State of Nature in the Preface to the *Discourse on the Origin of Inequality* as 'a state which no longer exists, which perhaps never existed, which probably never will exist.' *Oeuvres complètes* (Paris: Plelade, 1964), 3:123; trans. R. and J. Masters, *The First and Second Discourses*

(New York: St. Martin's, 1964), p. 93. The reading of Rousseau in relation to Levinas and Derrida only hinted at here was developed in a lecture delivered at Duquesne University in March 1982 under the title 'The Origin of Language.'

See also:

Critchley (3.5)
Belsey (4.5)
Benjamin (5.2)
Derrida (10.3)

'POST-STRUCTURALISM, THE ETHICAL RELATION AND THE LAW'

Drucilla Cornell

I will suggest that the entire project of deconstruction, one of the major strands of post-structuralism under anyone's definition, is driven by an ethical desire to enact the ethical relation. By the ethical relation I mean to indicate the aspiration to a nonviolent relationship to the Other, and to otherness more generally, that assumes responsibility to guard the Other against the appropriation that would deny her difference and singularity. I am deliberately using a broad brush here in defining the ethical relation, so as to include a number of thinkers who share the aspiration to heed the call to responsibility for the Other, but who would otherwise disagree on the philosophical underpinnings of the ethical relation and on its precise definition. I am, then, defining the ethical relation more broadly than the thinker Emmanuel Levinas, with whom the phrase is usually associated.[1] I will, however, return again and again to Levinas' specific formulation of the ethical relation as the 'beyond' to ontology,[2] because it is Levinas' own understanding of the ethical relation that Derrida interrogates. As we will see, one way to approach the ethical desire of deconstruction is by examining Derrida's engagement with Levinas' ethical philosophy of alterity.

But perhaps the ethical desire of deconstruction is never more evident than in Derrida's encounter with Hegel. When we confront our desire to 'escape' from Hegel, to put him to rest once and for all, we need to ask why we are trying to get out from under his shadow; or, more precisely, in the name of what do we make our escape. One answer, of course, is that the deconstruction of Hegel simply

Source: Drucilla Cornell, 'Post-structuralism, the ethical relation and the law', *Cardozo Law Review*, August 1988, pp. 1587–1628.

puts into operation 'the truth' that speculative reason will always turn against its own pretenses if it cannot come home to itself in Absolute Knowledge. On this reading, the motor of deconstruction is speculative reason, even if now turned against itself. But there is, as I have suggested, an alternative reading that locates the drive behind deconstruction in an ethical desire. (I want to note, however, that I am not advocating that the 'ethical' as opposed to the 'true' is the 'proper' entry into deconstruction: I am only suggesting that an emphasis on the 'ethical' as opposed to the 'true' yields a very different encounter with deconstruction.) On the ethical reading I offer here, we ask ourselves the opening question of Derrida's Glas[3] – a kind of wake for Hegel, with all the implications of both death and salvation that a wake implies – 'what, after all, of the remain(s), today, for us, here, now, of a Hegel?'[4] in the name of the elusive residuum left over once the relentless machinery of the Hegelian dialectic has finished its work? The subtle phrasing of Derrida's opening question acknowledges that we cannot separate the question of what remains of Hegel from the question of the remains of Hegelianism. What of the rest that has been pushed out of the system? To ask the question is already a kind of tribute to the forgotten Other, whose remains have been scattered. Glas attempts the only salvation of the rest that remains possible through the work of mourning itself. Indeed, for Derrida, it is only through the work of mourning that we can remember the remains because there has never been, nor can there be, a gathering of the rest that makes fully present what has been shut out: For what has been shut out is literally not there for us. Even so, the work of mourning remains demands the mimetic persistence to scrape through the debris left over from Hegel's system at the same time that we recognize that '"[t]he rest, the remain(s), is unsayable."'[5] Glas does rather than says. Derrida may well be our best salvage man, our ultimate Chiffonnier. Yet deconstruction as allegory in action can neither testify to its own faithfulness to 'things'[6] nor name the law or prescriptive force it so carefully follows.

Even if, however, Derrida practices Walter Benjamin's redemptive criticism only through parody and irony, that is still the way he practices redemptive criticism.[7] It is precisely the silence before the name of the prescriptive or ethical force heeded in deconstruction that has misled many readers to argue that deconstruction has to do with the radical indeterminacy of meaning and, therefore, with the impossibility of ethics. The asserted impossibility of naming the 'Law' of its own ethical desire, however, should not be confused with the complete rejection of the ethical. If anything unites deconstructive critics it is, ironically, their insistence not only on the inevitability of the ethical in reading but also in what Paul de Man would call unreadability.[8] But my suggestion is not only that deconstructive critics recognize that we cannot escape from the ethical. Instead I want to argue that Derrida, in particular, theoretically clears the space for the elaboration of the nonviolent relationship to otherness that Levinas describes as proximity,[9] a relation that is prior to the subject and to contractual consent and yet not encompassed within a unity. Derrida, however, is always careful to preserve the distance that respect for the otherness of the Other implies – which is not to contrast Derrida with Levinas necessarily, because Levinas' conception of proximity is based on the temporal distance that inheres in the precedence of the Other to me. Deconstruction practices Nietzsche's action at a distance in the name of responsibility to the Other.[10]

Derrida is often mistakenly understood to criticize Levinas for his inevitable fall back into the language of ontology, the language that Levinas supposedly thought he had moved beyond in his philosophy of the ethical. Derrida recognizes, however, that Levinas himself understands that he can only disrupt metaphysics from within the tradition. I will suggest that *Glas* is not a critique at all, but a deconstructive exercise that *does* show the inevitable dependence of Levinas' project on the language of ontology, but not, however, to resist Levinas' conception of the ethical relation; rather, to salvage it from potential degeneration into the very violence toward otherness that the philosophy of alterity attempts to guard against. In other words, Derrida's deconstruction of Levinas can itself be read ethically. Instead of simply preferring one to the other, we need to read Derrida and Levinas together to heed the call to responsibility and to enact a nonviolent relation to otherness.

Nor should we simply pit Levinas' philosophy of alterity against Hegelian-ism. I will suggest that neither Levinas' ethical philosophy nor the practice of deconstruction can be allowed to displace the Hegelian notion of reciprocity within the sphere of law. Within law we are fated to be 'unfaithful' to otherness, as we are forced to make comparisons which inevitably call for an analogy of the unlike to the same. Law classifies, establishes the norms by which difference is judged. If classification in and of itself is thought to be violence against singularity, then law inevitably perpetuates that violence. But we are also fated 'to fall' into law; for as Levinas himself reminds us, we are never just in a relationship to the Other, there is always the introduction of the third. With the introduction of the third we are forced to make comparisons, to weigh the competing demands of different individuals. The very process of weighing competing demands calls for a scale, a basis for comparison, what we would think of as a principle of justice. For Levinas, we are called to justice by our responsibility to the Other, even as we recognize that the synchronization of competing demands that justice calls for can never be adequate to the ethical relation. We cannot then simply surpass the synchronization of one to the Other that Levinas associates with Hegel's conception of relations of reciprocity. As a result, I will argue that Hegelianism remains valid for us within the sphere of law. Once we are within the realm of law, it is no longer desirable to seek to surpass the Hegelian 'ideal' of relations of reciprocity as a limiting principle for legal interpretation. It is a mistake, in other words, to attempt to directly translate the ethical philosophy of alterity into a new description of justice as the recognition of difference.

But let me turn now, first to Levinas' rejection of Hegelianism for its replication of the logic of identity, and then to Derrida's interrogation of both

Levinas and Hegel. By the logic of identity, I mean to indicate the unity of meaning and being that is disclosed in Hegel's *Logic*, as the 'truth' of the actual. To understand the interrogation of the logic of identity, then, we must move within the circle of Hegel's *Logic*. What I offer here is a conventional reconstruction of the *Logic* that does not attempt to defend a reading of the *Logic* that might meet the opposition of Hegel's post-structuralist challengers.

In Hegel, the category of Being is the necessary starting point of all thought. Things manifest themselves in and through Being. Reality appears to the thinking subject as an object of thought only because first and foremost things 'are.' Without the category of Being there would literally *be* no reality; we would instead be immersed in 'the night in which cows are all black.' Being is both the necessary starting point of all thought and the minimal determination of things. Being is, thus, the most universal, ontological category. And yet Being as a category is both abstract and empty. Certainly Being is 'nothing,' not just *a* being, because a thing presupposes many determinations other than its mere being. Being 'is' only in and through opposition to nothingness. We know 'Being' only by what is not; nothing. The copula affirms the inevitability of the is, the category of Being, yet at the same time, Being can be conceived neither as a predicate nor as a subject of the sentence. As copula, Being exists as something other to itself in which it is united to the diversity of determinations. It includes, therefore, that which is not: non-being. Of course, non-being is also not able to be what it *is*, non-being, unless it relies on its opposite, of which it is the inseparable complement. Hegel's opening moves in the *Logic* show that Being and non-being cannot be what they are unless they pass continuously into one another as Becoming. The unity of Being and non-being is their ceaseless changing into their opposite: an endless movement of becoming which is the onto-logical core of all movement and materiality. The interplay of Being and non-being signals the presence of Absolute as the very movement of the interpenetration of oppositional categories. Nothing is, unless it comes to be in and through the circle of Absolute Knowledge. Hegel's *Logic* culminates in the demonstration that thought and Being are the two opposite names of the Concept or Idea. The thinking which achieves Absolute Knowledge realizes that the self-movement of the Concept or Idea is its own essence, and grasps the full actualization of the structure of the logos in thought and reality itself. The unity of meaning and Being within the circle of the Absolute yields full knowledge of the truth of the essence of the actual. We come home to ourselves through the recognition of identity in nonidentity, of thought in Being. There is no remainder, no outside. Otherness is recaptured, and completely so, in the circle of the Absolute. Nothing escapes, for nothing is, only as non-being.

Within *Hegel's Philosophy of Right*[11] the realization of the truth of the actual yields the complete transparency of the determinations of *Sittlichkeit*, the collective ethics of modernity. For Hegel, we can know the universal language of democracy, the ultimate key to legal interpretation. Although Hegel himself retained the tension between any existing state of affairs and what the actualized concept of democracy demands – and, therefore, his account of *Sittlichkeit* cannot be simplistically condemned, as it often is by Hegel's 'liberal' critics, as merely an apology for the current social order – he did identify ethics with the actual. As a result, the dilemma of legal interpretation we are so troubled by today was resolved by the Hegelian identification of truth with history. The meaning of life in the strongest possible sense of meaning is revealed in the circle of the Absolute. The self-conscious recognition of the 'we that is I and the I that is we,' the coming home to oneself through the Other, is not only a description, but also a normative practice embodied in the institutions of right themselves. Hegel both justifies and interprets the modern law of property and of contract as abstract forms consistent with the actualization of relations of mutual recognition or reciprocal symmetry. As we will see, it is precisely the disjuncture of the ethical and the actual, the infinite from the totality of the Hegelian system, that is characteristic of the post-structuralist rebellion against Hegel.

For Emmanuel Levinas, Hegel's political philosophy exemplifies the thinking of totality he associates with ontology. The thinking of totality, for Levinas, carries within it the danger of totalitarianism because such a thinking would deny 'actuality' to the Other 'excluded' from the system. We are reminded, here, of Hegel's infamous statement that there is no place for Siberia in the philosophy of history. Siberia becomes the symbol of the otherness that has been squeezed out through the operation of the Hegelian dialectic. That which is left out and thus denied actuality does not count. Levinas' ethical subject called by the Other 'dispenses with the idealizing subjectivity of [Hegelian] ontology, which reduces everything to itself.'[12]

Levinas argues that Hegel's *Logic* reduces time to contemporaneous presence; the *Logic* unfolds in the moment that is eternity. But, in Levinas, time is diachronic; one moment pursues the other without ever being able to retrieve it. Levinas' diachronic view of time opens up the meaning of otherness and the otherness of meaning. The temporality of the interface, in which the Other confronts me, is forever beyond me – irreducible, as in Hegel, to the synchrony of the same. We are never together in the present. The Other is always before me. According to Levinas, relations of mutual recognition in Hegel's Absolute Knowledge are the example par excellence of the reduction of the Other to the synchrony of the same. There is always a trace of otherness that cannot be captured by my 'identifying' with the Other in relations of mutual recognition. The Other cannot be reduced in relation to me, by which I grasp her essence in the 'we that is I and the I that is we.' The basis of ethics is not identification with those whom we recognize as like ourselves, instead the ethical relation inheres in the encounter with the Other, the stranger, whose face beckons us to heed the call to responsibility. The precedence of the Other means that my relationship to her is necessarily asymmetrical. Reciprocity is, at the very least, the affair of the Other.[13]

In the asymmetrical and yet face to face relation with the Other, the stranger who calls to me, the subject first experiences the resistance to encapsulation of the 'beyond.' In the face to face relation we run into the infinity that disrupts totality. Levinas' account of the face to face is still a phenomenology, however, precisely because it is in and through our proximity to the Other in the interface that gives us the resistance of otherness. We encounter God as the transcendence inherent in the ethical relation itself. Transcendence in Levinas is temporal, not spatial. He does not point us to a 'beyond' that is 'there,' a someplace where we are not. Nor can infinity be reduced to the mere Other to the totality of what is, although there is a reading of Levinas on which infinity is completely 'beyond' history, a reading founded in the ambiguity of Levinas' own text. There is, however, clearly another reading, which understands Levinas to seek to displace the traditional oppositions of the inside and the outside, the imminent and the transcendent. The beyond, on this reading, is within totality as its very disruption, but not just as its negation. As Levinas himself explains, 'This "beyond" the totality and objective experience is, however, not to be described in a purely negative fashion. It is reflected *within* the totality and history, *within* experience.'[14] Yet on either reading, infinity cannot be reduced to actuality.

According to Hegel, on the other hand, the infinite must be infinite, and thus embodied in the actuality of what is. Otherwise, the finite would be the limit of the infinite. Differentiation then is the necessary condition for the infinite to be. Exteriority, therefore, is the inevitable result of the *presence* of the Absolute. The necessary estrangement of the Infinite from its self is overcome through the self-conscious recognition of exteriority as the manifestation of the Absolute. Nature, in this sense, is spirit. In Hegel, matter is purportedly redeemed, by being uplifted into the Hegelian system. Here, we have Hegel, as the eagle who struggles to lift 'the stone,' the dead weight of the remains, through the help of the machinery of the dialectic. For Derrida, Hegel's name gives the real nature of his enterprise away.

> His name is so strange. From the eagle it draws imperial or historic power. Those who still pronounce his name like the French (there are some) are ludicrous only up to a certain point: the restitution (semantically infallible for those who have read him a little – but only a little) of magisterial coldness and imperturbable seriousness, the eagle caught in ice and frost, glass and gel.[15]

What of the remains of Hegel then? In Hegel everything that counts, counts as part of a greater whole. Only the whole is actual. Truth is the whole, and once we have finished the *Logic*, we have the whole truth. We think God's thoughts.

NOTES

1. See E. Levinas, *Otherwise than Being or Beyond Essence* (A. Lingis trans. 1981) [hereinafter E. Levinas, *Otherwise than Being*]; E. Levinas, *Totality and Infinity* (A. Lingis trans. 1979).

2. See E. Levinas, *Otherwise than Being*, supra note 1.
3. J. Derrida, *Glas* (J. Leavey, Jr. & R. Rand trans. 1986).
4. Id. at 1.
5. Id. at 115.
6. I am using the word 'things' in Heidegger's sense. For a good definition of the Heideggerian usage of the word 'thing,' see J. Miller, *The Ethics of Reading* 104–05 (1987).
7. I am adopting the phrase redemptive criticism from Jürgen Habermas who uses it to describe Benjamin's project of salvaging the remains. Habermas, 'Consciousness-Raising or Redemptive Criticism – The Contemporaneity of Walter Benjamin,' 6 *New German Critique*, Spring 1979, at 30–59.
8. See J. Miller, supra note 6. But see P. de Man, *Allegories of Reading* (1979). As de Man himself explains 'Allegories are always ethical, the term ethical designating the structural interference of two distinct value systems. In this sense, ethics has nothing to do with the will (thwarted or free) of a subject, nor *a fortiori*, with a relationship between subjects. The ethical category is imperative (i.e., a category rather than a value) to the extent that it is linguistic and not subjective. Morality is a version of the same language aporia that gave rise to such concepts as "man" or "love" or "self," and not the cause or the consequence of such concepts. The passage to an ethical tonality does not result from a transcendental imperative but is the referential (and therefore unreliable) version of a linguistic confusion. Ethics (or, one should say, ethicity) is a discursive mode among others.' (Id. at 206).
9. It would be a mistake to read proximity as 'closeness' in the usual sense of the word. As Levinas explains: 'Proximity as a suppression of distance suppresses the distance of consciousness of . . . The neighbor excludes himself from the thought that seeks him, and this exclusion has a positive side to it: my exposure to him, antecedent to his appearing, my delay behind him, my undergoing, undo the core of what is identity in me. Proximity, suppression of the distance that consciousness of . . . involves, opens the distance of a diachrony without a common present, where difference is the past that cannot be caught up with, an un-imaginable future, the non-representable status of the neighbor behind which I am late and obsessed by the neighbor. This difference is my non-indifference to the other. Proximity is a disturbance of the rememberable time.' (E. Levinas, *Otherwise than Being*, supra note 1, at 89).
10. See F. Nietzsche, *The Gay Science* aphorism 60, at 123 (W. Kaufmann trans. 1st ed. 1974), in which action at a distance is associated with the aura and the power of the feminine. '*Women [Die Frauen] and their action at a distance* . . . The magic and the most powerful effect of woman is, in philosophical language, action at a distance, *actio in distans*; but this requires first of all and above all – *distance*.' Id.
11. G. Hegel, *Hegel's Philosophy of Right* (T. Knox trans. 1952).
12. Emmanuel Levinas & Richard Kearney, 'Dialogue with Emmanuel Levinas,' in *Face to Face with Levinas* 27 (R. Cohen ed. 1986).
13. As Derrida has argued in his latest essay on Levinas, 'At this Very Moment in this Work Here I Am,' the ethical relation can be read to demand radical ingratitude. J. Derrida, 'En ce Moment Même dans cet Ouvrage Me Voici,' in *Psyché* 159 (1987). Gratitude, as a kind of restitution, would again appropriate the Other to the same.
14. E. Levinas, *Totality and Infinity*, supra note 1, at 23.
15. J. Derrida, supra note 3, at 1.

See also:

9.4

'IN THE NAME OF ...'

Philippe Lacoue-Labarthe

Jacques, I would like to ask you a question. Or rather, I would like *to address* a question to you.

It is an old and an obscure question. Old, because it near enough dates from the time when I happened to read what was, I think, the first text of yours to be published (it was 'Force and Signification', in *Critique*). Obscure because it is not, at the outset, a truly philosophical question. However, it is indeed a question, but I do not know how to define – even if I feel it with an inexplicable precision – what it touches upon: perhaps it has to do with the idiosyncratic or idiomatic part of what you write, a certain climate, a strange aura, a style or a *tone*; also perhaps, but I say this without confidence (it is an impression, nothing more), it has to do with matters of profound, deep choices, tastes, a *habitus* or an *ethos* that are your own, let us say 'proper', but which one senses that you do not really master or calculate, that they are themselves brought about by carrying you along, that they inscribe you and write you when you write – or, which is the same thing, when you speak.

Today, I would like to attempt to elucidate this question. What settles it for me is, first of all, that I obstinately, that is to say passionately, believe in elucidation. I do not make myself clear, but I hear myself say, constantly: clarity is necessary. This must not – and cannot – simply be agreed.

Source: Philippe Lacoue-Labarthe and Jean-Luc Nancy, *Retreating the Political*, ed. Simon Sparks (London: Routledge, 1997), pp. 55–61.

But this is afterwards, because the occasion is here, the moment has come. I am not saying it in view of the singular circumstance of this colloquium or of your presence, here, now – which could, on the contrary, give the illusion that, addressing myself directly to you, I am enjoining or calling out to you; or that even, just about, I would be summoning you to appear and give an explanation. This is not the case at all. Moreover, if you were not there (and nothing assures me, whilst writing this text, that you will be there at the moment when I will deliver it, if I deliver it), it would be just the same, nothing would change. Basically, this address is (still) a letter – through which, still, I persist (or re-offend). It is a letter because what matters, both to my question and – I think – in general, is the second person utterance. But it is a letter to which I am not asking you, in any way, necessarily to respond (it is already, in many ways, a kind of response to your 'Envois', which are themselves one or many). Despite not really knowing what must be understood by this, I will simply say: considering the situation I am in, I would like for this letter to arrive at its destination in one way or another. Or, at the very least, I would like for it to arrive – whatever the risk that lies in this type of desire.

Moreover, as I know you have already realised (and for a long time), *destination* will be my question. Or at least it is what will remain in question in my question – being probably that which can only remain in question in every question. (Although you know this, I insist on pointing this out so that no one starts to think that this is what I am settling on or fixing, immobilising or maintaining as my 'subject'. In Latin: *destinata*.)

For this, already more or less double, question, I could have started off from one or other of your texts, quite indifferently. However, if I choose to take my point of departure from 'The Ends of Man', this is not simply to play the game of this colloquium, by respecting the theme or by underlining its intentions; in the first place it is because in this text, which is evidently not (since such was not its destination) among the most fundamental of your texts, but whose character, spirited and angry, in places terse, almost brutal, and, in short, absolutely clear, will, up to a point, make my task easier – because in this text, then, three things have kept hold of or struck me.

First: regarding the political, since your preamble is explicitly dedicated to it – and in view of the circumstances: an international colloquium, in the United States, during the Vietnam war, etc.; with regard to the political gesture that you insist on making and to which you speak of having suspended, your participation in this colloquium (and consequently the editing, the delivering and the publication of this text), the fate that you reserve for or the privilege that you accord to the concept – and to the fact – of 'nation'.

I see perfectly clearly, it is true, that, being careful to inscribe this gesture completely within a 'historical and political horizon', which you point out 'would call for a lengthy analysis', you also mention what is of the order of racial conflicts (the assassination of Martin Luther King) or social conflicts

(May '68 in France). Still better, I see that you deliberately date your text, but this also in enigmatic fashion, 12 May 1968, it being the eve (this is your final motif) of this demonstration, which, at the time, was itself symbolic, started by workers' organisations, left-wing parties and trade unions (what I myself persist in calling, since November '56, the workers' bureaucracies – but this matters little here) and which, whatever the revolutionary chances of the movements in May, will have in any case sounded the death knell of what, therefore, could still be interpreted and acted as a real social upheaval. But I do not know, deep down, what you thought of it all (I did not know you, and you have never spoken about it); and it only obscures what, in this preamble, comes to the fore, which is the nation (national styles, for example, the question of language, institutional diversity) and this is what, for a long time, has, let us say, 'intrigued' me.

This is not, as one says, a critique. But the account of a 'utopianism', mine, which has cracked quite a bit since the first time I read this text (this was the *destinal* utopianism of the 'final' struggle and of the international achievement of 'humankind'); and also, consequently, the account of a sort of 'realism' that I recognised in you, although your remarks were always very allusive, and whose validity, nonetheless, I *also* recognised; I could not avoid thinking, to take one of your examples, that those who had opened negotiations for peace in Vietnam, in Paris in '68, were – on one side *as* on the other – the same as those against whom I always thought it necessary to fight. And above all, in spite of not being a Marxist, and never having been one (I was, like many others, simply in solidarity, through a provisional ethic or, rather, through obedience to a kind of unspoken ethical commandment, a kind of revolutionary idea, and that is to say a kind of idea of justice), I did not understand that something other than this so very overdetermined concept of the nation was possible; one not accepted by you as self-evident (your text shows that it is nothing of the kind), but as offering you the possibility for one of the most explicit political or ethico-political gestures that you have ever made, in a piece of writing at least.

I did not understand it then, and I'm not sure, even today, that I understand it now. Let us say that it remains, to a not insignificant degree, within the parameters of the question that I would like to articulate here.

Second, and on another level: even if, from the outset, you recall 'that which has always bound the essence of the philosophical to the essence of the political', what struck me in the critical re-opening of the three great critiques or de-limitations of metaphysical humanism was the *extent* of your debate with Heidegger. In the two senses of this term: the place or the importance that you reserve for Heidegger, and the level of profundity at which you locate the adherence of the Heideggerean de-limitation to the anthropism or the anthropocentrism that it de-limits.

I do not want to insist on this now, except to underline the extreme importance that your *Auseinandersetzung* with Heidegger, the only one to have taken place in France, will have had for us ('us' means here: those, roughly of the same generation, that the reading and interpretation of Heidegger has decisively engaged in philosophy). I will return to this shortly. But it is clear, to me in any case, that you represent the only possible *practical study* of Heidegger. That is to say, the only possible practice of philosophy at its limit, insofar as one takes up the wager, as you put it about a year earlier in the same period, that Heidegger's thinking is the most recent of the West's 'great thinkings'.

In which case, however, the question for me remains (and not merely in regard to this text) the fact that, to the best of my knowledge, you have never said anything about the enormous weight nevertheless of the political in this 'philosophy'.

Third and finally: there is in this text – in accordance with a movement which, basically, is not uncommon with you, although, on the other hand, you might say that much of this comes from Heidegger – the relative univocity of your reading, of your critique.

And even if much has been said about Heidegger in the course of the last decade (but this had to be done), then that's just too bad; for, in turn, I am entering my question through him: both because I do not see any other way and because there is nothing that appears to me to be as decisive. If this is still obstinacy, I ask that you be kind enough to forgive me.

Obviously I am not resuming the whole thread of your demonstration, but I will simply retain this: despite the strict acknowledgement of what is due to Heidegger with regard to the question of man, the question of the relation between humanism and metaphysics or onto-theology, etc. ('It is not a matter here', you say, 'of enclosing all of Heidegger's text within a closure that he has delimited better than any other'); despite, in particular, the insistence that you bring very vigorously to bear upon the motif of ontological distance – and that is also to say despite all your respect for this intractable difficulty that Heidegger meets with when thematising under the name of 'thinking by examples' [*pensée par modèles*] and which refers to the necessarily ontic character of every example or to the obligation of going through this metaphorics, itself ontical, in order to say being (and this is a difficulty that, right up until 'The *Retrait* of Metaphor', you have made entirely your own); despite of all this, your argumentation happens to be fastened, formed and fixed upon two points:

1. On the one hand (and I am taking up your terms) 'the hold which the humanity of man and the thinking of being maintain upon one another', that you take or pick up, relieve or lift up [*relèves . . . lèves*] on the basis of the 'subtle' privilege attached to the position of the *we* (that is to say, of the 'we-men') in the Heideggerean discourse, and first of all in the breakthrough towards *Dasein* which opens *Sein und Zeit* and the question of the 'meaning of being'. And you rightly say on this subject, 'in the question of being such as it is put to metaphysics, man and the name of man are not displaced'.

2. On the other hand, what you call the 'magnetisation' of the Heideggerean text by the motif of the proper, which is not merely responsible for maintaining the question of essence or of the proper of man but which, going by way of the 'passage between the *close* and the *proper* [*le proche et le propre*]' (whose Latin element you nonetheless acknowledge: *prope/ proprius* is 'interrupted' in German), explains the constant and heavy valorisation of proximity and of proximity to self, of propriation (appropriation and reappropriation) – in brief, so as to speed things along, presence. In short, *Entfernung, l'é-loignement*, 'de-severing', at the end (and at the end of ends) always comes back down to the closest (as you write on the subject of Heidegger's trajectory: 'Everything happens as if it were necessary to reduce the ontological distance recognised in *Sein und Zeit* and to say the proximity of being to the essence of man'). Or indeed, since you also cite long passages from *Zeit und Sein, Ereignis* always bears upon *Enteignis*.

I do not believe this reading to be the only possible, strict and correct one, but I believe that it is still absolutely necessary. A necessity which is indissociably philosophical and political.

It touches, among other things, on the essentials of what (still today) founds Heideggerianism – and, this needs to be pointed out, of what founded the Heideggerianism of Heidegger himself. No one apart from yourself has – without recourse to external, simply empirico-anthropological criteria, criteria as such invalidated and disqualified in advance by the Heideggerian de-limitation – no one apart from yourself has been able to flush out from their truly philosophical depth, and from the very centre of the Heideggerian questioning, the secret weight of preferences, the metaphorical insistence, the insidious return of the ontic which (inevitably) does not cease to weigh down upon the pure thought of difference, and perhaps in the first place because this thought also wished to be so pure. All of which does not make of it, as it has become customary to say, an 'idolatry' (idolatry as such is explicitly denounced and dismissed, for example in the final lines of the inaugural lecture of 1929–). But which definitely, or almost – and considering the rigorous archaeology of the occidental eidetic (eidophilia or eidocentrism) as well as the extreme vigilance shown by Heidegger towards all of the metaphysical concepts derived from *eidos/idea, Gestalt* included – which makes of it, therefore, almost definitely, an *ideo-logy*. In spite of everything. And as you have shown, it is a fundamentally 'economistic' ideology, systematically organising itself on the basis of the values, themes and motifs of the 'house' and of the 'dwelling-place' or 'abode' (of the *oikos*), of 'dwelling' and of 'building', of the 'guard' and of the 'safe-guard' (of *Wahrheit*), of the closed peasant or artisan economy (shepherds and carpenters), of the 'homeland', of the 'native land', of the 'familiar', of the 'at home' – *Heimat, heimatlich, heimlich, heimisch*, etc. Turning, consequently, into the slightly biting, reactive and reactionary protestation against the entirety of modernity (not merely against all the forms of uprooting, of errancy, of *Befremdlichkeit* and devastation, but also, at the weakest moments, against technology in the sense of industrialisation, cities, mass culture, means of information, etc.). And, moreover, appealing, in a prophetic or messianic mode, to the hope of a mutation, a turning or renewal – the appearance of an 'other thinking' or, of course, a new God. In short, as Lyotard would have said some years ago (and as he still says today, perhaps), 'pious thinking' *par excellence*. I would say instead: pious *discourse*.

This reading had to be carried out, therefore – if only in order to save Heidegger from his 'faithful' interpreters or even from his own self-interpretation; if only, then, in order to restore to this thinking its impact, its irreducible force, and to undermine a certain propensity, which has not been sufficiently contested, towards idyllic inanity (or towards a manner of slightly outdated and vain aristocratism, which is not excluded from the former), with all the political consequences that this is, was, or will be capable of having.

This is why the deconstruction (the *Ab-bau*) of the proper will not have been simply critique but will have constituted, in its very difficulty, the stakes of what I was evoking before, deliberately making use of the Heideggerian term, as a real *Auseinandersetzung* – on the basis of which alone it seems to me possible thoroughly to engage the questioning of what, for convenience, I will continue to call the political or the ethico-political.

See also:
Readings (8.3)
Spivak (8.4)
Laclau (8.5)
Derrida (11.3)

9.5

'WHAT IS TO BE DONE?'

Jean-Luc Nancy

What is to be done, at present? The question is on everybody's lips and, in a certain way, it is the question people today always have lying in wait for any passing philosopher. Not: What is to be thought? But indeed: What is to be done? The question is on everybody's lips (including the philosopher's), but withheld, barely uttered, for we do not know if we still have the right, or whether we have the means, to raise it. Perhaps, we think more or less discreetly to ourselves, perhaps the uncertainty of 'what is to be done?' is today so great, so fluctuating, so indeterminate, that we do not need even to do this: raise the question.

Especially if the question were to presuppose that one already knows what it is right to think, and that the only issue is how one might then proceed to act. Behind us theory, and before us practice – the key thing is knowing what it is opportune to decide in order to embark on specific action. But this is what is presupposed most ordinarily by the question. And 'what is to be done?' means, in that case, 'how to act' in order to achieve an already given goal. 'Transforming the world' then means: realising an already given interpretation of the world, and realising a hope.

But we do not know what it is right for us to think, or even properly to hope. Perhaps we no longer even know what it is to think nor, consequently, what it is to think 'doing', nor what 'doing' is, absolutely.

Source: Philippe Lacoue-Labarthe and Jean-Luc Nancy, *Retreating the Political*, ed. Simon Sparks (London: Routledge, 1997), pp. 157–8.

Perhaps, though, we know one thing at least: 'What is to be done?' means for us: how to make a world for which all is not already done (played out, finished, enshrined in a destiny), nor still entirely to do (in the future for always future tomorrows).

This would mean that the question places us simultaneously before a doubly imperative response. It is necessary to measure up to what nothing in the world can measure, no established law, no inevitable process, no prediction, no calculable horizon – absolute justice, limitless quality, perfect dignity – and it is necessary to invent and create the world itself, immediately, here and now, at every moment, without reference to yesterday or tomorrow. Which is the same as saying that it is necessary at one and the same time to affirm and denounce the world as it is – not to weigh out as best one can equal amounts of submission and revolt, and always end up halfway between reform and accommodation, but to *make* the world into the place, never still, always perpetually reopened, of its own contradiction, which is what prevents us from ever knowing in advance *what* is to be done, but imposes upon us the task of never making anything that is not a world.

What will become of our world is something we cannot know, and we can no longer believe in being able to predict or command it. But we can act in such a way that this world is a world able to open itself up to its own uncertainty as such.

These are not vague generalities. I am writing these lines in January 1996. France's December strikes showed clearly the whole difficulty, not to say aporia, that exists in 'what is to be done?' once all guarantees are suspended and all models become obsolete. Resignation in the face of the brutalities of economic *Realpolitik* clashed with feverish or eager words that hardly took the risk of saying exactly what was to be done. But between the two, something was perceptible: that it is ineluctable to invent a world, instead of being subjected to one, or dreaming of another. Invention is always without model and without warranty. But indeed that implies facing up to turmoil, anxiety, even disarray. Where certainties come apart, there too gathers the strength that no certainty can match.

See also:

Marx (1.1)
Benjamin (1.4)
Spivak (8.4)
Ryan (8.1)

9.6

'GOD IS NOT DIFFÉRANCE'

John D. Caputo

AN IMPOSSIBLE SITUATION

The messianic tone of deconstruction was not at all evident at the start. Instead, in the midst of what looked more like a certain Nietzschean tone recently adopted in French philosophy in the 1960s, Derrida was visited with a suggestive 'objection' that occasioned his first encounter with theology. '[V]ery early on,' he says, 'I was accused of – rather than being congratulated for – resifting the procedures of negative theology' (*Psy.*, 537/DNT,74), of putting these procedures to work, it would seem, in the service of some *magnum mysterium* called *différance*.

As usual, his accusers/congratulators were only half right. For impossible things have on the whole always exercised a greater fascination over Derrida than the garden variety possibilities whose conditions philosophy is tradition-ally content to supply. So, it makes perfect sense that Derrida would 'have always been fascinated' (*Psy.*, 545/DNT, 82) by the impossible situation in which negative or apophatic theology finds itself, of denying that it is possible to speak of God even while, as theology, it keeps on speaking. As a good friend of mine once said, 'Of God I do not believe we can say a thing, but, on the other hand, as a theologian, I have to make a buck.' That is 'the impossible.'

Derrida was understandably fascinated with the syntactical strategies and discursive resources of negative theology, with a deployment of signs intent on

Source: John, D. Caputo, *The Prayers and Tears of Jacques Derrida: Religion without Religion* (Bloomington and Indianapolis: Indiana University Press, 1997), pp. 1–6.

the 'rarefaction of signs,' with a play of traces aimed at effacing the trace, with a language that is 'more or less than a language,' that 'casts suspicion on the very essence or possibility of language' (*Sauf*, 41/ON, 48), with a 'wounded' language, where the 'scar' of the 'impossible' has left its mark (*Sauf*, 63/ON, 59–60), with 'the most economical and most powerful formalization, the greatest reserve of language possible in so few words' (*Sauf*, 113/DNT, 321). He has long been fascinated by the 'experience of the impossible,' the possibility of this impossibility, by the absolute heterogeneity that the *hyper* introduces into the order of the same, interrupting the complacent regime of the possible. Derrida has always been interested in hyperbolic movements, in the whole family of *hyper*, *über*, *epekeina*, *au-delà*, and in movements of denegation, like *pas* and *sans*, which try to speak of not speaking.

Nonetheless, negative theology is worlds removed from deconstruction; the *mise en abîme* of deconstruction is separated by an abyss from the abyss of the Godhead beyond God. The paradox of negative theology – how to speak of the unspeakable transcendence of God – is at best provocatively analogous to the difficulty in which deconstruction finds itself – how to name *différance*, that word or concept that is neither word nor concept. So it is for substantively different albeit strategically analogous reasons that deconstruction, like negative theology, finds itself constantly writing under erasure, saying something without saying it, even deforming and misspelling it (*différance* being the most famous misspelling in contemporary philosophy).

That is why when, one day 'early on,' in the discussion following the original 1968 presentation of the famous paper '*Différance*' (which, for the most loyal deconstructionists, has a status something like the Sermon on the Mount), an interlocutor who had heard enough exclaimed with some exasperation, 'it [*différance*] is the source of everything and one cannot know it: it is the God of negative theology,' Derrida responded with the most exquisite precision and deconstructionist decisiveness, 'It is and it is not.' Yes and no.

As we will see, Derrida easily made the 'no' stick. He dispatched this accusation, or deferred this congratulation, effectively and efficiently, persuasively arguing that whatever their 'syntactical' similarities there is a deep 'semantic' divide between God and *différance*, that 'it,' *différance*, is not the God of negative theology. (We cannot fail to notice that 'God' here is not exactly Yahweh, not the God of prophets like Amos or Isaiah, a God who wants justice, but the God of Christian Neoplatonism.) However highly it is esteemed, *différance* is not God. Negative theology is always on the track of a 'hyperessentiality,' of something hyper-present, hyper-real or sur-real, so really real that we are never satisfied simply to say that it is merely real. *Différance*, on the other hand, is less than real, not quite real, never gets as far as being or entity or presence, which is why it is emblematized by insubstantial quasi-beings like ashes and ghosts which flutter between existence and nonexistence, or with humble *khôra*, say, rather than with the prestigious Platonic sun. *Différance* is but a quasi-transcendental anteriority, not a supereminent, transcendent ulteriority.

I will insist throughout that establishing that negation, getting that denial on the table, is only the beginning and not the end of the story of Derrida's encounter with theology. What Derrida has done is thoroughly misunderstood, I submit, if it is thought that deconstruction has somehow or other 'dispatched' negative theology, simply sent it packing, or shown it to be a transcendental illusion that has been done in by the metaphysics of (hyper) presence, so that our time would now be better passed reading Nietzsche on the death of God. Deconstruction is never merely negative; its desire is never satisfied with 'no, no.' Deconstruction is thoroughly mistrustful of discourses that prohibit this and prohibit that, that weigh us down with debts and 'don'ts.' Deconstruction is so deeply and abidingly affirmative – of something new, of something coming – that it finally breaks out in a vast and sweeping amen, a great *oui, oui* – *à l'impossible*, in a great burst of passion for the impossible. So over and beyond, this first, preparatory and merely negative point, deconstruction says yes, affirming what negative theology affirms whenever it says no. Deconstruction desires what negative theology desires and it shares the passion of negative theology – for the impossible.

Oui, oui. Sic et non.

What has become increasingly clear about deconstruction over the years is that, like negative theology, deconstruction has been taken by surprise, over-taken by the *tout autre*, the wholly other, about which it does not know how not to speak. Like negative theology, deconstruction turns on its desire for the *tout autre*. Derrida analyzes that desire, not like Doctor Derrida, his patient spread out on the couch before his clinical gaze, but with fascination and respect, with a little dose of *docta ignorantia*. For we do not know what we desire. Derrida has not been sent – who would have sent him? – to police negative theology and to tell it what it may desire. For he recognizes this desire for the *tout autre* as his own – yes, yes – indeed as a desire by which – if he is right – we are all inhabited. We are all dreaming of an absolute surprise, pondering an absolute secret, all waiting for the *tout autre* to arrive. So Derrida finds in negative theology a unique and irreducible idiom for answering the call by which we are all addressed, whether our discursive inclinations are theological, antitheological, or a/theological (or something else). For we are all – this is Derrida's wager – dreaming of the wholly other that will come knocking on our door (like Elijah), and, taking language by surprise, will tie our tongue and strike us dumb (almost), filling us with passion. That is why, with the passage of the years, Derrida's relationship with negative theology became more and more affirma-tive, more and more linked by the impossible. The difference is that in negative theology the *tout autre* always goes under the name of God, and that which calls forth speech is called 'God,' whereas for Derrida every other is wholly other (*tout autre est tout autre*). But the name of God is not a bad name and we can love (and save) this name (DLG, 62/OG, 42).

It is a serious misunderstanding, a little perverse, I would say, to think that there is something inherently atheistic about deconstruction, as if, lodged deep down inside *différance* or 'the trace' there were, à la Jean-Paul Sartre, some sort of negative ontological argument against God, against God's good name, as if what Derrida calls 'the trace' knocks out the name of God. On the contrary, Derrida, who 'rightly passes for an atheist,' is an atheist who has his own God, and who loves the name of God, loves that 'event' and what 'takes place' or eventuates in that good name. He has no desire, it goes against *everything* that deconstruction is and desires, to prevent the event of that 'invention.' Indeed, getting ready for the 'invention' of the other, covenanting (*con-venire*) with its in coming (*in-venire*), initialing a pact with the impossible, sticking to the promise of inalterable alterity, *tout autre* – that, says Derrida, 'is what I call deconstruction' (*Psy.*, 53/RDR, 56). That is his passion.

So Derrida follows with fascination the movements of what theology calls God, observing how theology speaks, and how it finds it necessary not to speak under the solicitation of the wholly other. When Meister Eckhart says, 'I pray God to rid me of God,' he formulates with the most astonishing economy a double bind by which we are all bound: how to speak and not speak, how to pray and not pray, to and for the *tout autre*. But in theology the *tout autre* goes (and comes) under the name of God.

Derrida is all along formulating a way to read negative theology, a way to hear it, be addressed by it, to be claimed and taken by surprise by it, which involves all along a way to 'translate' it. His reading makes negative theology of the utmost importance even to those who thank God daily in their temples that they do not believe in God, to those who have closed themselves off to the name of God (and this, often enough, in the name of resisting closure). But in 'translating' negative theology deconstruction has no part in the familiar, nineteenth-century ruse in which a clearheaded master hermeneut, striding to the podium, explains to misty-eyed theologians, their eyes cocked heavenward like that painting of Monica and Augustine in *Circumfession* (*Circon.*, 21/*Circum.*, 17), what they are talking about. Deconstruction is no Dupin deciphering theological self-mystification and showing theology plainly, scientifically, that if theologians could somehow, *per impossibile*, clear their heads ever so briefly they would realize that what they really meant all along by God was Man (Feuerbach), that what they really desired all along was their mommy (Freud), or even, *mirabile dictu*, *différance* itself, *sainte écriture* (the remarkable Mark Taylor, whose work I deeply admire, but who errantly missed the mark, 'early on,' in his first major brush with Derrida in *Erring*).

'Translating' in deconstruction is nothing reductionistic, and that is because *différance* opens things up rather than barring the door closed. Of itself, if it had an itself, *différance* does not tell for or against, does not say or gainsay, monotheism or atheism, even as it loves the name of God. It is no part of the business, or the competency, or the responsibility of deconstruction to decide *what* or *who* is calling in what theology calls God, in what calls theology to order. Theology and faith, all the theologies and their determinable faiths (*Sauf*, 86/ON, 71) – Christian, Jewish, Islamic, whatever – are the responsibility of whoever decides to venture out upon those stormy seas, a responsibility with laws and motivations of its own. The business of deconstruction is not to police theologians or anybody else, to maintain an unbroken Neokantian surveillance over the business of science or everyday life, but to keep things open. Its business is a certain quasi-analysis and affirmation of the trace, of the claims and exclamations that take shape in that place, there (*là*), where things are happening, language and everything else, *il y a du langue* (UG, 124/AL, 296). Its business is the trace, what the trace demands of us, what it inscribes upon us, and what we inscribe within it, whether that is theological or atheological – or perhaps something else, something we can only dream of, something of an absolute surprise.

Deconstruction is not out to undo God or deny faith, or to mock science or make nonsense out of literature, or to break the law or, generally, to ruin any of those hoary things at whose very mention all your muscles constrict. Deconstruction is not in the business of defaming good names but of saving them. *Sauf le nom*. Where would it get the authority? Who would have given it the power to wipe away the horizon, to dry up the sea, or to fill up the abyss with such a decisive, definitive result, such an unbelievable, unbelieving, atheistic closure? Would it mount a public campaign? Where would it get the funds? Would it expect support from the National Endowment for the Humanities? (Dream on!) Why would deconstruction want to associate itself with the *prevention* of the wholly other? What kind of madness would that be for something that arises from a pact with the *tout autre*?

Deconstruction is rather the thought, if it is a thought, of an absolute heterogeneity that unsettles all the assurances of the same within which we comfortably ensconce ourselves. That is the desire by which it is moved, which moves and impassions it, which sets it into motion, toward which it extends itself.

But let there be no mistake: 'early on' deconstruction *does* delimit the *metaphysical* side of theology. Still, is that not an honorable and hoary religious project? Does it not have an honorable name, the name of 'dehellenizing Christianity,' more generally of 'dehellenizing biblical faith'? Is it not an idea as old as Luther, and older still, tracing its origins back to the first chapter of First Corinthians, and older than that, given that the prophets never heard of the science that investigates *to on he on*? Is it not in step with Abraham Heschel's remarkable extrication of the prophets from the grips of metaphysical theology? By inscribing theology within the trace, by describing faith as always and already marked by the trace, by *différance* and undecidability, deconstruction demonstrates that faith is always *faith*, and this in virtue of one of the best descriptions of faith we possess, which is that faith is always through a *glas* darkly.

Even early on, the effect of deconstruction on theology – by which I mean the attempt to bring faith to discursive form – and in particular on negative theology, is not to defame theology but to reinscribe it within the trace and, by putting 'hyperessentialism' in its place, to resituate negative theology *within faith*. For the 'hyperessentialism' of negative theology, which Derrida delimits, would shatter faith and turn it into union, into oneness with the One, 'but then face to face,' which is to get impatient with *glas* and jump the gun. That hyperousiological high for Derrida has always been so much hype. But on the view that I take, a deconstructive theology would find it necessary to deny hyperessentialism in order to make room for faith. *Il faut croire* (MdA, 130/ MB, 129).

Deconstruction saves apophatic theology from telling a bad story about itself, about how it speaks from the Heart of Truth, and how the rest of us had better get in line with it. Or else! That kind of Truth always implies a threat, a dangerous triumphalism. Deconstruction saves the name of negative theology by subjecting it to the same necessity that besets us all, the same *il faut* (*Psy.*, 561/DNT, 99), which is to pull on our textual pants one leg at a time, to forge slowly and from below certain unities of meaning in which we put our trust, understanding all along the mistrust that co-constitutes that trust, the undecidability that inhabits and makes possible that decision. Deconstruction saves negative theology from closure. Closure spells trouble, which is why *différance* cloaks itself in a misspelling. Closure spells exclusion, exclusiveness; closure spills blood, doctrinal, confessional, theological, political, institutional blood, and eventually, it never fails, real blood *Salus in sanguine. Pro deo et patria* spells big trouble, with big words, master words, that need deconstructing.

I pray God to rid me of God, said a master of *Lesen und Leben*.

ABBREVIATIONS

AL	*Acts of Literature*
Circon	'Circonfession'
Circum.	'Circumfession'
DLG	*De la grammatologie*
MB	*Memoirs of the Blind: The Self Portrait and Other Ruins*
MdA	*Memoires d'aveugle*
OG	*Of Grammatology*
ON	*On the Name*
Psych.	'Psyche: Inventions of the Other'
RDR	*Reading De Man Reading*
Sauf	*Sauf le nom*
XUG	*Ulysse gramaphone*

See also:

Norris (3.1)
Royle (4.4)
Bennington (5.1)
Hartman (7.1)

PART 10
THE WORK OF MOURNING

10.1

'(IN MEMORIUM) PAUL DE MAN'

Jacques Derrida

Forgive me for speaking in my own tongue. It's the only one I ever spoke with Paul de Man. It's also the one in which he often taught, wrote and thought. What is more, I haven't the heart today to translate these few words, adding to them the suffering and distance, for you and for me, of a foreign accent. We are speaking today less in order to say something than to assure ourselves, with voice and with music, that we are together in the same thought. We know with what difficulty one finds right and decent words at such a moment when no recourse should be had to common usage since all conventions will seem either intolerable or vain.

If we have, as one says in French, 'la mort dans l'âme,' death in the soul, it is because from now on we are destined to speak *of* Paul de Man, instead of speaking *to* and *with* him, destined to speak of the teacher and of the friend whom he remains for so many of us, whereas the most vivid desire and the one which, within us, has been most cruelly battered, the most forbidden desire from now on would be to speak, still, to Paul, to hear him and to respond to him. Not just within ourselves (we will continue, I will continue to do that endlessly) but to speak to him and to hear him, himself, speaking to us. That's the impossible and we can no longer even take the measure of this wound.

Speaking is impossible, but so too would be silence or absence or a refusal to share one's sadness. Let me simply ask you to forgive me if today finds me with the strength for only a few very simple words. At a later time, I will try to find

Source: Jacques Derrida, '(In memoriam) Paul de Man', *Yale French Studies*, 69, 1985, pp. 323–6.

better words, and more serene ones, for the friendship that ties me to Paul de Man (it was and remains unique), what I, like so many others, owe to his generosity, to his lucidity, to the ever so gentle force of his thought: since that morning in 1966 when I met him at a breakfast table in Baltimore, during a colloquium, where we spoke, among other things, of Rousseau and the *Essai sur l'origine des langues*, a text which was then seldom read in the university but which we had both been working on, each in his own way, without knowing it. From then on, nothing has ever come between us, not even a hint of disagreement. It was like the golden rule of an alliance, no doubt that of a trusting and unlimited friendship, but also the seal of a secret affirmation that, still today, I wouldn't know how to circumscribe, to limit, to name (and that is as it should be). As you know, Paul was irony itself and, among all the vivid thoughts he leaves with us and leaves alive in us, there is as well an enigmatic reflection on irony and even, in the words of Schlegel which he had occasion to cite, on 'irony of irony.' At the heart of my attachment to him, there has also always been a certain beyond-of-irony which cast on his own a softening, generous light, reflecting a smiling compassion on everything he illuminated with his tireless vigilance. His lucidity was sometimes overpowering, making no concession to weakness, but it never gave in to that negative assurance with which the ironic consciousness is sometimes too easily satisfied.

At some later time, then, I will try to find better words for what his friendship brought to all of those who had the good fortune to be his friend, his colleague, his student; but also for his work and especially for the future of his work, undoubtedly one of the most influential of our time.[1] His work, in other words, his teaching and his books, those already published and those soon to appear – because, to the very last and with an admirable strength, enthusiasm and gaiety, he worked on ever new lectures and writing projects, enlarging and enriching still further the perspectives he had already opened up for us. As we know already but as we shall also come to realize more and more, he transformed the field of literary theory, revitalizing all the channels that irrigate it both inside and outside the university, in the United States and in Europe. Besides a new style of interpretation, of reading, of teaching, he brought to bear the necessity of the polylogue and of a plurilinguistic refinement which was his genius – not only that of national languages (Flemish, French, German, English) but also of those idioms which are literature and philosophy, renewing as he did so the reading of Pascal as well as Rilke, of Descartes and Hölderlin, of Hegel and Keats, Rousseau and Shelley, Nietzsche and Kant, Locke and Diderot, Stendahl and Kierkegaard, Coleridge, Kleist, Wordsworth and Baudelaire, Proust, Mallarmé and Blanchot, Austin and Heidegger, Benjamin, Bakhtin and so many others, contemporary or not. Never content merely to present new readings, he led one to think the very possibility of reading – and also sometimes the paradox of its impossibility. His commitment remains henceforth that of his friends and his students who owe it to him and to themselves to pursue what was begun by him and with him.

Beyond the manifest evidence of the published texts – his own as well as those that make reference to his – I, like many others, can attest to what is today the radiance of his thought and his words: in the United States, first of all, where so many universities are linked and enlivened by the large community of his disciples, the large family of his former students or colleagues who have remained his friends; but also in Europe at all the universities where I had, as I did here at Yale, the good fortune and the honor to work with him, often at his invitation. I think first of Zurich, where we came together so many times, with Patricia, with Hillis; and naturally I think of Paris where he lived, published and shared editorial or academic responsibilities (for example, for Johns Hopkins or Cornell – and again these were for us the occasion of so many encounters). I also know the impression his passage left on the universities of Constance, Berlin and Stockholm. I will say nothing of Yale because you know this better than anyone and because today my memory is too given over to mourning for all that I have shared with him here during the last ten years, from the most simple day-to-dayness to the most intense moments in the work that allied us with each other and with others, the friends, students and colleagues who grieve for him so close to me here.

I wanted only to *bear witness* as would befit the sort of admiring observer I have also been at his side in the American and European academic world. This is neither the time nor the place to give into indiscreet revelations or too personal memories. I will refrain from speaking of such memories therefore – I have too many of them, as do many of you, and they are so overwhelming that we prefer to be alone with them. But allow me to infringe this law of privacy long enough to evoke two memories, just two among so many others.

The last letter I received from Paul: I still don't know how to read the serenity or the cheerfulness which it displayed. I never knew to what extent he adopted this tone, in a gesture of noble and sovereign discretion, so as to console and spare his friends in their anxiety or their despair; or, on the contrary, to what extent he had succeeded in transfiguring what is still for us the worst. No doubt it was both. Among other things, he wrote what I am going to permit myself to read here because, rightly or wrongly, I received it as a message, confided to me, for his friends in distress. You'll hear a voice and a tone that are familiar to us: 'All of this, as I was telling you [on the phone], seems prodigiously interesting to me and I'm enjoying myself a lot. I knew it all along but it is being borne out: death gains a great deal, as they say, when one gets to know it close up – that "peu profond ruisseau calomnié la mort" [shallow stream caluminated as death].' And after having cited this last line from Mallarmé's 'Tombeau for Verlaine,' he added: 'Anyhow, I prefer that to the brutality of the word "tumeur"' – which, in fact, is more terrible, more insinuating and menacing in French than in any other language [tumeur/tu meurs: you are dying].

I recall the second memory because it says something about music – and only music today seems to me bearable, consonant, able to give some measure of what unites us in the same thought. I had known for a long time, even though he

469

spoke of it very rarely, that music occupied an important place in Paul's life and thought. On that particular night – it was 1979 and once again the occasion was a colloquium – we were driving through the streets of Chicago after a jazz concert. My older son, who had accompanied me, was talking with Paul about music, more precisely about musical instruments. This they were doing as the experts they both were, as technicians who know how to call things by their name. It was then I realized that Paul had never told me he was an experienced musician and that music had also been a practice with him. The word that let me know this was the word 'âme' [soul] when, hearing Pierre, my son, and Paul speak with familiarity of the violin's or the bass's soul, I learned that the 'soul' is the name one gives in French to the small and fragile piece of wood – always very exposed, very vulnerable – that is placed within the body of these instruments to support the bridge and assure the resonant communication of the two sounding boards. I didn't know why at that moment I was so strangely moved and unsettled in some dim recess by the conversation I was listening to: no doubt it was due to the word 'soul' which always speaks to us at the same time of life and of death and makes us dream of immortality, like the argument of the lyre in the *Phaedo*.

And I will always regret, among so many other things, that I never again spoke of any of this with Paul. How was I to know that one day I would speak of that moment, that music and that soul without him, before you who must forgive me for doing it just now so poorly, so painfully when already everything is painful, so painful?

NOTE

1. Jacques Derrida will soon publish an essay in homage to Paul de Man (Univeristy of Minnesota Press) and a longer work on the oeuvre of Paul de Man (Columbia University Press), the result of conferences held at the University of California at Irvine in April 1984 (editorial note).

'TEXT READ AT LOUIS ALTHUSSER'S FUNERAL'

Jacques Derrida

I knew, in advance, that today I would be incapable of speaking, of finding the words, as it were.

Excuse me, therefore, if I read, and for reading not what I believe I must say (does one ever know what one must say in such a moment?), but simply enough to not let silence win out over everything else – just a few shreds of what I was able to tear away from the silence in the depths of which I would, like you, doubtlessly, have been tempted to close myself at this instant.

I learned of Louis' death within the last twenty-four hours, upon returning from Prague – and the name of that city already seems to me so violent, almost unpronounceable. But I knew that upon my return I had to call him: I had promised him I would.

Someone present here, who was near Louis when I last spoke to him on the telephone, probably remembers: when I promised to call him and to come and see him when I came back from this trip, his last words, the last words I will have heard Louis pronounce were, 'if I'm still alive, yes, call me and come over, hurry.' I had answered him in a jocular tone in order to hide somewhere above my anxiousness and sadness, 'OK, I'll call and go over.'

Louis, that time is no longer with us, I no longer have the strength to call you, to talk to anyone – even to you (you are at once too absent and too close: in me, inside me), and even less have I the strength to speak to others about you even if they be, as is the case today, your friends, our friends.

Source: Michael Sprinkner (ed.), *The Althusserian Legacy* (London: Verso, 1994), pp. 241–5.

I haven't the heart either to recount anything or to pronounce a eulogy: there would be too much to say and this is not the moment. Our friends, your friends who are present here know why it is almost indecent to speak now – and to continue to direct our words to you. But silence is just as unbearable. I cannot stand the idea of silence, as if, within me, you too could not stand the idea.

On the death of someone close or of a friend, when one has shared so much with him (and, here, I have been lucky in that, for thirty-eight years, my life has been linked in a thousand strange ways with that of Louis Althusser, since 1952, when the *caïman* received into his office the young student that I was then, and since the time when, later, in the same place, I worked by his side for nearly twenty years), when one remembers just as well the light moments and the carefree laughter of days that pass by as one does the moments spent in intense work, teaching, thinking, in the philosophical and political *polemos*, or further, the wounds and the worst wrenching moments, the dramas and the mournings, at the death of this friend, there is, you all know, as always that pang of guilt, egotistical, to be sure, narcissistic also, but irrepressible, consisting in complaining to oneself and taking pity, that is, taking pity oneself upon oneself, and saying (and I am doing just this, because this conventional phrase never fails, nonetheless, to tell the truth of this compassion): 'a whole part of my life, a long and intense coursing of my living self has been interrupted today, concludes and thus dies with Louis in order to continue to accompany him as in the past, but now without return and to the limits of absolute obscurity.' What ends, what Louis takes away with him is not only this or that thing here or there that we would have shared at some time or another, it is the world itself, a certain origin of the world – his world, of course, but also the one in which I have lived, in which we had lived a unique story, one that is, in any case, irreplaceable and which will have had some sense or another for either one of us, even if this sense could not be the same either for him or for me. It is a world that is for us *the* world, the only world, one that sinks into an abyss from which no memory (even if we keep the memory, and we will do so) can save it.

Even though I detect some intolerable violence in this movement consisting in complaining about one's own death upon the death of a friend, I have no desire to abstain from it: it is the only way remaining to keep Louis in me, to conserve myself by conserving him in me just as, I am sure, we are all doing, each with his memory, which itself only exists with this movement of mourning, with its piece of torn-off history – and this was such a rich and singular history, a murderous and still unthinkable tragedy so inseparable too from the history of our time, so heavy with the whole philosophical, political, geopolitical history of our time – a history that each of us still apprehends with his own images. And there have been so many images – the most beautiful and the most terrible – but all forever indissociable from the unique adventure which carries the name of Louis Althusser. I think I can speak for everyone here today when I say that our belonging to this time was ineradicably marked by him, by what he searched for, experimented with, risked at the highest price, by means of all movements:

determined, suspended, authoritarian and personally concerned at the same time, contradictory, consequential or convulsive, extraordinarily impassioned as he was – a passion that left him no respite because it spared him nothing (with its theatrical rhythms, its deserts, its great spaces of silence, vertiginous retreats, those impressive interruptions themselves interrupted in their turn by demonstrations, forceful incursions, and powerful eruptions of which each of his books preserves the burning trace for their having first transformed the landscape around the volcano.

Louis Althusser traversed so many lives – ours, first off – so many personal, historical, philosophical, and political adventures, he marked, inflected, and influenced so many discourses, actions, and existences by the radiating and provocative force of his thought, his manners of being, speaking, teaching, that even the most diverse and contradictory testimonials could never exhaust their very source. The fact that each of us had a different relationship with Louis Althusser (and I am not only speaking of philosophy or politics), the fact that each of us knows that, through his or her singular prism, he or she only caught a glimpse of but one secret (an inexhaustible secret for us, but also, and in an altogether different way, fathomless for him), the fact that Louis was altogether different for other people, in these times and in others, within academia and without, at the rue d'Ulm and everywhere else in France, in the Communist Party, the other parties and beyond all parties, within Europe and without, the fact that each of us loved a different Louis Althusser, at some time, in some decade or another (as it was my fortune till the very end) – this generous multiplicity, this very overabundance that was his creates an obligation for us not to totalize, not to simplify, not to stop his step, not to fix a trajectory, not to seek some advantage, not to cross things out or to get even, and especially not to make calculations, not to appropriate or reappropriate (even if it be through that paradoxical form of manipulating or calculating reappropriation that is called rejection), not to seize what was inappropriable and must remain so. Each of us has a thousand faces, but those who knew Louis Althusser know that, in him, this law found a glittering, surprising and hyperbolic example. His work is, in the first place, great by what it attests to and by what it risks, by what it traversed with that plural, shattered, and oftentimes interrupted flash, by the very high risk taken and the endurance accepted: his adventure is singular, it belongs to no one.

I have no difficulty speaking (as I must here) about the things that tended to separate him and me, even to oppose us (implicitly or not, sometimes harshly, on both small and important matters) because they never chipped away at a friendship that was the dearer to me on account of those differences. For at no time could I consider that what was happening to him or what was happening through him, in these places where I still dwell with him, as anything other than upheavals in series, earthquakes or awakenings of volcanos, the singular or collective tragedies of our times – the time that I will have, like you, shared with him. Never, in spite of everything that might have distanced us from each other or separated us, never was I able or did I wish to observe (that is, with a spectator's neutrality) what was happening to him or what was happening through him. And for everything which by his means or through him occupied my whole adult life, even as far as the wrenching trials that we are all thinking of, I will always remain, at the bottom of my heart, grateful. The same goes for that which is irreplaceable. And of course, what remains the most present to my eyes, the most alive today, the closest and the most precious, is his face, Louis' handsome face with its high forehead, his smile, everything which in him, in the moments of peace (there were moments of peace: many of you here know that there were) – everything that radiated kindness, the gift and demand of love, manifesting an incomparable attentiveness to the youth of that which is coming, curiously vigilant for the dawn of signs still waiting to be understood, as to everything that upset the order, the program, facile consonance and previsibility. What to me remains today most alive is what in the light of that face bespoke a lucidity at once implacable and indulgent, by turns resigned or triumphant, as was sometimes the case with the verve of certain of his outbursts. What I love the most in him, probably because this was him, what fascinated me through what others probably knew better than I, and from much closer than I, was the sense and taste of grandeur – a certain grandeur, of the great theater of political tragedy where the greater-than-life engages, deviates or pitilessly shatters the private body of its actors.

When it arranges the echoing of proper names like so many direction arrows or trails upon a territory to be occupied, public discourse about Althusser allows the names of Montesquieu, for example, or Rousseau, Marx or Lenin to resonate. Those who, sometimes behind the great curtains of that political theater, approached Althusser, those who approached the hospital room and the bedside know that they owe it to truth to also name Pascal, for example, and Dostoyevsky, and Nietzsche – and Artaud.

Deep down inside, I realize that Louis doesn't hear me: he only hears me inside me, inside us (we are, however, only *ourselves* from that point within us where the other, the mortal other, resonates). And I know that within me his voice is insisting that I do not pretend to speak to him. I also know that I have nothing to teach you who are here, *since* you are here.

But above this tomb and above your heads, I dream of addressing those who come after him, or after us already, and whom I see (alas, by several signs) as too much in a hurry to understand, to interpret, to classify, fix, reduce, simplify, close off, and judge, that is, to misunderstand that, here, it is a question of an oh-so-singular destiny and of the trials of existence, of thought, of politics, inseparably. I would ask them to stop a moment, to take the time to listen to our time (we had no other one), to patiently decipher everything that from our time could be ratified and promised in the life, the work, the name of Louis Althusser. Not only because the dimensions of this destiny should command respect (also the respect of the time from which emerge these other generations, our generation), but also because the yet open wounds, the scars or hopes that they will recognize in it and which were and are our scars and hopes, will certainly teach them something essential of what remains to be heard, read, thought, and done. As long as I live, that is, as long as the memory remains with me of what Louis Althusser gave me to live with him, near him: this is what I would like to recall to those who were not of his time or who will not have taken the time to turn toward him. This is what I would hope one day to express more eloquently, without bidding adieu, for Louis Althusser.

And now I want to give him back or lend him the floor. For another last word: his again. Rereading some of his works late into last night, the following passage imposed itself upon me more than I read it or elected it to be resaid here. It is from one of his first texts, *Bertolazzi et Brecht* (1962):

> Yes, we are first united by that institution that the spectacle is, but we are more deeply united by the same myths, the same themes that govern us without our admitting it, by the same spontaneously lived ideology. Yes, even though it is *par excellence* that of the poor, as in *El Nost Milan*, we eat the same bread, experience the same angers, the same revolts, the same deliria (at least in memory, where this imminent possibility haunts us), not to mention the same despondency over a time that no History can move. Yes, like Mother Courage, we have the same war at our doorstep, a hairsbreadth away, even inside us, the same horrible blindness, the same ashes in our eyes, the same earth in our mouths. We possess the same dawn and the same night: our unconsciousness. We share the same story – and that is where everything begins.

10.3

'ADIEU: EMMANUEL LEVINAS'

Jacques Derrida

For a long time, for a very long time, I've feared having to say *adieu* to Emmanuel Levinas. I knew that my voice would tremble at the moment of saying it, and especially saying it aloud, right here, before him, so close to him pronouncing this word of *adieu*, this word '*à-Dieu*,' which in a certain sense I get from him, a word that he will have taught me to think or to pronounce otherwise. By meditating upon what Emmanuel Levinas wrote about the French word '*adieu*' – which I will recall in a few moments – I hope to find a sort of encouragement to speak here. And I would like to do so with unadorned, naked words, words as childlike and disarmed as my sorrow.

Yet whom would one be addressing at such a moment? And in whose name would one allow oneself to do so? Oftentimes, those who come forward to speak, to speak publicly, thereby interrupting the animated whispering, the secret or intimate exchange that always links one deep down inside to the dead friend or master, those who can be heard in a cemetery, end up addressing *directly*, *straight on*, the one who, as we say, is no longer, is no longer living, no longer there, who will no longer respond; with tears in their voice, they sometimes speak familiarly [*tutoient*] to the other who keeps silent, calling upon him without detour or mediation, apostrophizing him, greeting him even or confiding in him. This is not necessarily out of respect for convention, not always simply part of the rhetoric of oration. It is rather so as to traverse speech at the very point where we find ourselves lacking the words, and because all

Source: Jacques Derrida, 'Adieu: Emmanuel Levinas', *Critical Enquiry*, 23, Autumn 1996, pp. 1–10.

language that would return to the self, to us, would seem indecent, a sort of reflexive discourse that would end up coming back to the stricken community, to its consolation or its mourning, to what is called, in this confused and terrible expression, 'the work of mourning.' Concerned only with itself, such speech would, in this return, run the risk of turning away from what is here our law – and the law as *straightforwardness* or *uprightness* [*droiture*]: to speak straight on, to address oneself directly *to* the other, and to speak *for* the other whom one loves and admires, before speaking *of* him. To say to him *adieu*, to him, Emmanuel, and not merely to recall what he will have first taught us about a certain *Adieu*.

This word *droiture* – 'straightforwardness' or 'uprightness' – is another word that I began to hear otherwise and to learn when it came to me from Emmanuel Levinas. Of all the places where he speaks of uprightness, what comes to mind first is one of his *Four Talmudic Readings*, since it is there that uprightness names that which is, as he says, 'stronger than death.'

But let us also keep from trying to find in everything that is said to be 'stronger than death' a refuge or an alibi, yet another consolation. To define uprightness, Emmanuel Levinas says in his commentary on the 'Tractate *Shabbath*' that consciousness is the 'urgency of a destination leading to the Other and not an eternal return to self,'

> an innocence without naivete, an uprightness without stupidity, an absolute uprightness which is also absolute self-criticism, read in the eyes of the one who is the goal of my uprightness and whose look calls me into question. It is a movement toward the other that does not come back to its point of origin the way diversion comes back, incapable as it is of transcendence – a movement beyond anxiety and stronger than death. This uprightness is called *Temimut*, the essence of Jacob.[1]

This same meditation also set to work – as each meditation did, though each in a singular way – all the great themes to which the thought of Emmanuel Levinas has awakened us, that of responsibility first of all, but of an 'unlimited' responsibility that exceeds and precedes my freedom, that of an 'unconditional yes,' as this text says, of a '*yes* older than that of naive spontaneity,' a *yes* in accord with this uprightness that is 'original fidelity to an indissoluble alliance.'[2] And the final words of this Lesson return, of course, to death, but they do so precisely so as not to let death have the last word, or the first one. They remind us of a recurrent theme in what was a long and incessant meditation upon death, but one that set out on a path that ran counter to the philosophical tradition running from Plato to Heidegger. Elsewhere, before saying what the *à-Dieu* must be, another text speaks of the 'extreme uprightness of the face of my neighbor' as the 'uprightness of an exposure to death, without any defense'.[3]

I cannot find, and would not even want to try to find, a few words to size up the oeuvre of Emmanuel Levinas. It is so large that one can no longer even see its edges. And one would have to begin by learning once again from him and from

Totality and Infinity, for example, how to think what an 'oeuvre' or 'work' is – as well as fecundity. Moreover, one can predict with a certain confidence that centuries of readings will set this as their task. Already, well beyond France and Europe – and we see innumerable signs of this every day in so many works and in so many languages, in all the translations, courses, seminars, conferences, and so on – the reverberations of this thought will have changed the course of the philosophical reflection of our time, and of the reflection *on* philosophy, on that which orders it according to ethics, according to another thought of ethics, responsibility, justice, the state, and so on, another thought of the other, a thought that is newer than so many novelties because it is ordered to the absolute anteriority of the face of the Other.

Yes, ethics before and beyond ontology, the state, or politics, but also ethics beyond ethics. One day, on the rue Michel Ange, during one of those conversations whose memory I hold so dear, one of those conversations illuminated by the radiance of his thought, the goodness of his smile, the gracious humor of his ellipses, he said to me: 'You know, one often speaks of ethics to describe what I do, but what really interests me in the end is not ethics, not ethics alone, but the holy, the holiness of the holy.' And I then thought of a singular separation, the unique separation of the curtain or veil that is given, ordered and ordained [*donné, ordonné*], by God, the veil entrusted by Moses to an inventor or an artist rather than to an embroiderer, the veil that would *separate* the holy of holies in the sanctuary. And I also thought of how other *Talmudic Lessons* sharpen the necessary distinction between sacredness and holiness, that is, the holiness of the other, the holiness of the person, who is, as Emmanuel Levinas said elsewhere, 'more holy than a land, even a holy land, since, faced with an affront made to a person, this holy land appears in its nakedness to be but stone and wood.'[4]

This meditation on ethics, on the transcendence of the holy with regard to the sacred, that is, with regard to the paganism of roots and the idolatry of place, was, of course, indissociable from an incessant reflection upon the destiny and thought of Israel, yesterday, today, and tomorrow. Such reflection consisted in a requestioning and reaffirmation of the legacies of not only the biblical and talmudic tradition but of the terrifying memory of our time. This memory dictates each of these sentences, whether from close or from afar, even if Levinas would sometimes protest against certain self-justifying abuses to which such a memory and the reference to the Holocaust might give rise.

But refraining from commentaries and questions, I would simply like to give thanks to someone whose thought, friendship, trust, and 'goodness' (and I ascribe to this word *goodness* all the significance it is given in the final pages of *Totality and Infinity*) will have been for me, as for so many others, a living source, so living, so constant, that I am unable to think what is happening to him or happening to me today, namely, this interruption or a certain nonresponse in a response that will never come to an end for me as long as I live.

The nonresponse: you will no doubt recall that in the remarkable course he gave in 1975–76 (exactly twenty years ago) on *Death and Time*, there where he defines death as the patience of time, and where he engages in a grand and noble critical encounter with Plato as much as with Hegel, but especially with Heidegger, Emmanuel Levinas there often defines death, the death that 'we meet' 'in the face of the Other,' as *nonresponse*; 'it is the without-response,' he says. And elsewhere: 'There is here an end that always has the ambiguity of a departure without return, of a passing away but also of a scandal ("is it really possible that he's dead?") of non-response and of my responsibility.'[5]

Death: not first of all annihilation, nonbeing, or nothingness, but a certain experience for the survivor of the 'without-response.' Already *Totality and Infinity* called into question the traditional 'philosophical and religious' interpretation of death as either 'a passage to nothingness' or 'a passage to some other existence.'[6] To identify death with nothingness is what the murderer would like to do, Cain for example, who, says Emmanuel Levinas, must have had such a knowledge of death. But even this nothingness presents itself as a 'sort of impossibility' or, more precisely, an interdiction. The face of the Other forbids me from killing; it says to me 'you shall not kill,' even if this possibility remains presupposed by the interdiction that makes it impossible. This question without response, this question of the without-response, would thus be underivable, primordial, like the interdiction against killing, more originary than the alternative of 'to be or not to be,' which is thus neither the first nor the last question. 'To be or not to be,' another essay concludes, 'is probably not the question par excellence' ('C,' p. 151).

I draw from all this today that our infinite sadness must shy away from everything in mourning that would turn toward nothingness, that is, toward that which still – even potentially – links guilt to murder. Levinas indeed speaks of the guilt of the survivor, but it is a guilt without fault and without debt; it is, in truth, an *entrusted responsibility*, entrusted in a moment of unparalleled emotion, at the moment when death remains the absolute ex-ception. To express this unprecedented emotion, the one I feel here and share with you, the one that our sense of propriety forbids us from exhibiting, and so as to make clear without personal avowal or exhibition how this singular emotion is related to this entrusted responsibility, entrusted as legacy, allow me once again to let Emmanuel Levinas speak, he whose voice I would so much love to hear today when it says that the 'death of the other' is the 'first death,' and that 'I am responsible for the other insofar as he is mortal.' Or else the following, from this same course of 1975–76:

> The death of someone is not, in spite of what it appeared to be at first glance, an empirical facticity (death as an empirical fact whose induction alone could suggest its universality); it is not exhausted in such an appearance. Someone who expresses himself in his nakedness – the face – is in fact one to the extent that he calls upon me, to the extent that he

places himself under my responsibility: I must already answer for him, be responsible for him. Every gesture of the Other was a sign addressed to me. To return to the classification sketched out above: to show oneself, to express oneself, to associate oneself, *to be entrusted to me*. The Other who expresses himself is entrusted to me (and there is no debt with regard to the Other – for that which is due cannot be paid: one will never be even) [further on it will be a question of a 'duty beyond all debt' for the I who is what it is, singular and identifiable, only through the impossibility of being able to be replaced, even though it is precisely here that the 'responsibility for the Other,' the 'responsibility of the hostage,' is an experience of substitution and sacrifice]. The Other individuates me in that responsibility that I have for him. The death of the Other who dies affects me in my very identity as a responsible I . . . made up of unspeakable responsibility. This is how I am affected by the death of the Other, this is my relation with his death. It is, in my relation, my deference toward someone who no longer responds, already a guilt of the survivor. [*MT*, pp. 14–15; quotation in brackets, p. 25]

And a bit further on:

The relation to death in its ex-ception – and, regardless of its signification in relation to being and nothingness, it is an exception – while conferring upon death its depth, is neither a seeing nor even an aiming towards (neither a seeing of being as in Plato nor an aiming towards nothingness as in Heidegger), a purely emotional relation, moving with an emotion that is not made up of the repercussions of a prior knowledge upon our sensibility and our intellect. It is an emotion, a movement, an uneasiness with regard to the *unknown*. [*MT*, pp. 18–19]

The unknown is here emphasized. The unknown is not the negative limit of some knowledge. This nonknowledge is the element of friendship or hospitality, for the transcendence of the stranger, the infinite distance of the other. 'Unknown' is the word chosen by Maurice Blanchot for the title of an essay, 'Knowledge of the Unknown,' which he devoted to the one who had been, from the time of their meeting in Strasbourg in 1923, the friend, the very friendship of the friend. For many among us, no doubt, for myself certainly, the absolute fidelity, the exemplary friendship of thought, the *friendship* between Maurice Blanchot and Emmanuel Levinas was a grace, a gift; it remains as a benediction of this time, and, for more than one reason, the good fortune that is also a blessing for all those who have had the great privilege of being the friend of either one of them. In order to hear once again today, right here, Blanchot speak for Levinas, and with Levinas, as I had the good fortune to do when in their company one day in 1968, I will cite a couple of lines. After having named that which in the other 'ravishes' us, after having spoken of a certain 'rapture' (the word often used by Levinas to speak of death), Blanchot says:

But we must not despair of philosophy. In Emmanuel Levinas's book [*Totality and Infinity*] – where, it seems to me, philosophy in our time has never spoken in a more sober manner, putting back into question, as we must, our ways of thinking and even our facile reverence for ontology – we are called upon to become responsible for what philosophy essentially is, by welcoming, in all the radiance and infinite exigency proper to it, the idea of the Other, that is to say, the relation with *autrui*. It is as though there were here a new departure in philosophy and a leap that it, and we ourselves, were urged to accomplish.[7]

If the relation to the other presupposes an infinite separation, an infinite interruption where the face appears, what happens, where and to whom does it happen, when another interruption comes at death to hollow out with even more infinity this prior separation, a rending interruption at the heart of interruption itself? I cannot speak of the interruption without recalling, like many among you no doubt, the anxiety of interruption that I could feel in Emmanuel Levinas when, on the telephone for example, he seemed at each moment to fear being cut off, to fear the silence or disappearance, the 'without-response,' of the other whom he tried to call out to and hold on to with an 'allo, allo' between each sentence, and sometimes even in midsentence.

What happens when a great thinker becomes silent, one whom we knew living, whom we read and reread, and also heard, one from whom we were still awaiting a response, as if such a response would help us not only to think otherwise but also to read what we thought we had already read under his signature, a response diet held everything in reserve, and so much more than what we thought we had already recognized in that signature? This is an experience that, I have learned, would remain for me interminable with Emmanuel Levinas, as with all thoughts that are sources, for I will never stop beginning or beginning anew to think with them on the basis of the new beginning they give me, and I will begin again and again to rediscover them on just about any subject. Each time I read or reread Emmanuel Levinas, I am overwhelmed with gratitude and admiration, overwhelmed by this necessity, which is not a constraint but an extremely gentle force that obligates and obligates us not to bend or curve otherwise the space of thought in its respect for the other but to yield to this other heteronomous curvature that relates us to the completely other (that is, to justice, as he says somewhere in a powerful and formidable ellipsis: the relation to the other, that is to say, justice), according to the law that thus calls us to yield to the other infinite precedence of the completely other. It will have come, like this call, to disturb, discreetly but irreversibly, the most powerful and established thoughts of the end of this millennium, beginning with those of Husserl and Heidegger whom Levinas in fact introduced into France some sixty-five years ago! Indeed, this country whose hospitality he so much loved (and *Totality and Infinity* shows not only that 'the essence of language is goodness' but that 'the essence of language is friendship and hospitality'),[8] this hospitable France, owes him, among so many other things, among so many other significant contributions, at least two irruptive events of thought, two inaugural acts that are difficult to measure today because they have been so much incorporated into the very element of our philosophical culture after having transformed its landscape.

There was first, to say it all too quickly, beginning in 1930 with translations and interpretative readings, the initial introduction to Husserlian phenomenology, which would in turn irrigate and fecundate so many French philosophical currents. Then, and in truth simultaneously, there was the introduction to Heideggerian thought, which was no less important in the genealogy of so many French philosophers, professors, and students. Husserl and Heidegger at the same time, beginning in 1930. I wanted last night to reread a few pages from this prodigious book that was for me, as for many others before me, the first and best guide. I picked out a few sentences that have made their mark in time and that allow us to measure the distance he will have helped us cover. In 1930, a young man of twenty-three said in the preface that I reread, and reread smiling, smiling at him: 'The fact that in France phenomenology is not a doctrine known to everyone has been a constant problem in the writing of this book.' Or again, speaking of the so very 'powerful and original philosophy' of 'Mr. Martin Heidegger, whose influence on this book will often be felt,' the same book also recalls that 'the problem raised here by transcendental phenomenology is an ontological problem in the very precise sense that Heidegger gives to this term.'[9]

The second event, the second philosophical tremor, I would even say the happy traumatism that we owe him (in the sense of the word *traumatism* that he liked to recall, the 'traumatism of the other' that comes from the Other), is that, while closely reading and reinterpreting the thinkers I just mentioned, but so many others as well, both philosophers such as Descartes, Kant, and Kierkegaard, and writers such as Dostoyevsky, Kafka, Proust, and so on – all the while disseminating his words through publications, courses, and lectures (at the École Normale Israélite Orientale, at the Collège Philosophique, and at the Universities of Poitiers, Nanterre, and the Sorbonne) – Emmanuel Levinas slowly displaced, but so as to bend them according to an inflexible and simple exigency, the axis, trajectory, and even the order of phenomenology or ontology that he had introduced into France beginning in 1930. Once again, he completely changed the landscape without landscape of thought; he did so in a dignified way, without polemic, at once from within, faithfully, and from very far away, from the attestation of a completely other place. And I believe that what occurred there, in this second sailing, in this second time that leads us even further back than the first, is a discreet but irreversible mutation, one of those very powerful, very singular, and very rare provocations within history that, for over two thousand years now, will have ineffaceably marked the space and body of what is more or less, or in any case something different than, a simple dialogue between Jewish thought and its others, the philosophies of Greek origin or, in the tradition of a certain 'here I am,' the other Abrahamic monotheisms. This happened, this mutation happened, *through him*, through Emmanuel Levinas, who was conscious of this immense responsibility in a way that was, I believe, at once clear, confident, calm, and modest, like that of a prophet.

One of the indications of this historical shock wave is the influence of this thought well beyond philosophy, and well beyond Jewish thought, in various circles of Christian theology, for example. I cannot help but recall the day when, during a meeting of the Congrès des Intellectuels Juifs, as we were both listening to a lecture by André Neher, Emmanuel Levinas turned to me and said with the gentle irony so familiar to us: 'You see, he's the Jewish Protestant and I'm the Catholic' – a quip that would call for long and serious reflection.

Everything that has happened here has happened through him, thanks to him, and we have had the good fortune not only of receiving it while living, from him living, as a responsibility entrusted by the living to the living, but also the good fortune of owing it to him with a light and innocent debt. One day, speaking of his research on death and of what it owed Heidegger at the very moment when it was moving away from him, Levinas wrote: 'It distinguishes itself from Heidegger's thought, and it does so in spite of the debt that every contemporary thinker owes to Heidegger – a debt that one often regrets' (*MT*, p. 8). Now, the good fortune of our debt toward Levinas is that we can, thanks to him, assume it and affirm it without regret, in the joyous innocence of admiration. It is of the order of this unconditional *yes* of which I spoke earlier and to which it responds 'yes.' The regret, my regret, is not having said this to him enough, not having shown him this enough in the course of these thirty years, during which, in the modesty of silences, through brief or discreet conversations, writings that were too indirect or reserved, we often addressed to one another what I would call neither questions nor answers but, perhaps, to use another one of his words, a sort of 'question, prayer,' a question-prayer that, as he says, would be anterior even to the dialogue. This question-prayer that turned me toward him perhaps already shared in this experience of the *à-Dieu* with which I began earlier. The greeting of the *à-Dieu* does not signal the end. 'The *à-Dieu* is not a finality,' he says, thus challenging this 'alternative between being and nothingness,' which 'is not ultimate.' The *à-Dieu* greets the other beyond being, in 'what signifies, beyond being, the word glory.' 'The *à-Dieu* is not a process of being; in the call, I am referred back to the other human being through whom this call signifies, to the neighbor for whom I am to fear' ('C,' p. 150).

But I said that I did not want simply to recall what he entrusted to us of the *à-Dieu* but first of all to say *adieu* to him, to call him by his name, to call his name, his first name, such as he is called at the moment when, if he no longer responds, it is because he responds in us, from the bottom of our hearts, in us but before us, in us right before us – in calling us, in recalling to us: 'à-Dieu.'

Adieu, Emmanuel.

NOTES

1. Emmanuel Levinas, *Ouatre Lectures Talmudiques* (Paris, 1968), p. 105; trans. Annette Aronow cz, under the title 'Four Talmudic Readings,' *Nine Talmudic Readings* (Bloomington. Ind., 1990), p. 48.

2. Ibid., pp. 106–8; pp. 49–50.

3. Levinas, 'La Conscience non-intentionnelle,' *Entre nous: Essais sur le penser-à-l'autre* (Paris, 1991), p. 149; hereafter abbreviated 'C.'

4. Schlomo Malka, interview with Levinas, *Les Nouveaux Cahiers* 18 (1982–83): 1–8; trans. Jonathan Romney, in *The Levinas Reader*, ed. Seán Hand (Cambridge, Mass., 1989), p. 297.

5. Levinas, *La Mort et le temps* (Paris, 1991), pp. 10, 13, 41–42; hereafter abbreviated *MT.*

6. Levinas, *Totalité et infini* (The Hague, 1961), pp. 208–9; trans. Alphonso Lingis, under the title *Totality and Infinity* (Pittsburgh, 1969), p. 232.

7. Maurice Blanchot, *L'Entretien infini* (Paris, 1969), pp. 73–74; trans. Susan Hanson, under the title *The Infinite Conversation* (Minneapolis, 1993), pp. 51–52.

8. Levinas, *Totalité et infini*, p. 282; Levinas, *Totality and Infinity*, p. 305.

9. Levinas, *Théorie de l'intuition dans la phénoménologie de Husserl* (1930; Paris, 1970), pp. 7, 14–15; trans. André Orianne, under the title *The Theory of Intuition in Husserl's Phenomenology*, (Évanston, Ill., 1973), p. xxxiv. As the translator notes, Levinas's short preface, or 'Avant-Propos,' was omitted from the translation and replaced by the translator's foreword so as to include a series of 'historical remarks more specifically directed to today's English reader' (p. xxvii).

This text was delivered as the funeral oration for Emmanuel Levinas on 28 December 1995.

We would like to thank the members of the 1996 Levinas Seminar at DePaul University for their generous help with the preparation of this translation. Unless otherwise noted, all translations, and all notes, are our own. This essay is being published simultaneously in *Philosophy Today* 40 (Fall 1996). Many thanks to David Pellauer.

'I'M GOING TO HAVE TO WANDER ALL ALONE: GILLES DELEUZE'

Jacques Derrida

So much to say, and I don't have the heart for it today. So much to say about what has happened to us, about what has happened to me too, with the death of Gilles Deleuze; so much to say about what happens with a death that was undoubtedly feared – we knew he was very ill – but yet so much to say about what happens with this death, this unimaginable image which in any event would still hollow out, if it were possible, the sad infinity of another event. More than anything else, Deleuze the thinker is the thinker of the event and always of this event in particular. From beginning to end, he remained a thinker of this event. I reread what he said concerning the event, already in 1969, in one of his greatest books, *The Logic of Sense*. He quotes Jos Bousquet, who says, 'For my inclination toward death which was a failure of the will I substituted a longing for dying which is the apotheosis of the will.' Then Deleuze adds, 'From this inclination to this longing there is, in a certain respect, no change except a change of the will, a sort of a leap in place of the whole body which exchanges its organic will for a spiritual will. It wills now not exactly what occurs, but something *in* that which occurs, in accordance with the laws of an obscure, humorous conformity: the Event. It is in this sense that *Amor fati* is one with the struggle of free men.'[1] (One could go on quoting endlessly.)

I have so much to say, yes, like so many others of my 'generation,' about the time that was allotted to me to share with Deleuze, so much to say about the chance to think, thanks to him, by thinking about him. From the very

Source: Jacques Derrida, 'I'm going to have to wander all alone: Gilles Deleuze', *Philosophy Today*, Spring 1998, pp. 3–4.

beginning, all of his books (but first of all *Nietzsche and Philosophy*, *Difference and Repetition*, *The Logic of Sense*) have been for me not only, of course, strong provocations to think but each time the flustering, really flustering, experience of a closeness or of a nearly total affinity, concerning the 'theses,' if we can use this word, across very obvious distances, in what I would call – lacking any better term – the 'gesture,' the 'strategy,' the 'manner' of writing, of speaking, of reading perhaps. Therefore as regards these 'theses' – but the word doesn't fit – notably the one concerning an irreducible difference in opposition to dialectical opposition, a difference 'more profound' than a contradiction (*Difference and Repetition*), a difference in the joyously repeated affirmation ('yes, yes'), the taking into account of the simulacrum – Deleuze undoubtedly still remains, despite so many dissimilarities, the one among all those of my 'generation' to whom I have always judged myself to be the closest. I have never felt the slightest 'objection' arising in me, not even potentially, against any of his works, even if I happened to grumble a bit about one or another of the propositions found in *Anti-Oedipus* (I told him this one day while we were driving back together from Nanterre, after a thesis defense on Spinoza) or perhaps about the idea that philosophy consists in 'creating' concepts. One day, I would like to try to provide an account of such an agreement in regard to philosophic 'content,' when this same agreement never does away with all those deviations that I do not know, today, how to name or situate. (Deleuze had agreed to publish at some point a long improvised talk between us on this problem and then we had to wait, we had to wait too long.) I only know that these differences never left room for anything between us but friendship. There was never any shadow, any sign, as far as I know, that might indicate the contrary. This is rather rare in our milieu, so rare that I want it to go on the record here right now. This friendship was not based only on the fact – and this is not insignificant – that we had the same enemies. It's true, we didn't see each other very often, especially in the last years. But I still hear the laughter of his voice, which was a little raspy, saying to me so many things that I like to recall exactly as they were. He whispered to me, 'Best wishes, all my best wishes,' with a sweet irony in the summer of 1955 in the courtyard of the Sorbonne when I was about to fail the examinations for the *agrégation*. Or with a concern like that of an older brother: 'It pains me to see you put so much time into this institution [the International College of Philosophy], I would prefer that you write . . .' And then, I recall the memorable ten days at the Nietzsche conference at Cerisy in 1972, and then so many other moments, along with, of course, Jean-François Lyotard (who was also there), which make me feel so alone, surviving and melancholy today in what we call with that terrible and a little misleading word, a 'generation.' Each death is unique, of course, and therefore unusual. But, what can one say about the unexpected when, from Barthes to Althusser, from Foucault to Deleuze, it multiplies like a series all these uncommon ends in the same 'generation'? And Deleuze was also the philosopher of serial singularity.

Yes, we will have all loved philosophy, who can deny it? But, it is true – he said it – Deleuze was the one among all of this 'generation' who 'was doing' philosophy the most gaily, the most innocently. I don't think he would have liked me using the word 'thinker' earlier. He would have preferred 'philosopher.' In this regard, he was making himself out to be 'the most innocent' (the least guilty) 'of doing philosophy.'[2] Undoubtedly, this was the necessary condition in order to leave on the philosophy of this century the incomparably deep mark that will always be his. The mark of a great philosopher and of a great professor. The historian of philosophy, who conducted a kind of configuring election of his own genealogy (the Stoics, Lucretius, Spinoza, Hume, Kant, Nietzsche, Bergson, etc.), was also an inventor of philosophy who never enclosed himself within some philosophic 'field' – he wrote on painting, cinema and literature, Bacon, Lewis Carroll, Proust, Kafka, Melville, etc.

Next, next I want to say *even here* [in *Liberation*] that I loved and admired the way – which was always fair – he treated images, magazines, television, the public stage and the transformations that it has undergone during the last decades. Economy and vigilant retreat. I felt in complete agreement with what he was doing and saying in this regard, for example, in an interview for *Liberation* (October 23, 1980) on the occasion of the publication of *A Thousand Plateaus* (in the vein of his 1977 *Dialogues*).[3] He said, 'It is necessary to come to understand what is really going on in the field of books. We've been going through a period of reaction in all fields for several years. There's no reason for it not to have affected books. People are setting up a literary space, along with a legal space, and an economic and political space, that's completely reactionary, artificial, and crippling. I think it's a systematic process, which *Liberation* should have investigated.' It is 'far worse than censorship,' he added; but 'this sterile phase won't necessarily go on indefinitely.'[4] Perhaps, perhaps. Like Nietzsche and like Artaud, like Blanchot, others whom we both admired, Deleuze never lost sight of this connection of necessity with the aleatory, chaos, and the *untimely*. When I was writing on Marx, at the very worst moment in 1992, I was reassured a little by finding out that Deleuze intended to do the same thing. And I reread this evening what he said in 1990 on this subject: 'I think Felix Guattari and I have remained Marxists, in two different ways, perhaps, but both of us. You see, we think any political philosophy must turn on the analysis of capitalism and the ways it has developed. What we find most interesting in Marx is his analysis of capitalism as an immanent system that's constantly overcoming its own limitations, and then coming up against them once more in a broader form, because its fundamental limit is Capital itself.'[5]

I am going to continue – or begin again – to read Gilles Deleuze in order to learn, and I'm going to have to wander all alone in that long interview that we should have had together. I think my first question would have concerned Artaud, Deleuze's interpretation of the 'body without organs,' and the word 'immanence,' which he always held onto, in order to make him or let him say something which is still for us undoubtedly secret. And I would have tried to say to him why his thought has never left me during nearly forty years. How could it from now on?

NOTES

1. Gilles Deleuze, *La Logique du sens* (Paris: Minuit, 1969), p. 174; English translation by Mark Lester with Charles Stivale, edited by Constantin V. Boundas (New York: Columbia University Press, 1990), p. 149.
2. Apparently, Derrida is referring to comments Deleuze made in 'Lettre à un critique severe,' in *Pourparlers* (Paris: Minuit, 1990), pp. 12–14; English translation by Martin Joughin as 'Letter to a Harsh Critic,' in *Negotiations*; *1972–1990* (New York: Columbia University Press, 1995), pp. 4–6.
3. Gilles Deleuze and Calire Parnet, *Dialogues* (Paris: Flammarion, 1977); English translation as *Dialogues* by Hugh Tomlinson and Barbara Habbedam (New York: Columbia University Press, 1987).
4. Deleuze, *Pourparlers*, p. 41; *Negotiations*, pp. 26–27.
5. Deleuze, *Pourparlers*, p. 232; *Negotiations*, p. 171.

FRIENDSHIP-ABOVE-ALL [AMITIÉ-À-TOUT-ROMPRE]: JEAN-FRANÇOIS LYOTARD

Jacques Derrida

I do not have the strength, I feel unable to fit public words to what has just happened, and which leaves speechless all those who had the chance to become acquainted with the great thinker – whose absence, I am certain, will remain for me forever unthinkable: the unthinkable itself, shrouded in tears.

Jean-François Lyotard remains one of my closest friends, in as much as one is anxiously seeing that these words retain some meaning. It is as if, in my heart and in our thought, we have been friends forever – a word which, to me, translates more than 40 years of reading and 'discussion' (he always preferred this word, which he used as the title of a great text on Auschwitz – and on other things). A 'discussion' which was watchful, therefore, without complacency, a bemused provocation, always in the breath of a smile, I think, a smile which was both tender and mocking, an irony ready to yield in the name of something we had no name for at the time, and whose nickname now is 'friendship-above-all' ['Amitié-à-tout-rompre']. An overall tone which was both light and solemn, as well as the burst of philosophical laughter which all of Jean-François's friends no doubt can hear, deep inside themselves, today. A peculiar combination of curt laughter (judgement) and infinitely considerate attention which I always loved and thought I could recognise even at those – rare and difficult to pinpoint – times of 'differend', throughout the common grounds we had (phenomenology to start with, and an admiring and indispensable reference to Lévinas, although, once again, it wasn't the same reference – that is to say, it was one

Source: Jacques Derrida, 'Amitié-à-tout-rompre': Jean-François Lyotard', *Liberation*, 22 March 1988.

among so many other landmarks thus inscribed in the same landscape). But I couldn't and I don't want to recall here all the pathways on which we crossed and accompanied each other. To me, these encounters will remain forever uninterrupted. They have taken place but will continue to search for their place in me, until the end. Friends' memories are not identical, they certainly don't resemble each other. And nonetheless, today I remember having shared too many things with Jean-François throughout this life to even try to fit it all in a few words. I didn't know him at the time of *Socialisme ou Barbarie* but it seemed to me I could recognise its unfailing mark in all his great books (for example, to cite only a few, *Discours Figure*, *La Condition Post-Moderne*, *Le Differend*, which I am re-reading today, in admiration), and up to his last writings on childhood and tears: immense treatise on total disarmament, on what links thought and infinite vulnerability. The now world-wide application of 'post-modern' thought owes him, as we know, its initial elaboration. But there are so many other breakthroughs. I would say the same about the work which in our day and time (proper name and metonymy: 'Auschwitz') was meant to shake the philosophical tradition, its testimony on the testimony. Lyotard moved forward in this area, as always, with a courage and an autonomy of thought which I have rarely met elsewhere. No one will be able to think of this disaster, in the history of this century, without engaging in a dialogue with him, without reading and re-reading him. Students world-wide know this. I can confirm this to you from the remote place where I am writing to you, and where I have for many years shared a house with Jean-François and where I am grieving alone today.

Two more words before I give up.

Among the things that I love having loved with him there was more than one institutional impertinence. For example the College International de Philosophie – which he animated, which owes him so much and which still remains unbearable to the rearguard of resentment. One of the last times I saw him, Jean-François was laughing at the sad grimaces of those informers lying in ambush. He looked determined, as always, to respond. But he was also laughing to put my mind at rest about his health: 'stupidity protects me' or something of the kind.

When Deleuze died you also asked me, alas, to try, without waiting, still overcome by sadness, to write a kind of testimony. I think I remember saying that I felt we were getting really lonely, Jean-François Lyotard and me, only survivors of what one believes to be a 'generation' – of which I am the last child, the most nostalgic of the group, no doubt (they were all more joyful than me). What could I say today? That I love him, Jean-François, that I miss him, like I miss the words, and even beyond words: myself alone as well as his family, and our common friends miss him. For our best friends, in thought as much as in life, were our common friends. This is something quite unusual. I shall seek refuge in the texts which he wrote here, I shall listen to him, on the Pacific Wall and in order to think about childhood.

Translated by Ramona Fotiade

PART II
CLOSING STATEMENTS

II.1

'OPEN LETTER TO BILL CLINTON'

Jacques Derrida and Pierre Mendès France

President William Jefferson Clinton
Mrs. Hillary Rodham Clinton

The White House
1600 Pennsylvania Ave, NW
Washington, DC 20500
United States of America

Paris, November 15 1996

Mr. President, Madame First Lady,

At a time when the entire world welcomes the reelection of the President of the United States and the reaffirmation of his place in the highest office, permit us to address ourselves directly to you, and to do so on a personal level, at once public and private. For, in speaking the language of the heart as much as that of the law and right, we appeal to you above all out of duty and in the name of justice in order to beseech you, Mr. President, Madame First Lady, to make your voice heard.

In effect, a terrifying tragedy runs the risk of leading an innocent man to his death. Imprisoned for fifteen years, judged and sentenced under conditions that

Source: Jacques Derrida and Pierre Mendes France, 'Open letter to Bill Clinton', *Les Temps Modernes*, 52, 592, 1996, pp. 179–82.

appear more than suspect to the entire world, there is a chance that an American will pay with his life tomorrow for what could only be a police conspiracy and a miscarriage of justice. It is common knowledge today, in your country and everywhere else, that the trial of Mumia Abu-Jamal has been marred, from the very beginning, by many serious procedural irregularities. Countless violations of the rules have been the focus of credible and meticulous publications (dossiers, interviews, books, films). Irrefutable testimony has demonstrated that the conduct of his trial was led astray by pressure groups and a partial judge (recently affirmed in his position and notorious for holding the record for death sentences among American judges); and all this in order to punish at all costs, without sufficient proof or evidence, the past of a political activist (in the 70s, a young 'Black Panther', then a radio journalist, 'the voice of the voiceless'). Since then, Mumia Abu-Jamal has often been considered, justifiably, alas, a political prisoner under threat of death in a democracy.

Holding ourselves to but the last episode in a long series of police brutalities and judicial violences, we will be content to recall that last October 1st (1996), one of the principal eyewitnesses for the defense, Veronica Jones, was arrested on the stand right in the middle of the hearing, on a minor charge, having nothing to do with the trial, at the very moment she was giving decisive testimony. This testimony not only contained information capable of clearing Mumia Abu-Jamal (who, as everyone knows, has insisted upon his innocence from the very start). It also mentioned, under oath, the police threats under which, fifteen years ago, Veronica Jones was constrained to alter her initial testimony given just after the unelucidated death of a Philadelphia police officer.

As we, along with thousands and thousands of citizens from numerous democratic countries, appeal to you, Mr. President, Madame First Lady, it goes without saying that we are also eager to show our respect for the principles of the political and judicial institutions of your country, for the separation of power and the independence of justice. Moreover, it is in this spirit that numerous organizations (Amnesty International, the International Parliament of Writers, the Pen Club, the Movement Against Racism and For Friendship Between Peoples) have come forward to ask only for a rehearing of the trial. It is also in this spirit that certain Heads of major friendly nations, for example Chancellor Kohl and President Chirac, have publicly intervened. The latter, as you know, empowered the French Ambassador, on August 3rd, to 'take, in a strictly humanitarian capacity and in accordance with American law, all necessary steps that might contribute to saving the life of Mr. Mumia Abu-Jamal.'

After having, for some years, closely studied all the accessible information concerning this trial, we are, for our part, like so very many others, without a doubt deeply convinced that a horrifying injustice threatens to lead an innocent man to his death in the worst tradition of the biggest judicial errors in history. But as we are not in the position of judges, as we accept, by definition, that our profound, private conviction may not be unanimously shared, as we respect, on principle, every other sincere conviction, our request, though insistent and urgent, remains limited: let the trial finally be reheard. We ask that a new trial be conducted under appropriate and transparent conditions, that the logic of 'reasonable doubt' be rigorously taken into consideration in favor of a defendant who is presumed innocent, and that, whichever it may be, any judgement to come at least be founded on indisputable evidence. (Allow us to add, in passing, that this retrial would not only be an act of justice, it would no doubt prevent new outbursts of anger, foreseeable indignant reactions that could have unforeseeable consequences.)

Once again, Mr. President, Madame First Lady, we would never dare ask you to intervene contrary to the democratic principles of your institutions and to the independence of judicial proceedings, whether it be in the state of Pennsylvania or at the federal level. We turn to you today in order to beseech you only to declare, loudly, with the strength of your legitimate authority and a renewed confidence, words of justice that would recall to democracy the spirit of law and human dignity. We believe that the influence of your voice will be able to carry these words where a final realization appears urgent, that these words would enable the relevant authorities to reopen the trial, in complete independence, and thus to avoid the dangers, all the dangers of an inexcusable and irreversible injustice.

With our most sincere respects,

Mme Pierre Mendès France
Jacques Derrida

PS. Of course, if you think it appropriate, we may make this letter public, at the opportune time and under the title 'open letter', only after having taken account of your reply and your opinion on this subject.

(This letter, received by the 'Federal Priority Issues Office' at the White House remains unanswered. – ed. *Les Temps Modernes*)

Translated by David Kammer

'TELEPATHY'

Jacques Derrida

9 July 1979[1]

So, what do you want me to say, I had a premonition of something nasty in it, like a word, or a worm, a piece of worm which would be a piece of word, and which would seek to reconstitute itself, slithering, something tainted which poisons life. And suddenly, precisely there, only there, I started to lose my hair, no, to lose some hair which was not necessarily mine, perhaps yours. I was trying to keep it by making knots which, one after the other, came undone only to re-form themselves further on. I felt, from a distance and confusedly, that I was searching for a word, perhaps a proper name (for example Claude, but I do not know why I choose this example right now, I do not remember his presence in my dream). Rather it was the term which was searching for me, it had the initiative, according to me, and was doing its best to collect itself by every means, for a period of time which I could not measure, all night perhaps, and even more, or else an hour or three minutes, impossible to know, but is it a question here of knowing? The time of this word remains, does it not, especially if it were a proper name, without comparison with everything which might surround it. The word was taking its time, and by dint of following it   you ask me, I ask myself: where is this leading us, towards what *place?* We are absolutely unable to know, forecast [*prévoir*], /foresee, foretell, fortune-tell/.[2] Impossible anticipation, it is always from there that I have addressed myself to you and you have never accepted it.

Source: Jacques Derrida, 'Telepathy', *Oxford Literary Review*, 10, 1988, pp. 3–41.

You would accept it more patiently if something wasn't telling us, behind our backs [*par derrière*] and in order to subject us there, that this place, it, knows us, forecasts our coming, predicts us, us, according to its code [*chiffre*]. Suppose that an anachronism which resembles no other unwedges [*décale*] us, it lifts or displaces the blocks [*les cales*], brakes or accelerates as if we were late with respect to that which has already happened to us in the future,/the one which foresees us/ and by which I sense us predicted, anticipated, snapped up, called, summoned from a single casting, a single coming. Called, you hear? you hear this word in several languages? I was trying to explain it to him [or her], to translate it to him the other day, at his first smile I interrupted

and I ask myself, I ask myself how to deform the syntax without touching it, as at a distance. At stake here is what I'd like to call the old-new phrase, as they say over there, you remember, the old-new synagogue. I ask myself, not myself, it is not myself that I ask, it is myself that I ask for when I ask myself, you that I ask. But you cannot answer for the moment, only when I have met up with you again. Incidentally do you know that you saved my life again the other day when with an infinitely forgiving movement you allowed me to tell you where the trouble [*le mal*] is, its return always foreseeable, the catastrophe coming in advance, called, given, dated. It is readable on a calendar, with its proper name, classified, you hear this word, nomenclatured. It wasn't sufficient to foresee or to predict what would indeed happen one day, / forecasting is not enough/, it would be necessary to think (what does this mean here, do *you* know?) what would happen by the very fact of being predicted or foreseen, a sort of beautiful apocalypse telescoped, kaleidoscoped, triggered off at that very moment by the precipitation of the announcement itself, consisting precisely in this announcement, the prophecy returning to itself from the future of its own to-come [*à-venir*]. The apocalypse takes place at the moment when I write this, but a present of this type keeps a telepathic or premonitory affinity with itself (it senses itself at a distance and warns itself of itself) which loses me on the way and makes me scared. I have always trembled before what I know in this way, it is also what scares the others and through which I disturb them as well, I send them to sleep sometimes. I suffer from it. Do you think that I am speaking here of the unconscious, guess[3]   I ask myself – this, I ask you: when it plays, from the start, the absence or rather the indeterminacy of some addressee which it nevertheless apostrophises, a published letter provokes events, /and even the events it foresees and foretells/, what is going on, I ask you. Obviously I am not talking about all the events to which any writing or publication at all gives rise, starting with the most effaced of marks. Think rather of a series of which the addressee would form part, he or she if you wish, you for example, unknown at that time to the one who writes; and from that moment the one who writes is not yet completely an addressor, nor completely himself. The addressee, he or she, would let her/himself be produced by the letter, from its programme, and, he or she, the addressor as well. I can no longer see very clearly, I am stalling [*je cale*] a bit. Look, I'm trying [*je m'exerce*]: suppose that I now write a letter without determinable address. It would be encrypted or anonymous, it doesn't much matter, and I publish it, thus using the credit I still have with our publishing system, along with all that supports it. Now suppose that someone replies, addressing her/himself first to the presumed signatory of the letter, who is supposed by convention to merge with the 'real' author, here with 'me' who is supposedly its creator. The publisher forwards the reply. This is a possible route, there would be others and the thing which interests me can happen even if the aforesaid reply does not take the form of a missive in the everyday sense and if its despatch is not entrusted to the postal institution. So I become the signatory of these letters that are said to be fictive. When I was only the author of a book! Transpose that to the side of what they still call the unconscious, transpose in any case, it is transference [*transfert*, also 'transfer'] and telepoetics which, deep down, are weaving away. I encounter the other on this occasion. It is the *first time*, apparently, and even if according to another appearance I have known the other, like you, for years. In this encounter the destiny of a life is knotted, of several lives at the same time, certainly more than two, always more than two. A banal situation, you will say, it happens every day, for example between novelists, journalists, their readers and their audience. But you haven't got the point. I am not putting forward the hypothesis of a letter which would be the external occasion, in some sense, of an encounter between two identifiable subjects – and who would already be determined. No, but of a letter which after the event seems to have been lauched towards some unknown addressee at the moment of its writing, an addressee unknown to himself or herself if one can say that, and who is determined, as you very well know how to be, on receipt of the letter; this is then quite another thing than the transfer [*transfert*] of a message. Its content and its end no longer precede it. So then, you identify yourself and you commit your life to the program of the letter, or rather of a postcard, of a letter which is open, divisible, at once transparent and encrypted. The program says nothing, it neither announces nor states anything, not the slightest content, it doesn't even present itself as a program. One cannot even say that it 'looks like' a program, but, without seeming to, *it works*, it programs. So you say: it is I, uniquely I who am able to receive this letter, not that it has been reserved for me, on the contrary, but I receive as a present the chance to which this card delivers itself. It falls to me [*Elle m'échoit*]. And I choose that it should choose me by chance, I wish to cross its path, I want to be there, I can and I want – its path or its transfer. In short you say 'It was me', with a gentle and terrible decision, quite differently: no comparison here with identifying with the hero of a novel. You say 'me' the unique addressee and everything starts between us. Starting out from nothing, from no history, the postcard saying not a single word which holds. Saying, or after the event predicting 'me', you don't have any illusion about the divisibility of the destination, you don't even inspect it, you let it float (committing yourself to it even for eternity – I weigh my words – and you ask yourself if I am describing or if I am committing what is taking place at this very moment), you are there to receive the division, you gather it together without reducing it, without harming it, you let it live and everything starts between us, from you, and what you there give by receiving. Others would conclude: a letter thus *finds* its addressee, him or her.[4] No, one cannot say of the addressee that s/he exists before the letter. Besides, if one believed it, if one considered that you identify yourself with the addressee as if with a fictional character, the question would remain: how is it possible? how can one identify with an addressee who would represent a character so absent from the book, totally mute, indescribable?[5] For you remain indescribable, unnamable, and this is not a novel, or a short story, or a play, or an epic, all literary representation is excluded from this. Of course you protest, and I hear you, and I accept that you're right: you say that you begin by identifying with me, and, in me, with the hollowed-out figure of this absent [female] addressee with whom I myself dawdle along. Certainly, and you are right, as always, but it is no longer to you that I say this, or with you that I wish to play at this, *you* know it's you, so put yourself in the place of another reader [*lectrice*], it doesn't matter who, who may even be a man, a female reader [*lectrice*] of the masculine gender. Anyway what happens here, you well know, my angel, is so much more complicated. What I am able to extract from it in order to speak about it could not in principle measure up to it, not only because of the weakness of my discourse, its poverty, chosen or not: in truth it could only ever add a further complication, a leaf [*feuillet*], a further layering [*feuilleté*] to the structure of what is happening and across which I hold you against me, kissing you continuously, tongue deep in the mouth, near a station, and your hair in my two hands. But I am thinking of a single person, of the one and only, the madwoman who would be able to say after the letter 'it is I', it was already I, that will have been I, and in the night of this wagered certainty commits her life to it without return, takes all possible risks, keeps upping the stakes without trembling, without a safety net, like the trapeze artist that I have always been. All that can be done gently, must even entrust itself to gentleness, without show and as if in silence. We must not even speak of it together, and everything would be in ashes up to this letter here.

9 July 1979

You know my question: why do the theoreticians of the performative or of pragmatics take so little interest, to my knowledge, in the effects of the written object, the letter in particular? What are they scared of? If there is something performative in a letter, how is it that it can produce all kinds of events, foreseeable and unforeseeable, and even including its addressee? All that, of course, according to a properly performative causality, if there is such a thing, and which is pure, not dependent on any other consequentiality extrinsic to the act of writing. I admit I'm not very sure what I mean by that; the unforeseeable should not be able to form part of a performative structure *stricto sensu*, and yet ... ; it would still be necessary to divide, to proliferate the instances: not everything is addressee in an addressee, one part only, which compromises with the rest [*compose avec le reste*]. Yourself for example, you love me, this love is greater than yourself and above all greater than myself, and yet it is only a very small part that one thus names with this word, love, my love. That doesn't stop you from leaving me, day after day, and indulging in these little calculations, etc.   I give up [*je cale*].

I will have to make enquiries and clear this thing up: start from the fact that, for example, the /*big bang*/ would, let us say at the origin of the universe, have produced a noise which one can consider as still not having reached *us*. It is still to come and we will be given the chance to tap it, to receive it according to (anyway I will explain to you, the main thing is that from this moment on you draw out all its consequences, for example from what I said to you so many years ago – and then you wept   I heard the news, but I already knew, by telephone. This wasn't the end of the transfer and it will continue until the end of time, in any case until the end of the Cause   what did she want to give me or take away from me in this way, to turn away from him or in view of him, I don't know and I don't much care, what followed confirmed me in this feeling

in short, it was not a sign of a break but the last written sign, a little before *and* a little after the break (this is the time of all our correspondence): in short a postcard that he sent to Fliess on 10 October 1902. The *Ansichtskarte* [picture postcard] represented the *Tempio di Nettuno* at Paestum: '*Einen herzlichen Gruss vom Höhepunkt der Reise, dein Sigm.* [A warm greeting from the high spot of the trip, Yours Sigm.]' The history of this transferential correspondence is unbelievable: I'm not talking about its content, about which there has been plenty of gossip, but of the scenario – a postal, economic, even financial, military as well, strategic scenario – to which it has given rise and you know that I never separate these things, especially not the post and the bank, and there is always the training at the centre. Fliess's wife, the 'malicious woman', sells Freud's letters, and he had destroyed her husband's. The purchaser S. sells them to Marie Bonaparte (yes, she of 'The Purloined Letter' and 'The Purveyor of Truth'):[6] 100 pounds in 1937, so in English money, although the transaction took place in Paris. As you will see, our entire account of Freud also writes itself in English, it happens crossing the Channel, and the Channel knows how to keep quiet. During her training, this time in Vienna, Bonaparte speaks of the matter to the master who is furious and who tells her a Jewish story, a story about digging up and throwing away a dead bird a week after the burial (he has other bird stories, you know) and tries to palm her off with 50 quid! in order to get back his rights on his letters, without explicitly saying so. A little training, then, in exchange for some pieces of my old transference which has made me talk so much. The other – I've told you she wasn't such a fool – refuses. What goes on in her head I don't know, but talk about having a hold that won't let go (it is, says poor old Jones, out of 'scientific interest' that she 'had the courage to stand up [*tenir tête*] [ah! you see why I often prefer the

{French} translation] to the master'). Then it's the Rothschild bank in Vienna, the withdrawal of the letters in the presence of the Gestapo (only a princess of Greece and Denmark was capable of that), their deposit at the Danish legation in Paris (all in all /thanks to/ von Choltitz who wasn't just a general like any other!), their crossing the mine-sown Channel, 'in waterproof and buoyant material', as Jones goes on to say, as a precaution [*en prévision*] against a shipwreck. And all that, don't forget, *against* the desire of the master; all this violence ends up with Anna, for whom the letters are copied and who selects from them for publication! And now we can pick up the scent of lots of things and give lectures [*faire des cours*] on their stories about noses. And the other – one will never know what he wrote – there are others and it is always like that.   there is only tele-analysis, they will have to draw all the conclusions like us, get their concept of the 'analytic situation' to swallow a new metrics of time (of the multiplicity of systems, etc.) as well as another reading of the transcendental imagination (from the *Kantbuch* and beyond . . . , up to the present [*jusqu'à present*] as one dares to say in French). You and me, our tele-analysis has lasted for such a long time, years and years, 'the session continues',[7] eh, and yet we never see each other outside the sessions (and the fact that we employ the very long session doesn't change things in the slightest, we punctuate quite differently). So, never outside sessions, that's our deontology, we're very strict. If they did the same, all of them, as they ought, would grass grow again in the salons? We would have to come back to masks that is if at least   the last postcard was sent to Fliess, it seems, at the end of a journey which should have taken Freud (him too!) to Sicily. He seems to have given up on the idea, but it is from Amalfi that he goes to Paestum. Remember that he is travelling with his brother, Alexander, and that between two postcards he sees his double ('not Horch,' he says, 'another' double).[8] He recognizes in this an omen of death: 'Does this signify *Vedere Napoli et poi morire?*' he asks. He always associated the double, death and premonition. I'm not making anything up with regard to the two postcards, before and after the encounter with the double. The first, 26 August 1902, to Minna, his sister-in-law. He sends it to Rosenheim. The other, after Venice, and Jones writes: 'The following day, at half past two in the morning, they have to change trains at Boulogne, in order to get the Munich express. Freud finds the time to send another postcard.'   Meanwhile, for the reasons I have told you, I am leafing through the *Saga* rather absent-mindedly, without seeing very clearly whether I'll get anything out of it on the side of – of what? Let us say the England of Freud in the second half of the last century. The *Forsyte Saga* begins in England in 1886, and its second part, which Galsworthy entitles *A Modern Comedy*, comes to an end in 1926. Coincidence? 1926, that's when Freud shifted, with regard to telepathy; he comes round to it and that terrifies friend Jones, who in a circular letter declares on this point (Freud's so-called 'conversion' to telepathy), that his, Jones's, 'predictions have unfortunately been verified'! He had predicted (!) that this would encourage occultism.

Freud's circular letter in reply, 18 February 1926: 'Our friend Jones seems to me to be too unhappy about the sensation that my conversion to telepathy has made in English periodicals. He will recollect how near to such a conversion I came in the communication I had the occasion to make during our Harz travels. Considerations of external policy since that time held me back long enough, but finally one must show one's colours and need bother about the scandal this time as little as on earlier, perhaps still more important occasions.'[9]

At the start of the 'modern comedy' there's a magnificent /Forsyte family tree/ spread out over five pages. But I reread the Forsyth-Forsyte-von Vorsicht-foresight-Freund-Freud business [*histoire*] in the *New Introductory Lectures*, I read it and reread it in three languages but without results, I mean without picking up, behind the obvious, any scent I can follow.

There is, between us, what do you want me to say, a case of /fortune-telling book/ stronger than me. Often I ask myself: how are /fortune-telling books/, for example the Oxford one,[10] just like fortune-tellings, clairvoyants, mediums, able *to form part of* what they declare, predict or say they foresee even though, participating in the thing, they also provoke it, let themselves at least be provoked to the provocation of it? There is a meeting here of all the *for*, *fore*, *fort*'s, in several languages, and *forte* in Latin and *fortuna*, *fors*, and *vor*, and *forsitan*, *fr*, *fs*, etc.   Then I dozed off and looked for the words of the other dream, the one which I'd started to tell you. In a half-sleep I had a vague presentiment that it was something to do with a proper name (at any rate, there are only ever proper names there), of a common name in which proper names are entangled, a common name which was itself becoming a proper name. Untangle a little the hairs of my dream and what they are saying as they fall, in silence. I have just linked it to that photograph by Erich Salomon which I talked to you about yesterday, *The Class of Professor W. Khal* (almost 'bald' [*kahl*] in German).[11]   already a long time I drowned myself. Remember. Why, in my reveries of suicide, is it always drowning which imposes itself, and most often in a *lake* [*lac*], sometimes a pond but usually a lake? Nothing is stranger to me than a lake: too far from the landscapes of my childhood. Maybe it's literary instead? I think it's more the force of the word [*lac*]. Something in it overturns or precipitates (*cla*, *alc*), plunging down head first. You will say that in these words, in their letters I want to disappear, not necessarily in order to die there but to live there concealed, perhaps in order to dissimulate what I know. So *glas*, you see, would have to be tracked down thereabouts (*cla*, *cl*, *clos*, *lacs*, *le lacs*, *le piège*, *le lacet*, *le lais*, *là*, *da*, *fort*, *hum* [cla, cl, closed, lakes, snare, trap, gin, the silt, there, yes, strong, hum ...]). Had I spoken to you about 'Claude'? You will remind me, I must tell you who this name is for me. You will note that it is androgynous, like '*poste*' [post]. I missed it in *Glas* but it has never been far away, *it* has not missed me. The catastrophe is of this name.   Suppose I publish this letter, withdrawing from it, for incineration, everything which, here and there, would allow one to identify its destination. Of course, if the determined destination – determination – belongs to the play of the performative, this might conceal a childish simulacrum: under the apparent indeterminacy, having taken account of a thousand coded features, the figure of some addressee takes shape quite distinctly, together with the greatest probability that the response thus induced (asked for) come from one particular direction and not another. The place of the response would have been fixed by my grids – the grids of culture, of language, of society, of fantasy, whatever you like. Not just any old stranger receives just any old 'message', even by chance, and above all doesn't reply to it. And not to reply is not to receive. If, from you for example, I receive a reply to this letter, it is because, consciously or not, as you wish, I'll have asked for this rather than that, and therefore from such and such a person. As this seems at first, in the absence of the 'real' addressee, to happen between myself and myself, within myself [à part moi], a part of myself which will have announced the other to itself [qui se sera fait part de l'autre],[12] I will clearly have to have asked myself … What is it that I ask myself, and who? You for example but how, my love, could you be only an example? You know it, yourself, tell me the truth, o you the seer, you the soothsayer. What do you want me to say, I am ready to hear everything from you, now I am ready, tell me

It remains unthinkable, this unique encounter with the unique, beyond all calculation of probability, as much programmed as it is unforeseeable. Notice that this word 'calculation' [calcul] is interesting in itself, listen to it carefully, it comes just where the calculation fails perhaps … 'to have callus [du cal] in one's heart,' writes Flaubert. It is to Louise, from their very first letters (ah those two!), he is afraid that she is afraid, and there was good reason, on both sides: 'Oh! don't be afraid: he is no less good for having callus in his heart …'. Read all. And the next day, after recalling: 'I told you, I believe, that it was your voice especially that I loved', without telephone, this time he writes 'lake [lac] of my heart': 'You have come with your fingertips to stir up all that [cela]. The old sediment has come back to boiling point, the lake of my heart has thrilled to it. But the tempest is made for the Ocean – Ponds, when you disturb them give off nothing but unwholesome smells – I must love you to be able to say that.' The next day, /among other things/: 'it is now ten o'clock, I have just received your letter and sent mine, the one I wrote last night. – Only just up, I am writing to you without knowing what I am going to say.' Doesn't that remind you of anything? It is there that the correspondence communicates with 'the book about nothing'. And the message of the non-message (there's always some) consists in that. To say that 'OK? – OK' ['Ça va? – Ça va'] doesn't carry any message is only true from the point of view of the apparent content of the utterances, and one must acknowledge that I am not expecting information in response to my question. But that doesn't stop the exchange of 'OK's remaining eloquent and significant.   From cal to lac is enough to make one believe that that fellow also had a limp [sa claudication]. By the way, I have come across a claudius in Glas, next to glavdius (p.60).

How would this /fortune-telling book/ have reached me, reached you whom I do not yet know, and it is true, you know it, you with whom I am nevertheless going to live from now on?   'Something shoots [*tire*]! Something hits the target! Is it me who hits the target or the target which shoots me?', that's my question, I address it to you, my angel; I have extracted [*tirée*] this formula from a *Zen* text on the chivalrous art of archery. And when one asks the rabbi of Kotzk why the time when the Torah was *given* to us is called Shavuot and not the time when we received it, he gives the following reply: the gift took place one day, the day we commemorate; but it can be received at all times. The gift was given equally to everyone, but not all have *received* it. This is an Hassidic story from Buber. This is not the Torah, oh no, but between my letters and the Torah, the difference requires both in order to be thought.

10 July 1979

when you asked me the other day: what changes in your life? Well you have noticed it a hundred times recently, it is the opposite of what I was anticipating, as one might have expected: a surface more and more open to all the phenomena formerly rejected (in the name of a certain discourse of science), the phenomena of 'magic', of 'clairvoyance', of 'fate', of communications at a distance, of the things said to be occult. Remember
and we, we would not have moved a step forward in this treatment of the dispatch [*envoi*] (adestination, destinerrance, clandestination) if among all these tele-things we did not get in touch with Telepathy in person. Or rather if we didn't allow ourselves to be touched by her. Yes, touch, I sometimes think that thought   before 'seeing' or 'hearing', touch, put your paws on it, or that seeing and hearing come back to touch at a distance – a very old thought, but it takes some archaic to get to the archaic. So, touch with both ends at once, touch in the area where science and so-called technical objectivity are now taking hold of it instead of resisting it as they used to (look at the successful experiments the Russians and Americans are doing with their astronauts), touch in the area of our immediate apprehensions, our pathies, our receptions, our apprehensions because we are letting ourselves be approached without taking or comprehending anything and because we are afraid ('don't be afraid', 'don't worry about a thing', it's us all right), for example: our last 'hallucinations', the telephone call with crossed lines, all the predictions, so true, so false, of the Polish musician woman … The truth, what I always have difficulty getting used to: that non-telepathy is possible. Always difficult to imagine that one can think something to oneself [*à part soi*], deep down inside, without being surprised by the other, without the other being immediately informed, as easily as if it had a giant screen in it, at the time of the talkies, with remote control [*télécommande*] for changing channels and fiddling with the colours, the speech dubbed with large letters in order to avoid any misunderstanding. For foreigners and deaf-mutes. This puerile belief on my part, of a part in me, can only refer to this ground – go on, the unconscious, if you like – from

which there arose objectivist certainty, this (provisional) system of science, the discourse linked to a state of science which has made us keep telepathy at bay. Difficult to imagine a theory of what they still call the unconscious without a theory of telepathy. They can be neither confused nor dissociated. Until recently I imagined, through ignorance and forgetfulness, that 'telepathic' anxiety was contained in small pockets of Freud – in short, what he says about it in two or three articles regarded as minor.[13] This is not untrue but I am now better able to perceive, after investigation, how numerous these pockets are. And there's a lot going on in them, a great deal, down the legs. (Wait, here I interrupt a moment on the subject of his 'legacy' and of everything I'd told you about the step [*pas*], the way [*voie*], viability, our viaticum, the car and *Weglichkeit*, etc., in order to copy this for you, I came upon it yesterday evening: '... we have being and movement, because we are travellers. And it is thanks to the way, that the traveller receives the being and the name of traveller. Consequently, when a traveller turns into or sets out along an infinite way and one asks him where he is, he replies that he is on the way; and if one asks him where he has come from, he replies that he has come from the way; and if one asks him where he is going, he replies that he is going from the way to the way. [...] But be careful about this [oh yes, because one could easily be careless, the temptation is great, and it is mine, it consists in not being careful, taking care of nothing, being careful of nothing [*prendre garde, garde de rien, garde à rien*], especially not the truth which is the guarding itself, as its name suggests]: this way which is at the same time life, is also truth.' Guess [*devine*], you the soothsayer [*devine*], who wrote that, which is neither the *tô* (path and discourse) nor Martin's *Weg*;[14] guess what I have missed out. It is called *Where is the King of the Jews?* Despite the tautological viability of the thing, there are addresses, apostrophes, questions and answers and they put themselves on their guard!). So the pockets are numerous, and swollen, not only in the corpus but also in the 'Movement', in the life of the 'Cause': there was no end to the debate on telepathy and the transmission of thought, rather one should say 'thought transference' (*Gedankenübertragung*). Freud himself wished to distinguish (laboriously) between the two, firmly believing in this 'thought transference' and for a long time pussy-footing [*pratiquant longtemps la valse-hesitation*, lit., 'for a long time practising the hesitation-waltz'] around 'telepathy' which would signify a warning [*avertissement*] as regards an 'external' (???) [*sic*] event. An interminable debate between him and himself, him and the others, the other six in the band [*bagués*: 'beringed']. There was the Jones clan, stubbornly 'rationalist', Jones making himself even more narrow-minded than he already was because of the situation and ideological tradition of his country where the 'obscurantist' danger was stronger; and then the clan of Ferenczi who rushes into it even faster than the old man – to say nothing of Jung, obviously. He had two wings, of course, two clans and two wings. If you have the time, this vacation, reread the 'Occultism' chapter at the end of the Jones, it's full of things, but make allowance for this other Ernest: too heavily implicated to be serious, he trembles. You see, one cannot skirt around England, in our story. From the /fortune-telling book/ in *Sp* right up to the *Forsyte Saga* and Herr von Vorsicht, passing through the Jones's and the Ernests (the little one, who must be nearly 70 years old, continues to play with the bobbin in London where he is a psychoanalyst under the name of Freud – Ernst W. Freud, not William, Wolfgang, but Freud and not Halberstadt, the name of the father or of the son-in-law, poor sons-in-law). Of course, there were all the risks of obscurantism, and the risk is far from having disappeared, but one can imagine that between their thought of the 'unconscious' and the scientific experimentation of others who verify psychic transference from a distance, a meeting-point is not excluded, however distant it may be. Besides, Freud says it, among other places, right at the start of 'Psychoanalysis and Telepathy', the progress of the sciences (discovery of radium, theories of relativity) can have this double effect: to render thinkable what earlier science pushed back into the darkness of occultism, but simultaneously to release new obscurantist possibilities. Some draw authority from sciences which they do not understand as an excuse for anaesthetizing into credulity, for drawing hypnotic effects from knowledge. What you will never know, what I have hidden from you and will hide from you, barring collapse and madness, until my death, you already know it, instantly and almost before me. I know that you know it. You do not want to know it because you know it; and you know how not to want to know it, how to want not to know it. For my part, all that you conceal, and because of which I hate you and get turned on, I know it, I ask you to look after it in the very depths of yourself like the reserves of a volcano, I ask of myself, as of you, a burning *jouissance* which would halt at the eruption and at the catastrophe of avowal. It would be simply too much. But I see, that's the consciousness I have of it, I see the contours of the abyss; and from the bottom, which I do not see, of my 'unconscious' (I feel like laughing every time I write this word, especially with a possessive mark) I receive live information. Must go via the stars for the bottom of the volcano, communication by satellite, and disaster, without its for all that reaching its destination. For here is my final paradox, which you alone will understand clearly: it is because there would be telepathy that a postcard can not arrive at its destination. The ultimate naïvety would be to allow oneself to think that Telepathy guarantees a destination which 'posts and telecommunications' fail to provide. On the contrary, everything I said about the postcard-structure of the mark (interference, parasiting, divisibility, iterability, /and so on/) is found in the network. This goes for any tele-system – whatever its content, form or medium.

BETWEEN 10 AND 12 JULY (PROBABLY)

/My sweet darling girl/ to organize with Eli our meeting on Saturday and to smuggle through this audacious missive as contraband. But it seems to me impossible to postpone the sending of my letter

and yet I couldn't bring myself to take advantage of the few moments when Eli left us alone together. It would have seemed to me to be a violation of hospitality   am I going to receive the letter you told me about? You are going away – and it is essential that we correspond. How to proceed in such a way that no one knows anything about it?

I have drawn up a little plan. Just in case a man's handwriting [*une écriture masculine*] would look strange in her uncle's house, Martha [there, you know what smuggler wrote this letter, on 15 June 1882] might perhaps trace her own address on to a certain number of envelopes with her gentle hand, after which I will fill up these miserable shells with some miserable contents. I cannot do without Martha's replies ... End of quotation. Two days later she offers him a ring which has come from her father's finger. Her mother had given it to her but it was too big for her (she hadn't lost it, like I did with my father's, on a day that was so singular   ). Freud wore it but had a copy made of it! while telling her that the copy was to be the original. F. the wise. And here is the first archive of his telepathic sensibility, a ring-story of the type so frequent in the *Psychoanalysis and Telepathy* material (the woman who removes her wedding-ring and goes to see a certain *Wahrsager* [fortune-teller] who, according to Freud, did not fail to notice *die Spur des Ringes am Finger* [the mark left by the ring on the finger].   ): 'I have to ask you some serious, tragic questions. Tell me, in all honesty, whether last Thursday at eleven o'clock you loved me less or I had annoyed you more than usual, or else perhaps even whether you were "unfaithful" to me, to use the poet's word [Eichendorff, *The Little Broken Ring*]. But why this formal entreaty and in bad taste? Because we have a good opportunity here to put an end to a certain superstition. At the moment of which I have just spoken, my ring cracked, at the point where the pearl is set. I must admit, my heart did not tremble at it. No presentiment whispers to me that our engagement is going to be broken off and no dark suspicion makes me think that you were at that exact moment in the process of driving my image out of your heart. An impressionable young man would have felt all that, but I, I had only one idea: to have the ring repaired and I was also thinking that accidents of that sort are seldom avoidable ...'. So little avoidable that twice he breaks this ring and twice in the course of a tonsil operation, at the moment when the surgeon was plunging his scalpel into the fiancé's throat. The second time, the pearl could not be found. In his letter to Martha, you have the entire program, the entire contradiction to come already gathered together in the 'but I ...'. He too hears voices, that of Martha when he is in Paris (the end of the *Psychopathology of Everyday Life*) and 'each time I got the reply that nothing had happened'.[15] Just try to find out if that reassures him or disappoints him.   As is customary for me to do, I have collected all the fetishes, the notes, the bits of paper: the tickets for the Ringtheater in Vienna (the night of the great fire), then each visiting card with a motto in Latin, Spanish, English, German, as I love to do, the cards marking the place of the loved one at table, then the oak leaves on the walk at the Kahlenberg, so well named.

Between 10 and 12 July (probably)

skill in diverting the address from the words [*l'adresse à détourner des mots l'adresse*]. 'Ah! my sweet angel, how grateful I am to you for my skill [*mon adresse*]!' I leave you to discover the context all for yourself, it is in *The Spleen of Paris* ('Le galant tireur') and in *Fusées* (XVII).

12 July 1979

for his lectures on telepathy – what I'd like to call fake lectures because he confides in them so much, poor man – were for us as imaginary or fictive as Professor W. Khal's class. Not only did he have all this difficulty reaching a decision [*se prononcer*, 'reaching a verdict'] on telepathy, but he never made any pronouncement [*il n'a jamais rien prononcé*] on this subject. Nor wrote anything. He wrote with a view to speaking, preparing himself to speak, and he never spoke. The lectures which he composed on this subject were never delivered but remained as writings. Is this insignificant? I don't think so and would be tempted to link it up in some way with this fact: the material which he uses in this domain, especially in 'Dreams and Telepathy', is almost always written, literal, or even solely epistolary (letters, postcards, telegrams, visiting cards). The fake lecture of 1921, 'Psycho-Analysis and Telepathy', supposedly written for a meeting of the International Association, which did not take place, he never gave it, and it seems that Jones, with Eitingon, dissuaded him from presenting it at the following congress. This text was only published after his death and his manuscript included a post-script relating the case of Dr Forsyth and the Forsyte Saga, forgotten in the first version out of 'resistance' (I quote). The fake lecture of 1922, 'Dreams and Telepathy', was never given, as it was supposed to be, to the Society of Vienna, only published in *Imago*. The third fake lecture, 'Dreams and Occultism' (30th lecture, the second of the *New Introductory Lectures*), was of course never given and Freud explains himself on this in the foreword to the *New Introductory Lectures*. It is in this last text that you will find the *Vorsicht Saga* with which I would like to reconstitute a chain, my own, the one I'd told you on the telephone the day that you put your hand on the phone in order to call me at the same moment that my own call started to ring through   he says that he has changed his views on thought transference. The science considered (by others) 'mechanistic' will be able one day to give an account of it. The connection between two psychic acts, the immediate warning which one individual can seem to give another, the signal or psychic transfer can be a physical phenomenon. This is the end of 'Dreams and Occultism'. He has just said that he is incapable of trying to please (come off it, you've got to be joking), like me
) the telepathic process would be physical in itself, except at its two extremes; one extreme is reconverted (*sich wieder umsetz*) into the same psychic [*le même psychique*] at the other extreme. From that moment

on the 'analogy' with other 'transpositions', other 'conversions' (*Umsetzungen*), would be indisputable: for example the analogy with 'speaking and listening on the telephone'. Between rhetoric and the psycho-physical relation, within each one and from one to the other, there is only translation (*übersetzung*), metaphor (*übertragung*), 'transfers', 'transpositions', analogical conversions, and above all transfers of transfers: *über*, *meta*, *tele*: these words transcribe the same formal order, the same chain and as our discourse on this passage is taking place in Latin, add *trans* to your list as well. Today we give greater importance to the electric or magnetic medium in order to think this process, this process of thought. And the telematic *tekhnè* is not a paradigm or materialised example of another thing, *it is that* (compare our mystic writing-pad, it is an analogous problematic, it all communicates by telephone). But once again, a terrifying telephone (and he, the old man, is frightened, me too); with the telepathic transfer, one could not be sure of being able to cut (no need now to say /hold on/, *don't cut*, it is connected day and night, can't you just picture us?) or to isolate the lines. All love would be accumulated and dispatched by a central computer like the Plato terminal produced by Control Data: one day I spoke to you about the C.I.I. Honeywell-Bull software called Socrates, well I've just discovered Plato. (I'm not making anything up, it's in America, Plato.) So he is frightened, and rightly so, of what would happen if one could make oneself master and possessor (*habhaft*) of this physical equivalent of the psychic act, in other words (but this is what is happening, and psychoanalysis is not simply uninvolved, especially not in its indestructible hypnotic tradition) if one had at one's disposal a *tekhnè telepathikè*   but my love, this is to lose one's head, no more no less. And don't tell me that you do not understand or that you do not remember, I'd made it known to you right from the first day, then repeated it at each expiry date [*échéance*]. Plato is still the dream of the head accumulating and guaranteeing exchanges (a software plus a teachware [*didacticiel*], as one now says, the only thing missing is a dialectic-ware). But then one would have to kiss Plato himself goodbye (that is what we have been doing all the time we have loved each other and you told me about this terrifying parricide, you came since I killed him within myself, in order to finish him off, and there's no end to it, and I forgive you, but he within me finds it difficult ...). 'In such cases as these, it's only the first step which counts' ['*Dans des cas pareils, ce n'est que le premier pas qui coûte*'], he says in French at the end of 'Psy and Tele'. And he concludes: '*Das Weitere findet sich*' ['The rest sorts itself out']. No, for us, it counts at every step. Reread this final paragraph. Having had the cheek to say that his life has been very poor in terms of occult experiences, he adds: but what a step beyond it would be if ... (*welch folgenschwerer Schritt über ...*). So he envisages the outcome and adds the story of the guardian of the Saint-Denis basilica. Saint-Denis had walked with his head under his arm after his beheading. He had walked for quite a long time (*ein ganzes Stück*). And you know what he had done with his head, to put it under his arm? He had lifted it up [*relevée*] (*aufgehoben*). Tell me, you will lift me up, eh, you will walk with my head under your arm? I would like that. No. 'In such cases as these,' concludes the *Kustos*, 'only the first step counts.' In the *Gesammelte Werke*, the text that follows, the title of which you read immediately after the 'first step', is *Das Medusenhaupt*   Imagine that I am walking like him, to his rhythm: between fifty and sixty years old (roughly until 1920) I remain undecided. I send them to sleep, allowing them to think what they want: telepathy, you won't know, and I tell you that I don't know myself whether I believe in it. You see the doves in my hands and coming out of my hat, how do I do it, mystery. So everything in my life (sorry, in our life) organizes or disorganizes itself according to this indecision. One lets Plato or his ghost live without knowing whether it is him or his ghost. Then comes the last stage, the one which is still before us but which I see seeing us coming and which, softwarily [*logiciellement*], will have anticipated us right from the start. In this way a life totally transformed, converted, paralysed by telepathy would await us, given over to its networks and its schemes across the whole surface of its body, in all its angles, tangled up [*embobinée*] in the web of histories and times without the least resistance on our part. On the contrary we would take on a zealous participation, the most provocative experimental initiatives. People would no longer have us round, they would avoid us as if we were addicts, we would frighten everybody (so *fort*, so *da!*). For the moment I scare *myself*, there is one within me who has begun and who plays at frightening me. You will remain with me, won't you, you will still tell me the truth.

13 JULY 1979

I am only interested in the *saga*, first on the mother's side (Safah, the name of the 'lip' and of my mother,[16] as I told you in October) at least as far back as the great-grandfather who today has more than 600 descendants. Then hypnosis and I often told you last year: 'it is as if I were writing under hypnosis' or 'were making one read under hypnosis'. Although I don't believe in wakefulness [*la veille*], I must prepare for the great awakening, just in order to change sides, in short, like turning over in a bed   and so my first period, that of indecision. In the fake lecture entitled 'Dreams and Telepathy', my rhetoric is priceless, really incredible. Incredible, that's the word, for I play on credibility or rather acredibility as I did a short while before in *Beyond* . . . I do everything I can so that this audience (that I've set things up so as not to have, finally, to allow myself to be spirited away by poor old Jones with his political scientism advice) cannot either believe or not believe, in any case come to [*arrêter*] its judgment. That will make them work and transfer during this period, because belief and judgment halt [*arrêter*] work; and then, a secondary benefit, they will doze off and remain suspended on my lip [*lèvre*]. Mustn't know (and there I am strong because in this domain it is no longer a question of 'knowledge' [*savoir*]. Everything, in our concept of knowledge, is constructed so that telepathy be impossible, unthinkable, unknown.

If there is any, our relation to Telepathy must not be of the family of 'knowledge' or 'non-knowledge' but of another type). I will therefore do everything so that you cannot believe or not believe that I myself believe or do not believe: but the point is that you will never know if I am doing it intentionally. The question of the *intentional* will lose all meaning for you

will be astounding to you: in its ruse and naïvety (that's me all right, isn't it?), both equally probable and improbable, distinct and confused, as with an old monkey. In the first place I pretend to disappoint fictive listeners and aleatory readers: ah! there is a lot of interest in the occult today, and because I've put Telepathy on the bill, here you are, all excited about it. You have always taken me, like Fliess, for a 'mind reader'. Mistaken [*Mépris*]. You are waiting holding your breath. You are waiting on the telephone, I imagine you and speak to you on the telephone, or the teleprinter seeing that I've prepared a lecture which I will never give (like a letter which one doesn't send in one's lifetime, which I allow to be intercepted by Jones and the friends of the Cause, I may as well say by my lieutenants). Well, you are wrong, for once, you will discover nothing from me as regards the 'enigma of telepathy'. In particular, I will preserve this at all costs, you will not be able to know 'whether or not I believe in the existence of a telepathy.' This opening could still allow one to think that I know, myself, whether or not I believe, and that, for one reason or another, I am anxious to keep it secret, in particular to produce such and such a transferential effect (not necessarily on you [*toi*] or on you [*vous*], but on this public within myself which does not let go of me). And again, at the end of the fake lecture, when I take up the word 'occult' once more, I pretend (more or less, as my father used to say) to admit that I do not myself know. I know nothing about it. I apologize: if I have given the impression of having secretly 'taken sides' ['*pris parti*'] with the reality of telepathy in the occult sense. I am sorry that it is so difficult to avoid giving such an impression. Tell me, who do you think I'm talking to? What do I take them for? If I don't want to give the impression, I have only to do what is necessary, don't you think? For example not to play with German. In saying that I would like to be entirely '*unparteiisch*', I do not say '/impartial/' in the sense of scientific objectivity, but rather without bias [*sans parti*, 'without party', 'without option']. That's how I want to appear: not to take sides [*Partei nehmen*] and to remain 'without bias'. And I will have concluded as in *Beyond* . . . , without concluding, by recalling all the reasons I have for remaining without bias. It really is the first step which counts. There you are, asleep, propped up [*calée*] in your armchair. I have no opinion, you understand, 'no judgment'. This is my last word. At my age, 'I do not know anything on this subject'. From the first sentence to the last, from the moment that I said, 'you will know nothing about it, whether I believe it or not', up to the moment of concluding, 'anyway I do not know anything about it myself', you would think that therefore nothing is happening, that there's no progress here. But you don't think that I might be dissimulating at the start? And again at the end when I say that I do not know anything about it? Through diplomacy and concern for 'foreign policy'? You don't have to take my word for it. It's like you when I ask you in the evening: tell me, the truth, my little comma [*dis-moi, la verité, ma petite virgule*]. Do you believe that one can talk about lying in philosophy, or in literature, or better, in the sciences? Imagine the scene: Hegel *is lying* when he says in the greater *Logic* ... or Joyce, in some passage from *F.W.*, or Cantor? but yes [*mais si*], but yes, and the more one can play at that, the more it interests me. Basically, that's it, discourses in which lying is impossible have never interested me. The great liars are imperturbable, they never mention it. Nietzsche, for example, who unmasks them all, he can't have been much of a liar, he can't really have known how, poor chap ...

So, not a step further [*pas un pas de plus*], apparently, in the course of 25 closely-written pages. The delimitation of the problem, the strict railing [*garde-fou rigoureux*] (but then what am I frightened of? who is making me frightened?) – this is the relation between telepathy and dreaming, and 'our theory of the dream'. Above all don't speak of anything else, it's that, our theory of the dream, which must be protected at any price. And in order to save a dream, one only, a single dream-generator in any case, to save it against any other theory. What a strategy, don't you admire it? I neutralize all the risks in advance. Even if the existence of telepathy (about which I know nothing and about which you will know nothing, especially not whether I believe in it and whether I want to know anything about it), were attested with all its require-ments, even if it were assured, *sichergestellt*, there would be no need to change anything in my theory of the dream and my dream would be safe. I am not saying whether I believe in it or not but I leave the field open to every eventuality (just about), I appropriate it in advance as it were. My theory of the dream, ours (the first, the second, it matters little) would be able to adapt to it and even still control it. And the two scenes of 'Dreams and Telepathy' are too obvious to be pointed out, one more time. *First scene*: even while denying [*me défendant*], that is the word, that I know anything or that I am concluding anything, I speak only of myself, say I. Totally autobiographical, if not auto-analytical, text, and which devotes itself to constant speculation. *Second scene*: my fake lecture allowing itself, if you like, to be led from start to finish and to be driven by a trace, *Spur*, of a facial wound which I have from my childhood and which, don't you think, opens the text, holds it open, open-mouthed, the analytic material come from elsewhere, in my dossier on telepathy, remains *epistolary* through and through.

13 JULY 1979

What will I have told them! that my material is lightweight, that this time I am sorry not to be able to put a personal dream on display as in my *Traumdeu-tung*, that I have never had a single telepathic dream. You think they'll believe me? There will surely be at least one who'll have a premonition (with the exception of you, of course, soothsayer, you know everything in advance) that it is less simple and that, at the moment of demonstration, the dreams which I recount to bring out their ultimately non-telepathic nature, my dreams, then, could well be the most interesting thing and the main subject, the real secret [*la vraie confidence*]. When I say 'But I have never had a telepathic dream', there will be at least one who'll ask: what does he know about it? and why should I believe him? She's the one I'd like to wake up with one day and start everything afresh. Moreover I have clearly recognized, from the beginning, that I'd kept from certain dreams the impression that a certain definite event, *ein bestimmtes Ereignis*, was playing itself out in the distance, at such-and-such a place, at the same moment or later. And this indeterminacy allows enough play for them to start asking themselves slightly more complicated questions; those which I suggest to them in their sleep are never valid in themselves   calmly, I know it, calmly, another time, one more time. It is necessary to see 'double', over towards the dead brothers (beautiful brothers [*beaux frères*]), towards homosexualities more or less foreclosed, with the telepathy-calls (so much for changing the number every year, pay for it to be /unlisted/) the majority of which come to me from great-greats and grand-grands, etc. (fathers, uncles, aunts, my grandfather able on occasions to be my great-uncle *und so weiter*). Calmly, what do you want me to say, you've got to agree to wake up   then I leave the domain of the dream which I had nevertheless undertaken not to go beyond. I go out of it for a little bit, certainly, but already to speak about myself: even wide-awake I have often verspürt, sensed, experienced the presentiment of distant events. But these Anzeigen, Vorhersagen, Ahnungen, these premonitory signs and discourses are not themselves, wie wir uns ausdrücken, eingetroffen. In French one would say that they are not themselves, as we put it, realized [*réalisés*]. /Or in english that they have not come true/, which would be something else again, literally, because I hold that something can *turn out*, can be verified without *being realized*]. Now the fact that I emphasize, wie wir uns ausdrücken colon: nicht eingetroffen clearly shows that something bothers me about this expression which I nevertheless do not highlight in any other way. I would hesitate, for my part, to translate it by 'realized' ['*réalisés*']. Eintreffen does mean, in the broad sense, 'to be realized' but I would prefer to translate it by 'to happen', 'to be accomplished', etc., without referring to reality, especially (but not only) to that reality which we so easily assimilate to external-reality. You see what I'm getting at here. An annunciation can be accomplished, something can happen without for all that being realized. An event can take place which is not real. My customary distinction between internal and external reality is perhaps not sufficient here. It signals towards some event that no idea of 'reality' helps us think. But then, you will say, if what is announced in the annunciation clearly bears the index 'external reality', what is one to do with it? Well, treat it as an index, it can signify, telephone, telesignal another event which arrives before the other, without the other, according to another time, another space, etc. This is the *abc* of my psychoanalysis. Reality, when I talk about it, it is as if to send them to sleep, you will understand nothing of my rhetoric otherwise. I have never been able to give up hypnosis, I have merely transferred one inductive method onto another: one could say that I have become a writer and in writing, rhetoric, the production and composition of texts, I have reinvested all my hypnogogic powers and desires. What do you want me to say, to sleep with me, that is all that interests them, the rest is secondary. So the telepathic annunciation /has come true even if/ it is not itself eingetroffen in external reality, that is the hypothesis which I offer to be read at the very moment I foreclose it on the surface of my text.

Hypnosis, it is you who has made me understand it, hypnosis is you, slowly I wake up from you, I bring the circulation back to my limbs, I try to remember everything you made me do and say under hypnosis and I will not manage, I will be on the verge of managing only when I see death coming. And you will still be there to wake me. While I wait, I deviate, I use the power that you lend me – over the others   – 'foreclose' is a superb word, but only where it is valid just for me, my lip, my idiom. It is a proper name   on this hesitation between sleep and wakeful-ness. More precisely between the dream proper, the nocturnal one, and the presentiments of waking life, look under a microscope at the linking of my very first sentences. In three propositions I am saying(1) that I have never had a telepathic dream, except for those dreams which inform of a determinate event playing itself out at a distance and which leave it to the dreamer to decide if it is taking place now or later. To leave to decide, that's the great lever, I try to place the fictive listener, in short the reader in the situation of the dreamer where it's up to him to decide – whether he is asleep. (2) That in the waking state I have also had presentiments which, not coming to be 'realized' in 'external reality', had to be considered as just subjective anticipations. Now then (3) I start a new paragraph and say 'for example' in order to recount a story of which one doesn't know whether it illustrates the last proposition (premonitions in waking life) or the last but one (telepathic dreams). The content seems to leave no doubt, it is a question of nocturnal dreams, but the rhetoric of linking trembles a little, listening to me you think you are dreaming.   It is so long since I wrote that to you, I no longer know   my two apparently telepathic dreams, which seem not to have been 'realized', are two dreams of death. I offer them as hors-d'oeuvres, supposedly to demonstrate negatively that I have never had a telepathic dream and to insist on the poverty of my material. Further on I add that in 27 years of analytic practice (you hear, this is certainly our number today) I have never been in a position to witness or take part in, miterleben a dream which is truly, precisely, 'correctly' telepathic, and I leave them to ruminate on the 'richtige'. That said, the hors-d'oeuvre, my two dreams of death, *you* have quickly understood, bears the essential points of my fake lecture. The material which follows and which reaches me *by corre-spondence*, it's sufficient to be vaguely alert or sophisticated to understand it: it is only there in order *to read* my two dreams of death or, if you prefer, so-that-not [*pour-que-ne-pas*], in order not to read it, in order, on the one hand, to divert attention from them, while on the other paying attention to them alone. From the moment I started talking about hypnosis and telepathy (at the same time), a long time ago now, I always drew attention to the procedures of diverting attention, just like 'mediums' do. In this way they provoke experiences of thought-divination or betrayal of thought (Gedanken erraten, Gedanken verraten). Here, my two dreams of death, one reads them without realizing, and above all through the rest of the material which has come by correspondence, apparently unconnected with my own dreams.   The material of the others, which comes to me by post, would, it seems, come only to decipher my two dreams of death, along with their whole system, deciphering at a distance, under hypnosis and by correspondence. It is as if I were speaking a language of diplomacy and cultivating double vision [*la diplopie*] in my patient reader. Always out of concern over 'foreign policy', but where does foreign policy begin? where are the borders? Naturally, I let it be clearly understood that I am capable of interpreting my two dreams; and in order to reassure those who are concerned (for me) to preserve the theory of the dream as fulfilment of desire (they make me laugh, these old-fashioned types), I declare with a wink that it is not particularly difficult to discover the unconscious motives of my two dreams of death (my son and my sister-in-law). But it won't have escaped *you* that I say nothing of the second dream, through I sketch a reading of the first one (Totsagen of my son in ski-costume), referral to a fall of this same son while skiing (Skifahrerkostum, Skiunfal), referral from this referral to one of my falls when as a child I was trying, having climbed up a ladder, to reach or bring down something nice, probably, from the top of a chest: a *fort/da* of me when I was scarcely two years old. Some jam, perhaps? Of this fall and the injury that ensued I still preserve the trace, *Spur*. I tell them then that to this day I can still show it, this trace. I tell it to them in a tone which they have trouble identifying (worried about proof? compulsive exhibition? confirmation that I need because I am not very sure?). All of these things, if it is really a question of the dream of 8 July 1915. Three days later I was sent a postcard by my elder son, it alluded to a wound which had already scarred over. I asked for details but I never got a reply. Naturally I didn't breathe a word of this in my fake lecture. This mark [*trace*] under my beard sets things going, gives the title and the tone: the lecture deals only with ghosts and scars. At the end of the *mise en scène* of the last case (this lady correspondent who tells me she is haunted by her dream 'as by a ghost', a dream which has nothing telepathic about it and which I bring to the fore for the only (and bad) reason that the dreamer writes to me telling me she has had, *moreover*(!), that she *believes* that she has had telepathic experiences ...), I recall that spontaneous cures, one might as well say auto-analyses, usually leave 'scars'. They become painful again from time to time. The word 'Narbe' comes twice from my pen, I know that the English had already used the word 'scar' to translate Spur, much earlier on. This translation may have put some people on the trail [*piste*]. I like these words Narbe, scar,

Spur, trace and cicatrice in French as well. They say what they mean, eh, especially when it is found under the bristles of some Bart or beard. Nietzsche already spoke about a scar under Plato's beard. One can stroke and brush back the bristles so as to pretend to show, that is the whole of my lecture. Of the second dream then, I have preferred to say nothing. It announced to me the death of my sister-in-law, the widow of my elder brother, at the age of 87, in England. My two nieces, in black, are telling me 'am Donnerstag haben wir sie begraben'. This Thursday of the funeral, apparently the most contingent detail of the story, I say nothing about it but isn't this the password? I know one woman to whom it won't be necessary to say it twice. I recognize that there is nothing amazing about dying at the age of 87 but the coincidence over the dream would have been unpleasant. Once again it is a letter which reassured me. In the introductory part of the lecture, already, a letter and a postcard come to refute the telepathic appearance of my two dreams – that ought to have troubled the reader. Then in the two cases described the post again officiates: two correspondents who are not 'personally' known to me

it's us then, who really only know each other by correspondence. The fact that we have often met (often is a feeble word) remains rather by the way. We have confided our telepathies by correspondence. Do we know each other 'personally'? it's very problematic. / What does that mean? / And when I say that I don't have the slightest reason for suspecting my correspondents' intention to mislead, in the lecture, I see you laugh, you could already see me coming

because you believe in me, you are always ready to not believe a word I say   I am a double, for you, not Horch, another

Take the dream of the twins, the first case. Fido, Fido,[17] remember, I speak of telepathy à propos the double, in *Das Unheimliche*, it's absolutely essential. Here's someone who writes to me: having dreamt that his second wife had twins, and was giving them her breast and some jam (follow the jam through all these stories), he receives from his son-in-law, oh yes, a *telegram* informing him that his daughter (first marriage) had just had twins. I recount all this in great detail (and another time, *more or less* in the same way in the *New Introductory Lectures* while dropping the story which my correspondent had added. It had no connection with any dream and to be consistent with the subject I should have dropped it from 'Dreams and Telepathy' as well. I preserved this supplement because of a postcard and a child's death: the moment the postman brings him a postcard, my correspondent realizes that it is to inform him of the death of his young brother, aged 9 and living alone with his parents. Sudden and unexpected death all the same but his three other brothers, whom he hasn't seen together for 30 years, apart from at his parents' funerals, told him that they had had an exactly similar experience (similar up to a point which is not clear to him, he admits).[18] In my new fake lectures, I insist as always on reestablishing the legitimate order: only psychoanalysis can teach something about telepathic phenomena and not vice-versa. Of course, for that it must integrate telepathy without obscurantism and some transformation may ensue for psychoanalysis. But it is not opportune to present things in this way for the moment. I'm desperately trying to distinguish between telepathy and 'thought transference', to explain why I have always had greater difficulty in accepting the first than the second, of which so little is said in the ancient accounts of miracles (I am now less sure about it; in any case that can mean two things: either that one considered this 'transference' as going without saying, the easiest operation in the world; or else, precisely because of the (scarcely advanced) state of the relationship to scientifico-technical objectivity, a certain schema of transmission was not thinkable, imaginable, interesting. In this way you would explain to yourself the constant association, at least in terms of the figures, comparisons, analogies, etc., between a certain structure of telecommunications, of the postal technology (telegrams, letters and postcards, telephone) and the material which is today situated at my disposal when I hear about telepathy. I have scarcely even selected for you

story of twins, I'm coming back to it. Yes, I have inserted the postcard about the young dead brother, although it has nothing to do with any dream and it's getting off the subject. After which, I collect everything together on a central 'Sie sollte lieber meine (zweite) Frau sein'. And admire my audacity, I say that (it is she whom I would rather have liked as a (second) wife) in the first person, in a mimetic or apocryphal style as Plato would say. Admire it, and don't forget that it was written, all in all, a very short time after Sophie's death. I ought to write one day on this speculation, these telegrams and the generation of sons-in-law. The clause on which I blocked the interpretation ('I would have preferred her as a second wife') would translate the unconscious thought of the grandfather of the twins, that is to say of my correspondent. And I preface all that with some innocent reflections on the love of a daughter for her father (I know that his daughter clings to him, I am convinced that during the pains of giving birth she thought of him a great deal, and moreover I think that he is jealous of his son-in-law for whom my correspondent has some derogatory remarks in one of his letters. The bonds between a daughter and her father are 'customary and natural', one should not feel ashamed of them. In everyday life, it expresses itself in a tender interest, the dream alone pushes this love to its final conclusions, etc.). You remember, one day I told you: you are my daughter and I have no daughter. Previously, I am going back still, I had recalled that the psychoanalytic interpretation of dreams lifts up [relève], suppresses and preserves (aufhebt) the difference between the dream and the event (Ereignis), giving the same content to both. In other words, if there should one day be someone of either sex to follow me, to follow what I still hold back in the inhibition of the too soon, it will be to think: from the new thought of this Aufhebung and this new concept of the Ereignis, from their shared possibility, one sees the disappearance of all the objections in principle to telepathy. The system of objections rested on a thousand naïveties with regard to the subject, the ego, consciousness, perception, etc., but above all on a determination of the 'reality' of the event, of the event as essentially 'real'; now that belongs to a history of grandad's philosophy, and by appearing to reduce telepathy to the name of a psychoanalytic neo-positivism, I open up its field. For that they must also free themselves from the massively Oedipal training-ware [*didacticiel*] by which I pretend to maintain law and order in my class. I wanted to delay the arrival of the ghosts en masse. With you it was no longer possible to drag it out. Their martyrdom is very close to its end   I leave you to follow on your own the details of my slalom. This is some high rhetoric – in the service of a hypno-poetics. I always talk of it in the first person (ah, if this were my second wife, and if my first wife were still alive it wouldn't be enough for her to have just one grandchild, she'd have to have at least twins: this is what I call, you know, Fido, the first one second [*la première seconde*] – double the stakes the grandfather wins). After which I play the three-card trick with the dream and telepathy, and this is the slalom:(1) if it is a dream with a slight difference between the oneiric content and the 'external' event, the dream is interpreted according to the classical ways of psychoanalysis; then it is only a dream, telepathy has nothing to do with it, any more than with the problem of anxiety for example: this is my conclusion. (2) The content of the dream corresponds exactly with that of the 'real' event; so, admire, I put the question: who says it is a dream and that, as often happens, you are not confusing two separate terms: sleeping state and dream? Wouldn't it be better to speak then, not of dream, but rather of telepathic experience in the sleeping state? I do not exclude that possibility but it remains outside the subject here. Well played, wouldn't you say? The subject is the reine telepathische Traum. And in its purity, the concept of telepathic dream appeals to the perception of something external with regard to which psychic life would behave in a 'receptive and passive' manner.

14 JULY 1979

I prepare absent-mindedly for the journey to Oxford. It is as if, crossing the Channel from the opposite direction, I were going to meet Socrates and Plato in person, they are waiting for me over there, at the bend, just after the anniversary. The voices which Socrates heard, the voice rather, what was it, *Telepathie* or *Gedankenübertragung*? And me when he inspires me, diverts me in the hollow of my ear, and you?   The other, when he says 'receptive and passive' without raising any further questions, one regrets that he hasn't read a certain *Kantbuch* which was being written just at the time that he himself was changing his views on the possibility of telepathy, between 'Dreams and Telepathy' and the *New Introductory* fake *Lectures*. I was not born but things were programming themselves.   As for what is 'outside the subject' (and telepathy, that's what it is, the outside-the-subject, he knows the score), the second case in 'Dreams and Telepathy' is not, any more than is the first, a case of a telepathic dream. It is not presented as such by his correspondent. She has only had, *on the other hand*, numerous telepathic experiences. Writes she, says he. Freud then deals only with a dream which comes back incessantly,

'like a ghost', to visit his correspondent. Completely outside the subject, isn't it?
So, before discussing it again, follow my clues. I do not have any new hypothesis
for the moment. Pick out and link up what you can on your side, I myself am
scanning separately to begin with, without grammar: the ghost, the inflamma-
tion of the eyes and double sight or double vision (*Doppeltsehen*) and scars
(*Narben*), clear-sightedness and clear-hearing (*hellsehen, hellhören*), the postcard, again, this time announcing the death of the brother who had called his
mother and which the correspondent claimed to have heard as well, then (again!)
the husband's first wife, the agrammaticality of symbolic language as he recalls it
at the moment of saying that the passive and the active can be represented in the
same image, through the same 'kernel' [*noyau*] (this word comes back all the
time, be it a question of the kernel of the dream, the 'kernel of truth' in telepathic
experiences and the centre [*noyau*] of the earth which couldn't possibly be jam, at
the beginning of the *N.I.L.*), the exact place where F. recalls that the psychoanalyst also has his 'prejudices', again the scars, the admission that in this second
case there has been a complete neglect of the question of telepathy (!), the point
which can be neither proved nor refuted, the decision to deal only with the
(epistolary) evidence of the daughter-sister, leaving the telepathic experience of
the mother completely out of play; then the strange return to the previous case
(the young dead brother, the older brothers equally convinced of the altogether
superfluous nature of the youngest, of his birth I mean; finally the eldest daughter
dreaming of becoming the second wife on the death of her mother (once again) –
and the brazenly Oedipal interpretation with no two ways about it . . . Lastly, I
am perhaps more mistaken than ever, I punctuate badly, but anyway place a grid
[*calque*] over it, pick out and tell yourself whatever story you like in the gaps,
tomorrow we play, or the day after, when I have done the same thing for our saga.
Do not forget the reversal at the end. He is not content with repeating that Ps
should be able to help in understanding telepathy, he adds, *as if this were his real
concern*, that Ps would help to isolate more effectively those phenomena which
are indubitably telepathic! Ps and Telepathy would then make a couple: a
telepathic message may not coincide with the event in time (understand: the
time of consciousness, or even of the ego, which is also the time naïvely thought
'objective' and, as he says, 'astronomical', in accordance with an old science),
that does not disqualify it in its telepathic power. It will have needed the time it
takes to reach consciousness. With the aid of psychic temporality, of its dis-
crepant [*décalée*] heterogeneity, its time differences [*décalages horaires*] if you
prefer, depending on the instances one takes, one can safely envisage the
probability of telepathy. The conversion to telepathy will not have waited until
1926. 'No problem', he says, if the telepathic phenomenon is an operation of the
unconscious. The laws of the unconscious apply to it and everything goes
without saying. Which doesn't prevent him from concluding as he had begun:
I know nothing, I don't have any opinion, behave as if I hadn't told you anything.
Bye now, OK   if you wish to understand this apparent
oscillation, it is essential to be more specific about this: even at the moment when,

some years later, around 1926, he declares his 'conversion to telepathy', he does not seek to integrate it in a definite or univocal way into psychoanalytic theory. He continues to make it a private affair, along with all the fog in which such a notion can be wrapped. 'The theme of telepathy', he will say in a letter to Jones, 'is in essence alien to psychoanalysis', or the 'conversion to telepathy is my private affair like my Jewishness, my passion for smoking and many other things ...'. Who would be satisfied with such a declaration coming from him? Not that it is false or worthless, and I have suggested it often enough, it was certainly necessary to read his propositions (including the theoretical ones) about telepathy in relation to his 'private affair', etc., but how does one accept this dissociation pure and simple on the part of someone who has struggled with the theorization of telepathy? And then, if it is foreign to psychoanalysis, like a foreign body precisely, as though 'off the subject', must psychoanalysis remain silent about the structure and the incorporation of the foreign body? At the end of 'Dreams and Occultism' (*New Introductory Lectures*), he indeed speaks of a foreign-body (*Fremdkörper*) story and it is true that he deals with a phenomenon of thought transmission in the face of which he acknowledges the failure of the analyst. The case is all the more interesting in that it is about the mother's childhood memory (a gold coin) which bursts in on the following generation (her son, aged 10, brings her a gold coin for her to put by on the same day she had talked about it in analysis). Freud, who hears the thing from Dorothy Burling-ham (the one to whom, I heard from M., he had wanted to offer two rings[19] but Anna had dissuaded him), admits to failure in the face of the foreign body: 'But the analysis reveals nothing, the act itself being that day introduced like a foreign body into the little boy's life'. And when, a few weeks later, the kid begs for the coin in order to show it to *his* psychoanalyst, 'the analysis is incapable of unearthing any access to this desire', once again. Failure, then, in the face of the foreign body – which takes the form here of a gold coin: *Goldstück*, value itself, the authentic sign of allegedly authentic value. Freud has such an awareness (or such a desire) of having himself thus arrived at the limit of psychoanalysis (inside or outside?) that he begins a new paragraph and in this way concludes the lecture (these are the last words and one doesn't know whether they mean that the return to Freudian psychoanalysis has just begun or remains to come: 'Und damit wären wir zur Psychanalyse zurückgekommen von der wir ausgegangen sind': 'And this brings us back to psychoanalysis, which was what we started out from'. Started out from? Distant from?   For finally if the theme of telepathy is foreign to psychoanalysis, if it is a private affair ('I am Jewish', 'I like smoking', 'I believe in telepathy'), why take public positions on this subject, and after devoting several studies to it? Can one take this reserve seriously? Now, take account of this fact as well: he doesn't say to Jones, 'it is a personal affair', he advises him to make that response in case he should have difficulty in publicly assuming Freud's positions, I quote the whole letter, because of the allusion to Ferenczi and to his daughter (Anna), it seems to me important (note in passing that he abandons the idea, on the subject of the said foreign body, of making peace with England): 'I am extremely sorry that my utterance about telepathy should have plunged you into fresh difficulties. But it is really hard not to offend English susceptibilities ... I have no prospect of pacifying public opinion in England, but I should like at least to explain to you my apparent inconsistency in the matter of telepathy. You remember how I had already at the time of our Harz travels expressed a favourable prejudice towards telepathy. But there seemed no need to do so publicly, my own conviction was not very strong, and the diplomatic consideration of guarding psycho-analysis from any approach to occultism easily gained the upper hand. Now the revising of *The Interpretation of Dreams* for the Collected Edition was a spur to reconsider the problem of telepathy. Moreover, my own experiences through tests I made with Ferenczi and my daughter won such a convincing force for me that the diplomatic considerations on the other side had to give way. I was once more faced with a case where on a reduced scale I had to repeat the great experiment of my life: namely, to proclaim a conviction without taking into account any echo from the outer world. So then it was unavoidable. When anyone adduces my fall into sin, just answer him calmly that conversion to telepathy is my private affair like my Jewishness, my passion for smoking and many other things, and that the theme of telepathy is in essence alien to psychoanalysis' (7 March 1926).[20] Even if one takes into account what he says about 'diplomacy' and the diplomatic advice which he again gives to Jones, this letter is contradictory from start to finish. Enough to make one lose one's head, I was saying to you the other day, and he himself once declared that this subject 'perplexed him to the point of making him lose his head'. It is indeed a question of continuing to walk with one's head under one's arm ('only the first step counts', etc.) or, what amounts to the same thing, of admitting a foreign body into one's head, into the ego of psychoanalysis. Me psychoanalysis,[21] I have a foreign body in my head (you remember As for Ferenczi and his daughter, and the 'experiments' which he apparently carried out with them, there'd be so much to say. I have said enough about his daughters, even though ... but for Ferenczi, the trail to follow is essential. One of the most startling moments consists again (from 1909 onwards) of a story of letters (letters between the two of them on the subject of the letters that a clairvoyant, Frau Seidler, appeared to be able to read blindfold. Ferenczi's brother mediates between them and the medium, he introduces them to her and passes on the letters, see Jones, III, 411–12). As regards Jones, who no doubt wasn't so 'hard'-headed about this as he said, why, in your opinion, does he compare, in 1926, the dangers of telepathy for psychoanalysis to the 'wolves' who 'would not be far from the sheepfold'?[22]

15 JULY 1979

a terrifying consolation. Sometimes I also approach Telepathy as if it were an assurance finally   Instead of muddling everything up, or complicating the parasitism, as I told you and as I believe, I hope for complete presence from it, fusional immediacy, a parousia to keep you, at a distance, in order to keep myself within you, I play pantheism versus separation, so you are no longer leaving, you can no longer even confront me with your 'determination', nor I   *Fort*: *Da*, tele*pathy* against tele*pathy*, distance against menacing immediacy, but also the opposite, feeling (always close to oneself, it is thought), against the suffering of distance that would also be called telepathy   I pass on to the second and last great epoch today, the turn has begun, I was starting to get wedged [*calé*], I am going to tip over, I am tipped over already. You can no longer do anything, I think, I believe   keep a little time, we'll re-read things together   here already, as toothing stone, my first punctuation for the *Forsyte Saga* ('Dreams and Occultism' in the *New Introductory Lectures*), I don't rule out that it miss or carry everything off, according to a bad time-lag [*décalage*]. It is *your* punctuation which interests me, you will tell me the truth. So I start from the 'kernels' (centre of the earth, kernel of truth, jam, *der Erdkern aus Marmelade besteht*, pointless to tell you that he doesn't believe in it, not as much as I do), then mediums and imposture, the kernel again, 'around which imposture (*Trug*) would, with the force of imagination (*Phantasiewirkung*), have spread out a veil which would be difficult to pass through', the 'everything happens as if she had been informed by telephone (*als ob … telephonisch*)', 'one could speak of a psychical counterpart to wireless telegraphy (*gewissermassen ein psychiches Gegenstück zur drahtlosen Telegraphie*)', 'I don't have any conviction in this respect'. 'It was in 1922 that I made my first communication on this subject', then the 'telegram' again and our 'twins', then 'in the unconscious this "like" is abolished', dead, the woman of 27 (!) who takes her ring off at 'Monsieur le Professeur's' (in brackets, on the subject of 7, 27 and of our 17, did you know he chose the 17th as the date of his engagement after choosing the number 17 in a lottery which was supposed to tell the nature of your character – and this was 'constancy'!),[23] a Parisian fortune-teller, the 'greatest preponderance of probability in favour of an effective thought-transference', the little card (*Kärtchen*) at the graphologist's, etc. Finally there's the arrival of David Forsyth, and Freud puts into play all the names which are linked with it, Forsyte, foresight, Vorsicht, Voraussicht, precaution or prediction, etc., but never makes a point of drawing our attention to (so it seemed to me, I will have to re-read) the supplementary fold of the too obvious, namely that the proper name itself speaks foresight. Forsyth, who had an appointment, leaves *eine Karte* for Sigi then in session with M.P., who that very day tells him how a certain virgin nicknamed him, M.P., Herr von Vorsicht because of his prudent or discreet reserve. Sigi seems to know a lot about the real motives of this reserve, he shows him the card and tells us without any transition about the Saga, that of the Forsytes whom M.P., alias von Vorsicht, had anyway led him to discover starting with *The Man of Property*! Naturally, you are taking account of the fact that Jones, who knew Forsyth, suspected Freud of having 'unconsciously touched up the story', reproached him for small errors in this instance, 'the slightest', which he has 'related' to us, you follow all the twists and turns of proper names, in passing through Freud and von Freund, you collect and file, classify all the visits, visiting cards, letters, photographs and telephone communications in the story, then you focus on two centres in this long ellipsis. First of all, the theme of interrupted analysis. There is interrupted analysis in there and I would like to say while stretching out the ellipsis: telepathy is the interruption of the psychoanalysis of psychoanalysis. Everything turns, in the Vorsicht case, around M.P.'s fear of seeing his analysis broken off, as Freud had given him to understand. The arrival of Dr Forsyth, the card-visitor [*le visiteur à la carte*], would have been the omen. Unless it is to do with another interruption of analysis, marked by another card, from another Dr F. One has to sniff around in that area. Next, another focal point, the mother/child couple, the case related by the friend of Anna (herself in analysis – with whom was it, now?) and the gold coin (*Goldstück*) leading from the 'foreign body', etc.   and naturally I'm following all that along an invisible fold-line: you pull it down, without reducing it, onto autobio-thanatography, you are looking for the foreign body on the side of the doctor   and in the *Gradiva* piece, in front of a woman who resembled a dead patient, he had said 'So after all it's true that the dead can come back to life'.[24] He thinks he is a pretty good medium himself and in 1925, at the period in which he dares to declare his 'conversion', he wrote to Jones: 'Ferenczi came here one Sunday recently. We all three [with Anna] carried out some experiments concerning the transmission of thoughts. They were astonishingly successful, especially those where I was playing the role of the medium and analysing my associations. The affair is becoming urgent to us' (15 March 1925). With whom were they speaking, that Sunday? Who was M.P.?[25] Plato, the master-thinker, the postmaster,[26] but still, soothsayer [*devine*], at that date ...   So psychoanalysis (and you're still following the fold-line) resembles an adventure of modern rationality set on swallowing *and* simultaneously rejecting the foreign body named Telepathy, for assimilating it and vomiting it without being able to make up its mind to do one or the other. Translate all that in terms of the politics – internal and external – of the psychoanalytic State (c'est moi). The 'conversion' is not a resolution nor a solution, it is still the speaking scar of the foreign body   half a century already,

    commemorates   the big Turn, it's going to go very quickly now. I am going to re-read everything trying out the keys one after the other, but I am afraid of not finding (or of finding) all alone, of no longer having the time. Will you give me your hand?   no more time to lose, ὁ γὰρ καιρὸς ἐγγύς, Telepathy comes upon us, *tempus enim prope est.*

Translated by Nicholas Royle

NOTES

[Jacques Derrida's 'Télépathie' was first published in *Furor* 2, February 1981, 5–41, and later appeared in *Cahiers Confrontation* 10 (Paris: Aubier), 1983, pp. 201–30. It has since been collected in Derrida's *Psyché: Inventions de l'autre* (Paris: Galilée, 1987), pp. 237–70. I would like to express my gratitude and indebtedness to Geoff Bennington and Rachel Bowlby for all the invaluable criticisms and suggestions made in the course of my working on this translation. I would also like to thank Jacqueline Hall and Samantha Penwarden for all their advice and support. Except for those specified otherwise, the footnotes which follow are the translator's.]

1. [J. D.'s note:] Such a remainder [*restant*], I am no doubt publishing it in order to come closer to what remains inexplicable for me even to this day. These cards and letters had become inaccessible to me, materially speaking at least, by a semblance of accident, at some precise moment. They should have appeared, as fragments and in accordance with the plan [*dispositif*] adopted at that time, in 'Envois' (Section One of *La Carte postale* (Paris: Flammarion, 1980)). In a manner which was also apparently fortuitous, I rediscovered them very close by me, but too late, when the proofs for the book had already been sent back for the second time. There will perhaps be talk of omission through 'resistance' and other such things. Certainly, but resistance to what? to whom? Dictated by whom, to whom, how, according to what routes? From this bundle of daily despatches which all date from the same week, I have extracted only a part for the moment, through lack of space. Lack of time too, and for the treatment to which I had to submit this mail, sorting, fragmentation, destruction, etc., the interested reader may refer to 'Envois', p. 7ff.

2. Derrida's text is very much concerned with questions of translation and transmission within, across and between languages. I have used slashes (/. . ./) to isolate those words which appear in English in the original.

3. 'Devine' is both an imperative of the verb 'deviner' ('to guess') and a noun meaning a '(feminine) soothsayer'. The word is used recurrently in *The Post Card: From Socrates to Freud and Beyond*, trans. Alan Bass (Chicago: Chicago Univ. Press, 1987).

4. This is in part an allusion to 'The Purveyor of Truth' (*The Post Card*, pp. 411–96), and its famous 'disagreement' with Jacques Lacan's 'Seminar on "The Purloined Letter"' (in *Yale French Studies*, 48 (1973), 38–72).

5. 'Inqualifiable': literally, 'of whom it is impossible to predicate a quality'.

6. For the story which follows, see Ernest Jones, *Sigmund Freud: Life and Work*, 3 vols., (London: Hogarth Press, 1953–57), I, 316–17; and for the context of Marie Bonaparte's role here, see also Jeffrey Moussaieff Masson's Introduction to *The Complete Letters of Sigmund Freud to Wilhelm Fliess 1887–1904* (Cambridge, Mass.: Belknap Press of Harvard Univ. Press, 1985), pp. 3–11.

7. 'La séance continue': this phrase recurs frequently in *The Post Card*; see in particular p. 320ff. Besides (psychoanalytic) 'session', 'séance' has the sense of 'meeting' and 'performance' – as well as perhaps playing, here, on to the more specifically 'occult' English usage. In 'To Speculate – on "Freud"' (*The Post Card*, pp. 259–409) it is linked to notions of repetition, generation and legacy.

8. See Jones, II, 19.

9. See Jones, III, 422.

10. This is a reference to Matthew Paris's *Prognostica Socratis Basilei*, the book in the Bodleian Libary, Oxford, which contains the 'original' 'post card' from which Derrida's 'envois' derive and on which they are allegedly written.

11. See *The Post Card*, p. 205.

12. Here and elsewhere in this text there is play on 'faire-part'. As a verb 'faire part' means 'to inform, to notify, to announce, to confide'. As a noun, 'faire-part' is a card or letter of announcement, especially of a wedding, birth or death.

13. Derrida is referring in particular to the following texts: 'Psycho-Analysis and

Telepathy', in *The Standard Edition of the Complete Psychological Works of Sigmund Freud*, trans. James Strachey (London: Hogarth Press), vol. XVIII (1955), 173–93; 'Dreams and Telepathy', in vol. XVIII, 195–220; 'Some Additional Notes on Dream Interpretation as a Whole', which includes a section on 'The Occult Significance of Dreams', in vol. XIX (1961), 135–38; and 'Dreams and Occultism', in *New Introductory Lectures*, trans. James Strachey, The Pelican Freud Library, vol. 2, ed. James Strachey, assisted by Angela Richards (Harmondsworth: Penguin, 1983 rpt.), 60–87.

14. For the notion of Martin Heidegger's 'Weg', see for example *The Post Card*, p. 31.

15. See *The Psychopathology of Everyday Life*, trans. Alan Tyson, Pelican Freud Library, vol. 5, ed. James Strachey, assisted by Angela Richards and Alan Tyson (Harmondsworth: Penguin, 1978 rpt.), 324–25.

16. 'Lèvre' is used on numerous occasions in *The Post Card*. It has the sense of 'lip', but also (in Hebrew) 'tongue'. See also Derrida's 'Des Tours de Babel', in *Difference in Translation*, ed. Joseph F. Graham (Ithaca: Cornell Univ. Press, 1985), p. 167.

17. For the significance of the name 'Fido', especially in terms of notions of nomination in the work of Bertrand Russell and Gilbert Ryle, see *The Post Card*, pp. 98, 244.

18. See 'Dreams and Telepathy', p. 203: 'In October I had a visit from my three brothers. We had not all been together for thirty years, except for quite a short time, once at my father's funeral and once at my mother's. Both deaths were expected, and I had had no "presentiments" in either case. But about twenty-five years ago my youngest brother died quite suddenly and unexpectedly when he was ten …'

19. [J.D.'s note:] 'Dorothy Burlingham also came to Freud and psychoanalysis as Anna's close friend. Leaving her disturbed husband, she moved to Vienna from America with her four children. She was first in analysis with Theodor Reik and then Freud […] A member of the Tiffany Family, Dorothy Burlingham could afford to pay for the treatment of her whole family; her children were among Anna Freud's first patients. Freud was happy when Anna found Dorothy as a friend; to him it meant she was now in safe hands. In 1929 he wrote "our symbiosis with an American family (husbandless), whose children my daughter is bringing up analytically with a firm hand, is growing continually stronger, so that we share with them our needs for the summer" [to Binswanger]. And in 1932 Freud noted that Anna and "her American friend (who owns the car) have bought and furnished … a weekend cottage" [to Zweig]. Anna Freud loved dogs, and in his old age Freud would play "with them as he used to play with his ring" [Sachs]. Dorothy … was the main source not only of Freud's dogs but also of the chows that went to others in Freud's circle […] Anna became a second mother to her children, and Dorothy was recipient of one of Freud's rings.' Paul Roazen, *Freud and His Followers*, New York, 1975, p. 448. (Note added to proof-corrections, 22 January 1981.)

20. See Jones, III, 423–24.

21. This phrase inevitably recalls Derrida's 'Me – Psychoanalysis: An Introduction to the Translation of "The Shell and the Kernel" by Nicolas Abraham', trans. Richard Klein, in *Diacritics*, March 1979, pp. 4–12.

22. Here, as elsewhere, Derrida is citing the French translation of Jones. In his circular letter of 15-2-1926, Jones quotes from an article in a recent issue of the journal, *Psyche*, as follows: '"A few years ago the analysis of dreams must have seemed to many adherents of the Viennese school to be developing into a not altogether inexact science … But to-day the wild men are once more not far from the fold – for if Telepathy be accepted the possibility of a definite oneiric aetiology recedes some decades, if not centuries, into the future"' (Jones, III, 422).

23. See Jones, III, 406.

24. *Art and Literature: Jensen's 'Gradiva', Leonardo da Vinci and Other Works*, trans. James Strachey, Pelican Freud Library, vol. 14, ed. Albert Dickson (Harmondsworth: Penguin, 1985), 95.

25. It has in fact recently been argued that 'M.P.' was none other than the 'Wolf Man': see Maria Torok's 'Afterword' to *The Wolf Man's Magic Word: A Cryptonymy*, by Nicolas Abraham and Maria Torok, trans. Nicholas Rand (Minneapolis: Univ. of Minnesota Press, 1986), p. 85.
26. For this characterization of Plato, see also *The Post Card*, for example, pp. 200, 207.

'THE DECONSTRUCTION OF ACTUALITY: AN INTERVIEW WITH JACQUES DERRIDA'

Jacques Derrida

This interview was conducted in Paris in August 1993, to mark the publication of Derrida's *Spectres de Marx* (Paris, Galilée, 1993), and was published in the monthly review *Passages* in September. This English translation appears in *Radical Philosophy* with permission.

Passages: From Bogota to Santiago, from Prague to Sofia, not to mention Berlin or Paris, your work gives people an impression of being in touch with the moment, with actuality. Do you share that feeling? Are you a philosopher of the present? Or at least one of those who think their time?

Derrida: Who knows? How could anyone be sure? And anyway, being 'in touch with actuality' and 'thinking one's time' are not the same thing. Both of them imply *doing* something, over and above establishing facts or offering descriptions: taking part, participating, taking sides. That is when you 'make contact', and perhaps change things, if only slightly. But one 'intervenes', as they say, in a time which is not present to one, or given in advance. There are no pre-established norms which can guarantee that one is 'making contact with actuality', or 'thinking one's time' as you put it. And you often get one without the other. But I don't think I am capable of improvising an answer to this kind of question. We must stick to the time of our conversation – and of course time is limited. Now more than ever, thinking one's time – especially if there is a danger, or a hope, of speaking about it in public – means recognising and exploiting the fact that the time of this speaking is produced artificially. It is an

Source: Jacques Derrida, 'The deconstruction of actuality: An interview with Jacques Derrida', *Radical Philosophy*, 68, 1994, pp. 28–41.

artifact. In its actualisation, the time of such a public act is calculated and constrained, 'formatted' and 'initialised' by (to put it briefly) the organisations of the media – and these alone would deserve an almost infinite analysis. These days, anyone who wants to think their time, especially if they want to talk about it too, is bound to pay heed to a public space, and therefore to a political present which is constantly changing in form and content as a result of the tele-technology of what is confusedly called news, information or communication.

But your question referred not only to the present, but to actuality. Very schematically, let me quickly mention just two of the most actual features of the moment. They are too abstract to capture the most characteristic features of my own experience of 'actuality', or any other *philosophical* experience of it, but they do point to something of what constitutes actuality in general. I will try to designate them by two portmanteau terms: *artifactuality* and *actuvirtuality*. The first means that actuality is indeed *made*: it is important to know what it is made of, but it is even more necessary to recognise that it is made. It is not given, but actively produced; it is sorted, invested and performatively interpreted by a range of hierarchising and selective procedures – *factitious* or *artificial* proce-dures which are always subservient to various powers and interests of which their 'subjects' and agents (producers and consumers of actuality, always interpreters, and in some cases 'philosophers' too), are never sufficiently aware. The 'reality' of 'actuality' – however individual, irreducible, stubborn, painful or tragic it may be – only reaches us through fictional devices. The only way to analyse it is through a work of resistance, of vigilant counter-interpretation, etc. Hegel was right to tell the philosophers of his time to read the newspapers. Today, the same duty requires us to find out how news is *made*, and by whom: the daily papers, the weeklies, and the TV news as well. We need to insist on looking at them from the other end: that of the press agencies as well as that of the tele-prompter. And we should never forget what this entails: whenever a journalist or a politician appears to be speaking to us directly, in our homes, and looking us straight in the eye, he or she is actually reading, from a screen, at the dictation of a 'prompter', and reading a text which was produced elsewhere, on a different occasion, possibly by other people, or by a whole network of nameless writers and editors.

Passages: Presumably there is a duty to develop a systematic critique of what you call *artifactuality*. You say we 'ought' ...

Derrida: Yes, a critical culture, a kind of education. But I would not speak about this duty of ours as citizens and philosophers – I would never say 'ought' – without adding two or three crucial qualifications.

The first of these is about the question of *nationality*. (To respond briefly to one of the connotations of your first question, it sounded as if, coming back from abroad, you had fished it out of your diary for some reason: 'here's what they say about you abroad: so what do you make of that?' I would have liked to comment on this; but let it pass.) Amongst the filters which 'inform' the moment – and despite the accelerating pace and increasing ambiguity of internationalisation – nations, regions and provinces, or indeed the 'West', still have a dominance which overdetermines every other hierarchy (sport in the first place, then the 'politician' – though not the political – and finally the 'cultural', in decreasing order of supposed popularity, spectacularity, and comprehensibility). This leads to the discounting of a whole mass of events: all those, in fact, which are taken to be irrelevant to the (supposedly public) national interest, or the national language, or the national code or style. On the news, 'actuality' is automatically ethnocentric. Even when it has to do with 'human rights', it will exclude foreigners, sometimes within the same country, though not on the basis of nationalist passions, or doctrines, or policies. Some journalists make honourable attempts to escape from this pressure, but by definition they can never do enough, and in the end it does not depend on the professional journalists anyway. It is especially important to remember this now, when old nationalisms are taking new forms, and making use of the most 'advanced' media techniques (the official radio and TV of former Yugoslavia are only one example, though a particularly striking one). And it is worth noticing that some of them have felt it necessary to cast doubt on the critique of ethnocentrism, or (to simplify greatly) on the deconstruction of Eurocentrism. This is still considered acceptable, even now: it is as if they were completely blind to the deadly threats currently being issued, in the name of ethnicities, right at the centre of Europe, within a Europe whose only reality today – whose only 'actuality' – is economic and national, and whose only law, in alliances as in conflicts, is still that of the market.

But the tragedy, as always, lies in a contradiction, a double demand: the apparent internationalisation of sources of news and information is often based on the appropriation and monopolisation of channels of information, publication and distribution. Just think of what happened in the Gulf War. It may have represented an exemplary moment of heightened awareness, or even rebellion, but this should not be allowed to conceal the normality and constancy of this kind of violence in conflicts everywhere, not just the Middle East. Sometimes, then, this apparently international process of homogenisation may provoke 'national' resistance. That is the first complication.

A second qualification: this international artifactuality – the monopolisation of the 'actuality effect', and the centralisation of the artifactual power to 'create events' – may be accompanied by advances in 'live' communication, taking place in so-called 'real' time, in the present. The theatrical genre of the 'interview' is a propitiation, at least a fictive one, of this idolatry of 'immediate' presence and 'live' communication. The newspapers will always prefer to publish an interview, accompanied by photographs of the author, rather than an article which will face up to its responsibilities in reading, criticism and education. But how can we carry on criticising the mystifications of 'live' communication (videocameras, etc.) if we want to continue making use of it? In the first place, by continuing to point out, and *argue*, that 'live' communication and 'real time' are never pure: they do not furnish us with intuitions or transparencies, or with perceptions unmarked by technical interpretation or intervention. And any such argument inevitably makes reference to philosophy.

And finally – as I just mentioned – the necessary deconstruction of artifactuality should never be allowed to turn into an alibi or an excuse. It must not create an inflation of the image, or be used to neutralise every danger by means of what might be called the trap of the trap, the delusion of delusion: a denial of events, by which everything – even violence and suffering, war and death – is said to be constructed and fictive, and constituted by and for the media, so that nothing really ever happens, only images, simulacra, and delusions. The deconstruction of artifactuality should be carried as far as possible, but we must also take every precaution against this kind of critical neo-idealism. We must bear in mind not only that any coherent deconstruction is about singularity, about events, and about what is ultimately irreducible in them, but also that 'news' or 'information' is a contradictory and heterogeneous process. Information can transform and strengthen knowledge, truth and the cause of future democracy, with all the problems associated with them, and it must do so, just as it often has done in the past. However artificial and manipulative it may be, we have to hope that artifactuality will bend itself or lend itself to the coming of what is on its way, to the outcome which carries it along and towards which it is moving. And to which it is going to have to bear witness, whether it wants to or not.

Passages: A moment ago you mentioned another term, referring not to technology and artificiality, but to virtuality.

Derrida: If we had enough time I would want to stress another aspect of 'actuality' – of what is happening now, and what is happening *to actuality*. I would emphasise not only these *artificial* syntheses (synthetic images, synthetic voices, all the prosthetic supplements which can be substituted for real actuality) but also, and especially, a concept of *virtuality* (virtual images, virtual spaces, and therefore virtual outcomes or events). Clearly it is no longer possible to contrast virtuality with actual reality, along the lines of the serene old philosophical distinction between power and act, *dynamis* and *energeia*, the potentiality of matter and the determining form of a *telos*, and hence of *progress*, etc. Virtuality now reaches right into the structure of the eventual event and imprints itself there; it affects both the time and the space of images, discourses, and 'news' or 'information' – in fact everything which connects us to actuality, to the unappeasable reality of its supposed present. In order to 'think their time', philosophers today need to attend to the implications and effects of this virtual time – both to the new technical uses to which it can be put, and to how they echo and recall some far more ancient possibilities.

PLAYING FOR TIME

Passages: Might we ask you to come back to something rather more concrete?

Derrida: You think I have been wandering from the point? Avoiding your question? I admit I am not answering it directly. And people may think: he's just wasting time, ours as well as his. Or he's playing for time, putting off his answer. And that would not be entirely false. The one thing that is unacceptable these days – on TV, on the radio, or in the papers – is intellectuals taking their time, or wasting other people's time. Perhaps that's what needs to be changed about actuality: its rhythm. Time is what media professionals must not waste – theirs or ours. And often they can count on success. They know the price of time, if not its value. Before denouncing the silence of the intellectuals yet again, don't we need to investigate this new situation in the media? Don't we need to consider the effects of this difference of rhythm? Some intellectuals are reduced to silence by it – those who need a bit more time, and are not prepared to adapt the complexity of their analyses to the conditions under which they would be permitted to speak. It can shut them up, or drown their voices in the noise of others – at least in places which are dominated by certain rhythms and forms of speech. This different time, the time of the media, gives rise to a different distribution – different spaces, rhythms, intervals, forms of speech-making and public intervention. But what is invisible, incomprehensible or inaudible on the most public of screens can still be actively effective, either immediately or eventually. It is wasted only for those who confuse actuality with what can be seen, or done, on display in the mediatic superstore. In any case, this transformation of public space calls for work: and I believe that the necessary work is already being done, and is more or less accepted, in the obvious places one would expect. The silence of those who read the papers, or watch or hear the news, and analyse it too, is nothing like as silent as it sounds at the place where news is produced – which is deaf to everything that does not speak in conformity to its own law. So it becomes necessary to reverse the approach: there is a kind of mediatic noise about pseudo-actuality which falls like silence, which imposes silence on everything that speaks and acts. But it can be heard elsewhere, provided one knows how to train one's ears on it. This is the law of time. It is terrifying for the present, but it still leaves room for hope, that is to say for reckoning with the untimely. Here it would be necessary to consider the effective limits of the right of reply (which are the limits of democracy too). Quite apart from any question of deliberate censorship, they point to the appropriation of public time and space, and their technical distribution by those with power in the media.

If I still indulge myself in a pause – or a pose, a manner or mannnerism just like any other, since these really are manners of thinking one's time – it is because I really am trying to respond in every possible manner: responding to your questions, while taking responsibility for an interview. In order to take on such responsibilities it is necessary at least to know who and what the interview is for, especially when it is with someone who also writes books, teaches, or publishes in other ways, in a different rhythm, in different situations, and weighing words in different ways. An interview is supposed to be like a snap-shot, a film-still, the capturing of an image: Just look how he flailed around like a frightened animal, on that day, in that place, with those interviewers. I'll give you an example: they talk to this guy about actuality, about what happens in the world every day of the week, and ask him to summarise his opinions very briefly: and off he goes, back into his lair like a hunted animal: laying false trails, drawing you into a maze of qualifications, of fits and starts. He rings the changes on 'but no, it's more complicated than that' (thus earning mockery and dissatisfaction from the fools who think that things are always simpler than one supposes); or 'it is true that complication can be a strategy of avoidance, but so is simplification, and in fact it is a far more reliable one.' So you get your virtual photograph: confronted with a question like the one you just asked, that is my most likely response. It is not exactly impulsive, but it is not entirely deliberate either. It consists not in refusing to answer a person or a question, but on the contrary trying to attend to their indirect presuppositions or invisible twists and turns.

For instance, you made a distinction between 'philosophers of the present' and 'philosophers who think their time.' According to you, I belong with the latter rather than the former. But this could mean several different things. Some philosophers may concern themselves with the present, with what presents itself at the present moment, without bothering themselves with bottomless questions as to the value of presence and what it may signify, presuppose, or conceal. Are they philosophers of the present? Yes – and no. Others may do exactly the opposite: they could immerse themselves in meditations about presence or the presentation of the present, without paying the slightest attention to what is at present going on around them or in the world. Are they philosophers of the present? No – and yes. But I am sure that no philosopher-worthy-of-the-name would accept the way this choice is framed. Like anyone else who tries to be a philosopher, I do not want to give up either on the present or on thinking the presence of the present. Neither do I want to give up on the experience of what both conceals and exposes them – through what I was just calling *artifactuality*, for example. How are we to broach this theme of presence and the present? What are the presuppositions of an inquiry into this subject? What commit-ments do these questions involve? And this stake, this commitment – is this not the law which ought to govern everything, directly or indirectly? I try to adhere to it myself, but by definition it is always inaccessible, it lies beyond everything.

You may say that this is just another evasion, another manner that I have put on in order not to speak about what you yourself call actuality or the present. The first question, the one I should have returned to you, like an echo, is therefore: what does it mean to speak about the present? Of course I could easily try to show that in reality I have only ever been concerned with problems of actuality, of institutional politics, or simply of politics. We could pile up examples – references, names, dates, locations – (don't ask me to do it though). But I don't want to go along with that mediagogical form. Nor do I want to use this platform for the sake of self-justification. I don't feel I have any right to do so, and whatever I may do to avoid running away from political responsibilities, it will never be enough, and I will always reproach myself for this.

But at the same time I try not to forget that it is often the untimely intrusions of so-called actuality which are most 'preoccupied' with the present. Being preoccupied with the present – as a philosopher for example – perhaps means avoiding the constant confusion of presence with actuality. An anachronistic manner of encountering actuality need not necessarily miss out on what is most present today. Difficulties – risks and opportunities, and perhaps incalculabil-ities – may take the form of an untimeliness which arrives exactly on time: precisely this one and no other, and which comes *just-in-time*. *Just*, because it is anachronistic and ill-adjusted (like justice itself, which always lacks measure, and has nothing to do with justness in the sense of nice exactitude, or with adaptive norms, and which is different in kind from the legal systems over which it is supposed to preside). It will be more present than the presence of actuality, more in tune with the individual enormity which marks the irruption of the other into the course of history. These irruptions always take an untimely form, prophetic or messianic, but they have no need for clamour or spectacle. They can stay almost concealed. For the reasons mentioned a moment ago, it is not the daily papers which tell us most about the plu-present of the day (not that we get it every day in the weeklies and monthlies either).

So any answer which is responsible to the needs of actuality has to involve itself in qualifications of this kind. It requires the dissension, dissonance, and discord of this untimeliness, just the right disadjustment of the anachronism. It is necessary to defer, to take one's distance, to tarry; but also to rush in precipitately. And we need to get it right in order to get as close as possible to what is happening throughout actuality. Every time and all at once, and it's a different time each time, the first as well as the last. At least, actions which unite hyper-actuality with anachronism give me pleasure (rare as they are, even impossible, and anyway non-programmable). But my preference for the allying or alloying of these two styles is of course not just a matter of taste. It is the law of answering, of answerability, the law of the other.

DIFFERENCE AND THE EVENT

Passages: What relation would you see between this anachronism or untime-liness, and what you call différance?

Derrida: This takes us back, I think, to a more philosophical level of response, and to what I was saying earlier about the theme of the present or of presence. This is also the theme of différance, which is often accused of encouraging procrastination, neutralisation, and resignation, and therefore of evading the pressing needs of the present, especially ethical and political ones. But I have never seen any conflict between différance and the pressing urgency of present need. I am even tempted to say: *quite the opposite*. But that would also be a simplification. Différance points to a *relationship* (a 'férance') – a relation to what is other, to what differs in the sense of alterity, to the singularity of the other – but 'at the same time' it also relates to what is to come, to that which will occur in ways which are inappropriable, unforeseen, and therefore urgent, beyond anticipation: to precipitation in fact. The thought of différance is also, therefore, a thought of pressing need, of something which, because it is different, I can neither avoid nor appropriate. The event, and the singularity of the event – this is what differance is all about. (This is why I said that it means something quite different from the neutralisation of events on the grounds that they are artifactualised by the media.) Even if it also and inevitably involves an opposite movement 'at the same time' (this 'same time' about which sameness disagrees all the time, a time which is 'out of joint', as Hamlet says: disturbed, distracted, dislocated, and disproportionate) – an attempt to reappropriate, divert, loosen, and deaden the cruelty of the event, or simply to deaden the death towards which it is bound. So différance is a thought which wishes to yield to the imminence of what is coming or about to come: to the event, and therefore to experience itself, in so far as it too has an inevitable tendency, 'at the same time' and in the light of 'the same time', to appropriate whatever is going to happen: the economy of the other and the aneconomy of the other, saving and dispensing, both at once. There would be no différance without urgency, emergency, imminence, precipitation, the ineluctable, the unforeseen arrival of the other, the other to whom both reference and deference are made.

Passages: In that connection, what does it mean, for you, to speak of 'the event'?

Derrida: It is a name for the aspect of what happens that we will never manage either to eliminate or to deny (or simply never manage to deny). It is another name for experience, which is always experience of the other. The event is what does not allow itself to be subsumed under any other concept, not even that of being. A 'there is' or a 'let there be something rather than nothing' arises from the experience of an event, rather than from a thinking of being. The happening of the event is what cannot and should not be prevented: it is another name for the future itself. Not that it is good – good in itself – that everything or anything should happen; nor that we should give up trying to prevent certain things from coming to pass (in that case there would be no choice, no responsibility, no ethics or politics). But you do not try to oppose events unless you think they shut off the future, or carry a threat of death: events which would end the possibility of events, which would end any affirmative opening toward the arrival of the other. This is why thinking about the event always opens up a kind of messianic space, however abstract, formal, deserted and desolate it may be, and however little it may have to do with 'religion'. It is also why messianism is inseparable from justice, which again I distinguish from law (as I already attempted to do in *Force of Law* and *Spectres de Marx*,[1] where it is perhaps the basic claim). If the event is what arrives or comes to pass or supervenes, it is not sufficient to say that this *coming* 'is' not, that it cannot be reduced to any of the categories of existence. Nor do the noun (*la venue*) and the nominalised verb (*le venir*), exhaust the 'coming' that they come from. I have often tried to analyse this sort of performative summons, this appeal which refuses to bow to the being of anything that is. Such appeals are addressed to the other, and they do not simply express desires, or orders, requests, or demands, though they may make them possible subsequently. The event must be considered in terms of the 'come hither', not conversely. 'Come' is said to another, to others who are not yet defined as persons, as subjects, as equals (at least in the sense of any measurable equality). Without this 'come hither' there could be no experience of what is to come, of the event, of what will happen and therefore of what, since it comes from the other, lies beyond anticipation. There is not even any horizon of expectation in this messianics without messianism. If there were a horizon of expectation, of anticipation, or programming, there would be neither event, nor history (a possibility which, paradoxically and for the same reasons, can never be rationally ruled out: it is almost impossible to think the absence of a horizon of expectation). There would be no event, no history, unless a 'come hither' opened out and addressed itself to someone, to someone else whom I cannot and must not define in advance – not as subject, self, consciousness, nor even as animal, God, person, man or woman, living or dead. (It must be possible to *summon* a spectre, to appeal to it for example, and I don't think this is an arbitrary example: there may be something of the revenant, of the return, at the origin or the conclusion of every 'come hither'.) The one to whom 'come hither' is addressed cannot be defined in advance. This absolute hospitality is offered to the outsider, the stranger, the new arrival. Absolute arrivals must not be required to begin by stating their identity; I must not insist that they say who they are, and whether they are going to integrate themselves or not; nor should I lay down any conditions for offering them hospitality, for whether or not I shall be able to 'assimilate' them into the family, the nation, or the state. With an absolute new arrival, I ought not to propose contracts or impose conditions. I ought not; and in any case, by definition, I cannot. That is why, although this may seem to be no more than the morals of hospitality, it actually goes far beyond morality, and even further beyond law and politics. The kind of absolute arrivals I am trying to describe are similar to births, the arrival of babies, but they are not really equivalent. The family anticipates and forenames its new arrivals, it prepares the way so that they are caught up in a symbolic space which muffles the novelty of the arrival. But despite all the anticipations and prenominations, the element of chance cannot be eliminated: the child that arrives is always unforeseen. It speaks of itself from the *origin* of a different world, or from a *different* origin of this one.

I have been struggling with this impossible concept of messianic arrival for a long time now. I have tried to define the basic principles in my forthcoming book on death (*Apories*),[2] as well as in the short book on Marx that I have just finished. But it is difficult to give a justification, even a provisional, pedagogical one, for the term 'messianic'. Messianic experience is *a priori*, but it is *a priori* exposed, in its own expectation, to what will be determined only *a posteriori*, by the event. A desert within a desert, one signalling to the other, the desert of a messianics without messianism and therefore without religious doctrine or dogma. This dry and desolate expectation, this expectation without horizon, has one thing in common with the great messianisms of the Book: the reference to an arrival who may turn up – and may not – but of whom, by definition, I can know nothing in advance. Except one thing: that justice, in the most enigmatic sense of the word, is somehow at stake. And therefore revolution too, through the connection between the event, justice, and this absolute fracture in the foreseeable concatenation of historical time. Eschatology breaks teleology apart: the two have to be kept distinct here, difficult though this always is. It is possible to give up on revolutionary imagery, to abandon all revolutionary rhetoric; it is possible to give up revolutionary politics of certain kinds, perhaps of all kinds; but it is impossible to give up on revolution without abandoning both justice and the event.

An event cannot be reduced to the fact of something happening. It may rain this evening or it may not, but that is not an absolute event. I know what rain is; so it is not an absolutely different singularity. In such cases what happens is not an arrival.

An arrival must be absolutely different: the other that I expect to be unexpected, that I do not await. The expectation of an arrival is a non-expectation; it lacks what philosophy calls a horizon of expectation, through which knowledge anticipates the future and deadens it in advance. If I am sure that something will happen, then it will not be an event. It will be someone I have arranged to meet – Christ perhaps, or a friend – but if I know they are going to arrive, and am sure that they will, then to that extent it will not be an arrival. But of course the arrival of someone I am waiting for may also, in some other way, astonish me every time; it can be an amazing surprise, new every time, and so it can happen for me over and over again. And the arrival, like Elias, may never arrive at all. It is within the ever-open hollowness of this possibility, the possibility of non-arrival, of absolute disconvenience, that I relate to the event: it is what may always fail to come to pass.

Passages: So there can be no event without surprise?

Derrida: Exactly.

NATIONALISM

Passages: To take a recent example, have you been surprised by the fact that there has suddenly turned out to be a mingling between the extreme right and certain strands of left-wing thought?

Derrida: A brutal return to 'actuality'! But you are quite right, and in the light of what I have been saying, the question ought not to be dodged. The 'mingling' you speak of is complicated, though perhaps less improbable than it might seem. We need to proceed with great care here, and this is difficult when improvising. There are so many facts and problems that have to be taken into account: which extreme right, which 'left-wing thought', etc., what kind of 'mingling', who, where, when, within what limits, etc.? And before turning to individual, untypical actions, which are as usual the most interesting and innovative, we ought to remind ourselves of certain chains of general intelligibility, programmes or logics which contain no surprises. This is not the first time that far-right positions have been able to ally themselves, on certain issues, with those on the far left. Though based on quite different motivations and analyses, opposition to Europe can encourage nationalistic strategies on both left and right. Doubts about the policies of the dominant states in Europe – legitimate doubts, very likely, about their economism, or simply their economic or monetary policies – may lead parts of the left straight into positions which are in objective alliance with the nationalism and anti-Europeanism of the far right. Le Pen is currently parading his opposition to 'free trade' and 'economic liberalism'. This opportunistic rhetoric may turn him into an 'objective ally', as they used to say, of those on the left who also criticise the capitalistic and monetarist orthodoxies in which Europe is getting itself bogged down, though with quite different motives. Vigilance and clarity in action and in thought are required if these amalgams are to be dissolved or analytically resolved. The risk is ever-present, more serious than ever, and sometimes 'objectively' unavoidable: in an election, for example. Even if you sharpen the divisions and distinctions, which you should always be trying to do, through inquiries, records, and electoral analyses, with all that they entail, and in all the sites of publication, demonstration, and action associated with a given electoral conjuncture (but given by whom, exactly, and how?), the anti-European votes of left and right will still be added together in the end. And the pro-European votes too, of course.

But as you know there have been left revisionisms (to be specific, as one should always try to be: the negationist revisionisms over the Shoah) which have slipped into anti-Semitism (if indeed they weren't inspired by it in the first place). Some of these grew, more or less confusedly, from a basic anti-Israelism or, more narrowly, from opposition to the politics of possession, of the *fait accompli*, as practised by the State of Israel over a long period, in fact throughout the whole history of Israel. But these confusions can surely be subjected to bold and honest analyses. It must be possible to criticise specific policies of particular governments of the State of Israel without fundamental hostility to the existence of this State (I would even say: quite the opposite!), and without either anti-Semitism or anti-Zionism. I would also suggest that even for Jews who are committed to the Zionist cause, a willingness to wonder and worry about the historical foundation of the State, its conditions and what it has brought into existence, need not imply any betrayal of Juadaism. The logic of opposition to the State of Israel or its politics of possession does not entail anti-Semitism, or even anti-Zionism; nor does it have anything to do with revisionism, in the sense I defined earlier. There are some very great examples (such as Buber, in the past). But, to stick with general principles, surely you would agree that our duty today is to denounce confusion. And to protect ourselves from it in each of two ways. *On the one hand*, there are the nationalist confusions of those who veer from left to right and confound every possible European project with the actual current policies of the European Community, and the anti-Jewish confusions of those who cannot see any dividing line between criticising the Israeli State and anti-Israelism, anti-Zionism, anti-Semitism, and revisionism, etc. There are at least five possibilities here, and they must be kept absolutely distinct. These metonymic slides are all the more serious – politically, intellectually and philosophically – because they pose threats on *both sides*, so to speak: both to those who yield to them in practice, and to those who, *on the other hand*, denounce them whilst adopting their logic in perfect symmetry: as if you could not do one without the other – for example, oppose the actual policies of Europe without being opposed to Europe in principle; or worry about the State of Israel, its past and present policies, the conditions of its foundation and of what it has been possible to build upon them for the past half century, without thereby becoming anti-Semitic, anti-Zionist, or indeed revisionist-negationist, etc.

This symmetry between enemies forges a link between obscurantist confusion and terrorism. And it takes tenacity and courage to resist such occult (or occultising, occultist) strategies of amalgamation. In order to stand up to this double intimidation, the only responsible response is never to give up the task of distinguishing and analysing. And I would also say: never to give up on the Enlightenment, which also means, on *public* demonstrations of such discriminations (and this is less easy than you might think). This resistance is all the more urgently necessary since we are in a phase where renewed critical work on the history of this century is getting into dangerous waters. It is going to be necessary to re-read and re-interpretation, is going to be automatically associated with negationist-revisionism, if every question about the past, or more generally about the constitution of truth in history, is going to be accused of paving the way for revisionism? (In *Spectres de Marx* I quote a particularly shocking example of this idiocy, from a leading American newspaper.) What a victory for dogmatisms it will be, if prosecutors are constantly getting to their feet to make accusations of complicity with the enemy against anyone who tries to raise new questions, to disturb stereotypes and good consciences, and to complicate or re-work, for a changed situation, the discourse of the left, or the analysis of racism or anti-Semitism. Of course, in order to keep the risk of such accusations to a minimum, it is necessary to take extra care in our discussions, analyses, and public interventions. And of course absolute assurance can never be promised, let alone delivered. Several recent examples could be given to illustrate this.

But to come back to your question: Were you surprised, you asked me, by this mingling? I have offered only a very general and abstract answer: certain models or schemes of intelligibility may make the mingling less surprising than it would at first appear; but they also show why the issues ought to be kept separate. As regards the most interesting particular cases, we would need more time and a different situation in order to analyse them. This is where you meet with surprises and syncopations. In between the most general kinds of logic (with the greatest predictability) and the most unpredictable singularities, comes the intermediate schema of *rhythm*. Ever since the fifties for instance, people have known what was wrong with the totalitarianisme of the East, and how it was bound to lead to their eventual collapse: for my generation, it was our daily bread. (Together with that old theme, recently patched up in the style of 'F-ukuyama', of the supposed 'end of history', 'end of man', etc.) What could not be anticipated was the rhythm, the speed, the date: for example that of the fall of the Berlin wall. In 1986–7, no one in the entire world could have had even the vaguest idea of it. Not that the rhythm is inexplicable. It can be analysed in retrospect, taking account of new causalities which earlier experts ignored (in the first place, the geo-political effects of telecommunication in general: the whole sequence in which a signal like the fall of the Berlin wall gets inscribed would have been impossible and incomprehensible without a given density of telecommunication networks, etc.).

IMMIGRATION

Passages: To develop your point in a different direction: immigration is no higher now than it was half a century ago. But now it takes people by surprise: it seems to have surprised the social body and the political class. The discourses of both right and left, in turning against illegal immigration, seem to have careered into xenophobia in a quite unanticipated way.

Derrida: In this respect, at least in the discourse of the two republican majorities, the differences are mainly a matter of emphasis. The overt political lines are more or less the same. The common axiom, or the consensus as they say, is always: stop illegal immigration, and put an end to excessive, unpro-ductive or destabilising levels of immigration. The manipulation of this con-sensus is more vigorous now and the atmosphere has changed; and this is an important difference. But the principles remain the same: that the national community has to be protected from any excessive effect on the national body, that is to say on the consciousness it supposedly ought to have of the integrity of its own body (an axiom which, by the way, implies that all kinds of biological or cultural transplants ought to be banned, which would of course lead us a long way – unless it led nowhere, or to death itself). When François Mitterand spoke about the threshold of tolerance (and some of us protested publicly against those words, whereupon he at least had the courage, honour or agility to withdraw them), his careless lapse spoke the truth of a discourse which is common to the republican parties of the left and the right, indeed the far right: we must not allow any new arrivals, in the sense I was just speaking of; we must control their arrival, and we must filter the flow of immigration.

I realise, I promise you, that what I am saying about new arrivals is politically impracticable, at least as long as politics is based, as it always is, on the idea of the identity of a body known as the State-nation. There is no State-nation in the world today which would simply say: 'We throw open our doors to everyone, we put no limit on immigration'. As far as I know – and I would be interested if you could think of a counter-example – every State-nation is based on the control of its frontiers, on opposition to illegal immigration, and strict limits to legal immigration and right of asylum. The concept of the frontier, no less than the frontier itself, constitutes the concept of a State-nation.

On this basis the concept can be treated in various way but these different policies, however important they may be, are subordinate to the general principle of politics, that the political is national. This is then used to justify the filtering of population flows and stamping out of illegal immigration, even though it may also be recognised that this is actually unachievable, and indeed (a supplementary hypocrisy) that in certain economic circumstances it is quite undesirable.

What I have been saying about the absolute arrival cannot generate a politics in the traditional sense of the word: a policy which could be implemented by a State-nation. But whilst I realise that what I have been saying about the event and the arrival is impracticable and unpolitical from the point of view of this concept of politics, I still want to claim that any politics which fails to sustain some relation to the principle of unconditional hospitality has completely lost its relation to justice. It may retain its rights (which once again need to be distinguished from justice), and its right to rights, but it will lose both justice and the right to speak of it with any credibility. This is not the place to go into it, but it is important to distinguish between immigration policy and respect for the right of asylum. In principle the right of asylum (in the form in which it is still recognised in France, at least for the time being and for political reasons) is, paradoxically, less political, because it is not based in principle on the interests of the body of the State-nation which guarantees it. But, apart from the fact that it is difficult to distinguish between the concepts of immigration and asylum, it is almost impossible to delimit the properly political grounds for exile – those which, under our constitution, are supposed to justify an application for asylum. After all, unemployment in a foreign country is a malfunction of democracy and a kind of political persecution. In addition, and this is the role of the market again, the rich countries always share in the responsibility (if only through foreign debt and everything it symbolises) for the political and economic situations which push people into exile or emigration. Here we run against the limits of the political and the juridical: it is always possible to show that the right of asylum may be either meaningless or infinite. Thus the concept always lacks rigour, though this may not bother anyone except in times of global turmoil. It would have to be completely reworked before we could understand or in any way alter the current debate (between constitutionalism on one side, for example, and, on the other, the neo-populism of those who, like Charles Pasqua [Minister of the Interior], want to change the Constitution so as to adapt the article on right of asylum to the supposed wishes of a new or ancient 'French people' which is apparently different from the one which voted for the constitution in the first place). But I ought to try to come back to the point of your question. You were saying that it seems that 'the social body and political class' of today have been taken by surprise. Do you mean by immigration, or by xenophobia?

Passages: Xenophobia.

Derrida: What the political class has been adapting to – both the class which came to power in 1981, and the one which is now taking over from it – is not so much xenophobia itself as new ways of exploiting it, or abusing it by abusing the citizens. They are quarreling over an electorate, roughly speaking that of the security-conscious (the '*sécuritaires*' as they are called, rather like the 'health-conscious', the *sanitaires*, since what is supposed to be at stake is the security and health of a social body which needs to be protected, as they say, by a *cordon sanitaire*). The National Front electorate, which is dominated by an image of the quasi-biological hygiene of a proper national body (*quasi*-biological because nationalist fantasy, like the rhetoric of the politicians, makes frequent use of such organicist analogies).

Parenthetically, take for example the rhetoric of a recent intervention by Le Pen (*Le Monde*, 24 August 1993) – remarkable, as always, for his somnambulistic lucidity. Le Pen now prefers the analogy (both apt and threadbare) of 'a living membrane which is permeable to what is benign, but impermeable to everything else'. If an organism could regulate this filtration in advance, then I suppose it might achieve immortality, but first it would have to die in advance, kill itself or let itself be killed, for fear of being *altered* from outside, by the other in fact. Hence the theatre of death which is common to so many kinds of racism, biologism, organicism, and eugenicism, and to certain philosophies of life as well. And – to continue the parenthesis – let me once again stress a point which is unlikely to please anyone. All of those on the left or right who say they favour immigration controls 'like everyone else' and call for a clamp-down on illegal immigration and tighter immigration controls, are – in fact and in principle, and whether they like it or not, and with varying degrees of elegance and gentility – subscribing to Le Pen's organicist axiom. They are accepting the axiom of a national front (the front is a skin, a discriminating 'membrane': it only lets in what is homogeneous or capable of being homogenised, what is assimilable, or at most what is heterogeneous but considered 'benign': the appropriable immigrant, the proper immigrant). We should not close our eyes to this ineluctable complicity: it is rooted in the political, to the extent that the political is and remains linked to the State-nation. And since we had better recognise, like everyone else, that we have no choice but to protect what we take to be our own body, then let us be spared all these pure souls who appeal to high principles and put on a high moral tone and start lecturing us on politics as soon as we propose to control immigration and asylum (a proposal which is anyway accepted unanimously by the left as much as the right). Just as Le Pen will always have the most terrible problems in justifying or regulating the filtration of his 'membrane', so there is a permeability between these supposedly opposite concepts and logics which is far more difficult to regulate than is usually recognised. Today we have a neo-protectionism of the left and a neo-protectionism of the right, both in economics and in matters of demographic flows; a commitment to tree trade both on the left and on the right; we have both right neo-nationalism and left neo-nationalism. All these 'neo-' logics pass straight through the protective membrane of their concepts, without any chance of control, and they create shady alliances both in discourse and in political and electoral activities. Recognising this permeability, this combinatory, and these complicities does not mean adopting an apolitical stance, or believing in an end of the division between right and left or an 'end of ideologies'. On the contrary: it means calling for a courageous thematisation and formalisation of this terrible combinatory, as an essential preliminary not only to a different politics, but to a different theory of politics, and a different delimitiation of the *socius*, especially in relation to citizenship and State-nationhood in general, and more broadly to identity and subjectivity as well. How am I supposed to discuss all that in an interview, and in an aside? And yet, as you know, these questions are at present anything but abstract or speculative. So, to return to France, the majorities are in the range of 1 or 2 per cent in presidential elections, 10 to 15 per cent in others. So the problem, as I was saying, is how to attract, motivate, and seduce (both trouble and reassure) a fraction of the potential xenophobes who vote for the National Front.

This points to some other questions: why is the National Front able to exploit this fear or aggravate this impatience? Why is it that, instead of doing what is needed (in education and socio-economic policy) to defuse these feelings, people are trying either to take over the positions of the National Front, or to exploit the split which it is creating within the so-called republican right? Meanwhile the level of immigration has, as you said, remained very steady: apparently it has not changed for decades, or it may even have gone down a bit. Is this surprising or not? Analysis always tends to dissolve surprise. 'It was only to be expected', as we say in retrospect, when we can finally see the elements that our analysis had overlooked, or we have developed a different analysis (for example, higher levels of unemployment, increasing permeability of European borders, the revival of religions and of claims to identity – religious, linguistic, and cultural – amongst the immigrants themselves: all this means that the same rate of immigration gets to seem more threatening for the self-identification of the host social body).

But an event which remains an event is a happening, an arrival: it is a surprise, and it resists even retrospective analysis. With the birth of a child – the obvious image of an absolute arrival – you can analyse the causalities, the genealogical, genetic and symbolic conditions, and all the wedding preparations as well, if you like. But even if such an analysis could ever be complete, you would never be able to eliminate the element of chance which constitutes the place of this taking-place: there will still be someone who can speak, someone unique, an absolute beginning, a different origin of the world. Even if it ought to yield to analysis, or return to ashes, the clinker of the absolute arrival refuses to break up and dissolve. The history of the immigrations which have constituted the culture, religions and languages of France is in the first instance the history of these children – children of immigrants or others – who were such absolute arrivals. The task of a philosopher – and therefore of anyone, a citizen for example – is to take the analysis as far as possible and try to make the event intelligible, up to the point where a new arrival takes place. What is absolutely new is not this rather than that; it is the fact that it only happens once. It is marked by a date (a place, a moment), and it is always births or deaths that are marked by a date. Even if it had been possible to predict the fall of the Berlin wall, it still happened on one particular day, there were a few more deaths (both before the collapse and during it) – and this is what makes it an irremovable event. What refuses to yield to analysis is birth and death: as ever, the origin and the end of a world.

JUSTICE AND REPETITION

Passages: Can what resists analysis be equated with the undeconstructable? Is there such a thing as the undeconstructable, and if so, what is it?

Derrida: If anything is undeconstructable, it is justice. The law is deconstructable, fortunately: it is infinitely perfectible. I am tempted to regard justice as the best word, today, for what refuses to yield to deconstruction, that is to say for what sets deconstruction in motion, what justifies it. It is an affirmative experience of the coming of the other as other: better that this should happen than the opposite (an experience of the event which cannot be expressed simply as an ontology: that anything should exist, that there should be something rather than nothing). The openness of the future is worth more than this: that is the axiom of deconstruction – the basis on which it has always set itself in motion, and which links it, like the future itself, to otherness, to the priceless dignity of otherness, that is to say to justice. It is also democracy as the democracy of the future.

It is easy to imagine the objection. Someone might say: 'But surely it would sometimes be better if this or that did not happen. Justice requires us to prevent certain events (or "arrivals") from coming to pass. Events are not good in themselves, and the future is not unconditionally desirable.' Of course that is true. But it will always be possible to show that what we are opposing, what we would hypothetically prefer not to happen, is something which, rightly or wrongly, is thought of as obstructing the horizon, or simply forming a horizon (the word means *limit*) for the absolute coming of what is completely other, for the future itself. This involves a messianic structure (but not messianism – in the book on Marx, I make a distinction between the messianic, as a universal dimension of experience, and every particular messianism) which unites the promise of the new arrival with justice and the inscrutability of the future, and knits them indissolubly together. I cannot try to reconstruct the argument now, and I realise that the word 'justice' may seem equivocal. Justice is not the same as law, and it is broader and more fundamental than human rights; nor is it to be equated with distributive justice; nor is it the same as respect for the other as a human subject, in the traditional sense of that word. It is the experience of the other as other, the fact that I permit the other to be other, which presupposes a gift without exchange, without reappropriation, without jurisdiction. Here I meet up with several different traditions, whilst also slightly displacing them, as I have tried to show elsewhere.[3] There is an inheritance from Levinas, when he defines the relation to the other simply as justice ('the relation with the Other – that is, justice').[4] There is also that paradoxical thought, Plotinian in its first formulation, but which also surfaces in Heidegger, and then in Lacan: giving not only what one has, but what one has not. Such excess overflows the present, propriety, restitution, and no doubt law, politics and morality as well, though it ought also to inspire and encourage them.

Passages: But doesn't philosophy also discuss the idea that anything, perhaps the worst, can always return?

Derrida: Yes, it precisely 'discusses' this return of the worst, and in more than one way. In the first place, everything that prepared the way for a philosophy of Enlightenment, or that has become its heir (not rationalism as such, which is not necessarily associated with it, but a progressive, teleological, humanistic and critical rationalism) does indeed struggle against such a 'return of the worst', which education and an awareness of the past are supposed to be able to prevent. Although this Enlightenment struggle can often take the form either of denial or of conjuration and incantation, one has to play one's part in it and reaffirm the philosophy of emancipation. I personally believe in its future, and I have never gone along with these proclamations about the end of the great emancipatory and revolutionary discourses. Nevertheless the very act of affirming them pays tribute to the possibility of what they oppose: the return of the worst, the incorrigible repetition-compulsion in the death drive and radical evil, history without progression, history without history, etc. And the Enlightenment thought of our time cannot be reduced to that of the eighteenth century.

Then there is another manner, still more radical, in which philosophy can 'discuss' the return of the worst. This consists in misrecognition (denial, exorcism, incantation, each form requiring analysis) of what might constitute a recurrence of evil: a law of spectres, which is resistant both to ontology (a ghost or a revenant is neither present nor absent, it neither is nor is not, and it cannot be dialecticised either) and to any philosophy of the subject, of the object, or of consciousness (of being-present) which, like ontology and philosophy itself, will also be committed to 'expelling' spectres. And hence also to not attending to the lessons of psychoanalysis either about ghosts, or about the repetition of the gravest threats to historical progress. (To which I would quickly add that on the one hand it is only a particular concept of progress which is under threat, and that there would be no progress at all in the absence of that threat; and that on the other hand psychoanalytic discourse, starting with Freud, has always been dominated by something which entailed a certain misrecognition of the structure and logic of spectres – a powerful, subtle and unstable misrecognition, but one which it has in common with science and philosophy.) Yes indeed: a ghost can return, as the worst can return, but without such revenance, and without some acknowledgement of its ineradicable originality, we would be stripped of memory, inheritance, and justice, of everything that has value beyond life, and by which the dignity of life is measured. I have made suggestions about this elsewhere, and it is hard for me to schematise them right now. But I suppose that when you spoke of the 'return of the worst' you were thinking, more immediately, of what took place in Europe before the war?

Passages: Yes.

Derrida: And not only in Europe, let's not forget. In this context, each country has its own original history, and its own economy of memory, its own way of being economical with it. My immediate feeling is that what took place in France well before World War II, and during it, and still more, I think, during the Algerian war, has imposed, and therefore overdetermined, several layers of forgetting. The capitalisation of silence is especially dense, resistant and dangerous here. Through a slow, discontinuous and contradictory process, this compact of secrecy is being replaced by a movement towards the liberation of memory (especially of public memory, so to speak, and its official legitimation, which never proceeds in the rhythm either of historical knowledge or of private memory, if such a thing can exist in its purity). But if this process of unsealing is contradictory, both in its consequences and in its motivations, this is due to the effect of ghosts. The moment at which the worst threatens to return is also the moment when the worst is being remembered (out of respect for memory, for truth, for victims, etc.). One ghost recalls another. Often it is because of signs of the resurgence or quasi-resurrection of the one, that an appeal is made to the other. The pressing need for official commemoration of the round-up of Jews at the Vélodrome d'Hiver [in Paris on 16 July 1942], or for recognition that the French State bears some responsibility for the 'worst' that happened under the occupation, is recalled because the signs of a return of nationalism, racism, xenophobia and anti-semitism are becoming visible, though in a very different context, sometimes with the same aspect, sometimes with different features entirely. The two memories relaunch each other; they provoke and invoke each other; and of necessity, again and again, they do battle with each other, always on the brink of every possible contamination. When the abominable ghosts return, we recall the ghosts of their victims, not only in order to preserve their memory but also, inseparably, for the sake of the current struggle: especially for the promise which commits it to a future without which it would have absolutely no sense – to a future, beyond every present life, beyond every living being who can already say 'me, now.' The question of ghosts is also the question of the future as a question of justice. This double return encourages an irre-pressible tendency to confusion. Analogy is confused with identity: 'Exactly the same thing is being repeated, exactly the same thing.' But no: a kind of iterabil-ity (difference within repetition) means that what returns is nevertheless a completely different event. The return of a ghost is always a different return, on another stage; it takes place under new conditions, which we must study with as closely as possible, unless we don't care at all what we are saying or doing.

Yesterday a German woman, a journalist, telephoned me. (It was about that 'appeal' from European intellectuals for 'vigilance', to which I felt I ought to lend my signature, on and about which there would be so much to say – but there is no time to do that seriously now.) Noticing that many German intel-lectuals were welcoming this action, and calling it opportune, for obvious reasons, especially in the current situation in Germany, she was wondering whether this was a revival of the tradition of 'J'accuse!' Where is Zola today? she wanted to know. I tried to explain to her why, despite my enormous respect for Zola, I was not sure that he was the best or only model for a new 'J'accuse!' Everything is so different now – the public space, the channels of information and authority, the relation between power and secrecy, the figure of the intellectual, the writer, the journalist, etc. It is not 'J'accuse!' which is out of date, but the form and space in which it was written. Of course the Dreyfus affair should not be forgotten, but we must also realise that it will never be exactly repeated. What happens may be worse, of course, but it certainly will not be the Dreyfus affair over again.

In short, in order to think (but what does 'thinking' mean here?) what you were calling the 'return of the worst', it is necessary to go beyond ontology, beyond philosophies of life or death, beyond a logic of the conscious subject, and enter into the relations between politics, history and the revenant.

MARX

Passages: Hadn't you already spoken about all this in *Of Spirit: Heidegger and the Question?*[5]

Derrida: From the very first sentence, in fact, that book was moving towards a disruptive logic of spirit as spectre. The matter is treated differently, but I hope consistently, in the book on Marx. This book is no more pro-spiritualist than the one on Heidegger was anti-spiritualist. But the need for a strategy of paradox did push me, at least in appearance, to distrust a certain kind of spirit in Heidegger and to *defend* spirit, a certain kind of spirit, a particular spirit or spectre, in Marx.

Passages: You spoke about Marx in a course at the Ecole Normale Supérieure in the seventies, but only allusively.

Derrida: They were more than allusions, if I may say so, and it was in more than one course. But apart from such references, my book is an attempt to explain that situation, that relative silence, and the difficult but, I believe, intimate connections between deconstruction and a certain 'spirit' of marxism.

Passages: What has led you to speak about Marx now?

Derrida: It is hard to answer that question in a few improvised words. But the book on Marx began as a lecture delivered in the United States in April, to open a conference entitled 'Whither Marxism?' – which also asked, through a play on words, whether Marxism was in the process of 'withering away'. I sketched out an approach to Marx's writings, to everything in them that can be subordinated to the problematic of the spectre (and so also of exchange value, fetishism, ideology, and much else besides). But I also tried, mainly as a political act, to mark, as I think it is now necessary to do, a point of resistance to a dogmatic consensus on the death of Marx, the end of the critique of capitalism, the final triumph of the market, and the eternal link between democracy and the logic of economic liberalism, etc. I tried to show where and how this consensus has become dominant and often obscene in its troubled but grinning euphoria, triumphal but manic (I make deliberate use of the language which Freud uses to describe one phase of the work of mourning: the essay on spectres is also an essay on mourning and politics). It is urgently necessary to rise up against the new anti-marxist dogma, don't you think? I consider it not only regressive and pre-critical in most of its manifestations, but also blind to its own contra-dictions, and deaf to the creakings of ruination, of the ruinous and ruined structure of its own 'rationality', a new 'colossus with feet of clay'. And I believe that it is all the more urgent to combat this dogmatism and this politics, as this urgency itself seems to me to be syncopated, to go against the rhythm. (Another theme of the essay is syncopation in politics, and anachronism, untimeliness, etc.) Clearly, this is connected with what I was saying earlier about the messianic and the event, about justice and revolution.

The responsibility for rising up comes back to everyone, but especially to those who, without ever being anti-marxists or anti-communists, resisted a certain kind of marxist orthodoxy as long as it remained hegemonic, at least in certain circles (and this was a long time for most of my generation). But apart from this position-taking, and also in order to sustain it, I started up an argument with Marx's writings. The argument is organised by the question of the spectre (networked with those of repetition, mourning, and inheritance, the event and the messianic, of everything that exceeds the ontological oppositions between absence and presence, visible and invisible, living and dead, and hence above all of the prosthesis as 'phantom limb', of technology, of the teletechnological simulacrum, the synthetic image, virtual space, etc.; and so back to the themes I have already discussed: *artifactuality* and *virtuactuality*). Remember the opening sentence of the *Communist Manifesto*: 'A spectre is haunting Europe, the spectre of communism.' Well I investigate, I roam around a little with all the spectres which literally obsessed Marx. Marx really was persecuted by them: he chased them everywhere, he drove them away, but they followed him around as well. It happens in the *18th Brumaire*, in *Capital*, but above all in the *German Ideology* where, as you know, he set out an interminable critique (interminable because fascinated, captivated, shackled) of Stirner's hauntings, a hallucination which is already critical, and which Marx found extremely difficult to shake off.

So I have tried to decode the logic of the spectre in the work of Marx. I aimed to do this in relation, so to speak, to what is taking place in the world today, in a new public space which has been transformed by what is summarily called the 'return of the religious' as well as by tele-technology. What does the work of mourning mean when it comes to marxism? What does it attempt to invoke, to conjure up? The word and concept of *conjuration*, highly ambiguous as they are (at least in French, English and German) play an important role in this essay, no less important than that of heritage or inheritance. To inherit is not essentially to *receive* something, a *given* which one then *has*. It is an active affirmation, a response to an injunction, but it also presupposes initiative, the endorsement or counter-signing of a critical choice. To inherit is to select, to sift, to harness, to reclaim, to reactivate. I also believe, though I cannot argue the point here, that every assignment of inheritance harbours a contradiction and a secret. (This is the thread which runs through the book, and which ties the genius of Marx to that of Shakespeare – whom Marx loved so much and quoted so often, especially from *Timon of Athens* and *Much Ado about Nothing* – and to Hamlet's father, who is perhaps the main character in the essay.)

Hypothesis: there is always more than one spirit. To speak of spirit is immediately to evoke a plurality of spirits, or spectres, and an inheritor always has to choose one spirit or another. An inheritor has to make selections or filtrations, to sift through the ghosts or the injunctions of each spirit. Where assignations are not multiple and contradictory, where they are not sufficiently cryptic to challenge interpretation, where they do not involve the unbounded dangers of active interpretation, there is no inheritance. Inheriting implies decisions and responsibilities. Without a double-bind, there is no responsibility. An inheritance must always include an undecidable reserve.

If inheriting means reaffirming an injunction, if it is not a possession but an assignment which needs to be decoded, then we are nothing but what we inherit. Our being is inheritance, and the language we speak is inheritance too. Hölderlin said, more or less, that language has been given us so that we may witness the fact that we are our inheritance: not an inheritance that we have or receive, but one that we are, all the way down. What we are, we have inherited. And we inherit language, which witnesses the fact that we are what we inherit. There is a paradoxical circle here, a circle within which we have to struggle, and then strike out with choices which not only inherit their own norms, but invent them too, in the inevitable absence of programmes and fixed norms. Saying that an inheritance is not a commodity that one acquires and that we are inheritors all the way down is therefore not traditionalist or antiquarian at all. And we are, amongst other things, inheritors of Marx and marxism. I try to explain why this involves an event which nothing and no one can eradicate, not even – in fact especially not – the monstrosity of totalitarianism (all the various totalitarianisms, and there were several of them, which were in part linked to marxism, and which cannot be seen as mere perversions or distortions of the inheritance). Even people who have never read Marx, or so much as heard of him, are Marx's heirs, and so are the anti-communists and anti-marxists. And then, you cannot inherit from Marx without also inheriting from Shakespeare, the Bible, and much else besides.

COMMITMENT

Passages: To take this point a little further: would you be surprised if there were some kind of return of communism, though in a different form and with different applications – communism simply coming back, though perhaps with a different name? And if what brought it back was a need within society for the return of a little hope?

Derrida: But this is what I was calling justice. I do not believe in a return of communism in the form of the Party (the party-form is probably disappearing more generally from political life, though it may be hard for it to die), or in the return of everything that was so dispiriting about certain kinds of marxism and communism. At least I hope it won't come back: it is very unlikely to, but still it's necessary to be vigilant. But what is bound to return is an insurgence in the name of justice, which will give rise to critiques which are marxist in *inspiration*, in *spirit*. And there are signs. It's like a new International, but without a party, or organisation, or membership. It is searching and suffering, it believes that something is wrong, it does not accept the 'new world order' which is currently being imposed, and it finds something sinister in the discourses to which this new order is giving rise. And this insurgent dissatisfaction will be able to recover various forces from within the marxist inspiration, for which we do not even have any names. Although in some respects it will resemble the elements of a *critique*, I try to explain why it is or ought to be more than a critique, or method, or philosophy, or ontology. It needs to take a completely different form, and this may mean that Marx has to be read in a completely different way – though it's not a matter of a reading in an academic or philological sense, or of rehabilitating a marxist canon. There is a certain tendency, which I take issue with in this essay, which is gently trying to neutralise Marx in a different way: now that marxism is dead and its apparatuses disarmed, so they say, we can at last settle down to read Marx and *Capital* calmly, theoretically; he can be given the recognition he deserves as a great philosopher whose writings belong (in their 'internal intelligibility', as Michel Henry puts it) to the great ontological tradition. No: I try to explain why we should not be satisfied with such a mollifying re-interpretation.

Passages: You have always claimed that the experience of deconstruction entailed an ethico-political responsibility. How does this differ from the old idea of the 'committed intellectual'?

Derrida: I don't feel I have either the right or the inclination to disparage what you call the 'old idea' of the committed intellectual of the past, particularly in France. I continue to find Voltaire, Hugo, Zola and Sartre admirable and exemplary. Such models can inspire us; but often they are inaccessible and we certainly ought not to try to imitate them now that the situation is, as I was saying, structurally altered. With that reservation, it seems to me, very roughly, that their couragaeous stands presupposed that there were two identifiable partners in a kind of confrontation: on one side a given socio-political field, and on the other the intellectuals with their language, their rhetoric, their literary output, their philosophy, etc., who came along and 'intervened' or *committed* themselves to a field in order to take sides or adopt positions. From that point on they had to refrain from trying to alter either the structure of their public space (press, media, modes of representation, etc.) or the nature of their language and the philosophical or theoretical axioms of their interventions. In other words, they committed their culture and authority *as writers* (and the very French examples I mentioned were popular mainly for their literary rather than philosophical work); they put them at the service of a political cause – sometimes a legal issue, but often one which went beyond legality: a matter of justice. I am not saying that Hugo or Sartre never questioned or transformed the forms of involvement available to them. I am only saying that it was not a constant theme for them, or a major preoccupation. They did not think it appropriate to begin, as Benjamin would have suggested, by analysing and transforming the apparatus, instead of simply entrusting their messages to it, however revolutionary they might be. The apparatus in question comprises technical and political authorities, and procedures of editorial and mediatic appropriation, and the structure of a public space (and hence of the audience that one is meant to be addressing); and it also involves a particular logic, rhetoric, and experience of language, and the entire sedimentation which that presupposes. Asking oneself questions, including ones about the questions that are imposed on us or taught to us as being the 'right' questions to ask, even questioning the *question-form* of critique, and not only questioning, but thinking through the commitment, the stake, through which a given question is engaged: perhaps this is a prior responsibility, and a precondition of commitment. On its own it is not enough of course; but it has never impeded or retarded commitment – quite the reverse.

Passages: We would like, if we may, to ask you a rather more personal question. There is one thing that is coming back in some parts of the world, especially in Algeria with its religious aspect. Politicians and even intellectuals have a way of talking about Algeria, which consists in saying that it has never really had an identity, unlike Morocco or Tunisia, and that the death and destruction which are now taking place there are due to this absence of identity, this lack. Beyond all the emotional turmoil, how do you see what's happening there?

Derrida: You say it's a personal question, but I wouldn't dream of comparing my own distress and anguish with that of most other Algerians, whether in Algeria or France. I am not even sure that I could claim that Algeria is still my country. But I should perhaps say that I never left Algeria in the first nineteen years of my life, that I have been back regularly, and that something in me never left at all. It is true that the unity of Algeria seems to be under threat. What is happening there is not far from resembling a civil war. The news media in France are only slowly beginning to realise what has been going on in Algeria for some years now: preparations for taking power, assassinations, guerrilla groups; and in response, repression, torture, and concentration camps. As in all tragedies, the crimes are not all on one side, or indeed on two. The FIS [Islamic Salvation Front] and the state would not have been able to confront and pursue each other in the classic cycle (terrorism/repression; the social and popular diffusion of a movement which has been driven underground by a state with both too little power and too much; the impossibility of sustaining a process of democratisation, etc.), and this infernal duet, which has already claimed so many innocent victims, could never have taken place, without a simple and anonymous third factor: that is to say, without the country's economic and demographic situation, its unemployment and the development strategy it adopted long ago. These conditions tend to favour a kind of duel; but perhaps it is not so symmetrical as I have been suggesting. (Some of my Algerian friends disagree with this symmetrisation: they regard the state's violent reaction and the suspension of the electoral process as its only possible response to a well-prepared long-range plan to take over power, which was hostile to democracy itself; they have a point, but still it's going to be necessary to devise some means of consultation or exchange which will get people to lay down their arms and enable the processes that have been broken off to be resumed.) If we consider this nameless third partner, it is clear that responsibility goes back much further, and that it is not purely algero-algerian either. This is connected to what I was saying earlier about the emblematic foreign debt, which is a heavy burden on Algeria. I mention it not in order to level accusations, but in recognition of our responsibility. Without in any way diminishing what is primarily a matter for the citizens of Algeria themselves, every one of us is involved and responsible, especially – for obvious reasons – those of us who are French. We cannot be indifferent, particularly to the fate and the efforts of all those Algerians who are trying to stand up to fanaticism and all sorts of intimidation. (Many of the victims of recent assassinations have been intellectuals, journalists and writers, though we must not forget all the other unknown victims; it is in this spirit that some of us have come together, on the initiative of Pierre Bourdieu, to form CISIA, the International Committee in Support of Algerian Intellectuals, some of whose founder members, it must be said, have already received death threats.)

You said that some people regard the identity of Algeria not merely as problematic or endangered, but as something that never really existed in an organic, natural or political fashion. There are several ways of responding to this. One would be to invoke the fractures and partitions of Arab-Berber Algeria, the divisions between languages, ethnic groups, religious and military authorities, and perhaps to draw the conclusion that it was basically colonisation which, in this as in many other cases, created the unity of a State-nation so that when formal independence was at last achieved, its struggles took place within structures partly inherited from colonisation. I cannot get into lengthy historical analyses here, but I think that this is both true and false. It is certainly true that Algeria as such did not exist before colonisation, with its present frontiers and in the form of a State-nation. But that in itself does not undermine such unity as has been forged through, within and against colonisation. All State-nations have this kind of laborious, contradictory and tortuous history of decolonisation and recolonisation. They all originated in violence, and since they constitute themselves by establishing their own law and legitimacy, they cannot base it on any prior legitimacy, notwithstanding all their protestations and inculcations to the contrary. You cannot object to a unity simply because it is the result of a process of unification. Unification and legitimacy never establish themselves successfully except by making people forget that there never was any natural unity or prior foundation. The unity of the Italian State is also very recent, and it is going through a good deal of turbulence at present. But does this mean that it has to be cast into doubt, on the grounds that it is a recent foundation and that, like every other State-nation, it is an artifact? Some people are certainly being tempted to suggest as much, and from motives which are more than just historiographical. But there are no natural unities, only more or less stable processes of unification, some of them solidly established over a long period of time. All these state stabilities, all these familiar steady states, are only stabilisations. Israel is another example of a state which was founded recently and, like every other state, founded on violence; and this violence is bound to seek retrospective justification for itself, provided that national and international stabilisation manage to wrap it up at least in provisional and conditional oblivion. But that is not the current situation. These are seismic times for all State-nations, and correspondingly favourable to this sort of reflection – which must also be a reflection on what may (or may not) link the idea of democracy both to citizenship and to nationality.

The unity of Algeria is of course in danger of being ruptured, but the forces which are tearing it apart are not, as is often supposed, those of the West as opposed to those of the East, or of democracy against Islam, as if these were two homogeneous units. Various different models of democracy, representativeness, and citizenship are involved – and above all, various different interpretations of Islam. So part of our responsibility is to pay careful attention to this multiplicity; and to plead unceasingly against the confounding of the confusion.

NOTES

1. *Force of Law: 'The Mystical Foundation of Authority'* (bilingual text) in *Deconstruction and the Possibility of Justice*, Cardozo Law Review, New York, July–August 1990 – English text reprinted as a book with the same title, edited by Drucilla Cornell *et. al.*, Routledge, New York & London, 1992; *Spectres de Marx*, Paris, Galilée, 1993.
2. Paris, Galilée, 1994
3. See especially *Donner le temps 1: La fausse monnaie*, Paris, Galilée, 1992.
4. Emmanuel Levinas, *Totalité et Infini: Essai sur l'extériorité*, The Hague, Nijhoff, 1961, p. 62; translated by Alfonso Lingis, *Totality and Infinity*, Pittsburgh, Duquesne University Press, 1969, p. 89.
5. *De l'esprit, Heidegger et la question*, Paris, Galilée, 1987, translated by Geoffrey Bennington and Rachel Bowlby, Chicago, Chicago University Press, 1989.

BIBLIOGRAPHIES

BIBLIOGRAPHY 1: JACQUES DERRIDA

One day someone will produce a definitive bibliography of all of Derrida's work in both English and French. In the interests of economy here, I have tried to avoid listing essays by Derrida which appear in books also listed, except at the beginning of the list, where I wished to give a sense of the history of Derrida's writing. I have also avoided repeating details of French publications which are now available in English. While this bibliography is not exhaustive, I hope it reflects the varied interests of this collection and will stimulate readers to explore the variety of Derrida's texts for themselves.

'Introduction', *Edmund Husserl: L'origine de la géométric*, trans and intro. Jacques Derrida (Paris: Presses Universitaires de France, 1962).
De la grammatologie (Paris: Minuit, 1967).
L'écriture et la différence (Paris: Seuil, 1967).
La Voix et le phénomène: Introduction au problème du signe dans la phénomènologie de Husserl (Paris: Presses Universitaires de France, 1967).
'Discussion', *The Structuralist Controversy: The Languages of Criticism and the Sciences of Man*, eds Richard Macksey and Eugenio Donato (Baltimore: Johns Hopkins University Press, 1970), pp. 265–72.
'D'un texte à l'écart', *Les temps modernes*, 284, 1 July 1970.
La dissémination (Paris: Seuil, 1972).
Marges – de la philosophie (Paris: Minuit, 1972).
Positions: Entretiens avec Henri Ronse, Julia Kristeva, Jean-Louis Houdebine, Guy Scarpetta (Paris: Editions de Minuit, 1972).
'L'archéologie du frivole', introduction à l'essai sur l'origine des connaissances humaines de Condillac (Paris: Galilée, 1973).

Speech and Phenomena, and Other Essays on Husserl's Theory of Signs, trans. David B. Allison (Evanston, IL: Northwestern University Press, 1973).

'Letter of Jacques Derrida to Jean-Louis Houdebine (excerpt)', *Diacritics*, 3 (3), 1973, pp. 58–9.

Edmund Husserl, 'L'origine de la géométrie' (Paris: Presses Universitaires de France, rev. 2nd edn, 1974).

Glas (Paris: Galilée, 1974).

'Linguistics and grammatology', *Sub-Stance*, 10, 1974, pp. 127–81.

'Mallarmé', *Tableau de la littérature française*, vol. 3: *De Madame Stael à Rimbaud*, ed. Dominique Aubry (Paris: Gallimard, 1974), pp. 368–79.

Valerio Adami: Le voyage du dessin (Paris: Maeght, 1975).

'A-coup', Jacques Derrida et al., 'Trente-huit réponses sur l'avant garde', *Digraphe*, 6, 1975.

Of Grammatology, trans. Gayatri Chakravorty Spivak (Baltimore: Johns Hopkins University Press, 1976).

'Fors: The anglish words of Nicolas Abraham and Maria Torok', *Georgia Review*, 31 (1), 1976, pp. 64–116.

'Signature event context', *Glyph I*, 1977, pp. 172–97.

Edmund Husserl's Origin of Geometry: An Introduction, trans. John Leavey, Jr. (New York: Harvester Press, 1978). Includes the text of 'The origin of geometry' trans. by David Carr.

Gérard Titus-Carmel: The Pocket Size Tlingit Coffin [Exhibition March 1-April 10, 1978 at the Centre National d'Art et de Culture Georges Pompidou, Musée National d'Art Moderne] (Paris: Centre Georges Pompidou, 1978).

Writing and Difference, trans. Alan Bass (London: Routledge & Kegan Paul, 1978).

'Becoming woman', *Semiotext(e)*, 3 (1), 1978, pp. 128–37.

'Coming into one's own', *Psychoanalysis and the Question of the Text*, ed. Geoffrey Hartman, trans. James Hulbert (Washington DC: Johns Hopkins University Press, 1978).

'Restitutions of truth to size', *Research in Phenomenology*, 8, 1978, pp. 1–44.

'The retrait of metaphor', *Enclitic*, 2 (2), 1978, pp. 5–34.

'Speech and writing according to Hegel', *Man and World*, 11, 1978, pp. 107–30.

Spurs: Nietzsche's Style/Eperons: Les styles de Nietzsche, trans. Barbara Harlow (Chicago: Chicago University Press, 1979).

'Ce qui reste à force de musique', *Digraphe*, 18–19, 1979, pp. 165–74.

'Living on: Border lines', in Harold Bloom, Paul de Man, Jacques Derrida, Geoffrey Hartman and J. Hillis Miller, eds, *Deconstruction and Criticism* (London: Routledge & Kegan Paul, 1979), pp. 75–176.

'Me – Psychoanalysis: An introduction to the translation of *The Shell and the Kernel* by Nicholas Abraham', *Diacritics*, 9 (1), 1979, pp. 4–12.

'Scribble (writing/power)', *Yale French Studies*, 58, 1979, pp. 116–47.

'The supplement of copula: Philosophy before linguistics', *Textual Strategies: Perspectives in Post-Structuralist Criticism*, ed. Josué V. Harari (London: Methuen, 1979), pp. 28–120.

The Archeology of the Frivolous: Reading Condillac, trans. John Leavey, Jr. (Pittsburgh: Duquesne University Press, 1980). [Reprint: Lincoln: University of Nebraska Press, 1987].

'The law of genre', *Critical Inquiry*, 7 (Autumn), 1980, pp. 55–81.

Dissemination, trans. Barbara Johnson (London: Athlone Press, 1981).

Positions, trans. Alan Bass (London: Athlone, 1981).

'Economimesis', *Diacritics*, 11, 1981, pp. 3–25.

'Title (to be specified)', *Sub-Stance*, 31, 1981, pp. 5–22.

Margins of Philosophy, trans. Alan Bass (Brighton: Harvester Press, 1982).

'All ears: Nietzsche's otobiography', trans. Avital Ronell, *Yale French Studies*, 63, 1982, pp. 245–50.

'Choreographies', *Diacritics*, Summer, 1982, pp. 66–76.

'Letter to colleagues, May 18, 1982', *Sub-Stance*, 35, 1982, pp. 2 and 80–1.

'Letter to John P. Leavey, Jr.', *Semeia*, 23, 1982, pp. 61–2.

'Sending: On representation', *Social Research*, 49 (2), 1982, pp. 294–326.

'Critical relation: Peter Szondi's studies on Célan', *Boundary 2*, 11 (3), 1983, pp. 155–67.

'Geschlecht: Sexual difference, ontological difference', *Research in Phenomenology*, 13, 1983, pp. 65–83.

'The principle of reason: The university in the eyes of its pupils', *Diacritics*, 13 (3), 1983, pp. 3–20.

'The time of a thesis: Punctuations', *Philosophy in France Today*, ed. Alan Montefiore (Cambridge: Cambridge University Press, 1983). *Signéponge/Signsponge*, trans. Richard Rand (New York and Guildford: Columbia University Press, 1984).

'Deconstruction and the other: Interview with Richard Kearney', in Richard Kearney, ed., *Dialogues with Contemporary Thinkers* (Manchester: Manchester University Press, 1984).

'Eidos et télévision: Questions à Jacques Derrida. Entretien avec Bernard Stiegler', *Digraphe*, 33, May, 1984.

'An idea of Flaubert: Plato's letter', *Modern Language Notes*, 99 (4), 1984, pp. 748–68.

'Languages and institutions of philosophy', *Semiotic Inquiry/Recherches Semiotiques*, 4(2), 1984, pp. 91–154.

'My chances/Mes chances: A rendezvous with some epicurean stereophonies', in Joseph H. Smith and William Kerrigan, eds. *Taking Chances: Derrida. Psychoanalysis, and Literature* (London: Johns Hopkins University Press, 1984).

'No apocalypse, not now (Full speed ahead, seven missiles, seven missives)', trans. Catherine Porter and Philip Lewis, *Diacritics*, 14 (2), 1984, pp. 20–31.

'Of an apocalyptic tone recently adopted in philosophy', *Oxford Literary Review*, 6 (2), 1984, pp. 3–37.

'Two words for Joyce', trans. Geoffrey Bennington, in Derek Attridge and Daniel Ferrer, eds, *Post-Structuralist Joyce: Essays from the French* (Cambridge: Cambridge University Press, 1984).

'The unoccupied chair: Censorship, mastership and magistriality', *Semiotic Inquiry*, 4 (2), 1984, pp. 123–36.

The Ear of the Other: Otobiography, Transference, Translation: Texts and Discussions with Jacques Derrida, trans. Avital Ronell and Peggy Kamuf, ed. Christie V. McDonald (New York: Schocken Books, 1985).

'Deconstruction in America: An interview with Jaques Derrida', *Critical Exchange*, 17 (Winter), 1985, pp. 1–33.

'Des tours de Babel', *Difference in Translation*, ed. J. F. Graham (Ithaca and London: Cornell University Press, 1985).

'(In memoriam) Paul de Man', *Yale French Studies*, 69, 1985, pp. 323–6.

'Letter to a Japanese friend', in Robert Bernasconi and David Wood, eds, *Derrida and Difference* (Warwick: Parousia Press, 1985).

'Racism's last word', *Critical Inquiry*, 12, 1985, pp. 290–9.

Altérites, eds Pierre-Jean Labarri and E. Gravere (Paris: Osiris, 1986).

Antonin Artaud: Dessins et portraits, Jacques Derrida et Paule Thévenin (Paris: Gallimard, 1986).

Glas, trans. John P. Leavey, Jr. and Richard Rand (Lincoln and London: University of Nebraska Press, 1986).

Parages (Paris: Galilée, 1986).

'The age of Hegel', *Demarcating the Disciplines: Philosophy – Literature – Art*, ed. Samuel Weber, trans. Susan Winnett (Minneapolis: University of Minnesota Press, 1986).

'But beyond . . .', trans. Peggy Kamuf, *Critical Inquiry*, 13(1), 1986, pp. 155–1.

'Interpreting signatures (Nietzsche/Heidegger): Two questions', trans. Philippe Forget, in Diane P. Michelfelder and Richard E. Palmer, eds. *Dialogue and Deconstruction: The Gadamer-Derrida Encounter* (New York: SUNY, 1986).

'Literature and politics' and 'Declarations of independence', *New Political Science*, 15 (Summer), 1986, pp. 5, 7–15.

'On the university (Interview with Imre Saluzinski)', *Southern Review (Adelaide)*, 19 (1), 1986.

'Proverb: He that would pun . . .', *GLASsary*, ed. John P. Leavey Jr. (Lincoln: University of Nebraska Press, 1986).

— with J. Ch. Rosé, *Caryl Chessman: L'écriture contre la mort*, film, TFI-INA-ministère de la Culture, 1986.

— and Bernard Tschumi, *La case vide: La villette*, eds. Jacques Derrida and Anthony Vidler (London: Architectural Association, 1986).

Cinders, trans. Ned Lukacher (Lincoln: University of Nebraska Press, 1987).

The Post Card: From Socrates to Freud and Beyond, trans. Alan Bass (Chicago and London: University of Chicago Press, 1987).

Psyché: Inventions de l'autre (Paris, Galilée 1987).

The Truth in painting, trans. Geoffrey Bennington and Ian McLeod (Chicago: Chicago University Press, 1987).

'*Geschlecht* II: Heidegger's Hand', trans. John P. Leavey Jr., in John Sallis, ed., *Deconstruction and Philosophy: The Texts of Jacques Derrida* (Chicago: University of Chicago Press, 1987).

'Interview with Imre Saluzinski', in Imre Saluzinski, ed., *Criticism in Society* (London: Methuen, 1987).

'The laws of reflection: Nelson Mandela in admiration', trans. Mary Ann Caws and Isabelle Lorenz, in Jacques Derrida and Mustapha Tilli, eds, *For Nelson Mandela* (New York: Henry Holt, 1987).

'Les mots autobiographiques: Pourquoi pas Sartre?', *Revue de la pensée d'aujourd'hui*, 15–18, 1987.

'L'oeuvre chorale: Une participation à Vaisseau de Pierres 2', in I. Auricoste and H. Tonka, eds, *Parc-Ville Villette* (Seyssel: Champ Vallon, 1987).

'Some questions and responses', in Derek Attridge, Nigel Mapp, Alan Durant and Colin MacCabe, eds, *The Linguistics of Writing* (Manchester: Manchester University Press, 1987).

'Women in the beehive' and 'Reply', in Alice Jardine and Paul Smith, eds, *Men in Feminism* (London: Methuen, 1987).

Limited Inc., ed. Gerald Graff, trans. Samuel Weber (Evanston, IL: Northwestern University Press, 1988).

'The deaths of Roland Barthes', in Hugh Silverman, ed., *Continental Philosophy I: Philosophy and Non-Philosophy since Merleau-Ponty* (London: Routledge 1988).

'Derrida-Bourdieu: Débat', *Libération*, 29 March 1988, p. 19.

'Fifty-two aphorisms for a foreword', trans. Andrew Benjamin, *Deconstruction: Omnibus* (London: Tate Gallery/Academy Forum, 1988).

'Friendship-above-all: Jean-François Lyotard', *Liberation*, 22 March 1998.

'Interview with Jean-Luc Nancy', *Topoi*, 7, 1988, pp. 113–21.

'Une lettre de Jacques Derrida', *Libération*, 3 March 1988.

'Like the sound of the sea deep within a shell: Paul de Man's war', *Critical Inquiry*, 14 (Spring), 1988, pp. 590–652.

'The new modernism: Deconstructionist tendencies in art', *Art & Design*, 4 (3–4), 1988.

'A number of yes (Nombre de oui)', *Qui Parle*, 2 (2), 1988, pp. 120–33.

'On reading Heidegger: An outline of remarks to the Essex Colloquium', *Research in Phenomenology*, 17, 1988, pp. 171–88.

'The politics of friendship', *Journal of Philosophy*, 75 (11), 1988, pp. 632–45.

'Telepathy', *Oxford Literary Review*, 10, 1988, pp. 3–41.

Mémoires for Paul de Man, Revised Edition, trans. Cecile Lindsay, Jonathan Culler, Eduardo Cadava (New York: Columbia University Press, 1989).

Of Spirit: Heidegger and the Question, trans. Geoffrey Bennington and Rachel Bowlby (Chicago: Chicago University Press, 1989).

'Biodegradables: Seven diary fragments', *Critical Inquiry*, 15 (4), 1989, pp. 812–73.

'Desistance', in Philippe Lacoue-Labarthe, ed., *Typography: Mimesis, Philosophy, Politics* (London: Harvard University Press), 1989.

'The ghost dance: An interview with Jacques Derrida', *Public*, 2, 1989, 60–74.

'How to avoid speaking: Denials' and 'Post-scriptum: Aporias, ways and voices', in Harold Coward and Toby Foshay, eds, *Derrida and Negative Theology* (Albany: SUNY Press, 1989).

'How to concede, with reason?', *Diacritics*, 19 (3–4), 1989, pp. 4–9.

'On colleges and philosophy', in Lisa Appignanesi, ed., *Postmodernism: ICA Documents* (New York: Columbia University Press, 1989).

'Rights of inspection', *Art & Text*, 32, 1989, pp. 19–97.

'Some statements and truisms about neologisms, newisms, postisms, parasitisms, and other small seismisms', in D. Carroll, ed., *The States of Theory* (New York: Columbia University Press, 1989).

'Psyche: Inventions of the other', trans. Catherine Porter, in Wlad Godzich and Lindsay Waters, eds, *Reading de Man Reading* (Minneapolis: University of Minnesota Press, 1989).

Du droit à la philosophie (Paris: Galilée, 1990).

Le problème de la gnèse dans la philosophie de Husserl (Paris: Presses Universitaires de France, 1990).

'Force of law: The mystical foundation of authority', *Cardozo Law Review*, 'Deconstruction and the possibility of justice', 11 (5–6), 1990, pp. 920–1045.

'Let us not forget – psychoanalysis', *Oxford Literary Review*, 12, 1990, pp. 3–7.

'A letter to Peter Eisenman', *Assemblage: A Critical Journal of Architecture and Design*, 12 August 1990.

'Louis Althusser: Texte prononcé à la mort de Louis Althusser', *Les Lettres Francaises*, 4, 1990.

'On rhetoric and composition (Conversation with Gary Olson)', *Journal of Advanced Composition*, 10 (1), 1990, pp. 1–21.

'The philosopher sees (or doesn't see)', *The Art Newspaper*, 1 (1), October 1990.

'Sendoffs', *Yale French Studies*, 77, 1990, pp. 7–43.

'Subverting the signature: A theory of the parasite', *Blast Unlimited (Boston)* 2, 1990, pp. 16–21.

'Videor', in R. Bellour, ed., *Passages de l'image* (Paris: 1990).

'At this very moment in this work here I am', trans. Ruben Berezdivin, in Robert Bernasconi and Simon Critchley, eds, *Re-Reading Levinas* (Bloomington: Indiana University Press, 1991).

'Che cos'e la poesia', in Peggy Kamuf, ed. and trans., *A Derrida Reader: Between the Blinds* (New York: Columbia University Press, 1991).

'Interpretations at war: Kant, the Jew, the German', *New Literary History*, 22, 1991, pp. 39–95.

'Interventions', in Ingeborg Hoesterey, ed., *Zeitgeist in Babel: The Postmodernist Controversy* (Bloomington: Indiana University Press, 1991).

'[Interview with] Jacques Derrida', in Raoul Mortley, ed., *French Philosophers in Conversation* (London: Routledge 1991).

'Sight unseen', *Art in America*, 79 (April), 1991, pp. 47–53.

'Summary of impromptu remarks, 58 minutes, 41 seconds', in Cynthia C. Davidson, ed., *Anyone* (New York: Rizzoli, 1991).

'This is not an oral footnote', in Stephen A Barney, ed., *Annotation and its Texts* (Oxford: Oxford University Press, 1991).

Penser la folie: Essais sur Michel Foucault (Paris: 1992).

The Other Heading: Reflections on Today's Europe, trans. Pascale-Anne Brault and Michael B. Naas (Bloomington: Indiana University Press, 1992).

'L'atelier de Valerio Adami: Le tableau est avant tout un systéme de mémoire', *Rue Descartes*, 4, 1992.

'Invitation to a discussion', *Columbia Documents of Architecture and Theory*, vol. 1 (D), 1992, pp. 7–27.

'Mochlos, or The conflict of the faculties' and 'Canons and metonymies', in Richard Rand, ed., *Logomachia* (Lincoln: University of Nebraska Press, 1992).

'Nous autres Grecs', *Les Stratégies contemporaines d'appropriation de l'Antiquité*, ed. B. Cassin (Paris: 1992).

'Onto-theology of national-humanism: Prolegomena to a hypothesis', *Oxford Literary Review*, 14 (1–2), 1992, pp. 3–24.

'Passions: An oblique offering', in David Wood, ed., *Derrida: A Critical Reader* (Oxford: Blackwell, 1992).

'Philosophy and communication: Round-table discussion with Paul Ricoeur (1971)', in Leonard Lawlor, ed. and trans., *Imagination and Chance: The Difference between the Thought of Ricoeur and Derrida* (New York: SUNY, 1992).

'Schibboleth', in Aris Fioretis, ed., *Word Traces* (Baltimore: Johns Hopkins University Press, 1992).

'This strange institution called literature' and 'Ulysses gramaphone: Hear say yes in Joyce', in Derek Attridge, ed., *Acts of Literature* (London: Routledge, 1992).

Aporias (Stanford: Stanford University Press, 1993).

Given Time I: Counterfeit Money, trans. Peggy Kamuf (Chicago: University of Chicago Press, 1993).

Memoirs of the Blind: The Self Portrait and Other Ruins, trans. Pascale-Anne Brault and Michael Naas (Chicago: Chicago University Press, 1993).

'Back from Moscow, in the USSR', trans. Mary Quaintaire, in Mark Poster, ed., *Politics, Theory, and Contemporary Culture* (Columbia University Press 1993).

'Circonfession', in Geoffrey Bennington and Jacques Derrida, *Jacques Derrida* (Chicago: University of Chicago Press, 1993).

'Heidegger's ear: *Geschlecht* IV: Philopolemology', in John Sallis, ed., *Reading Heidegger: Commemorations* (Bloomington: Indiana University Press), 1993.

'Le sacrifice', *La Metaphore – Revue I*, 1993, pp. 51–65.

'Talking about writing' (with Peter Eisenman), *Anyone*, 1 (0), 1993, 18–21.

'Le toucher: Touch/to touch him', *Paragraph*, 16 (2), 1993, pp. 124–57.

Specters of Marx: The State of the Debt, the Work of Mourning, and the New International, trans. Peggy Kamuf (London and New York: Routledge, 1994).

'The deconstruction of actuality', *Radical Philosophy*, 68, 1994, pp. 28–41.

'Foreword', in Susan Sellers, ed., *The Helene Cixous Reader* (London: Routledge, 1994).

'Nietzsche and the machine (Interview with Richard Beardsworth)', *Journal of Nietzsche Studies*, 7, 1994, pp. 7–66.

'Text read at Louis Althusser's Funeral', in Michael Sprinkner, ed., *The Althusserian Legacy* (London: Verso, 1994), pp. 241–5.

'The time is out of joint', in A. Haverkamp, ed., *Deconstruction Is/in America* (New York: New York University Press, 1994).

'Maddening the subjectile', trans. Mary Ann Caws, *Yale French Studies*, 84, 1994, pp. 154–71.

'The spatial arts: An interview with Jacques Derrida', in Peter Brunette and David Wills, eds, *Deconstruction and the Visual Arts: Art, Media, Architecture* (Cambridge: Cambridge University Press, 1994).

The Gift of Death (Chicago: University of Chicago Press, 1995).

On the Name (Stanford: Stanford University Press, 1995).

Points: Interviews 1974–1994, ed. Elisabeth Weber, trans. Peggy Kamuf (Stanford: Stanford University Press, 1995).

'Archive fever: A Freudian impression', trans. Eric Prenowitz, *Diacritics*, 25 (2), Summer, 1995, pp. 9–63.

'Geopsychoanalysis: . . . and the rest of the world', trans. Donald Nicolson-Smith, *New Formations*, 26, 1995, pp. 141–62.

'Tense', in Kenneth Maly, ed., *The Path of Archaic Thinking* (Albany: SUNY 1995).

Negotiations: Writings, eds. Deborah Esch and Thomas Keenan (Minneapolis: University of Minnesota Press, 1996).

'Adieu: Emmanuel Levinas', *Critical Enquiry*, 23, Autumn 1996, pp. 1–10.

'The philosopher and the architects' and '(No) point of folly – maintaining architecture now', in Dorothea Eimert, ed., *Deconstructivist Tendencies* (Ostfildern: Cantz Verlag, 1996).

'Remarks on deconstruction and pragmatism', trans. Simon Critchley, in Chantal Mouffe, ed., *Deconstruction and Pragmatism* (London: Routledge, 1996).

Cosmopolites de tous les pays, encore un effort! (Paris: Galilée, 1997).

Du droit à la philosophie du point du vue cosmopolitique (Paris: Verdier, 1997).

Institutions of Philosophy, eds. Deborah Esch and Thomas Keenan (London: Harvard University Press, 1997).

Politics of Friendship, trans. George Collins (London: Verso Books, 1997).

— and Anne Duformantelle, *De l'hospitalité* (Paris: Calmann-Levy, 1997).

— and Peter Eisenman, *Chora L Works*, eds. Jeffrey Kipnis and Thomas Leeser (New York: Monacelli Press, 1997).

— Bernard Schneider, Mark C. Taylor and Kurt Forster, eds, *Radix-Matrix: Daniel Libeskind* (New York: Prestel, 1997).

'Architecture where the desire may live (interview)' and 'Why Peter Eisenman writes such good books' and 'Point de folie – maintenant l'architecture', in Neil Leach, ed., *Rethinking Architecture: A Reader in Cultural Theory* (New York: Routledge, 1997).

'. . . et grenades . . .', in Hent de Vries and Samuel Weber, eds, *Violence, Identity and Self-Determination* (Stanford: Stanford University Press: 1997).

'Fourmis', trans. Eric Prenowitz, in Helene Cixous and Mireille Calle-Gruber, *Helene Cixous: Rootprints: Memory and Life Writing* (London: Routledge, 1997).

'History of the lie: Prolegomena', *Graduate Faculty Philosophical Journal*, 19/20 (2/1), 1997, pp. 129–61.

'"On responsibility": An interview', *Responsibilities of Deconstruction: PLI Warwick Journal of Philosophy*, Summer, 1997, pp. 19–86.

'"Perhaps or maybe": Jacques Derrida in conversation with Alexander Duttman', *Responsibilities of Deconstruction: PLI Warwick Journal of Philosophy*, Summer, 1997, pp. 1–18.

'A silkworm of one's own', *Oxford Literary Review*, 18, 1997, pp. 3–65.

'The Villanova Roundtable: A conversation with Jacques Derrida', in John D. Caputo, ed., *Deconstruction in a Nutshell* (New York: Fordham University Press 1997).

'Writing proofs', *Responsibilities of Deconstruction: PLI Warwick Journal of Philosophy*, Summer, 1997, pp. 38–50.

Monolinguisime of the Other, or, The Prosthesis of Origin, trans. Patrick Mensah (Stanford: Stanford University Press, 1998).

Recontres de Rabat avec Jacques Derrida: Idiomes, nationalités, deconstructions (Paris: Editions de l'aube, 1998).

Resistances of Psychoanalysis, trans. Peggy Kamuf, Pascale-Anne Brault and Michael Nass (Stanford: Stanford University Press, 1998).

— and Catherine Malabou, *Jacques Derrida: La contre-allée* (Paris: La Qunizaine litteraire/Louis Vuitton, 1999).

— Paul Thevenin and Georges Paster, eds, *The Secret Art of Antonin Artaud*, trans. Mary Ann Caws (Boston: MIT Press, 1998).

— and Hélène Cixous, *Voiles* (Paris: Galilee, 1998).

'Faith and Knowledge', in Jacques Derrida and Gianni Vattiamo, eds, *Religion* (Cambridge: Polity, 1998).

'I'm going to have to wander all alone: Gilles Deleuze', *Philosophy Today*, Spring 1998, pp. 3–4.

L'animal autobiographie: Autour de Jacques Derrida, ed. Jacques Derrida (Paris: Galilee, 1999).

Manifeste pour l'hospitalite: Autor de Jacques Derrida, ed. Jacques Derrida (Paris: Grigny Editions paroles d'aube: 1999).

'Marx & Sons', trans. G. M. Goshgarian, in Michael Sprinkner, ed., *Ghostly Demarcations: A Symposium on Jacques Derrida's Spectres of Marx* (London: Verso: 1999).

Le Touche, Jean-Luc Nancy (Paris: Galilée, 2000).

— and Maurice Blanchot, *The Instant of my Death, Demeure: Fiction and Testimony*, trans. Elizabeth Rottenberg (Stanford: Stanford University Press, 2000).

— and Bernard Steigler, *Television: Echographies* (Cambridge: Polity, 2000).

BIBLIOGRAPHY 2: KEY PUBLICATIONS OF CONTRIBUTING AUTHORS

This bibliography only lists the work of those authors anthologised in this volume. It specifically lists monographs and edited collections, but it also includes the full reference for any essay or chapter as it appears in this volume. A complete bibliography of all texts on deconstruction relevant to the concerns of this book would prove to be a lengthy undertaking. I suspect that it would be as long as this book itself. However, I hope that the publications of the selected authors here will provide a starting point for all those interested in carrying their reading beyond the confines of this volume. Useful lists of texts on deconstruction can be found in Geoffrey Bennington, *Jacques Derrida* (1993), William B. Schultz and Lewis L. B. Fried, *Jacques Derrida: An Annotated Primary and Secondary Bibliography* (1992), and Julian Wolfreys, *The Derrida Reader: Writing Performances* (Edinburgh: Edinburgh University Press, 1998). For all sorts of useful information on Derrida and deconstruction I particularly recommend Peter Krapp's web-site 'Deconstruction on the net', available at www.hydra.umn.edu/derrida

Abrahams, Nicholas, and Maria Torok, *The Wolf Man's Magic Word*, trans. Richard Rand (Minneapolis: University of Minnesota Press, 1986).

Abrahams, Nicholas, and Maria Torok, *The Shell and the Kernel: Renewals of Psychoanalysis* (Chicago: University of Chicago Press, 1994).

Abrahams, Nicholas, and Maria Torok, *Questions to Freud* (Cambridge, MA: Harvard University Press, 1996).

Abrahams, Nicholas, and Maria Torok, *Rythms: The Work, Translation, and Psychoanalysis* (Stanford: Stanford University Press, 1998).

Attridge, Derek, *Peculiar Language: Literature as Difference from the Renaissance to James Joyce* (London: Methuen, 1988).

Attridge Derek, ed., *Acts of Literature* (London: Routledge 1992). [A Derrida Reader, contains: 'This strange institution called literature', 'Mallarmé', 'Before the law', 'The law of genre', 'Ulysses gramaphone', 'Aphorism countertime' and extracts from *Dissemination, Of Grammatology, Signspogne*, 'Psyche: Inventions of the other' and 'Shibboleth'.]

Attridge, Derek, 'Ghost writing', in *Deconstruction Is/in America: A New Sense of the Political*, ed. Anslem Haverkamp (New York: New York University Press, 1995), pp. 223–8.

Attridge Derek, *Joyce Effects: On Language, Theory, and History* (Cambridge: Cambridge University Press, 2000).

Attridge, Derek, Geoffrey Bennington and Robert Young, eds, *Post-Structuralism and the Question of History* (Cambridge: Cambridge University Press, 1987).

Attridge Derek, and Vincent Cheng, eds, *Joyce, Race and Empire* (Cambridge: Cambridge University Press, 2000).

Attridge, Derek, and Daniel Ferrer, eds, *Post-Structuralist Joyce: Essays from the French* (Cambridge: Cambridge University Press, 1984).

Bataille, Georges, *Literature and Evil: Essays* (London: Marion Boyars Publishers, 1988).

Bataille, Georges, *The Accursed Share: An Essay on General Economy*, Vols 1, 2, 3, trans. Robert Hurley (New York: Zone Books, 1993).

Bataille, Georges, *Eroticism: Death and Sensuality*, trans. Mary Dalwood (New York: City Lights Books, 1996).

Bataille, Georges, *Inner Experience* (SUNY, 1998).

Bataille, Georges, *Theory of Religion*, trans. Robert Hurley (New York: Zone Books, 1998).

Bataille, Georges, *Visions of Excess: Selected Writings 1927–1939* (Minneapolis: Minnesota University Press, 1999).

Beardsworth, Richard, 'Thinking technicity', *Cultural Value*, 2(1), 1988, pp. 70–86.

Beardsworth, Richard, *Derrida and the Political* (London: Routledge, 1996).

Belsey, Catherine, *Critical Practice* (London: Methuen, 1986).

Belsey, Catherine, *The Subject of Tragedy* (London: Methuen, 1987).

Belsey, Catherine, *Desire: Love Stories in Western Culture* (Oxford: Blackwell, 1994).

Belsey, Catherine, 'Hamlet's dilemma', from *Shakespeare and the Loss of Eden: Family Values in Early Modern Culture* (London: Macmillan, 1999).

Belsey, Catherine, *Theory* (Oxford: Blackwell, 2000).

Benjamin, Andrew, *What Is Abstraction?* (London: Academy Editions, 1988).

Benjamin, Andrew, 'Derrida, architecture and philosophy', *Architectural Design*, 58 (3/4), 1988, pp. 8–12.

Benjamin, Andrew, *The Problems of Modernity: Adorno and Benjamin* (London: Routledge, 1989).

Benjamin, Andrew, *Translation and the Nature of Philosophy* (London: Routledge, 1989).

Benjamin, Andrew, *Art, Mimesis, and the Avant-Garde* (London: Routledge, 1990).

Benjamin, Andrew, *Object/Painting* (London: Routledge, 1992).

Benjamin, Andrew, ed., *Judging Lyotard* (London: Routledge, 1994).

Benjamin, Andrew, *The Plural Event* (London: Routledge, 1996).

Benjamin, Andrew, *Present Hope: Philosophy, Architecture, Judaism* (London: Routledge, 1997).

Benjamin, Andrew, *Philosophy's Literature* (Manchester: Clinamen Press, 2000).

Benjamin, Andrew, and Peter Osbourne, eds, *Walter Benjamin's Philosophy* (Manchester: Clinamen Press, 2000).

Benjamin, Walter, *Illuminations*, trans. Harry Zohn (London: Fontana, 1973).

Benjamin, Walter, *The Origin of German Tragic Drama*, trans. John Osborne (London: Verso, 1985).

Benjamin, Walter, 'Critique of violence', in *One Way Street and Other Writings* (London: Verso: 1985).

Benjamin, Walter, *Reflections: Essays, Aphorisms, Autobiographical Writings*, ed. Peter Demetz, trans. Edmund Jephcott (New York: Schocken Books, 1986).

Benjamin, Walter, *Selected Writings*, eds Marcus Bullock and Michael Jennings (Cambridge, MA: Harvard University Press, 1996).

Benjamin, Walter, *The Arcade Project*, trans. Howard Eiland and Kevin McLaughlin (Cambridge, MA: Harvard University Press, 2000).

Bennington, Geoffrey, *Sententiousness and the Novel: Laying Down the Law in Eighteenth-Century French Fiction* (Cambridge: Cambridge University Press, 1985).

Bennington, Geoffrey, *Lyotard: Writing the Event* (Manchester: Manchester University Press, 1988).

Bennington, Geoffrey, 'Deconstruction is not what you think', *Art and Design*, Vol. 4 (3/4), 1988, pp. 6–7.

Bennington, Geoffrey, *Dudding: Des noms de Rousseau* (Paris: Editions Galilée, 1991).

Bennington, Geoffrey, *Legislations: The Politics of Deconstruction* (London: Verso, 1994).

Bennington, Geoffrey, 'Genuine Gasché (perhaps)', *Imprimatur*, 1(2/3), Spring 1996, pp. 252–7.

Bennington, Geoffrey, and Jacques Derrida, *Jacques Derrida* (Chicago: Chicago University Press, 1993).

Bernasconi, Robert, 'The trace of Levinas in Derrida', in Robert Bernasconi and David Wood, eds, *Derrida and Différance* (Evanston, IL: Northwestern University Press, 1988), pp. 13–29.

Bernasconi, Robert, and Simon Critchley, eds, *Re-Reading Levinas* (Bloomington: Indiana University Press, 1991).

Bernasconi, Robert, *Heidegger in Question* (Atlantic Highlands: Humanities Press, 1992).

Bernasconi, Robert, *The Relevance of the Beautiful and Other Essays* (Cambridge: Cambridge University Press, 1996).

Bernasconi, Robert, *The Question of Language in Heidegger's History of Being* (Atlantic Highlands: Humanities Press, 1999).

Bernasconi, Robert, and David Wood, eds, *The Provocation of Levinas* (Bloomington: Indiana University Press, 1990).

Bhabha, Homi K., ed., *Nation and Narration* (London: Routledge, 1990).

Bhabha, Homi K., 'Of mimicry and man', in *The Location of Culture* (London: Routledge, 1994), pp. 85–92.

Bhabha, Homi K., *Identity* (London: ICA, 1999).

Blanchot, Maurice, *The Gaze of Orpheus and Other Literary Essays*, trans. Lydia Davis (New York: Station Hill, 1981).

Blanchot, Maurice, *Writing the Disaster*, trans. Ann Smock (Lincoln: University of Nebraska Press, 1986).

Blanchot, Maurice, *Infinite Conversation*, trans. Susan Hanson (Minneapolis: Minnesota University Press, 1991).

Blanchot, Maurice, *The Space of Literature*, trans. Ann Smock (Lincoln: University of Nebraska Press, 1992).

Blanchot, Maurice, *The Work of Fire*, trans. Charlotte Mndell (Stanford: Stanford University Press, 1992).

Blanchot, Maurice, *The Blanchot Reader* (Oxford: Blackwell, 1996).

Blanchot, Maurice, *Awaiting Oblivion*, trans. John Gregg (Lincoln: University of Nebraska Press, 1998).

Blanchot, Maurice, *The One who Was Standing apart from me*, trans. Susan Hanson (New York: Station Hill, 1998).

Blanchot, Maurice, *The Station Hill Blanchot Reader* (New York: Station Hill, 1998).

Blanchot, Maurice, *The Most High*, trans. Allan Stoell (Lincoln: University of Nebraska Press, 1999).

Blanchot, Maurice, *The Step Not Beyond*, trans. Lycette Nelson (New York: SUNY, 1999).

Blanchot, Maurice, 'Friendship', *Friendship*, trans. E. Rottenberg (Stanford: Stanford University Press, 1999), pp. 289–92.

Blanchot, Maurice, *Ressassement Eternel* (New York: Gordon & B, 2000).

Blanchot, Maurice, and Michel Foucault, *Foucault/Blanchot*, trans. Jeffrey Mehlman and Brian Massumi (New York: Zone Books, 1990).

Botting, Fred, *Gothic* (London: Routledge, 1997).

Botting, Fred, *Sex, Madness, and Navels: Fiction, Fantasy and History in the Future Present* (Manchester: Manchester University Press, 1999).

Botting, Fred, *Making Monstrous* (Manchester: Manchester University Press, 2000).

Botting, Fred, *Scenography* (London: Routledge, 2000).

Botting, Fred, and Scott Wilson, eds, *The Bataille Reader* (Oxford: Blackwell, 1997).

Botting, Fred, and Scott Wilson, eds, *The Bataille Critical Reader* (Oxford: Blackwell, 1998).

Bowlby, Rachel, *Still Crazy after All These Years* (London: Routledge, 1992).

Bowlby, Rachel, 'Domestication', in Diane Elam and Robyn Wiegman, eds, *Feminism besides itself* (London: Routledge, 1995), pp. 72–4.

Bowlby, Rachel, *Shopping with Freud* (London: Routledge, 1996).

Bowlby, Rachel, *Feminist Destinations* (Edinburgh: Edinburgh University Press, 1999).

Butler, Judith, *Gender Trouble: Feminism and the Subversion of Identity* (London: Routledge, 1990).

Butler, Judith, *Bodies that Matter: On the Discursive Limits of 'Sex'* (New York: Routledge, 1993).

Butler, Judith, *Excitable Speech: A Politics of the Performative* (New York: Routledge, 1997).

Butler, Judith, *The Psychic Life of Power: Theories in Subjection* (Stanford: Stanford University Press, 1997).

Caputo, John D., *Radical Hermeneutices: Repetition, Deconstruction and the Hermeneutic Project* (Bloomington: Indiana University Press, 1987).

Caputo, John D., *The Prayers and Tears of Jacques Derrida: Religion without Religion* (Bloomington: Indiana University Press, 1997).

Cixous, Hélène, *The Exile of James Joyce*, trans. Sally Purcell (London: John Calder, 1976).

Cixous, Hélène, *To Live the Orange/Vivre l'orange*, trans. Ann Liddle and Sarah Cornell (Paris: Des Femmes, 1979).

Cixous, Hélène, *Angst*, trans. Jo Levy (London: John Calder, 1985).

Cixous, Hélène, *Reading with Clarice Lispector*, ed. and trans. Vera Conley (Ann Arbor: University of Michigan Press, 1990).

Cixous, Hélène, *The Book of Promethea*, trans. Betsy Wing (Lincoln: University of Nebraska Press, 1991).

Cixous, Hélène, *'Coming to Writing' and Other Essays*, ed. Deborah Jenson, trans. Sarah Cornell, Deborah Jenson, Ann Liddle and Susan Sellers (Cambridge, MA: Harvard University Press, 1991).

Cixous, Hélène, *Three Steps on the Ladder to Writing*, trans. Sarah Cornell and Susan Sellers (New York: Columbia University Press, 1993).

Cixous, Hélène, *The Hélène Cixous Reader*, ed. Susan Sellers (London: Routledge, 1994).

Cixous, Hélène, *Manna, for the Mandelstams for the Mandelas*, trans. Catherine MacGillivray (Minneapolis: Minnesota University Press, 1994).

Cixous, Hélène, 'What is it o'clock? or The door (we never enter)', from *Stigmata: Escaping Texts* (London: Routledge, 1998), pp. 57–84.

Cixous, Hélène, and Mireille Calle-Gruber, *Helene Cixous: Rootprints: Memory and Life Writing* (London: Routledge, 1997).

Cixous, Hélène, and Catherine Clement, *The Newly Born Woman*, trans. Betsy Wing (Minneapolis: University of Minnesota Press, 1986).

Cornell, Drucilla, *Beyond Accommodation: Ethical Feminism, Deconstruction, and the Law* (New York: Routledge, 1991).

Cornell, Drucilla, *The Philosophy of the Limit* (New York: Routledge, 1992).

Cornell, Drucilla, Michael Rosenfield and David Gray Carlson, eds, *Deconstruction and the Possibility of Justice* (New York: Routledge, 1992).

Cornell, Drucilla, *Freedom, Identity and Rights: Selected Essays* (New York: Rowan and Littlefield, 1994).

Cornell, Drucilla, *At the Heart of Freedom: Feminism, Sex and Equality*, (Princeton: Princeton University Press, 1997).

Cornell, Drucilla, ed., *Hegel and Legal Theory* (New York: Routledge, 1997).

Cornell, Drucilla, *The Imaginary Domain* (New York: Routledge, 1998).

Cornell, Drucilla, 'Post-structuralism, the ethical relation and the law', *Cardozo Law Review*. August 1988, pp. 1587–1628.

Cornell, Drucilla, *Transformations: Recollective Imagination and Sexual Difference (New York: Routledge, 1999)*.

Cornell, Drucilla, and Seyla Benhabib, eds. *Feminism as Critique: On the Politics of Gender* (Princeton: Princeton University Press, 1995).

Critchley, Simon, 'Black Socrates? Questioning the philosophical tradition'. *Radical Philosophy*, 69, January/February 1995, pp. 17–26.

Critchley, Simon, *Very Little . . . Almost Nothing* (London: Routledge, 1998).

Critchley, Simon, *The Ethics of Deconstruction: Derrida and Levinas* (Edinburgh: Edinburgh University Press, 1999).

Critchley, Simon, *Ethics-Politics-Subjectivity: Essays on Derrida, Levinas and Contemporary French Thought* (London: Verso, 1999).

Critchley, Simon, and Peter Dews, eds, *Deconstructive Subjectivities* (Albany: SUNY, 1996).

de Man, Paul, *Allegories of Reading: Figural Language in Rousseau, Nietzsche, Rilke, and Proust* (New Haven and London: Yale University Press, 1979).

de Man, Paul, *Blindness and Insight: Essays in the Rhetoric of Contemporary Criticism* (Minneapolis: University of Minnesota Press, 2nd edn rev. 1983).

de Man, Paul, 'Autobiography as de-facement', in *The Rhetoric of Romanticism*. (New York: Columbia University Press, 1984).

de Man, Paul, *The Resistance to Theory* (Minneapolis: University of Minnesota Press, 1986).

de Man, Paul, *Critical Writings: 1953–1978*, ed. Lindsay Waters (Minneapolis: University of Minnesota Press, 1989).

de Man Paul, *Wartime Journalism 1940–1942*, ed. Thomas Kennan (Lincoln: University of Nebraska Press, 1989) [See also: Thomas Kennan, ed., *Responses to Paul de Man's Wartime Journalism 1940–1942* (Lincoln: University of Nebraska Press, 1989)].

de Man, Paul, *Aesthetic Ideology*, ed. Andrzej Warminski (Minneapolis: University of Minnesota Press, 1996).

Duttmann, Alexander, *The Gift of Language: Memory and Promise in Adorno, Benjamin, Heidegger and Rosenzweig*, trans. Nicholas Airline Lyons (London: Athlone, 1994).

Duttmann, Alexander, *The Memory of Thought: On Heidegger and Adorno*, trans. Nicholas Walker (London: Athlone, 1996).

Duttmann, Alexander, 'Recognising the virus', from *At Odds with Aids: Thinking and Talking about a Virus*, trans. Peter Gilgen and Conrad Scott-Curtis (Stanford: Stanford University Press, 1996), pp. 70–1.

Duttmann, Alexander, *Between Cultures* (London: Verso, 1999).

Elam, Diane, *Romancing the Postmodern* (London: Routledge, 1989).

Elam, Diane, 'Unnecessary introductions', *Feminism and Deconstruction: Ms. en abyme* (London: Routledge, 1998), pp. 1–11.

Elam, Diane, and Robyn Weigman, eds. *Feminism besides itself* (London: Routledge, 1995).

Freud, Sigmund, 'A note upon the "mystic writing-pad"', from *The Standard Edition of the Complete Psychological Works of Sigmund Freud*, Vol. 19, pp. 225–32, trans. James Strachey (London: Hogarth, 1957).

Gasché, Rodolphe, 'Deconstruction as criticism', *Glyph*, 6, 1979, pp. 177–215.

Gasché, Rodolphe, *The Tain of the Mirror: Derrida and the Philosophy of Reflection* (Cambridge, MA: Harvard University Press, 1986).

Gasché, Rodolphe, *Inventions of Difference: On Jacques Derrida* (Cambridge, MA: Harvard University Press, 1994).

Gasché, Rodolphe, *The Wild Card of Reading: On Paul de Man* (Cambridge, MA: Harvard University Press, 1999).

Gasché, Rodolphe, *On Minimal Things* (Stanford: Stanford University Press, 2000).

Hartman, Geoffrey, *Beyond Formalism: Literary Essays, 1958–1970* (New Haven: Yale University Press, 1970).

Hartman, Geoffrey, *The Fate of Reading and Other Essays* (Chicago: Chicago University Press, 1975).

Hartman, Geoffrey, *Criticism in the Wilderness: The Study of Literature Today* (New Haven: Yale University Press, 1980).

Hartman, Geoffrey, 'Psychoanalysis: The French connection', *Saving the Text: Literature/Derrida/Philosophy* (Baltimore: Johns Hopkins University Press, 1981), pp. 96–118.

Hartman, Geoffrey, *Easy Pieces* (New York: Columbia University Press, 1985).

Hartman, Geoffrey, *A Critic's Journey* (Cambridge, MA: Yale University Press, 1994).

Hartman, Geoffrey, *The Fateful Question of Culture* (New York: Columbia University Press, 1994).

Hartman, Geoffrey, *The Longest Shadow: In the Aftermath of the Holocaust* (Bloomington: Indiana University Press, 1996).

Hartman, Geoffrey, *Minor Prophecies: The Literary Essay in the Culture Wars* (Cambridge, MA: Harvard University Press, 1997).

Hartman, Geoffrey, Harold Bloom, Paul de Man and J. Hillis M iller, eds, *Deconstruction and Criticism* (New York: Continuum, 1987).

Hartman, Geoffrey, and Patricia Parker, eds, *Shakespeare and the Question of Theory* (New York: Routledge, 1992).

Heidegger, Martin, *Existence and Being*, ed. Werner Brock (Chicago: Henry Wegner Company, 1949).

Heidegger, Martin, *What Is Philosophy?*, trans. William Kluback and Jean Wilde (New Haven, CT: College and University Press, 1956).

Heidegger, Martin, *The Question of Being*, trans. William Kluback and Jean Wilde (New Haven, CT: College and University Press, 1958).

Heidegger, Martin, *An Introduction to Metaphysics*, trans. Ralph Manheim (Garden City, NY: Doubleday-Anchor Books, 1961).

Heidegger, Martin, *Discourse on Thinking*, trans. John Anderson and E. Hans Freund (New York: Harper & Row, 1966).

Heidegger, Martin, *What Is a Thing?*, trans. W. B. Barton, Jr. (Chicago: Henry Regnery Company, 1967).

Heidegger, Martin, *What Is Called Thinking?*, trans. Fred D. Weick and J. Glenn Gray (New York: Harper & Row, 1968).

Heidegger, Martin, *The Essence of Reasons*, trans. Terrence Malik (Evaston, IL: Northwestern University Press, 1969).

Heidegger, Martin, *Identity and Difference*, trans. Joan Stambaugh (New York: Harper & Row, 1969).

Heidegger, Martin, *Hegel's Concept of Experience*, trans. J. Glenn Gray and Fred D. Weick (New York: Harper & Row, 1970).

Heidegger, Martin, *Poetry, Language, Thought*, trans. Albert Hofstadter (New York: Harper & Row, 1971).

Heidegger, Martin, *Early Greek Thinking*, trans. David Krell and Frank Capuzzi (New York: Harper & Row, 1975).

Heidegger, Martin, *The Piety of Thinking*, trans. James Hart and John Maraldo (Bloomington: Indiana University Press, 1976).

Heidegger, Martin, *On the Way to Language*, trans. Peter Hertz (New York: Harper & Row, 1977).

Heidegger, Martin, *The Question concerning Technology and Other Essays*, trans. William Lovitt (New York: Harper & Row, 1977).

Heidegger, Martin, *Basic Problems of Phenomenology*, trans. Albert Hofstader (Bloomington: Indiana University Press, 1982).

Heidegger, Martin, *Metaphysical Foundations of Logic*, trans. Michael Heim (Bloomington: Indiana University Press, 1984).

Heidegger, Martin, *History of the Concept of Time: Prologomena*, trans. Theodore Kisiel (Bloomington: Indiana University Press, 1985).

Heidegger, Martin, *Hegel's Phenomenology of Spirit*, trans. Parvis Emad and Kenneth Maly (Bloomington: Indiana University Press, 1988).

Heidegger, Martin, 'The task of destroying the history of ontology', *Being and Time*, trans. John McQuarrie (Oxford: Blackwell, 1988).

Heidegger, Martin, *Kant and the Problem of Metaphysics*, trans. Richard Taft (Bloomington: Indiana University Press, 1990).

Heidegger, Martin, *The Principle of Reason*, trans. Reginald Lilly (Bloomington: Indiana University Press, 1991).

Heidegger, Martin, *Basic Writings, Revised Edition*, ed. David Krell (London: Routledge, 1993).

Jabes, Edmond, *The Book of Question: Yael Elya Aely El, or The Last Book*, Vol. 2, trans. R. Waldrop (Boston: University of New England Press, 1990).

Jabes, Edmond, *From the Book to the Book: An Edmond Jabes Reader* (Boston: University of New England Press, 1991).

Jabes, Edmond, *The Book of Questions*, Vol. 1, trans. R. Waldrop (London: Wesleyan University Press, 1992).

Jabes, Edmond, 'The moment after', *The Book of Margins*, trans. R. Waldrop (Chicago: University of Chicago Press, 1993), pp. 33–48.

Jabes, Edmond, *The Book of Shares*, trans. R. Waldrop (Chicago: Chicago University Press, 1995).

Jabes, Edmond, *The Foreigner Carrying in the Crook of his Arm a Tiny Book* (London: Wesleyan University Press, 1996)

Jabes, Edmond, *If There Were Anywhere but Desert*, trans. K. Waldrop (New York: Station Hill, 1998).

Jabes, Edmond, *A Little Book of Unsuspected Subversion*, trans. R. Waldrop (Stanford: Stanford University Press, 1999).

Johnson, Barbara, *The Critical Difference: Essays in the Contemporary Rhetoric of Reading* (Baltimore: Johns Hopkins University Press, 1980).

Johnson, Barbara, 'Gender theory and the Yale School', *Genre*, 1984, Vol. 17 (1–2), pp. 101–12.

Johnson, Barbara, *A World of Difference* (Baltimore: Johns Hopkins University Press, 1984).

Johnson, Barbara, ed., *Freedom and Interpretation* (New York: Basic Books, 1993).

Johnson, Barbara, *The Wake of Deconstruction* (Oxford: Blackwell, 1994).

Johnson, Barbara, *The Feminist Difference: Literature, Psychoanalysis, Race, and Gender* (Cambridge, MA: Harvard University Press, 1997).

Johnson, Barbara, and Jonathan Arac, eds, *Consequences of Theory* (Baltimore: Johns Hopkins University Press, 1992).

Kamuf, Peggy, *Signature Pieces: On the Institution of Authority* (Ithaca: Cornell University Press, 1988).

Kamuf, Peggy, ed., *A Derrida Reader: Between the Blinds* (New York: Columbia University Press, 1991) [Contains: 'Différance', 'Signature event context', 'Tympan', 'Che cos'e la poesia', 'Des tours de Babel', 'Living on: Border lines', 'Letter to a Japanese friend', 'Geschlecht: Sexual difference, ontological difference', 'At this very moment in this work here I am', 'Ulysses gramaphone: Hear say yes in Joyce', and extracts from *Speech and Phenomena, Of Grammatology, Dissemination, The Truth in Painting, Spurs, The Post-Card*].

Kamuf, Peggy, *The Division of Literature or the University in Deconstruction* (Chicago: Chicago University Press, 1997).

Kamuf, Peggy, 'The ghosts of critique and deconstruction', first appeared in *Tympan*, www.tympanum.usc.edu/Kamuf

Laclau, Ernesto, and Chantal Mouffe, *Hegemony and Socialist Strategy* (London: Verso, 1977).

Laclau, Ernesto, *Reflections on the Revolutions of our Time* (London: Verso, 1988).

Laclau, Ernesto, ed., *The Making of Political Identities* (London: Verso, 1991).

Laclau, Ernesto, 'Why do empty signifiers matter in politics?', *Emancipations* (London: Verso, 1996), pp. 36–46.

Laclau, Ernesto, *The Politics of Rhetoric* (Colchester: University of Essex Department of Government Publications, 1999).

Lacoue-Labarthe, Philippe, *Typography: Mimesis, Philosophy, Politics* (Cambridge, MA: Harvard University Press, 1989).

Lacoue-Labarthe, Philippe, *Heidegger, Art, and Politics: The Fiction of the Political*, trans. Chris Turner (Oxford: Blackwell, 1990).

Lacoue-Labarthe, Philippe, ed., *The Subject of Philosophy*, trans. Thomas Trezis (Minneapolis: University of Minnesota Press, 1993).

Lacoue-Labarthe, Philippe, *Poetry as Experience*, trans. Andrea Tarnowski (Stanford: Stanford University Press, 1995).

Lacoue-Labarthe, Philippe, 'In the name of', in Philippe Lacoue-Labarthe and Jean-Luc Nancy, *Retreating the Political*, ed. Simon Sparks (London: Routledge, 1997).

Lacoue-Labarthe, Philippe, *Musica Ficta: Figures of Wagner*, trans. Felicia McCarren (Stanford: Stanford University Press, 1998).

Lacoue-Labarthe, Philippe, and Jean-Luc Nancy, *The Literary Absolute: The Theory of Literature in German Romanticism* (New York: SUNY, 1993).

Lacoue-Labarthe, Philippe, and Jean-Luc Nancy, *The Title of the Letter: A Reading of Lacan* (New York: SUNY, 1995).

Levinas, Emmanuel, *Otherwise than Being: or, Beyond Essence*, trans. Alphonso Lingis (The Hague: Matinus Nijhoff, 1981).

Levinas, Emmanuel, *Collected Philosophical Papers*, trans. Alphonso Lingis (Dordrecht: Kluwer Academic Publishers, 1987).

Levinas, Emmanuel, *Ethics and Infinity: Conversations with Phillipe Nemo*, trans. Richard Cohen (Pittsburg: Duquesne University Press, 1987).

Levinas, Emmanuel, *Time and the Other*, trans. Richard Cohen (Pittsburg: Duquesne University Press, 1987).

Levinas, Emmanuel, *Existence and Existents*, trans. Alphonso Lingis (London: Kluwer Academic Publishers, 1988).

Levinas, Emmanuel, *The Levinas Reader*, ed. Sean Hand (Oxford: Blackwell, 1989).

Levinas, Emmanuel, *Totality and Infinity: An Essay on Exteriority*, trans. Alphonso Lingis (London: Kluwer Academic Publishers, 1991).

Levinas, Emmanuel, 'Jacques Derrida: Wholly otherwise', from *Proper Names* (Stanford: Stanford University Press, 1997), pp. 55–62.

Lyotard, Jean-François, *Driftworks* (New York: Semiotexte, 1984).

Lyotard, Jean-François, *The Postmodern Condition*, trans. Geoffrey Bennington and Brian Massumi (Manchester: Manchester University Press, 1984).

Lyotard, Jean-François, *The Libidinal Economy*, trans. Ian Hamilton Grant (London: Athlone, 1988).

Lyotard, Jean-François, *Peregrinations: Law, Form, Event*, trans. Geoffrey Bennington (New York: Columbia University Press, 1988).

Lyotard, Jean-François, *Postmodernism Explained for Children* (Minneapolis: University of Minnesota Press, 1988).

Lyotard, Jean-François, 'Discussions, or phrasing "After Auschwitz"', in Andrew Benjamin, ed., *The Lyotard Reader* (Oxford: Blackwell, 1989), pp. 386–9.

Lyotard, Jean-François, *The Differend: Phrases in Dispute*, trans. Georges Van Dee Abbeele (Minneapolis: University of Minnesota Press, 1990).

Lyotard, Jean-François, *Heidegger and 'The Jews'*, trans. Georges Van Dee Abbeele (Minneapolis: University of Minnesota Press, 1990).

Lyotard, Jean-François, *Political Writings*, ed. Bill Readings (London: Routledge, 1990).

Lyotard, Jean-François, *The Inhuman: Reflections on Time*, trans. Geoffrey Bennington and Rachel Bowlby (Stanford: Stanford University Press, 1994).

Lyotard, Jean-François, *Postmodern Fables*, trans. Georges Van Dee Abbeele (Minneapolis: University of Minnesota Press, 1994).

Lyotard, Jean-François, *Lessons on the Analytic of the Sublime* (Stanford: Stanford University Press, 1995).

Lyotard, Jean-François, *Phenomenology*, trans. Brian Beakly (New York: SUNY, 1996).

Lyotard, Jean-François and J.-L. Thebaud, *Just-Gaming*, trans. Wlad Godzich (Manchester: Manchester University Press, 1985).

McQuillan, Martin, and Eleanor Byrne, *Deconstructing Disney* (London: Pluto, 1999).

McQuillan, Martin, Graeme Macdonald, Robin Purves and Stephen Thomson, eds, *Post-Theory: New Directions in Criticism* (Edinburgh: Edinburgh University Press, 1999).

Maley, Willy, *Salvaging Spenser* (London: Macmillan, 1996).

Maley, Willy, 'Spectres of Engels', in Peter Buse and Andrew Stott, eds, *Ghosts: Deconstruction, Psychoanalysis, History* (London: Macmillan, 1999), pp. 23–50.

Marx, Karl, *The German Ideology*, trans. W. Lough, C. Dutt and C. P. Magill (London: Lawrence and Wishart, 1970).

Marx, Karl, *The Complete Works of Karl Marx*, ed. T. Borodulina (Moscow: Progress Publishers, 1972).

Marx, Karl, *Capital*, trans. Ben Fowkes (Harmondsworth: Penguin, 1977).

Marx, Karl, and Frederick Engels, *The Communist Mannifesto*, trans. B. Fowkes (Harmondsworth: Penguin, 1988).

Miller, J. Hillis, *The Disappearance of God: Five Nineteenth-Century Writers* (Cambridge, MA: Belknap Press, 1963).

Miller, J. Hillis, *Fiction and Repetition: Seven English Novels* (Oxford: Basil Blackwell, 1982).

Miller, J. Hillis, *The Linguistic Moment: From Wordsworth to Stevens* (Princeton: Princeton University Press, 1985).

Miller, J. Hillis, *The Ethics of Reading: Kant, de Man, Eliot, Trollope, James, and Benjamin* (New York: Columbia University Press, 1987).

Miller, J. Hillis, 'An open letter to Professor John Wiener', in Thomas Kennan, ed., *Responses to Paul de Man's Wartime Journalism 1940–1942* (Lincoln: University of Nebraska Press, 1989), pp. 334–42.

Miller, J. Hillis, *Tropes, Parables, Performatives: Essays on Twentieth-Century Literature* (Hemel Hempstead: Harvester Wheatsheaf, 1990).

Miller, J. Hillis, *Versions of Pygmallion* (Cambridge, MA: Harvard University Press, 1990).

Miller, J. Hillis, *Hawthorne and History* (Oxford: Blackwell, 1991).

Miller, J. Hillis, *Theory Now and Then* (Hemel Hempstead: Harvester Wheatsheaf, 1991).

Miller, J. Hillis, *Victorian Subjects* (Durham, NC: Duke University Press, 1991).

Miller, J. Hillis, *Ariadne's Thread: Story Lines* (New Haven: Yale University Press, 1992).

Miller, J. Hillis, *Illustration* (Cambridge, MA: Harvard University Press, 1992).

Miller, J. Hillis, 'Derrida's Topographies', *South Atlantic Review*, 59 (1), (1994), pp. 1–25.

Miller, J. Hillis, *Topographies* (Stanford: Stanford University Press, 1994).

Nancy, Jean-Luc, *The Birth of Presence*, trans. Brian Holmes (Stanford: Stanford University Press, 1992).

Nancy, Jean-Luc, *The Inoperative Community* (Minneapolis: University of Minnesota Press, 1992).

Nancy, Jean-Luc, *The Muses*, trans. Peggy Kamuf (Stanford: Stanford University Press, 1996).

Nancy, Jean-Luc, *The Gravity of Thought*, trans. François Raffoul and Grégory Recco (Atlantic Highlands: Humanities Press, 1997).

Nancy, Jean-Luc, 'What is to be done?' in Philippe Lacoue-Labarthe and Jean-Luc Nancy, *Retreating the Political*, ed. Simon Sparks (London: Routledge, 1997), pp. 157–8.

Nancy, Jean-Luc, *Sense of the World*, trans. T. S. Librett (Minneapolis: University of Minnesota Press, 1998).

Norris, Christopher, *Deconstruction: Theory and Practice* (London: Methuen, 1982).

Norris, Christopher, *The Contest of the Faculties: Philosophy and Theory After Deconstruction* (London: Methuen, 1985).

Norris, Christopher, *Derrida* (London: Fontana, 1987).

Norris, Christopher, *Paul de Man, Deconstruction and the Critique of Aesthetic Ideology* (New York: Routledge, 1988).

Norris, Christopher, *Deconstruction and the Interests of Theory* (Norman: University of Oklahoma University Press, 1989).

Norris, Christopher, 'Deconstruction, postmodernism, and the visual arts', in Christopher Norris with Andrew Benjamin, *What is Deconstruction?* (London: Academy Editions, 1989).

Norris, Christopher, *Against Relativism: Philosophy of Science, Deconstruction, and Critical Theory* (Oxford: Blackwell, 1990).

Norris, Christopher, *Uncritical Theory: Intellectuals and the Gulf War* (London: Lawrence and Wishart, 1992).

Norris, Christopher, *New Idols of the Cave: On the Limits of Anti-Realism* (New York: St. Martin's Press, 1994).

Norris, Christopher, *What's Wrong with Postmodernism: Critical Theory and the Ends of Philosophy* (Baltimore: Johns Hopkins University Press, 1994).

Norris, Christopher, *Quantum Theory and the Flight from Realism* (London: Routledge, 1996).

Norris, Christopher, *Reclaiming Truth* (London: Lawrence and Wishart, 1997).

Norris, Christopher, *Resources of Realism* (London: Macmillan, 1997).

Readings, Bill, 'The deconstruction of politics', in Lindsay Waters and Wlad Godzich, eds, *Reading de Man Reading* (Minneapolis: University of Minnesota Press, 1989), pp. 223–44.

Readings, Bill, *Introducing Lyotard: Art and Politics* (London: Routledge, 1991).

Readings, Bill, *The University in Ruins* (Cambridge, MA: Harvard University Press, 1993).

Readings, Bill, and Bennet Schaber, eds, *Postmodernism: Across the Ages* (Syracuse, NY: Syracuse University Press, 1993).

Ronell, Avital, *The Telephone Book: Technology, Schizophrenia, Electric Speech* (Lincoln: University of Nebraska Press, 1989).

Ronell, Avital, *Finitude's Score: Essays for the End of the Millenium* (Lincoln: University of Nebraska Press, 1994).

Ronell, Avital, 'Towards a narcoanalysis', *Crack Wars: Literature, Addiction, Mania* (Lincoln: University of Nebraska Press, 1995), pp. 47–65.

Rorty, Richard, 'Philosophy as a kind of writing', *New Literary History*, no. 10, 1978, pp. 141–60.

Rorty, Richard, *Consequences of Pragmatism: Essays 1972–1980* (Minneapolis: University of Minnesota Press, 1982).

Rorty, Richard, *Philosophy and the Mirror of Nature* (Oxford: Blackwell, 1988).

Rorty, Richard, *The Linguistic Turn: Essays in Philosophical Method* (Chicago: University of Chicago Press, 1989).

Rorty, Richard, *Philosophical Papers* (Cambridge: Cambridge University Press, 1992).

Rorty, Richard, *Contingency, Irony, and Solidarity* (Cambridge: Cambridge University Press, 1994)

Rorty, Richard, *Truth and Moral Progress* (Cambridge: Cambridge University Press, 1996).

Rorty, Richard, *Achieving our Country* (Cambridge, MA: Harvard University Press, 1998).

Royle, Nicholas, *Telepathy and Literature: Essays on the Reading Mind* (Oxford: Basil Blackwell, 1991).

Royle, Nicholas, ed. *Afterwords* (Tampere: Outside Books, 1992).

Royle, Nicholas, 'The remains of psychoanalysis (i): Telepathy', *After Derrida* (Manchester: Manchester University Press, 1995).

Royle, Nicholas, *E. M. Forster* (Plymouth: Northcoate House, 1999).

Royle, Nicholas, and Andrew Bennett, *Introduction to Literature, Criticism and Theory* (Hemel Hempstead: Prentice Hall, 2nd edn, 1999).

Royle, Nicholas, ed., *Deconstruction: A User's Manual* (London: Macmillan, 2000).

Ryan, Michael, 'Derrida and Marx', *Marxism and Deconstruction: A Critical Articulation* (Baltimore: Johns Hopkins University Press, 1982).

Ryan, Michael, *Politics and Culture: Working Hypotheses for a Post-Revolutionary Society* (Baltimore: Johns Hopkins University Press, 1989).

Ryan, Michael, and Douglas Kellner, *Camera Politica: The Politics and Ideology of Contemporary Political Film* (Princeton: Princeton University Press, 1986).

Spivak, Gayatri, *In Other Worlds: Essays in Cultural Politics* (New York: Routledge, 1988).

Spivak, Gayatri, 'Practical politics of the open end', *Canadian Journal of Political and Social Theory/Revue canadienne de théorie politique et sociale*, 12 (1–2), 1988, pp. 104–11.

Spivak, Gayatri, *The Post-Colonial Critic: Interviews, Strategies, Dialogues*, ed. Sarah Harasym (New York: Routledge, 1990).

Spivak, Gayatri, *Outside in the Teaching Machine* (New York: Routledge, 1993).

Spivak, Gayatri, *The Spivak Reader*, ed. T. Laubs (London: Routledge, 1995).

Spivak, Gayatri, *A Critique of Postcolonial Reason: Toward a History of the Vanishing Present* (Cambridge, MA: Harvard University Press, 1999).

Tschumi, Bernard, 'Violence of architecture', *Artforum*, September 1981, 20 (1), pp. 44–7.

Tschumi, Bernard, *Architecture and Disjunction* (Boston: MIT Press, 1988).

Tschumi, Bernard, *Architecture in/of Motion* (Amsterdam: Netherlands Architecture Institute/Nai Uitjevers Publishers, 1989).

Tschumi, Bernard, *Questions of Space* (New York: Architecture Association, 1989).

Tschumi, Bernard, *Space, Event, Movement* (New York: World Microfilms Publications, 1990).

Tschumi, Bernard, *Event-Cities* (Boston: MIT Press, 1996).

Tschumi, Bernard, *The Manhattan Transcripts: Theoretical Projects* (New York: Moncelli Press, 1999).

Tschumi, Bernard, and Nigel Coates, *Discourse of Events* (New York: Architecture Association, 1997).

Tschumi, Bernard, and Hugh Dutton, *Glass Ramps/Glass Walls: Deviations from the Normative* (New York: Architecture Association, 1998).

Tschumi, Bernard, and Pierre Le Fresnoy, *Architecture in/between* (New York: Moncelli Press, 1992).

Valéry, Paul, 'In praise of water', trans. Christine Izzary, *Oeuvres* (Paris: Gallimard, 1957–60), vol. 2, pp. 202–3.

Valéry, Paul, *Monsieur Teste (Collected Works of Paul Valery)*, trans. Jackson Matthews (Princeton: Princeton University Press, 1990).

Valéry, Paul, *War, Power, and Civilization* (Toronto: Canadian Scholars Press, 1999).

Weber, Samuel, 'The sideshow, or: Remarks on a canny moment', *Modern Language Notes*, 88, 1973, pp. 1102–33.

Weber, Samuel, *Unwrapping Balzac: A Reading of La peau de chagrin* (Toronto: Toronto University Press, 1979).

Weber, Samuel, *The Legend of Freud* (Minneapolis: University of Minnesota Press, 1982).

Weber, Samuel, ed., *Demarcating the Disciplines: Philosophy, Literature, Art* (Baltimore: Johns Hopkins University Press, 1986).

Weber, Samuel, *Institution and Interpretation* (Minneapolis: University of Minnesota Press, 1987).

Weber, Samuel, *Return to Freud: Jacques Lacan's Dislocation of Psychoanalysis*, trans. Michael Levine (Cambridge: Cambridge University Press, 1991).

Weber, Samuel, *Mass Mediauras: Essays on Art, Technics and Media* (Stanford: Stanford University Press: 1996).

Weber, Samuel, and Hent de Vries, eds, *Violence, Identity, Self-Determination* (Stanford: Stanford University Press, 1997).

Weber, Samuel, Slavoj Zizek, Philippe Despoix and Edith Seifret, eds, *Perversion der Philosophie: Lacan und das unmögliche Erbe* (Köln: Bittermann, 1992).

Wills, David, *Prosthesis* (Stanford: Stanford University Press, 1995).

Wills, David, and Peter Brunette, eds, *Deconstruction and the Visual Arts: Art, Media, Architecture* (Cambridge: Cambridge University Press, 1994).

Wills, David, and Peter Brunette, eds, *Screen/Play: Derrida and Film Theory* (Princeton: Princeton University Press, 1994).

Young, Robert, ed., *Untying the Text: A Post-Structuralist Reader* (London: Routledge & Keagan Paul, 1981).

Young, Robert, 'The same difference', *Screen*, 28 (3), 1987, pp. 4–11.

Young, Robert, *White Mythologies: Writing History and the West* (London: Routledge, 1990).

Young, Robert, *Colonial Desire: Hybridity in Theory, Culture and Race* (London: Routledge, 1995).

Young, Robert, *Postcolonialism: A History* (Oxford: Blackwell, 1999).

INDEX